THE WRITER'S HANDBOOK

The
Writer's
Handbook

Edited by A. S. BURACK
Editor, *The Writer*

Boston   THE WRITER, INC.   *Publishers*

FOREWORD

The Writer's Handbook has long been considered a standard reference work and is regularly revised and enlarged. Part IV, *The Writer's Markets,* is brought up-to-date annually to include current addresses and editors' names and the latest editorial requirements of magazines, book publishers, etc.

The articles in this collection were originally published in *The Writer* Magazine. I have always felt that in addition to their appearance in the magazine, these valuable articles should be available in book form for study and permanent reference.

It has not been an easy task to make a selection from the hundreds of excellent pieces which have appeared in the magazine. In many cases it was not a matter of which we should select but rather which we must eliminate because of space limitations.

To make the scope of the editorial material in The Writer's Handbook as comprehensive as possible, I have included chapters on a wide variety of literary forms and fields. Application of the techniques presented in the text will help writers develop their writing ability, and use of the up-to-date manuscript market lists should greatly increase the writer's opportunities to sell.

I wish to thank the authors who have so generously given us permission to reprint their articles in this book. It is my hope that the material they present will be read and re-read as a continuing source of inspiration and instruction.

A. S. BURACK

Boston, Mass.

CONTENTS

PART I—BACKGROUND FOR WRITERS

PART II—HOW TO WRITE: Techniques

FICTION

CONTENTS

CONTENTS

PART I

BACKGROUND FOR WRITERS

1

CREATIVE WRITING

By Richard Martin Stern

I have a proposal that may raise a few eyebrows and even some hackles, but I will brave the result. It is this: Let us take the word "creative" out of writing courses. Let us put the word back in the dictionary where it belongs, to be brought out only rarely and in exceptional circumstances. Let us, in short, hack away at some of the pretentiousness that has invaded the craft, or the business, or the work of writing.

My reasons?

That one word "creative" has done and is doing more harm to potential writers than all the rejection slips that have ever been mailed. And it hasn't done practicing writers any good, either. Let me explain.

The beginning writer, faced with that word "creative," tends to believe that he must *create*. Not construct. Not narrate. Not simply tell the story he has in mind. *Create.* Somehow—and how can he ever find the handle?—he is supposed to rear back and produce a miracle, bring into being the heaven and the earth and all of the creatures thereof, breathe life into emptiness, *create*.

It goes deeper than that. The senior trade editor of one of the old established publishing houses tells me that each summer he is inundated by bright young college graduates, male and female, who have edited college papers and who want jobs doing something *creative*. They can't spell, punctuate or write a simple, declarative, unambiguous sentence, but that is besides the point. Those minor skills are for hired help.

All of these young hopefuls have taken *creative* writing courses, and all that stuck was that one blasted word with all that implies. If you can't *create*, you're dead, you're nobody, you're strictly

3

tuned out. And *create* means to fly, to soar above such mundane matters as grammar or syntax or that clarity of thought without which clarity of expression is impossible. *Create* means "like you know what I mean and if you don't you're square man you're worse you don't you know *communicate* you aren't *relevant!*"

I submit that that single word ****** must bear its share of the responsibility. I submit that its effect goes even deeper than I have said. It distorts vision almost to the point of blindness.

A syllogism must go something like this: Hemingway (or Proust or Dickens) was a *creative* writer. I am studying *creative* writing. Therefore, I must write like Hemingway (or Proust or Dickens). Not for me the kind of story or novel I really like to read, and therefore might be able to write, because, ugh!, secretly I am devoted to Mickey Spillane, and how in the world could I turn in that kind of thing in a *creative* writing course?—Now do you see my point?

There is an open secret that is known to every professional writer, but, strangely, it is almost never discussed. It is that the form of writing, the *genre*, if you will, is not what restricts the quality of writing; the strictures are only within the ability of the writer himself. Do you think I exaggerate? Then consider:

The quality of work in confession magazines? Colette wrote confession stories, what else? Adventure stories? How about Kipling's *Kim*? *Treasure Island*? Go back and have another look at *Beowulf*. Children's stories? Re-read the *Jungle Books, Alice in Wonderland,* even, so help me, *Huckleberry Finn*. I have saved the best for the last: Mystery-suspense? What else is *Hamlet* in *form*? The substance is something else (again) but because it was a fellow named Shakespeare, and not R. M. Stern, wielding the pen.

Have I strayed from my thesis? I think not. That single word *create* and its adjective *creative* have planted false seeds that grow into mighty oaks of confusion. Only certain forms, certain *genres*, are considered *creative*: all others must be avoided like the plague. It takes more courage and more perseverance (and perhaps more luck) than most who hope to write possess to break through this barrier of nonsense, and so they give it all up as a bad job and live their lives as bankers or lawyers or ribbon clerks.

How many men, or women, who might have settled down happily to stretching to new heights the "uncreative" forms of romance, mystery, suspense, adventure, child's tale, have battered their egos into bloody confusion trying to write the kind of navel novel or without-end short story that at the moment is considered *creative*? How many Kiplings or Dickenses or Steinbecks or Faulkners, yes, or Shakespeares have we never known and never will know because they tried desperately to write the kind of thing that was not for them to write well? And how many second-rate writers have we had who might have been superb had they written what they really felt, enjoyed? How many literary tragedies, yes, crimes, can we lay in the lap of that monstrous academic invention, the phrase "creative writing"?

The point is, of course, that no one is going to write well something he does not care about, does not feel, cannot laugh with or cry over—and the operative word in that sentence is *write*. To be in any way successful, books and stories of fiction must carry emotion and must by some magic no one can really explain break through the artificial barriers of paper and ink and print to convey that emotion to the reader. Unless the feeling, the caring, the emotion is there in the writer's mind in the first place, the entire process is impossible.

Write what you will, write what you want, write what you yourself like to read. Never mind what is considered *in*, what is thought this year or this decade to be *creative*. Write what you can write, and if there is within you—and I hope there is—that once-or-twice-in-a-generation spark that ignites the reader's emotions and makes him captive to your tale, then no matter what *genre* you have chosen *because you preferred it*, you will carry it to new heights. Then, *after the fact*, let them apply the word *creative*.

I rest my case.

2

THE BATTLE OF FICTION AND NON-FICTION

By Elizabeth Janeway

WHY has non-fiction become so much more popular than fiction? Why is non-fiction so much more widely read? Except for phenomena like *Love Story*, it is generally true that non-fiction sells much better than fiction. Why?

This is an interesting topic, and because it is germane to our present social situation, it is a trend you can expect to continue, rather than just a fashion of a few years. A basic reason is that fiction is much harder for people to follow than non-fiction.

Fiction, you see, is not about facts, but about relationships. In that sense, it's like algebra instead of arithmetic. Fiction isn't a straightforward statement; it's a comment on something the author believes the reader knows something about already. But today in a very heterogeneous society like ours, it's rare for people to have the sort of common background of assumption which permits fiction to speak movingly, evocatively and clearly to its audience.

As everyone knows, our society is shifting; it's much more mobile than in the nineteenth century when there was a common, bourgeois, middle-class sense of relationships—of the world being more or less the same, of standards being more or less accepted within it. This is not so today. Consequently, it is much, much, harder to write the sort of book which assumes that the reader will feel as the writer does about a given personal relationship, a given moral situation.

People are much more isolated—and that includes emotional isolation. We tend to find it harder to feel our way into other people's emotions because they are more various and less familiar. People come from other parts of the world. The reading audience now comes from many, many more different kinds of childhood than potential readers in 1850 or 1870.

For this audience non-fiction spells things out. You know how

6

children ask you to tell them a story and want to know if it's true. And by that they don't mean is it fictionally true, is it true to a level of plausible emotion? They mean, did it really happen? Non-fiction is able to answer, yes, it did happen; or else, at least, to *pretend* that it did happen.

Of course, as we all know, history is often rewritten from generation to generation, as historical attitudes and views on life change, but historiographers and their readers still assume the facts they are discussing are the same. It takes a fairly sophisticated critic to realize how emphasis and interpretation change our map of the world—or (as I suggest in my book *Man's World, Woman's Place*) how they rework our "social mythology."

But fiction, unlike history or biography, openly and overtly requires from the reader some prior knowledge of the way life works, some sense of what's plausible and possible. Fiction—and, of course, I am talking about good fiction—demands that a society should seem to be knowable to the audience living within it. The writer and the reader have to agree that they are talking about the same facts and the same rules. We have a very bad situation for agreement today, not only because fiction writers are isolated from their possible readers, but also because social change takes place so fast. This is one place where the generation gap is wide indeed, for young people and their parents seldom read the same writers.

Fiction is about personal relationships. These relationships must seem to the readers out there to carry the same moral overtones that the author feels as being present and significant in them. But since so much of the common background of social and emotional and cultural experience has vanished, this similarity of response can't be taken for granted. Take an obvious example. One hundred years ago it was a tragedy if an unmarried girl had a baby. An author writing about such a situation could assume that this is what his readers would also feel. They might sympathize with her and they might feel that her plight was unjust, but they would feel, nonetheless, that it was a tragic situation. Today this isn't true. Our moral judgments have shifted and become much more diverse, and fluid.

An author can still set up a situation that involves the girl, her lover, the man she might have married and didn't, the child, the

parents, the whole village, but his readers won't react in a predictable way. Some people will say, "Right on," and others will say,
"What about the population explosion?" Some people will say her
parents are callous pigs, and the tragedy lies in their anger with the
girl. In short, there will be all kinds of reactions to the situation,
and not just one you can count on.

In other words, the symbols and the meanings which are the tools
of fictional communication have ceased to carry a significance
which will be commonly agreed upon. Fiction is becoming an archaic
and special language. It is no longer a *lingua franca* that everyone
can understand. I don't, myself, think that fiction will die out; but
it will have to change.

Meanwhile, non-fiction reaches the readers, but, again, the writer
can't take this for granted. This book of mine, *Man's World, Woman's Place*, is the first long work of non-fiction I have written and,
in doing it, I had to learn quite new techniques. One of the things I
discovered was that I had to know who my audience was. I had to
think consciously about whom I was writing for. In fiction, I always
assumed that I was writing for people who would understand me
because we shared the same assumptions about the world.

In more stable times, when people have a better idea of what's going on around them, they turn to fiction for an interpretation;
whereas, in times like these, people turn to non-fiction just to find
out what's going on. When people lived in tiny communities and
knew each other extremely well, and could tease each other, and
joke about relationships, you had communication by poetry. You
didn't have to set up inter-personal relationships. You could assume
that everyone knew what you meant if you wrote in lyrical form.
Fiction and poetry both demand an intimate knowledge and a
shared experience, based on the size and intimacy of the community,
and on the rate of social change.

Fiction should be about recognizable people. That, to me, makes
it very difficult to read certain writers who are enjoyed by other
people. For instance, I'm not very fond of Kurt Vonnegut and
Joseph Heller, writers who are difficult for me to read because their
characters too often fall toward stereotypes and toward a kind of
allegorical presentation of themselves in what seems to me a flat

situation. A situation where right and wrong are too easily determined.

I find this unexciting and lacking in tension. I understand why writers do this: they are looking for the moral agreement that I spoke of earlier. We can no longer expect it when we're talking about an unmarried girl having a baby. But it's assumed that we will all agree that war is hell, and we shouldn't have bombed Dresden and all Air Force generals were nitwits, etc., etc.

To people my age, this is dull partly because it is hellishly oversimplified. Also, being oversimplified it seems to us false in many respects. Vonnegut and Heller and many of their followers are like Irving Berlin—they can only compose in the key of C. Berlin has had a special keyboard made that transposes his key of C tunes into B minor or F sharp for him. I wish allegorically inclined writers could do this too, and have their stereotyped situations enriched by doubt and diversity.

I suspect that another effect on fiction that we're experiencing comes out of television. McLuhan, though out of fashion today, is perfectly right about his basic premise: what is important about television is not just what it says but—much more—how it says it, how it picks up experience and processes it and passes it to the viewer.

Television speeds up the processes of life. You look at the tube long enough and you'll begin to believe that every problem can be resolved in a time span of half an hour or, at most, an hour. Leonard Woolf writes in his marvelous autobiography that when he gave up his job as editor of *The New Statesman* he found a heavenly relief. *The New Statesman* is a weekly, and he'd begun to count everything in the world, political processes, news events, human life in seven-day spans. In television everything happens, reaches a climax and is resolved in an hour at most. Of course, art and fiction compress experience, but that is not the effect that television gives.

It's difficult to know what's going to come from television. I can't be completely hopeless about it because there's a great deal of talent there. But again, I think factual documentaries are at present a good deal better than the fiction shown. When you really had some plausible and complicated fiction shown, as in *The Forsyte Saga*, you found the television audience very much moved and involved.

Now, it's certainly true that anyone my age has seen film turn into an art form in the past thirty or forty years. Perhaps television will too. As yet it hasn't achieved a depth of experience which permits art to grow, permits diversity, suspense, surprise. Art needs this richness of possibility to hold its audience. When it doesn't exist, the creator too often falls back on seeking to grab hold of the audience by a shock effect. But shock effects wear off. They can't be used too often because you begin wondering what else for an encore.

It's interesting today to see how many writers want to grab the reader via sex; and of course it works—for a while. But sex novels defeat themselves in the end, because they cease to be novels. They reach for the reader at the level of involvement which produces heavy breathing; and Janeway's law on critical appreciation declares that heavy breathing breaks down the brain cells.

In other words, personal involvement at this level wipes out critical ability. Instead of understanding the word through art, the reader experiences sensations. Now it happens to be psychologically true that the more you want something, the less you can tell how good it is until you've had it.

The remarks on this situation by a great author of former times sum it up pretty well:

> The expense of spirit in a waste of shame
> Is lust in action; and till action, lust
> Is perjur'd, murd'rous, bloody, full of blame.
> Mad in pursuit, and in possession so;
> Had, having and in quest to have, extreme;
> A bliss in proof—and prov'd, a very woe;
> Before, a joy propos'd; behind, a dream.

Which brings us directly to the question of pornography and censorship. I'd better begin by saying that I'm totally opposed to any kind of censorship from anyone: from the local police chief, from the courts—which means that I support the publication of pornography, including hard-core pornography. But I warn you not to get pornography mixed up with literature, which it isn't.

It's more like "How to Fix the TV" and "Everything You Always Wanted to Know About Air Conditioning, Hair Setting, or Septic Tank Repair." It aims at hard breathing and no thinking at all. It is a substitute for action, not a comment on it.

Pornography purports to be fiction, but it really isn't about personal relationships, and relationships are the stuff of fiction. Pornography is only about relationships within the self. It is deeply narcissistic and claustrophobic. So, though I support the publication of pornography for those who want it, I can't call it literature.

Part of the confusion about pornography arises from the fact that literature can be written and art created around pornographic situations. But this requires the introduction of human relationships into the closed world of pornography. Henry Miller is a good example. In his books, we find recognizable human beings who are caught in pornographic situations which become both comic and tragic because the characters know they are trapped, and their emotions are moving and effective. In such scenes, publication of pornography has opened the door to a wider area of consideration for fiction. To this extent literature itself may be said to have profited by it.

I have cited this example both because it is so common today and because it illustrates clearly how writing may extend its range. Humanity suffers when there are areas of experience and emotion which cannot be discussed, which are cut off by barricades of taboo. Such hidden, denied emotions are the breeding ground of neurosis, fear and compulsion. For the artist, there should be nothing human that is alien. Part of his job, his obligation, is to show his audience the reality of other people's experience. And so, the wider the range of life that can be used as material for art, the better for all of us, readers and writers alike.

3

MY RELUCTANT MAGICIAN

By Richard Powell

SOMEWHERE in the upper part of my head, in a Victorian tangle of attics and dormers and cupolas, there is a locked room for which I do not have a key. In it lives the Reluctant Magician who produces my ideas for stories.

He does not, unfortunately, combine all the better qualities of Merlin, the genie of the lamp, and the Wizard of Oz. If he did, life would be much easier for me. I would simply snap my fingers whenever I needed an idea. That would make R. M. materialize, ready to do my bidding, in a puff of pleasantly-scented smoke. (None of this brimstone odor for me; look what happened to Faust.)

"You called, sir," R. M. would say.

"Ah, yes," I murmur. "I'm ready for an idea for my next story."

"Here it is, sir," R. M. says, giving me a handsomely-illuminated parchment scroll. "I hope it's satisfactory, sir."

I open the scroll and glance at the contents and perhaps yawn slightly. "It's not your best," I say, "but it will do." Then I go to my typewriter and begin writing a novel for which the book clubs and movies will later scramble.

Things don't work out that way. When I need an idea for a story, I climb painfully up the steep creaking stairs to Reluctant Magician's locked room. I rap politely. There is a puff of smoke— neither pleasantly scented nor like brimstone; just cheap cigar smoke—and a small furious gnome pops out through the keyhole, carrying an armful of signs. He plasters these all over the door, and pops back in again. The signs announce: OUT TO LUNCH, GONE FISHING, DO NOT DISTURB, CLOSED BY ORDER OF U.S. MARSHAL, ILL-NESS IN FAMILY, NO TRESPASSING, BEWARE OF THE DOG. I stand outside the door begging for help, but R. M. does not give any hint that he hears me or would care if he did. So I go wearily downstairs and spend days and weeks and often months trying to work out a new story. Sooner or later Reluctant Magician will appear, bringing an idea. Sometimes he will be in a grumpy mood and tell me I'm more bother than I'm worth. Sometimes he will rush in, shouting, "Got a great idea, boss! Wait till you hear this!"

I don't know whether or not my experience is typical of fiction writers. Ordinarily I avoid talking about how I get ideas for stories. I pretend that I always have dozens of lovely ideas lolling around in my head awaiting attention, like harem beauties hoping that the sultan will call. This protects me from people who want to give me an idea for a book. I don't want other people's ideas, no matter how good. I can find good ideas by the score in the morning newspaper, but either I can't or don't want to use any of them. An idea is worthless to me unless I am not only capable of handling it but also excited by it.

The answer to whether or not I am capable of turning an idea into a story depends on how much I know or can learn about the subject involved. Long ago, Reluctant Magician gave me a lesson in writing about things I know. The year was 1936, and I had yet to sell my first story. I decided that, as part of my training, I ought to write an animal story. I told R. M. about my decision, and we had the following talk:

ME: I'd like to write a story about lions and tigers in Africa. They're big, important, glamorous animals and they appeal to me.

R. M.: Pick an animal you know better. You never saw a lion or tiger outside a zoo.

ME: I can do research on them, can't I?

R. M.: Among the things you'll learn is that there are no tigers in Africa.

ME: Then how about dogs? Everybody loves dog stories.

R. M.: You never owned a dog.

ME: But I don't know any animals well except house cats! Who wants to read about house cats? To the best of my knowledge, nobody ever sold a short story about a house cat.

R. M.: Then you can be the first.

ME: I won't write about house cats. The idea is humiliating.

R. M.: It's even more humiliating that you haven't sold any stories.

ME: Very well. I'll write the story, but it's a waste of time.

Four months later, *Woman's Home Companion* bought a story

from me titled, "The Cat Named George." This established Reluctant Magician as a genius, and made him insufferable. It also made him lazy, and he kept suggesting more cat stories instead of digging up new ideas for me. I wrote and sold nine more George the Cat stories (all to *This Week* Magazine) before taking a firm stand with R. M. and telling him no more cat stories. He sulked for weeks and wouldn't bring me any ideas. But finally he came rushing up to me one afternoon when I was mowing the lawn.

R. M.: Got a great idea, Boss! You're gonna start writing magazine serials! Lots of money in it! Less work for both of us! One idea gets us a book-length manuscript instead of just a short story!

ME: What do I write a serial about?

R. M.: We got this hero, see, who keeps getting drawn into crimes and solving them, and—

ME (*Groaning*): Oh no! Not another private eye story!

R. M.: He's not a private eye. He's an antique dealer who plays detective.

ME: What's so great about that? There have been lawyers who played detective, orchid fanciers, ministers, old maids . . . I could name dozens.

R. M.: This guy is different. He doesn't want to play detective. He hates the idea. Crime scares him. Crooks give him the jitters. He just wants to live a quiet, calm, safe life, but this dizzy blonde he married keeps digging up trouble that he can't avoid.

ME: Maybe you've got something there. A Reluctant Hero, hm-m? Where did you get the idea for him?

R. M.: From you. I just started thinking how you'd react if you were forced to solve crimes and play around with thugs and gunmen, and hooray, we got a scared hero, and you can write about him from firsthand knowledge.

ME: Your suggestion is insulting, humiliating—

R. M.: You said it was humiliating when I told you to write a cat story, didn't you?

Well, yes, I remembered, and, come to think of it, the idea of a timorous hero was appealing. I could make him sensibly cautious, the way I was; it was ridiculous to talk about me being scared. I wrote a story called "Don't Catch Me." *American Magazine* ran it as a serial. Simon & Schuster published it as an Inner Sanctum Mystery. Orson Welles bought the film rights (although he never made the picture). My hero's name was Andy and the heroine's name was Arab, short for Arabella. R. M. lazed in his room smoking his cheap cigars after I finished the story and simply suggested more Arab and Andy stories. I wrote four more. I might have gone on writing them if an editor at either *Collier's* or *The*

Saturday Evening Post (they were sort of taking turns buying the Arab and Andy stories, at that point) hadn't said to me, "We've decided we can't buy any more of these unless you find a way to get more romance into them. It was all right when Arab and Andy were new, but my gosh, they've been in five books now and millions of magazine readers have met them, and they're old, settled married folks now. Maybe you could introduce a secondary couple and let them have a romance, huh?"

I didn't like that idea, and there was a simpler solution. I *unmarried* Arab and Andy, gave them different names and new backgrounds, and wrote five more mysteries. Then I sat down to do a little inventory work on myself. For one thing, magazines were starting to disappear, and whenever a *Collier's* or an *American* vanished, I lost a market. For another thing, I was tired of writing to magazine formulas. If I was ever going to write a serious novel, I'd better get at it. I made my usual pilgrimage upstairs and rapped on R. M.'s door:

ME: May I have another idea, please?
R. M.: Sure. Write a mystery serial.
ME: I'm tired of them.
R. M.: Dig up your own ideas if you don't like mine.
ME: I want to write a serious novel.
R. M.: Ah! The clown wants to play Hamlet.
ME: I want to write a novel that will explore the traditions, customs and beliefs of Philadelphians. I'm a native Philadelphian and have been studying the place for years. So I know my subject.
R. M.: Cities are big, sprawling places. You'll need a plot that can pull the sprawl into a sharp, tight pattern.
ME: I know. That's why I came to you. What do you suggest?
R. M.: I suggest that you stop bothering me.

So I went downstairs and for a year tried to find a solution. There didn't seem to be any way to write my novel about the city. I kept putting the subject aside in despair and trying something else, and failing with other things, too. One night my thoughts wandered away from their chores, and I began thinking about a friend of mine who had just died in office, as Philadelphia's first city manager. I wondered who might be appointed to the job. I ran the names of some well-qualified men through my thoughts and tried to decide if all of them would take the job if offered it. In each case, taking the job would mean his giving up glittering prospects in some business or profession in exchange for the dirt and uncertainty of politics. I realized that the decision would not be a simple one for any of the Philadelphians I had in mind, and that any decision would be affected not only by the man's own life but also by the lives of his Philadelphian ancestors.

Cigar smoke billowed beside my chair, and R. M. stood there, smirking at me.

R. M.: You will title your novel *The Philadelphian*. As the book opens, your hero, a man who is just achieving the material and social success in Philadelphia that he has fought hard to win, is offered a chance to run for District Attorney. That would mean giving up his nice corporation law practice and maybe losing his cool and lovely and very social Philadelphia wife. What will your hero decide? Every bit of his past life will influence his decision. The lives of his mother, grandmother and great-grandmother will affect what he does. His great-grandmother, Margaret, is an Irish girl who comes to Philadelphia in 1857 after the potato famines in Ireland, and becomes a housemaid in the home of a leading family. She and her descendants have a burning urge to get ahead in the world . . . and their whole world is Philadelphia. How do you like it?

ME (*Almost knocking* R. M. *down on my way to the typewriter*): I believe it will just about do.

This is, almost literally and exactly, the way I got the theme and basic plot for *The Philadelphian*. All through my adult life I had wanted to write such a book and had been thinking about it off and on. I'd been trying vainly to develop a theme and plot for a year, putting in hundreds of hours of work. Suddenly, in five minutes, the story blueprinted itself in the way I described. I'm sure that psychologists would smile pityingly at my story of a Reluctant Magician, and would point out that my subconscious had been working on the problem all this time and at last produced the answer. All right, let them talk about the subconscious; I'm a writer who likes to personify things and create characters, and it pleases me to substitute, for my subconscious, a tough little cigar-smoking gnome. When I have trouble writing, let the experts say I have writer's block; I prefer to blame the lazy habits of my Reluctant Magician.

This whole matter of how writers get ideas for stories is very complicated. Little has been written about it in textbooks, perhaps because it isn't a subject that lends itself to neat analysis. I know only three things about how to get an acceptable idea for a story. The first is that I have to work at it. Unless I seek ideas deliberately and actively, I get no ideas at all. Inspiration never comes uninvited to my door, and comes very seldom even when I beg and nag and coax and threaten and plead. The second thing I know is that I have to be very well informed on a subject before I can use it as the background for a book; if I ever wanted to write a novel about a doctor, probably I'd have to attend medical school in preparation for it.

The third thing I know is that the idea for a story has to excite me and keep me excited. Why does one idea do this and another fail? I haven't the faintest notion. Reluctant Magician has a pet idea for a story that he keeps trying to sell me whenever I need a new one. He knows that I think women's clubs are fascinating, and worth exploring in a novel. So he will materialize by my chair, crying, "Got a great idea, boss! Wait till you hear this! The background is women's clubs, see? There's this club that wants to put on a lecture program, and they write to a big lecture bureau for speakers. The first lecturer who shows up at the club is dark, handsome, suave, kinda mysterious. Now get this, boss. The guy is really the Devil, see, and he starts playing hell with all these women and . . . you're not listening, boss."

No, I'm not listening. R. M. has tried too many times to deal that one to me. In the past, I've actually carried the plot through many chapters, but somewhere along the way the excitement fades, and I give up.

R. M. has a lot of possible story ideas, like the women's club novel, that he keeps in his room. These are not ideas that he originated; he never originates an idea; I have to do this. I will get a few ideas for stories, and work on them with poor results, and tote the bedraggled things upstairs and leave them outside his door, perhaps with a note saying, "Will appreciate your comments." His usual comment is to throw the ideas out with the trash, but sometimes the idea for a story disappears, and I know he has kept it. I suspect that in most cases he drops it in a corner and forgets about it.

Back in the late 1940's, I left a story idea outside his room.

I'd been living in Fort Myers, Florida, and watched the development of a situation that interested me. The State Road Department built a bridge to nearby Pine Island, and in the process created some new land by filling in a wide causeway across shallow water. People began squatting on this new unclaimed land, and putting up little shacks and making a living by selling bait and renting boats and providing other services to fishermen. In a way, it was like frontier pioneering. I felt sure there was a novel in it, but after several tries I gave up and left the idea outside R. M.'s door. Eighteen years later—yes, *eighteen!*—R. M. appeared beside me in his cloud of cheap cigar smoke:

R. M.: I like the title *Pioneer, Go Home!* for that book.
ME: What are you talking about?
R. M.: That book about the Pine Island bridge. We have this family of New Jersey Pineys, see, who start some modern pioneering beside a fine new bridge in Florida, but they run into all kinds of trouble because nowadays Big Government doesn't believe in pioneering.

So, after eighteen years, I wrote the book. Fortunately for me, ideas don't always take so long to develop. In fact, the idea for my most recent novel, *Tickets to the Devil,* developed in a time span of about sixty seconds. I was relaxing in a chair reading a book on the bidding systems in duplicate bridge (I happen to be a duplicate bridge nut) when R. M. began kicking me in the shins:

R. M.: Why don't you get to work?
ME: I just had a book published. It's doing very nicely. I don't have to write another yet. R. M., did you ever play bridge?
R. M.: I consider it a sickening waste of time.
ME: No, it isn't, in my case. A writer needs to study human nature, correct? Well, a major bridge tournament is the finest laboratory for the study of human nature that I've ever found.
R. M.: Then you'd better write a bridge novel, and justify all the time and money you spend on the game.

The moment that thought was uttered, I had my next book. True, characters had to be developed, and their lives intertwined during a Spring Nationals of the American Contract Bridge League, but that part was easy and exciting. My head was already filled with notes about the fascinating people I had played bridge with and against, and my imagination had long been at work speculating about their motivations and their private lives. So the material for a bridge novel was already stacked up in my head. All that was needed was for R. M. to point to the material and say, "It's a book."

I hope he will do as well for me next time. In a little while, I will have to climb those steep creaking stairs again and pause outside R. M.'s door. I always listen for a moment or two before knocking, hoping to hear a distant rumbling that means R. M. is conjuring up thunder and lightning. My hopes, however, are not very high. Whenever I have heard distant rumbling from his room in the past, the source of the noise has been all too evident. I regret to say that R. M. snores very loudly.

4

PRIVACY AND PRODUCTION

By Peggy Simson Curry

PRIVACY, to the writer, usually means *place,* a corner where he may shut away interruptions of the world and do his work. In terms of production, he also relates to place, thinking of physical surroundings; if his output has fallen off, he complains that he lacks a room of his own.

Although a place to write is important, there is another and, to me, more significant concept of privacy and its relation to production: I refer to privacy of mind, that personal and secret room that too many beginning writers refuse to open. Here is the material that sometimes goes into the locked diary. And here is the material of the imagined dialogue, the monologue, and the many shapes, sounds and colors of the writer's conscious dreams. There are other things in this room of mind's privacy: memories of how a train whistle sounds on a rainy night; the color of March willows just before the green comes on; the texture of old wood under the fingers; fragrance of rose petals in a jar; shapes of roads and rivers and streets.

It is in this particular privacy that the writer confronts fear, sorrow, loneliness, hope, courage. Here, he comments to himself on people, places, ideas. And this is where he may laugh silently when he is hesitant to laugh aloud.

Sometimes, in this place of hidden emotions and thoughts, we examine those sweeping statements we make that are neither true nor reasonable. We may ask ourselves, "Now, why did I say that? Why did I get so angry I spoke without thinking?" And we begin to uncover our motivations.

All this secret material, pleasant and unpleasant, we don't bring out in casual conversations. It is seldom a subject for discussion with family and friends. Often it is knowledge we don't wish to share with anyone.

But in this realm of privacy of mind are fragments and whole sections of the most vital experience we have known. Because it is so vital, memory has preserved it for us. We add to it each day we live, for in privacy of mind, we are all uninhibited, and promptly and honestly record what we think and feel. There is no lack of material in this carefully guarded mental room. Indeed, if we were to fling wide the doors and let everything come pouring out, we'd have more material than we could possibly write about in a lifetime.

Why are we so guarded with the most valuable material we possess? Because it *is* private. We are not sure we want people to really know what we think and feel. Why lay ourselves open to scorn, ridicule, curiosity? After all, we can write without going *that* deep.

A question immediately arises: Is there a valid reason for exposing our guarded material? There is indeed—if we wish to consider a definition given to me years ago by a talented editor, Keith Jennison (at that time, with Viking Press): "A good book," he said, "should expose the privacy of the writer's mind and invade the privacy of the reader's mind." One may carry this definition on and say that the same should be true of a memorable short story, poem or article. Today's article writing demands all the techniques of fiction, and many articles may be given an added impact by a small private touch from the writer.

"Expose" and "invade" are strong verbs, but strong writing has always been in demand, and by strong I mean writing that involves the reader, challenging his imagination, stirring his memory, refreshing his mind.

If we wish to do our best writing, we must expose the privacy of our minds. We must attempt to get to our readers in such a way that they will become involved with what we've written. This is the best kind of communication, for it means participation —living *into* and *out of* what is read.

Today, as never before, people search for meaningful communication. Much of the entertainment offered us does not provoke creative participation. There is nothing to challenge our privacy of mind. As a result of this lack in the entertainment world, the literary magazines are flourishing as never before. This is simply because the unsatisfied person may go to such magazines and read stories, articles and poems that involve him, challenging emotions, intellect, and imagination. Such magazines are printing, as they always have, stories that expose the privacy of the writer's mind and invade the privacy of the reader's mind.

Nor is this kind of "deep" writing restricted to the literary magazines. In the "slick" or large-circulation magazines, we see more and more and more stories of the kind that used to appear only in literary publications. Such stories are neither casual nor surface writing. Their writers scorn the too-neat plot, the tired phrasing, the tidy ending. Instead, the authors are saying, "This is how life is. This is what life is about. This is the way people really think and act and feel." Even in the confession magazines, which I frequently study because some of my students write for them, I find a definite trend toward realism and realism of considerable variety. While in many instances the *way of writing* differs from the slick treatment, being less subtle and more emotional, the basic situations are very believable.

By way of summation of this brief glimpse at markets, we must recognize that people are demanding more meaningful fiction. Editors, keeping always the needs of the people in mind, are also demanding stories that have something worth saying and are saying it in the best possible way. Neither readers nor editors of magazines are satisfied with fiction that doesn't have the ring of truth. The best and most basic truth that you or I know is readily accessible in the privacy of our minds.

There is another realm of privacy of mind besides the one we have discussed. This one we scarcely know at all, except when suddenly it is revealed to us in dreams while we sleep or in sudden flashes of what we call intuition or inspiration. This mysterious and intriguing private kingdom is, of course, the subconscious. Here is the most significant material any writer can ever find. This we must learn to use, even as we use the surface privacy of our minds. We get to it more easily if we are willing to acknowledge the surface privacy of thought and emotion that we can easily recognize. We help ourselves to use it if we try to remember our dreams when we waken and try to understand them. Above all, we must learn to trust the subconscious. Many of us do this in our daily tasks. We say, "I won't make up my mind tonight. I'll sleep on the problem and decide in the morning." Or, "I can't handle this situation today. I'll set it back in my mind and forget it for a day or so. Then I'll look at it again." We should do the same thing when we hit a snag in our writing, trusting the subconscious to help us. Picasso best explained this in one of his best-known quotations: "When I paint a passage that is pretty, I wipe it out, and after a while it comes back beautiful."

Not only should we deliberately search our privacy of mind, but we should also be alert to any words or combinations of words that startle us to awareness. Once in my writing class, a student was reading a story so dull the class had lapsed into a state just short of coma. I struggled to listen, to keep my eyes open, silently scolding myself for not checking the manuscript before giving her permission to read and subject the class and me to such torture. Then I heard, wonderfully clear and sharp, a single sentence: "We were gathering wild fruit on the sand hills of Nebraska." I jolted awake. *Wild fruit!* Glancing quickly over the class I was astonished to note each of them was also awake and staring at the reader.

"Stop," I said to the reader. "I want to know why we all reacted to that line about gathering fruit on the sand hills."

"Because," one of my students said, "it catches my imagination. I'm glad she didn't say what kind of fruit. I just like to think of it as wild."

For a time we were quiet, each of us running through our private associations with the two words "wild fruit." Then the student who had been reading said, "I know how dull all the rest of it is. It took me so long to get to anything worth remembering—and I didn't especially want to remember it. We were so poor—other people got fruit from—from the store in town."

"That's what you should be writing about," I told her. "All the pride and pain and beauty connected with gathering wild fruit in the sand hills. Think of the tension in that single sentence, too— fruit in sand hills—not in the cultivated garden—fruit in dry country."

The next week we had some excellent reading in the class. I am certain it was because minds were jarred open by that one sentence, brought painfully out of the mind's privacy. I hope one day that student may be able to put down all that's there to be said about gathering the wild fruit. No matter how many technical mistakes there may be, her work will have a ring of authenticity that will make it worth revising into the best form she can achieve.

As for myself, I was grateful for her single sentence, for it opened a number of private doors that had been long closed. It gave me a lot of notebook material that will one day find its way into poetry or prose—or even into an article.

There still may be those who are reluctant to delve into the mind's privacy. They may hesitate because they think what they bring out will be shocking, foolish or even childish. I can only say that one *must take the risk*. Without taking such a risk we have nothing fresh or meaningful to say. We should realize, also, that no writer has ever lived who didn't at some time do work inferior to his best. It may be some consolation to know that brilliant people can say foolish things, too. For instance, the great Aristotle, whose works are still read and praised, said some foolish things. Children, he said, should be conceived in winter when the wind is from the north. He also declared that a pig was the only animal likely to get measles.

Remember, too, that while the most private experiences are traced as firmly and rhythmically in memory as the rings that form the age record of a tree, telling the seasons of its growth, you will never use these experiences exactly as they happened. The writer works and reworks his material in the light of his imagination, until the finished product is as near perfect as the writer can make it. Sometimes only a small seed of the original "privacy" of experience is left. And even that small seed is often so transformed as to become most impersonal in its setting. As writers, we offer the mind's privacy not as a monotonous recitation of self but as a projected creation that involves other people, other places, other worlds of thought and emotion. We give what we are away to our characters and in the very act of giving alter the original material into something greater than it was while we kept it captive. It is really the act of imagination that sets our private thoughts and emotions free. In this freedom they become more significant, more enduring, more memorable.

In writing what we know best, what is most private to each of us, we are offering the most meaningful experience we have known. And we are dealing with those basic emotions that men have dealt with through the ages—fear, love, joy, sadness, pity, pride. Handling emotions such as these is the challenge of a lifetime. Many people never find a way to handle them. We, as writers, have the privilege—and the obligation—of our writing. This is our way of defining ourselves and our existence.

In an article in *Harper's Bazaar*, architect Frederick Kiesler said, "The artist must learn only one thing in order to be creative: not to resist himself, but to resist without exception every factor that prevents himself from being himself."

By turning aside from exposing the privacy of your mind, you *are* resisting yourself, and you cannot be truly creative. Your privacy of mind, conscious and subconscious, is most genuinely you. You owe it to yourself to resist everything that might keep you from exploring this unique privacy. Out of it you have the best you can offer your reader. And while few of us will become great artists, we can all do the best we can with what we have. That's no small contribution.

Why not start now to use what is in your particular private world? By this rich and reckless exposure you may contribute to the enlightenment of your fellowman. Gather your "wild fruit" while you may on the "sand hills" that you know. The flavor of that fruit is in demand in the markets of the printed word.

5

AIM FOR THE HEART

By Paul Gallico

IF I wished to write a novel for my own edification, which really is just another way of saying for my own vanity—most of those books that writers are always telling you they are going to write someday just for themselves are indicative of narcissism—I suppose I could delve backwards into what was actually a reasonably happy childhood and find dark moments of anguish or self-induced terrors. I could manage to exploit weaknesses of my elders, sexual experiments, and produce an adequate panopticon of unpleasant subsidiary characters who frightened, harassed or disliked me at one time or another, or made me aware of my inadequacies, to be able to come up with a fair facsimile of what seems to be the modern novel and the aim of the young writer. It might even draw me one of those two-column, analytical reviews, or unwarranted praise.

But if I wanted to write a novel that would sell, I would sit down at my desk and try to think of some human and likable characters, for whose makeup I would borrow here and there from the personalities of people I had met—men, women and children—and I would then attempt to invent a situation that would try them almost beyond endurance.

I would endeavor to make you care deeply about these people, and hence I would have to care deeply about them myself first. In each one I would have to find some echoing chord of my own being: the kind of person I am, the kind of things I like, my fears, my hopes, so that these would be recognizable as genuine fears and hopes, the longings and appetites and the ambitions that might be found in any of us.

I would give these people spiritual strength coupled with near fatal flaws, good luck and bad, and a meed of cowardice, but a greater gift of courage. In the course of the trials I would prepare for

them, they would have need for all of these things and love besides—
love in the sense that it is the one emotion capable of mounting
guard over our natures. I would wish you to feel at one with someone, if not with several of the people in this book, to the point where
you entered into their adventures and lost yourself in them. And I
would try to tell my story and their story, and vicariously your story,
in such a way that once you began, once you had recognized yourself
in either the characters or the situation, you would not be able to put
it down.

I would want to tell you the story of people under adversity who
struggled and won or lost, according to their capabilities, but without too great an emphasis on victory, so that those who lost might
even be thought to have won something beyond those who seemed to
triumph.

It would be a story of man against nature, or man against man;
man the supreme being on earth, or man the infinitesimal speck. But
a story it would be, with a beginning, a middle and an end, and at
that end, after you had followed with me the travail and strivings of
these persons, I would hope that I would leave you not quite the
same as you had been before you started. That is the kind of book I
would try to write, if I wanted it to sell.

"Wanted to sell"—or just "sell" alone—has a harsh sound and
some of the stink of the market place.

Yet to sell is what the honest writer wants to do, to sell to earn a
living to feed his family, or even for the pure satisfaction of selling,
of having written something good enough to cause the largest number of people to reach into their pockets and give over money they
have earned, for the privilege of spending some hours alone with
characters and narrative that the writer has created.

The highest form of flattery comes not from the reviewer, however
erudite or complimentary he or she may be, but from the man or
woman unknown to you who enters a bookshop, finds and fingers a
copy, tests a page or, listening to the bookseller tell what it is about,
says, "I think I'll have that one," and produces his wallet.

It is possible, I know, to do this today in many other ways—by
writing the kind of obscenity one only used to see on privy walls; by
lifting the lid on human sewage pits and letting the reader look
within at the horrors; by rewriting some well-known human folly or

personal disaster into fiction form. But the great storytellers of the past never needed these, nor will the great storytellers of the future. To sell, it is only necessary to capture the human imagination and touch the human heart.

Fashions in fiction come and go, but the storyteller will never go out of date. I remember when I was a young man and sold my first stories to *The Post*, I was summoned for a visit with its great Editor, George Horace Lorimer. Several of these were sports stories, and Mr. Lorimer said that the magazine had a great need for these and hoped that I would fill it. And I remember remarking, even through my awe of the great man, that I wanted to play Hamlet. He eyed me and said, "And what form does your Hamlet take?"

I said, "Stories with a d-d-different b-background, sir, not just sports—newspapers, circuses, other things. . . ."

When I had finished stammering, he said quietly, "Young man, I'll tell you something. I don't care what background you decide to use, just don't forget to tell me a story."

Around ancient campfires, or at court, the jester with the dirty joke could make them laugh for a few moments, but it was the storyteller who had his listeners spellbound, whether he twanged his lyre in song or spoke in poetry or prose of heroes who overcame great odds, and of lovers whom not even death could part.

The anti-hero is the prototype of despair. The hero flings aloft the banner of hope. The storybook ending isn't life, but life often enough provides the storybook ending to make it worthwhile to tell about. If we thought that there was nothing but misery, degradation and darkness and above all perpetual defeat, what would be the use of trying to feed or clothe ourselves, raise children, and put a penny by to purchase a book to refresh one's spirit and fortify one's hopes?

It isn't easy and everyone can't do it, but everyone can try. Tell a story in which you believe, about people with whom you sympathize or admire. Tell it simply and enthrallingly, and the pile of your books on the bookstore counter will melt away like the snows in spring. Aim for the heart.

6

WHEN THE WRITER
COMES OF AGE

By B. J. Chute

THERE is no royal road to maturity for any human being, and most certainly I know of none for the writer. Coming of age is not a chronological matter; it is a lifetime process. Fortunately, there are signposts along the way, and the signposts that guide the writer are really no different from the ones that guide everyone else.

The process of writing, like the process of growing up, is one of accepting, testing and rejecting, of "holding fast that which is good." It is a process of infinite curiosity, a seesaw process of vast enthusiasms opposed by discouraging failures. For a writer, as for anyone, there are days when anything seems possible, and there are days when everything seems hopeless. Gardeners know this feeling very well. The lawn, the flower bed are full of crabgrass and a multitude of weeds, and many things done once are all to be done over again.

The first thing one learns is that this is not nearly as wasteful a pattern as it appears to be. Out of the nonsense, wildness and despair, there is always left the fine growing ground which we label experience. Experience is a dull word; another dull word is discipline. I am going to use both.

I have very strong feelings about discipline, and especially about self-discipline. I have not found life at all permissive, either in the day-to-day process of living it or in the strict professional process of being a writer. This is no contradiction to my other strong feeling, which is that life should be enjoyed. I am also a firm believer in daydreaming, wasting time, staring into space or leaning against a wall while watching the snails whizz by. There are certainly times when one's mind should be as open, empty and placid as a millpond. Who knows what attractive bugs will come to skitter on the surface, or what wonderful white whales of the imagination will rise from its depths?

But self-discipline means doing one's work and doing it to the top of one's bent. I need hardly add that this often involves simple drudgery. There is no way to avoid it, whatever profession or calling you enter. There is drudgery in housework, in office work, in acting, painting, writing; it cannot be avoided, and the habit of self-discipline is the habit of doing what has to be done, even when dull. At any age, the ability to dodge disagreeable tasks comes naturally. I am not suggesting a permanent state of high-minded activity. I am merely urging you to avoid that intellectual curvature of the spine which results from lounging on the back of one's mental neck.

Mental discipline is like physical discipline. It becomes easier through practice. Any athlete knows that the first aching clumsy use of untrained muscles eventually gives way to flexibility and control. The mental muscles behave in the same way, so that knowledge, sensitivity and capacity all improve through exercise.

I need hardly say that other people's exercise will not improve *your* muscles. Here, the intellect has some advantage over the physique, since other people's knowledge can enlarge yours. But only if you use it. We are the heirs of and contemporary to worlds of experience so vast as to be limitless, but these are ours only through our own effort. Therefore, my next piece of advice has to do with what Langston Hughes meant when he said, "Listen fluently." This is an art which enlarges art; it is partly objective and partly subjective.

It is an objective art when it is derived from the world around you. In a recent book by Pamela Frankau, she writes, "There must come a time when . . . all your mirrors turn into windows." I could ask for no better definition of coming of age. When we are young, we are surrounded by mirrors, and wherever we turn we see ourselves. As we grow up, the mirrors dissolve, and the windows that replace them set our horizons free. We learn to see people as they see themselves, to understand the complexity, the shifting, the lights and shadows of other people's lives and emotions, and through understanding them to understand, in some measure, ourselves. We realize that nothing is as simple as it looked in the mirrors, but that everything is far more wonderful. And finally we learn the most marvelous truth of all: that, in the last analysis, we can never know the whole truth about anyone or anything, but that we are, like Tennyson's Ulysses, a part of all that we have met.

Now, necessarily, everything I have discussed so far applies to any kind of coming of age; but, since I am a writer, I would like to relate it to the specific problems of my own craft.

I never consciously planned to be a writer. I never pictured short stories in magazines with my name on them; I never imagined books that I would have written. I wrote because I wrote and, I suspect, also because I read omnivorously. (I will come back later to that splendid subject.) I was blessed with a grounding in grammar so solid, so stern, so basic that I have never had to think about the structure of the language at all in the purely grammatical sense. I learned it the hard way—by endless parsing, by drawing diagrams, by rote, by drill. If there is another way in which to become so firmly and surely rooted, I do not know it. I suspect there is not. Grammar is to a writer what anatomy is to a sculptor, or the scales to a musician. You may loathe it, it may bore you, but nothing will replace it, and once mastered it will support you like a rock. I have no quarrel whatever with the writer who breaks the rules of grammar intentionally, but I have a quarrel with the writer who breaks them because he has not been willing to learn them properly. The English language deserves more respect.

I learned something else from learning grammar. I learned not to mind working hard for the sake of control. I learned not to trouble myself about what appeared to be wasted pages, if through the producing of them I moved closer all the time to the thing I wanted to say in the way in which I thought it should be said. I am a confirmed re-writer. There is no especial moral virtue in re-writing; it merely happens to be my particular way of achieving an end, and if you can get your results on the first try, more power to your pen! What matters is not to be afraid of doing the same thing again, and again, and then again, if that is necessary. A writer will never be judged by his private vision, only by what shows of it on paper. It is no use sitting around admiring one's mental processes, however enchanting they may be. The reader is not sitting around in any such admiring state. His posture is "Show me!" and he is quite right to insist.

I can speak of drudgery casually, as a part of a writer's task, because I have learned there is no evading it. When I have finished a novel, taking it through as many drafts as needs be, to the point where I am almost satisfied, I expect to sit down at my typewriter and do the whole thing over once more from beginning to end, so that the words suit my ear, the effort to communicate has become the best effort of which I am capable, and the courtesy due the English language has been given to it as completely as I can. This is not a sign of nobility, but it is a matter of pride. I have no wish to encounter in print words I have written that should have been written better, and there is something very immovable about that thing called movable type, once the printer has locked it up. There is no time for reconstruction after the words lie in the bound book.

I began my writing career as a sports writer in the field of short stories for boys. I had no particular aims except to tell a story, in action and dialogue and description. I can look back now and see the growing process that took place, but I did not see it then. I could have gone on doing the same kind of writing for a professional lifetime, and I could probably have made a satisfactory living from it, but somewhere inside of me there lay a strong instinct to experiment.

The company is too noble for me, but I knew very well what John Keats meant when he described the experimentation of his new poem, *Endymion:*

I leaped headlong into the sea, and thereby have become better acquainted with the soundings, the quicksands, and the rocks, than if I had stayed upon the green shores, and piped a silly pipe, and took tea and comfortable advice.

George Bernard Shaw put it more acidly:

A man learns to skate by staggering about making a fool of himself. Indeed he progresses in all things by resolutely making a fool of himself.

I did not offer my own results in the public marketplace, because I did not need to be told what I was doing wrong. I threw them away, generally forgot them; sometimes, the effort would remain to plague me, to be taken up years afterwards when I had the skill to do what I had early wanted to do. These things will wait. The currently impossible, if one keeps on growing, becomes the possible, the probable, and at last the achieved. I urge you to be patient and to persist.

I have always loved language; I have always loved style. I had a serviceable enough style, founded on good grammar. I had an ear trained by reading, so that at least I knew when I was wrong, if not always how to make it right. I had a strong sense of respect and affection for the tools that help a writer to write well. But, above all, I think, I had the wit to know that it was no use forcing myself into writing more effectively unless that effort went hand in hand with having something to say.

So I wrote, for quite a long time, stories for young people—stories about football, track, ice hockey and almost every other sport. Later, I moved into the field of adult fiction—boy-meets-girl stories and stories about young married life, which were purchased regularly by major magazines and were very popular with their readers.

And then, one day, I wanted suddenly to write a story about a ten-year-old boy whose Air Force pilot brother had been reported missing in action. I wanted to write about how a child in a child's safe world felt when he was catapulted into a dangerous adult world of loss and misery and fear. There, for the first time, I tried something which I had not tried before, and which later became a necessary way of working for me. I consciously sought the style which would mirror and encompass the thing itself. Straight action writing was impossible; the requirements of this story were subjective, inner. The story idea, for the first time in my writing career, demanded of me an entirely new way of writing.

I remember that story as being exceedingly difficult to write, and I also remember it as being curiously exciting to write. I found I could do things I had not expected to be able to do, and I found that I knew why I did them and why they were right. It was not a particularly original idea for a short story, but, when I finished it, no one except myself could have written it in just that way. Someone else could have done it and made it his story (and perhaps a better one), but I had done it in my way, an invented way, if you like, and it was particularly my own.

It was called *Come of Age,* and I sold it to *The Saturday Evening Post.* It was not the first adult story I had sold, but it was the first time I had plunged into an entirely new way of writing, and ever since it has been my way.

By that, I do not mean that subsequent stories were written by me in that style. I mean that I had found it possible to seek out my own individual way for each story and, later, for each novel. It is just as difficult for me to do now as it was then, perhaps more so. The difference is that I have slowly acquired the skills, the techniques, and most of all the understanding that make it, if still not always possible, much more probable.

When I wrote a novel called *Greenwillow* and, later, one called *The Moon and the Thorn*, I needed everything I had learned, and then I had to learn even more than I thought I needed. Both novels depended entirely on mood and manner of telling. Both first chapters nearly defeated me, and I remember the problem of *Greenwillow* with these depressing statistics: I wrote the first chapter sixteen times; the first page, more than thirty times. *The Moon and the Thorn* was almost as exasperating, but I wrestled with it as patiently as possible, since I knew that, in each novel, the opening chapter would set the tone for the whole. If I could get this right, I would be—if not on safe ground—at least not adrift, and I used up yellow paper with a fine frenzy that must have cheered the corporate hearts of the yellow paper manufacturers. (Parenthetically, yellow paper is a boon and a blessing; it is so easy to tear up, so expendable. I recommend it to you as the most prudent extravagance in the world.)

I have not arrived as a writer; I will never arrive. No writer really does; we only travel. But I have learned that, however elusive or difficult the dominating idea of a story, there is some way to put it into a form that approaches achievement.

There is one other writing problem I would like to mention briefly: the problem of success. If you wish to write, there is only one kind of success possible. It has nothing to do with money or reputation. The only success worth having for a writer is to put on paper what you have wished to put on paper. There is a wonderful story told about a small child who watched a sculptor working on a slab of marble. Day after day, the child watched, and the sculptor worked. And then, at last, there came a day when the child drew in his breath and looked at the sculptor in amazement and said, "But how did you know there was a lion in there?"

That is success for a writer. To know there is a lion in one's mind, and finally to produce it. Compared to that, money and fame are really very negligible returns.

Now, I want to revert to that one subject I only touched on earlier: reading. Reading is only another way of "listening fluently."

My first advice to any would-be writer is that he read—creatively, passionately, chronically. I am impatient with the idea of sugar-coated reading. I do not believe in padding about timidly in the tepid waters of the merely entertaining, the placidly simple. Reading is a joint creative process between writer and listener. It is a multi-level process, more than mere ability to recognize and interpret words. It is also more than mere familiarity with contemporary fiction or a dutiful sampling of the classics. The real reader needs to have a mariner's knowledge of those myriad minor writers of past centuries who compose the vast ocean of literature.

Some writers of the past are not easy to understand. They speak in idioms not always clear to us; they reflect ways of life that are now alien. They make heavy demands on the reader to respond to their strangeness. The ear complains, "But this is old-fashioned"; the mind replies, "It was modern once." Even the classics sometimes fall heavily on the senses, and after a few chapters one's attention falters and lags, and it is tempting to say, "This is not for me," and turn to the familiar.

I think part of the trouble here rises from the theory that one is a reader because one has learned to read. One would not think of himself as a tennis player because he had mastered the elements of tennis playing, or as a skier because he was able to go downhill without collapsing in a snowbank. We willingly train our muscles to the mechanical difficulty of a powerful serve, to the controlled rhythm of stem turns, but we do not as willingly train our minds to follow the involutions of an unfamiliar way of writing. This is a pity. Batting a ball earnestly back and forth, going downhill soberly and arriving upright—this is neither tennis nor skiing. They are both exciting sports, and we work hard to become adept in them so we can know their real excitements. Yet what Baudelaire called "the heavenly mechanics of the mind" is the source of an infinity of excitement, compared to which Wimbledon and the Alps seem very small indeed.

I know readers whose whole literary world seems to be related to the so-called "modern" literary world. They are experts on the Twentieth Century of prose and poetry, widely read, subtle; but, except for the great mountain peaks of Shakespeare, Homer, Dante (the names that leap to the mind), they have none of that accumulation of reading which would illuminate, broaden, deepen every modern book they read.

I think we often fail to recognize how a wide range of reading enlarges literature. Let me take two quotations from Shakespeare, a writer with whom we all have a bowing acquaintance, to show how one kind of writing, even the greatest, can be affected by all the other kinds.

The first, from *Antony and Cleopatra,* said of the great Egyptian queen herself, beautiful in death as she was in life:

> . . . she looks like sleep,
> As she would catch another Antony
> In her strong toil of grace.

This is a marvelous bit of poetry, in and of itself. You need not be deep-rooted in literature to know that. But suppose your reading roots *do* go deep, so that the description of Cleopatra wakens within your mind a memory of other beloved women stricken by untimely frosts—Villon's "Flora, the lovely Roman," Tolstoy's achingly tragic Anna Karenina, Robert Herrick's country girls like daffodils. For the wide-ranging reader, who is not intimidated in his reading, a host of perilous and immortal women join hands. Where are the snows of yesteryear, if not imprisoned forever in the minds of the "fluent listeners"? The color from each spreads to the others, and the passage from Shakespeare, most beautiful in itself, is made more beautiful through association, through links and echoes.

The second quotation, then, from *The Winter's Tale.* A small boy is invited to tell his mother a tale "of sprites, and goblins." He is an artful storyteller, and he begins magically:

> There was a man . . .
> Dwelt by a churchyard: I will tell it softly,
> Yond crickets shall not hear it.

This is the perfect invitation to the listener, hushed, mysterious, full of shadows. The immediate echo it wakes is the childhood one of "Once upon a time." But for the skilled reader other echoes cry like bells, calling us to come, to come and listen. I think of a modern chime in that wonderful line of Scott Fitzgerald's—"Draw your

chair up close to the edge of the precipice and I'll tell you a story." I
think of the legends and the ballads—"There dwelt a man in fair
Westmoreland," "The king sits in Dumferling town." I remember
that deceptively simple opening of Dickens' which pulls us into the
world of his Curiosity Shop: "Although I am an old man, night is
generally my time for walking." And I am even moved to remember
the harsh, dark texture of *Beowulf*, which in high school I studied so
resentfully, only to know now that its granite lies in the pit of my
mind forever.

Neither writer nor reader can quite talk of coming of age until
these echoes and links begin to crowd into the mind. George Eliot is
too alien, too Victorian? She is one of the most modern and civilized
writers on earth, with a sharp wit and a broad compassion and a
capacity to translate life that you will pass by at your peril. Chaucer's Middle English makes him unreadable? But his *Troilus and
Criseyde*, though written in poetic form, is one of the finest psychological novels ever written, and Criseyde is as enchanting a woman
as ever a great poet loved.

Stretch, I implore you, in your reading. The words are unfamiliar
to your ears? The passions are foreign to your own? Reach up to
them; do not wait until they reach down to you, because they will
not. When Horatio said, "But this is wondrous strange," Hamlet replied, "And therefore as a stranger give it welcome." Leap to your
place in reading. Bruise your mind, fracture your old ideas, stretch
your muscles until they shriek in protest. I offer you no sympathy. I
offer you, instead, the kind of delight that comes from effort, a delight you will never have unless you step out dangerously.

What I am saying then is, simply, that the mind grows in use. "Art
was given for that," Robert Browning tells us. "God uses us to help
each other so,/Lending our minds out."

Discipline and experience cannot be separated from the whole
bright process of coming of age. Every writer, every reader, indeed
every human being, knows in his heart that he has a capacity for
growth that would astound a redwood tree. In one sense, none of us
ever comes of age—not at twenty-one, not at fifty-one, not at ninety-
one.

But, oh, the journey! And I wish you Godspeed.

7

THE MAGIC OF WORDS

By Richard Powell

Of course it will never come true, but I keep having this dream in which the President of the United States sends a message to Congress demanding civil rights for words. In it, he points out how badly words are abused, and calls attention to the fact that our language is a national resource that is being mistreated even more than our rivers and air. It is only a dream, however, and I do not look for the War on Poverty to be extended to the spoken and written word.

The trouble is that the poverty pockets in this case are too hard to get at, because they are not in city slums or Appalachia but inside people's heads. People are willing to use their brains on many difficult problems—avoiding income taxes, beating the horses, sneaking an extra coffee break—but apparently most of them couldn't care less about the problem of how to use words clearly and dramatically. Among these people are scientists, educators, lawyers, government officials, doctors, businessmen and housewives.

Is it possible that there are also writers among them? Yes, friends, there are writers among them.

Let us skip the problem of writers who do not know how to use words clearly. Nobody can help them, and perhaps the published writers among them do not even want to be helped, because a murky style of writing may sometimes win critical acclaim. Let us, instead, take up the problem of writers who use words clearly but with no more impact than that of a wet dishrag dropped on the floor. There are many such writers. They may do a fine job on plotting and characterization, but they handle words like a cook ladling out alphabet soup: the first collection of letters that comes out of the pot goes into the dish. Here is an example of alphabet-soup writing:

I got up this morning as happy as a lark and, as usual, ate breakfast like a horse. I sat at my desk and worked like a mule all day and ended dog-tired.

38

I have given you a lot of information about my day, have I not? I have also given it clearly. But how many people would be interested in hearing about my zoological day? I have used words that bored you stiff and were dull as dishwater, including the expressions I used in this sentence. I have used old worn-out groupings of words. I have used words in a lazy, thoughtless way, picking up expressions once new and shiny, but now so overworked that they have no power to hook reader attention. The sad thing about this is that there is magic in words when they are used with a touch of imagination. What I should have done, if I wanted anybody to pay attention to a very ordinary collection of facts, was to call on the magic of words. Perhaps I might have written:

When I got up this morning I felt like the bubbles in champagne, and breakfast tasted as if I were just coming off a diet. I spent the day beating a typewriter ribbon to rags, and ended as tired as the clichés I was trying not to use.

Now I have dressed my dull facts in bright clothes, and so people might pay attention. I have thrown out my collection of zoological clichés and developed some new expressions. A cliché is an expression that, when it was new, sketched a vivid picture for people. The first man who used the expression "dog-tired" no doubt impressed his audience; they would have pictured how a dog looks when he is panting and his tongue hangs out and he flops down. But, with use, the term dog-tired lost its force. Nobody who reads or hears it for the tenth or hundredth or thousandth time gets a vivid picture from it. It has become a cliché. It is now merely a crutch for lame brains; it is a mental sleeping pill. It is a way to avoid thinking. There is no word magic in a cliché.

I don't want to pretend that, when I developed some new expressions to replace the zoological clichés, I simply made a flourish and pulled them out of a hat. In the first place, I wouldn't pull them out of a hat because that's another cliché, perhaps invented soon after the first magician pulled the first rabbit out of the first hat. New expressions do not come easily to me; my brain is lazy, too, and approaches the idea of work like a teen-ager asked to do the dishes. But I have learned that if I play the harsh parent with my brain, it will go to work, even though grudgingly. It took me an hour to work out those new expressions, and if I had spent two hours on them they would undoubtedly be better. I don't advise writers to spend an hour on every sentence they write, because they might never finish a story or article. But, when you need to grab attention, you must spend time and thought on the job.

It is not difficult for a person of normal intelligence to write in a colorful and dramatic way. One summer, several years ago, I taught a writing course at Syracuse University. Included in the homework I assigned were some problems in colorful writing. I explained to my students that one method of colorful writing is to describe Item A in terms of Item B: for example, describe a mountain as if it were a living creature. (It could be an old lion crouched in the distance, or a vulture hovering over the valley.) None of my students were professional writers, and none had previously known any tricks of colorful writing. But, when given a method of doing it, they produced such examples as these:

A. (*Describe a young girl, at her first dance, in terms of another type of living thing.*) "Jane sat in the small gilt chair beside the dance floor, thin, angular, unmoving, eyes carefully blank, legs straight out before her like knobby stems. She seemed as much a fixture as the potted palms."
B. (*Describe a society matron in terms of another type of living thing.*) "Mrs. Cheyney was, he thought, like a faded rose, even to her hands with their thorns of fingernails."
C. (*And the same.*) "Mrs. Culpepper looked for her name in the society column, eager as a St. Bernard sniffing at a hydrant."

This is good writing. It is professional. Anybody who can do this on demand could have a successful career in some form of writing. The trick of describing one thing in terms of another is much used by good writers. Carl Sandburg wrote a complete poem by using this trick merely one time. The poem contains six lines and twenty-one words, and has been reprinted in many anthologies of American poetry. It is titled "The Fog," and Sandburg described the fog as if it were a cat.

Some years ago, in writing a story, I wanted to describe gulls flying, and I wrote of them in terms of ice skaters: "Gulls figure-skating against the sky." This happens to stick in my memory because *Reader's Digest* used my words on its "Picturesque Speech" page and paid me ten dollars, the first of many delightful checks from the magazine and Reader's Digest Condensed Book Club. While writing this article I wanted to see if I had exhausted the ways of describing gulls in terms of something else, and I came up with these descriptions:

The gulls went tobogganing down the snowy clouds.
The gulls did a waltz in the ballroom of the sky.
High up, a gull wheeled and curved, writing a message against the blue paper of the air.

This experiment seems to hint that there may be as many ways of describing gulls in flight as there are gulls.

When does a writer use such colorful expressions? Always? No. That might be like a steady diet of fruitcake. Colorful writing is used to create a needed effect—perhaps of mood or atmosphere or character—and when the effect has been achieved, it is a waste of time to do it over and over. Nor should colorful writing be used merely to show off. It must contribute to achieving the writer's purpose in his piece of fiction or article or poem or speech or whatever. I would not use colorful words to describe the ringing of a telephone bell, unless I needed to create a certain mood; if the mood had already been created, I would simply say that the telephone rang, and then get on to more vital things. But if the call was going to be important and I had to get the reader into the right mood for it, I might write:

I reached for the ringing telephone as if getting my first lesson in snake charming.
The telephone bell echoed in my head like a dentist's drill.
The telephone bell made a little apologetic murmur.
The telephone jingled pleasantly, like an old hurdy-gurdy.

Each of these sentences contributes to the establishment of a different mood or atmosphere. They could not be used interchangeably.

The same method, of course, can be used in describing people. In my novel, *Don Quixote, U.S.A.*, I wanted to describe my hero's physical appearance, and at the same time create a mood and tell something of his character. This called for colorful writing and for the expenditure of several hours of mental sweat to produce two sentences. As I say, these things do not come easily to me; getting them out of my head is often like trying to shake the last dime out of a piggy bank. After four hours, I had these two sentences:

Mine is not the grim strong face of the typical Goodpasture. Such a face is spare and angular, as if welded from steel plowshares, whereas my features look as if they had been hastily whittled out of balsa wood.

In those two sentences, I provided a good deal of information about my hero's physical appearance, the family from which he came, and his character. I doubt that it would have been interesting to readers if I had merely written: "All my family have strong grim faces, but mine is rather weak and nondescript."

Another way to write colorful language is to exaggerate to achieve an effect. It is not very striking merely to write that somebody is thin. If you want to create a dramatic effect, use exaggeration. Draw a word picture of how thin the person is. For example:

She was so thin she could have taken a bath in a fountain pen.

He was so thin he could have lurked behind a needle.

He was so thin he could have crawled through a pencil sharpener . . . and with a pencil in his pocket, too.

In trying to make magic with words, however, it is wise to beware of the adjective. Nouns are good words to use in sentences. They are like bones, providing the needed skeleton. Verbs are good words. They are like muscles, providing the action. But adjectives are in most cases merely the clothing or ornaments of a sentence, and it is easy to overdress a sentence. Let me quote the beginning of a famous speech, and count the adjectives in it:

Friends, Romans, countrymen, lend me your ears;
I come to bury Caesar, not to praise him.
The evil that men do lives after them,
The good is oft interred with their bones;
So let it be with Caesar.

How many adjectives in those opening lines of Mark Antony's speech? Shakespeare didn't use any.

So, in trying to put magic into your words, don't think that a piling up of adjectives will do the job. One well-chosen adjective may be perfect, like a diamond ring on the hand of a pretty woman. Too many adjectives may be like too many diamond rings: not only does the display seem crude, but also it may hide the fact that the woman has lovely fingers.

Words should be a source of never-ending mystery and delight to any writer. All of us should be forever curious about how words were invented and evolved and what they used to mean and what they mean now. Another term for a cliché is a hackneyed expression. Think a moment about that word "hackneyed." Do you know how it originated? Well, back in the days of horses and carriages, a horse that was kept for hire was called a hackney. Such animals were over-worked, and were often tired and slow and thin. Somebody started applying the term to phrases that were also tired and slow and thin: hackneyed phrases. When first used, the term was colorful, and called up a picture in the reader's mind. But how good a picture does it evoke now?

Are you the sort of writer who can look up a word in the dictionary without ever being lured into looking up others? Can you run across such words as "boycott" without digging out the sad tale of Captain Charles Cunningham Boycott? Can you hear the term "halcyon days" without discovering the pleasant old Greek myth from which it comes? If you are not fascinated by words, I feel sorry for you, because you must find the use of them a dull and tiring job. To make magic with words, a writer must know what they mean. And, if he hopes to use words in a new and colorful way, he must be able to recognize the old drab ways in which they have been used.

Words are like Cinderella: sad little drudges, wearing rags and dirtied by soot. It is in the power of writers to play Fairy God-mother, and make these drudges into shining creatures. Words can sing and dance, growl and roar, tiptoe and march. They will do all these things for any writer who is willing to wave the magic wand of his imagination over them.

8

CHANGES AND CONSTANTS IN A WRITER'S LIFE

By Margaret Culkin Banning

One of the great satisfactions—and sometimes boasts—of a writer is that he belongs to one of the few privileged professions which has no fixed retirement age. He can write as long as he wants to. He does not have to fear the exposure of footlights or the ambitions of younger men in the office. But he has a problem of time nonetheless. Will he be read as long as he wants to be read, which is, of course, as long as he continues to write?

The established writer of historical novels does not have to worry about this. Fiction material is practically inexhaustible in the chronicles of the past, and a writer who can make bits of it come alive in the imagination of readers has a permanent audience. But the fiction writer who deals with contemporary life is in a far more precarious situation. He can be trampled into oblivion by changes in social interest, variation in habits of living, an increase in public tolerance, and by new methods of presentation of stories.

This can happen very fast, and it does happen, even to talented writers. Suddenly a novel, as well-written and well-organized as the author's last successful novel, fails in the market. Readers are not interested in it. The writer can hardly be blamed if he is resentful. He will argue to himself and to his publisher that he is writing as well as he ever did, that his theme is sound. He is probably right. But the probability is that he has lost contact with contemporary life, and argument or scolding will not bring back his readers.

If a writer wants to write about today's world, he must keep in touch with it. He must understand the mood and taste—also the lack of taste and indifference to it—of those with whom he wants to communicate. I personally think he must like the world he lives in or he had better not try to write for it. He does not have to approve of all

44

its habits, and he may endeavor to have a hand in changing some of them. But basically he must have sympathy—empathy, at any rate —for the world which contains his audience.

If he wants to write about contemporary life, he must be aware of the influences that are playing upon people, the causes of their immediate excitements and interests, and the subtle changes in ambitions. He must go along with the questions in the public mind, the new exciting experiments, the bewilderment. None of these things has ever been static, but they have changed incredibly in the last fifty years and at a rate of speed which accelerates every day. The fiction writer must quicken his own pace of observation.

I do not think that a writer should search the horizon for contemporary problems, choose the one that is farthest out or most publicized and try to write about it. He should choose the situations in which he is personally interested, about which he has some special knowledge, or with which he has a natural link. Most important of all he should try to relate change to what is constant, both in the needs and emotions of life and the needs and desires of readers. This is one of the great responsibilities of a writer of fiction or nonfiction, and especially now, when so many people want something to tie to and doubt that there is anything strong enough to hold them fast.

It is embarrassing to be personal. But it is impossible to deal with this subject without being autobiographical. I only know my own experience. I have written and been published without too many defeats for nearly half a century. During all that time I have hewed to a few interests that were important to me but constantly changing. These were politics at all levels, the relation and adjustment of women to their domestic and career lives, the problems of laymen in the Catholic Church, such as their attitudes toward divorce and birth control, and what used to be called social service.

Obviously each of these basic subjects must be considered today in a completely different environment from that of the thirties. I wrote a great many political stories in the thirties and forties and most of them were published in *The Saturday Evening Post*. They would be too pallid and too unsophisticated to interest today's reading public, which has been hardened by continual war or threat of war, has developed deep international interests and has turned from the political rally to the often erudite television panel discussion.

The novel which I am writing at present touches on how modern industry is affected by political strategy, and I must be well enough informed to be sure my facts are up-to-date in my fiction.

Social service, when I first wrote about it, was just emerging as a profession. It was always a good subject for fiction because there is an element of heroism in it. But it has become over the years a far more profound subject and wonderfully dramatic. I wrote a novel a few years ago called *The Quality of Mercy,* which tried to show the changes from a casual personal charitableness to the days of riots and the efforts of statesmen everywhere to build a great society. This is becoming the most important thing in the world, and I have watched it become important. That would have been impossible without taking a small personal part in the growth.

What has happened to women's share of life since I began to write is almost incredible and continually fascinates me. In the early decades of this century, a woman who worked outside her home, unless she was in domestic service, the schoolroom or a sweat shop, was an oddity. A divorce was a scandal. A woman supporting a husband or a family was a pitiable creature. That has all changed. I wrote a novel called *The Dowry* not very long ago on the theme that a woman today is apt to bring her husband, not a featherbed or a farm as a dowry, but instead, her earning capacity. And I wrote frankly that this is useful and necessary, but it arouses competition and jealousy and resentment in a marriage. This belongs in today's fiction because it is true. But in that same book my characters showed—I hope— that love is as indestructible as it ever was in the past, when women were usually homebodies.

When my publisher suggested that I should write a novel on birth control, nothing could have interested me more, for I knew the obedient attitude of some Catholic women, the rebellion of many young Catholic wives, and the reasoning of those Catholics and non-Catholics who believe in the necessity of planned parenthood. It was a truthful story, and because this was one of my books which the Reader's Digest Condensed Books published, it was translated into many languages. I was not writing about the same bigotry that I had dealt with in *Mixed Marriage* thirty years before, although I was writing about the same Church and the same devotion to it.

In each of these cases I have gone along with change and progress as well as I could and as fast as I could, not because I wanted to sell a piece of fiction but because the subjects involved were part of my life, up my own street. None of it was deliberate and heaven knows I do not state this with the slightest vanity. My forte has been to keep up with the times. But I know that many writers become more profound by ignoring the passing scene and studying only the eternal verities. What a writer does must depend on his temperament and, of course, on the circumstances of his life.

Nonetheless, all fiction writers have some things in common, some constants that they must respect. They must tell a story. The subject may be contemporary, but its treatment must never be a thinly disguised tract. If you cannot make your characters do the work, say what must be said, quarrel, suffer, try for solution—and do all these things believably—it does not matter whether you are abreast of your times, behind them, or avant-garde. The good story is the indestructible core of fiction and that has not changed through the centuries.

Your characters must be believable enough to make the narrative credible. This is not quite so easy to achieve as it used to be—and it never has been very easy—because the readers of today are in no mood to be soothed by unlikely happy endings. If the ending of your story chances to be happy, your characters have to prove to a pretty skeptical public that happiness is possible under the circumstances of today. Probably no reading audience has ever doubted this more.

The only way to do this is to convince yourself of it in the first place. I have seen—and here I go with autobiography again—several wars at close range, watched their terrible aftermaths, known poverty and wealth. I have been scorned by many cynics. But always I have seen happiness rear its head somewhere. Joy has harder going than it did in a simpler society, but it is indestructible. Even the young people who are most confused chant that it is what they want most. There is certainly a waiting audience for a fiction writer who is great enough to tell such groups a truthful, satisfying story and give them the lift of believing in the possibility of fidelity and love.

Readers have never been so hungry for stories or for reader identification with fictional characters. Why did *Night Falls on the City*, a novel of wartime Vienna, rise to the top of the best seller lists? Not because it is history, although it is that, but because the woman who is the central character loves and suffers, and the readers go along with her, knowing that is the way life is. Here there is loss of happiness but that does not deny its existence. Why do terrible tales like *The Thousand Day Week* and *The Night of the Generals* reach great audiences? It isn't because of the cruelties they reveal but because the characters are often capable of tenderness and love among horrors.

Fiction writers today have an obligation to tell the truth. That obligation has been growing more binding during my long writing life. Their eyes must be clearer than ever before, and the eyes of good storytellers more penetrating. The task of fiction writers is just the same as it has always been, to swing the imagination of readers into the lives of other people. But not now for escape from reality, rather for better understanding of it. The reader must live in the world as it is, a violently political world, a social world that is undisciplined to the point of being disorderly, a world that is critical of religion but cannot leave it alone. The writer must live in the same world as the reader and not deny nor falsify any part of it. His hope must be that he can interpret it fearlessly and with complete understanding of both change and permanence. He has never had better material to work with or such great possibilities of usefulness.

9

A MAP IS NOT A JOURNEY

By Phyllis A. Whitney

It is of course a truism that a teacher cannot teach without learning from his students. The eleven years I spent teaching juvenile writing at New York University were rewarding to me in many ways. I found that as I talked about the techniques of writing, I was put on my mettle as a writer and made increasingly aware of weaknesses in my own work. In the give-and-take of the classroom, shared experience encouraged and improved us all. But for me the most important thing to come out of those teaching years was the development of a method of work so useful that I have been able to step up my own writing output and improve its quality at the same time. This method has proved useful to other writers as well as to me in avoiding that occupational disease, the "dry spell," and any writer can adapt it to his own individual needs.

A word first about the sometimes controversial matter of a writer's productivity. Some editors and critics and other non-writers in the book trade seem to regard it as slightly disgraceful if a writer has written a large number of books or stories. They claim that if the author wrote less, he would write better. I don't believe this is true and find any attempt to keep writers from writing "too much" regrettable, and possibly even harmful, since this would discourage the writer from what is his real business—putting a great many words on paper.

In this connection, I like something John Creasey (the prolific mystery story writer who has more books published every year than any other author) once said during a radio interview. He pointed out the fact that in order to learn his craft an actor acts, a composer composes, a painter paints. Everyone in creative work improves by "producing."

As we write we learn. For one thing, we gain a facility with words.

From a state of wooden awkwardness, where our thoughts outrace our ability to express them on paper, we develop a skill for saying what we mean. Gradually, we may even come to say it with some grace, as we come to have a keener appreciation of the versatility of the English language. This learning should go on for our whole writing lives. We cannot do justice to our craft unless we spend a great deal of time writing. Reading and learning from other writers is fine —as far as it goes. But putting enough of our own words on paper and examining them critically is the best way to improve all aspects of our writing.

Still, there are times when the words won't come. What happens when we want very much to write, and the well fills so slowly that a steady flow of words seems impossible? This was my own experience in the beginning. Fortunately a solution to the problem was forced upon me.

When I began teaching, I was a one-book-a-year writer and had published some six or eight books. Before long the students in my classes began to ask how I worked on a book—a question I found embarrassing. My "planning" of a book amounted to keeping a folder in which I dropped odds and ends of characterization, bits of narrative, stray story ideas, as they occurred to me. There was never enough of anything, and it was never at my fingertips. When I got to the writing, I was always faced with long blank periods in which my story would not move, simply because I was not yet ready to write it and had no idea how to push the work along. A great deal of time was wasted and I did not seem able to speed up the process. The fact that I was working slowly did not mean that I was doing more careful, painstaking work. It meant that there were gaps when I did not work at all. Blank sheets of paper remained blank for long stretches of time.

In order not to lose face with my classes, I decided that I had better develop some sort of sensible plan for writing a book —something I would not be ashamed to tell others about. Of course it had to be practical, and it had to work for me. I began with a simple, commonsense organizing of my working time and my material. I gave up the idea that I must spend my three hours a day of creative work at my typewriter actually writing. As my plan began to grow, I realized that I had to do a great deal in those working hours before I was ready to put a word of the story on paper. Only when I had planned *thoroughly* would words flow with ease. Since I had been a non-planner, this took some reconditioning. I soon found, however, that being able to keep busy on the progress of the book, whether I was writing or not, was a wonderfully comforting thing. The dry periods vanished and eventually my actual output of words was more than doubled. At that time I was doing one juvenile book a year, of approximately two hundred pages. Now I do, each year, a 200-page juvenile and a 300-page adult suspense novel as well.

Sound planning, I quickly discovered, pays off in stepped-up production and elimination of blank spaces of time in which nothing happens. The organization of a notebook was the main factor in helping me to achieve this increased output.

The novice is eager to start writing much too soon. In an excellent book, *How to Write a Novel,* Manuel Komroff says this:

> The experienced novelists know that to launch out on an idea that is only half conceived will prove disastrous. The inexperienced writer plunges in quickly and often manages to write several good chapters before the story begins to wither and die. In such instances the creative flight is broken because of incomplete preparation.

The notebook, with which I started out some fifteen years and thirty books ago and am still using, is a loose-leaf binder with big rings that will hold a thick stack of pages. I prefer paper in the 5½ x 7½ size. It is simpler to handle than large sheets, tucks into a pocket or purse if I want to carry a few sheets around, and is easier to fill in pencil script—as I often like to do during the planning period when I "think" with a pencil. For my indexing, I purchased some good-sized linen tabs, attached these to some divider pages, and was ready to organize my new plan for writing a book.

It is a flexible plan even now. Sometimes I discard labels because I've grown away from using them. Or I insert new labels for sections that now seem more valuable to me. It is simply a commonsense plan for organizing one's work. Each individual writer can fill in his own variations and take the direction that most appeals to him. Probably most professional writers develop something of the sort for themselves, but the novice who is tackling his first book may not know where to begin.

I will simply list and explain the labeled sections of my own note-book, and if you're interested, you can take it from there.

My first label is *Work Calendar*. This is important because it shows me my target dates as well as where I am in my schedule at any given period along the way. Here I set down a six-month sched-ule, with definite dates. Perhaps I will start the active plotting on November 2 (ideas were of course stirring around in my mind, even while I was working on the last book). I allow myself two months and no more for the plotting, with December 31 as my deadline. An-other two months for the writing of the first draft—say to the end of February. Revision and typing of the manuscript to be completed by the end of March. And more revision in April after my editors have read the story. (While they're reading, I get busy on initial planning for the next book.) The dates I set down never run exactly as I intend. Sometimes the plotting goes faster than I expected. Often, when my plan is right, the writing takes less time than I counted on. Revision may take more time than usual. But in any event, where I should be, and where I actually am, are set down, and nothing serves as a better spur for not falling behind and wasting time.

When it comes to the actual writing, I draw a line down the center of my calendar pages and enter in the left-hand column exactly how many pages I should write each day for some two weeks ahead. My writing speed runs about eight pages a day at 250 words a page, though when all is going well, I may write ten or twelve pages. In the right-hand column, I enter the actual number of the page I have reached on this particular date, and the approximate number of words written. Thus I can keep a stern eye on whether or not I lag behind schedule.

I also play a sneaky little psychological trick on myself in this calendar department. I ask of myself only five days' writing time each week (about three morning hours for me), but I actually work six days a week, which keeps me nicely ahead of schedule. However, I've learned not to plan more than two weeks at a time, because sooner or later the writing falters, and I borrow from my revision time and start rereading what I've written from the beginning and working it over. This gives me the impetus to continue when I reach the sticking place, and I can usually get over the hump. Sometimes I can write for a straight month without any difficulty at all. But I've

never gone all the way through without stopping for revision somewhere. If I know a great many things are piling up wrong behind
me, I feel better when I go back.

The next section is *Title Ideas*. If I hit a blank period in plotting,
I turn to titles: I study *Bartlett's Quotations* or read poetry which
may help. Sometimes getting the right title will open new windows on
my plotting and produce all sorts of new story ideas.

The next heading is *Chronology*. Here I list the dates of historical
events that may have a bearing on my story so that I can be sure of
having things happen at the right time. On a second page I list the
actual time sequence of the story action as it develops in each chapter. This is a little trick that saves me much confusion later on. By
the time I reach Chapter Five I may not know what day of the week
it is, or how many days or weeks have passed since the beginning. I
may not even know whether a scene can be set for night or morning,
unless I keep constant track of where I am, timewise, in each
chapter.

The next section is a double one: *Situation* and *Theme*. My first
entries when it comes to plotting are usually under *Situation*. Here I
state in some detail the difficulties that have brought my heroine to
the situation she is in—or is about to be in. This has to do with past
action and enables me to be sure of what has happened before the
opening chapter. Characters don't spring into being with nothing but
the present to live in. Unless you have a situation of conflict, or rising conflict that is already in motion, you will have nothing to lead
you into a story.

Under *Theme* I talk to myself about what I am trying to say. In
the beginning I am seldom sure. Significance, meaning, grow out of
character, and before I write I need to know what my characters are
going to learn, how they are going to grow—or deteriorate. A story
that says nothing leaves the reader with little satisfaction.

Problem is a most important section. It is one I have added in
recent years. At first I took it for granted that the heroine's problem
would automatically appear under other headings. Often, oddly
enough, it didn't. There were *problems*, yes. Most of my characters
were stirring around in a mess of trouble, but all too often that trouble was not the primary trouble of the main character. Her emotions
might be engaged, she might be sympathetically involved in the

troubles of others, but the big life-or-death struggle to solve a problem, beat the adversary, avoid disaster, and win through to victory (which is what my heroines, both adult and juvenile, must do) was not specifically *hers*. This serious weakness, by the way, is a common fault in many stories that don't come off. Not only must the heroine be faced by a serious problem: We must go one step farther and make sure it is one she can *do* something about. If she doesn't *take action*, fling herself headlong into *working* toward a solution, the going will be pretty dull.

Theoretically, I suppose this is something we all know. Yet in every book I write I face the difficulty of putting the problem on my heroine's doorstep and finding a way to put her into action in order to solve it. So now I have a section in which I deal with *Problem* itself and all that is inherent in that tricky word.

Development is one of my most useful headings. Often I will wind up with sixty pages or so of random notes jotted down concerning all possible angles of the story as they occur to me. At first these ideas may be unrelated to each other, but I never let the slightest item get away. Its value, or lack of value, cannot be judged when it first appears. Sometimes I can spend an hour or more simply jotting down bits and pieces that occur to me haphazardly. Choosing at random from my current plot pages I find such entries as this:

> Make it a long raincape with a hood. Navy blue, dark. Get it into the story earlier. Maid sees.
>
> Leila has notion that by doing the things Catherine did she can keep her alive. This can take on a sense of the eerie as Jessica watches.
>
> Get in something about Catherine's sensitivity to pain.

These are short entries. Others go on for pages and do just what the label says—*develop* my story. When I come to the outlining of the book I return to these pages every day, reading a few of them, scratching out what I can discard, or anything I am able to place in my outline. Otherwise, the whole thing becomes unwieldy and I lose track of good ideas.

Next we come to an obvious department: *Characters*. First, as the people emerge from the original plot situation, I choose and list my characters' names. These are often changed until I can feel they are right and won't conflict with one another. After that follows an individual full-length sketch of several pages for each character. These sketches are not a mere listing of possible traits. They show the characters-in-action, expressing themselves about other characters, stating their individual likes and dislikes, clarifying their "goals." These sketches bring the characters out of the "type" class and turn them into individuals whom I will know thoroughly before I begin to write. These character sketches grow constantly as I work and are often drastically changed and improved.

Now one of the advantages of this notebook system becomes evident: I am going to spend two months, three hours a day, on planning my story—in my mind and in rough pencil jottings in my notebook. This is the point at which I used to waste time because the story wouldn't move. But when I have a notebook full of sections that need to be filled, there is always something to do. As I write about a character, a wonderful plot idea occurs to me and I jot it down in the *development* section. As I make plot jottings, a new idea for a character, or for my theme, or for any of the other sections, may pop into my mind. I can easily fill the three hours of planning time moving about in my notebook. That blank feeling is gone.

Eventually, when my story has begun to emerge to quite an extent, and my characters are pretty well worked out, I begin to *Outline*. This section begins very sketchily at first. I can't plot a mystery (or any kind of story) from a standstill position. I can develop its complications only bit by bit. Thus my first outline may consist of putting chapter numbers down on several pages, with only a couple of inches of space between. I know that something or other is going to happen in Chapter One, and in the space allowed I set down words that are clues to the action; note something that might happen around Chapter Four, and again I enter a few clue words. Perhaps there will be a beach scene in Chapter Eight, but all I know about it now is the one word "beach," so I set it down. Making this sort of arbitrary arrangement of action and possible settings gives me something to build on, though I may change it completely before I'm through. Gradually this skeleton begins to fill up with action "clues," usually many more for the beginning part of the book, since I am not one of those who thinks from the climax backwards.

When there seem to be enough such clues in the early chapters, I begin a detailed outline of the action for these chapters. I write deliberately in present tense so that I won't feel that I'm writing the story. I spend sessions lying down thinking, "watching" the action, then I get up and outline. By taking plenty of time for this part of the story planning, I can iron out a lot of the difficulties that would otherwise arise to plague me later on in the writing. Sometimes I outline in detail all the way through. Sometimes I don't need to write as completely about the final chapters, because the early outline makes the rest of the story become so clear in my mind that only jottings are needed to keep me on the track.

My next heading is *To Be Checked*. This is merely an aid in keeping track of all the unanswered factual questions that keep cropping up as I work. There are always things I must ask about or look up. I must not forget any of them.

Additional is a section that saves me a lot of grief once I am actually writing. The best rule of keeping production high is not to keep going back every day over all that you've written. I reread only the pages I wrote the day before, in order to gain a push into today's writing. But I am apt to find while writing Chapter Three that an important change or addition needs to be made in Chapter One. Instead of going back to make it then and there, I enter a note about the needed change in this section and go back to it later when I get to revision. Usually I have several pages of this very important and easily overlooked material before my book is finished.

Bibliography is just what it says. A list of the books I have read during my research. I may need to know where I have been.

Research is a section that varies, depending on the story background. If I am writing about South Africa, for instance, I may need a separate notebook for material on that country. (Three writing hours in the morning, remember, but the rest of the day is for all the other chores that beset a writer.) Currently, I have in my research section several pages of notes about disturbed teen-agers, a page or two about skin diving, and a lot of information about shells. The section may contain anything at all that might be of use to me (and if it gets too full I move it over into another book).

We're getting toward the end. Under *Background* I list scenes I may use in the story. When I've made a trip to some unfamiliar place, I keep a list of specific places I visited in Rhodes, or Istanbul, or Charlotte Amalie. When I am outlining a book, I find it helpful to run down this list for possible settings of specific chapters. Of course I have more detailed background notes, made in a pocket notebook at the time of my actual visit to a new place.

Last of all—and sometimes this is left empty—is a section I've borrowed from Manuel Komroff's book, previously mentioned. I label it *Diary*. If I am faced by a character who refuses to come to life, I sit that particular character down at the typewriter and let him talk to me in first person, as if keeping a diary. He can tell me anything he pleases—what he thinks of the other characters in the story, what was going on in his mind during that last scene I put him into, or what plans he has (unknown to me!) for future action. This little exercise always serves to get me under the skin of a balky character. Thank you, Mr. Komroff!

There are some outside helps as well that keep this notebook work moving steadily ahead. I keep a number of small slips of paper handy wherever I am, and on these I enter all the questions about my story that I can't answer. In the beginning there are dozens of these. As I find the answers, I throw the slips away. Such a listing gives me specific things to think about and keeps my mind from skittering all over the place during the times when I "just think."

Sooner or later I may have an irresistible urge to start writing. This usually comes long before I am ready. But when it comes, I give in to it. I know very well that I won't get far, but I will at least bring my characters onstage and thus see them more clearly in action. So I go to my typewriter and let the opening pages run along as they like. By about page five or so, I've had enough. The urge has been satisfied, and I'm content to go back to my planning. In the meantime, I may have written a good opening scene that will help me over the self-conscious moments of getting a new book started.

Of course the moment the book is finished I take out all my notes and file them away. Then I put in a stack of clean empty sheets and I'm in business again for the next book.

This then is my plan for organization as it has evolved over the years. When I had tried it out for a year and had written two books using it, I began to present it to my writing classes. Some of the students adapted it to their own use. By now it is one of the most popular lectures I give when I teach at a writers' conference.

To the writer who recoils from the slightest suggestion of planning for fear he will take the "edge" off his writing, let me point out that a map is not a journey. When it comes to the actual writing, there will be all sorts of pleasant surprises never dreamed of in the planning stage. But if you leave New York, heading for Boston, at least you will get there with a map. You won't wind up in Miami instead and find that you must retrace your steps and start all over.

10

FOLLOWING ONE'S INSTINCTS

By E. B. White

STUART LITTLE, himself quite a traveler, came into being as the result of a journey I once made. In the late Twenties, I took a train to Virginia, got out, walked up and down in the Shenandoah Valley in the beautiful springtime, then returned to New York by rail. While asleep in an upper berth, I dreamed of a small character who had the features of a mouse, was nicely dressed, courageous, and questing. When I woke up, being a journalist and thankful for small favors, I made a few notes about this mouse-child—the only fictional figure ever to have honored and disturbed my sleep.

I had eighteen nephews and nieces. As a young bachelor-uncle I used to be asked now and then to tell a story. At this task I was terrible. Whole minutes would go by while I tried to think of something. In self-protection I decided to arm myself with a yarn or two, and for this I went straight to my dream-mouse. I named him Stuart and wrote a couple of episodes about his life. I kept these stories in a desk drawer and would pull them out and read them on demand. As the years went by, I added to the tale. Book publication never crossed my mind. These were the golden days before television, when children got their entertainment not by twisting a dial but by twisting an elder's arm.

In 1938, having decided to quit New York, I began tidying up what I called my "affairs." One of these was the Stuart Little adventures, now grown to perhaps a dozen episodes. At the suggestion of my wife, I carried them to a publisher (not Harper) and left them, to see whether they might be acceptable if expanded. The answer came back No, and I left for Maine, taking my rejected child along.

Seven years later, in the winter of 1944–45, I returned to New

York to spend a few months in a furnished apartment and do some work for *The New Yorker*. I was almost sure I was about to die, my head felt so queer. With death at hand, I cast about to discover what I could do to ease the lot of my poor widow, and again my thoughts strayed to Stuart Little. My editor at Harper's, Eugene Saxton, had been urging me to finish the narrative, and I determined to put it off no longer. Mornings I sat at a top-floor window looking out into West 11th Street and there I completed the story. I turned it in to Harper and then took a train for San Francisco, to join Stettinius, Molotov, Lawrence Spivak, and that crowd, for the formation of the U.N. Another springtime, another journey!

Harper accepted the book, and Stuart was off at last, after a pardonable delay of some fifteen years. Garth Williams was brought into the enterprise and began turning out the drawings that were to give shape to my diminutive hero.

A few weeks later, back home in Maine, a letter arrived for me from Anne Carroll Moore, children's librarian emeritus of the New York Public Library. Her letter was long, friendly, urgent, and thoroughly surprising. She said she had read proofs of my forthcoming book called *Stuart Little* and she strongly advised me to withdraw it. She said, as I recall the letter, that the book was non-affirmative, inconclusive, unfit for children, and would harm its author if published. These were strong words, and I was grateful to Miss Moore for having taken the trouble to write them. I thought the matter over, however, and decided that as long as the book satisfied me, I wasn't going to let an expert talk me out of it. It is unnerving to be told you're bad for children; but I detected in Miss Moore's letter an assumption that there are rules governing the writing of juvenile literature—rules as inflexible as the rules for lawn tennis. And this I was not sure of. I had followed my instincts in writing about Stuart, and following one's instincts seemed to be the way a writer should operate. I was shook up by the letter but was not deflected.

Stuart was published in October, and other surprises were in store for me. Miss Moore's successor at the Library had some misgivings of her own about the book, and Stuart met with a cool reception. He got into the shelves of the Library all right, but I think he had to gnaw his way in. The press, to my astonishment, treated the book almost as though it were adult fiction. The daily *Times* gave it a full-scale review by Charles Poore, who praised it. Malcolm Cowley, in the Sunday *Times,* said it was a good book but disappointing— should have been better. This exactly expressed my own feelings about it.

A couple of days after the book appeared, Harold Ross, my boss at *The New Yorker,* stopped in at my office. His briefcase was slung over his shoulder on a walking stick and he looked unhappy. "Saw your book, White," he growled. "You made one serious mistake."

"What was that?" I asked.

"Why the mouse," he shouted. "You said he was born. Goddamn it, White, you should have had him adopted." The word "adopted" boomed forth loud enough to be heard all down the corridor. I had great respect for Ross's ability to spot trouble in a piece of writing, and I began to feel uneasy. After he left the room I sat for a long while wondering whether Miss Moore had not been right after all. Finally I remembered that Harold Ross was not at home in the world of make-believe, he was strictly for the world of 43rd Street, and this cheered me and revived my spirits.

My next encounter was with Edmund Wilson, who stopped me in the hall. "Hello, hello," he said, in his wonderfully high and thrilling voice that sounds like a coaching horn. "I read that book of yours. I found the first page quite amusing, about the mouse, you know. But I was disappointed that you didn't develop the theme more in the manner of Kafka."

I thanked Edmund and wandered back to my room to chuckle at the infinite variety of *The New Yorker;* the editor who could spot a dubious verb at forty paces, the critic who was saddened because my innocent tale of the quest for beauty failed to carry the overtones of monstrosity. What a magazine. There's never been anything like it.

Despite the rough time the author was having, Stuart himself seemed to be doing all right. The book drew generally favorable reviews, and by October 24th Harper had sold 42,000 copies.

The next thing that happened was that three fellows turned up claiming that *their* name was Stuart Little, and what was I going to do about that? One of them told me he had begun work on a children's story; the hero was a rat, and the rat's name was E. B. White. I never learned how far he got with this splendid project, but I know he phoned Ursula Nordstrom at Harper's to alert her.

The real returns came when letters began arriving. Some were from children. Some were from teachers. They expressed pleasure, along with a fairly steady stream of abuse about the book's ending, which fails to tell whether Stuart found the bird. The letters have not stopped coming. Of the many thousands I've received, only two, I believe, questioned the odd fact of Stuart's arrival in this world and the propriety of an American family's having a boy that looked like a mouse. After twenty years, I am beginning to relax.

I learned two things from the experience of writing *Stuart Little:* that a writer's own nose is his best guide, and that children can sail easily over the fence that separates reality from make-believe. They go over it like little springboks. A fence that can throw a librarian is as nothing to a child.

11

ON WORDS

By Rumer Godden

Words are in my blood: my great-great-grandfather was Professor of Comparative Grammar (Philology) at the University of London.

He wrote, too, a book *Languages and Their Origin,* and I like to think that a little of his love of words has come down to me. It is this that drives me to make this plea for words, because it would seem that their values are in danger of being lost.

I am not, here, writing of journalists whose work is meant to make an immediate effect and then be forgotten, nor am I writing of poetry which safeguards itself, because if a poet loses his sense of words, he is no longer a poet, and cannot practise. I am writing of the serious novelist whose book, he hopes, will last for a little span at least, will bear rereading, even be read over and over again, be reprinted, find new editions. That is what every novelist hopes of every novel—but does he earn this love and respect?

Novels can be written helter-skelter in shoddy English full of clichés, and have a temporary success, but they seldom last. If books were Persian carpets, to assess their value one would not look only at the outer side, the pattern and colourings, one would turn them over and examine the stitch, because it is the stitch that makes a carpet wear, gives it its life and bloom. The stitch of a book is its words.

It seems obvious to say that a book is made of words, but is it quite as obvious to say that it is the words that make a book? Yet this is true. It is in its words that its ultimate value lies. Authors fuss about looking for ideas, but ideas hardly matter. There are very few of them anyway; it is the way they are told that makes a book original, and it is here that words play their extraordinary part.

The words in novels meant to be taken seriously should, of course, be good English, and more than that: They should "belong," bind together to make a whole, because through every good book runs an

integral and unobtrusive rhythm (if it is obtrusive, it is overdone)
a rhythm made of words. This English should be fresh (slang, if it
"belongs" in a novel, can be transformed into good English), original, free from cliché, as if this particular eye had seen freshly, this
ear caught something new, even in old, old situations. The reader
feels the power of this unconsciously. As I have said, if he is conscious of it, the writing is overdone. It is the writer who must be
conscious of every word, weighing and feeling each one, trying as far
as he can to predict its power. Words are unpredictable because one
never quite knows their effect until they are read or heard in context.
"Words, unfortunately, have meanings," said Tagore. They have
more than that; shades and shades of meaning—and countless
shades of sound.

Once upon a time, all books were meant to be read aloud; then for
a long while only children's books fell into this category; now, with
the increasing number of books read on radio, or adapted for television, this need for rhythm in sound is becoming recognised again;
but the writer should always have had an ear for these shades, as he
should have a mind for the infinite variations of meaning.

This has always been recognised as a poet's pre-occupation—his
perpetual battle with shades of sound and meaning—but it extends
to prose as well, and a writer who never explored words, never
searched, seeded, sieved, sifted through his knowledge and memory,
his dictionaries, the thesaurus, poems, favourite paragraphs, to find
the right word, is like someone owning a gold mine who has never
mined it, someone living near a mountain who never walks to the top
of it to see the view, someone putting his gift into a cage when it
might fly free. Yet so many writers today do just this.

Why? I think there are several reasons. The chief one, to me, is
the speed at which much writing is now done. Many serious authors
work directly onto a typewriter, and the typewriter is too fast for
thought, except for a few inefficient creatures like myself who type
painfully with three fingers; the typewriter is too fast, the dictaphone too easy. It is not possible to brood in thought with either of
them, and a writer needs to brood. No one can advocate going backwards in time, but it is a sobering thought that every new invention
to make writing easier—each tempting tool—has taken us further
away from thoughtfulness, from appreciating our heritage of words.

Once we wrote with quills, which meant always breaking off to sharpen them—"I have to mend my pen"—and every writer knows how doing something with one's hands, not mechanical but manual, releases thought. Sharpening pencils had the same effect, but now we have gadget pencil sharpeners. The pen came after the quill, but a pen that had to be dipped, that at least needed the nib changed. All these small needs made pauses that gave valuable time in which to think. The pen became the fountain pen—even that, now and again, ran out and had to be filled. Now we have perpetual ball points and the typewriter and dictaphone.

Another robber has been simplified spelling, though I expect no American will agree with this, but to me "color," for instance, has not the same weight and richness as "colour"; "center" is more diffuse than "centre" with its tightly coiled ending. A proof of what has been lost is that a great many writers will not understand what I mean by these differences; they will neither see nor hear them; and here, too, one has to indict the magazine "house style": an edited style to which all its writers must conform. Take the word "grey" or "gray." One magazine that I know will allow only the first, yet "gray" is not the same shade as "grey"; one can write "gray eyes" with truth, but "gray twilight" is unpleasing, even wrong—it must be "grey twilight." This is not fanciful thinking. Words were originally chosen to fit the things they describe, to give the essence of them, often onomatopoeically. Think of the word "shadow" with the harder first syllable, the open "a" rising to the "d," then falling away with the soft "ow" with its longer sound. It gives the feeling of a shadow, as does the French word "ombre," again with the falling away of the soft "bre." The expressive beauty of certain words runs through all languages; one akin to "shadow" is "twilight": twilight, crépuscule, crepusculo . . . "dämmerung," which seems to glimmer.

It is paradoxical that magazine editors spend large sums and much energy to find writers who are unusual, have a new flavour, and then proceed blindly to destroy much of their subtlety by making their style conform. This conformity, this editing, is creeping into book publishing even more disastrously (not my publishers, thank God).

Jargon, too, has spread like a miasma over modern writing: technical jargon from psychiatry and science, pressurized jargon from advertisements; pep jargon from radio and TV commercials. You—Americans—invent turns of phrase that are original—and horridly memorable. They certainly put new vigour into English but they are boomerangs: They come back and hit the word that has been so invigorated that it often loses its intrinsic meaning and becomes a parody of itself. The true writer is continually having to rescue words.

This does not mean of course that only the odd words are acceptable. Language is a living thing, and all that lives must grow and change. I believe there are over 20,000 new words waiting for admittance to Britain's *Oxford English Dictionary*, which with its 450,000 words is the biggest in the world. Some old words fall out of use, but every year there are more. That does not mean the writer has to use more—to be called "wordy" ("verbose") is always to be condemned—but it does mean that the writer has to be more discriminating, and it is precisely in his choosing, his judgment of these shades, and the fine-tuned power of his eye and ear, that his value as a writer lies.

> Words are living beings
> Held within your spell;
> All of them are chosen,
> Guard them very well.

(Translated anonymously from the German of Martin Beheim-Schwarzbach.)

12

A WRITER'S SERMON

By Storm Jameson

Two or three years ago I was asked to help a young English writer, author of one book, a volume of short stories, to get a so-called travelling fellowship offered by a generous patron of letters. I was happy when he was awarded it—that is, I was happy that he had not been disappointed. About the principle of travelling fellowships for the very young writer, and all such aids to beginners, I am far from happy. Nothing could be more delightful than a year's free travel when one is very young. And perhaps, if the chosen young man—the choice rarely falls on a young woman—is able to turn himself into a camera walking down the street (in a phrase that was more fashionable in the experimental thirties than it is now), watching people, recording gestures, looks, scenes, and listening to the familiar talk of strangers, his year will not, humanly speaking, have been wasted. Perhaps, too, it will have the additional advantage and merit of postponing for a year the moment when he sits down, with pen or typewriter, to begin writing his novel.

This sounds frivolous but is meant in dead earnest. For one genius, one writer born, who writes as naturally and inevitably as a bird sings or a tiger kills, an uncounted number of talented young writers are ruined by the haste with which they rush into authorship. Almost any device which serves to delay them is an unmitigated good.

I am almost ready to add that any device—such as a degree course in creative writing—which serves to hurry them on their way, and make it seem a pleasant respectable way, is an unmitigated evil. I was once, for one gloriously happy year, the most incompetent teacher of creative writing in the United States. I had not the haziest idea how a genuine professor teaches the subject (and never had time to find out, because my ignorance forced me to spend all day "tutoring"—that is, talking to—each of my pupils separately). My total inability to train them in the acrobatics of writing had at least a negative merit—I did not do any damage.

But surely, someone cries at this point, writing is a trade *like any other?* This is one of the platitudes we all utter at least once in our lives, and assent to, happily, without reflection, when we hear it. And if it meant no more than that a writer must work at his job at least as hard as any other serious craftsman, it would be harmless. The harm, the illusion, lies in the words *like any other.* The trade of an artist is not like any other. A baker who makes superlatively good bread and brings it to the notice of the public is 99% sure of making a modest fortune. A writer's superlatively good book has no certainty, none at all—not even if he is also a superlative self-advertiser (though this helps)—of bringing him in a living. We all know this, *and we do not draw the necessary conclusion,* which is that a young man (or a young woman) must be either a hero or a madman to bet his whole life on such a risk. The folly of starting too soon is only less heroic (blind, reckless, ignorant—choose your own adjective) than the rashness of starting at all. I am not talking cynically; I am only saying (in effect) that the forces and circumstances which have turned the highly individual craft of writing into a vast industrial enterprise, heavily capitalised, employing an immense army of editors, publicity experts, professors of creative writing, and, by a strange necessity, writers (who, unlike the other labourers, are paid by results, like commercial travellers on a commission basis) are, on balance, a public and personal disaster.

If I had the moral courage, I should have said to the young man I helped to his travelling fellowship: "Take your year abroad by all means. But use it to learn a language or two, which will fit you to take a job as consul (like Stendhal), or a schoolmaster (like Mallarmé), or a foreign correspondent (like X, Y, and Z), and write your first five novels in your spare time, and God be with you. You may have the luck to make a killing with your very first book (like Norman Mailer), in which case God be even more with you, because the pressures that will be applied to you to do it again make a child's toy of the thumb screw. To resist them will demand greater will power, a cooler head, than most young writers possess."

Let us suppose that you have arranged your life so prudently that you need not hurry to finish a book by five o'clock next Wednesday, but can take your time. What, even before you sit down to write, is the first discipline you ought to teach yourself? (The word *discipline* is the correct one, since there is or should be a good deal of the monk in your make-up.) Not—believe me—not how to begin, how to end, how to use dialogue: these are skills you must dredge out of your soul for yourself, if they are to be sound. No—the first thing you should have guessed is that there is no value in the emotions, the spiritual writhings, started in you by the sight, smell and touch of your fellow human beings. You cannot avoid having emotions about them, but you can avoid boring us with them. To analyse your feelings for our attention is inexcusable clumsy egoism. When I catch sight in the novel I have just opened of a paragraph beginning, "It is difficult to say what my feelings were when I . . . ," I shudder and close the book hurriedly.

And direct analysis of the feelings of your characters is just as clumsy. Tell us what they did, what they said, and (not too often) what they thought, and from that let us infer the state of their hearts and minds. If you will take the time to read, slowly, Pasternak's *Doctor Zhivago*, you will be astonished how seldom, in this long, subtle, and subtly emotional book, he tells you anything directly about the emotions of his people. Yet their feelings are as vividly present to us as their looks and background. I am not saying—it would be evidently absurd—that no great writer ever indulges in the prolonged unravelling of an emotional web. There was, after all, Proust. I am saying that it is a weapon for the hand of a genius. If you who are reading this happen to be a genius, stop reading at once: you can look after yourself and you are a law unto yourself.

There is another good reason, apart from the probability that you will bore us, why a great deal of self-indulgent chat about your characters' emotions will be an error. The task of the serious novelist today is quite hideously difficult and complicated, demanding of him the greatest breadth of knowledge with the greatest clarity and skill in compression. His essential concern is with men and women *in their times*. He has to portray, as vividly as he can, a social landscape, a social climate, which seems to dwarf the human beings moving about in it. This is one of the moments in the history of our planet when what is personal to a man is no more important than the fears and hopes, the impulses he shares with a great many of his fellows. I do not mean that the task of the serious novelist is to write only or directly about the danger we all lie under of mass suicide, or about communism, or about the need for God. Heaven forbid! But I do mean that unless he is sharply aware of these things, unless his ears are always open to the frightened or clamorous voices coming from every corner of modern society, he cannot even write honestly a simple novel about two young people who fell in love, married and had children. Jane Austen could ignore entirely the dark impulses to murder which exist in all our hearts, because these were on the periphery of her comfortable world. We, unless we can remember their existence even while we are writing about spring and babies and calf love, had better give up writing and take to gardening or jam-making, harmless and honest occupations.

The convulsive movements going on everywhere now, wherever we turn our eyes, form the harsh country of the contemporary novel. Whether we notice it or not—but the writer *must* notice it—something which is essentially a revolution has started. In the old trite phrase, humanity has struck its tents and is on the march God knows where. In one way or another, the meaning, the energy, of this revolution must lie behind the novelist's simplest words. Or else he is not telling the truth about life in his time. This has nothing to do with putting politics in the novel, nothing to do with propaganda. Propaganda—that is, deliberate propaganda—is one use for words, but it is not the artist's use of them. And politics is only one of the activities of men and women. If it appears in a novel, it must do so not as politics but as a human impulse, expressed through passions and deeds, part of the great net in which men and women work, suffer, rejoice, and die, like fishes in water.

There never was a moment in the history of the human race so baffling to the novelist, so abominably exacting. The novelist does, or ought to do, something more than draw characters in action. Before he even begins to write, he has to form a conception of life and human nature—that is, he has to be able to answer to his own satisfaction the question: Why was I born, what does my life mean? (If he is an honest writer, the answers he finds will never satisfy him completely; he will always be asking the question afresh.) And the conception he forms for himself *is* his novel. It is the inner compulsion from which the events, the story, grow and the characters, in turn, spring from these events. These characters affect these events, or try to, and are affected by them. Before Pasternak put pen to paper, he had already decided for himself what human life meant at a given period in Russia, and his sense of its meaning colours his every word. In the same way, an English or an American novelist who is moved to write about the inhabitants of a small obscure town needs to see their story in the light of all he knows, all he can find out, about where humanity itself is going.

"Dear me," I hear at this point, "this is all very solemn and alarming. But all I want to do is to amuse and interest as many readers as possible; I want to take their minds off their dull, unromantic lives, I don't want to disturb them in any way." All right. Then forgive me if I say that although your innocent impulse to exhibit yourself in the role of entertainer bears no relation to literature, it does, in fact, bring you into the same highly competitive world in which serious writers are struggling to keep their footing. It does entangle you in the great industrial machine of modern publishing. It does compel you, if you are relying on your entertainment value for your sole living, to keep on doing your tricks before an audience which is all the less likely to be loyal to you, that is being bombarded on every side by inducements to form new tastes, to try a newer product of the machine.

And this finally is why I view with dismay all the methods, from literary prizes to three-year courses in creative writing, by which we try to stimulate the production of writers and more writers. The risk of a genius being left to die of hunger in a garret is less horrible than the glut, the ever-rising flood, of novels and novelised biographies, pouring through the mill wheels of modern publishing. This is why I feel, with guilt, that I did no kindness to a talented young man when I helped to push him out into the treacherous stream instead of saying to him: First secure to yourself a modest living, and then take all the time you really need—years, if necessary—to think through, to live through, the novel, the short stories which, for all I know now, may reveal you as the modern Dickens, the modern Faulkner, the modern Chekhov. You may write much less than you would otherwise have done, but what you write will be infinitely more satisfying.

13

TEN TIPS FOR WRITERS

By Max Shulman

The oldest cliché in the writing business is "Write about what you know about." Like all clichés this is true.

Your own life is your largest source of material. This is not to say that you must live everything you write; as you learn your craft, as you acquire technique, you will be able to handle all kinds of plots and situations of which you have no personal knowledge.

But in the beginning, write about yourself, your family, your friends, your home, your neighborhood. Shape the material—give it form and direction. Arrange it as your story requires—but basically write about yourself.

• A plot is simply this: a problem and a solution. Be sure your people are in a real problem. Be sure the solution is plausible.

• What you're after in popular fiction is not truth but plausibility. Motivate carefully. Make each event in your story an inevitable outgrowth of preceding events.

• If finding names to suit your characters is difficult, the telephone book is a big help.

• I am never without a notebook in my pocket—nor should you be. You never know when a bright notion for a story will strike you. The mind, being a capricious organ, often lets you forget some truly valuable ideas. If you have a notebook and make your notes instantly, you don't have to rely on your memory.

• Don't show your manuscript to anyone at frequent intervals during its composition. You cannot expect a baby to be born if you pull it out every few hours and pass it around. There may come a point in the composition of a story when you are stuck and need help—but try your best to lick your problem by yourself. As a general rule it's wise not to show a story until it is completed.

• In my early years I was hell-bent on becoming a humorist and so I read the humorists—read them and studied them. I knew every word of Lardner, Benchley, Perelman, Thurber, Ade, Twain and all the rest.

I had always thought that the joke was the building block of humor, but today I know that the joke is the enemy of humor. Jokes piled end on end—and I have done it; oh brother, have I done it!—do not make a work of humor. Humor is not jokes; it is reality, it is familiarity, it is identifiability seen through a comic lens. To construct a humorous work, you do not compound incongruities; you tell a story—a serious story about real people—and you infuse it with the comic spirit. . . .

Find the people who write as you would like to and study them. Today my style, such as it is, is formed and I no longer have to read for instruction—I can read for pleasure.

The authors I enjoy most now are Dostoevsky and Shakespeare. These are two more writers I would recommend to a beginning writer because they illuminate every corner of the human soul.

• If you are using a character from real life, change him enough so that he can't be identified.

In fact, the very changing of factual characters is an integral part of the writer's art and should give you pride and satisfaction.

• There is always an unseen attendant looking over my shoulder when I am at the typewriter. He represents the reader I am trying to reach. When I have to make a decision between my taste and his, I always yield to his.

• The background of your story can be of enormous added value. If you can paint an exotic picture, if you can evoke a nostalgic mood, you cannot help but captivate a reader. Beware, however, of piling up detail for the sake of detail. Never let description get in the way of your story.

The writing of humor in television is not stringing a lot of jokes together; it is telling a story which is plausible, believable, well-motivated, well-plotted and funny. The rules of composition, the rules of fiction, the rules of dramatic writing all continue to apply when you're writing humor. Besides, you have the additional problem of making your story funny.

PART II

HOW TO WRITE: TECHNIQUES

14

THE ONLY WAY TO FLY

By Cecilia Bartholomew

LIFE today is real and earnest, we are told.

Fiction can no longer compete with it, we are told.

But that's not where the trouble lies. Fiction is the only way to treat the real and earnest. Fiction is the only way to fly.

The trouble lies not with fiction, but with the writers of fiction. They are giving us the dull for "the real." They are giving us the boring for "the earnest." The result is fiction that is pompous. Fiction can withstand anything but the pompous.

We *are* living in serious times, in violence, in continuing war, in total destruction, including the destruction of space. All the more reason to create something else. I don't mean escape. I mean the very opposite.

Man has been described (perhaps erroneously) as an animal who has been successful in carrying over from infancy and childhood the ability to play. Play is man's unique contribution. Play is the essence of life. And we have stopped playing. For true play is creative. We have even stopped playing love. What has become of flirting? First, in the fifties there was going steady, which was deadly serious. Then in the sixties came sexual freedom, which ought to be play if anything is, but somehow we have managed to turn it into solemn posture. Play is not something you do to impress. Call that by some other name. Play is indulged in for your own enjoyment. What has become of enjoyment? Total earnestness is death. We have killed joy in work, and we are now working at killing joy in play.

Flirting is dead. Unnoticed, unmourned, it is gone. I am not being frivolous. If one thing more than any other has been responsible for its death, that thing is nudity. It is impossible to flirt in the nude. The only thing you can in any decency do when nude is copulate. Everything else is indecent. There is, when all is said and done, a limit to the number of ways to copulate, as there are limitations to the body. Copulation is for real and earnest; it produces babies. But there is an endless number of ways to flirt. Flirting is an art. There are no limitations to art. I say, let's restore art to our lives, and expand our minds. But art requires work.

Today we reject work. We reject the world bequeathed to us, we have retired from the Establishment, and we turn our backs to it, in cynicism or in contemplation—take your pick. We wrap ourselves in the philosophic cloak of aphorism, superbly unaware that it is as invisible on us as aphorisms generally are, as the emperor's new clothes. And when we are able to see our nudity, we flaunt it. We congratulate ourselves that we are, indeed, naked— saggy-breasted, pot-bellied, varicose-veined, hairy, freckled. As if to be naked were an accomplishment. As if we created the naked body. The only thing we can create is the decoration that we put upon the body. And the bruises.

Appearances count. It is the puritan in our ancestry who denies appearance, and preaches doom. Doom is death, and of course the puritan sets his course by death. But appearances count more than anything else. What doesn't show can be denied. Perhaps it doesn't even exist. Life *is* serious; anybody who tries to live it knows that. But we can put any face on it that we choose. "Any face that we choose." That's the power of fiction! And that's its role. What makes life livable is suspense. "Anything can happen" is more than a phrase. Read on and find out.

It is no accident that nudity is given such a large part of the "scene" today. And it is no accident that the word "scene" has replaced the other words for here and now, for life. People are being pushed back into the woodwork. Life is being made as static as a stage setting. We need less nudity, and more striptease.

"Take it off, take it off" was crude, but it was art. Striptease partakes of the "and then . . . and then . . ." of story. Striptease is a becoming, like life. A becoming undressed is no great aim, but there is effort, and elaboration; and there is play. Even poorly done, there is movement, there is suspense. At the moment of complete revelation, the lights flash on, and then there is the blackout. The blackout is very important.

For some, there may be shock in nudity. But shock is short-lived. Nothing is more fickle than the senses. Whereas true suspense is as endless and retreating as space, as versatile as the mind of man, which can provide an endless supply of food for the senses. Familiarity need not breed contempt, but total round-the-clock familiarity will breed boredom. Man needs challenge. He needs the mysterious, the unknown. He needs the closed door, the veil. Questions are the beginning of creativity. Man does not live by knowledge alone. He needs suspense. "What if?" is a magic key.

In the days of the pulps, the writer was paid by the word. The longer the story, the bigger the check. Sometimes, at its worst, that resulted in a thinly spun-out story. At its best, the effort to lengthen the story by valid complication and motivation developed the writer's craft. There is no substitute for craft. On the television screen when the camera dawdles over a skyline, or travels slowly from wall to wall of a room, you can bet that there isn't enough story; but there could be if the writer knew his craft. I recall a successful western writer who created a continuing hero who stuttered, and every time he got stuck on a word (but-but-but-but) the author got paid four times, not once. This is not to be recommended generally, but too many stories today leave out the stuttering, and some even leave out the stutterer.

Curiosity is what separates the members of the animal kingdom from vegetables. It is an instinct, as basic as survival. Rebecca West has suggested in one of her books that it is a reflex, built in, as predictable as the one that makes the foot jump when the knee is tapped by the doctor's little hammer. When that knee reflex doesn't work, the man is in a bad way. When the curiosity reflex doesn't respond, mankind is in a bad way. We are so in earnest today that we have anesthetized the curiosity instinct. Curiosity is not operating any more in space: science is. What can be known, must be known, Oppenheimer said in the fifties. And the mind thrills to that. But let's keep a few unknowns to be curious about. We know more about the moon now, but where has the wonder gone?

Laurence van der Post, writing about the bushman in the interior of Africa, relates that this nomadic prehistoric people, depending upon the rains for survival, will share even water with the encountered stranger; but what they will not share until the stranger becomes the friend, are their stories. They know the value of the "and then . . . and then . . ."

This is a basic rhythm of life. We have discovered (prodded by Marshall McLuhan) that life is simultaneous as well as consecutive, and like children we have seized the new and want to throw away the old. If we throw away the consecutive, we throw away the baby with the bath water.

In stressing the simultaneous to the exclusion of the consecutive, we have made life static. We have turned stories into photographic shots. I would not be surprised to see us go back to the stereopticon. It is no accident that this is a time that has seen the revival of the one-act play. We are reducing art, and we are naïvely delighted with what we have done. Life isn't static. The only thing in life that is static is death. Fiction isn't dying: we are killing it.

Pompous, I said above. We are preachers, mouthing platitudes, clichés, moralities, aphorisms. Every generation has to find its morality for itself, but let's not be self-congratulatory. Let's not reduce art to a proclamation.

Preachers have their role. Cassandras have their role. But neither preachers nor Cassandras are curious. They are sure. The writer's role is a different one: it is to be curious, and to be hopeful.

To prove that today's Establishment relegates old people to the trash can, the play *Endgame* by Samuel Beckett literally upends the old people into a trash can right on stage. And that is called subtlety.

To prove that life is a metaphor for waiting, the same playwright in *Waiting for Godot* asks us to watch his characters on stage wait. Life *is* a metaphor. And there is something noble and ennobling about man's endurance. But not when he stands and waits. Only when he lives as fully as he can. Someone has said that man cannot change his fate, but he can change how he reacts to his fate.

We are all acquainted with the man who yearns to be a writer and never gets around to it, who has a notebook full of good titles, but never writes the stories. That man has bided his time, and now he has us at his mercy. He has found a use for all those titles. He is pawning them off on us, in lieu of the stories themselves.

Are we lazy? Is that all it is? Well, inertia is the last tie between man and the rock from which he came. But man's history has been his efforts to overcome laziness. Inertia is to be overcome. "I think I can. I think I can. IthinkIcan. IthinkIcanIthinkIcan," said the little red engine as it pulled its long load over the mountain.

Disaffection is convenient. It allows you to be self-indulgent, and a Demonstrator at the same time. You can be distinguished, even a martyr, and your lazy inert self. You can get paid, as Hildegarde once sang, for doing what you like best to do. But the non-hero is a contradiction in terms. We have to go back to the hero. And a hero is a man who acts for himself. In life, fate may happen to your advantage, but fate may not happen to the advantage of your hero. What fate has in store for him is bruises.

He must also speak for himself. We are growing so lazy that we cannot even stir ourselves to speak in words. Slogans suffice. The shorter the better. "Love!" "Peace!" You've said it, man, when you've said that. Breathe in on "om," breathe out on "pah." Obscenity, man, that says it. Yeah, right on. But if we are not careful, we are like going to like ruin those four-letter words. They are going, going, gone. They have already become trite, the clichés of today, not tomorrow. The reader is always from Missouri. The man sitting there cross-legged and nude may be wise, but we are not going to believe it until we hear him speak.

We are growing so lazy as writers that we are substituting happenings for art. It began with the development of movie cameras light enough in weight to be hand-carried. You could walk with them; you could even run with them. The faster you run, the lower the cost of the movie. All you have to do is run around with a movie camera in your hand, and you've got a work of art. At first it seemed that we were moving into a marvelous new dimension in moviemaking. But to pretend that anything and everything that the camera picks up is art, or even good enough to show to one's friends, is really giving in to inertia. Someone should have nerve enough to say that the emperor is naked. Beautiful things come out of happenings; boring, meaningless things do also. We are being given self-conscious, self-congratulatory happenings instead of story; we are being given platitudes instead of insight, aphorisms for originality, shock for suspense.

Some congratulations are in order. It is not surprising that the accidental (that is what a happening is) results in the mediocre and the boring. What is surprising is that anything at all results. It proves how instinctive, how basic, is man's urge to form. Prehistoric man drew paintings on his cave walls before he even bothered to make a bowl to eat out of. He had two tools—rocks and flints—and at that point in his development, he had a very sophisticated art.

By its very definition, art is not life. It is a lie, a magnificent lie, that can be truer to our hopes and our destiny than life. A man's eye can learn something from a camera, but it can see deeper than a camera, it can go far beyond the range of the camera's eye. Let's stop trying to be a lens. And let's start the train moving, ourselves, with our own efforts. And with a hero. Under the guise of involving the audience, under the novelty of the new, we are being self-indulgent. Call it something else, if you want it; but don't call it art.

The writer's job is not to quote universal truths, but to flesh them out with individuality. The art is in the clothes, in the elaboration of character. What is happening in fiction is the melting down of individuality into types; and worse, into archetypes. Yes, we are an earnest, humorless, moral generation. There is no paradox in the juxtaposition of morality and nakedness. These times breed men who do not see themselves in the variety of their clothes, but naked. These times breed bigots.

A good play about old age would say not a word about trash cans, and certainly there would be no trash cans on stage. But the audience leaving the theater would be compelled to say, in horror, or in amusement, if they could speak at all under the impact, "Why, they might as well dump all the old people into the trash can." That is truly involving the audience. All you can say coming out after a morality play is smothered in a yawn.

A good play about the meaning of life would not forget that life is to be lived. We must make life (and art) a way, not a wait.

Leave the moral, the aphorisms, yes and the profanity to the reader. A reader has no responsibility to be creative. He can be dull. He doesn't have to find the right word. We will accept swearing from him. Even the essayist may preach. But not the storyteller. The fiction method is by implication.

It is time for writers to shift back to entertainment. Entertainment is not solely frivolity, though, God help us, there is nothing wrong with frivolity either. But entertainment is a worthy aim. It will help us get through our lives. Growing pompous on the one hand, or retreating into inertia on the other hand, will only make the waiting long.

Put the story back into fiction. Put the conventions back into art, or new conventions, but there must be conventions, there must be something for the artist to work against. There must be opposition before there can be growth. Before there can be a work of art.

Put the hero back. I trust him. If he is given the slightest chance, I am confident that he will prove himself interesting, worth reading about. He will prove himself a man who can play, who can think, who can act, who can create. Anyway, he will try. Bruised and shaken, he will get on his feet. Laughable, weak, scared, ridiculous, he will be in there fighting, living.

Fiction is the only way to fly.

15

IN THE BEGINNING . . .

By Eva Ibbotson

My Lords, if you would hear a high tale of love and death. . . ."

If? There's no "if" about it. Of course we would, nothing better. We've been buttonholed, compelled by one of the great opening sentences in literature; by the romantic conjunction of "love" and "death," by the promise contained in the word "high."

Nor does the author cheat. For this is the beginning of *The Romance of Tristan and Iseult* by Charles Bedier, perhaps the most poignant and unforgettable love story in the world. The spell, in a dozen words, has been woven, and the spell, as we progress through ungovernable passion, betrayal and the death of kings, is gloriously maintained.

And of course the great authors do *not* cheat. "It is a truth universally acknowledged that a single man in possession of a good fortune must be in want of a wife," wrote Jane Austen, beginning *Pride and Prejudice*, and again in the first sentence we already have the balanced style, the gentle irony, and the subject matter of the best novel on the hallowed art of husband-hunting ever written.

Or the famous beginning of *Anna Karenina:* "Happy families are all alike; each family is unhappy in its own way. . . ." (And if you're tempted to say, no, that's not a fair opening, it doesn't give an inkling of the tragic fate which awaited the love-racked heroine, reread, as I did recently, the book. It is a book about *families;* about those who struggle to break the mold of responsibility and obligation and so perish, and those who accept its disciplines and survive, and there are fifty-four unspectacular pages after that great Russian train has crushed poor Anna.)

Or to come to a modern novel, a best seller to end all best sellers, Daphne du Maurier's *Rebecca*. "Last night I dreamt I went to

Manderley again. It seemed to me that I stood by the iron gate leading to the drive and for a while I could not enter. . . ."

There follows a whole chapter describing the heroine's dream of Manderley, that fabulous Cornish house with its valley of azaleas and whispering woods, and *Rebecca,* of course, *is* about Manderley, about the almost obsessive love the hero had for it and the power this gave his evil first wife, Rebecca.

An opening, then, is a seed, a fat, well-nourished seed, like the opening to Dickens' *A Tale of Two Cities:* "It was the best of times, it was the worst of times, it was the age of wisdom, it was the age of foolishness. . . ." And so on for three, rolling, euphuistic paragraphs, a leisured opening for a leisured age. Or the exotic seed of some strange, dark orchid like the beginning of William Golding's *Free Fall:* "I have walked by stalls in the marketplace where books, dog-eared and faded from their purple, have burst with a white hosanna." Or a seed of wheat because from it we make bread, in St. John's, "In the beginning was the Word and the Word was with God. . . ."

A seed, then; a promise, something which encapsulates what follows. But for the writer it is also something very different. An arrow—no, something tougher—a pickax with which he embeds himself in his material, a stick of dynamite with which he opens a new seam in the darkness of the coal face.

There can be few writers who haven't had living hell in doing their openings. I myself, though I write the lightest, airiest of short stories, produce manuscripts which look like the blood-stained survivors of some medieval massacre. And if the "body" of each story has been rewritten five, six, seven times, the opening (and closing) paragraphs have been through countless more metamorphoses.

And who am I to complain? Plato rewrote the opening sentence of *The Republic* fifty times. Nor is it a particularly startling opening: "I went down to the Piraeus yesterday with Glaucon, the son of Ariston. As this was the first celebration of the festival I wished to make my prayer to the goddess and see the ceremony. . . ." No buttonholing here, no explosion of images, but obviously this fiftieth attempt had a quality in the original Greek of . . . immediacy? of projection? which was necessary to carry him forward into, arguably, one of the most influential works ever written.

The ideal opening, then, will instantly beguile and interest; it will be direct and concise; it will make promises which later are made good; it will plummet you into the story in the author's wake. And to my mind all these conditions are marvelously fulfilled by the classic, traditional beginning of all fairy stories: "Once upon a time . . ."

"Once upon a time there lived a king and queen who were grieved, more grieved than words can tell because they had no children. . . ." So begins "The Sleeping Beauty"—a beautiful, elegiac opening, touching in passing, and with dignity, on the universal theme of a childless couple's longing for children. Or: "Once upon a time there lived a woodcutter who had seven children, all boys . . ."—and we know at once that Tom Thumb, the youngest of these, must be a robust and enterprising child to whom a giant is mincemeat.

It is, I suppose, because I myself am a writer of fairy stories that I admire so much the brevity and directness of this kind of beginning. My fairy stories, admittedly, are disguised as stories for magazines, women's magazines as often as not, stories to be read lightly by people in a hurry or reading in a crowd. Stories, therefore, with a promise: that the princess will get her prince (but my goodness what she'll have to go through first!), that the poorest, shabbiest of the suitors will guess the riddle. . . .

As everyone who writes professionally knows, short stories are short and daily getting shorter. So not only must my opening paragraph beguile and buttonhole, interest and intrigue, but it must do so *very quickly* and without (and here comes the rub) sacrificing the special atmosphere, the patina which makes that particular story unique and therefore salable.

Recently, for example, I was asked to write a story for Britain's *Woman's Journal* with the title of "Tangle of Seaweed." Two other authors were commissioned to write on the same theme, all three stories to appear in consecutive issues. Since the other two authors were using seaside settings, I decided to set my story in an aquarium. Briefly, the idea was that a young man came into the darkness of the aquarium with the "wrong" girl and came out with the "right" one. A further twist was added by the fact that the "right" girl is *behind* the aquarium, glimpsed as a mysterious mermaid, sea-witch figure, though in fact simply a loopy girl who has taken a holiday job in the zoo and is always losing her engagement ring inside the tanks. (A fish eventually swallows it, as in all good fairy stories, so that *Redbook*, when they bought the story, changed the title to "Why Is This Fish Smiling?".)

I needed, therefore, very quickly to establish the heroine, and I began: "She was always reading, Nell. Well, that is when she wasn't stroking the sooty London leaves of plane trees or laying her cheek against cool window panes or loving—ecstatically—unsuitable young men. You could have started any Chinese couplet from the Golden Dynasty of Tang, and she'd have finished it for you. Dostoevsky was her brother, Victorian children's books her passion, and though she lived, when in funds, mainly on avocados, she took her bath each night with a different cookery book."

And that's all the space I can allow myself for describing Nell. I've said "Once upon a time there lived a princess," but I've said, too, that she was sensual, passionate, intelligent, lived in London and was a bit of a kook (see the word 'unsuitable'), the kind of girl who has to be rescued from her messes in the time-hallowed way by the love of a good man.

Or another story, "The Little Countess," which appeared recently in *Ladies' Home Journal*. This story has a very romantic and conventional theme: a little Russian countess at the turn of the century is engaged, at sixteen, to a dissolute prince but loves her impoverished young tutor. Because the atmosphere was so richly emotional, the characters so passionate and highly-charged, I wanted to treat the story at one remove, through the eyes of the little countess' English governess whose Victorian common sense tempers the events and puts everything in order. So I began not with the limitless steppes of Central Russia, the mighty Volga, the country estate where the little countess lives; I began: "In the early years of this century, my grandmother, whose name was Laura Petch, became engaged to a Mr. Alfred Fairburn. A month later she set off for Russia to be a governess." No prim spinster, you see, but a woman of determination and patience who will make short work of the Russian mania for self-torture and despair.

Or take a Christmas story bought recently by *McCall's:* "Vicky and the Christmas Angel." This story is set in Vienna before the First World War and is based on the true story of a little girl (my own mother, in fact) who believed, as all Viennese children used to do, that the Christmas tree and presents were brought down from heaven by the Christmas Angel. She is persuaded on Christmas Eve to look through the keyhole—only to find the despised and shabby "poor relation" fixing the tree. Her shock and disillusionment and the reassembling of the myth for the benefit of her two little sisters is the real theme of the story, the old theme of the transition into adulthood made in an instant. Initially I began with a description of the radiant Vicky sitting on the lid of a great mahogany toilet seat and telling the story of the Christmas Angel to her spellbound little sisters in the bath. But because this story depended so much on the setting—Vienna at a time when a child's upbringing protected her so much more than today—my opening moved on to the bathroom through a description of the winter streets: "It was mid-December and a night of snow. All day the thick, soft flakes had fallen quietly, covering the nymphs and satyrs on Vienna's innumerable fountains; blanketing the bronze rumps of the rearing horses on which dead warriors of the Hapsburg Empire rode forever. . . ."

Even now, as I finish this article, I'm searching in my mind for my next pickax, arrow, tube of gelignite. . . . The story floating in my mind is set in old St. Petersburg. It is about two English governesses exiled to this exotic city, at first friends, then after a quarrel over the imagined attentions of the English chaplain, violent enemies. While the governesses are friends, their charges—a diminutive princess, a sailor-suited little count—play together; when they quarrel they forcibly separate the children—a Montague and Capulet situation which keeps alive the children's affection for each other, enabling it, years after the revolution, to renew itself as adult love.

I've thought for months about this story, decided to keep the emphasis, for humor's sake, on the eccentric governesses, to use the little boy recollecting the story in old age as narrator. I've read everything I can lay hands on about St. Petersburg and could lead you blindfold down Nevsky Prospect. And so I pick up my pen (because my opening paragraphs are far too labile for a typewriter), and I begin: "A love story set in a bygone, snowflake world of crystal light, of pale palaces and glittering ice—that's what I'd meant to write in telling of my childhood in St. Petersburg. . . ."

No. Affected and self-conscious. Try getting straight down to the "heroine," the tiny, seven-year-old Princess Anna Grazinsky. "I saw her first, fur-trussed and patient and hardly bigger than the muff she carried, trudging behind her governess along the snowbound English quay. . . ."

Not bad, perhaps, but really I want the first confrontation of all the four characters, the two relentless governesses with their reluctant, trailing charges. How about: "It was only the children with English governesses who had to go for walks in the winter in St. Petersburg. Those with mademoiselles stayed snugly. . . ."

No. Not enough atmosphere.

Don't worry. Another forty-seven attempts and I'll almost certainly be there. . . .

16

HARBINGERS

By George P. Elliott

A LOT of people are saying that fiction is in the doldrums these days, and they have some discouraging symptoms to point to, no doubt of that. There are fewer magazines than there were twenty years ago, and the total number of stories published in them is a mere fraction of what it used to be. Moreover, editors of magazines complain that it is harder than ever to find good stories. In graduate creative writing workshops, there are as many talented poets as formerly but many fewer talented fiction writers. Critics and reviewers keep announcing the death of the novel, as they have been for the past half century—foolish, to be sure, but also depressing. I keep hearing literary people say they read much less current fiction than they used to, or none. There is a whole school of American "anti-fiction" writers, of whom John Barth and Donald Barthelme are much the cleverest; "anti-fiction" is parasitically literary, being especially given to parody and allusion, and it gives the impression of getting its nourishment from the corpse of fiction, with not much longer to go. And of course there is pseudo-fictional journalism feeding on the body, too—"the nonfiction novel," "the novel as history." Worst of all, there are doomsters who, outcrying McLuhan, promise an electronic takeover of narrative which will leave printed fiction an elitist pastime about as "relevant" as string quartets and stained glass windows.

Any way you look at it, that's enough to lower a writer's spirits at least a little. The 1960s marked the end of a great many things; and, as always when there is a big cultural shift, much good has been swept away with the bad, or at least relegated to a minor place. Among these, it seems to me, is realistic fiction, short and long, as an important cultural phenomenon.

My guess is that the age that began with the Enlightenment in the mid-eighteenth century waned with the 1960s, and so did its chief literary form, realistic fiction. Sociology and psychology between them dealt hard blows to such fiction, and so did journalism and photography; but even harder has been the loss of faith in the scientific, rational view of the world which lent realism its apparent objectivity and impersonality. Of course seldom does a vigorous literary form disappear from the world completely; the sonnet, for instance, despite all predictions keeps popping back full of vitality age after age. Realistic stories and novels will continue to be written, some of them excellent, no doubt; but it is very unlikely that such fiction will be dominant in the foreseeable future.

Nevertheless, I am not too discouraged, for I see not the slightest sign that love of story is diminishing, and I think of myself as a storyteller (who sometimes writes realistically, but sometimes not). Let TV and movies and the rest have all the narrative they want: there is plenty to go around, the more the merrier. What I cannot ever imagine disappearing, since I think it is rooted in our deepest nature, is the impulse, *Tell me a story*. In words. One word after another, whether spoken or printed. Realistic fiction pretended to retire the storyteller off into the wings, but just about all the other kinds of narrative have had him front and center: the bard at the fireside, the ancient mariner, "once there was a woman who . . . ." A storyteller who amounts to much has his own "voice": Dickens, Twain, Lawrence, Faulkner. He lets you know he is in charge of the story and of your reactions. He enjoys astonishing you (this is one of the reasons science fiction is big these days). He likes to play and assumes you do, too. He has opinions about life and is not afraid to tell you them. He is entertainer as much as artist.

I think this is not just self-serving optimism on my part, for there have been plenty of signs of excellent tale-telling around for a couple of decades. Thomas Mann's last, and to my mind best, novel, *The Confessions of Felix Krull* (1955), is a splendid, preposterous tale. Hesse. Tolkien. Dinesen and the gothic tale. Science fiction. "Black humor" (insofar as it is satire and not just a kind of nihilism). You know from the outset of Frederick Exley's *A Fan's Notes: A Fictional Memoir* (1968) that you are in the hands of an enormously gifted, old-fashioned storyteller with a new-style story to tell. What does John Cheever ever do but delight and amaze in all his best stories? Or John Fowles in his jazzy up-to-date (1969) Victorian novel, *The French Lieutenant's Woman*? And here are the opening sentences of the most delightful novel (i.e., long story in prose) I have read in a couple of years, *One Hundred Years of Solitude* by Gabriel Garcia Márquez (published in 1967 in Spanish, 1970 in English).

Many years later, as he faced the firing squad, Colonel Aurelian Buendia was to remember that distant afternoon when his father took him to discover ice. At that time Macondo was a village of twenty adobe houses, built on the bank of a river of clear water that ran along a bed of polished stones, which were white and enormous, like prehistoric eggs. The world was so recent that many things lacked names, and in order to indicate them, it was necessary to point.

And he keeps it going like this for 422 pages without asking you to believe a word of it.

These are not "new novels" or anti-fictions, pallid fungi of a decaying era, decadent and essentially frivolous. These are harbingers of a new (and, I dare to hope, a rich) age coming. How dare I hope that the age we are entering will be rich in fiction? Because so many vigorous storytellers are doing what unperverted artists usually do when a tradition has exhausted itself as the "modernist" tradition has done. That is, they turn to the old for inspiration and models, knowing very well that to tell even an old story in your own voice is to make something new in the world and that most of the modes of storytelling are ancient, primitive in fact, ultimately rooted in *listen to what happened to me the other day*.

This presupposes that people are interesting—in what they do and the ways they are connected. Granted that, everything else about telling and listening to stories comes naturally—and that's why I believe they will keep on coming.

17

PLOT, PLOT—WHO'S GOT A PLOT?

By Robert L. Fish

It seems to me there are enough occupational hazards to being a professional mystery writer—starvation not being the least—so that some form of protection should be provided against the more non-essential fortuities. Among others, I refer to the interrogations one is forced to face at social gatherings, and which—no matter how they start—inevitably end up taking the form of the query: "Where on *earth* do you *manage* to get your *plots?*"

My main objection to the question, however, is not that it is fatuous, or even that it is invariably a lead-in to a very boring discussion. My objection is that it is a very difficult question to answer, or at least to answer honestly, and cocktail parties are no place for this sort of thing. Where does one get one's plots? Well, about the only positive answer is that one very seldom gets them from questioners at cocktail parties.

A friend of mine gets most of his plot ideas from newspaper stories, usually involving some macabre or outlandish event in some far-off place, preferably with an exotic name. A mine disaster in Chiang Mai, a mass suicide in Cachinal de la Sierra, a ship burning off the coast of Tamantave—one of these is all he needs to begin working out all sorts of dishonorable motives for all sorts of unprincipled people to have brought about the macabre or outlandish event. The major problem he faces is that he sweats blood during the writing of the book in fear that someone else will beat him to press with a book based on the same news event. Actually, this has never happened, since other writers face the same fear. His novels, therefore, are safe, but his constant worry has left him with an ulcer and a tendency to leap at unexpected noises, scarcely recommendations for his method.

We are forced to conclude, therefore, that writers get their ideas from various sources, and that it is impossible to set down any rigid rules for unearthing plots. My own favorite method—and I merely mention it in passing, since it is not the point I wish to make in this article—is to dream up some inexplicable occurrence. For example: A man is murdered for a package which contains nothing but a dead coral snake. A man legally sells diamonds at a price far below what he legally paid for them, and manages a very nice profit as a result. A man absconds from the United States with a briefcase chained to his wrist, supposedly filled with money but actually containing worthless blocks of newsprint. At great expense in time, money and trouble, a man goes into a jungle to destroy a bridge that leads nowhere. Now, having established the illogical nature of the situation, the idea is to proceed to explain it in a manner that not only defends the logic of the seemingly illogical situation, but proves it to be inevitable. Out of the explanation, a book evolves.

But, as I said before, this is not the point I wish to make. The most important thing for beginning writers to recognize is that plot in itself is probably the least important element making up a fictional work. More important by far is characterization—and *most* important, of course, is the ability to write the English language in a manner that makes other people want to read what you've written. Plot alone will never induce anyone to turn a page, and getting people to turn pages is the true definition of successful writing.

There was a time—and I speak now of the mystery field, with which I am most familiar—when the discovery of a new method of slaughter, supposedly undetectable, was considered by many writers to be sufficient in itself to carry a book. The injection of air bubbles in the bloodstream, the icicle dagger, etc., etc. For anyone who still holds to this theory, I would recommend John Dickson Carr's deservedly famous essay on the subject. I honestly believe the only murder method not used to date is boring people to death at cocktail parties, and I'm exposing that one right now.

There was also a time when involved plotting was the be-all and end-all of mystery stories; when the phrase "Who-Dun-It?" meant exactly that, and the reader was being challenged directly by the author to match wits. (I have always considered this contest basically unfair. After all, the author had months and months to solve the problem, and the reader is given only minutes to arrive at the same conclusion.) In any event, today such mysteries are few and far between, and the authors who continue to write them are all old professionals of excellent skill who can depend for their success more on their ability to write convincingly and interestingly, and to characterize superbly, than on the eventual unmasking of the butler.

Today the old "Who-Dun-It?" has largely been replaced by what might be called the "Where-Did-He-Go-And-More-Important-How-Did-He-Get-There?" (I have a feeling the title will never catch on, but the idea remains.) These are the adventure-suspense novels and concern themselves to a very large degree with the chase, the oldest—and possibly still the best—suspense device in the fictional bag of tricks. Yet these books really have no plot at all, and certainly not in terms of those convolutions once considered essential. It is extremely simple: our Hero must get from place A to place B—usually a good distance apart—in a very limited time and for any one of a number of good reasons: to warn the settlers, to deliver a vital message to headquarters, to bring the last fragile vial of antidelirium tremens serum to the plague-stricken village, to lead the natives to safety before the volcano erupts, to get the mortgage payment to the bank before the moment of foreclosure, etc., etc. In addition to the stormy weather and the treacherous terrain across which he must travel, there are also bad men who are being paid to prevent the success of his mission. This they attempt to do: by crippling his horse, by dynamiting the rope bridge over the chasm, by changing road-markers, by drugging his sarsaparilla, by decoying him with sensuous sirens, by sniping at him from ambush, and—if all else fails—by physically molesting him.

Ludicrous? Corny? Only if the author makes it so. The most successful suspense novels of the past few years have had no more plot than those mentioned above. But the writing was good and exciting, and the people in them were human beings with human reactions, whose motivations were understandable, both hero and villain, and were not wooden puppets being put through the motions. When we read a series suspense novel, for example—meaning one in which the same hero appears in book after book—we know even before he climbs out onto that crumbling two-inch ledge skirting the eighteenth floor of the murderer's hideout that he isn't going to fall. But if the situation is presented to us properly, our hands will still sweat as we fearfully peak at the next page.

There are many other examples of non-plot writing; the entire so-called "slice-of-life" school prefers to take a section from everyday living and describe it with skill which translates itself into an emotional response on the part of the reader. This type of writing continues to produce quite successful and often great, blockbusting novels, as well as to find a market at some of the higher-paying magazines. Actually, how much plot is there in great symphonic music? Still, it manages to communicate, which is the important thing. It gets us, in effect, to turn the page.

I suppose my advice to the beginning writer, in the matter of plot, is to put it into its proper perspective and not allow it to become an insurmountable obstacle to a successful writing career. Someone once said there was only one basic plot: Boy Meets Girl, Boy Loses Girl, Boy Finds Girl. In general it's a correct concept, and what makes one book different from another is the quality of the characterization and the writing.

And think how lovely it would be if this obsession with plot were eliminated and replaced with more important concerns. I dream of the day when someone comes up to me at a cocktail party and asks, "Where on *earth* do you *manage* to get those weird *characters*?" Think how simple it would be to look them right in the eye and tell them where I got one of them, at least. . . .

18

INSIDE URIAH HEEP

By Nina Bawden

There are two kinds of fictional characters, the flat and the round. "Flat"—that is, seen objectively, with no intrusion by the novelist into his character's skin—is not a dismissive adjective. Most of the memorable characters in literature are "flat." We don't know what it would be like to be inside Uriah Heep, or Mr. Micawber, or Mr. Collins, and they would be less "real," perhaps, less effective, if we did. Detail would blur the sharpness of the picture.

Flat characters are, of course, the supporting cast in most novels, the backdrop against which the heroes and heroines, the "round" characters, act out their bigger parts. And "act" is the word, because the novelist is inside them, impersonating another human being who may be quite unlike himself: handsome where he is ugly, or a different age, a different sex.

Success depends on the skill and imagination employed. But sometimes one gets the impression, however great the writer's skill, that the impersonation is a kind of gymnastic exercise, a contortion that has been forced on the writer simply because it is no longer possible to write straightforwardly—that is, in the tradition of the old novels when the novelist was omnipotent and could speak with his own voice. He could be inside his characters but outside them, too—writing about, as well as through them.

This is a freedom we have lost. Without it, a writer can do one of two things. He can, like Françoise Sagan, whose heroines grow older as she grows older, write only about himself, under one or another thin disguise. Or he can perform what amounts to one virtuoso ventriloquist act after another.

This "internal" method of characterization may be bewildering for the reader who opens a book by a young man in his twenties

97

and finds himself inside the consciousness of a middle-aged woman going through the menopause, but it is almost always fun for the writer. Learning to see through someone else's eyes, to speak with his voice, is a fascinating and challenging experience. But it has its dangers, too.

The only person you can really know is yourself. You can observe how other people look and behave, listen to what they say, guess how they think and feel—but you can only guess. The young man cannot know how it feels to be a middle-aged woman: he can only impersonate her.

It might seem to follow from this that the most successful characters in fiction must be those the writer has been closest to, the ones whose ideas and feelings match best with his own. It would explain, certainly, why so many modern novels seem to be a voyage of self-discovery, a sort of private joke, or game. As an illustration of what I mean, my last novel was about two women, one a timid ninny, a fanatasist; the other cheerful and extroverted, a kind of female buccaneer. Both these women were me—or rather, aspects of them were in me—and often, as I wrote about them alternately, slipping slyly from one personality to the other, I found myself shaking with silent laughter at some contradiction, or absurdity, that no one but myself would ever see.

Writing this novel, and the one before it, I became aware of the difficulties (for me) of writing through someone too much like myself. Although her situation was different from mine, Elizabeth, the heroine of *A Woman of My Age,* was my own sex, my own age, and came from the same educational and social background. As I wrote about her, I found we intruded on each other—not just I on her, but she on me. She was a frustrated woman with an overbearing husband; I became so involved with her, so indignant on her behalf, that I lectured my husband one suppertime on how badly he was treating me, how constricting my life was. My family listened, putting down their forks and watching me with mild, astonished faces. When I had finished—worked up, by this point, into a fine, righteous rage—my son said gently, "But you're not talking about *yourself,* are you?"

Elizabeth and I had grown too close. I had to remove myself from her, stand back to see her clearly. I managed to do this—at least, I hope I did—by making her physically different from myself: large-framed instead of small, long-haired instead of short—a simple, idiosyncratic trick, but one that worked in this case and prevented confusion of identity.

It is important, if you do not want to gaze Narcissus-like into the mirror, to distance yourself from your characters, who might, otherwise, become no more than vehicles for your thoughts, your perceptions. Your "round" characters will be bound to have a bit of you in them—and since we are all many-sided, infinitely complex, this is not as limiting as it sounds—but they must have their independence as well, their own life. I have found that one way to achieve this is to write as a man: it seems, in some ways, less inhibiting, and gives a broader focus. Or to write as a child or young adolescent. There is an additional freedom in this method because the child is naturally distanced from us in years, and yet, if our memory is good, we know him well.

To be at a distance from, and yet to know. That is the ideal, I think. To be far enough away to see objectively and still be able, without too much trickiness, too much contortion, to get inside the skin of someone who is quite different from you.

Which brings me to what is—paradoxically, perhaps—another danger for the novelist who is writing not just for and about himself, but for and about other people. Again I can best explain it through an example from my own work. Twelve years ago I wrote a book, *Devil by the Sea,* about a nine-year-old girl who became obsessively involved with a child murderer. She was a perverse child with what school teachers call an "unfortunate manner." She had a pretty younger brother, and somewhat insensitive parents, but she was not, in any objective sense, neglected: she simply wanted more love and attention than came her way, and, not getting it, felt it must be her own wickedness that deprived and isolated her. As a result of this fairly common, childish belief, she identified herself with the murderer whom she thought of, for reasons too complicated to go into here, as the Devil.

I have recently written a script of this novel in collaboration with a film director who was worried about the psychological exactness of the child's behavior. Would this type of child have reacted quite like this to this situation, or, if she did, shouldn't she be a different sort of child? There were one or two textbooks which contained accounts of the child who is "accident-prone," likely to be a victim in this kind of crime. Wouldn't it be a good idea to read them? I did read them. The result, to my gratification, was confirmation, not confusion: *my* child, established both in my mind and on paper, was more real than any number of case histories. And why shouldn't she be? Nothing that happened to her had ever happened to me, but I knew what it was like to *be* her: an awkward, difficult, greedy child, not worth loving. But if I had read those case histories (and taken them into account) before I wrote my novel, would she have been more convincing, more "real"? At the risk of sticking my neck out, I'd like to say I don't think so. I might easily have been overawed by the opinions of people who seemed to know more than I did, and constructed a sterile, composite character. An Identikit Child. . . .

We know so much now: psychiatrists and sociologists have taught us to take people apart like clocks. And to put them in categories: The Graduate Wife, The Organization Man, The Status Seeker. As if, fitting ourselves into slots, we could understand ourselves better.

But do we? There are no individuals in a statistical sample. If there is anything in the complaint that the modern novelist no longer writes about "real" people—and how many characters from recent fiction can you remember as clearly as you remember Anna Karenina, or Fagin, or Huck Finn?—it may stem from the fact that we have lost, not only the old, sure sense of our place in society, but also our belief that the individual is important within it. Or if we have not lost this belief, we are half-afraid to assert it. We do not wish to appear trivial. And so we write "important" novels about this Problem or that; put in a lot of sex (because in bed we are all alike, the sense of character is lost); try to expand the narrow world of the particular into some grander, more diffuse design.

It is no good, of course. The novelist's business is with the particular. You cannot inject universal significance into a novel about the old man next door who is dying of cancer by writing about The Problem of Terminal Illness in Old People in Suburban Communities. If you tried, your book would be stillborn, because you would be writing from the outside in, letting the tail wag the dog. There are no Old Men for you, just one old man. He is a retired merchant sailor, let's say, who keeps a collection of wood and ivory elephants in the front room of his bungalow and grows roses and vegetable marrows in his garden. His wife has been dead ten years, and he doesn't miss her as he misses his mother who now seems younger, in his thoughts, than his wife. He has a daughter who is married to a truck driver and a son who is a professor of mathematics. He is jealous of his son but pretends to be proud of him. He has tufts of hair growing out of his ears and a wart on his right index finger which bothers him when he ties his shoelaces. He doesn't know about the cancer, which he thinks of as "his old stomach trouble," but he is frightened sometimes when he wakes in the night.

Of course, you cannot know exactly what it is like to be that old man, but you will know *something:* who hasn't been jealous, who hasn't, at four in the morning, been afraid of death? Stick with your old man. Look and listen, both for the exterior and the interior truth about him, and you may, if you have paid attention and are honored with talent, end up by finding that the universal has been there all the time, looking out from the particular.

19

WRITING THE MYSTERY SHORT STORY

By Joe Gores

A mystery story," Stanley Ellin wrote a few years ago, "is a short prose fiction which is, in some way, connected with a crime."

Brief and simple as this is, it successfully spans the immense variety of the short mystery since Poe and makes you want to hustle over to the old portable and peck one out. Just lift a crime from today's newspaper, dream up a couple of side-of-the-mouth characters, crank out a few pages of one-sentence dialogue in the Hammett manner. . . .

It didn't come out so well? Didn't . . . hold together?

Defining the short mystery story doesn't make us able to *write* one. Especially when the definition seems, at first glance, to give us only a single element to set apart the mystery (whether novel or short story) from the mainstream of fiction: a crime.

Let's begin with our crime, then, be it art forgery or stealing someone's good name or murder. We immediately see that the crime leads us logically and inescapably to a new element: a solution. If we have a crime, we must have a solution. This is absolute bedrock to the short mystery.

I can see the boys flicking open their switchblades to cut me up. How straight can you get, man? Don't you dig obscure? Don't you dig the anti-hero and black humor and existentialism?

I dig. But despite the fact that fiction can probe deeper and talk dirtier than ever before, can, since Sigmund Freud, glibly mouth *psychosis* and *id* and *ego,* the successful story still must have a resolution. No resolution, no story, whatever other merits it may have as a piece of prose. And if it is a mystery story, implicit in that resolution must be some solution to the crime. It doesn't matter if your bad guy triumphs over your good guy, or even if your bad guy *is* your good guy; there still must be some sort of solution.

After the crime and its solution, however, the mystery short story starts getting tricky. ˙(Here it comes, folks, all those whodunits and howdunits and whydunits, and suspense and thriller and crime stories, and private-eye caper and procedural and formal mystery and locked room and spy story and gothic. . . .)

Not at all.

By getting tricky I don't mean all the possible ways to make a reader believe the butler dunit—or didn't dunit. We are going to get tricky by making the necessary distinction between *telling* a story and *plotting* a story. It is precisely here that the "serious" writers who condescend to walk down our dingy little street of crime so often step on the banana peel. They have never learned how to plot.

This distinction between storytelling and story plotting is simple—and vital. E. M. Forster once defined a story as "a narrative of events arranged in their time sequence."

It might now be helpful to analyze a mystery short from first conception to finished manuscript, to show how a story originally conceived as a straight fiction tale became a mystery short story through a deliberate building-in of suspense elements.

As a junior in college, I wrote a story, "Epitaph," in 1952 following the lingering death of a deeply loved and respected grandfather. The story, which contained a good deal of youthful anger and sorrow, opened with a doctor walking downstairs from a sickroom in which Chris Miller's father lies dying of cancer:

"Well?"

"Your father—he—he's very ill." His moon face was drawn up into what was supposed to be condolence, and his fat gut still quivered from the stairs.

I shrugged. "Ya, ya, cut the crap. Is he going to live or die?"

Chris is an inarticulate man in his mid-twenties, a ne'er-do-well who spends his time hunting and fishing. As a result, neither his mother, his two sisters, nor his brother Rod, who works at the local bank, understand his deep unspoken emotion at his father's terminal illness. A few days after the old man's death, Chris and his brother go up to the casket at the funeral home to view the body:

"Looks just like old dad, doesn't it?" Rod said with a quaver in his voice. "No, it looks like hell to me."

Afterwards, the mourners follow the casket out to the cemetery ("moving at a proper funeral pace, to show the world that we were sad"). As they return to town, Chris looks back: the snow "had stopped melting on the coffin; it laid a soft blanket over it and . . . would cover the old man up from this shallow mess of humanity that had carried him out here." Chris skips the wake; he knows that no one will miss him there.

No more jump-shooting mallards down in the bottoms or deer-shining out of season in the hardwood belt across the creek . . . (But) I knew a good rabbit woods across the highway from my shack, where the snow wouldn't be too deep for the dog. The old man would like that, I thought. He always loved rabbit hunting.

My writing teacher at Notre Dame, after reading "Epitaph," told me that funeral stories were hard to sell, and suggested that I put it away for a while. I did. For fifteen years, in fact. But the story kept bugging me; there was a wealth of honest emotion in it despite my college boy hostilities and shallow philosophizing. Later, I tried a rewrite with Chris as an older man, about thirty-five now, an ex-convict returning home after his release from prison. I blue-penciled his sisters, gave Rod a wife, and began the story with Chris's arrival in town:

I got off the Greyhound and stopped to draw icy Minnesota air into my lungs . . . I caught my passing reflection in the window of the old-fashioned depot: a tall, hard man with a white and savage face . . .

Chris, who calls the old man "Pops" inside himself, remains at his father's side for the thirty-seven hours until the death, despite open hostility from the family.

I could see the old man's arm hanging limply over the edge of the bed . . .The upper arm, which once had measured an honest 18 and had swung his small tight fist against the side of my head a score of times, could not even hold a cigarette up in the air. It gave me the same wrench as finding a good foxhound that's gotten mixed up with a bobcat.

As the image suggests, Chris has retained the earlier version's love of the outdoors. His father's eyes, "translucent with imminent death," are to Chris the "pure, pale blue of birch shadows on fresh snow"; and when he and his father reminisce, the old man goes "way back . . . to the big white tail buck that followed him through the woods one rutting season until he whacked it on the nose with a tree branch."

Chris goes to the funeral home and the grave, but leaves "when the preacher starts his scam." He gets a long-barreled .22 target pistol from the house ("Pops and I had spent thousands of hours with that gun"), takes the jeep to drive down into the woods.

> There was a flash of brown as a cottontail streaked from under a deadfall toward a rotting woodpile I'd stacked years before. My slug took him in the spine . . .
> I left him there and moved out again, down into the small marshy triangle between the hills . . . Finally a ringneck in full plumage burst out . . . I squeezed off in mid-swing, knowing it was perfect even before he took that heart-stopping pinwheel tumble . . .

Chris returns to the cemetery and, in the dusk, lays the dead rabbit and pheasant on top of the casket. He stands in silent contemplation for a minute or two ("The wind must have been strong, because I found that tears were burning on my cheeks"), then leaves town (again by bus), taking the .22 with him because "Pops would have liked that."

I began submitting the story, to find my ex-teacher's judgment still valid: stories about funerals don't sell. Finally, despite the lack of crime in the story, I sent it to *Ellery Queen's Mystery Magazine*. After all, I rationalized, I had a criminal. Ellery Queen's editorial reaction was swift, crisp, and pointed.

> It is (not) a crime story simply because it has a criminal in it. A detective story is not necessarily that simply because it contains a detective. There would need to be some detection.
> Suppose Chris managed a prison break in order to get to see his father before he dies . . . (It) will have much more suspense if the cops are after him . . . He would need to leave some sort of red herring that would send the cops off in a different direction . . .

I decided to revise the story along the lines suggested. Into the opening paragraph, for instance, went a second reflection in the bus depot window:

. . . one that froze my guts: a cop in uniform. Could they already know it was someone else in that burned-out car?

That was my red herring. An old farmer (with whom Chris hitched a ride after the break) has been killed when the car has gone off an icy road. Chris has poured gasoline on him and lighted it, so the police will think that the body is Chris. But Queen still was dissatisfied.

You're missing the point . . . Your red herring throws the cops off completely . . . The dramatic situation can't just be left hanging; it needs to be resolved to make the story complete . . .

On reflection I knew Queen was right; so revision included references to the search Chris knows must be fanning out behind him. My ending was dramatic, with Chris dodging downhill between the tombstones for a presumably fatal shoot-out with the arriving police.

Ellery Queen's Mystery Magazine offered to buy this version. But now the essential difference between a great editor and an editor who merely buys stories from writers became apparent. He wrote:

I will, of course, run the present version if you wish me to. But I still think that the last scene is not as strong and dramatic as it could or should be . . . He should . . . turn to leave—and see the cops and/or detectives standing there, waiting for him. I think this stark, sudden, final ending is what this particular story needs.

Please think it over, Joe, and if you agree, send a revised last page.

I thought it over, and sent a revised last page to them. It read like this:

I turned away, toward the jeep—and stopped dead. I hadn't even heard them come up . . . I tensed, my mind going to the .22 pistol that they didn't know about in my overcoat pocket. Yeah. Except that it had all the stopping power of a fox's bark. If only Pops had run to hand guns of a little heavier caliber. But he hadn't.

Very slowly, as if my arms suddenly had grown very heavy, I raised my hands above my head.

A straight short story that wouldn't sell had become a mystery short that would, and did. But one other change first was neces-

sary. "Epitaph" no longer fit the tone of the story. Out of the
ending of the 1952 version I had constructed what may be the
best paragraph I have ever written; and from it came *the* absolutely perfect title.

Goodbye, Pops. Goodbye to deer-shining out of season in the hardwood belt
across the creek. Goodbye to jump-shooting mallards down in the river bottoms.
Goodbye to woodsmoke and mellow bourbon by firelight and all the things that
made a part of you mine. The part they could never get at.

In May, 1970, my story, "Goodbye, Pops" was given the Edgar
Allan Poe Award by Mystery Writers of America as the best mystery short published in America during 1969. But whenever I notice that statuette glowering from the bookshelf, I have the nagging
feeling that I should somehow share my Edgar with Ellery Queen.
Because it was he, as editor, who reminded me, as writer, that only
when the mystery short follows the simple formula of crime, solution and logical plot can it be wholly successful.

20

THE USES AND ABUSES OF DIALOGUE

By Bill Pronzini

PERHAPS the most important technique a fiction writer must master in order to achieve any degree of lasting success in today's highly competitive magazine and book markets is the art of writing believable and appropriate dialogue. Without that mastery, he is foundering in heavy seas, and, like as not, he'll go down and fail to come up again.

Many beginning writers tend to de-emphasize the importance of dialogue. They believe that narrative is the key to salability, and hence, to success. But, in my opinion, the argument that characterization, mood, and plot line should be set forth primarily in expository passages in which the author alone does the talking is not valid. The characters themselves *must* have a voice—a strong voice. They have to corroborate the author's statements about them, about their qualities, temperament, eccentricities, etc.; they have to reflect and intensify the established mood in their spoken words as well as by their actions; they have to advance and reaffirm and assist in clearly establishing the plot line by what they say and how and why they say it. In short, and in a very literal sense, if the characters aren't able to speak for themselves—if the reader can't believe them simply on the basis of what they *say* —then the author has failed to do his job properly.

The best-selling novelists in all fields—for example, mystery-suspense, science fiction, westerns, mainstream—are to a man (or woman) highly capable practitioners of the art of dialogue. Prime examples are found in the mystery-suspense genre, into which perhaps 75% of my own writing output is channeled. Evan Hunter, whom most everyone knows is also Ed McBain of 87th Precinct fame, is perhaps the best writer of realistic dialogue. You can learn almost everything that needs to be learned about composing believable, moving, suitable colloquy from reading and studying his work. Chandler and Hammett and Erle Stanley Gardner became giants because all were able to write superb fictional conversation. Other contemporary craftsmen who come to mind are Donald Westlake, John D. McDonald, Thomas B. Dewey, and Ross Macdonald.

The following ideas have for some time governed my own writing of dialogue. They certainly aren't intended to be hard-and-fast rules, for they are what works best for one *individual* author, but I hope that in some small way they might prove helpful to beginning writers.

There are, basically speaking, two schools in the writing of dialogue. One is the "short dialogue" school; the other is the "exposition dialogue" school (some writers, though I'm sure not many, believe in a composite of both—and all writers, of necessity, are members of both schools at times—but as a general rule you can place any author into one or the other category merely by examining his work). Both schools are perfectly tenable, and have their distinct advantages, but I belong—heart and soul—to the "short dialogue" school.

This is to say that I believe conversation in a fictional endeavor should be short and crisp between speakers whenever possible. When you consider it, this is normally the way you and I converse with friends, relatives, business associates every day of our lives. When an individual asks a question, it is most often a single, brief question; and having asked his single, brief question, he will usually wait for an answer before asking another question or continuing on to something else. And the answer, more often than not, will be as succinct as the question—a single, concise sentence, or perhaps two concise sentences. For example:

"Where were you?"
"At the park."
"Which one?"
"Oak Hill."
"What were you doing there?"
"I went to find Jack."
"Did you find him?"
"No. He'd already gone home."

A brief answer follows a brief question, a simple corroboration or negation follows a simple statement. This kind of dialogue flows quite nicely, for both the reader and the writer. And the reader is not overloaded with ideas, questions, or factual material presented in blocks. There is time for him to assimilate each detail before going on to the next.

Unless a writer is accomplished technically, expository dialogue (in which each speaker is given several sentences, some of which may take on the characteristics of straight narrative, before he relinquishes the floor to the next speaker) can be very difficult to write. The progression has to be planned *ahead* of time, rather than allowing questions, answers, statements to flow naturally from one speaker to the next and back again. Of course, there are times when I'm forced to write expository dialogue—these are unavoidable, especially when unraveling a complicated plot—but I've found that people simply do not, on the average, speak in intricate, verbose sentences and paragraphs. Most individuals run out of ideas (if not inclination) after three successive statements and wait to be led on by someone else's comments.

People generally speak idiomatically. All of us utter clichés, overwork certain words, use double negatives, preface ten sentences in a row with the word *well*, swear, and pretend that we've forgotten every grammatical axiom we ever knew. We seem to have an affinity for words and phrases like *sure, uh-huh, right, well, O.K., listen, look, why not?, all right, yeah, huh, oh, ah, um-m, hm-m,* etc. Should fiction be any different?

I am not advocating that every character's dialogue should be idiomatic or exhibit all of these features, or that these speech traits should be used indiscriminately. But a sprinkling of them will make any piece of dialogue seem more real, less stilted and contrived. The following example, while perhaps *too* idiomatic, will serve to illustrate my point:

"Listen, let's go to a movie."
"Why not?"
"Which one you want to see?"
"Oh, I don't care."
"How about John Wayne?"
"Yeah, he's good, all right."

"Or maybe Rod Steiger."

"Sure."

"Well, which one?"

"It makes no difference to me."

You *can* go overboard with this kind of thing, especially if you follow the methods of some writers to reveal lack of intelligence and/or education, and of other writers hung up on backwoods dialect. These are the authors who write phonetically, combine words and phrases, drop g's, and so on—perpetrators of the *gonna, wanna, c'mon, whyain'tcha, yer, ya, lessee, whazzat, whozzit, dunno, comin', goin',* etc., school.

While fictional characters should be made to speak as realistically as possible, there are limits. A reader can grow very weary of page after page of lousy English, and if he is forced continually to decipher elided words and phonetic spellings, he can very easily lose the flow of the story. And, ironically, this kind of writing does not establish lack of intelligence or lack of education—nor is it particularly representative of the backwoods. I've known educated men who went around saying "gonna" and "wanna" and dropped their g's; and I've known some "down-home" types who spoke clear, grammatical English.

Writers who persist blithely in this sort of thing are largely responsible for fictional stereotypes: a back-country sheriff saying ponderously, "Wal, Sam, them there fellas ain't goin' ta get away, I'm tellin' ya that"; a criminal raised in a slum district saying out of the side of his mouth, "Less'n ya want dat dere cement overcoat, bud, ya'll keep yer yap buttoned up, see?"

Careful, sparse usage of such devices is permissible, of course, but there are simply better ways of accomplishing the same purpose. To show that a character is uneducated or unintelligent, for example, the author can give him a limited vocabulary, have him repeat favorite words or phrases, or stumble over words of more than one or two syllables and seem not to understand words and phrases whose meanings should be apparent—and so on. In this way, stereotyping is eliminated and, at the same time, character is effectively revealed.

Slang and dialect should be employed by the fiction writer to achieve realism as long as he keeps three things in mind: 1) Don't use slang that is out of character (i.e., having a sheltered spinster say, "He's groovy" or "She's up tight" or "They're really cool"). 2) Don't overuse dialect or slang; there's nothing more irritating to a reader than to be confronted by one slang expression after another, especially unfamiliar ones. 3) Don't use slang expressions or jargon that is likely to go out of date. What is an "in" phrase today may become passé tomorrow. If a supposedly hip character uses slang which is obsolete and the reader is more hip than the author, the author is in trouble.

Dialogue, as I mentioned earlier, must be an integral part of a story. Dialogue which does not move the story along, or add to the mood of the story, or have an easily definable reason for being there at all (such as to establish important characterization), should be considered superfluous and therefore cut.

As a means of telling the story itself—moving it from Point A to Point B to Point C—dialogue is invaluable. In many instances, when the author has a choice of writing a scene in narrative or in dialogue, he would do well to choose the latter. Conversation is a superb way to build tension and suspense between two or more characters—and, at the same time, to build tension and suspense for the reader. Character A speaks, and the effect of his words on Character B is reflected in B's response as well as in B's actions. The effect of B's response on A is then reflected in A's subsequent response as well as in A's subsequent actions. The impact is therefore *doubled*. That is why scenes with more than one individual can be (if the conversation is skillfully handled) much more exciting, can move much more swiftly, than scenes involving only a single character and his actions, or two or more characters who do not exchange words and their actions. And that is why stories and novels using well-written dialogue can be more exciting, more rapidly paced, than stories and novels written primarily in narration.

Without conversation that flows smoothly, a story can noticeably drag; it can lose some or all of its impact on the reader; it can be divested of mood, characterization, even plausibility. If the dialogue is stilted, illogical, overwritten, patronizing, condescending or consistently inappropriate or unsuited to setting and situation, it does not matter how well the plot or the narrative is constructed;

chances are that the story or the novel will not sell "as is" in to-day's market.

There is nothing wrong with the word "said." Some writers, especially beginners, seem to spend more time thinking up synonyms for that perfectly good word than they do in plotting their stories or novels. There is no good reason for this. Words are *spoken;* they are not *ejaculated, flung, rasped, gurgled, expostulated, hissed, grated, sneered, predicated, heaved, gulped, vociferated, wheezed, blatted, pontificated, croaked, bubbled, fumed, proclaimed,* or *asserted.* Indiscriminate use of such substitutes can weaken otherwise acceptable dialogue, and make a scene less than effective—perhaps even ludicrous.

Certain *said*-substitutes may be used now and then to avoid constant repetition. Such words as: *agreed, admitted, replied, answered, asked, muttered, whispered, shouted, told* (him, her or it), etc., are all excellent synonyms. But in two out of three instances, a simple "said" is sufficient.

Some writers seem to feel the need to use *said*-substitutes to convey manner or emotion. All a writer needs to do to show that a character does more than simply "say" something is to add an appropriate adverb after the word *said* (or *asked* or *answered,* etc.); *slowly, warily, evenly, happily, cheerfully, argumentatively, solicitously,* and so on.

One thing to keep in mind, however, is that no one makes a statement or asks a question with particular inflection or emotion or purpose *every time.* Most often, we simply make statements and ask questions. Adverbs are fine as long as they're used sparingly, and when genuinely necessary.

To illustrate the foregoing, I offer the following two passages of dialogue. Which would you consider the most effective?

"Where's the money, Harry?" Jack asked.
"I don't know," Harry said.
"You stole it, didn't you?"
"No."
"Don't lie to me," Jack said.
"I'm not lying!"
"I can always tell when a man is lying," Jack said coldly.

Or

"Where's the money, Harry?" Jack hissed.
"I don't know," Harry ejaculated.
"You stole it, didn't you?"
"No."
"Don't lie to me," Jack blatted.
"I'm not lying!"
"I can always tell when a man is lying," Jack iced out.

Almost any kind of fiction can be effectively written if the dialogue is properly constructed and used. The best sex scene and the best tender love scene I have ever read were both done entirely through dialogue. There were no graphic bits of narrative in the former, and no "shining eyes of love, and palpitating heartbeats" in the latter. Both were memorable—real—because all the elements of humanism and emotion were inherent in the words which were spoken by the characters.

Mastery of the art of dialogue truly *can* make the difference between sales and rejection slips.

21

BIRTH OF A SAGA

By R. F. Delderfield

Let me make my position clear at the outset. Nobody, in my belief, has ever taught anyone how to write a novel, and nobody ever will. It was therefore with some hesitation that I accepted the Editor's invitation to offer beginners technical advice on the craft, and I might have declined the invitation had he not used a certain noun and prefaced it with a certain adjective, both commonplace words in themselves but somehow inducing second thoughts. The noun was "guidelines." The adjective was "certain" . . . "*Certain guidelines* on the subject of storytelling and story planning. . . . to help beginning writers create a convincing story." The terms of reference were broad. I decided to do an honest, earnest best.

For the benefit of those (almost surely a majority) who have never set eyes on a work of fiction written by me, I admit to dealing mainly in sagas, or three-deckers, as our grandfathers called them. I also admit (very cheerfully) to something else. Weaned on the novels of a century ago, I am cast in an old-fashioned mould—which even American critics who are very kind to me always say in their reviews—and about this I am unrepentant. Hence, I am qualified to give only old-fashioned advice: For what it is worth, here it is.

I do not see the professional writer as a prophet, a sage or a missionary. A majority of novels published since World War Two have little to offer me. The best of them, as I see it, are brilliant fireworks displays. The worst of them are pretentious and boring, shot through with a gloom and defeatism that override any storytelling virtue they might conceivably have possessed had the author sat down and learned his craft before lifting the cover from the typewriter. Some, and these include the dreariest, are deliberate attempts to shock. Others, even those that are plotted, are so larded with misery, suffering, degradation, and self-pity that the unsuspecting reader who picks them up in the hope of being entertained is a man seeking relaxation on a bed of nails.

I like to think that I regard the fiction writer's function more modestly. He is, after all, the lineal descendant of the man who once sang for his supper in a baron's hall, and his main concern should be to interest and entertain. If he also succeeds in making his customers think, then that is a bonus.

Forty years ago, when I was eighteen, a London playwright gave me a laconic piece of advice that I heeded—possibly the only literary advice I ever did heed. He said, glumly, "For God's sake, don't try to please the public! Write what you like and at least you'll please yourself. There is a hundred to one chance you will also please others. By accident." Only now, after getting on for half a century at the game, do I see the wisdom of that remark, and this gives me guideline No. 1: *Unless you feel delirious with excitement over the prospect of telling a story, don't tell it!*

For secondary guidelines I draw on my own experience. Every writer, even every saga writer, approaches his task in an individual way and perhaps mine is slightly more individual than the majority. I invariably begin a three-decker with a map of the kind Stevenson used in *Treasure Island,* for it is essential to me to know not only where I am going but where my characters are going. By this I do not mean north or south but something far more precise.

When I began the three-year stint that resulted in *A Horseman Riding By,* I drew a corner of the English West-country where every river, hill, wood and farm was marked. I then named the farms. It was only when the topography of the Sorrel Valley was starkly clear in my head that I invented characters to live in those farms, and sometime after that when I fixed the span of years the story was to cover, 1902–40.

I went to work in precisely the same way with *The Avenue,* the story of a suburban road outside London, but here I numbered the houses and marked out a dozen as rallying points for the narrative. The story, in this case, covered the period 1919–1947, and I was able, well in advance, to use those rallying points for social aspects of the decades. Thus, No. 22 harboured a militant Socialist, and No. 17 a small-time Fascist. Further along the street, I had other houses I intended to people with jazz musicians, a cinema pianist, a suburban adventuress and a slick tradesman to be earmarked for easy money in the black market period between 1940–45.

And this leads me to another important guideline. In the name of God and Charlie Dickens, *never make a firm plan for your storyline.* In a book of this type, it is absolutely essential to keep the narrative fluid and to let the characters behave as they want to behave and not as you hoped they would behave when you started out.

I can give a good example of the advantage of flexibility. In *Horseman,* I had every intention of allowing the hero, Paul Craddock, to spend his life, and raise a large family, in partnership with Grace, an attractive and very intelligent woman he met the first night he set foot in the Valley. Alas, it was not to be. Grace's temperament made it quite intolerable that she should bury herself alive in a remote rural backwater, and I was obliged, like it or not, to enlist her in the suffragette movement and offer Paul a divorce. In this way, he married Claire, a far more suitable partner for him, and Claire (a walk-on part in the first section of the book) ultimately became its most important female character.

I can give another example. In *The Avenue,* I invented twin brothers, Berni and Boxer, and grew very fond of them, as one does when one spends years in the company of fictitious characters. It was my intention, however, to let Boxer, the lumbering twin, learn to stand on his own feet at the age of about twenty-eight after Berni had been killed at Dieppe in 1942. Five times I tried to bring a mortar shell down on Berni, and five times the page went into the wastepaper basket. In the end, I came to terms with the strength of the bond. I was physically incapable of destroying Berni Carver and compromised by depriving him of an arm. He lived on, a repatriated prisoner-of-war, and played a useful part in the final third of the book.

The reading public are incurably inquisitive about an author's source materials. I rarely give a talk on the subject without being asked, "Do you create characters or do you lift them from life?", so that I have pondered this innocent-seeming question for years.

Now I think I can give an honest answer. Every character I have ever created has not *one* living prototype but any number up to a dozen. In writing the R. A. F. comedy, *Worm's Eye View*, I went so far as to compose a list of the airmen who had contributed to the five major characters. When I toted up, there were nineteen names on the slip.

I ramble on. How are we doing for guidelines? We have so far three vital ones: *enthusiasm, familiarity with background,* and *flexibility*. To sum up, write only of places, themes, and people *capable* of generating excitement in you; get to know the background well in advance; and, above all, let the characters, once created, follow their own inclinations, even if they lead you straight up the gum tree. Suppose we poke about for other guidelines, not so vital, perhaps, but each contributing something material to the strength and structure of the story. Period research, for instance, and a word of warning about that.

Do not imagine that however well researched your saga is you will not be caught by some triumphant smart aleck at least once a chapter. Every day, from all over the world, letters arrive on my desk beginning, "I enjoyed your book immensely, but. . . ." There is always a "but," and many of them make my ears burn. In the first chapter of *Horseman*, for instance, I awarded a C. B. E. to a doctor fifteen years before the honour was initiated here in Britain.

You cannot research every line of a saga. If you did, you would never get it started, let alone finished. Every now and again you have to take chances and make inspired guesses, particularly if you are writing of a period in which you have not lived, but do not let this depress you. You are giving someone somewhere immense satisfaction. *He* knew, and *you* didn't, and if he took the trouble to write, at least he read the book and read it carefully. Research a period, of course, but never let it frighten you. It is far more important to get the *feel* of a period than note down its trivia, and perhaps the best way to do this (and get away with it) is to learn to love your characters as you go along, even those you project as unsympathetic characters. Galsworthy began his *Forsyte Saga* loathing Soames. He ended up by making him the true hero of the series. I found this hard to believe until I worked on Archie Carver and Elaine Frith in *The Avenue*, both greedy, heartless people. After 400 pages I found myself warming towards them in a way I could not begin to do as respects far worthier characters, so I eventually married them to one another and was cock-a-hoop one morning when a reader wrote, "I found all the honest people in that *Avenue* prigs! The book was saved by Archie and Elaine!"

And now discipline as it concerns the writer. How can I throw out a guideline on this without sounding outrageously priggish myself? For of all the guidelines this, surely, is the mainstay of any literary creation, especially one running to several hundred pages. As a professional writer, I think it is essential to work regular hours, no matter how uninspired you feel when you roll the first sheet into the typewriter. The reading public have a fixed idea that most writers sit about waiting for inspiration. Poets may, for all I know, but saga writers don't. They slog away, six to eight hours a day, seven days a week and sometimes 365 days a year. More reflective work comes with revision, and it is a good idea not to begin revision until you have a pile of manuscript at least twenty pages thick. There is a great deal of truth in that assertion that ninety-nine per cent of any creative job is the result of perspiration rather than inspiration, and this is not simply a figure of speech. On the coldest days, after a stint resulting in some 5,000 words, I have been drenched in sweat.

Writing a book, I sometimes think, is rather like preparing a good, substantial meal, and writing a saga is like cooking a ten-course banquet. To do it at all, you must, of necessity have a well-stocked larder, and let me hasten to add that I do not mean to imply you have to be particularly well-informed or generously endowed with brains. What you need far more is a retentive memory that enables you to distill material from the attics of the brain to the blank page. The professional writer should train himself never to forget anything but to file it away for future use. Conversations overheard in a bus or train, an unfamiliar scent, a cloud pattern, a physical sensation, a trick of expression on the face of a stranger, the sound of distant thunder—all these things must be hoarded, for there is not one of them that will not prove useful, and the odd thing here is that they tend to pop out of the attic filing cabinet the moment they are needed.

The rewards for this back-breaking toil? They are many and

often unlooked for. Financially, if you succeed, it can provide a reasonably good living and, what is more important to the artist, personal independence. Then again, once a book is in print, readers will seek you out by mail from every corner of the globe, and the letters almost always give you a queer satisfaction, for you feel, somehow, that you have contributed something to their lives and have not wasted your time in a back-alley occupation. But the real reward is in the job itself, in the exhilaration of plucking something out of nothing, fashioning it, perfecting it—at least to your own satisfaction—and sending it out into the world to earn its living. In this instance a comment of the British novelist Ernest Raymond comes to mind: he once wrote regarding the craft of fiction, ". . . some of its ways are plenteousness and all its ways are joy." Which returns me to what is, I suppose, the central theme of this piece. *Enjoy your work. For if you don't nobody else will.*

22

PEN TO PAPER

By Catherine Aird

Guy de Maupassant, the famous French writer of short stories, had a phrase which described the work of writing more aptly than any other I know. He called it "the getting of black on white." Now, where in the wide field of the detective story do you, the writer, start getting black ink on white paper?

I would suggest that you, if you want to write detective fiction, should begin by first reading the acknowledged experts in the field. After all, if you were making a study of almost any other subject, you would begin with what is often called "required reading." So read those who have written about writing detective stories—Howard Haycraft, Dorothy Sayers (in her classic introductions to various collections of stories of detection, mystery and horror); Ronald Knox (his "Detective Story Decalogue" is very useful reading); G. K. Chesterton; and anyone else who has written well about detection. I am sure that they all have something to teach.

In addition to helping you with their accumulated wisdom, this practice may well save you the embarrassment of coming up with a cry of "Eureka" and a discovery of your own, only to find that "your" idea has been in cold print for a very long time. Remember that the detective story convention is a well-established one.

It is also an exacting one.

It requires, for instance, that the criminal must be mentioned early on in the story and that he must continue to appear throughout. [In this context, read "he or she" for "he"; as the lawyers' clerks say, "The male embraces the female."] The great G. K. Chesterton held that the real criminal must be suspected at least once in the course of the story. Time spent on thinking this out is not wasted, and you will save yourself a good deal of rewriting if, right at the outset, you cast the criminal in a major role in the story.

This, incidentally, is much easier said than done. You have to write the scenes in which the murderer appears with that much extra care, but it is important. If he doesn't appear often enough, your reader will feel cheated. And this is probably the most important tenet of all in the whole detective story concept: the reader must not feel cheated. Puzzled, misled, teased, intrigued, mystified —it is permissible to inflict the whole gamut of bewilderment upon your reader, provided only that he isn't left with the feeling of having been cheated.

This does not mean to say that you can't put a false emphasis somewhere. Or put the clues in the wrong order, so that the real significance of the first clue becomes apparent only after the second clue. Or allow someone in the story to make the wrong assumption. Or use the well-tried technique of saying something truly important just before or just after a matter which is made to seem extremely significant when it isn't at all. Or let your detective make misleading inferences—in moderation, of course. He is still the hero!

Or allow your character to make ambiguous remarks, and let everyone else (except the detective) choose the wrong one of the double meanings offered.

Or steer suspicions towards a character whom everyone knows isn't the murderer because they're cleverly suspecting someone else. He isn't the murderer either. You could call this the Crime Writer's Rule of Three.

Or—and this is one of the oldest and simplest deceits of all—allow someone to display knowledge which he wouldn't have if he were innocent.

There is also a great deal to be gained from reading good examples of crime fiction. Take your own favorite crime fiction writer and then ask yourself exactly what makes him—or her—your favorite. Now read his latest book once for pleasure and then a second time, more slowly, to take a look at the mechanics of his story.

How often does he bring the criminal into his tale? How exactly does he make you suspect the wrong character? Was it a fair way? Could you have improved upon it? How does he introduce his red herrings, and how many of them are there? More importantly, perhaps, how neatly does he convey the real clues?

Mark, learn and inwardly digest how well he delineates the area of his story both in time and place. This is more important in a detective story than in other forms of writing. The whole world cannot be suspect—observe, therefore, how he defines those open to suspicion and how expertly he rules out whole groups of people as above suspicion.

And how well does he weave his invaluable subplot in and out of the main warp and weft of his story. Subplots *are* invaluable. They give the writer a chance of changing the scene, which is always useful, of working in his personal speciality, of riding his own particular hobbyhorse, perhaps. All of these things can be inconvenient in the burden of the main plot. As small interwoven threads in the tapestry of your real story, they can make for light relief.

A good tale by an acknowledged favorite, read in a truly analytical frame of mind, with a pen and paper beside you, should certainly set your mind working along the right lines.

If you were indeed at a school desk studying the writing of crime fiction, you might very well be required by your teacher to do more than just read the main textbooks on the subject. You might, for instance, be asked to do some exercises. You might be asked, for example, to write for practice a dialogue between two strong, relatively silent men conveying, say, some bad news. Then, to write a dialogue between one garrulous woman and one timid girl who is trying to get a word in edgeways, conveying the same bad news.

Then to try doing it all over again without using a single adverb. Or taking, for example, some statistics and turning them into dialogue. The facility to do this is important because it is one of the ways in which you utilize background knowledge of all kinds and incorporate it into your writing.

The most likely place for murder is in the home. The most dangerous place (statistically) in the home for the woman is the bedroom; for the man, the kitchen; and for the child, the bathroom— where they are (still statistically) most likely to be strangled, knifed and drowned in that order. Could you serve this up—so to speak—as lugubrious dialogue between two policemen? Then throw in the hoary old joke about the statistician who was drowned in a river whose average depth was six inches and make your dialogue into cheerful chitchat, even though you are using the same facts? Try it—and see if you don't come up with some ideas of your own about working facts into your story. (And deduct marks if you've used the same adverb more than once.)

Looking at facts in this way should also lend savor to the background reading which is also part of the business of writing detective stories. Consider for a moment the "homework" a course on crime writing might reasonably require. A rough working knowledge of the "fringe" subjects of ballistics, forensic medicine, the history of crime, law, pharmacology, penology, famous criminal case histories, and police procedure will all come in handy. The mere studying of these varied arts and sciences should provoke a few good ideas.

Go to the squirrel as well as the ant. Do make and hoard useful notes from your reading as you go along. Paradoxically, though, if you write them down, don't let that be an excuse for forgetting them.

There is one useful exercise which any aspiring crime writer can practice with advantage; that is, the writing about the discovery of a dead body. Sooner or later, as you cannot fail to have noticed, a victim crops up in almost every detective story, and at least once. Try your hand, then, at finding one in a hundred words, in fifty words, in twenty-five.

Thrillers, where the body is found between one sentence and the next, so to speak, have just one pace. Fast. In the detective story you have the valuable option of alternating the pace, so do try varying it from the staccato, where no paragraph has more than two sentences, and no sentence more than twenty-five words, to the rather more—but not too—wordy. Even so, however leisurely the pace of your choice, make it a cardinal rule that every chapter in your story has some action in it.

Let us take the school analogy to its ultimate conclusion and assume that you would be expected to take an examination at the end of your course. The questions for crime writers might read something like this:

1. How many Holmes/Watson syndromes can you recognize in contemporary writing?

2. List the characteristics of a successful detective hero.

3. Select ten detective story titles from the works of Shakespeare. (Senior students omit quotations from *Hamlet*.)

4. Give an example of a forensic clue.

5. Enumerate the police hierarchy starting at the bottom.

6. Name a famous trial at which, in your view, the wrong verdict was reached. Give reasons.

7. List ten names for characters in an imaginary novel. Go to the bottom of the class if any of them look or even sound faintly alike!

8. John Webster, the Jacobean dramatist, says in his play *The Duchess of Malfi*,

> Death has ten thousand several doors
> For men to take their exists.

Name a round dozen.

There are, of course, some things which no one person, however well-intentioned, can teach to another person.

One is what Anthony Trollope called "the habit of industry." I take this to mean actually writing something every day, come rain, come shine, and preferably at the same time of day. Discipline and staying-power (which I suspect go together) are very much personal matters.

Another is the ability to observe. This is a quality which novelists share with poets and painters and sculptors. They must all be acutely aware of what they see—and see so much more than the casual observer.

If all this sounds like very hard work—which it is—remember the credit side: that it is not everyone who can be said to be putting in a good evening's work settling down with a new detective story by his favorite author.

23

SIX WAYS TO SUCCESSFUL CONFESSIONS

By Florence K. Palmer

"To my surprise—" an English professor at a large university said of the magazines I'd sent her, "the confession is just a good story that makes use of every basic principle of short story writing, but with stronger emotional overtones."

It's also a capsule of life, relived vicariously by millions of housewives, schoolgirls, working women—and yes, some men—who read the thirty-odd confession magazines currently published for information and guidance, as well as entertainment.

For serious freelancers both of these facts are important, particularly for those writers struggling to get into a sadly shrunken fiction market, at the same time condemning unread today's liveliest short story medium.

Actually, although the confessional tone has been preserved, titles and blurbs are all that remain of the once shoddy confession. Inside the flamboyant covers now there is a concerned searching into, and compassionate understanding of *human behavior*. The modern confession writer analyzes motivating factors, and relates them to the effect on, or problem of a story narrator.

Besides a genuine love of people, however, three things are absolute—*first-person viewpoint, reader identification*, and a *hold-nothing-back discussion* of the narrator's mistaken course of action in resolving her problem. This calls for strong characterization, and as the writer, you must feel every doubt and fear exactly as if you were that person—your typewriter keys are the bridge between a heart that listens, and a heart that reveals. If there's any secret to writing confessions, this is it!

Perhaps you've never suffered the agony of a child's death, nor known the heartbreak and disillusion of marital discord. How then can you write convincingly of emotions outside your personal experience?

The surest way is to go back in your mind and heart to your childhood. Relive the moment a favorite doll was broken, feel again the utter hopelessness of cradling those bits of shattered china, knowing full well that no other doll will ever be quite so precious. Put that same feeling into the heart of a bereaved mother, and you'll find it possible to express her deeper, more elemental grief with verisimilitude.

And remember the time a flip little newcomer to junior high walked off with your steady boyfriend? The outrage, the bitterness, and frustrating inability to do anything about such piracy isn't too different from a rejected wife's reaction!

Yes, by all means write about what you know, but don't underestimate the depth of your own knowledge either. Somewhere in your life there is a counterpart of almost every human emotion, but you must have the insight and imagination to recognize the analogy.

But—and watch this—all people are different, and no two persons will react in quite the same way to the same problem. So, in creating a confession character, work with universal traits and emotions. Let the individual reader apply your solution in her own fashion to the similar problem she herself faces, for these first-person problem stories aren't intended as add-water-and-mix advice, but rather to help others help themselves.

Keep in mind, too, that good fiction begins and ends with people, not plot. Whatever the story germ, it can be told only through the words, actions, and emotions of real people in conflict with real problems. You must, therefore, climb inside your narrator. For the space of twenty to thirty typed pages, you see, hear, taste, and feel only through her senses. You must, or the confessional tone is lost, and with it, that all-important reader identification.

So, how are those basic short story principles applied to confession writing?

1) *You must confront your narrator with a problem.*

Is her husband unfaithful? Do her parents refuse to believe a teen-ager is capable of mature, lasting love? Has she gone into debt for the material possessions her more secure neighbors take as a matter of course? Is she afraid to bear a child because her own mother died in childbirth? Has she allowed a mistaken concept of religion to channel her life?

Your choice is limitless. It can be swift and dramatic, or seemingly trivial, but in general, the problem is a common one that could trouble you, or a family down the street. Once the problem is selected, however, something must happen to set the action in motion—something that leads inevitably, incident by complicating incident, to a resolution which will have a marked influence on the narrator's whole future.

This brings us to the kind of character defect most likely to trigger things. Perhaps your narrator is bedeviled by envy, or maybe only discontented with the monotony of dishes and diapers seven days a week. To make her sympathetic to readers, though, you go into the whys and wherefores of her particular flaw, or mistaken attitude. A woman doesn't hate her children, or make the drug scene, or suffer an emotional collapse overnight—and that convenient phrase, "I don't know what made me do it!" won't satisfy anybody. You must know and transmit the underlying reasons, which is merely another way of saying that there must be sound motivation or your story will fall flat on its tear-stained face!

And what about the incident or situation that pinpoints the problem and creates a necessity for the narrator to take decisive action? This is the *narrative hook*, and can be in the form of dialogue, action, or a bit of philosophy—all are good confession openings, so long as they stress the problem's immediacy. For example:

The mother with teen-age youngsters and an after-forty baby on the way has the problem of family adjustments. She begins her story like this:

Honestly, I could practically hear Betsy already. "Oh, Mom, what's everybody going to say—how'll I tell the kids at school?"

She may go on to say that her son won't act as if she were a freak, or doing something downright indecent. But she'd "see the flush of scarlet creep into his ears, catch the way his eyes avoided mine."

At least her husband would feel differently about a belated addition to their family:

Joe's a darling, and loves children as much as I do, only the trouble is, he'll start working twice as hard to earn more money. Probably keep on wearing his shabby old topcoat, and cutting down on cigarettes, or lunch. . . .

And here's the immature wife, who becomes involved in what she thinks is an innocent affair:

If it hadn't wound up another scorcher that day, a lot of things might've been different. I don't know, I really don't, because maybe it wasn't the weather at all, maybe I was just spoiling for trouble.

Anyhow, with the temperature nosing 80 before noon, I was dripping wet even thinking of the ironing left to do, and that bucket of soft, purple salal berries still to jell. And if that wasn't plenty, Timmy picked the hottest day of the year to get active enough for twins, let alone one small three-year-old!

All the same, I should've known when I married Kale what it'd be like—living in a logging camp, I mean. So what was I kicking about? He was a lumberjack, wasn't he? And loggers have to live where they work—in the woods!

In both of these, the problem is presented, a hint of the narrator's background, the other characters involved, and in one, you also learn the locale. This is done, you'll note, in less than a page, or about 150 words.

2) *The format of your story is the next consideration.*

Will it be told by flashback, or chronologically? The full flashback, or opening at the so-called "dark moment," is no longer very popular, although some stories demand this method to get background material and motivation in at the outset.

The following is an example of the full flashback:

They started coming while we were still elbow-deep in scrubbing out the house, curiosity plain on their faces, and paper-thin excuses at the tip of every tongue.

"Knew you'd need a chair or two until you're settled," that was Mrs. Grunwald, the old crow! "We got an attic full of Ma's stuff; no reason you shouldn't have it."

"That's how they are!" I stormed to Shep when he protested my curt refusal of the furniture we really did need badly. "Shoving their charity at me the same as they did after Mom died, and Dad—"

The narrator is now back to the time when her father went completely to pieces, "not giving a hoot for anything except the rot-gut he began to drink morning, noon, and night." That was bad enough by itself, but then the "do-gooders" pitched in to make them a sort of neighborhood project:

Little kids aren't particularly touchy that way, only I was older, a string-bean twelve, and rawly aware of a humiliating undertone to their generosity.

Oh, sure, we needed the things all right . . . but with nothing to give in return it amounted to outright charity, and that's one thing I wasn't taking from anybody if I could help it. . . .

Here is the *cause* of the narrator's character flaw, which motivates everything that comes later. But its warping *effect* should be lived, not just told. By using this "happening right now" treatment of the flashback, you show your reader the opening scene again without his feeling that he has been taken on a round trip into the past, and the story can then move forward without any interest-losing break.

But since confession editors prefer the chronological form, fragmentary flashbacks are an effective means of speeding the pace of a story. Such flashbacks are woven into dialogue and narration as the story is happening, without slowing the forward movement: "I hadn't even thought of Rick Bradley in years, not since his folks moved to Denver our junior year of high," tells in one sentence what would otherwise take a paragraph or two. Then, you can bridge the time between like this:

I stared up at the tall, laughing-eyed man incredulously, remembering how red he'd gotten, and the way he had stammered asking me for a dance at our class stomp. "My gosh, are you the Richard Bradley that's headlining that big show at the Palace?" I exclaimed.

Each of these transitions from past to present, however, should be preceded by a sentence (as I've done above) to justify a situation that might seem illogical, and indicate the upcoming incident's purpose.

3) *With your story now underway, write in scenes—live the action and conflict, don't just tell it.* And, since the confession is intended to be informative as well as entertaining, use specific locales whenever possible. The Puget Sound area, for instance, provides a colorful setting, by which the reader learns something about the rugged Cascade Mountains, or Seattle's busy seaport where vessels from all over the world take on cargo.

Your own part of the country may be equally interesting, or draw on memories of that trip out west, or weekend at the beach.

Regional backgrounds are always a plus, but they must never dominate the story. It must be capable of standing alone, without the aid of any crutch.

The same applies to the narrator's occupation. Weave in the information about particular types of work through dialogue and action, but don't make your story a textbook on how to repair TV sets, or the daily routine of a dance instructor!

Incidentally, there is no confession vocabulary per se. Just sit over coffee with an intimate friend, and talk your problem out, breathlessly, urgently. Use action verbs—race for hurry; whirl rather than turn—and the contractions—I'm, he's, would've—to create this illusion.

But avoid purple writing or breast-beating—they're only an emotional veneer, and slapdash writing doesn't get by in today's confession. Which reminds me, let's not hoard lovely bits of imagery for "something better"—they can make your story sing, and be the difference between a standard three-cents-a-word sale, and the five-cent rate paid by top confession magazines.

4) *How does your narrator go about solving her problem?* As in real life, because of that motivating character flaw, she'll see only one way out of her predicament—and, of course, her warped judgment will prompt the wrong decision, which plunges the narrator into the *dark moment.*

5) *The climax.* This is a tricky point in the confession story, and its challenge can't be wrapped up with a flimsy, "Suddenly I realized—!" Instead, the narrator, faced by an apparently hopeless situation, begins to understand the *why* of it. She examines her mistaken attitude, delves into the past for its basic causes, and is determined somehow to overcome that troublemaking character flaw. In other words, your narrator has actually been in analysis all along, and her story is "the couch in print."

6) *The theme.* Up to this point, confessions follow the general pattern of every other short story, but their endings are peculiarly confessional. They go one step beyond the climax, because here the problem's resolution is also an exemplification of your theme—*and the theme is always the lesson to be learned.*

The true purpose of this tagged-on ending isn't to preach, but to offer the reader reassurance that she is not alone, and that God is still in His heaven. "Here is my life," the narrator, in effect, says, "I was just as mixed up, too . . ."

Speaking of themes, did you know that scores can be found in Aesop's Fables? *Happiness cannot be bought, Pride goeth before a fall, Greed can cost your all*—confession themes, and yours for the writing.

Then for a real treasure trove of story ideas, what about the Bible? With no irreverence meant, "The Prodigal Son" is one of the greatest confessions ever written. "The Story of Ruth" parallels the attitude of many a wife today, and "Jephthah's Daughter" underscores the tragic consequence of a promise rashly given.

Daily newspapers are another excellent source, as are your friends and own family. Wherever you find the idea originally, however, it is wise for you to keep some sort of memo. The date of a news item, or what sparked your story is enough, and may save a lot of bother if there's ever any question of its being public property.

There is one drawback to writing for the confession market—you are bound to get rather harsh comments from less informed freelancers, those who haven't looked inside the cover of a *True Story*, or *True Confessions*, or *Modern Romances* since they were kneehigh to a cricket.

"You'll never be able to write anything worthwhile," they sniff. "Confessions are a literary limbo—trash!"

Yet, some of the finest documentaries on medical achievements and sociological advances have used the pages of a confession magazine to reach the widest possible audience. Some of the most moving stories presented on movie or TV screens were first printed in a confession magazine. And some of today's most honored by-lines have been made by writers who learned to create flesh-and-blood characters for the confession market.

Will confessions harm your other writing? Not if you write sincerely, and with perception. Then, the facility gained through this person-to-person handling of human problems and emotions is far more likely to enrich whatever you may write, fiction or nonfiction.

24

STORYTELLING, OLD AND NEW

By Elizabeth Spencer

BEING a Southerner, a Mississippian, had a good deal to do, I now believe, with my ever having started to write at all, though I did not have any notion about this at the time it all began. Having had stories read to me and having listened to them being told aloud since I could understand speech, I began quite naturally as soon as I could write to fashion stories of my own. I now can see that my kind of part-country, part-small-town Southerners *believed* in stories and still remain, in my own experience, unique in this regard. They believed, that is, in events and the people concerned in them, both from the near and distant past, and paid attention to getting things straight, a habit which alone can give true dignity to character, for it defeats the snap judgment, the easy answer, the label and the smear. Bible stories, thus, which were heard at home and in church, were taken literally, and though the Greek and Roman myths which were read aloud to me, along with Arthurian legends and many others, were described as "just" stories, the distinction was one I found easy to escape; maybe I did not want to make it. And we heard oral stories, too—Civil War accounts and tragic things, some relating to people we could actually see uptown, almost any day. All ran together in my head at that magic time—I trace any good books I have written, or stories, right back to then.

Starting at the other end of things, however, is what the writer who daily faces the blank sheet must do: that is to say, O.K. about childhood, what about now?

The work of fiction begins for the writer and reader alike, I feel, when the confusing outer show of things can be swept aside, when something happens which gives access to the dangerous secret pulse of life. What is really going on? This is the question that continually tantalizes and excites. For the fiction writer, the way of getting the answer is by telling the story.

Right back to stories. You see how quick it was.

A story is a thing in itself. It has a right to *be* without making any apology about what it means, or how its politics and religion and pedigree and nationality may be labeled. The writer can be guessed at by the stories he puts down, but the writer is not the story any more than an architect is a building. The events in a true—that is to say a real, or honest-to-God—story are a complex of many things, inexhaustibly rich, able to be circled around like a statue or made at a touch to create new patterns like a kaleidoscope. Such a story may be absorbed sensually or pondered about reasonably; it may be talked about by friends or strangers in the presence or the absence of the writer. The story should be allowed to take in all its basic wants. It may want discipline, but it may not get it, depending upon how greedy it is or how obsessed the writer is about it. A story has the curious, twofold quality of seeming all in motion and at times even in upheaval while it is being told, but when finished, of having reached its natural confines and attained repose. Many times characters seem to have life outside the story in which they engage. So much the better; the story will not question this.

Each story I have written commenced in a moment, usually unforeseen, when out of some puzzlement, bewilderment, or wonder, some response to actual happening, my total imagination was drawn up out of itself; a silent magnetism, without my willing it, had taken charge. What was it all about? It is just as well for the writer to pause here and consider. Not that the writer will take the imprint, literally, of people and event—though for some writers the main worry falls here. To me, it is rather the power of the story that one should be warned about: Don't enter that lion's cage without knowing about lions. For the writer enters alone. He may be eaten up, or mauled, or decide to get the hell out of there, but even if all goes splendidly and ends in fine form, the person who comes out is not the same as the one who went in.

Anyone who takes stories as an essential part of life is only recognizing the obvious. Religion, love, psychiatry, families, nations, wars and history have all become deeply mixed up with stories and so find no way to shed them without violating or even destroying their own natures. Every human being is deeply involved with at least one story—his own. (The Southern tendency to get involved with family stories has accounted for the larger part of Southern fiction—if we add to this hunting stories and war stories, then we have just about accounted for all of it.) The present faint-hearted tone which some critics now adopt when discussing the future of fiction is surprising, for stories, being part of the primal nature of human expression, are in one way or another going to continue to be told. What disturbs us all, I believe, is the debasement of the story into something mass-made, machine-tooled, slick and false. (The lion was stuffed or drugged or doctored some way.) At its highest level, a story is a free art form, daring to explore and risk, to claim that it recognizes truth and that even when inventive, what it imagines is, in terms it can splendidly determine, true.

At a level short of this highest fiction, but shared by it, many group stories exist, the bulk of which never get written down. They are told every day, repeated, embellished, continued, or allowed to die, and some are better than others; inventive and factual at once, both commonplace and myth-like, they grow among humanity like mistletoe in oaks. They are much better than average TV fare, and anyone who wants to write should start collecting everyday accounts that are passed about offices, campuses, neighborhoods, or within family situations, noticing whatever there is to be found of humor and terror, character, achievement, failure, triumph, tragedy, irony and delight. The modern theme of self-exploration with heavy emphasis on the private sexual nature and fantasy has been done to the point of weariness. Can we think of ourselves again in communion with others, in communities either small, medium or large, which may be torn apart disasterously or find a common note, an accord? One word for it, maybe, is love.

25

PEOPLE AND CHARACTERS

By Borden Deal

A NOVELIST's stock in trade is people . . . characters. A novelist deals not with intellect, but with emotion. Even when he's trying to spring an idea on an unsuspecting public—and this is a sin committed by most writers at one time or another—he must do so in emotional rather than intellectual terms. It is the very foundation of the human psyche that nothing, not even the most abstract and rarefied of intellectual conceptions, means anything until you feel it in the gut.

Emotion is the basic characteristic of the human individual. So the novelist must embody his ideas and emotions in the form of characters. We have, in this day and time, a great proliferation of fact and, consequently, a major emphasis on non-fictional writing. I, as a novelist, have a massive distrust of facts, of data, of rationality and the scientific approach. Scientific rationalism is a fraud and a delusion, and the vaunted scientific method that we're all so proud of is only the dogwork of small minds plodding in the giant footsteps of greater men.

The great discoveries of science are reached by the same intuitive process as that employed in the creation of fiction; a quantum leap into the unknown. Einstein did not arrive intellectually at the idea of relativity. He tells us himself that he first perceived it emotionally, in a sudden flash of insight—and later spent years of work devising experiments and equations to justify it in scientific terms.

And yet, science has become such a powerful force—emotional as well as rational—in our lives that our moralists no longer warn us that smoking cigarettes or using the oral contraceptive is sinful, and therefore displeasing to God; they tell us, instead, that it will give us cancer and is, therefore, displeasing to Science!

I am greatly interested in what is called the documentary novel —the book that enters one of the many separate little worlds of modern life in an attempt to get at its meaning for us all. For my last novel, *Interstate,* I devoted a full year to researching the background of highway building.

But too many documentary novels stop there, failing to go on to the inevitable human equations, the meaning and impact of that special world on the people touched by it—in other words, on us all. In writing *Interstate,* I was acutely aware of the necessity of getting on beyond the documentary facts to the people involved—and so, during that year of research, I watched the people as much as I listened to them. I sought the shape of their minds, the slant of their feelings, as much as I sought the facts of their profession.

For the truth can be told *only* in emotion. Character is the vehicle for emotion. A novelist is, if you will pardon the expression, something of a creative relativist. A person himself, he must look inward and outward at one and the same time. People—characters —are a novelist's way of life, his hobby, his delight . . . and his job. When he doesn't understand what he sees, he looks inside himself for the key, for we are all living branches of the same immortal tree and there dwells in each of us the murderer, the lover, and the saint. You don't have to look deep or hard, either, to find the fool.

There is one infallible sign of the true writer: a constant listening to the sound, the movement, of people. That listening is not only practiced, it is automatic and instinctive. What I am trying to describe is an openness, a vulnerability, to the meaning and impact of people. When a writer closes himself against this vulnerability, he closes off the truest and best part of himself.

A writer can move—must move—on every level of society. Something of an outsider wherever he goes, he can yet make himself one with any group he chooses to join. A writer can never be a snob, for he knows no boundaries of class. He can learn as much— sometimes more—from a truck driver or a whore as from another professional writer. Indeed, I think it's dangerous for writers to huddle together in coteries, to spend too much time in listening to each other, for that is only another way of closing oneself against humanity.

One never knows from where the word will come. Nathanael said, "Can there any good thing come out of Nazareth?" and he was about as wrong as one can get. Indeed, it is in the *unlikely* places that a shard of the truth can most often be found. And, above all, a writer must learn to allow a man a style . . . both in life and in fiction. It is style—manner, slant of mind—that makes an individual unique.

I treasure the moments of many people in my memory—I save them as a miser saves gold. Sometimes it is an individual in his wholeness; sometimes it's only a word, a gesture, a way of walking . . . maybe the tilt of a head, the slope of cheekbone, or simply the shape of a hand. One never knows what small clue, what large understanding, will trigger a characterization or illuminate an entire book.

This should not be taken to mean that fictional characters are, or should be, based on real people. Far from it. The facts of a real person are constricting to the novelist's creative imagination. What the novelist seeks is the key, the catalyst, the distillate of human nature.

My wife, Babs H. Deal, in her last novel, *High Lonesome World,* derived what many people consider the most memorable character in the book, a Cajun guitar player, from a momentary glimpse of a young Cajun man in overalls, standing alongside the Louisiana highway on which we were driving one day. Something in his face, his posture, his whole air, set off a constellation of meanings in her mind, which resulted in a total imaginary human being holding only a tenuous connection—if that—with that real Cajun boy.

A writer must believe that every man has a meaning—and that that meaning can be arrived at not through rational processes, but through the primordial process of unconscious thought and feeling that a writer has learned to trust far more than he trusts his conscious mind. Sometimes that meaning is learned through the years of a close, intense relationship—sometimes it is revealed in a glance, a betrayal of gesture, a moment of passing. All these meanings, which one gleans as a harvest of his days and his years, serve to feed that primordial process of creativity, to emerge days or months or years later, at the moment of need, as shaped forms of fiction. For a writer must also understand that his books are not the products of his ego, his rational mind, but of processes deep within of which he is only partially aware, and which he cannot completely control. A book, a novel, is, above all, an act of faith.

Allow me to revert here, very briefly, to my principal thesis: The truth can be told only in emotion. Emotion can be set forth only in terms of character. So the novelist feeds whatever meager talent he has with observation of habit ar ' manner and speech, and with whatever understanding he can find in other people and within himself. The novel can never move far away from the teeming multitude that is man, and the novelist learns in his early years this unalterable truth: You can always count on people . . . to be people.

All the great novels are based on people—characters—and story. When you think of the great novels, you remember them in terms of the characters—Micawber, Huckleberry Finn, Soames Forsyte, Becky Sharp, Raskoinikov, Long John Silver. These characters are not presented as ideas, even when—especially when—they embody ideas, but as living, breathing people, based on their creators' long and intense scrutiny of humanity. This intense and unremitting observation, I emphasize again, operates inwardly as well as outwardly; for the author must never forget that he is as human as the characters he writes about.

Story is important, too. But all story derives from character. At present, storytelling itself is denigrated by the critics. If a writer tells a story, it is considered "nothing but a story." We have forgotten the knowledge that story itself was the first, the original, and still the most powerful symbol that mankind has ever invented out of his collective unconscious. In tales, in stories, in legends, mankind has capsuled over and over again the ever-recurring experiences of his mind and soul.

A novel must, above all else, add up to a total greater than the sum of its parts. If a book doesn't do this, it may be a number of things, but it is not a novel. I have stated many times what I consider the simplest and best definition of a novel: a character in collision with a truth.

You will note that I say *a* truth, not *the* truth. No man can claim to know *the* truth. But when a man, a character, comes into conflict with *a* truth, then drama, story, inevitably develops. Distilled and capsulated, a piece of the great story of mankind can be told.

That is my endeavor; it is also, I believe, the endeavor of every true fiction writer—to begin with character, and progress through story to a final meaning that is larger than the surface events that have been recounted. This is, to my mind, the true place and function of the novelist—not just in this age, but in all ages, in the future as well as the past. And it will continue to be his function until the endlessly repetitive and infinitely varied story of mankind is finished.

26

CHOOSING DETAILS THAT COUNT

By Elizabeth Taylor

I HAVE been asked to write something about the building of character and situation from the use of detail, and to illustrate it by referring to my own novels. It would be easier for me—and a more interesting exercise—to work on examples of other people's books; but if there is the slightest use to anybody in tracing finished things back to origins, then I can probably do it only by turning inwards on myself, by trying to catch my own self unawares.

I suppose all writers know the experience of having an idea come winging to their aid, of at first wondering if it came from outer space, and then deciding that, no, it came after all from the lumber room of the mind. I know that it is unfashionable to believe in inspiration, but it is the only word I can use to describe the method of dispatch of such ideas, and the complex of storage, selection, fusion that preceded it. One really does feel that one has breathed it in from the air, that it has come from outside oneself, and by itself, and without reference to anything that has gone before.

However, that is, for most of us, a brief reward for the other hours of rather grim concentration, when nothing is yielded up from the lumber room, from the ragbag of details. And what are details? My dictionary informs me that they are minute parts or particular facts. In a novel, I see them as strokes of reality, highlights, dashes of colour; breath to the abstract, death to the vague.

Some great writers can dispense with such minutiae. I. Compton-Burnett does so: none appears in her books, unless it has relevance to the plot. But for most novelists, details (of clothes, belongings, gestures, settings) give reality. I don't mean descriptions of wardrobes, or lists of furniture, for I believe that these cancel themselves out; but there is usually *one* thing from all that is known, implied and omitted that it might be illuminating to include. The word "illuminating" is important; for if the detail is not this, it is not carrying weight.

Appearances are tricky. In my last novel, *The Wedding Group,* for instance, I wanted to describe some waifish girls in an artists' colony. This description had to be briefly done, for it was a recollection in another character's mind, and if this kind of thing goes on too long, it can grind the story to a halt. "All had pale faces and long, pale hair. Their brown feet, in clumsy, homemade sandals were rough and scuffed. All bit their fingernails." Later in the book, when I could expand a little more, I added chilblains. I intended that the repeated vowel-sound—"clumsy," "rough," "scuffed"— should have a cumulative effect, so that each word does a little more than its call of duty.

Frugality is to be aimed at. Compression is important in describing the appearance of characters, and the best of all compression is not to set out flatly a few features, as I did in the passage above, but to bring them in *en passant,* obliquely glanced at while sketching in some action. For instance, here is a description I did of a man in a pub in *The Soul of Kindness:*

He covered his mouth with one hand, and with the other worked with a pick among his gold or rotting teeth, eyeing every woman who came in.

We have to learn to be receptive, and then to know how and when to go to work on what we receive—sorting out, discarding, having hunches about what can be left lying idle in the mind to wait for its fusion with some other chance material. Some days when we are dull, and not on any wave-length, nothing comes in: we can go anywhere, see all kinds of people, but nothing assails us; there is nothing to be recognized or picked up, not a gesture, or a look, not a hat to be borrowed or a habit to be copied.

On other days, things seem to come flying out of the blue, in the manner of a dream, and seem to fasten themselves to us as if drawn to a magnet.

Sometimes a small detail heralds a whole book. I was told of a long-ago bride who, at her wedding reception and while the bridegroom was making his speech, threw crumbs of wedding cake out of the marquee for the birds on the lawn outside. For some reason, this small action fascinated me, and I began to wonder about such a character. I sensed a vague sweetness of disposition, charm, simplicity. The more I wondered, the more Flora in *The Soul of Kindness* came into being, and opened the novel with that very gesture:

> Towards the end of the bridegroom's speech, the bride turned aside and began to throw crumbs of wedding cake through an opening in the marquee to the doves outside. She did so with gentle absorption, and more doves came down from their wooden house above the stables. Although she had caused a little rustle of amusement among the guests, she did not know it; her husband was embarrassed by her behavior and thought it early in their life to be so, but she did not know that either.

And there was once a blind man I saw on a bus. From watching him, wondering about him, I built up a whole story. The thing to do, I have found, is to fasten to some detail, and then let the mind wander down any corridor it fancies, opening doors or ignoring them. One must be capricious in this exercise, and not dogged. It is in this way the details will build up into the whole character, the whole situation, and the scene.

Sir Laurence Olivier has described the building up of a character, and it seems to me to be equally valuable to a writer:

> I sometimes on the top of a bus see a man. I begin to wonder about him. I see him do something, make a gesture. Why does he do it like that? Because he must be like *this*. And if he is like this, he would do—in a certain situation—that. Sometimes months later, when I am thinking about a bit of business, I hit on a gesture, or a movement or a look, which I feel instinctively is *right*. Perhaps not till later, perhaps weeks after I have been making that gesture, I realize where it came from—the man on top of the bus. Then I realise, again, that the gesture looks right because it *was* right, and that it was right because it was real.

After all, our material is all about us. Sometimes it claims us, rather than the other way round. At the moment, I am haunted by a seedy man with a ragged moustache I sat opposite in a train. I don't want him. I have other characters to concentrate on, without being bothered and bored by this disembodied moustache; but it will not go away, and I know at the back of my mind that it will overcome me in the end.

Buses and trains seem to be particularly good places for the snapping up of details; also pubs and cafés and strange hotels and railway stations. In a relaxed way, one can sit and eavesdrop, watch people drinking and eating, examine food. Here is a plate of cakes over which two characters sit in a café in *The Soul of Kindness:*

"These awful cakes," he murmured. They were large, bright yellow, some covered with shaggy coconut. One had green marzipan leaves, shaped like a cauliflower; a rock cake was pitted with holes where burnt currants had fallen out.

Above the table lurks despair, and the cakes lie in the glare of it, and reflect it.

Food is important, I think. It brings people together. It can be a sacrament: it can be an expression of character. It can make a world more real.

But no detail is of any use if it is buried under what is called "descriptive writing." I even like the actual *look* of a page to be broken up. One dense page of print is very daunting to a reader.

Descriptive writing can be a trap. The enlivening detail comes better on its own, glancing, allusive, stirring. When I praised frugality I meant that a little should be made to do its utmost; not that much should be made of it.

In *A Berlin Diary*, Christopher Isherwood wrote:

I am a camera with its shutter open, quite passive, recording not thinking. Recording the man shaving at the window opposite and the woman in the kimono washing her hair. Some day, all this will have to be developed, carefully fixed, printed.

This seems to describe very well all of us, the writers, as we sit in trains or in restaurants, as we listen and observe, as we humbly record the passing scene. I feel like murmuring, every time I step onto a bus, "For what I am about to receive, may the Lord make me truly thankful."

27

DO-IT-YOURSELF FICTION WRITING

By Jane Hinchman

Because I got into the writing business as a second career, without any formal training and after my children were older, I wonder if I am really qualified to offer advice to new writers.

But it may be that my message *is* exactly that: If I could write and sell short stories and a novel under those discouraging circumstances, you can do it, too—provided, of course, that you don't mind rewriting a story twenty times if it takes that to get it right; that you have a strong stomach and a sense of humor to help you endure the rejections; and that you're willing to persist, no matter how dim the prospects are.

When I began, I was such an amateur that I did not even know how to submit a manuscript. But with the help of books like this one, and your local library, you should know better. There are any number of really good books on writing a beginner should read. If I had found them earlier, I would have saved much time and misdirected effort.

So, now that you've read the books and dug out the typewriter from your college years, it's time to begin.

What to write about? Almost any subject will do for a starter. The point is to put down words and sentences, which will grow into paragraphs and, with luck, will gradually shape into a story. You may be surprised to discover how many different characters you had locked away in the attic of your mind all these years.

I have two different methods of beginning. When I'm broody and expectant with a new piece of writing but not yet sure what it's going to be, I sometimes start with a simple character sketch. This is how my novel, *A Talent for Trouble,* began. I hadn't the vaguest glimmering of a plot in mind. I was sure only that I wanted to write something cheerful and that, as an antidote to the ghastly gloom of the mid-sixties, this story would end on a hopeful or even —of all things!—a happy note.

At the time, our house was full of adolescent children, so I began with a character sketch of a girl who combined in herself the traits of several boys and girls I knew, along with some characteristics of a mother who had herself once been fifteen.

By the time I reached page eleven, I knew Ann Bonney, or Calamity Ann, fairly well. I could foresee what mistakes she was going to make and even the sort of person she would choose to fall in love with the first time. The story grew. Each small incident, or accident in Ann's case, arose out of what had gone before and developed in an easy, natural sequence. My only real problem came when I had to think of a way for Ann to capture the pair of finches she'd been hired to sit with. When I had finches loose in my own house, I turned eight teen-agers out after them with nets and handkerchiefs in a wild, funny romp, but that wouldn't do for the book. It took me three weeks to think of letting them be trapped in a dish of fudge that never hardened, the only kind of fudge my inept heroine would have been able to make.

My other method is to wait with my arms extended for one of those marvelous moments when an idea for a story floats down from heaven like manna.

The idea for "The Day They Gave Hamsters Away," a short short that appeared in *Redbook* recently, came to me that way, complete with the housewife heroine and her two children, the time sequence, and even the right form—a monologue. Where the idea had lain during the five years since our family had hamsters I don't know, or even why it finally germinated and bore fruit. I wrote the story rather quickly, for me, but in its original form it was not quite right. It took some suggestions from a kind *Redbook* editor to put it into final focus.

Speaking of editors, you will find that they are not dragons, but your very best friends. When they reject a story with a note pointing to its major flaws, they don't do it because they are cruel and unsympathetic, but rather in the hope that you will avoid making the same mistake another time and that your next story will be one they can buy with cries of joy. If many patient editors had not taken time to send me personal notes during my learning years, I am sure I would have given up long ago.

As a do-it-yourself writer, then, who has never been fortunate enough to study creative writing, or to meet a live editor or be invited to a writers' conference, and who still sends stories to magazines without benefit of agent and sometimes sells them, I have several suggestions I hope you'll find useful.

First, please understand that I don't recommend doing it my way. Take all the courses you can find, meet editors (don't ask me how), attend conferences, and above all, read constantly, not only the magazines you hope to sell to, but everything, indiscriminately—newspapers, biography, how-to books, the Bible, even your old school yearbooks (you'll be amazed at how many ghosts straggle out of their pages like moths out of an old letter-sweater).

Second, but most important, make yourself write something every day, even if it is only a long letter or an entry in a diary, a character sketch or an essay. Like any athlete, a writer who wrestles with words has to practice regularly in order to keep himself in shape.

A third rule is one I swear by, although its origin is lost to me. However, here it is: Test every word and sentence in a story against this standard: Does it directly affect the action of the story? If it doesn't, cut it out.

You'll protest that you need it to develop character or paint in background or build up symbolism, but if you're honest, once you get over the deadly insult and force yourself to reread your recently rejected story, you'll find that the story failed because you became infatuated with the beauty of your own words and forgot that the *sine qua non* of a good story is keeping your audience interested. You may curl up around the edges like a sizzling oyster at your own description of sensitive Gloria's rejection of her parents' materialism, but if this takes more than a sentence or two, the editor who is reading it will lay it aside, and you've undone the good you meant to do, since you've lost your sale and your projected audience.

For writers who have gone stale and are desperate, I have a

desperate remedy. I understand it works for some people, though I've never had any luck with it myself. It originated with G. B. Shaw, I believe, who said he did it to grab the reader's attention quickly.

The trick is to think up a preposterous sentence that still makes sense, like: "Andrew lay very quietly on his bed and watched the pigeons parade across his room, cooing." After that you write the rest of the story, explaining to your own satisfaction what the pigeons were doing there and whether Andrew finally got rid of them or decided to keep them; or were they a part of his drugged dream or did one pigeon stay behind and become his pet and help him recover from his nearly fatal illness?

This one last bit of advice I would offer isn't easy to put into words. Bluntly, it's this: Find out who you are, and then tell your stories in your own special way. Most writers are competent. To set yourself apart, you need to cultivate the individual approach to life which is yours alone and to write from that point of view.

As with singers, our voices are all pitched differently. Try to develop your own unique sound. If it turns out to be a high squeak rather than a thunderous bass like Tolstoy's, maybe you can use it to make people laugh, a not unsatisfactory goal, after all. James Thurber did not disdain it, nor did Mark Twain, and the only way Jane Austen could have written *Pride and Prejudice* was with tongue in cheek.

Never be ashamed to write about the homely little things that happen. Often it's just the small, homely detail described expertly that makes a reader think: Yes, this could happen to me, or, it's just the way things happened yesterday.

Our thunderous Tolstoy was not too proud to write about family life. Is there anyone who does not know his opening sentence in *Anna Karenina:* "Happy families are all alike; every unhappy family is unhappy in its own way." The families he describes have moments of both happiness and unhappiness, as most of us do, although you'll hardly believe me if you read much modern fiction with its insistence on unrelieved despair.

I wish I could guess what changes the future will bring.

Seen in retrospect, the sixties were masculine years filled with the clamor of war and violence; they left very little behind in the way of memorable fiction. For fictional women, the sixties were a lost decade during which they appeared only at the hearth or hopping in and out of beds. Hopefully, a change seems to be coming now.

While I'm not a Lib member, owing to my fondness for so many male chauvinists, I believe women need and deserve a literature of their own. Publishers seem to forget that women get tired of reading about complaints they don't share, such as Portnoy's, or about the ubiquitous and totally unbelievable character, the prostitute with the heart of gold. Bank account, yes, but heart? No.

I am sure that women do genuinely enjoy reading what is so often, and unfairly in many cases, labeled "soap opera," the reason being that from the time we begin to baby-sit with our younger brothers and sisters, we are more interested in the reasons why people behave as they do than in abstract ideas. Women consider themselves experts in human relationships, but they're always willing to learn more; witness the success of Dr. Spock's book. I think anyone who writes with some originality about family life should be able to find a market for his work in the coming years, if only because we are tired of being outraged and are ready for a change.

I'm more optimistic than most about the future of magazine fiction because I can remember that radio was once given up for dead but, because it filled a need, it survived and prospered, as I believe magazines will once again. Television or no, there will always be people who love to read, and, I hope, magazines to serve them.

And in spite of the trend toward factual writing, I think fiction will always be with us. In fact, we need it more now than ever before. Researchers working on a study of human sleeping habits discovered that people deprived of the opportunity to dream developed neurotic symptoms. I wonder if our whole population, deprived of something to believe in and forbidden fantasy, isn't showing similar symptoms. Thank goodness for science fiction and mystery; it's all the imagination we're allowed to taste freely.

I sometimes wonder if writers are not partly to blame for the low esteem in which fiction is held today. Maybe if we leave it to the pamphleteers to reorganize the social and political face of the country, and get back to our own real business, which has always been to entrance and entertain, we can coax our audiences back once again. I just hope it isn't already too late.

28

A STORYTELLER'S CREED

By Frank G. Slaughter

Since the Stone Age, storytellers have occupied a favorite niche in the affections of the people. Cave drawings in Spain show that even without a written language some men sought to portray events through pictures at least thirty thousand years ago. And one of the oldest written documents in the world, the Epic of Gilgamesh, is an exciting and revealing historical novel. If storytelling has fallen into disfavor in modern times, as the rise in nonfiction sales seems to indicate, the cause lies not in a fickle reading public, but in a deterioration of the product—a crime that can be laid to the door of television more than to any other source.

Like medicine, storytelling is both a science and an art. The techniques can be learned; the sources of ideas can be defined; the methods of their development can be set down in words; sales gimmicks have been devised by enterprising authors and publishers whereby even an inferior product can be made to catch on with the reading public. And yet, unless a storyteller possesses the same vivid imagination that made the *jongleur* of old welcome at the nobles' table—though "below the salt," it was true—sustained success is impossible.

Creative imagination is a gift that cannot, I believe, be acquired, though it can be stimulated by various psychological techniques. Being a gift, it places an obligation upon the owner to be sincere, whether he is writing a play for television, a suspense-novelette for *Cosmopolitan,* or a serious novel of the present or the past. Long ago in my own career as a weaver of tales, I formulated a personal creed which I have always followed. With the purchaser of a book that bears my name, I make an unwritten contract guaranteeing him: (1) A story that is interesting and exciting from start to finish; (2) an authentic historical and cultural background, whether the time is today, the Civil War, or 4,000 B.C.; (3) a minimum of my own personal philosophy.

I am by profession a storyteller, a literal, if not lineal, descendant of the first cave man who came home from the hunt empty-handed and had the imagination to weave a tale about the "one that got away." Luckily, this prehistoric ancestor of mine found others so enthralled by his story that they willingly contributed to his larder. His next discovery was that if his tales were exciting enough, he didn't have to go out to hunt any more but could stay home and entertain the women. Just that, in fact, is largely what those of us who are sometimes called "popular" novelists do today, since by far the greater number of our readers are on the distaff side.

But entertaining the women, pleasant and sometimes profitable though it may be, is not without its responsibilities. Women are quick to detect an implausibility. They read more and, with an intuitive instinct for getting their money's worth, demand a product that gives it to them. More important, women are essentially romantic—and thereby hangs one important key to success as an author. All romance and no plot makes pretty dull reading, after the first "heart-stopping" embrace has been described; conversely, all plot and no romance drives women readers away, and sends the author back to teaching school, writing newspaper stories or—in my case—the practice of surgery. The trick is to achieve a balance of the two ingredients, not always an easy task.

In lectures, I often describe a successful story as "exciting things happening to interesting people under colorful circumstances." Excitement implies anticipation and doubt concerning the outcome of a particular situation, in itself a definition of suspense, the essential ingredient of plot and the *sine qua non* of the storyteller's art. For unless the reader is vitally concerned with the fate of the story people, his attention wanders, and failure results. Makers of old-time movie serials carried this principle to its ultimate conclusion —absurdity; producers of daytime soap opera use a somewhat more sophisticated approach, with enormous success in terms of the looking and listening public. The successful novelist must emulate their principles but on a much higher level of quality. Nevertheless, he can also learn much from their methods.

It is a far cry from the soap opera hero and his vicissitudes to the struggles of young Oliver Twist, but the principle involved, as far as storytelling is concerned, is the same—exciting things happening to interesting people.

Moving from the ridiculous to the sublime, let us look for a moment at *To Kill A Mockingbird,* by Harper Lee. Ostensibly, this is a rambling story of a little girl, her family and friends, in the day-to-day life of a small southern town. But from the very first scene, a succession of events is set in motion, an excitement of suspense is generated, which is only resolved in the final scenes of the story. In other, less truly artistic, hands the same plot might have resulted in a polemic, one of the most difficult of all novels to write successfully because the author usually lets his personal feelings turn the story into a rostrum from which to expound them. Without the discipline of a definable plot, Miss Lee also might have wandered into fruitless byways of description and personal experience. That she did none of these is the mark of highly practical, yet nonetheless inspired, literary artistry.

It is not happenstance that many promising new writers founder and go down into obscurity after a widely-hailed first novel. Such stories are almost always autobiographical and, told with feeling and understanding, the transition from childhood to adulthood is inherently exciting. Not only is this true because the chronological pattern forms a natural plot, but because, having walked the same paths, the reader finds a natural suspense and interest in the writer's personal experience. But having once written their own stories, many young writers find themselves at sea. Not having taken the time and the trouble to learn their trade, they lack the techniques necessary to unblock imagination, to cement down the cornerstone of a plot, and build a structure upon it complete to the final shingle of the cupola. Here, I think, is the point that, to use a colloquialism, "separates the men from the boys." My personal creed, my contract with the reader, would not be binding, if I did not guarantee to him an exciting story.

Two decades ago, historical novels were all the vogue. Almost any hackneyed plot, with a sketchy historical background and an equally sketchy costume adorning the heroine on the jacket, could be sure of book club acceptance and a substantial sale. The result was predictable: a flood of inferior stories. In spite of the declining sales of most historical novels, I continue to write them because the challenge of creating a broad tapestry of an ancient era is exciting and rewarding to me. These novels take roughly twice as long to write as a story of medicine today, much of it spent in patient research, but I welcome each new expedition into the past as an adventure in learning.

After twenty years in medical practice and study, medical backgrounds pose few problems, but the task of recreating the vast panoply of the Roman Empire in the first years of the Christian Era, as seen through the eyes of a Greek physician named Luke, required six months of study before a word was written and another year of continuing research during the writing. Even more challenging was the problem of picturing faithfully the Middle East of 854 B.C., when the Assyrian invader was halted in an obscure battle at a place called Karkar in the valley of the Orontes River, and Israel was saved from destruction for nearly two centuries.

The cliché that "history is stranger than fiction" is far more truth than truism. And historical characters are often much deeper and more complex than any novelist would depict them in fiction. There was a day when a writer with an interesting fictional situation might deliberately lay it against an historical background to increase sales. But with the decline in popularity of the run-of-the-mine historical story, such a device frankly isn't worth the trouble any more. The better historical novels spring from history itself, as witness Mary Renault's fascinating picture of ancient Crete in *The King Must Die,* and many others.

All this means that a successful historical novelist today must be at least as much student as he is writer, a constant searcher through the past for colorful and exciting situations and people. What is more, in plotting his story, he is duty bound to remain as nearly as possible within the limits of historical truth, since he is dealing with what I consider to be a true art form in which sincerity and accuracy of portrayal are vitally necessary. Usually this requires an intensive use of the creative imagination, which can be exhausting and often very frustrating, yet tremendously rewarding. An equally interesting by-product is the privilege of associating in the close intimacy of a biographer with some of the most interesting people the world has ever known. All of which, of course, is part of the second clause of my contract with the reader, assuring him that the historical and cultural background of my story will be as accurate as I can make it by drawing upon my own large library, as well as the finest university and other collections in the country.

The final clause of my creed is, to my mind, the least important, since I consider myself a storyteller and not a philosophical novelist. Every novel has a theme, it is true; without it, the lack of sincerity in a story is immediately apparent. But in a professionally produced product, the theme is inherent in the actions and speeches—preferably short—of the characters, not in the sermons and fulminations of the author. As a physician with many years of experience, I could not have failed to develop some understanding of human nature; the only place where people let their hair down more often than a doctor's office is in a beauty parlor. But as a student of history and people through the ages, I can see little change in the basic facts of human nature, or human relationships and ambitions. Like the ancient Greek philosophers, I am sure most men basically desire to live decent, honorable lives. And the only sermon I ever preach to a reader, in as few words as possible, is one preached long ago: *"A new commandment I give unto you, That ye love one another, as I have loved you."*

29

THE FINE ART OF
EAVESDROPPING

By The Gordons

For many years now, we've been eavesdropping. It's a part of our work, a very profitable part, to hear what people around us are saying. We've trained our ears so that unconsciously they scan with radar swiftness the surrounding area at a party. If anything interesting turns up, the built-in recorder in our brain takes over.

Our best dialogue has come from our eavesdropping. There was that time at the Hollywood Bowl when a row of teen-agers sat behind us. Now, we have no teen-agers of our own. We wish we did, a whole pack of them. Our friends who do tell us we would commit suicide. But we wouldn't because they would be making us so much money. We'd have tape recorders going all over the house.

This night they were chattering away like mad. Not rock-and-roll dialogue but spontaneous talk that crackled like a string of firecrackers going off. We don't know what the attraction was in the Bowl that night. We were too busy jotting down snatches of conversation that eventually found their way into the talk of the Hayley Mills character in *Undercover Cat,* the novel that became the Disney movie, *That Darn Cat.*

"... *I'm going in and tell Mr. Hopkins he's simply, absolutely got to give me another home room teacher, and if he doesn't I'm going to try tears. I'm going to cry my heart out. ... You're learning, Babs, you're learning fast. ... That school does everything except put numbers on our backs. ... Isn't she the most? Don't you like her an awful lot? ... Did you see that movie with John Davidson? I think he's a living doll. My pulse was going 150 a minute. I get these crushes on people I don't know and never will. ...*"

These are the bits of conversation that we used. But in getting them we discarded pages of dialogue that we wrote down that night.

Much of it was repetitious. Virtually all talk is. Much of it was inane, and only amusing because the person talking made it so.

Shortly after we took up eavesdropping, we discovered how boring a conversation can be when set down verbatim—and how exciting it can be after having been edited. So we turned city editor, searching for those words and phrases that would characterize someone, that would bring him alive. Soon we realized that no dialogue we manufactured could compare with edited, condensed, highlighted conversation, both heard and overheard.

"I was so mad. The next morning I told him, why didn't you tell me? I pulled him in, that's what he needs. It was terrible but damn it, he doesn't have to fix her tire. He's got plenty to do here at home. She could've called the auto club but she talks him soft and he does what she wants."

We overheard that one-way conversation while waiting for a phone at a market. There were five minutes more of the same. We kept only the first paragraph. Funny, but people usually say all they have to say in a few sentences and then can't turn the record off.

Occasionally, of course, we want to give the impression of a garrulous character without letting her actually ramble on paper, which for us would be devastating. William Faulkner could get by with it but few writers can.

In *Undercover Cat Prowls Again,* the sequel to *Undercover Cat,* a young couple catch a snoopy old woman next door spying on them from behind a hedge. She says, "What a turn you gave me, you did. Didn't know a soul was about. Thought I was all by my lonesome. Oh, Mr. Kelso, good evening. Didn't see you there. My eyesight's failing me. Was to the doctor twice last week and he told me I was no spring chicken, and I'd have to—but I'm glad to see you, Mr. Kelso. Always does my heart good when I see you. . . ."

This is an actual conversation, but when we heard it, the party kept repeating, "What a turn you gave me," and told in detail about her failing eyesight and going to the doctor. If we had put it all down, we would have lost some impatient readers.

Aside from unedited rambling, we resist another hazard in this business of eavesdropping, the temptation to use new slang. Six months from now it may sound as dated as "the cat's meow." This is especially true of high school and college slang. Such expressions as "dig" and "cool it" have become fairly well established, but every year there is a plethora of new words that won't last until fall.

While we scan for unusual words and phrases, we are more interested in how people put them together. Most of us use at best a few hundred basic words, but we have endless ways of stringing them together. In the above conversation, where the woman doesn't want her husband to fix the neighbor's tire, it's the way she shuffles ordinary words around that characterizes her, that makes for interesting dialogue. She could have said, and most of us would, "I told him I didn't think he had any business fixing her tire when there were so many things he had to do at home."

In this tricky matter of dialogue writing, we went through several phases. First, our characters all talked the same—exactly like us. So, of course, the dialogue sounded wonderful—to us. It had such a natural ring! Without question, this is the easiest way of writing conversation, and we're not saying it will ruin your fiction. One very famous novelist writes this kind of talk. Everyone speaks the same: old men, children, suburban housewives. And people buy her books by the millions.

Nevertheless, when a kindly editor eventually tapped us on the shoulder to tell us what we were doing, we decided to reform. We then took to writing dialogue the way we *thought* people talked. Most of it we picked up unconsciously from the movies. And this wasn't always bad. Most of Hollywood's film and television writers work diligently at coming up with good conversation. The only trouble was that it was secondhand by the time we used it. And it sounded like it.

Next we turned to manufacturing the kind of talk that we thought would characterize our people. By this time we were on a characterization kick. Sometimes we were devastatingly clever. You know the kind of dialogue. Now and then you'll hear it on the stage and say, "How'd anybody ever think up all that brilliant conversation?", not realizing, of course, that the playwright has cribbed from George Bernard Shaw and Abe Burrows. This type of chatter may be entertaining, but people just don't talk that way.

Eventually, we discovered there was more conversation floating in the air around us than we could ever use. All we had to do was to jot it down and *edit* it. In our files, which look like magpie nests, and where our two cats love to sleep while we are working, we have pages headed, TEEN-AGE TALK, 80-YEAR-OLD CONVERSATION, BOY-TWELVE, PLUMBER, MURDERER, MEXICAN-AMERICAN, etc. We should hasten to add that the file listed MURDERER was accumulated while covering a trial. We regret that we have no killers among our friends. This necessitates our making long, weary journeys to courtrooms where we sit bored for hours on end waiting for that electrifying moment when a witness or attorney comes alive. Nowhere do you need to edit more than in a courtroom, but the little that is left after the blue-penciling may make the trip worthwhile.

We have found better spots: cafés where we eavesdrop on the people in the next booth, sports events where there's always one character close by giving vent to his feelings, movies during inter-mission, and neighborhood gatherings in the summer when everyone is more relaxed than at formal parties.

As writers, we owe a great deal to the teen-age and college crowd. They do inject new words into our speech—they and the sports writ-ers and a few others in occupations that seem to call for expressive vocabularies. They keep English a living, vibrant tongue. For the most part these are words that accurately peg a feeling or thought. If it weren't for the teenagers and sports writers and truck drivers and such, English might become a pretty staid, dull language. We get a terrific boot when we hear some youngster come up with a word that hits an emotion or thought right on target, what we call a real *wallop* word.

We find it great sport to eavesdrop. We'll come home from a party and one of us will say to the other, "Did you hear anything?", and the other will say, "Yeah, were you around when So-and-so was tell-ing about getting the parking ticket?" And then one of us will say, "We ought to invite her to dinner some night. She's got a terrific way of putting things."

And then months later, when a book or piece of ours comes out in print, we chortle, "Old Sam said that." Strangely enough, none of our friends has ever recognized any of his own dialogue. And grate-ful as we are, we don't dare thank them. They might clam up—and put us out of business!

30

THE IMPORTANCE OF IRRELEVANCIES

By Cecilia Bartholomew

Pick up any book or magazine about writing, and I'll wager that you will read something about the importance of unity of effect, of the careful selection of only those details that contribute toward an organic whole, of the ruthless blue-penciling of the non-essentials. Without disputing this, because I also have written it, I'd like to put in a word here for an important element of stories that never seems to get its due, an element not inorganic, but rather non-organic.

Stress has always been laid upon the relevancies, and, of course, if you don't have the relevancies, you run the risk of not having a story at all. But we don't want merely a story, we want a good story, and in my opinion what breathes life into characters, and drama into situations, are the irrelevancies.

In his autobiography, *Act One,* Moss Hart speaks with affection and gratitude of his Aunt Kate, who introduced him to the theater. In describing Aunt Kate I think he may have said what color her hair was, how tall she was and how much she weighed, but for the life of me, I can't remember now. Naturally I remember how she loved the theater, and how she blackmailed her relatives for enough money to get her to every performance she yearned to see. But what I will never forget, no matter how long I live or write, is that, according to her nephew, Aunt Kate had a "fine eye for irrelevancies."

There it is, in as nicely turned a relevant phrase as you could wish for. Every teller of stories needs two eyes with which to see the relevancies and a third one, an especially fine one, for the irrelevancies.

In life we pay homage to irrelevancies in such references as "the straw that broke the camel's back." Every story should be as lumpy as a camel's back, and every story should contain within it a straw strong enough to break it.

Sometimes an entire story, an entire novel, is in itself an irrelevancy. Stephen Crane's *Red Badge of Courage* is such a novel. The characters in that story thought they were fighting the Civil War, they thought that they had won it, but on their tired but victorious return from the battle, they learned that what they had been involved in was merely an irrelevancy, an unessential skirmish. The real war was being fought somewhere else, over beyond those hills.

A number of years ago Lillian Ross did an excellent profile in *The New Yorker* on the making of the movie of *Red Badge of Courage*. The big running controversy between John Huston, the director, and Max Reinhardt, the producer, was over this matter of relevancies *vs.* irrelevancies. They didn't call it that, but that's what it was. Huston wanted to play the movie by ear, without a script; Reinhardt said you had to block out the scenes, otherwise how did you know you would get anywhere; you had at least to write some dialogue. The controversy seemed to me to be so exciting with all that it had to say about the creative process, that I hastened to track down the movie at a neighborhood theater.

I came out of the theater with not a little sympathy for Max Reinhardt, and the feeling that one could become too irrelevant, particularly in treatment. But there was in this movie one memorable irrelevance: the brief shot over which the battle waged hotly between director and producer. This was a shot of a dying soldier who in the moment just before death reaches for the eyeglasses that have been knocked off his face by the shell that has mortally wounded him, and having adjusted them with care on his nose, breathes his last breath.

It is such irrelevancies that give to art the look and feel of life. I won't forget that small oblique glimpse of the human spirit. As William Blake has said, "The road of excess leads to the palace of wisdom." In my book, better too much irrelevancy than too little.

Ernest Hemingway's *For Whom the Bell Tolls* is another example of the novel whose entire action is an irrelevancy; this time it is played against the canvas of the Spanish Civil War. Some of the characters were fully conscious of the irrelevancy of what they were doing even when they were bending every energy to its gratification. But the full impact of this irrelevancy is for the survivors to note and attest as they view the years since that struggle.

There is great pathos in irrelevancies. I suppose it is because man feels how puny he is in the universe, how he is at the mercy of fate, that is to say, the irrelevancies of nature. Nature, red in tooth and claw. Man feels himself caught and ground between the paradoxes of existence: finiteness in infinity; time clocks in eternity. Life with a capital L may be related to some Great Scheme, man allows, but he sees that *individual* life is not essential to this Scheme. He has only to read the pages of the morning newspaper. He has only to look at himself. One can even wonder whether Life itself isn't an irrelevancy. Who has endowed it with a capital L but man out of his need? Yet he goes on endowing it thus, accepting his irrelevance. The courage of man in the face of this irrelevance is one of the great moving themes of stories, with infinite variations. If you want to see what this courage is, if you can look upon it, observe the people queuing up patiently with their groceries behind the cash register in the supermarket, or observe the man on the other side of the counter in the small corner grocery. Boris Pasternak has said it in the poem, *Hamlet:* "To live life to the end is not a childish task."

Life is lived on the level of irrelevancies, of incidental action, no matter how high we strain, or how wide our view. A woman may have lost her husband, but she mustn't lose her appointment at the beauty parlor because it will only have to be made again, and probably at greater inconvenience. Inconvenience is the motivating force of life, the handmaiden of irrelevance. Mother Earth, according to pagan mythology, was born out of Chaos.

When we can't bear the realities, we busy ourselves with the certain small details of everyday living. In great deprivation, what we may miss the most is our toothbrush. In jeopardy, we may feel that the last straw is a false accusation of always burning the carrots. In agony, what we find intolerable is the itch between the shoulder blades that can't be reached. And because of that unscratchable itch, a man might commit violence. We may go through great tragedy dry-eyed and then weep over a broken fingernail.

The event that turns a man's career is often small and unrelated to all his preparation. How many times do we hear someone say that he got into his line of work "by accident." By an irrelevancy. A woman may live with her husband for years enduring debasement and cruelty, and in the end it is the way he eats artichokes that prompts her finally to leave him.

In catastrophes, it is often the non-essentials that people choose to take with them: an empty bird cage, a jar of peanut butter, a pair of frivolous high-heeled sandals. What would you rush to save if your house were on fire? My husband and I were living in southern California at the time of a flood. We had to evacuate our home, were allowed to return to it when the immediate danger was over, but were cautioned that a dam might break north of us and in that case the fire siren would sound the warning, and we would have ten minutes to get out of the area. Our first desire back in our home was to get clean. I was just out of the shower when the fire siren screamed the alert. I recall that it was of the greatest and first importance that I find and don my brassiere, before I even thought of my baby.

At a funeral we want to feel grief, but all we can hear is the soprano's quaver on the high notes. The essence of the tragedy of modern warfare is caught not by the burning earth or the flaming sky, not even by the mushrooming bomb, but by a passing shot as the camera records a baby girl whose upraised arms come no higher than the knees of the crowds that race around her.

Nothing characterizes so instantly or so brilliantly as the seemingly unimportant trait: the big man who carries his change in a snap pocket purse; the bookkeeper who has too many teeth; the murderer who feeds the pigeons; the villain who plays chamber music; the banker who laughs without sound, his mouth open but showing no teeth.

The irrelevancy can also be used as a symbol. Queeg's eternal handling of the steel balls in *Caine Mutiny* is such a symbol. I remember a short story by Mark Schorer where a child's repetitious unsuccessful assault on a Bach Fugue is the background against which is played an unhappy scene between the people next door whose efforts to communicate result over and over again in failure. In *The Risk*, if I may take an example from my own work, there is the chapter where Dave has decided he must tell his children about the accusation that has been made against him, and is forced to wait while his young daughter protracts a typical adolescent telephone conversation with her girl friend.

Another aspect of the irrelevant that pleases me is that it may work poetic justice. The murderer who is finally caught and identified with that major offense when he pilfers a woman's purse, illustrates this well. And substantiates my claim that the irrelevant is, in the long run, most relevant.

When I first suggested the idea for this piece to the editor, he replied that he liked the phrase, "the importance of irrelevancies", but, he added in parentheses, "or seeming irrelevancies." Seeming is as seeming does. Is there any validity inherent in anything, or is it only what it seems to the observer? Well, of course, some things seem quite obviously (sic) to be "seeming irrelevancies." For instance, a young girl leaves home because her father sends her away from the dinner table to wipe off her lipstick. Obviously, she has been unhappy in her relationship at home before this episode. This is, then, a seeming irrelevancy. But there are others that are pure irrelevancies, not in themselves, but with reference to the central event.

I call this Quantity X, or if I didn't make up that name, I could have. Two men get together to settle a business deal. "A," thinking that it has all been arranged except for the formalities, plunges ahead on that assumption, and meets with sudden opposition. What he does not know is that "B" has been up all night with a bad stomach (Quantity X). "B" himself does not credit his resentment and distrust to his bad night; he says "A" has revealed a selfish aggression that he had not known he possessed, that he could not work with such a man, and he breaks off the deal. (An upset stomach is certainly not an irrelevancy to the sufferer, but it is, in relation to the business deal.)

I have wondered how many times the stories we submit to editors are rejected not because they lack merit, but because the editor has had a fight with his wife, or because his child is sick, or his son wants a car, or some other irrelevant factor. I recall several years ago arranging a lecture program with two women, each an excellent writer in her own field, but writing in different fields. "Madame A" spoke first and made some slighting allusions to Madame B's field. Alarmed, I wondered if I should pass up to the speakers some explanatory notes. The only man on the platform with us calmed me saying, "Don't worry. Madame B is far too sophisticated to respond

in kind. She will realize that the slight is unintentional." What neither of us knew was that Madame B had just come from a wedding
and was in a highly emotional state (Quantity X), sophistication had
deserted her, and her response drew blood and fire. The result was,
of course, of enormous interest to everyone in the audience, except
me. But Quantity X will always add this excitement and drama to
characters and stories.

Mystery and detective story writers have always made full use of
the irrelevant clue which in the end provides the solution to the
crime. Writers of all good stories do also, even if they aren't aware of
it. But how can you do it, if you aren't aware of it? Some writers
profess to scorn the mechanics of writing, the pasted-up little rules.
But in an art where there is so little conscious technique, it is such
phrases as "a fine eye for irrelevancies" that we must hang on to. I
will even go so far as to say that if there is any chance of your forgetting this phrase, frame it and hang it over your typewriter.

In the final pages of *Homage to Catalonia*, George Orwell is returning to England from the war in Spain, and he lists some of the
things that mean England. These are not population figures, statistics on industry, geographical places, or even names of Englishmen
of fame. They are: ". . . the larkspurs in the cottage gardens, the
barges on the miry river, the posters telling of cricket matches and
royal weddings, the men in bowler hats, the pigeons in Trafalgar
Square, the red buses, the blue policemen. . . ."

In other words, the irrelevancies.

31

PERSON AND PLOT

By Seymour Epstein

To write a novel, one must *want* to write a novel. This is, I hope, not as obvious as it sounds. A writer may conceive of a character or a story, and the novelistic virtues of this character or story may be perfectly apparent to the professional senses of the writer, but while he holds this potentiality in the incubator of his mind, a writer may find it equally apparent that it will never hatch. There are no stirrings within. All the ingredients of life are there, but the writer instinctively knows that he cannot supply the fertilizing seed.

Weeks and months may be lost in groaning over the sacrifice of such excellent material, but in the end the writer will not attempt the novel because he does not want to. What he thought would be vital stuff simply did not, on closer approach, send out the long, restless agitations which create wave after wave of insight and situation, situation and insight—and I do believe that a writer who embarks on a novel without its possibilities seeming endless, shortchanges himself from the start.

But if the writer's instinct can serve him with negative cautions, it should serve him positively as well. In other words, when the restless agitations *are* there, he should have no difficulty in recognizing them.

The question now arises whether the writer wishes to reveal a person, or persons, by means of a fictional story, or to tell a story by means of a cast of enacting characters? Or both? Or is there a preferential order? In short, is the person more important than the story, or the story more important than the person?

Let us say that a writer wishes to tell a story of Pompeii, and he chooses as his main character a volcano on the point of erupting. He may describe the fulminations, the explosion, the massive flow of lava, and the fiery inundation of a city, but unless he gives the volcano anthropomorphic qualities or switches over to the sinful Pompeians caught in their final acts of lust and self-indulgence, his novel will fail. A geologist, or a volcanist, or whatever the specialist is called, can have told the volcano's story better, with more authenticity of detail. The novelist's job is to see the volcano with human eyes—his own or those of the observer he creates—and the moment he does so he commits himself to a certain kind of terror and action and hope of salvation.

Or the writer may wish to tell a story of crime and retribution. The nephew of a fratricidal king, for example, who feels called upon to avenge his father's death. What about the plot? Shall the murderer's identity be concealed until the end? Shall a ghost appear and confirm the nephew's suspicions? Shall the nephew plunge a sword into his uncle's body, or shall he hesitate because of some scruple, some ambiguity of temperament? Frankly I don't see how the author can begin to solve the problem of plot until he has solved the problem of person.

One man—call him Harry Hotspur—might fly to his revenge, catch the vile king standing, kneeling or lying down, and put an end to the business right there. The author with a character like Harry Hotspur in mind could have him do no other. His next worry would be what to do with Harry after the deed. He would undoubtedly have him take the throne, probably send his mother to a nunnery, and possibly make a morganatic marriage with a girl by the name of Ophelia—or else take his royal pleasure and provide for the poor girl's illegitimate offspring.

But if the author has another sort of man in mind, then the revenge might take much longer, and out of the hero's vicissitudes will occur many more deaths, the making of madness, and much coming and going. The story still remains one of crime and retribution, set in a particular time of human history, and told in a language suitable to the characters and their station in life, but the difference in protagonist will change the sequence of events so that the two stories will bear only the most coincidental relationship.

In advancing these same ideas before a group of creative writing students, I have been asked whether the writer is supposed to do no plotting at all but simply to allow his character, or characters, to go stumbling through a novel, creating events out of the special quality of their natures. The answer to that was no, of course not; the novelist must still decide what will happen, and then create the context in which it can happen believably.

But what will happen to a particular person is to a large measure controlled in fiction, as it is in life, by the person himself. A person who fears to travel by airplane will not meet his death by falling from the sky, but since all men are subject to accident, that person might conceivably die as the result of a plane crashing on his house. This is, of course, a gross oversimplification of detail selection, but the principle applies, I think, even to the finest shadings of action and sequence. The principle also applies to the creation of other characters who shall affect the protagonist, and upon whom the protagonist shall have effect. I think I can best illustrate what I mean by personal example.

In writing my novel, *Leah,* I knew pretty well the kind of woman I wanted to write about before setting down the first word. Her main problem (at least from her own point of view) was that she was unmarried, and problem it was at the age of 37. . . . Right here it would be well to pause and consider the possibilities arising from this bare beginning. If my heroine is unmarried at the age of 37, then there must be a reason. Since I intend to have her be a fairly attractive woman with no sexual problems other than infrequency, the answer could conceivably lie with mama and papa. Here, then, is a perfectly valid reason for stocking my novel with two more characters.

Now another writer with another heroine in mind (she could still be a woman living alone in a city like New York) might choose an entirely different problem for his heroine. He might wish to concentrate on her sex life, or her passionate commitment to a cause, or her addiction to liquor, drugs, whatever, and mama and papa could, for him, be more an encumbrance than a help. In any event, the shape of the novel he projects in his mind would not include two such major figures. If any mention of their existence becomes necessary, he will dispose of the necessity as quickly as possible. They will live in a different city, meet an early death, or possibly break with their erring daughter well before the beginning of the story.

So again, bearing in mind the woman I wish to create, other characters present themselves out of the single postulation I have made. Consider the age of my protagonist. The great bulk of available men

are not available to her. Too much discrepancy. Those who make
themselves available must, perforce, appear with problems, the most
obvious of which is that they are already married. And if not married, why not? The "why not?"—an unavoidable question—channels my thoughts in directions which, when you come to think of it,
are surprisingly few in number. Homosexuality, impotence, the silver cord. Confirmed bachelors and my heroine exercise a mutually
repelling force on each other. Quite naturally, my heroine's socially
anomalous position will excite attention from the wrong, or at any
rate inefficacious quarters, complicating a situation that would cause
trouble even in its simplest state.

I can't say how delimiting an influence on my novel my heroine
exerted at the time I fashioned her in my mind, but certainly some
astringencies had come into the picture. I can distinctly recall—before coming to grips with my characters—having more grandiose
ambitions. I wanted to do much with the influence of place on person. If I could capture the manner and rhythm in which the attractions of a great city are transformed into moments of sterility, I
might contribute something artistically significant to the picture of
urban life. If I could show how a city like New York can paralyze a
human being by its very multiplicity, I would, perhaps, add that
extra precious level to my novel that would attract the interest of the
high-rise critics. Because, you see, like most other writers humbled
before the awesomeness of art, I not only wanted to make a million
dollars but to make it with the tortured blessing of the quarterlies.

Unfortunately the writing of a novel has little to do with ambition,
critics, or a million dollars. No matter how much one may be moved
by these motivations, they have to be put aside at least during that
relentless time that it takes to write the thing. I don't believe that
anyone can get an incisive glimpse into character with the bulk of a
million dollars obstructing his vision, or while worrying whether that
vision will be in accord with Alfred Kazin's. It isn't that the writer
undergoes a self-imposed purification for the sake of high purpose,
but that in the most practical way he has learned that when he stops
thinking about his book he stops writing it, and dreams of glory are
just another way to stop thinking.

That is why in thinking about the book I was writing, I began to
trim the fancy edges of my literary dream just as I continually

trimmed the edges of my story. The sense of appositeness which operates in selecting proper people also operates in selecting proper circumstances. The breadth of vision I entertained while reflecting on the book I intended to write became circumscribed by the breadth of vision imposed on me by the people I was trying to create. All avenues are open to the writer when he begins, but I believe it is a sign of professional craft to recognize the natural limits of a novel once it has taken form.

I know that this sounds like a contradiction of a previous statement I made concerning the highest intentions of the writer at the outset of his novel, but in making the distinction between work-in-contemplation and work-in-progress I do not at all mean to imply that one partakes of a lofty illusion and the other of a sustaining practicality. The writer must have a framework of values within which to work, or else, at the first sign of trouble, he is likely to fall back on the faddish and false. At the same time, the organic integrity of the novel he is writing demands that proportion be maintained. The writer must unfailingly try for the most intense and true, the deepest insight, the final word, but these literary virtues have to be applied with discretion. If the scope of the writer's original intention has been shrunk by the natural action of person and plot, then it is on the side of wisdom and professionalism to recognize this and make the necessary accommodation. To force feed one's literary child is much more likely to result in obesity than strength.

But despite this exercise of discretion, a novel is a long, long undertaking, and a conscious effort for organic integrity makes it seem longer still. I have no idea how absolute a connection other writers make with their material, but it is hard for me to imagine that there does not come a time for every writer when he scratches his head and, like the letter-writing boy in Danny Kaye's song, muses: "*Now* what do I say?" He has been faithful to person and plot, the fate of his hero or heroine is far from decided, there are people waiting to enter and others for whom a credible exit must be arranged, but the thread has been snipped and there he is, holding on to one end while groping for the other in a pitch-dark brain. It has happened to me, I know, many times.

I can recall one such point in the writing of another novel. I had introduced all the people who were to play a major role in the novel;

I had established their relationship to my principal character—and then I found myself without the slightest clue to continuation. . . . No, that isn't quite true: what I found was that I had a multitude of choices. I could take up at random any one of the relationships, carry it forward to the next stage; and then perhaps advance another relationship, and so on. But it was the very randomness of these choices that stopped me. Surely a novel that was to have the tight, inevitable development that I hoped to see in mine could not be handled like a game of Parcheesi. If one choice would do as well as another, where was the inevitability? And not only did this flaw apply to the particular point at which I was stuck, but it must also apply to all that had gone before, since I could not have reached such an impasse if I were properly meshed with the gears of my story.

This last supposition is, of course, not true. A writer can proceed in a perfectly honest, craftsmanlike, sensitively felt way and still come to a dead halt. The people he is creating are—to him, at least—unique. There are no guidelines, precepts, or previously recorded histories to advise him how to continue with their story. But having created the story of my people as far as I had, I think I assumed that a certain causality must now exist, and what I was doing was gazing into a blank crystal ball to see if I could discover clues to continuation.

The sad and sweaty fact, however, is that while the novelist must always be conscious of causality, he can't borrow five cents worth of prose from its operation. Since he must create both cause and effect, he is in the position of the Prime Mover who must continually bring natural law into being without being able to pause long enough to enjoy its benefits.

It would be impossible for me to retrace the exact convolutions of mind, the attempts and rejections that went on before I found myself confronting my principal character in much the same way that I had at the beginning of the novel, but that is what finally did happen. It was as if I had brought her in on a consultative basis to help me decide how to go on with this story of hers. What followed was a chapter in which my heroine—therapeutically alone—therapeutically for *my* sake—walks in a bitter cold evening with only her recent mood for company. Mood and evening conspire to evoke an episode from the past (much as it might for me if I were in a similar situation), and in recalling a wretched and frightening affair, she emerges at the end of the chapter in another mood—or rather, she rebounds from that memory in another direction, and that direction was the one I had been looking for. I could then continue with my story.

What I am saying is that I again had recourse to person in order to determine plot. In varying subliminal ways, I do this during the writing of any book, any short story, and I believe other writers do, too. It is not a question of technique, really, but a question of proclivity. This is the way I work, because this is the way I move closest to what Henry James called the quality of "felt life."

Determining plot through person might be the death of another writer, but I don't hesitate to recommend it to those who have not yet crystallized their methods. It may still not work, but if it does, it will go far toward the creation of people who will remain in the reader's mind for at least a little time after he has turned the last page.

32

TICKET TO TIMBUKTU

By Norah Lofts

THIS article is not directed at the well-to-do, or the footloose, or written for anyone whose imagination can only be sparked off by something that his physical eyes have seen. I am writing it specifically for people who are bound to a job, or to a family, or even to a wheelchair and have an impulse to tell a tale set against a background with which they are unfamiliar. Such people are often inhibited because they have been overexposed to the theory that one can only write about what one knows at firsthand, and are a little too ready to believe that only Mr. X, who has spent a lot of time and a lot of money in Timbuktu, can possibly use it as a setting. This simply isn't true. Given the story, enough curiosity and determination, enough time and enough exercise of what Wordsworth called "that inward eye", you can, without losing a day at the office, without being unfaithful to the kitchen sink, write your book about Timbuktu; and presently people will write to you and say, "When were you there? I lived there for twenty years and, believe me, your book made me positively homesick."

So far as I know, nobody has yet come up with any real evidence that Shakespeare was ever in Denmark or Venice or Padua. There is a strong likelihood that he was hobbled in London, earning his bread, saving his money for his old age, and keeping his eyes and ears open. In the Thames-side taverns, he probably talked to sailors who had visited far places; and it is true that his audience was less critical and less well-informed than ours. To balance this, we have wider resources: all those books by Mr. X, accurate maps, pictures, films, television documentaries.

The thing is not to be timid. Maugham once said—I can't give the actual words, but this is the gist—you don't go out and find stories, stories come and find you. A story about Timbuktu may have found *you,* seemingly the least likely person to write it, tethered as you are by all these Lilliputian strings, some so frail as the question, "But what will happen to my dog?" The thing is that this story has found *you.* You are the one to do it. Stories are wiser in their generation.

Another thing is not to think for a moment that to write about a far place without seeing it is easy. The material has to be found, studied and checked with more care than is required when you write of what you know. Two accounts of the same place may vary wildly; then you must find two more, find, if possible, someone who has been there and is willing to talk. Quite recently I met, on a train journey, a woman who had spent twenty-six years behind the Iron Curtain; she was talkative and fair-minded, and told me many things, both good and bad, about the regime. I was all ears, though at the time I had no intention of using anything she told me; but later on, two stories found me and I wrote them; both have been published and so far I have had no complaints. And if you are by this time thinking that nobody would bother to correct a blatantly ignorant writer, think again. The world is full of frustrated schoolteachers who are, like God, "extreme to mark what is done amiss." Ironically enough, the harshest reprimand I ever invited, and a well-deserved one, came after I had written something that I really did know about—or thought I did. Born and reared a Methodist, I thought I was safe with a Methodist hymn, quoted it without checking, and presently was slapped down in a letter from Malaya.

I know that the method I advocate and practice is often denigrated by the term "armchair traveling." I contend that the armchair traveler is a far more cerebral creature than the man on the spot whose mind is subject to physical concerns: will his money last out, has the last train gone, what was in that queer-looking dish that now lies so uneasily in his stomach, could that really be a bedbug? It is all too possible to look upon the Bridge of Sighs or the Leaning Tower and to be preoccupied with the site of the nearest lavatory. The books of genuine travelers often reflect this physical preoccupation which the reader can afford to skip or minimize. I remember one travel book through which the sentences, "We harnessed the yak," and "We unharnessed the yak," ran as recurrent themes. I had no responsibility for the animal and, after noting that in this particular place the yak is a form of transport, could afford to concentrate upon the scenery.

There is this, also, to be considered: If armchair traveling were not a pretty adequate substitute for firsthand experience, how would historical writers fare? So little of the physical past remains, and most of what remains has changed so much, that an effort of imagination is required to give even a glimpse of what it formerly was.

Once, in the company of a member of the you-must-go-and-see school, I traveled all the way to Spain to see a certain palace. There were bits of ruined wall, shoulder high in places, but the site was a pleasure garden, full of people, noisy with children, bright with kiosks selling ice cream. True, we stood on the spot where something had actually taken place, there was that satisfaction; but there was little to be learned, the atmosphere was wrong. For me, at least, a contemporary description, a picture, even the words "a castle in Spain," would have been much more productive.

I sorely disappointed—and this I regret—the kind person who took me to Rome and said, as proudly as though he had just built it, "There is the Colosseum!" I said, "I know. It is exactly as I imagined it." That was true, in a way, yet profoundly untrue in another, because in my imagination the marble facing had still been in place, and the seats had been filled with avid spectators, the gladiators' quarters occupied, the lions complaining of hunger.

I have to confess that when the time came for me to abandon armchair traveling for the other kind, my immediate reaction to any place was—I have been here before, and it was better then.

And to clinch this argument, let us think for a moment about my own home town. It grew up around a great Benedictine Abbey, the second largest north of the Rhine. St. Edmund, King and Martyr, was enshrined here, kings patronized and endowed it, it was a place of pilgrimage. Somewhere, sometime a story concerning its two most famous Abbots, Baldwin and Sampson, or its best known scribe, Jocelyn de Brakelond, may find somebody behind a desk or a counter or a cooking stove in Oklahoma. This chosen person may be one of the go-take-a-look practitioners. He will come to Bury St. Edmund's, which is well worth a visit, and he will receive a warm welcome. With his own eyes he will see the Abbey Gate, a Norman tower, two splendid churches which were once chapels to the Abbey and survived the Dissolution as parish churches and have been practically rebuilt in the intervening years; and he will find a public pleasure ground with lumps of grey ruin here and there. He will see only one thing which conveys the size and magnificence of the Abbey in its prime and that is a picture which hangs inside the Abbey Gate. This picture is a reconstruction, based upon actual measurements and upon contemporary or near-contemporary documents. From that picture the traveler will learn something that his own eye, however imaginative, could hardly have told him as he stared at the flowerbeds, the tennis courts and bowling green—that the buildings still standing are, compared to the Great Abbey Church, as a matchbox is to a two-floored house. In fact, with this picture and a few books, this would-be writer has a far more certain entry to the Abbey as Brakelond knew it than his actual visit could confer.

This is an age of realism; there may be some danger that the imagination, underexercised, will take the way of the appendix and end with nothing but a nuisance value. Publishers delight in announcing on a book's jacket that Mr. X spent four years in Timbuktu and that the book was ten years in preparation; they feel that this adds to its worth. If Mr. X has done a sound job, his book has worth, not least to those of us who need the information he imparts. But this kind of approach, used often enough, tends to make the writer who is unable to travel feel inferior, incapable of writing about anything but his own backyard. And this may mean a loss to the reading public, for a book's most real and lasting value is the pleasure that it affords to the reader. Remember this and be bold.

As a postscript this may sound frivolous, which is a pity, for everything I have so far written has been sincere and borne out by my own experience. But if, having studied books and maps and pictures, talked to people and done all that you can to provide your story with an authentic background, you still feel hesitant about launching it upon a critical world, call your place Gimbuktu; the story will not suffer; the initiate will know what you mean, and you are insured against any small slip or omission. Trollope did it: there is no English county called Barsetshire.

33

THE SECOND MILLION WORDS

By William E. Barrett

There are many writers' conferences in the United States each year, with study periods ranging from an intense three days to a leisurely three weeks. A conference is not only a stimulating approach to writing: it is ideal for the study of writers. We come in all sizes, all shapes, and in all degrees of aspiration. The most tragic figure in a conference is the author who was successful too soon, who failed to repeat his success and who has come to a gathering of writers out of grim desperation; the second most tragic figure is the writer who writes very well, more eloquently than most professionals, and who has never been published, who comes close to the target but who perpetually misses.

One of the prematurely successful authors was in my class one year when I conducted a workshop on the novel at a large university. His first novel had been a widely acclaimed book club choice; his second novel had been received without praise by the critics and not accepted by the public; his third novel had been rejected by every publisher to whom he had submitted it. He stubbornly insisted that it was the best thing he had written. I read it. The reasons for its history of rejections were obvious.

The third novel wore all of the cliché badges of current box office: bizarre sex situations, failures in communication between older and younger people, four-letter words in profusion, rumbling background discords of racial conflict and one violent racial incident. The novel had not one glint of humor, one ray of light. There wasn't a person in the book whom anyone could like, or for whom anyone could feel sympathy; the piling up of misery, violence and sexual degeneration was unrelieved and hence unconvincing. I knew that the author had had a bad time so I tried to be gentle to him. I pointed out the fact that he needed variation, color, contrast to hold a reader's interest, that he lost his point when he buried it under solid masses of unvarying sameness. He rejected everything that I tried to tell him with one bitter line: "I am writing literature, not slop."

The author walked out of my class and I never heard of him again. As far as I know, he has never had another book published. There are probably many possible explanations for his failure, but his own attitude toward his work, and toward the work of others, was wrong. No man can sit at a typewriter with the vow that he is going to produce literature. The angel must visit us unawares. Many men, and women, who write self-consciously, convinced that they are producing great art, succeed merely in writing drivel, while many others who have written desperately under the whiplash of debt and illness have produced books for the ages. Intellectual snobbery, like all forms of snobbery, is creatively sterile. The greatest fiction is written out of compassion for mankind, never out of contempt for it.

In the beginning, we authors are all very much alike. We dramatize ourselves, our inadequacies, our hopeless dreams, our frustrations, our desires to be great, to be heroic, to be noticed. Life, however, demands growth of us. The self-dramatization of our extreme youth should be modified by the impact of life; the sensitivity should remain.

What happens when we strive hard, when we do grow, when we still fail of publication with our most carefully wrought works? Why doesn't some mysterious law take care of us when we obey the rules? A simple, easy answer to that is not possible. So many fine manuscripts come to a writers' conference, unpublished and destined to remain unpublished. Such manuscripts baffle an editor, too. He does not know quite what to say about them. These stories, from all sections of the country, have an odd identity.

Beautifully written, these stories are actually voices from another world, voices out of yesterday. The people and the situations are oddly dated. It does not seem quite accurate to call them "old-fashioned", but they are not of today, nor are they placed definitely in any other period of history; they seem to hang in time. It is rather amazing that we writers can move through our own world without seeing it. The well-written rejects in editorial offices demonstrate the fact that we do exactly that, or that, at best, we see with clouded eyes.

Our world is one in which big, staunch, sturdy old houses are being torn down every day while small, flimsy houses are being built. It is the world of the two-paycheck family, of the two-automobile household, of married people working different hours and living in a suburb. It is a world of junior and senior proms in grade school and of courting which starts at an earlier age and reaches an earlier climax. It is, then, inevitably a world of teen-age marriages which are not self-supporting. It is a world in which medical science is prolonging life, and social science is forcing early retirement to an unwanted leisure, leisure in many cases which cannot be supported. That is the world that we must see, and that we must interpret, if we want to write successful fiction; but it is not enough to see it.

If we love old things, old customs, old ways of life, we may deplore the changes that we see, but if we resist and deplore in our writing we are dated again; we are dousing our manuscripts with the perfume of nostalgia. To write of our world we must accept it and sympathize with the people in it. We must try to see with the eyes of people born to this time, those who have not known another world in other years.

When we open our eyes there are stories all around us. Authors live in the same world as other people, hearing and seeing the same things. The difference is, and forever should be, that the author is not satisfied with saying: "How interesting!" or "How shocking!" The creative mind constantly asks: "Why?"

Some years ago, a favorite editor of mine was Eleanor Stierhem (now Eleanor Rawson). She was fiction editor for *Today's Woman* and later for *Collier's*. Eleanor sought creatively for stories although she did not write them herself. She would have lunch with an author and throw out leads or challenges without being too obvious about it. One luncheon she commented to me that she had seen a news story in that morning's *New York Times*. A girl had disappeared from an exclusive girls' school, an attractive girl from a background of wealth and social standing, a girl who seemed to have everything that anyone would want. There was no indication of foul play. It was rather obvious that she had merely run away.

Eleanor said: "I have heard of many similar cases. What would make a girl do that?"

I ventured the opinion that there were many reasons that one could easily imagine. She said immediately: "All right. Imagine one! Give me an answer in a short story."

At another time she was chatting over the luncheon table and she said: "I receive many short stories about men breaking off with women. They are usually adult people, a man and wife, a man and mistress. Everyone from Maugham down has written such a story. I have never seen it on a young and innocent level. If a boy and a girl have grown up together and have always taken it for granted that they will be married some day, and the boy changes his mind, how does he handle the breaking off?"

I said that I would have to think about that one, and again she said: "Tell me in a short story how he handles the problem."

I wrote both of those stories, and many more that were responses to ideas of Eleanor's. They were not significant stories, not earth-shaking, but they represented my honest response to creative challenge; they were stories about people facing aspects of the human predicament. Without an editor across a table, we can find stories in the papers every day which ask questions of us, questions which can be answered fictionally. We write stories without considering art, motivated perhaps by no stronger reason than our need for experience in writing stories; if we are paid for such stories by some editor, they are still what they were when we wrote them and not "commercialized products." Money enters into the writing equation as it enters into everything, but if the writer has integrity, he places the writing first and merely hopes for the money.

The impulse to write is a creative drive. It demands satisfaction. Ability that is not used makes the soul sick. I know that if I inherited a million dollars tomorrow, it would make little difference in my writing schedule. I would still write through long hours. I would have to do that. I am not unique. In making that statement I speak for many authors, a great many authors.

If the writing urge is a creative drive, where does it originate? Why do some people feel it and others live full lives without experiencing it? It is not enough to speak of imagination or of "restless imagination." There are writers, highly successful authors in the field of fiction, who have no imagination, as there are writers without a sense of humor. Imagination, however, is a fascinating subject.

Many people confuse daydreaming with imagination. There is no relationship. Anyone can daydream. The daydream is an idle device, while imagination can be trained and directed; imagination is capable of growth. In the daydream, the dreamer is always wonderful. A boy lying on the grass can hit a home run with the bases full and trot around those bases, tipping his cap to an applauding multitude. A girl can go on as understudy to a star in a play and be famous immediately, or she can come down a staircase with an entranced group, mostly men, waiting for her eagerly because she is vaguely marvelous. The dialogue in a daydream, when there is dialogue, is appalling. You never realize how ridiculous it is until you write it down in whole or in part. Imagination is made of sterner stuff.

A great editor, Arthur Sullivant Hoffman, once tried to discover what imagination is by sending a questionnaire to one hundred authors. It was a clever questionnaire. One of the questions was, "When you dream, do you dream in color or in black and white?"

It took me a long time to answer that question. I tried to catch myself dreaming and steal a brief look at the screen before the picture faded. I found that difficult. As far as I can tell, I dream in a sort of photographic gray, never in technicolor, although I have, sometimes, flashes of color memory from a dream. By the same token, when a story is taking form in my mind, it is rarely in color. The color is added later. I can will myself to see color in a mental picture and see it.

One limitation of imagination that I have discovered is that imagination is never sharper in any human being than the quality of his observation. If you look at trees and see merely trees, your imagination will supply you with only vague tree outlines when it supplies you with an outdoor background; if you see willows and elms and stately oaks when you walk down a road, your imagination—even years later—will supply clear, rich detail for an imaginary road.

Most authors, of course, are good observers. We watch people and things, unconsciously recording gestures, facial expressions, mannerisms; storing them up in the memory file. It is a mistake, however, to assume, as so many people do, that authors are always looking for characters to put into their books. Some authors do. There are authors who are strictly autobiographical, who cannot write of anything that has not happened to them. Such writers naturally use the people around them, the people they know, usually without a hint of change or disguise. They are writers without creative ability, no matter how many writing skills they may acquire. The creative writer realizes his events creatively, events that have not happened in his own experience, and he realizes his people creatively, composites of many actual people but never portraits. In the long run, the creative writer may not be as successful as his non-creative, perhaps non-imaginative, contemporary. There are so many confusing bypaths along the road of authorship, so many strangely blended skills, impulses, drives and frustrations in those who strive to write.

When I was very young, wishful and unpublished, I attended a lecture by Albert Payson Terhune. He said, in effect, that an aspiring writer should write one million words and throw them in the wastebasket; that only after a million words was the aspirant qualified to make a beginning in the odd art of authorship. It was a frightening statement and, to me, a depressing one, a statement that I could not accept. Now, so many years later, I believe that Albert Payson Terhune was correct, that he did not exaggerate. The redeeming point about those million words, however, is the fact that he did not specify the quality of them; he merely laid down the dictum that one million words must be written in the process of learning to write. Many writers have had thousand of words from the first million published, and publication has encouraged them in the long task, but the work in any author's career that is worth the rereading will be found in his second million words, or his third million, or his fourth. So many words are rewritten, so many end in the wastebasket; but we have learned much in the writing of them, and there is no other way in which one can learn to write.

As he writes his words, the author may, occasionally, take comfort in what fellow authors have written of their own work, their feeling for art, their self-valuations. Frank Harris, for example, has left us one statement worth a place on the wall. "I am really a great author," he wrote. "My only difficulty is finding great readers."

That, of course, is our eternal quest.

34

USE THREEFOLD MAGIC

By Jean Z. Owen

A number of years ago I wrote a multiple-plot novelette that dealt with the problems of four women who, for one hour, were caught between floors in a department-store elevator. When I had it finished I took it to my friend.

She frowned as she read it.

"There's something not quite right about it," she told me. "The plot and characterization are sound enough, but there seems to be a lack of balance in the story that I find irritating. Perhaps you are trying to juggle too many major characters. Do you suppose you could eliminate one of them?"

I was aghast. Couldn't she see that the story needed all four of the problems if it were to say all I meant it to convey? I was positive that the deletion she suggested would ruin the story; I felt my opinion was vindicated when the story—just as it was—promptly sold to a top slick magazine, and then to television and to a number of foreign markets.

Several years went by, and I thought no more about it until the story finally appeared as an hour-long television drama. I had no part in the adaptation, and as I watched the play, I was astonished to observe that although the cast had been cut from four to three major characters, the play seemed complete and well-rounded. I went to my files and dug out the yellowing carbon of the story and read it with fresh perspective. Now—belatedly—I could perceive the lack of balance that had disturbed my critic. I recalled, too, that the magazine novelette, *A Letter to Five Wives,* had appeared on the screen as *A Letter to Three Wives,* and that *Four Secrets* had been changed to *Three Secrets.* Other motion picture titles came to mind—*The Three Faces of Eve, Three Smart Girls, Three Coins in a Fountain,* and many more.

It dawned on me, too, that I had begun to sell nonfiction pieces only after I learned that the most effective means of presenting factual material is via the classic threefold method—1) tell them what you're *going* to tell them, 2) *tell* them, 3) tell them what you *told* them.

The more I thought about it, the more convinced I became that a writer must pay attention to the Number Three. I don't know *why* this should be so. Some persons think it has a religious basis, while others point to mythology and to the Greek triads. Numerologists have their own explanation. I am inclined to suspect it may be a carry-over from our nursery-rhyme days when we learned to react emotionally to the vicissitudes of the three bears, the three little kittens, the three blind mice, the three little pigs, the three Billy Goats Gruff, the three little fishies, and Wynken, Blynken, and Nod.

I do not wish to imply, of course, that all stories can be forced into a three-sided mold. But I have found that in my own stories and in manuscripts other writers have asked me to evaluate the use of tricornered characterization frequently provides the solution to a stubborn problem of roughness or imbalance.

Once I became aware of the Number Three, I discovered that it can help a writer in many ways. Take the matter of *plants*, for instance. Just as language experts assure you that you can make any new word a permanent part of your vocabulary merely by using it three times, a triple repetition will firmly convey any information you wish your reader to retain.

Suppose, for example, that the climax of your story is going to involve the collapse of a bridge. Even a beginning writer knows that if you toss this at the reader "cold," with no preliminary build-up, you will have the word "coincidental" tossed right back at you. So you painstakingly plant the fact, early in the story, that the bridge may go down. And the best way to do it to make it seem a logical, inevitable part of the story (and a suspense-building factor, as well!) is to mention it three times, from three different viewpoints:

1) Your hero drives across the bridge and notices that it creaks and sways *dangerously* in the wind.

2) An old-timer remembers a storm of 1890 when the old bridge—sturdier, by cracky, than this newfangled flimsy one—washed away as if it had been made of matchsticks.

3) A fortuneteller warns of approaching peril; her crystal ball has revealed a glimpse of people falling into water from a collapsing structure.

This is an oversimplified example, of course. Most of the stories for today's market require less obvious repetition. A plant must be handled so subtly, so artfully, that the reader is not consciously aware of the fact that important information is being accented. The best way to find out how skillfully it can be accomplished is to read again some of the recent stories you have enjoyed. Look for the triple plants—they will be there!

The same principle holds true of characterization. If you describe Ellen, your heroine, as having *shy* brown eyes—if you have some other character mention the fact that it's a shame Ellen *can't seem to mix with people* as easily as her sister Kate—if you show Ellen *flushing with embarrassment as she makes a casual remark*—your reader will thereafter see Ellen as a quiet, retiring, indrawn young woman. If you belabor the point by excessive use of such phrases as "she said timidly" and "she glanced up shyly," the story will seem overdrawn and amateurish. Merely make certain that everything Ellen *says* and *does* and *feels* lies within the framework of a timid personality; your reader will automatically supply most of the stage directions far more effectively than you could possibly depict them.

Another area in which Number Three can help you is in smoothing out jarring sentences and rough paragraphs. There is a natural, euphonic cadence to three modifying words or three descriptive phrases that makes for a smooth, even flow. See what happens if you try adding to, or taking away from these examples: *Blood, sweat, and tears. Of the people, by the people, for the people. Three cheers for the red, white, and blue. Bell, book, and candle. Tom, Dick, and Harry. Morning, noon, and night. Tall, dark, and handsome. Love, honor, and cherish. Healthy, wealthy, and wise. We're having fun-fun-fun! See no evil, hear no evil, speak no evil. Faith, hope, and charity. Gold, frankincense, and myrrh.*

Very likely you have been utilizing three-word or three-phrase descriptions without realizing it. Just for fun sometime, hunt up the rough copy of one of your old stories—or, for that matter, take a look at the story or article you are working on right now. Find one of the paragraphs that sounded uneven, harsh, and amateurish as you first wrote it. So you wrote it again . . . and again and again. And finally, after switching sentences around, putting a phrase in here, pulling a word out there, you could get on with the story, secure in the knowledge that the difficult portion now has a polished "feel" to it. Look at it again; I'll give you odds that you'll discover much of the smoothness resulted primarily from using sequences of three words or three phrases.

(Notice the above paragraph. *Uneven, harsh, and amateurish. Again . . . and again and again. Switching . . . putting . . . pulling.*)

Perhaps the greatest asset Number Three gives a story is a natural, built-in suspense mechanism, free for the writer's taking, simply because in our culture we are geared to react with an automatic "This is *it*" feeling when we reach number three. Three strikes and you're out. One-two-three-*go!* The third time's the charm. Three on a match and evil will befall. Trouble comes in threes. A *three*-time loser is sentenced to life imprisonment.

When we wanted to prove to the world that our space program was something to be reckoned with, we sent John Glenn around for three orbits. Playgoers sit contentedly through Acts I and II, knowing that Act III will give them the same kind of emotional payoff that kindergarten children expect from the *third* wish the fairy queen has granted the poor woodcutter. And next time someone says to you, "Have you heard the one about—?" I'll give you odds that the punch line of the joke will directly follow two build-up lines.

For a writer, the awareness of the fact that the reader's *feeling of expectation* will automatically reach its highest pitch at the third climax of the story is like knowing that one's house is electrically wired. When the occasion calls for it, all you need to do is to plug in your story and the vitalizing current goes to work for you.

Again—an oversimplified example: Your hero wants to get the girl; he tries—and fails. He tries another approach—and fails again, more abjectly than before. So, from the depths, he rises to make a third attempt and *this* time . . . ! If he were successful on the second attempt, it would give the reader the same thudding sensation you get when you lift your foot to step up, only to find you've already reached the top of the stairs. Success on the *fourth* effort is very likely to make the reader bored and impatient. Three—and *only* three—climaxes give the reader his expected quota of emotional impact.

To those of you who protest, "But that's *formula* and I thought formula stories were *out!*", I can only refer you to the best of the non-formula stories that are being printed. For although *story formula* may be discarded, *story form* remains constant, and any fiction, whatever its type, is only as good as the emotional response it draws from the reader. If you will study the markets you will observe that the one-two-three-*payoff* principle works just as strongly in the artistic as it does in the strictly commercial story. The difference lies only in the subtlety of its presentation.

Why is Number Three so important? I haven't the faintest idea. I don't understand the principle of electrical refrigeration, either, but a few moments ago, as the California sun beat down on our house, I pushed the button that turns on our air conditioner—and I strongly suspect that the breezes now wafting through my study are just as cool as they would be if I had a degree in electrical engineering.

Think about Number Three. Note how often it appears in our culture—how frequently it is reflected in the work of writers you would like to emulate. It's only a minor bit of technique, perhaps—but for the writer who seriously seeks to perfect his craftsmanship it can be another tool that can help him create effectively.

35

BUILDING TENSION IN
THE SHORT STORY

By Joyce Carol Oates

THE most important aspect of writing is characterization—does a character come alive, is he memorable in some way? But the means of disclosing character is also important, for if a story lacks a strong narrative line, an editor or reader might not be patient enough to discover even the most stunning of fictional characters.

Novels are complex matters; the density of interest has to go up and down. Short stories, however, are generally based on one gradual upward swing toward a climax or "epiphany"—moment of recognition. A good chapter in a novel should probably be based on the same rhythmic structure as a short story. The novel, of course, can be leisurely while the average short story must be economical. Certain modern stories are so economical that single words or phrases are used to reveal the story's meaning—for instance, John Collier's "The Chaser," which ends with the words "au revoir" and not "goodbye."

While I think the best kind of contemporary story is much more rich and complex and daring than the Chekhovian-type stories so fashionable a few decades ago, still the writer must be careful to limit the range of his "secondary" material—descriptions, background. If he succeeds in winning the reader's attention by dramatic means, then the more important aspects of his story will be appreciated. We have all written wonderful little stories that are "hidden" somewhere in overlong, awkward, unsatisfactory masses of words.

Here are two examples of short story beginnings, each leading into a different kind of story:

1) "Let me tell you something about the Busbys," the old gentleman said to me. "The Busbys don't wash themselves—not adequately. And especially not as they grow older."

2) Just around the turn, the road was alive. First to assault the eye was a profusion of heads, black-haired, bobbing, and a number of straw hats that
looked oddly professional—

The stories following these beginnings are to be found in *Prize
Stories 1965: The O. Henry Awards,* edited by Richard Poirier and
William Abrahams. The first story, "There," by Peter Taylor, in-
vites the reader to listen in on a confidential, gossipy conversation:
the words "Let me tell you" are intriguing enough, but the surprise
comes in the second line. And we are introduced to a strange little
town, "There," where each family seems to have a peculiar trait all
its own—not washing properly, eating too much, narrow-minded
complacency—and dying. Peter Taylor, the author of many excellent short stories of a rich, complex type, builds tension in a highly
refined manner. We listen in on this old man's monologue, amused by
his portraits of people back "there," and gradually we become emotionally involved in the pathos of his love for a girl who belonged to
a family with a secret common trait—and then we find out, along
with the narrator, that this common trait is dying. The girl has died
young; the lover, now an aged man, has married someone else; there
is no tragedy here, everything is muted and understated. But the
story is unforgettable because Taylor has built so very gradually and
unobtrusively the tension that arises out of the girl's impending
death. Everything is past tense, but vitally alive.

The second beginning is from a story of mine, "First Views of the
Enemy." Beginning with a near-accident, this story relies on tension
building up within the main character's mind. A bus carrying mi-
grant fruit pickers has broken down at the roadside, and when a
young mother with her child drives by, one of the Mexican children
darts in front of the car to frighten her. The tension between the
young, American, rather materialistic woman and the socially-
marginal people is the theme of this story. The woman arrives home
safely, but she carries the image of this "enemy" with her into her
expensive home, which now seems to her vulnerable. Her realization
that she could lose everything she owns drives her to an orgy of selfishness as she locks things up, closes her drapes, even picks her most
beautiful flowers and forces food upon her child. The tension is psychological, not active; the "enemy" does not appear after the first

encounter. We see that the true "enemy" is the woman's hysterical selfishness, which she is forcing upon her child also.

Franz Kafka's classic, "The Metamorphosis," begins like this:

> As Gregor Samsa awoke one morning from uneasy dreams he found himself transformed in his bed into a gigantic insect.

Incredible, of course. Unbelievable. But Kafka's mild-mannered prose proceeds on as if an event of no great dimensions has taken place. You, the reader, find out about Gregor's metamorphosis at the same time he does. You are surprised, yes, but so is Gregor—a quite ordinary young man, devoted to his family and his work. This surrealistic story is much more "realistic" in its ability to convince and emotionally involve than most slick fiction with its easily-recognizable people. But Kafka thrives on tension. He builds it from his first sentence on. Kafka is always asking, "What happens next?" and then he asks, "After that, what happens?" Like Simenon, he drives his characters to extremes and tests them. "The Metamorphosis" is beautifully constructed in three sections, each dealing with the tense relationship between the stricken Gregor and his family, until Gregor dies in order to release his loved ones. Tension is achieved on the literal level—what is going to happen to the insect-man?—and on the symbolic level—what will be the outcome of the "love" between members of a family when one of them is mysteriously stricken and is no longer "human"?

These three stories, widely differing in technique, build up tension through an accumulation of detail. If violence erupts in fiction, it should be the outcome of tension; it should not come first, nor should it be accidental. Action stories are of interest to certain audiences, but quality stories usually refine action onto a psychological level. There is "action"—movement—but it takes place in a person's mind or in a conversation. If someone finally kills someone else, it is simply the climax of a rhythmic building of tension that lasts long enough to be convincing but is short enough to be interesting.

Remember that tension created for its own sake is cheap; no one will read your story more than once. The tension is part of your technique but technique is only a means to an end; it is never the end itself. That is why the French "new novel" is so boring—it has no capacity to move us—while older, stormy works like *Wuthering*

Heights (which could only be "camp" to today's *avant-garde*) will be interesting to all imaginable future generations. I think the stress placed today on technique is misleading. A writer should imagine his scenes dramatically, as if they were to take place on the stage. There, empty, wordy passages are found out at once. It isn't "words" or "style" that make a scene, but the content behind the words, and the increase of tension as characters come into conflict with one another. "Words" themselves are relatively unimportant, since there are countless ways of saying the same thing.

A final suggestion: be daring, take on anything. Don't labor over little cameo works in which every word is to be perfect. Technique holds a reader from sentence to sentence, but only content will stay in his mind.

36

PLANNING A MYSTERY

By Stanley Ellin

It took me ten long years of apprenticeship at my trade to learn that the closing lines of a mystery story are more important than the opening lines, which is why I was a haggard thirty when writing became my vocation, and not a fresh and bouncing twenty.

This hiatus between the time I first sat down, forefingers poised over an old Underwood, and the time I became what writers' magazines fondly call a "Selling Writer" was not altogether my fault. When I was twenty, we were still in the golden age of detective pulps (observe that they were "detective" magazines, not "mystery" magazines) and one was distinctly given to understand that the formula for cranking out a proper story in the genre was as rigid as that for a No play. The big thing was a Narrative Hook calculated to grip the reader's attention instantly and get the story's hero off to a running start, after which he was kept running through and around various plotted obstacles until, within five thousand words, he finally disposed of the villain.

If the hero's strong point was deduction, the deduction was frequently given a vital assist by the villain himself, who, when cornered at the story's climax, would immediately blubber out a full confession of his crime, including motive and method. Most professional criminals, as I have since learned, are inclined to be tight-lipped fellows, glad to have their lawyers do all their talking for them, but the detective magazine villains in the golden age rarely fell back on that kind of shoddy device. Lucky for the writers they didn't, or it would have ruined many an epic tale.

The fact is—and anyone who has plowed through enough back issues of the old pulps will verify it—the golden age of pulps was really much more brass than gold, which, if I may be forgiven a digression, sometimes has me wondering about the golden ages of

Greece, opera, and television. As far as pulp writing went, it had gone its limit very quickly after writers like Dashiell Hammett, Raymond Chandler, and James M. Cain turned away from it. What remained was a host of their admirers filling the pulps with imitations of them, and while imitation may be the sincerest form of flattery, it also means sure death to a literary form when it hardens into tired formula. Even without the entrance of paperback books and television on the scene to sweep the pulps out of existence, pulp detective story writing had already doomed itself to death anyhow, just the way slick magazine fiction doomed itself to death soon afterward by petrifying into formula.

But this is hindsight, of course, and does not change the fact that there I was in the mid-1930's, solemnly striving to master the art of the Narrative Hook, cooking up heroes and villains, and gory episodes for them to plunge through, making sure my stories ran to exactly five thousand words, often in the way of a tailor snipping off pieces of customer to fit the suit, and, for all of it, collecting rejection slips by the carload. Between times, I devoted myself to reading articles in the writers' magazines where authors who were successfully belting them out at the rate of a million words a year cheered me on by explaining that very often they started a story going without the least idea of its plot or complications. "Once I get going, the yarn just seems to tell itself," they would remark, snapping the rubber bands on their fat bankrolls. Obviously they had a point. If a story was merely a string of episodes linked by a thread of plot, there was no reason why it couldn't go in practically any direction at all with fine effect, providing you had that Narrative Hook just right to start with. Apparently, I never did have it just right.

It was ten years, as I have remarked, before I saw the light and started to consider the writing of a mystery story from the correct angle, which is back to front. The change was forced on me. There were no more detective pulps left. What was left was a constant reprinting of de Maupassant and Saki and stories like Hemingway's "The Killers" and Maugham's "The Letter" and Faulkner's "A Rose for Emily" and Anatole France's "The Procurator of Judaea", which remains just about the finest short story ever written. And, as time went on, there appeared among the fiction studies of exurbanite *Weltschmerz* in *The New Yorker* some stuff by somebody named

Roald Dahl and, great day, a story called "The Lottery" by a lady named Shirley Jackson. The Dahl and Jackson stories were as out of place in *The New Yorker* as a leopard would be in granny's parlor, especially since that magazine dislikes arrant shockers in fiction and regards the name of O. Henry as anathema; but these two writers, using the O. Henry shock-ending technique, were in *The New Yorker* simply because they were too good to be left out.

From the vantage point of my old age, I can say that O. Henry's technique can be studied with profit by any mystery writer. The trouble with O. Henry was never his technique, which is so frequently brilliant, but his tendency to use types instead of people, to depend too often on surprise for the sake of surprise, no matter how logically he built to it, and, above all, to lean toward open sentimentality. Even his occasional cynicism seems weak and hollow. Now, if it had been the healthy, believable cynicism of a Hammett or Chandler—!

In a world denuded of detective pulps, it was writers like Jackson and Dahl who suggested the direction to take if one still had an interest in writing stories about murder or robbery or swindle. And part of the lesson to be learned was that dealing with a story idea from back to front didn't mean adherence to just another kind of formula, but, in fact, meant freedom from formula. It meant that the climax of the story, its point and purpose, must dictate everything that goes into the narrative along the way. It meant that it's better to know where you want to go before you start. The scenery along the way will be just as interesting, and added to it will be a sense of direction which is far more effective, in intriguing the reader than the most violent, but purposeless, episode can ever be.

This process of working out a story idea from back to front is not as easy as it may seem at a glance. It usually demands a period of gestation—it can be weeks or months—where the writer goes around with the story idea developing in his brain until he can see just how it should move to its climax. That climax is the thing. The outlines of the narrative leading to it may remain nebulous in the mind, they may take on a different form every time the writer turns his attention to them, but once he knows in precise words what the final lines of the story will be, everything else starts to fall quickly into position.

When those final lines are set, it's good policy to write them down. Now, when the narrative—the whole body of the story—is reappraised, it must be strictly in terms of what has been written down. The infinite decisions on what must go into the story, what characters will play it out, what length it will be, what point it will start from in its opening line—all this is to be determined solely by the need to build logically to that pre-written finale. The objective is to use only the material and treatment which will establish the climax logically, at the same time providing the reader with a *frisson*, an impact, the shock of recognition one experiences when he finds that a logical sequence of events has led to a logical—but unpredictable—conclusion.

In this process, the story one has been carrying around in his mind as a sort of smoky substance will undergo its vital transformation into hard-knit, tightly structured drama. This does not mean the reduction of it to telegraphic form. A tightly woven story can be ten thousand words long and present twenty characters. What it does mean is that every line of narrative must contribute to the final effect. Digressions are out of order. Lingering descriptions are usually out of order. Dialogue should stick to the point while enlightening us as to the nature of the speakers. Revision of the completed manuscript must be ruthless under these conditions. A character, an episode, a single phrase which doesn't contribute to the progress toward the story's pre-written climax must be penciled out.

So it was that I finally won my first bout with the editors by treating a story idea from back to front. The idea concerned a restaurant where the customers themselves, when properly fattened like Hansel and Gretel by the solicitous restaurateur, were literally fed to each other, although without knowing it. The story treatment, I decided, would not make any great effort to conceal this shocking fact from the reader; the climax would simply be a sentence or two which would assure him that his macabre supposition about what was going on in that restaurant was gruesomely correct.

I got off to a dozen futile starts on the story, and then at last it dawned on me that I was in trouble because I didn't know exactly what my final climactic and revelatory lines were going to be. The solution, I decided, was to write those final lines before anything else, and it took a couple of weeks before I even understood exactly what

they had to set forth. It was the picture of a customer, a key character in the story, being happily led into that fatal kitchen by my restaurateur, and, without specifically stating it, I had to make it plain
that this customer was a lamb for the slaughter. The lines I decided
on read:

> The restaurateur held his kitchen door invitingly wide with one hand, while
> the other rested, almost tenderly, on his customer's meaty shoulder.

It was that word "meaty" which took the longest time to hit on
and which, I knew intuitively, locked up the story. From that instant, the restaurant owner, his doomed patron, the restaurant itself,
and the whole structure of the story started to take on form by themselves; an outline of episodes leading to the finale seemed to spring
magically to mind. It took much revision to get everything trimmed
down to its essence, but now that I knew exactly what I wanted to
say, the revisions, like the story's episodes, almost imposed themselves on the material.

The final draft was sent to *Ellery Queen's Mystery Magazine,* and
a few days later the editor let me know that the story's title was
henceforth to be "The Specialty of the House," and that I was now a
Selling Writer. And, since it seemed sound policy to stick with a winning system, I've followed the same principle of writing down the
closing lines of every story I've tackled since then, before even considering the opening lines, and I have had no cause to regret this
back to front approach.

Admittedly, this method of preparing a final polished draft of a
short story adds up to a slow and laborious time of it, especially
when one has a complicated story to tell. But time is no longer relevant in writing stories for mystery magazines. On that barren plain
filled with the bleached bones of the defunct detective pulps now
stands an impressive beacon, *Ellery Queen's Mystery Magazine,*
surrounded by a few lesser lights, perhaps a half-dozen in all. Once
upon a time, a capable and prolific story writer could make a living
from the detective pulps by flooding these magazines with acceptable
material. Today, he would simply flood himself right out of any market in a short time. So writing for the present market is best done
with tender, loving care as an avocation, not a vocation.

Ironically, despite the limited market, the demand for stories is greater now than it was during the palmiest days of the detective pulp. The scant dimensions of the market plus the editorial demand for quality instead of quantity seem to keep writers at bay and the result is a *shortage* of good stories.

From my experience, it is possible that planning and writing your mystery story from back to front will do much to alleviate the shortage.

37

THE BIOGRAPHICAL NOVEL

By Irving Stone

THE biographical novel is a true and documented story of one human being's journey across the face of the years, transmuted from the raw material of life into the purity of an authentic art form.

The biographical novel is based on the conviction that the best of all plots lie in human character; and that human character is endlessly colorful and revealing. It starts with the assumption that those stories which have actually happened can be at least as interesting and true as those which have been imagined. Alexander Pope said that the proper study of mankind is man; the biographical novel accepts that challenge and sets out to document its truth, for character is plot; character development is action; and character fulfillment is resolution.

The biographical novel attempts to fuse not only its parent sources of biography and the novel, but that of its grandparent, history, as well. It must tell the story of its main character, not in the bulk of millionfold detail, but in essence; it must recreate the individual against the background of his times, with all of its authentic historical flavor; and it must live up to the exacting demands of the novel structure.

Let me joyfully proclaim that basically the biographical novelist is a yarn-spinner, and the biographical novel a vigorous medium that has been created in order to tell the fine stories that have been lived. The form is fortunate in its opportunity to utilize the single greatest virtue of the novel: growth of character. This growth may be into good or evil, into creativity or destruction; it cannot be static. There are few joys for the reader to surpass that of watching an interesting story unfold through growth of character; and in this field no form surpasses the biographical novel, which by the very definition of its nature is always about people rather than impersonal forces.

The biographical novelist has a greater freedom to interpret than has the biographer, and the reader has a greater chance of coming away with a more personal understanding of human motivation. If there is a tendency to oversimplify, it is in the same fashion that man's memory does as he looks back on his span of time, forgetting nine-tenths of the bulk, remembering only the distillation which has meaning. For the biographical novel is based not merely on fact, but on feeling, the legitimate emotion arising from indigenous drama. Facts can get lost with almost too great a facility, but an emotional experience, once lived, can never be forgotten. Nor can this emotion be artificially induced for the sake of raising the reader's temperature. While a biography can be written purely out of a life's worthiness, with details of important names, places and dates, the biographical novel must emerge naturally and organically from the conflicts of man against himself, man against man, or man against fate.

Now that the biographical novel has come of age, a few ground rules can perhaps be laid down for its practitioners.

The first of these must surely be that history is not the servant of the biographical novelist, but his master. No biographical novel can be better than its research. If the research is deep and honest, the novel will be deep and honest; if the research is sleazy, shallow, evasive or sensation-seeking, the novel will be sleazy, shallow, evasive, sensation-mongering.

Not every life will fit into the form of the biographical novel. There are specific dramatic elements that must be present, recurrent themes of conflict and accomplishment woven through its entirety, an overall, perceivable pattern into which the parts can be fitted to make an organic whole. There are many lives, important and significant in their end results, which are nonetheless diffuse, their content and design antithetical to the nature of the novel; others seem to have been lived as though the subject himself were constantly aware that he was creating a dramatic structure.

While the biographical novelist is assuredly licensed to search out and select those lives which make good copy, the basic demonstrable truth cannot be pushed around to serve a plot purpose. The writer who must twist or pervert the historic truth to come out with what he thinks is an acceptable or salable story is a tragically misplaced person in his field. The biographical novelist, on the other hand, who becomes moralistic or political, turns into a pamphleteer. An integrated, successful, first-rate biographical novel can emerge only from a union of the material chosen and the author of the choice.

The author has a right to ask, as he looks at the outline of a human life, "Can this story serve my purposes?"—but only after he has demanded of himself, "Can I serve the purposes of this story?"

How is a reader unacquainted with the field to distinguish between the honest and dishonest biographical novel, the complete and the fractional? How can the question, "How much of this is true?" be answered? Only by insisting that the biographical novel must be as complete in its documentation as the most scholarly history and biography, and as honest in its interpretation.

If it takes four years to train a schoolteacher or engineer, five years to train a pharmacist, six a dentist, seven a lawyer, and eight a doctor, is there any reason to believe that it can take less time to develop a qualified and professional biographical novelist?

He must become experienced in the writing of imaginative novels, wrestling with this form in order that he may come up against the challenging complexities of structure, mood, master scenes, dialogue, with its accompanying lyricism of language, the mounting involvement and suspense of the fictional tale. He would be well advised to write a half-dozen plays to absorb the superb economy of the form, and learn how to stage his tale under a proscenium instead of in the wings: for what the reader does not see with his eyes he never really knows.

He must be trained as a biographer, working at the assembling of materials about one man or group of men, mastering the technique of close-knit organization of these materials, the perceiving and the weaving back and forth of the life theme, evolving a style, personality, and manner of writing by means of which one man's story can be brought to life all over again by black hieroglyphs on white paper: the eternal miracle of literature: for each life has a distinctive face and figure; and this must be captured in order to differentiate this one special story from the hundreds of millions that have been lived.

Though research is as fascinating as the resolution of a crossword puzzle or a murder mystery, it is also hard work, thoroughly exhausting and unending in its demands. The researcher sometimes gets lost in his forest of facts. To change the metaphor, the biographical novel must be built like an iceberg, about one ninth of solid substance showing above the literary water line, and the other eight-ninths submerged, but giving a solid base to that which is permitted to appear. If the biographical novelist does not know nine times as much as he reveals, the substance of the print he spreads over the page will be painfully thin: for the eight-ninths which he does not reveal permeates the whole, giving to the pages a discernible bouquet, a subtle emanation which enables the reader to feel comfortable and secure.

I would like to outline some specifics.

Having determined that he is going to write a biographical novel about the life of Leonardo da Vinci or Alexander Hamilton, the biographical novelist must put out of his mind for six months or a year any illusion that he is a writer, and become a library mole. He must read all the books and articles written by his subject, study the works created by him, be they art or engineering, read every findable word that has been written about the man or work. He must read all the letters that have passed between the hero and his contemporaries, as well as his private notes, journals and memoirs; or, in the case of a heroine, those wonderfully confiding diaries that are kept locked in the middle drawer of a desk. If the subject is of recent times, there will be a need to interview or correspond with everyone who has been involved in the drama, no matter how slightly.

Having grasped more fully the outlines of his story, the biographical novelist then takes to the road, seeing with his own eyes the places his hero has lived, the quality of the sunlight, the native earth beneath his feet, the personality of the cities and the feel of the countryside: for only then can he write with the intimacy and knowledgability of tactile experience.

This is the first and direct line of attack. The second is equally important: the biographical novelist must now begin the study of his hero's times, its fads and fancies, its majority and minority ideas as well as the prevailing conflicts in religion, philosophy, science, politics, economics and the arts; in short, the overall social, mental, spiritual, esthetic, scientific and international climate in which his characters lived and evolved their codes of conduct. He must read the source books of the period in order to absorb its background, the old newspapers, pamphlets, magazines, the novels, plays and poetry of the times, in order to learn the uncountable thousands of illuminating details which he must have at his fingertips in order to recreate the period: what people wear, the architecture of their houses as well as the fabric on their furniture, how they heat their homes, cook the foods they eat at the various hours of the day; what they are buying in the shops and why, how much it costs as well as how it tastes and smells and feels; what ailments they are suffering and how they are treating them; what colloquialisms they are using to enrich their conversation; what their preachers are preaching on Sunday morning and their teachers teaching on Monday morning.

If the biographical novelist has any feeling for his job he will eventually find emerging out of this seemingly vast and inchoate mass of material certain recurrent patterns, strains of character and action that provide a dominant motif and rhythm for the story he will tell, even as the dominant strains of a symphony are enunciated early. Above all, the biographical novelist is looking for those interwoven designs which are perceivable in every human life: for nearly every life works out its own tightly woven plot structure. Any action forced upon the participants which does not arise indigenously, which arises instead from the author confusing motion with direction, tears the fabric of the story.

Yet by the same token the biographical novelist must be the master of his material; the craftsman who is not in control of his tools will have his story run away with him. For after his research labors, the biographical novelist must then expend as much time and energy as the writer of fiction to create a novel structure which will best project his material, and be unique to the particular story to be told.

And all this new knowledge must never come between the reader and the narration. In the biographical novel a basic tenet is that the author must stage his story as though it were happening right now; he may not emerge at intervals to inform the reader of what will happen two or twenty or two hundred years later. The reader may never be in possession of information which is not available to those who are acting out the day-by-day passion of their lives. The story must unfold for the reader even as the pageant of events unfolds for the participants. There are few soothsayers; the biographical novelist may not turn himself into an *a posteriori* prophet. Whatever the reader may divine about what lies ahead must arise from his own perception, and not from the biographical novelist fudging on time sequence. If there be wisdom in the author (and God grant that there may sometimes be!) it will emerge from the nature of the story he wants to tell, from his selection of materials within the framework of that particular story, from his understanding of what motivates his people, and from the skill with which he shapes the unassimilated raw action of human life.

Since I did not know how much I did not know about the writing of a biographical novel, I sat down to my first morning's work with a little calling card in front of me on which I scribbled four strictures: 1. Dramatize. 2. Plenty of dialogue. 3. Bring all characters to life. 4. Use anecdotes and humor.

Beyond the specifications for any one particular book, I found the following *obiter dicta* to be essential to all biographical novels:

No use of names because they later become important elsewhere. No asides, or smart whisperings. No fixations, no prejudices carried over from past feelings or readings. No harpings, or preconceived "theories, into which all history and happenings must fit." No name-calling; let the reader call the proper names. No fiery passions, for or against; they cloud judgment. No assumptions as to the reader's tastes, opinions, ideas, education. No writing for any one class, age or geographic group. No condemnations of people or events; give them their rightful place in the story, and let God judge them. No seeking the sensational for its own sake; and no philosophizing. No concealing of important evidence, no lies, cheating or defrauding the reader. No dullness; throw out the slow, meaningless passages. No striving for effects, no manifest anger or hatred, no browbeating. Watch comparative materials and balance them; no disproportions about materials where I happen to know more. No inheriting of other people's prejudices, hatreds, blindness. No details that illuminate little but themselves. No posturing, no exhibitionism: "See what I know!" No striving for novelty for its own sake. No doctrinairism, or fitting material into one school or pattern. No destructivism, nor defeatism. No pugilism or blind spots. No lethargy. No weasel

phrases; all space is needed for direct lines. No meandering down
pleasant paths. No use of material that does not tie into focal core of
book.

Because of the tender youth of the biographical novel there has as
yet been little discussion of its particular character, of its strengths
as well as its limitations. Is it a history, a biography, or a novel? Is it
none of these? Or perhaps all three? If here I presume to provide a
beginning critique, standards of judgment against which the biographical novel may be viewed, it is done with the happy reassurance
that all such strictures will be altered, expanded and materially improved by later practitioners of the craft.

The biographical novel has suffered from an excess of good taste
and respectability, perhaps because the biographical novelist has
been awed by the fact that his characters once actually lived, and
hence were endowed with certain inalienable rights, not of conceal-
ment, but of privacy and decorum. Bedroom scenes of which critics
complain in the lurid, so-called historical novels are not to be found
in the biographical novel, a sometime limitation to the sale of the
genre, but one which calls forth the subtlety of the biographical novelist if he is to convey to the reader the all-important love and sex
life of his subject.

The biographical novelist is a bondsman to the factual truth; yet
he will succeed very little if he remains a mere reporter. As Robert
Graves said to me, "The biographical novelist who does not have
strong intuitions about his subject, and later finds from the documents that his intuition has been substantiated, is not likely to get
far in understanding his subject."

Inside the skeletal outline imposed on him, the biographical novelist is free to soar to any heights which his own inner poetry and
perception will allow him. There are few if any differences of structure between the two types of novel; with the biographical novel the
reader asks, "Did this happen?" and with the fictional novel, "Could
this happen?" Therein lies the major distinction between them.
Credibility lies at the base of both. A chance reader, unacquainted
with the material, setting and character of the two stories, should
not be able to tell them apart; he should be able to think that the
fictional novel actually happened somewhere, or that the biographi-

cal novel was invented by the author. I remember with considerable satisfaction the day in September 1934 when Mrs. Stone asked the telephone operator in her office how she had liked *Lust for Life,* and the girl replied, "Fine, but why did Irving have to kill off the poor man?"

The historical novel is the closest to the biographical novel in its nature and scope; again the difference is not of form but of approach. In the biographical novel all of the characters have lived; in the best historical novels, such as *War and Peace,* only the history has actually happened, while the characters are invented, or built up by accretion, and then set in the authentic framework of the period and the action being written about. The main characters of the historical novel become the apotheoses of their times; they are true in that such characters did live in this particular period, and this dramatic series of events did take place, but to other people, perhaps half a hundred of them, in modified form and sequence. Sometimes the historical novel will be close to the biographical novel.

The differences between the straight biography and the biographical novel are considerable, not in substance, since both draw their nourishment from the same source, but in structure, manner, attitude, and relationship between the author and the reader.

The biography has traditionally been in indirect discourse, a chronicle told by a second party, the writer, to a third party, the reader. The biographer, for example, relates what his principals have said; the biographical novelist enables the reader to listen to the conversations as they develop. The biographical novelist, in order to recreate a character, must not only understand his every motivation, but must write of it from behind the eyes of his protagonist. Only then can the reader feel everything that he feels, know everything that he knows, suffer his defeats and enjoy his victories. The biography has been expected to be objective; too often it has been written in cool blood. The biographical novel must be written in hot blood.

What are the criticisms that have been and still are, in some unconvinced corners, levied against the biographical novel? It is said to debase the biography and the novel, discrediting both and adding to the stature of neither. Allegedly it mines biography without regard for the verities, strains history through the author's personality, reshapes that history to fit the novel form, oversimplifies, prevents the reader from separating fact from fiction, chooses only those subjects which allow for a lively sale, violates the privacy of people long dead, and makes character the victim of plot.

All of these criticisms have sometimes been true, and probably a good many more of which the critics happily have not yet thought. But to decide that any art form is untenable because of its weakest example or its potential for error is similar to saying that the human race should be obliterated because of the shortcomings of its least admirable percentage.

One of the assets of the human race is said to be that it can learn from experience; history and biography constitute the greatest mine of lived experience; and it is the fond dream of the biographical novelist to bring the wisdom of that experience to the problems and complexities of the modern world.

My own biographical novels have had two motivations: I have hoped to feel deeply about simple things; and I have wanted to tell the story of man, against obstacles, for man.

38

STORY PLOTS AND THEMES

By Marlene Fanta Shyer

In my "Hopeless" file, I've accumulated at least a dozen clinkers, stories that have flopped here and abroad and represent more than a year's work which will never see print. I keep them for sentimental reasons; these are the efforts that carried me from the Bridge of Sighs to the Bridge of Sales; they've taught me how to sell, if not how to write.

Before I unburden myself with one more word of self-pity about how long it took and how difficult it was to get there, let me stress that there would have been no transition without persistence. In the years preceding my first sale, I gave up writing a half dozen times, the result of overdoses of failure, but each time I crept back. Persistence is to selling what will power is to diets; only one writer I've ever heard of sold a first story to the slicks, and she admitted that the next twenty were rejected! So endure the rebuffs, tolerate the rejections and faithfully read the stories that the slick magazines have chosen instead of yours. Like dieting, it becomes easier with time.

Watch a pattern emerge. Some things are *in* at the slicks and some are *out*. To mitigate the frustration of your apprenticeship I've capsuled some bylaws that distinguish the commercial from the *non*, and include as case studies some of my hopeless cases, hopeless characters and hopeless themes to illustrate where I went wrong—as well as a few that made the grade.

Next to giving up smoking and learning to address your mother-in-law as "Mom", it seems to me the hardest hurdle in a writer's life is learning what makes a good plot.

I've written enough stories to know how to put together a hero and heroine and make it all come out all right in the end, but after all these years I still get the shudders when I sit down in front of a naked piece of paper with not an idea in my head. Where, I ask myself, are all these other authors coming up with the sort of clever and complicated story convolutions that add up to a check? I stare at the paper, secure in the knowledge that I'm a published writer with a strong will and a dandy style. So why haven't I got anything to say?

One reason is that every plot has to go steady with a theme. It took me a mountain of rejections to make this discovery. Nobody thought to warn me. Actually, I don't think I ever really knew what a theme was. Now, after a lot of wasted postage and a few years of crushed hopes, I know. A theme is the answer to the question that is raised when your story is finished: What does it all prove?

Pull your story together and let it *say* something, and you're in. For example, if, in your story, your daredevil hero gets hit by a street-cleaning truck, he must learn something in the end. If he learns to beware of street-cleaning trucks, that's no theme. If, on the other hand, he learns that he must temper his incaution because his life is valuable not only to himself but to others (like a good little wife and apple-cheeked children you've introduced earlier), *that* could be a theme.

Themes must be positive or forget the whole thing. If you take a jaundiced-eye view of humanity in real life, reform fast or go unsold. The slicks are not convinced that life is a drag; they want to hear about generosity, love and the bluebird of happiness—preferably subtly.

Don't spell it out in black and white, if grey and white will do nicely. The reader is getting wiser and likes to use a little imagination, like putting his own egg in the cake mix. Go easy on the "I suddenly realized" department. Dialogue can be more effective than narrative.

When I began I wrote delightful stories with beginnings, middle, and ends, full of wit and sprightly characters. I have these stories and enjoy a laugh over them now and then. They are themeless orphans and might have sold to the *Woman's Home Companion* in the forties, when fiction was not so serious. For now, they score minus ten with every editor. One of these, "Daddy's Girl," concerned a lively girl who disobeyed her father and ultimately fell in love with the man she rebelled against because he was her father's choice. Theme? Obey your father. But no one has to be told that!

A story in *Good Housekeeping*, "Life and Love Upstairs," probably less witty than "Daddy's Girl," brought me a large check. The plot is simple: A young family is badgered by the lady downstairs, who vociferously objects to the noise of their lives being lived above. The simple theme: The young must come to understand and to tolerate the forms of loneliness of those who are old and alone.

The theme is the stuff of which the story is made and is as important nowadays as the paper on which it appears. It must have a basic truth, perhaps even a message. It does not have to be spelled out at the end like an essay on ethics, but even a witty story should be sewed together with one serious thread.

"First Smile," quite a funny story I wrote and sold to a Canadian magazine, concerned the disastrous results when a brand-new mother is faced with her overly helpful mother and mother-in-law, who come to assist with the new arrival. The story was light from beginning to end, but the new baby's first smile brought in the happy ending, complete with theme: becoming a grandmother is every bit as difficult as becoming a mother.

So now you know you've got to have a theme as well as a plot and here you are, face-to-face with your Smith-Corona, without a thought in your head. In answer to the question, "Which came first —the plot or the theme?" I start with the chicken, the meat, the plot, usually. When I've worked out some characters and action, I ask myself what it all means. Often I sit shrugging my shoulders over this problem for days. It often doesn't mean a thing.

For example: I thought up the beginnings of a very tidy plot about a girl in a country hospital (*Good Housekeeping*, "Rx: One Mended Heart") and a boy in the next room. The rollicking possibilities seemed fine: an escalating romance in an offbeat setting peppered with bumbling doctors and erratic plumbing.

But what about the egg, the theme? In other words, so what? I wasn't going to touch the typewriter until I'd nailed the answer. Finally, little by little I began to build. Suppose this girl hated the country, had just come up to visit, had broken her leg and was now stuck in this rustic wasteland? I elaborated on this; I gave her a solid city past, a job, and an urban beau. Here she was, lying in the hospital and feeling desolate.

The boy in the next room also had a past, and a fiancée who coincidentally wanted him to move to the city.

Now I brought the boy and the girl together through the machinations of a country hospital telephone operator, and they fell in love. In the end, the girl is convinced that country life is exciting and wonderful. Note the formation of theme with plot. The theme: Happiness is where the heart is.

Where did I get my idea for a country hospital in the first place? I don't have a little notebook full of spontaneous jottings. I carry my ideas in my head and wait for them to pop up at propitious moments. Sometimes they do and sometimes they don't; one needs patience.

Not the kind of patience that means you go out on the town instead of sitting at the typewriter. I mean the kind required for sitting somewhere quiet and really trying to build a story from scratch.

I don't mean a whole story. It doesn't have to jell from A to Z before you begin, unless you're the fastidious outline type. It seems to me that some of my best stories begin with a vague outline, a theme, and a firm idea of the end. As I work, new ideas pop unexpectedly into my head. Suddenly, the story begins to zip along in its own clever way, independent as a ouija board. The outcome often surprises me. Occasionally even the theme is changed. Often the firm ending is not the one I originally had in mind. This writer's serendipity is one of the great pleasures of writing.

The country hospital idea came, as it happens, from nowhere. I've never been in one, I've never seen one. I made it up. That's really my job, as a writer. Often I have help; I get an idea from something real, something that's actually happened. Slick fiction should mirror ordinary life, so I try to garner everyday things from people's conversations, the very things they wouldn't report to a writer.

For example, my last few published stories dealt with 1) a pair of neighbors, grown very close, who are now to be separated; 2) a husband who is promoted and can't seem to cope with success; 3) a mother, laid low by a brief illness, who finds no one can substitute mother-love; 4) a gloomy, rainy Sunday that helps a young wife to realize how lucky she is to have a family.

All these plots are based on the most mundane, day-to-day experiences, easy for the reader to recognize as real, incorporating pleasant characters with which the reader can identify.

I listen, I observe and I think. Then I stick a few things together, change the end, revise, cut, and I'm all set. Easy, isn't it?

That part of a plot which is pivotal in a story, I have dubbed the "hinge": the point toward which the characters must move all along, the point in a plot once known as the climax. Climax, nowadays, is too strong a word for this pivot; it can consist of a word or a look, instead of a war or a first kiss, but it changes the direction of the story and the writer must have established this point before his fingers first touch the typewriter. He must have planned it with utmost strategy, sneaking in forecasts of it almost from the beginning.

My clinker, "Christmas Incident," ran as follows: Joe's daughter had alienated him by a forced marriage to a man of whom Daddy doesn't approve. Joe is lonely and bitter, but on Christmas Day, he decides he must accept his daughter's invitation to visit her and her new baby. On the way to his daughter's house, Joe drives past a frozen lake and notices some children trying out their Christmas ice-skates. The hinge: Just as he passes, a young girl ventures too far and falls through thin ice. The water is not deep, and she is quickly hauled out, but the moment of fear has shifted Joe's sentiments. He is reminded of his own daughter in childhood, the fragility of their present relationship and immediately realizes how precious she actually still is to him. With this fresh viewpoint, he continues to his daughter's, determined now to accept his son-in-law and make peace with his daughter.

This hinge is marred with the anathema of coincidence and is therefore unacceptable. It strains the reader's credibility to believe that Joe just happened by as someone was about to be drowned; it does not stem logically, in A-B-C order, from the structure of the plot. It is a trick, and sounds as if it had been stuck in as an afterthought.

An example of a thoroughbred hinge appeared in *Redbook,* in my story, "The Difficult Part." The story concerned a mother who was told that her young son had musical talent. Without consulting him, she forced piano lessons on the boy, and despite his lack of interest, she made arrangements with his teacher to have him appear at a students' recital. The hinge follows naturally: The boy, frightened and a poor beginner, plays some wrong notes and runs off stage in a panic. His humiliation changes the focus. His mother realizes that "children do not always fit into the tuxedos their parents weave for them in their imaginations."

Here is the natural outcome of a logical hinge that does not depend on chance or coincidence. The reader, finishing the story, might say, "I could have guessed that would have happened," without actually having more than a clue and certainly without making the story predictable.

Whitewash the heroine—and that goes for the hero as well. The editors of the women's magazines are unified in demanding a protagonist with whom the reader can identify. This does not mean Pollyanna and Little Orphan Annie rolled into one, but it does mean, *no big vices!* She never embezzles, gossips or has dirty fingernails, and if she has a questionable past, it wasn't her fault. She's allowed little shortcomings and may be given to shyness or absent-mindedness or disorderly ways, but she is Virtue Personified, like you. That goes for her husband, too, and all those people near and dear to her with whom she's going to mingle in her plot. Not too much unpleasantness anywhere, please, as there was in my ill-fated story, "New Boy."

Strictly speaking, the protagonist of this story, one I considered excellent before it came back and back and back, was a sensitive boy. He adored his dear and loving parents who were, unfortunately, jewel thieves. If the readership of *Good Housekeeping* were composed of gun molls, this would have gone over big; unfortunately in this case, the readers of women's slicks are ladies between the ages of eighteen and forty, and for all practical purposes, they do not steal. They prefer to identify with paragons rather than felons.

And "New Boy" taught me something even more important: aim for non-fiction fiction. Avoid, like rejection slips, the incredible. The response that the writer must aim for is, "This is real. It's just like what happened to me last year!" or perhaps, could happen tomorrow. Jewel thieves don't happen to anyone, but car mishaps do, as in my *Good Housekeeping* story, "All My Own":

A young wife wants a second car for her own use. Husband says no but finally relents long enough to buy, reluctantly, an old heap from a used car dealer. These things happen every day. The hinge: the car, containing our *pleasant* heroine and three children, stalls and dies in the middle of a traffic tie-up leading to a huge department store parking lot. Please note: The car does not explode or hiss fire or lose a couple of wheels. These things *could* happen, but the slicks are not interested in improbable catastrophes. They want everyday occurrences. Whose battery, after all, hasn't gone dead at some time or other? In short, the trick is to be original—in an *ordinary* way!

Of all the mistakes my clinkers made, lack of action is the most deadly. Narrative, like aspirin, is only effective in small doses, except, perhaps, in *The New Yorker*. If you aim for the slicks, make the story move—no—jump from scene to scene. Jump into the dialogue at the beginning, if possible; if not, keep your introduction short because it will amuse only you and those who love you enough to be bored by overdoses of your descriptions of the mountain flowers that grew on the west side of your heroine's house. A successful writer I know once told me that she plans her stories like scenes in a play. Put your reader into a time and place immediately and avoid heavy details that can flower through dialogue. In a story I wrote recently, for example:

Cass fumbled with the wrapping paper; I saw Dickie strain forward.
"A muff! A muff! Cass cried, stuffing both hands into the white fur. "Thank you, Grandma!"

This is the rewrite of the original:

Cass fumbled with the wrapping paper; I saw Dickie strain forward. She peered into the box, then pulled out a white fur muff. "Thank you, Grandma."

A slight difference, perhaps just a shade. But the rewritten paragraph jumps!

Unlike the slice-of-life fragments that are characteristic of small quarterlies, unlike the offbeat pieces that are occasionally seen now in such magazines as *Playboy,* the current high-paying slick market is oriented toward the sort of story which can best be described as optimistic. The jaundiced eye does not go over well here, and defeatist themes are generally unpopular. (There are exceptions.) This does not mean that you must tack a happy ending on everything; still, if things don't work out for the heroine at the finish, try for a ray of hope, at least. The experience you have put her through must have taught her a lesson or given her some insight, and at the end, things should be looking up.

Another criterion high on the editor's list is the predictability of the plot. If he can guess how it's going to end much before it does, you'll get the story back; the days of boy-meets-girl, loses girl, gets girl are over. And fantasy, slapstick, and farce went out with the mustache. The it-could-really-happen is very much *in*.

That goes for dialogue, double. No rhetoric, please. Characters must talk, not give Gettysburg Addresses. And, the briefer the better; it is amazing how many redundancies crop up in monologues, my own in particular. In real life, people tend to be repetitive; they don't dare to in fiction; still, they must sound real. "No!" is as effective as "No! No! No!" so learn to cut, even if it brings tears to your creative eyes.

And learn to stay on the track. Beware of those tempting extraneous details that derail your theme. Those beautifully written paragraphs about the heroine's life at the Sorbonne will have to go, unless they have a direct bearing on her situation right now. This is both the challenge and the limitation of writing for the slicks; plot first, style second. Don't let your own talent carry you away.

While you're cutting, be suspicious of double and triple adjectives. Sometimes they can't be helped, but consider trimming "She looked into a cold, flat, grey sky" to "She looked into a slate sky," and congratulate yourself on your economy.

Never, however, strain for an analogy or overdo a metaphor. This kind of overwriting is the mark of the neophyte.

Ready to begin? Of course you are. It's the middle of the story that sends the writer running, defeated, from the typewriter. The I-can't-go-on plateau is as common as a cold. Remember persistence? It's the only remedy.

39

STORYTELLERS' STREET

By Sanora Babb

Once in a faraway place in an evening of summer, I was wandering through an ancient narrow street, aware of its people in their odd mixture of Eastern and Western clothes, the unknown language, the sounds and smells and heat, and all around me an atmosphere that was the sum of these parts and yet something more, something intangible and powerful. It convinced me of the reality of my own experience, and remains in my memory to evoke the wonder of that evening.

Walking on, I came to a quieter street and turned in. Still under the spell of the atmosphere, I did not at first feel curious at this variation, but soon I became aware of a distinct difference, especially in the sounds: fewer voices, and islands of intense listening quiet surrounded by little seas of emotion. I was in Storytellers' Street.

This was not its official name but its *real* name, used by everyone for centuries.

The old men, for most of them were old, were telling their tales, and around them squatted boys and girls, men and women, who had worked all day and come into this street at evening to be entertained, or to expand their lives in the experiences of imagined tales freshly spun, or the old, known loved ones they had heard many times. They contributed their small coins, these "readers", and lost themselves to their living books.

Each storyteller had his following. There were omnivorous "readers" who sampled them all. Here and there, a young or a new "author" told his stories to a few adventuresome listeners. He was most likely starving and struggling like his fellow beginners everywhere in the world. But he had his own style, and perhaps he was telling the old themes in a fresh way, or adopting the formulas of popular-old tellers.

Some told stories that began and ended in one sitting, while others related episodes or chapters that charmed their audience back for more. By watching the faces of the listeners, I observed how expertly the storyteller aroused their desire to hear "what happened next"; how well he expressed himself, how lightly or how seriously he spoke; how deeply he involved their emotions. Their eyes shone with delight or sympathy or tragedy or nobility. And sometimes they were glazed with boredom or cool doubt, in which case the listener moved to another teller. Mostly, the audience showed respect, esteem, even affection for the storytellers.

The best storytellers evidently possessed a sense of character and story structure and evocation of emotion that caused their listeners to suspend their disbelief. When they rose to leave, many of them walked still in the world of the story.

That evening, I learned a great deal about writing, in spite of the fact that I could not understand the language. I, too, went along the street dreaming, overwhelmed and extended by my experience, and filled with first-hand knowledge and respect for the timeless role of the storyteller in the world.

Those men, all so unalike, and several of them obviously trusting their intuitive powers to create as they went along, skilled by prac-tice in their form, gave me the assurance to continue to follow my own way, write my own stories, which, in the end, were the only stories I *could* write. In my ignorance I had rejected technique, con-fusing it with formula. There, I saw emotional tension achieved by imagination disciplined and released through technical skill. I em-phasize discipline and rich release as opposed to the debris-filled flood of careless expression.

Storytellers' Street was an unforgettable experience, but I realized that only the experience of writing and writing and writing could develop my own talents. It seems to me that one writes first and learns after to estimate and comprehend the various inherent ele-ments of a good story. To begin too soon to appraise one's intangible emotion-idea or the sudden effulgence that often announces creative work, is to hamper its true growth. Writing requires infinite patience, and to hurry to apply the tools may be to mechanize or even destroy the pattern originating in another area of our minds to which we should give the utmost acceptance.

To take pride in a know-nothing attitude is to deny that writing has its craft. Every art is the more clearly and fully expressed by the excellence of its technique. Technique is a *way* of doing, and only when method dominates meaning (thought and feeling), does it fail its role, its subtle, integral role of bringing the whole to its best possible realization.

Every word should have a purpose. If it has none, it should be cut without regret. The purpose is not mere action, but story action, and this includes every value that contributes to the whole effect. The purpose of the story itself is to arrive at its destination. The journey may be one of soaring, or probing deeply, or traveling on the surface, but it must be a *journey*—within or without—of implied or dramatized conflict. Characters must live and change within a structured time. Change is the result of an encounter with an idea, emotion, person, animal, nature, circumstance, or any of these in combination; and it is the writer's artistic responsibility to show, to reveal, to dramatize, not tell about, this encounter.

A single point of view is far more than a formality. It is the difference between knowing one person well, sharing an experience, and wandering about among acquaintances or even strangers. It is true that it helps the reader to identify with the character, while acrobatic viewpoints scatter his attention and the story's unity, but very importantly, and first, the single point of view helps the author to identify with and more effectively give life to the character.

A pleasure in, a respect for, a love of language, though not always traits of the writer, would seem to be vital, since after all, language is the means for conveying the reality of the created experience. Few writers attain a distinctive style, as style is as much an expression of the writer's unique creative personality as it is his experience-trained language; or, perhaps it *is* the language of the writer's personality. Nevertheless, the exact word, the fresh phrase, the attempt *to say truly* what one means, lead toward coveted simplicity. Simplicity is not bony writing any more than a skeleton is a human being. And, "to say truly" gives individual scope.

But the story itself will excite or involve no one if it does not move. Life moves, everything is changing every moment. *Creative* is the opposite of *static*. And yet, movement alone does not insure life. Movement must *grow* out of the characters and not mechanically from the author's head, and these characters must be allowed to speak and act for themselves, which they will do if they are not fitted into arbitrary molds, the story ending in a lifeless concoction.

Evocation of emotion, that vital, living authority, may exist because the author has achieved all these things, but more likely because he has an indefinable ability to produce it, perhaps through intense feeling and heightened affinity for all that he creates.

If he is fortunate, his quantitative substance has metamorphosed into the qualitative state of form. Not by accident. Outwardly, form is shape, design, pattern, but totally, form is a coalescence of all the elements of internal reality projected into external reality. It is the climax of art, the aura of life of which one is deeply aware but cannot "see" and must not confuse with structure, its composed and inseparable associate.

In this subtle matter of art into life, it may be reassuring to remember that there can be no form without craft, and the writer does better to go respectfully about the business of writing his stories. By respectfully, I mean that the familiar techniques of the short story should not be imposed upon the material, but rather, that each story be permitted to make its particular claims upon its craft, to grow up an individual within its generic laws. Whether the story achieves the rare state of art or mortal excellence, or mere and often admirable competence, its organization and structure are vital. Organization may take place as a part of the mysterious creative process, or it may be consciously built, but it is not the proper fitting together of parts for the simple reason that there is no proper or correct story.

This is no contradiction of the story's integrity, no license for careless writing but an attempt to emphasize an imaginative approach to the *whole* story, to use technique, not be used by it. The exciting challenge of writing the short story is its demanding symmetry and the variety of possibilities within that symmetry, that balance.

My method may seem vague to the writer who functions best with a plan or outline or a thought-out story. But every writer writes as he can. My stories "arrive" when they are ready to be written. I have never been able to finish satisfactorily a story that arrived too soon. Of course, they do not appear from nowhere; they grow from experiences, some direct, others from a suggestion, both created through imagination. Once I write the first sentence, the story begins to unfold as I write, swiftly or slowly, being "worked out" within, as I go or long before. Who knows? I have a sense of destination, only a sense, without knowledge of events in between, and as I work, I am aware of the destination (event or meaning or both) as a reason for what I am writing down. It is as if, were more revealed to me, I should lose the sense and feel of the moment.

I write the whole story first, and later, go over and over it, checking its structure, cutting, revising, rewriting, polishing. Parts remain intact. Principles become, it seems, a part of the intuitive approach, as if my imagination uses techniques I have learned by practice. Revising, to me, is as creative as original writing, because once again into the mood of the story, I am creating, experiencing, being the characters.

All this may sound as if in some esoteric way my stories have been written for me and present themselves to be typed, which is far from the whole truth, and every writer knows this. E. M. Forster gave this valuable advice: "The act of writing is inspiring." True. The total act of writing is hard work, also. This is frequently said as a drawback, a threat, a warning. But, why not hard work? Why are we hesitant to admit what we all (or almost all) feel when working: the joy of work?

One part of this joy for me is the creation of atmosphere. While I recognize that it is only one element, and perhaps not a vitally important one at that, writing begins for me with a strong, almost overwhelming sense of the atmosphere of my story, whether it is weather or place or emotional climate. Characterization, dialogue, tension and the rest develop more easily within their felt state.

Excerpts from dramatic texture inevitably lose values of emotion and meaning, but the following may partially illustrate:

That evening the canyon was strangely quiet. Lights blazed from every window of the house on El Ramo Way. No shadows passed the bright panes. The city below was jeweled in faraway, deceptive elegance. One tall, white flowering yucca glowed on the dim hillside like the ghost of reality fled. At times a little wind came up Viento Road carrying a brief reminder of the sea. The night air was tropic-sweet with jasmine. A woman's crying drifted faintly through the evening under the cricket's song. ("Woman On A Balcony," *New Mexico Quarterly Review*.)

When the Santa Ana comes, blowing off the Mojave Desert two hundred miles away, people walking along the city streets are suddenly embraced by a lasso of warm soft wind. The air has a radiant clarity. The atmosphere becomes strange, subtly exciting. People begin to unwind, to gentle, to feel young, to delight in breathing, to be aware of being alive, and sad that they've been dully taking it for granted. The wind enfolds them and kisses them like petals, and they begin to feel in love—in love with being alive; and this is so rare, like a primeval sensation coming up through all the centuries, that they are a little frightened, but the wind soothes them, and a tender wily restlessness sets in. They aren't what they call *themselves* until the wind ceases and they can get back into their protective masquerades. The wind sometimes blows a day and a night. The time is enchanted with an alien beauty. It is as if love had come without a lover. ("The Santa Ana," *Saturday Evening Post* and *Best American Short Stories 1960*.)

. . . fascinated to see a woman's hat of another era hanging on the supporting frame of a dresser mirror. She knew at once that the hat had been placed there years ago and never removed; it had deteriorated with dust. A breath would scatter it! Under the bed were two high-heeled slippers whitened and warped with the time they had rested there. Old finery and cans of talcum lay on the chairs, and over everything was a coat of ancient dust. Holly imagined Mrs. Polk young and willowy, wearing the dress she had on today, entering the bedroom, kicking off her slippers, and with a wide lamenting gesture, placing the hat, looking at herself in the mirror; and in that moment, closing a door, a massive knobless door. Why? ("The Tea Party," *Seventeen*.)

For each writer, one element or another may act as a key. Atmosphere helps me to live in the world of my story. If the author lives there, perhaps the reader will live there, too. This is rather like the teller of tales and the listener to tales who live for a time on Storytellers' Street.

40

SHORT STORY OR NOVEL?

By Jean Rikhoff

A SHORT story ceases to interest me almost the moment I conceive of it. Already the people I have first envisioned have begun to grow; soon their proportions and problems are far more complicated than those which could be encompassed in the few pages of a short story. I begin dreamily to think in terms of something bigger, something that will give my people time to develop—in other words, a novel. This inability to keep a small set of characters in a localized setting in the center of one elaborated or elongated incident—which I more or less take as a definition of the short story—has been, in the end, my saving. No matter how many times it has been said before, it must be said again:

It is much easier to sell a novel than a short story.

Let's take an example I know well, my own. For years I hopefully sent out short stories and as near as I came to selling one was a nice, encouraging letter now and then cheering me on to try harder. Far more representative was the wastepaper basketful of printed rejection slips I set afire at the end of each week. It was tiresome, repetitious, unencouraging, certainly uneconomical, and—let's face it— self-defeating. What I wanted to do was break into print and I certainly had no evidence to show I had done so or was ever going to do so. And even if I had had a story or two a year accepted, the acceptance would probably have come from one of the little magazines, which, if they do pay, can hardly be accused of making a writer wealthy (they may, however, make him eventually famous, so think twice before turning up your nose at the little magazines).

If you want something done, do it yourself, the old maxim goes. Speedily, a group of us were organizing our own magazine and putting out announcements that we were interested in publishing fiction and poetry—let the academic reviews concentrate on criticism. Running *Quixote* for six years taught me a good deal more than I care to know about the impossible plight of the short story writer. We were a small literary quarterly, coming out of England first (later Spain), with a woefully small subscription list (we never had over five hundred *paid* subscriptions, but we still managed to make our influence felt, as is evidenced by the fact that a number of the stories were reprinted in the *Best Short Stories* of the year in which they were published and that Grosset and Dunlap still publishes an anthology of the best stories the magazine printed *), yet we were inundated by manuscripts. Sometimes it seemed to me everyone in the world was pouring out his heart on paper. From the letters that came into *Quixote* from writers whose material we did accept, we received a fairly accurate and dismaying picture of past discouragements, disappointments, utter disinterest from the publishing world at large. One would imagine that somewhere along the line the punishment-pleasure principle would have begun to operate, and these writers would have faced up to the fact that no matter how dedicated they were, the odds were against their publishing anything at all *ever* and that they would do better expending their energies in chicken raising.

I know of writers whose stories we accepted and with whom we entered into long, revelatory correspondence who had been sending out stories week after week, month in and out, year after year, *up to twenty years,* who had never come near seeing anything of theirs in print.

To be practical (just for a moment): Say a writer writes one story every two weeks (on the average). That's twenty-six stories a year, and over twenty years that would be upward of five hundred stories, equal in length to a considerable number of books if the effort had been put into the longer instead of the shorter form.

But books are too hard to write, they take too long: one hears that again and again. Very well. That means that those who do attempt a novel and manage to keep at it until the last word is set down have a nice mathematical advantage over their fellow short story writers. The majority of writers who even begin a novel don't have the stamina to carry through—and that is precisely the point. The writer who does finish a book has immediately been set apart from the vast ma-

---

* *The Quixote Anthology,* Grosset's Universal Library.

jority of writers—by more than half, I'd guess, though an awful lot of people write books, too, and a surprising amount of these are published. If you look at the number of bad books published as compared to the number of bad short stories, the inevitable conclusion seems to be that it is easier to publish a bad book than a bad short story, though I wouldn't want to defend this thesis in, say, *Publishers' Weekly*.

Granted, then, that the novel has it all over the short story as far as possibility of publication is concerned (provided, of course, that the writer has a modicum of ability), how do you finish a novel? Anyone, obviously, can begin one; the trick is to get through it and get into the publishers' offices.

I know only one rule for writing novels and it suffers no exception. How do you write a novel? Day by day. You must place yourself at a desk with the sole purpose of working on the novel and *nothing else* for at least two to three hours a day. No letter writing, no paying bills (if you can), no dabbling in your diary, no making project notes in your journal (you can do that later), no exceptions whatsoever, just you and the work in progress, and this means the *novel* in progress—not a new idea for a short story that has just popped into your mind, not a note to remind you to pick up some coffee and drop off the dry cleaning that afternoon, not a quick dip in the morning paper before you settle down to real work. It doesn't make any difference if, for a time, you don't write a word, if, in Simone de Beauvoir's felicitous phrase, "sentences wither at the tip of the pen." Don't give up. Sheer desperation will force you to make up something, and once begun, momentum will carry you along. After a few weeks you will sit down and begin to write out of a sense of preservation. Nothing is quite so nerve-racking as fifty minutes of staring at a blank sheet of paper, listening to noises sifting in from that outside world that tell you what you already too well know, that non-writers are a lucky breed who have escaped the crucible of composition.

And speaking about composition—how do you compose a novel? Some people use outlines. I loathe them, I think they are confining and take up too much time, and I have the suspicion that people who labor long over them are using their creative energies wastefully. I know there are some writers who do draw up elaborate outlines and specify for themselves every scene that will take place in a novel before they write down one word. I have never found this a workable plan. In the first place, characters have a tendency to insist upon lives of their own at certain points in a book and the outline must either be rigidly adhered to or thrown away, something that produces panic in either case. Secondly, there is something to be said for a freedom of feeling in attacking anything, and most particularly a book. The spontaneity and excitement of stumbling on a "great scene" gives energy and impetus to a writer; once outlined, the material is pretty much *déjà vu*.

I usually start with people in conflict. It's as simple as that. Plot is always conflict of one kind or another, a character at odds with his society, his fellowmen or himself. This is perhaps a simplified way of stating that people, of whom all books, even those of the new wave of anti-novels, are composed, have come a cropper with the values which hitherto they have acted on unconditionally, unconsciously, automatically. Character in the true sense of the word—that which makes up the beliefs of a man—is suddenly in a dilemma because the inner supports are threatening to give way or have given way. The things by which a man has always got along no longer serve; conflict means he must make some kind of fight to keep his life going or it will collapse under him. Therefore, plot—to use a somewhat old-fashioned word—is really people in situations which tax them beyond their resources so that they are called upon for new insights, new energy, greater understanding and undertakings in their lives. If they fail to make these, they are defeated—not always irrevocably, however. Tragedy shows us the voice of conscience able to verbalize its understanding of the overwhelming obstacles that are in the process of destroying the central protagonist of a story. By being able to put that understanding into powerful expression, the defeated triumphs, for he has, in his determination to assert values against inevitable defeat, once more pointed up the indestructibility of man and his beliefs. Thus, the defeated man fails in the name of something better; he is not defeated; he has reaffirmed (to use the old word) a better vision of the universe, has refined for us aspects of a better tomorrow. Rigidly speaking, plot is of no great importance, if we mean by plot the *events* of a book. What is of concern is the individual struggle. Or, to put it succinctly, people matter, not plot.

Thus, we begin with character in the deepest sense of the word, and in conflict. Often the unfolding idea for a novel is vague—why *did* these people who gave me so much pain act like that? Why did *I* act as I did? For most first novelists (and quite rightly) usually begin to go into old wounds. In this way, writing has been called therapy—or revenge. As the great psychiatrist Theodor Reik remarked on Ibsen's observation that writing means to sit in judgment on oneself, "It also means to acquit oneself."

I must say that I myself feel that writing is an act toward understanding. It is an attempt through tearing down, to rebuild, this time properly; to take apart and remove the pieces bit by bit so that the whole structure can be understood, from its smallest component. But we are most apt to understand the familiar house in which we have lived; hence the old and workable adage, Write about what you know. Most of us, if the truth were confessed, know little about anything, most especially the workings of the human heart; yet that is the novelist's territory, the contradictory, complex human heart. Without people of depth and concern, there is no book.

Certain limitations have already been imposed, then, before the writer even begins. Most obviously, shallow people are hardly of much universal concern. (A good case can be made for the fact there are no shallow people, only shallow see-ers. I would grant this, but the act of imagination and the gift of understanding are limited in all of us, and given these limitations, we are apt to get on better with some kinds of characters than with other kinds, generally those drawn from the people who have influenced our lives strongly.) For good or evil, the strongest characters in a novel are generally those which exert the most pull on the novelist. The writer, who comes finally to feel he has understood the whole love-hate relationship between his parents and himself, his mate and himself, his life and himself, is the one who draws a deeply moving portrait of these. It is only after the individual example has been explored that any universal connotation can be made. In these terms, then, the writer who concentrates deeply on—say—one love affair and all its aspects has a better chance of saying something universal about all love than the writer who starts out to write about Love with a capital L.

So far the formula for putting together a novel sounds deceptively simple. "Deceptively" is certainly the word. It is not "simple" to understand your characters' true motives for their acts (perhaps—

no, often—even unknown to them), nor is it easy to present human beings in their most prevalent attitudes, many of which are paradoxical and contradictory. The trouble arises from the fact few of us act on one instinct alone, nor do we live by a set of ethics that do not in themselves come into conflict; our lives are constant questionings and inner warfares. Often our actions appear absolutely inexplicable.

Think through your characters—your plot—your ideas, your theme—and then argue with yourself about what you think. Is this character only surface-explored? Is this *really* the way this character would act? Have I taken the easy, obvious way out in ending this episode? Is what I am writing as much of the truth as I am capable of seeing or is it only as much as, lazily, I've been willing to glance over? Am I *really* exploring a theme, or am I only using plot to pull me through? Do I really know my material? Have I dug down far enough to make discoveries? "It has been said," writes Koestler in *The Act of Creation,* "that discovery consists in seeing an analogy nobody had seen before"; he goes on to say that "this leads to the paradox that the more original a discovery, the more obvious it seems afterwards." In connection with this, there is a triumvirate of words that serves a writer well in testing every phase of his work:

Imagine

Argue

Act

The great pitfall in all this is that the writer begins to take himself too seriously. "Total absence of humor renders life impossible," says Colette; she might just as well have added it renders literature impossible, too. Instead of putting a character in a situation and letting him demonstrate the opposing sides of his nature, the novelist lets the action grind to a halt, the character fades into the background, the conflict is forgotten or hastily pushed aside, and the author jumps center stage and begins to talk. Unfortunately, the fatal flaw in most of this talk shows up at once. It is a lecture we must listen to, *the writer has something to say* (after all, haven't all of us heard ad infinitum that we must be instructive as well as entertaining?), and the promising scene is lost in a harangue about the good or moral or corrupt life. Humor, objectivity, action—all these desert the page in deference to high seriousness, and virtue, observes Bellow's Herzog, bores mankind. (Was it one of the Mauriacs who said there were few histories of happy loves, which means, I suppose, that where conflict does not exist, where placidity reigns, so does disinterest.) Therefore, perhaps the golden rule that ought to be embossed above all writers' desks is

SHOW, DO NOT SAY

But if you *must* say, at least say *some*thing. Nothing can be so paralyzing as the forum seized only to cover old arguments. Few of us need to be told (and certainly not at length), for instance, that war is hell, that children are more often ungrateful than not, that the loss of youth is some kind of tragedy we still do not understand.

To recapitulate for a moment: The novelist begins with a protagonist or a group of protagonists at odds and in conflict; brooding over the intricacies of these, he tries to understand. In the act of understanding, other ideas—often in the form of concrete scenes—suggest themselves; the novelist finds he is interested in writing a book about some human situation, which by its very nature participates in all human behavior. Tentatively, gropingly, he sits and begins to write (type, tape record, dictate). He has now embarked, and the only way the voyage will be made is day by day, bit by bit—what we are taught is "one step at a time"—the end does not come by the writer's telling himself that he *must* have a rest, that he will get a better perspective on the material if he goes off on a little vacation, that really the lawn must be attended to today and the book can wait one day while the grass is taken care of; or that it is such a perfect day that the only thing to do is throw everything up and rush out to hit a few around the links.

From the beginning it is best to be prepared for moments of insurrection and rebellion. The working writer cannot be blamed if he begins to feel he is skimping on his life, that he is denying himself the ordinary everyday pleasures most people take for granted, that he is nothing but a drudge for a lot of people—not even real—he has come to hate because they are robbing him of all the things he likes to do—skiing, seeing an old friend, reading, even going about the necessary business of life which must be attended to. A deep guilt springs up even when he is doing chores that simply must be done during the hours he knows he should be at his desk. Nothing can be worse than tidying up the daily dirt of our lives—which ordinarily we hate and credit with robbing us of so much valuable time we might be using toward "worthwhile" things—and then, instead of feeling righteous, being overcome by awful anxiety. That awful anxiety is the sign of the conscientious workman who has put away his tools before the job is done. There will be other beautiful days, other years in which to ski; the world will not crack if the lint collects a few hours longer under the bed; the friend will wait, but the book will never be done unless it is done day by day, and it can never be done day by day without an organized and determined discipline.

In other contexts, this might be called self-sacrifice.

41

SUSPENSE: RULES AND NON-RULES

By Patricia Highsmith

"Too much thought is bad for the soul, for art, and for crime. It is also a sign of middle age. . . ."

Patrick Hamilton wrote this in one of his novels about Gorse, a real-life criminal who started early and successfully, but later began to plan a bit. It was his doom.

I wrote Hamilton's words down in the back of my notebook, where I keep other people's remarks that I wish I had made myself. I do not set much store by logic, no doubt because nature did not give me much. Novels are products of emotion, and to my illogical mind Hamilton's statement seems doubly true, because a suspense writer must be at the same time an artist and a criminal. It is probably better to be young for this. Middle age does bring thought, alas, and looking before leaping. Not much can be done about middle age, but thinking and logic should be discouraged, except in minutiae of the plot: e.g., would X really have had time to wipe up the blood, make a telephone call, and get all the way from Hoboken to Grand Central in seven minutes?

People who don't write often ask writers where they get their ideas from, not knowing that writers get them out of thin air a good part of the time, and at other times from incidents so trivial and fleeting that the incident, or face, or phrase can hardly be recaptured and repeated as an answer as to where their novel came from. Is this logical? Of course not. The unconscious mind takes the germ of an idea and develops it, but usually this happens only when a writer has tried hard, and logically, to develop it himself. After he has given it up for a few hours, getting nowhere, a great advancement of the plot will pop into his head. I have been waked up in the night sometimes by a plot advancement or a solution of a problem that I had not even been dreaming about. Everyone functions like this to some extent, and it is what people mean when they say, "I don't want to make up my mind today, I'd better sleep on it."

I like a wild coincidence in a plot—as in *The Blunderer,* in which I had Walter guess the murderer (Kimmel) and his method of killing his wife, then attempt the same kind of attack upon his own wife, or rather contemplate it, because to give the plot a further twist, I had him not carry it out. His wife committed suicide. It looked like murder. And the similarity of the circumstances to Kimmel's tragedy exposed the guilt of Kimmel. *The Blunderer* has been made into a French film, *The Murderer.*

Wild implausibilities I highly recommend, too. My most celebrated —thanks to Alfred Hitchcock—is *Strangers on a Train,* which might be described as a series of almost incredible events. They were a little too incredible for the scriptwriters of the film (they cut out the second murder), just as the story, when presented as half the written novel and a synopsis of the remainder, was too incredible for six publishing houses which turned me down. They thought it could not be made convincing. The novel when finished was accepted by the next publisher I showed it to, Harper's, which shows the power of persuasion of illogical prose.

And I like harebrained schemes that must forever waver on the brink of discovery, as in *The Talented Mr. Ripley* (later the film *Purple Noon*), in which Ripley impersonates the man he has killed, though he does not look enough like him to pass for him among even his casual acquaintances. By an act of even greater audacity at the end of the book, Ripley allays any suspicion of himself, acquires his victim's income for life, and gets away with it all. Of course they couldn't have him get away with it either on television or on the screen, but the novel won a prize from the Mystery Writers of America in 1956 and in 1957 the Grand Prix de Littérature Policière in France.

Young writers often worry about pace and atmosphere. Pace is no problem if one has a story. If I find my pace slowing, it is because the story is vague in my mind and I am muddling about, getting stuck on details and overdescribing. A writer should be quite sure of his story for at least thirty pages to come, and as for myself, I like to rush ahead—in a way, as if I were narrating a story to someone and talking a little too fast. Some writers, I know, like to plan very carefully, make outlines before they begin, and I do not mean to say here how writers should write, I am only saying the way I prefer to write and probably the only way I can write. My headlong method often necessitates heavy revision and major changes and then a new plunge. But often it comes off, too, as it did in *The Talented Mr. Ripley,* certainly the fastest book I ever wrote (five months) and consequently the fastest of all my books to read. When I begin a book, I have no more than sixty pages clearly in mind, often much less, but I have an idea of the effect I want to create—tragedy, success, a sense of being hopelessly trapped, as in *This Sweet Sickness,* a plodding gloom, as in *The Blunderer.* And I do know what the end will be, therefore. After a few pages (it ought to be before the first line) the characters are alive and move, they have directions in which they move, or they have directions that circumstances prevent them from taking. Anyway, one has a dynamic situation, and from then on—certainly by page sixty—the book seems to write itself. When writers look through one of their printed books, see all the twists and turns, the speculations of harassed characters and their possible lines of action (all brilliantly set forth, of course, like spokes radiating from a wheel hub), surely many must say to themselves, "I don't remember thinking all that out in such detail. My goodness, I don't even remember writing it." This has already happened to me on looking through my book, *The Two Faces of January,* which I wrote only a few years ago.

Atmosphere? I am grateful to reviewers for saying that my books have it, but it is another thing I have never given any thought to until now. And it seems to me that laboring it, like laboring anything in a creative work, is fatal. If I have any suggestion as to the building of atmosphere, it is to let the characters react to whatever environment they are in. Thus one presents a setting through the senses (how does it smell, what color is it, how does the color strike the person looking at it?) and also reveals a great deal, effortlessly, about the character perceiving it. A formal garden in Italy may delight a spinster schoolteacher; she may want to sit for hours on a cold stone bench reading her favorite poems in it; it may make a young American football player want to scream, tear out the hedges with his bare hands, or at any rate get out of it as fast as possible. Either reaction gives "atmosphere." A melancholic scene, mist on a deserted beach at night, may please another character who (for some reason) has certain associations with such a place. Characters' reactions produce atmosphere more vividly than solid paragraphs of prose about places—though even solid paragraphs can be relieved and made more alive by one small "he felt . . ." in regard to colors, sounds and smells.

I disapprove of the word "discipline" in regard to writing—that is, in the grim way in which it is generally used. A young writer looks, I imagine (I once did), with wide-eyed and respectful bewilderment at the well-meaning teacher who advises him to get it and keep it, for without it he can do nothing. No wonder the young person does not understand—not completely, because he probably already has the makings of this severe and abstract thing called discipline. Writing is a way of life, and what teachers mean by discipline is the habit and necessity of writing. Discipline never made a writer. Discipline is for the armed forces. And I think distractions and non-writing never unmade a writer, because a real writer will chuck his obligations, shed them somehow, and get away by himself and write. Writing is a way of organizing experience, or of organizing something imagined, of making something perfect and beautiful—even something as small as one sentence—in a world that can be at times chaotic, wretched, ugly and upsetting.

The habit of writing often begins in adolescence, sometimes even earlier. In adolescence, when emotion is intense, when many emotions bring tears, and the teen-ager picks up a pencil or a pen and writes a poem or a paragraph about it, and feels better—that's the beginning of writing. And all art comes from the prolongation of this childlike intensity, which many people lose even at puberty. When writing becomes a habit and a necessity, the writer need never give a thought to discipline, because writing is a pleasure. Then friends and relatives will say, "Ah, what discipline!" on seeing the writer at work, not realizing that it would take more discipline than they dream of for him to spend the next few hours in their company. After a good day's work, when one is feeling rather godlike, it is a different matter, a writer looks on the human race with a new joy, and feels like saying even to the Fuller Brush man, "Come in! Got time to sit down for a few minutes?" Discipline may be needed later when a writer has to cut forty pages from a manuscript he already considers cut, for instance, or his editor tells him to get rid of his favorite minor character because he doesn't advance the plot.

Life can also be chaotic at forty, of course, and a writer can feel he is written out, that he has nothing to say—at least not at the moment. I have just had a letter from a writer friend saying this, that he's written out, and so forth. He hasn't been writing very long at fiction (he was formerly a newspaperman), and he has also rather recently been married, and his wife has had a baby. He writes that he is getting tired of little marital tiffs—among other things—but mostly he writes about not being able to get settled in the book he is trying to start. I suggested to him that his problem might be the sense of loss-of-importance of what he wants to write—a ghastly condition that can easily come when one is faced with marital tiffs, household bills, a sick child, a weekend shattered by a visit from the in-laws, or, above all, by lack of privacy. It is astounding how after days of being with people—sometimes out of necessity, social or economic—a good and exciting idea becomes pale and wan, vague, and not worth writing. It is just as outstanding and thrilling when, after a day or so of solitude, silence, daydreaming and loafing, the same idea comes alive again, beautiful and bright like a wilted plant that has been given a good soaking in the rain.

It takes a few years to learn this. It takes a lot of skill and scheming, make-believe and trickery, to preserve one's enthusiasm through the hideous periods of reality, of people, of obligations, of non-privacy. It is sometimes necessary to avoid thinking about one's story in the midst of people, because it can be crushed like a violet— a violet tossed on a subway platform in the rush hour. I so often think of young writers everywhere who are not able to have, yet, that most expensive commodity in the world—aloneness. I think of young writers who get married thinking that their wives will be so cooperative about their weekend stints at the typewriter, of writers whose wives are cooperative and who themselves are jangled by obligations that will not let their minds be at peace, or by interruptions their wives are not militant enough to prevent. The greatest service a wife can render her writer husband is not typing his manuscripts for him, but keeping people away from him. Of course, a husband might do the same, if his wife is the writer.

How to make psychopathic types attractive? I would suggest making them young, perhaps even rather handsome, tidy in their dress (heavens, what a picture of impropriety we could conjure up by remarking quietly that our psychopathic hero was wont to be untidy in his dress), or give them a nice trait or two, like being generous, or kind to old ladies and animals. A sense of humor is also of tremendous help. This, perhaps, does not always work. Tom Ripley was nice looking, though his face was thoroughly forgettable; he was tidy; he had a sense of humor, and many readers liked him; yet others said they disliked him, with an "Ugh-h!" and a shudder. But the likers and dislikers kept turning the pages, the dislikers with an attitude of "Good Lord, what's he going to do *next?*" What writer could ask for more? And I also feel sure it would be possible to write a book with an untidy, fat, sloppy psychopath as hero, if one only gave him enough fascinating and audacious things to do. His more repellent qualities might have to be introduced gradually, but if you introduce him in some kind of action, the reader will be drawn along. Good action and a good story are irresistible.

Of all my published books, two, I think, are decidedly dull. They are *A Game for the Living* and *The Cry of the Owl*. In the first, a psychopathic murderer-hero is missing; in fact the murderer is off-scene, unknown, so it becomes a mystery whodunit in a way—definitely not my forte. In *Owl*, the hero is too square, becoming a sitting duck for the more evil characters, a passive bore. In both, I tried to do something different from what I had been doing, but left out some elements vital for me: surprise, speed of action, coincidence, and the stretching of the reader's credulity—which I ordinarily do to excess and without scruple. The result was mediocrity. It would be easy for me to keep on writing stories with heroes like Bruno of *Strangers on a Train* and Ripley, but it would also be cowardly and unenterprising. My conclusion is that it is well for a writer to realize what he can do best: a frightened heroine, a mad hero, a chase; and what emotional elements he does best: anxiety, the destructiveness that is associated with the criminal mind, the playing off of good against evil —and use them as the strong points of his story. I believe that any story, about anything, in the suspense category, can be told using some of the writer's stronger points, if he takes the trouble to find out first what his strong points are. I did not in these two dull books, and it was unforgivable of me.

42

VERBS AND PEOPLE

By Frances Rickett

JUST as the mystery novel has, over the past several years, expanded in form from the whodunit (now usually referred to as the old-fashioned detective story) to the suspenseful who-is-doing-it-and-watch-out-hero-or-you-may-get-a-dose-of-"it"-yourself, so has its audience expanded from the hard-core detective fan to a wider group of readers—people who love a good story and who are turning, in ever-increasing numbers, to the mystery-suspense novel to find it.

What makes a good story? The first and obvious answer is a soundly constructed plot with plenty of action—so "first" and so "obvious" that a writer can be led to think it's the only answer. It isn't.

For about ten years (and if I had any pride at all, I wouldn't admit to being so thick-headed) I wrote and was rejected—and even, sometimes, accepted—laboring under the impression that when an editor said to me, "Your story is too thin," he or she meant my plot was at fault.

Please notice "laboring" under the impression, because that's what I did. I read the experts and badgered writer friends, I diagnosed and analyzed and—I tried harder. Editors still said to me, "Your story is too thin."

At about the time I was reaching the point of despair, I submitted two chapters and an outline of a *novella* to a woman's magazine. Telling an interlocking tale of the lives of three sisters, this small gem was one of the most intricately plotted stories imaginable. It came back. The editor happened to be a friend of mine, so I called her to ask why. "Your story is too thin," she said.

I said—no, I didn't say it, I wailed it—"Barbara, how can you *say* that? Look at that plot!"

"Who's talking about plot?" she said.

There followed a stunned silence, after which I wanted to know then what in the world was she talking about?

People.

People?

My story was too thin because the characters in it were treated superficially, they didn't come alive, they weren't real.

How curious, I thought later, that so many editors over such a long period of time had been using the word "story" to mean something altogether different. And yet, *was* it something altogether different?

Think of some of the novels you have read that have stayed with you long past the reading—novels which had a good, strong story. Is it the details of the plot you remember, or is it the people? If, for instance, the incident of the eagle in *The Adventures of Augie March* remains fixed in your mind, is it because of the incident *per se,* or because that incident lays bare the soul of Thea and, ultimately, of Augie?

If, as has been claimed, the mystery-suspense novel is coming ever closer to the so-called straight novel, it isn't because mystery-suspense writers are maneuvering puppet characters through increasingly complicated twists and turns of plots, but because they are writing better stories—stories about real people.

How, then, to make a fictional character seem like a real person? By setting him in the context of life the way a real person is.

You give him a background. What kind of family was he born into? Did he—or does he—have parents, grandparents, brothers, sisters, uncles, aunts, cousins? And what kind of individuals are they? (You don't, of course, have to supply a full complement, but enough to give him some kind of family background, or, conversely, if it's important to your story, a lack of it.) In what exact place was he brought up? Under what circumstances? With what education? On what social and financial level? Have some specific childhood experiences left their mark on his adult life?

You give him a physical description and, if possible, some physical attribute or mannerism which will distinguish your six-foot, blue-eyed, curly-haired blond from any other six-foot, blue-eyed, etc. Most important, you try to draw from his physical description those specifics which will reveal his character.

You determine his age, his intelligence, marital status, dependents, occupation, present abode, state of health, appearance.

You provide him with a personality. Is he gregarious? Ambitious? Kind? Generous? A bit tight with money? Sadistic? Does he have a sense of humor? Is he unable to bear criticism? Is he outspoken? Shy? And so on.

You figure out his relationship to all of the other major characters —that is, how he regards each of them and why, and how and why each of them regards him.

After you have devoted two or three or more pages in a notebook to all of the above, you—or I, at least—add a paragraph called Details, which, in some ways, is the most important paragraph of all.

Why?

Because from this paragraph will come those facts about your fictional character which, because they seem to have nothing to do with the story you want to tell about him, will help give him that sought-for air of reality.

When a person in real life is confronted by an absorbing, even a vital, problem, he does not come to it in a vacuum. If a man has had a lifelong aversion to turnips, the fact that he is involved in a murder does not mean that he now views turnips with a neutral eye.

Nor do the man and his problem exist in a vacuum. The rent must still be paid, clothes washed, meals eaten, business conducted, love made, quarrels quarreled, the boys taken to Cub Scouts, the flowers watered, the dog walked.

But what in the world can an aversion to turnips or a soft spot in his heart for the den mother have to do with how a man faces a murder charge or flees from danger? Maybe nothing. But these small details, along with others you devise—(1) he invariably keeps library books until they're overdue; (2) as an ardent stamp collector, he was incensed when the government threatened to make a stamp mistake worthless by flooding the market with that mistake; (3) when his dog died he stood in the backyard with the dog in his arms, sobbing and unable to bury him; (4) he loves practical jokes; and so on—these small details begin to give you the picture of a man with the kind of real concerns, petty or otherwise, which mark real-life people.

An oft-heard statement proclaims that your characters write your story, and they do, more or less. Certainly your characters define and limit your story. What kind of story you tell, what direction it takes, what its outcome will be depends upon the kind of people you have created and the capabilities or lack of capabilities with which you have endowed them.

But aside from that, your characters can create incidents which may make the plot forge ahead or, if not that, provide a richness of detail which makes your story stronger because it's more believable. And where do those incidents, that richness, come from? From that paragraph of seemingly irrelevant details you have devised for your main character. And not just for him, of course, but for all of the characters in your novel.

It is important to understand the difference between detail and wordiness. Detail helps to create reality in characters, locale, atmosphere, action. Wordiness helps to create boredom.

Wordiness can mean repeating something too often. It can also mean taking too long to say something in the first place.

Which brings us to verbs.

When I was in school, I was told somewhere along the line, and often enough to make an impression, that a too liberal, nondiscriminating use of adjectives was a prime cause of wordiness. This can be true. But I think writers more often overuse adverbs.

Written in my notebook is a sentence I picked up from somewhere, and if I remembered where, I would give the person credit. The sentence: "Remember the power of verbs to be at once descriptive and active."

It is a good thing to remember, and a couple of simple examples will suffice to demonstrate that:

> He walked slowly down the street.
> He ambled down the street.
> He ran quickly up the stairs.
> He raced up the stairs.

One apt verb not only says what you want to say more economically than a modified verb, it says it with more power, more picture, more mood.

The right verb can do more than eliminate an unnecessary adverb. It can sometimes knock out an entire phrase of unnecessary words.

For instance, a woman at the theater is rejoining her escort in the middle of a filled row. You could say, "I made my way past the other people in the row, all of whom had to stand up to let me get by." You could better say, "I skinned past the other people in the row."

Verbs and people may seem a queer combination for an article on how to write a good story, whether suspense-mystery or otherwise, but to me they are two basic and not unrelated essentials. To give your novel reality, concentrate on creating real people, not paper characters. To give your writing about those people power, vividness, and economy, concentrate on verbs.

43

WRITING THE GOTHIC NOVEL

By Phyllis A. Whitney

EVER since the name "Gothic" came to be used for a certain type of story, people have been asking, "What *is* a Gothic?" During their period of runaway popularity in the softcover field, the questions were often raised, "Who reads them, and why?" Since the genre continues to sell steadily, writers want to know what makes a good novel of this kind.

First, why the label, "Gothic"? I would like to make a switch in terms. "Gothic," for all its usefulness as a catchy term, is too limiting, with its gloomy-old-house atmosphere. Already the boundaries are being pushed out from the "true" Gothic. The writer need not feel restricted. I prefer a label which gives me more room in which to perform. I have always called my own books "romantic novels of suspense," and I ask that this descriptive phrase be used on the jackets by way of identification for the reader. The Gothic can easily be included in this larger category. The same readers like the broader horizon just as well, and the basic ingredients are similar.

The word Gothic has always carried darkly romantic medieval connotations, but it was an editor of paperbacks who first used the term in our time as a marketing label. Considering the long reprint life of Daphne du Maurier's *Rebecca,* he wondered if there were books of a similar type which had been published in hardcover and could be reprinted in a softcover series. He came upon my own hardcover *Thunder Heights* and decided to start his softcover venture with that title. The name he gave the series derived from the gloomy, arched and towered architecture so often described in these stories. The name caught on with the success of the series and has now come to stand for the romantic novel stamped by a brooding sense of mystery and terror.

Of course, stories of this type have been with us for a long time.

Even before the Victorian years the true Gothic novel was originated with romantic hair-raisers like the melodramatic *Castle of Otranto* (1764) by Horace Walpole, Mrs. Radcliffe's *Mysteries of Udolpho* (1794), and others. The Brontë sisters added psychological problems, depth of characterization, and greater credibility for the eerie doings. Since then, a great many writers, mainly women, have written romantic mystery novels in this tradition. They seem to be read by women of all ages, from teens to grandmothers—by schoolgirls, housewives and businesswomen. Men, too, read the more adventurous books of this type, such as those written by Mary Stewart. But it took the "Gothic" label and the selling excitement that followed in the softcover field to put them on the market as a distinct genre.

As to the *why* of the Gothic's popularity, one can only speculate. The women readers of these books appear to like stories with strong human problems and an avoidance of the police procedure that marks the more orthodox murder mystery. They find psychological action more interesting than the physical action of books aimed primarily at a masculine reader, though of course there must be a mixture of both. They enjoy the woman's viewpoint, and they like heroines who solve their problems. The anti-heroine who is destroyed by her problems has no place here! Women enjoy the sort of suspense that keeps them eagerly turning pages, and they want a love story as well. There is about these stories—and now I'm speaking as a reader —a certain wonderment. One steps into what Monica Dickens has called "a dear familiar landscape," in which anything at all may happen, romantically speaking. There is an entrancing promise, sure to be fulfilled by the skilled writer.

Gothic novels are not, as a rule, serious novels. They are entertainment—which does not bar you in the least from putting the best writing possible into them, or from bringing to them your own feelings and understanding about human beings and life. You must realize, however, that there is a performance involved. You are a magician standing on a stage. If your illusions are skillful, so that you both hold and fool your audience, you succeed. If you fumble and are caught, you fail. This skill takes a good deal of effort and practice to learn, but it is a lot of fun along the way. It takes a very real understanding and mastery of technique. In the course of writing some thirteen books in this field, I have had to learn something of my craft. There are definite ingredients involved in this type of story, and I would like to share what I have learned about these ingredients—learned both as a reader and a writer. Let's consider them:

BACKGROUND

There must be color and romance in the story setting. In the traditional Gothic this usually means a spooky old mansion set in a brooding landscape, whether up the Hudson River, on the coast of Cornwall, or wherever. Yet I have used the sunny island of Rhodes, with my characters living in a hotel, and the background still had romantic suspense. Background is basically used to create atmosphere and the writer can concoct this out of all sorts of things. The very period of the story can provide atmosphere. Victorian times lend themselves nicely to mood, and of course credibility is more easily achieved if the events take place in a distant time. But be careful not to sound exactly like a Victorian writer if you use that period. A blending with the modern is necessary, with an avoidance of strictly modern terms.

If you use the modern scene, you'd better remove your characters to some isolated spot where you won't have as much trouble with believability. Such isolation can even be achieved in an old brownstone in today's New York, if you can shut out the outside world to a sufficient extent. These books seldom concern themselves with the wider problems of the world. There are plenty of problems, but they are of a personal variety.

When I use a foreign background, I always make the story modern. I can do my research of the modern scene more easily than I can probe back into foreign history. It would be much too difficult to find out everything I would need to know about life in, say, Istanbul a hundred years ago.

ROMANCE, EMOTION

No feeling, no story—and that's a rule! Of course there must be a strong love story, though the ingredient of emotion may come in on several levels. In my *Window on the Square*, emotion arises from the presence in the story of a small boy who is supposed to have murdered his father. The heroine champions him against his mother and stepfather—while falling in love with the latter. This makes for complications, conflict and tension. A big, dramatic, hard-to-solve problem will contain plenty of emotion in itself, and has never hurt any kind of story.

There must be obstacles to true love, naturally, and the obstacles must be real and hard to surmount. The more difficult the corner you paint your characters into, the more interesting the story. And if you find a way out the reader never expects, you have successfully passed one of the principal tests.

One footnote on the matter of this obstacle: I have sometimes used an obnoxious wife or husband of the hero or heroine—who must, therefore, be disposed of by the end of the story. This is not supposed to be cricket, for some reason, though it provides a strong story situation. Of course the reader will realize—if he thinks about it—that if hero and heroine are to get together, the obstruction must go. But for someone caught up in the spell which a magician has cast, this doesn't seem to matter. You know that card didn't really vanish —but you believe it at the time. All sorts of variations can be played. In *Columbella* the wife dies two-thirds of the way through the book, but her evil influence continues after her death, so that the obstacle remains. The only rule is that the removal of the obstacle—whatever it is—must be credible; even better if in retrospect it seems inevitable.

SEX

Although there are never explicit details about sex in these books, and your hero and heroine may indulge (onstage) in no more than a warm embrace, don't think sex isn't there. Charlotte and Emily Brontë both knew about sex. It smolders in *Wuthering Heights,* and it is present in *Jane Eyre* as well. If you'll go back and look, you'll find that Jane possessed a strongly passionate nature, for all that she has been a much maligned heroine.

This is a tricky thing to handle. It is a good deal more difficult than to detail the act of lovemaking clinically. Yet it's worth the effort. A scene that is underplayed, suggested, rather than stated, can often have greater emotional effect because of the way the reader's imagination will work for you.

So physical and emotional attraction between hero and heroine

must certainly be present, even when they are fighting each other.
Perhaps especially then. In the true love scenes, there is always an
underlying tenderness that, for a woman, can be an exciting factor in
sex—James Bond to the contrary.

Sometimes men writers who are quite aware of this factor have
gone to the extreme of handling the love story element in too delicate
and supposedly ladylike a fashion. Catherine and Heathcliff would
turn in their graves! Look to the masters for the genuine physical
feeling that should be present, even though its consummation is postponed (as a rule) until after the last chapter.

DAMSEL-IN-DISTRESS

Although a damsel-in-distress is necessary, you can get into trouble here. We want a heroine with real spirit. She should be intelligent, too (as all Mary Stewart's heroines are). She may or may not
be pretty, and quite often she regards herself as plain. A wholly self-
confident beauty can lose the reader's sympathy fast. A beautiful
heroine will serve your purpose only if she is engaging enough to
overcome this dire handicap. The best of these heroines have a
touching vulnerability about them. They are brave, and sometimes
reckless, they meet adversity with courage, but they are fearfully
open to hurt, and the reader must feel this, believe in it. Perhaps this
is why the put-upon little governess in all her variations has done so
well. Max de Winter's young wife was vulnerable in *Rebecca*. So was
Mary Stewart's charming heroine in *Nine Coaches Waiting*. Victoria
Holt is a master at evoking this sort of openness to hurt. Our heroine
must be vulnerable because of her love, because of her involvement
with other characters, and because her initial position is one of help-
less unimportance. All this she overcomes in the end. She is in trouble, but it must not be trouble brought on because she is a total idiot.

Above all, make sure that your heroine is faced with a problem—
probably continuing problems—which she can *do* something about.
The problem must be largely hers, and she must not just sit and look
at it without taking any action until the end of the story. In every
chapter she must *act*, whether in a large or small way. Or she must be
planning action, so that the reader will know she isn't sitting still.
Just worrying is never enough.

A strong hero

Here we play all the variations possible, since this is the character most likely to be typed. In fact, I've never found a sure way to avoid this kind of typing entirely. Your hero is descended from some pretty distinguished ancestors, and the mark of his heritage is likely to show: Heathcliff, Mr. Rochester, Max de Winter—all driven, bedeviled, stern, dark men (dark in the sense of the dark brooding quality usually associated with this sort of man). He is generally older than your heroine by a number of years and has experienced a good deal of living. He is the sort of hero who seems to fascinate women readers, and of course he has a real need which the *right* woman can fill—and what satisfaction for any woman to find herself needed by such a man!

I've tried to get away from the type by giving all these qualities to the villain, and making my hero blond and cheerful, as well as strong, with the result that the villain became the more interesting character. Sometimes, of course, the hero may even appear to be the villain for a good part of the way through the story—which leads to even more desperation on the distraught heroine's part. Mary Stewart did this with as thrilling a chase scene as I've ever read in *Nine Coaches Waiting,* and Du Maurier frightened us badly about Max de Winter toward the end of *Rebecca.*

Play your own interesting variations, if possible, but don't wander too far afield. After all, this is the type of hero who will give you (and the reader) the best run for the money. His admiration and love are both worth the winning, but not to be easily won. He will never readily succumb to feminine wiles, and he will remain strong and perverse to the end—always the master.

Don't let your hero remain offstage for too long at a time. If he can't be actively present, we must at least think about him, and deal with him through the heroine's developing problems. An offstage hero who pops in at the beginning and then at the end of the story will do you no good at all. He must participate actively at the very center of your plot. He can't stand around on the outskirts trying to help without being himself caught up in the central involvement. He must *do* something. He may or may not come to the heroine's rescue at the end. It's rather nice if he does, but not absolutely essential, provided there is a wind-up to a romantic clinch at the end.

Your other characters should be "interesting," but don't make them all eccentrics or your story will lose believability. Some of your actors will be mainly good, others mainly evil, but all should be in-esting. What makes them the sort of people they are is important. When I am planning a story, I spend more time writing up dossiers about each character than I do on all the other preparation. You can't develop an interesting character in depth quickly and easily. You must give him time to grow. In this growth, you will discover useful events in his past—even back into his childhood—and you will know what his secrets are. You will work out the relationship between each character and every other character in the story, and know exactly how each thinks and feels about all the others. If you don't do your homework here, you'll come up with the shallow, the superficial, and your motivation may be too thin to carry real story interest.

Don't forget the importance of characterizing some of the people who are dead before your story starts. Rebecca was dead long before Max brought his nameless (what a trick for a writer to play!) young wife to Manderley, yet she is one of the strongest, most important characters in the book. So if you have a character who is no longer alive, but whose actions have set into motion all the trouble that is happening in the present, be sure you spend time getting to know that character as well as you know those who are performing on-stage.

A child can be enormously useful. So can an animal, if well charac-terized and important to the plot. Don't overlook either, but don't let either one take the story away from your main character. Both are notorious scene-stealers.

Suspense, mystery

Gothic novels are not simple romances. The mystery element, the building of suspense, is all important. How well this element is han-dled is the test of a good Gothic novel.

From the first, there must be a sense of urgency, of growing threat, of fear that mounts to terror. And there must be something *real* for the heroine to fear. This element can't be faked, or be "all a mistake." The sense of sustained terror that comes in certain scenes and builds to a climax at the end will make or break your story.

This sense of urgency must not come from outside forces alone. It should grow from the heroine's interrelationship with other characters. Equally important is the genuine feeling of evil, existing in some unknown form. In all good mystery stories, there must be the vital clash of good and evil. Before the end of the story, your heroine should feel thoroughly trapped, so that escape from her predicament, a solution to her problems, seems impossible both to her and to the reader. Out of such trappings will grow high suspense.

There must be mystery *right now*. From scene to scene, you make the reader ask questions, but you don't answer the last question until the final scene. Urgency—always urgency! Time is running out, the plight is desperate, all is about to be lost. In the beginning, curiosity will carry you for a while, but soon it must be the real character conflict that builds story interest.

Beware of the problem that gets stuck in one groove. Things that go bump in the night, and continue to do so with monotonous regularity, lead only to boredom. The problem must shift, grow, develop, or we lose interest.

There may or may not be a murder. I usually avoid an onstage murder because that brings in the police, and I don't want them cluttering my scene. I am not writing a detective story. If the reader can't add up the clues for himself, I'm not going to waste pages "deducting." I am playing a different sort of game. So, the death, if there is one, is often thought to be accident or suicide, and the police get out of the picture as fast as possible. Only the heroine, or some other character, begins to see past the easy answer to what may really have happened. Or it is possible that a real murder took place before the story started, and the murderer may be lingering around uncaught. Or evidence may come up to reopen an unsolved crime— reopen it by one of the story characters, if not by the police.

But there is danger in that past murder. One of my favorite ways of bogging myself down in a story is to have the past action so exciting and so interesting that it begins to take over, with very little present action resulting. A fatal disease for a story to develop is "past-itis." Your story is *now;* whatever effect past events may have, things must happen in the present.

Use your background, weather, season; use moonlight or glaring sunlight unhesitatingly to build suspense. Sometimes the gloomy atmosphere of a storm goes along with what is happening; sometimes it is equally effective if you use contrast.

When I was in the Virgin Islands doing research for *Columbella,* we had a hurricane scare. Of course I made notes all through it, and then used a near-hurricane in the climax of the story. In reviewing the book, one critic said I should never have used the device of a storm to help along the climax. Why not? I will use anything that enhances the feeling of terror, of mounting suspense, that seems to fit in properly with my scene. Don't cheat your reader of the drama he craves because you are afraid of being called corny.

Make surprises your stock in trade. Don't let a chapter, or even a scene, go by in which the unexpected doesn't happen. Once a reader knows exactly where you are taking him, he doesn't need to finish the book. Because you know your characters so well, you will know that they can take unexpected turns which the reader will never guess are coming.

Things, objects, will prove useful to you in this respect: a mirror that gives your heroine an eerie sense of the past, a seashell used in a strange way, an animal killed in a way that strikes terror into the heroine. Physical objects can often be used as symbols as well. The Columbella shell was a symbol for the evil Catherine. Almost everything has been done, of course, by other writers, which is all the more reason for you to try for unexpected variations to make your way different.

SOURCE OF EVIL

Of course there must be a villain, either male or female. There must be someone to provide the source of evil that sets everything in motion. Hiding the identity of this person is one of your main illusionary effects as a magician. As you trick and fool, while playing as fair as you dare, so will the reader be pleased. This is not a game which your opponent wants to win. All sorts of methods can be worked out for the role of the villain. Sometimes he's not a real villain, having caused trouble inadvertently or mistakenly. Sometimes his face is revealed ahead of time and the suspense lies in how the heroine is to escape the trap in which she is caught. I reveal the identity of the villain long before the end in *Seven Tears for Apollo,* but the suspense continues.

MEANING

Call it what you like—theme, moral, significance—it must be there. Not preached, but underlying. I've heard this element dismissed as being of no importance because readers of these books want only to be entertained. Of course no reader will tell you that he picks up such a book for anything but entertainment. But you, as a craftsman, had better understand why a reader is disappointed when the story doesn't add up to anything at the end.

All good fiction—being a reflection of the basic course of life—is an account of growth or deterioration. Because so much fiction these days deals with deterioration, a good many readers are turning in relief to the story which builds toward its main character's growth. If your heroine learns nothing at all in the course of the story, if she is the same at the end as she was in the beginning, the reader will have a sense of letdown, of disappointment.

A good story of this sort is about somebody who *grows.* Your heroine is human—she makes mistakes, she stumbles, she learns—and in the course of her maturing you cannot help but say something to the reader. Something worth saying about life, about living, about maturing. This is an element which leaves an intangible sense of satisfaction in the reader when the book is closed. Even your dark-browed, sardonic hero might be able to learn a few things by the end of the story. It wouldn't hurt him at all!

HAPPY ENDING

No other kind of ending will do. We read a story of suspense so that everything will stop hurting at the end. The final clinch should take care of that. But don't think you can tack on a whole chapter given to romance when the mysteries are all solved and the story is over.

There is always plenty of explaining to be done. The expert writer starts feeding in his explanations long before the end, holding out two or three items the reader really wants an answer to until the very end. Only then can the author hold his audience.

Make sure your heroine deserves her happy fate at the end. If she hasn't earned it, there will be no reader satisfaction.

A final word. I doubt that you can write Gothic novels unless you like reading them. You must be able to throw yourself genuinely into your performance as you write. While I am in the process of writing, I am submerged in my heroine and her problems—and having a wonderful time. Me and all those dark-browed heroes! I'm sure this is the first necessary ingredient, though I'm mentioning it last.

Not long ago at a meeting of the Authors' Guild, I heard a bookseller of many years' experience say something which is worth remembering. In a really good book, she said, "the juices must flow." But such juices cannot be produced synthetically. It is the writer's own feeling that must flow through his characters to bring his story to life and vitality.

44

THOSE MAGIC ONE-LINERS

By Eileen Jensen

You can pick up any magazine short story lying on your coffee table right now and give yourself an easy lesson in how to depict character. Leaf through the fiction. Read a little. Notice how quickly the people in the story spring to life, moving and acting in ways peculiar to them alone. Often they bloom in a single sentence.

Why?

Because a writer of magazine short stories must be a speedy fellow, darting between the recipes and deodorants, drawing his verbal pictures on the run.

Blurred images won't do. They must be sharp, exact, distinct—clear vignettes which register at once on the retina of the mind. I call these instant characterizations the one-liners. They're puzzlers—they're not easy—but you can learn to do it—and it's fun.

Try it.

Think of a character.

Walk all around him in your mind. Why is there a story in him? What makes this fellow unique and special, worthy of the reader's attention? What single fact can you think of which sets him apart as a recognizable and memorable person? Try to come up with the singular trait which reveals all. Do it in one sentence.

That's asking a lot, isn't it? But it can be done. And professional short story writers do it all the time.

Take my own story, "Androcles and the Librarian" (*Ladies' Home Journal*). I wanted to describe an elderly, unmarried woman —a spinster who lived by conventional moral standards but had an uninhibited mind. She read the Bible—but she read Faulkner, too. She was proper but she wasn't dull. I thought about her for a long time, and I finally hit on the one magic sentence which gave the reader the essence of this lonely old girl:

251

252 THE WRITER'S HANDBOOK

She had slept naked all her life and no one knew it.

In the same story I wanted to describe her rigid father who had prevented her from going into the life work she coveted. He was one of those old-fashioned autocrats who is sure he knows best. I said it in one sentence when I told you that:

Papa had put his foot down and said the Bohemian world of journalism, by God, was no place for the daughter of a decent man.

Notice that in both of these examples the characters are shown in *action*. Characters reveal themselves by acting and reacting. A whole page of purple prose describing a character will have less impact than one strong sentence showing him in a decisive action. The best action is that which reveals typical thoughts or traits which become important in the later resolution of the plot.

In "Who's Afraid of Love" (*Chatelaine*), I did a story about that hardy perennial among short story characters—a lonely career girl. I described her in one full-blown sentence:

It was Sunday evening and she had tidied up the apartment and gone to bed with her lapboard, a new novel, a glass of warm milk, a copy of *Women's Wear*, a fountain pen, and two unanswered letters—pretending to herself that she was resting.

Now, what do you know about this girl from that one sentence? Quite a bit! She's neat (tidied up the apartment), she stays abreast of current literature (a new novel), she's nervous and doesn't sleep well (warm milk), she's in the fashion business (reading *Women's Wear*, a trade paper), she has friends (two letters), she's busy (the letters are unanswered), and she isn't resting (she's pretending to herself that she's resting). I claim that's a blockbuster of a one-liner!

Let's go to the other extreme now. Suppose you wanted a man in your story to describe his love for his wife. You wanted to show that he had adored her for years, that he saw the sun, the moon, and the stars in this woman's glance, that she had made him happy throughout their long married life together, that she was everything to him. Can you do all that in six short words? Mark Twain did. He said of his wife:

Where she is, there is Eden.

You and I may never approach anything as sublime as that, but one must start somewhere. All moonshots begin on a launching pad. Let's orbit a simple one. An alcoholic, let's say. Call him Steve (since I don't know any alcoholics named Steve). This fellow drinks far too much. He's close to disintegration. How will you say it?

Steve had reached the hidden bottle stage.

I once read a story in *Good Housekeeping* Magazine written by Millie McWhirter, and I've forgotten everything about it except the skilled manner in which she described an early-rising mother-in-law through the eyes of her son's sleepyhead wife. The new daughter-in-law said that his mother was one of those women who

when dawn broke, believed in being there to pick up the pieces.

Good Housekeeping published my story, "Marry A Stranger." In that one I was writing about a henpecked son trying to break through an overly protective mother's dominance. He tells her:

"You've steam-rollered me all my life. . . . You don't weigh a hundred pounds, but it's all steel."

Do you know such a woman? I'll wager you do.

This same mother takes her son's bride (it was a secret marriage) out to lunch because the mother-in-law knows

you can tell a lot about a woman by the way she walks into a restaurant, unfolds her napkin, speaks to the waiter, notices—or ignores—the men going by.

Actually, you see, this sentence tells you quite a lot about the mother-in-law, not the girl. Writers are sneaky.

Redbook bought my story "Love Is Only A Beginning," in which I described a simple farm girl who after marriage found herself on the losing end of a triangle. I wanted to show the reader what a plain, wholesome, simple girl the heroine was. I let her tell it herself:

All I ever wanted to do was marry Jim Connors and have the children cleaned up and the chicken frying when he came home.

See how simple it is? To prove it even further, I have thought up some fresh one-liners to illustrate the point I've made. I did it by mentally ticking off a few people I know, and thinking of what one thing would describe them so you would understand a special facet of their personalities.

Take a rabid Republican of my acquaintance. This man is so opposed to the New Deal Democrats that to this day he won't carry a Roosevelt dime in his pocket.

I know a good-looking, young man-about-town, a professional model. He seems pleasant enough, but after a while you notice that his smile is on his lips but not in his eyes.

A harried young husband down the street fusses because his wife is so attached to her mother that even when the young couple spends a whole day with the folks—having Sunday dinner and a long evening—when he drives her home again, the moment she steps inside the house she goes to the telephone and rings her mother and says, "What's new?"

Newspaper columnists are good at one-liners, too. (They have even less space than short story writers.) In this morning's paper, I find Earl Wilson describing a wife who talks all the time:

Gabby? She's on the phone more than Shelley Berman.

I once spoke to a small creative writing class made up of members of the American Association of University Women. We discussed the magic of one-liners, and the group later turned in nine original characterizations done in the single-sentence form as an exercise in writing. One offering was in the adjectival style which is common to so many beginners:

The dignified, white-haired gentleman stood to his full, handsome height, to voice his authoritative opinion.

The writer of that sentence had a good character in mind—she saw him, she heard him—but she loaded him down with so much verbal gear that we can't get to know him. How much better if she had said something as simple as:

Uncle Joe was a quiet man, but when he spoke, everyone listened.

Or

When J.B. roars on the intercom, the whole staff turns up on the double in the board room.

Actually, you don't *see* the last two men as well—but you *know* them better.

Three very good sentences were turned in by the same group.

Mr. Benjamin doggedly swept up the last dead leaf, unaware of the autumnal glory still above him.

You know this man. He's a drone. You see him in action. You know what he is missing. But *he* doesn't.

Dr. Smith taught the class like a farmer ploughing a field, cutting through all obstacles to make a clean furrow.

You know this teacher. The writer also shows a sense of humor. And the simile lends interest.

With each quick click down the hall her thin spiked heels annnounced her determination not to let middle-age overtake her.

You hear this woman. You know how she walks, how she dresses, and how she thinks. There's a good strong verb—*announced*—and a definite state of mind: *determination*. This woman is more than a character. She's a whole plot.

That is the attractive bonus that carefully thought-out one-liners bring to the writer. The chances are better than good that when you have distilled your thinking to a point of clarity from which a character's true identity will emerge—you will have more than a sentence. You will have a story.

Try it. Start with a simple one. Embroider it with humor. Add a simile. Double it by bringing in a second character. It isn't easy, no—but you can do it anywhere—at the bus stop, in the shower, waiting at the cafeteria. Doodle a character. It's habit-forming. It might even pay.

45

BACKGROUND—THE MOST
IMPORTANT CHARACTER

By Elisabeth Ogilvie

NOVELISTS have always been intrigued and inspired by the power of environment to influence human lives. Since we're all readers, I don't have to list even a half dozen classic examples; you can name ten in as many minutes. And they all observe the rule for the background novel; whatever the situation may be, the cause, the working out, and the final effect are influenced by the milieu in which the characters experience their jealousy, hatred, love, adultery, greed, or sacrifice.

The word "background," in itself as flat as a backdrop on a stage, is a misnomer for the environment in which we live our lives. We are what we are because of it; if we are completely at home in it, we are shaped to it, but if we fight it, it becomes an impersonal yet hostile force that shapes us in another way. Or we have a love-hate relationship with it: we can't live with it and we can't live away from it, and that turns us into ambivalent creatures, never at home anywhere, always eaten with homesickness for we don't know what.

You have *your* background, which you know in every detail because you've been born to it, or else you've come to it with fresh and excited eyes, seeing things which the native doesn't even notice anymore. It can be a corrupt and fascinating old city in Europe, or a suburb full of status-seekers; or you may have a useful knowledge of steel mills, ranch empires, ocean liners, or research laboratories. Whatever and wherever the territory, as a writer you contemplate its citizens and its effect upon their personal lives. If there is an impressive physical setting to be described, so much the better. You are rich beyond the dreams of avarice, and you are going to spill these riches out on paper.

Now, where to begin, and how to get it all down on paper? You're not only spendthrift, you're like the enthusiastic new painter who wants to get every last twig of that enchanting scene onto canvas, not knowing that to leave out some of it is to strengthen the rest.

Or, you have people and their fundamental problems in human relations, and you want to use a rich and unique setting which you know well, but your problem isn't that of disciplining a mass of material, but of how to use it at all.

The rule in both cases is as essential and simple for you as it was for Emily Brontë, Thomas Hardy, and Mark Twain. In the novel of background, events must happen *because* of the background. Ask yourself this: Are these people acting the way they are because they live in a certain place, under certain conditions? Or could they be found anywhere? Could the whole action be picked up and set down somewhere else? If you say *yes* to these questions, you are not using your background correctly.

I write about fishing and lobstering people along the coast of Maine, more specifically about two islands. I live on one, which I used in my novels, *The Witch Door* and *There May Be Heaven.* The other is Bennett's Island which I used in my *Tide* trilogy, and in *The Dawning of the Day, The Seasons Hereafter,* and several juvenile novels. This island, twenty-five miles out in the Gulf of Maine, rugged and magnificent, turned me into a writer at the age of fifteen because I had to express my passionate emotions about it in some way. I still haven't finished exploring all the aspects of its disturbing influence on human beings.

Here is a world of stunning beauty and often of stunning brutality. Here are men making their living in an intensely physical way, on terms of truce with the elements. The women live accordingly. (Ask yourself, in what ways are the people in my setting different from other people? To what unique situations must they react in their daily lives?) The suburban woman whose husband is late getting home knows he has probably been caught in traffic on the freeway. The fisherman's wife, who may read the same magazines and whose children may be watching the same thing on TV as the children two hundred miles away in Newton, Massachusetts, knows that when *her* husband is overdue, his engine could be broken down and he may be drifting out there in the dusk, or he has lost his course in a surprise snow squall and piled his boat on a ledge. He may already be dead. She says nothing to the children, but lets out a long breath when she looks out at the harbor for the twentieth time and sees a moving light at his mooring.

In *The Seasons Hereafter,* as in the *Tide* books, I kept the strong rhythms of life beating like a counterpoint to a woman's private experience by the use of a few simple devices. To say that description and local color are combined with action may sound too simple:

She got frantically out of bed and saw Western Harbor Point and the breakwater washed bronze and rose with the sunrise. A boat was going out by the breakwater, and the man was putting on his oilclothes, now and then touching the wheel.

Vanessa is frantic with her own confusion, yet life goes on, there is a clear sunrise and the boats are going out. The harbor is the heart of the place, it dominates her. She keeps coming back to it:

The changeable harbor seemed curiously empty and lifeless this morning in spite of the skiffs at the moorings and the gulls picking through the fresh wet weed on the ledges. It was as if an invisible tide had gone out with the men and wouldn't return until they did.

In a quick sketch you get the look and feel of a fisherman's harbor when the boats are out.

They go out, they come in, no matter what happens to her. She has been waiting all day for her lover, "watching *White Lady* ride into the harbor on towering seas; Steve Bennett's *Philippa* rolled deep on one side, and Nils Sorensen came in behind, easing his boat when she slid downhill on the smoking green slopes. Charles rounded the breakwater after him, sinking out of sight in the trough. . . . When the family came in, it was an armada." This is the family whom she resents and tries to despise.

Walking to the store, what does Vanessa see that the farm or city woman doesn't see? "Seine dories newly painted buff and blue at the edge of the coarse grass, a graveyard of old hulls rotting beside a little pond." She smells a whiff of bait and wet lobster traps brought in to dry out. She recognizes the sound of trapnails being driven into a lath, oarlocks, an engine being tried out. And there are always the gulls that haunt the place like its familiar spirits. Vanessa is concentrating intensely on herself, yet you and she are forever conscious of messages from the outside.

"When she came into the house, Barry had been in and gone out again. His dinner box was on the table, and his rubber boots stood against the wall. He had cooked some lobsters and eaten a couple; the shells were in a sink." She takes two lobsters for herself, "breaking them open with quick professional twists of her hands and getting the meat out in big pink and white chunks."

The dinner box, the rubber boots, the fresh lobster bring Barry's work into the room; implicit are the long hours on the water in the rolling boat. The way Van handles the lobsters shows another of the small but significant differences that give validity to her and her background.

A child's accident can be of any kind, anywhere. Make the bad fall or burn something that could only have happened *here*. Don't miss any chance to strengthen the sense of apartness. A child in *Seasons* sees a starfish from a wharf, goes down over the ledges to get it, slips on wet rockweed, and falls in. Vanessa goes down a steep ladder to get him. Just as she casually handles lobsters live or dead, and can stuff salt herring into a baitbag, she is used to ladders at low tide. The suburban wife doesn't quiver at the thought of city traffic or the farmer's wife at helping a cow to calve.

In *The Seasons Hereafter,* the love affair begins and is carried on in secrecy only because it happens where it does. In the first confrontation, the man appears suddenly at Van's door looking for her husband to help him seine herring. In five minutes, simply because Owen Bennett heard herring "puddling" in the harbor, his and Vanessa's lives are changed, and they will never be the same again.

Because he is a lobsterman, it is perfectly legitimate for him to hire her to knit trapheads for him. This is a tiresome job many men don't want to do or have the time to do. It is a dying skill, and the person who can knit (actually *net*) can always be sure of work. When he brings her the twine and meshboards, the businesslike meeting is as intimate an encounter as exchanged glances over cocktails or dancing together at a party:

As he started to give her instructions for the heads, she said, "Wait a minute, I'd better write everything down." But she could find neither pencil nor paper, and she got very hot and her eyes stung. "Oh, damn it," she wailed softly, pawing without sense at magazines, and he called to her, "Never mind, I've got something in my pocket." . . . He was sitting at the table writing on the back of an envelope. She stood looking at the bulk of his shoulders and the back of his neck, at the way the wiry black hair grew down on it and at a small puckered scar, a white seam against the burnt-dark skin. She lit a cigarette after several futile attempts to scratch a match because her hand was unsteady.

They discuss technical details. Then, when he is about to leave, he tells her, apparently off-hand, that he'll be going around the shore in a dory looking for traps of his washed ashore:

"This morning I saw three down in Ship Cove."
"I'll bet your youngsters will enjoy going with you."
"I'm not taking them. They'll still be in school."
"Oh." The syllable floated between them, a leaf or a feather. . . .

As simply as this, the appointment is made; they can meet in a lonely cove because the island has so many such coves, and because he has a legitimate excuse to be out there at midday. She of course can take long walks without question. On an island with no automobiles, people still walk for recreation.

The nylon trapheads become a sexual symbol.

Soon they would be handled with careless expertise by those brown hands with the long thumbs which she could see so clearly as they wrote, gestured, lit a cigarette, and held out the meshboards.

The trapheads represent the way of life which has thrown these two together, and something more subtle. This is something his wife can't do. What other need can't she fill for him?

The familiar situation in which secret lovers are crowded in with other people and must hide their feelings can also contribute to authenticity. In this case, it's a severe gale when the men stay up all night to watch the boats. Van is upset at being in close quarters with Owen, her husband, and another couple. What makes it more agonizing is that Owen ignores her:

The scene around the table lacerated her nerves, yet she could not bear to go away from that oblivious black head. He could at least look in my direction once, it's his trapheads ruining my hands. . . . I wish all their damn boats would come ashore at once. Then you'd see some hopping and swearing. And I'd sit here and laugh. I'd laugh myself sick and never stop. She drove the needle hard through the loop and gave a vicious pull.

Just when she thinks she can stand no more, a boat is driven ashore, and the men fly out in a grand scramble of oilskins and rubber boots. She is saved by one of this salt-water world's particular disasters.

Another appointment is made, this time almost within earshot of his children, the girl knitting baitbags for pocket money, the boy gathering ballast rocks to help his father: a tiny design to help bring out the whole pattern of the fabric.

This date is for a weekend. The island makes such occasions for lovers, because there are twenty-five miles of water between it and the nearest dentist, doctor, lawyer, or income tax official. A couple of errands that could be done in one morning by a mainlander take up two or three days for the islander.

These lovers, each with a different errand (Van's is false), travel across the bay at the same time, speaking to each other only casually. On the mainland they meet again, they go away, and because they are what they are, they seek another island. The stolen time is spent in a place of great beauty, no sordid hideout, and they are bemused and betrayed into believing for the first time that they can have a life together. In this spot between sun and sea, where he could go on being the fisherman and the islander that he was born, everything seems possible.

At home, waiting for the time to make a move, she rows across the harbor to relieve tension, as a mainland woman might get in her car and go somewhere. She thinks, "Anyone could row all around Jessup's Island in a few hours. I would like a little dory like the one we went out there in." She sees herself watching for Owen's boat to come up the thoroughfare on that far coast; she sees herself painting buoys while he builds traps. She is always true to her background, even in her dreams.

And at the end, who is to say whether his wife holds Owen or Bennett's Island does? Vanessa doesn't know.

When you are planning your story, take into account the hazards, the rewards, the triumphs and terrors of the world you are trying to create. What in his professional life makes a rancher, a doctor, or a schoolteacher happy? What depresses him or, worse, terrifies him? The fire in *The Seasons Hereafter* doesn't ruin everyone, as it could have done with the right wind blowing, and the fire department twenty-five miles across the bay, but it is a catalyst for Vanessa and a disaster for squalid little Gina, whose struggles run parallel with Van's. The two of them are, each in her own way, victims of the most important character in the novel—the island.

The island has made its people what they are. It imposes a peculiar discipline on them, and they must obey if they are to survive and prosper. It exercises a Lorelei charm on men like Barry, stronger than his rage at Van's betrayal.

Here's a final sympathetic word if you're afraid of swamping hardboiled editors with masses of descriptive matter, but can't hold back. *Don't*. Put it all in that first draft; go madly poetical with description, or splash it on like thick paint. Don't refine as you go. Don't try to understate. Be free-swinging and uninhibited. But come back to it sternly a month later with a handful of sharp pencils, and *cut*. The essence will be there.

Without false emphasis but with a sure knowledge of your background and a meticulous attention to detail—from the games of children to the adults' tragedies, whether on a city block or a Maine island—you can make your reader *see, smell, hear,* and *feel* its presence below, above, and behind everything else.

46

THE HAND IS QUICKER
THAN THE "I"

By Wilma Shore

Q. *You wrote the stories in your book,* Women Should Be Allowed, *from a first-person viewpoint. Did you find that this posed any particular problems? What advantages did it offer? In general, do you think the first-person viewpoint is a good one for fiction?*

A. It's very hard to weigh advantages against problems; they're too closely interwoven. The advantages create the problems; in solving the problems other advantages are revealed.

I first used the first-person viewpoint when a story idea came to me in the bright, breezy words of the central character. There's the first advantage—the undiluted flavor of your character's idiom, the richness of regional speech, the fresh turns of phrase that your narrator can use although you, as author, cannot.

For example, in my story "Some Day I Have to Buy A Hat" (*Good Housekeeping*), I could not have described an overworked obstetrician the way his office nurse did:

It's brutal for the Doctor; I haven't seen him look so thumbed over since I been in this office. The poor guy doesn't have a chance to eat, sleep, or get a hair cut. Last week I had to give him a trim over the ears with the surgical scissors. Around twelve every day he runs downstairs to the drug store and takes a good look at somebody's egg salad sandwich and that has to do him till evening. Myself, I can make a nice meal off my cuticle.

Why the boom in maternity? The whole thing is on account of the war, of course. In the first place, what else can you really spend money on nowadays? . . . And lots of girls, their husbands are going away, and who knows when they'll see them again? You have to admit a baby's got it all over a camera portrait when it comes to souvenirs.

But, at the same time, there's your problem—you're stuck with that idiom, that flavor. A naïve character, for example, can't suddenly express a sophisticated insight. A very straight narrator can't make wisecracks.

In other words, *you* have to stay offstage. Still, this is really an advantage. A story told entirely through the medium of one character will have at least the unity of that character's personality.

Which brings us to another problem; as you must remain inside your narrator, you may not show him from the outside—you can't describe his appearance, manner, tone of voice. No "gently," "sadly," "belligerently"—your creature cannot gasp or murmur, whimper or purr.

How can this be an advantage? Because you have to think harder about the way people really speak—listen harder—work harder—so that we will know what we need to know simply from what he says.

It's exciting to see how much you can show by speech alone. For example, your narrator's age. If he is old he is likely to ramble and reminisce. The narrator in "May Your Days Be Merry and Bright," one of the stories in my book, *Women Should Be Allowed,* says:

> Most mothers, whatever the children do, it's not enough. They keep asking for more, the children keep making excuses. They know it's excuses, but they can't stop asking. Not me. Like I told this woman, some woman at the hotel, I didn't know her from Adam, I was only there two weeks, but she says, "Where's your daughter? Not here today?"
> You could have knocked me down. The woman didn't even know me. But I just said, "I told her, don't come. Or she would have. She's very attentive. I consider myself lucky." Which I did. Do. But it isn't luck, it's how I handle it. My mother, if we didn't come every day, pandemonium. We used to try and spread the burden. I made up my mind I would never be a burden.
> So then . . . But I'll tell you a funny thing, a month later I knew when anybody's daughter came. When they called on the phone, even. The news spreads.
> Well, anyhow, this Gleason . . .

A young narrator may exaggerate and romanticize, like Sheree Wallach, in "The Whole World Takes Off its Hat to Sheree Wallach" (another story in *Women Should Be Allowed*), who says:

> Sometimes the way I feel, if there wasn't a lock on the bathroom door I might as well die. I went back in and turned on the hot water to sound busy. When the sink got full I let it run out again. I felt overstuffed, like from too many waffles. Only it was from too much life. But you can stop *eating* waffles, whereas life just keeps coming at you, day after day.

A narrator's place of birth can be indicated, his education, his economic bracket. His state of mind will be expressed by the tempo and structure of his phrasing. Gloria MacAdoo, in "A Mammal in a Black Crepe Dress," describes her self-education like this:

> At first I figured on just reading my way through, like through a tunnel; then it began to seem more like a tree, with boughs off the trunk and branches off the boughs and twigs and et cetera. For instance, when I decided to find out something about the import-export business, in which I handled the switchboard, that brought me to the tariff. The tariff led me back to the War of 1812. And next thing I knew, there I was in the middle of Napoleon.

But at the climax of the story her style changes:

> And I ra₁ into the drugstore and into the phone booth and closed the door and got a dime out of my wallet and it went bong, bong, and my finger remembered Harry's number although it was six months since I dialed it and I thought, oh, God, let him be home, listen God, this is *Gloria,* Gloria in Excelsis Deo; and then he said, "Hello?" I mean, Harry Borderman.

And—here's another advantage—your story will come to the reader firsthand, with the immediacy of an actual account. As though he were hearing someone tell a story, your reader will draw his own conclusions. He will *earn* many insights that would otherwise be spelled out for him by the author.

The most interesting aspect of the first-person viewpoint arises from its greatest problem. The author has no editorial column, so to speak, in which to present his own beliefs and attitudes. Everything must be funneled through his narrator's consciousness, as Lardner did so brilliantly in "Haircut," giving us only the barber's words, showing us only what the barber considered significant, and yet leaving us with a judgment diametrically opposed to that of the barber. The barber has taken us on a guided tour, and yet we have seen something our guide did not even know was there and could not have imagined—Lardner's own point of view.

Between Lardner's attitudes and those of his narrator lies a thrilling area of irony. In "The Golden Honeymoon" his narrator is also his protagonist. It is his own story which he tells. We hear it, but we hear another story as well. The material has been selected and organized to function on two levels of reality at once.

To tell two distinct stories simultaneously is as fascinating for the author as a challenging puzzle; as intriguing for the reader as a magician's sleight of hand. But it is far more than a trick or an illusion; it is a means of expressing in literary terms the contradiction between subjective and objective—the world as seen by the narrator, the world as the author sees it.

How can this be done? As it happens in life. We often form independent judgments about the stories people tell us. We often sense things they are trying to conceal. Haven't you ever read an interview of a celebrity or a politician, or the transcript of a trial, and thought suddenly, "He's lying!"?

What made you think so? Perhaps the speaker's choice of words— a euphemism where a straightforward phrase would have been natural. Or perhaps the *way* he spoke—an overly abrupt answer, an evasiveness, a glibness that sounded rehearsed. Or did you catch an actual contradiction of something previously said?

These are a few of the clues that make us suspect the existence of a truth which the speaker is hiding from us, or even from himself. We respond, often without being aware of it, to a slip of the tongue, a hesitation, an inconsistency of style. When a speaker seems to jump haphazardly from one idea to another, our minds often supply the elided sections, and we can guess the unspoken train of thought. Sometimes we note a surprising burden of feeling in a supposedly casual phrase. Sometimes we note the repetition of a trivial comment, and question its apparent unimportance.

For example, in "May Your Days Be Merry and Bright," the narrator says:

The day Gleason left I was walking down Broadway. It was a terrible day, that kind of damp cold that goes right through to your bones. I'll tell you the truth, the only reason I was out in such weather was on account of Gleason. I just didn't feel like being in the lobby for the launching party. And anyhow that was the day Janet called to say she had to change the plans.

She is convincing herself that the only thing she is disturbed by is the weather, but we will mistrust that afterthought—*and anyhow*— and recognize that she has been very badly shaken by her daughter Janet's rejection at Christmas.

Sure, I was disappointed. Anyone would be . . . she continues, and for a whole paragraph pretends to herself that she understands why it had to happen that way, and is bearing the disappointment easily. Then she says:

> Anyhow, there I am on Broadway, and when I got down around Eighty-second I passed this florist's window. White poinsettias. Beautiful! And I thought, Janet would love it, I can get it now and take it up Christmas morning. So then I remembered I wasn't going Christmas morning.
> Well, anyhow, after a minute I look up, and who do I see . . .

She does not realize that she has momentarily forgotten the change of plan because it is too painful to remember. But we do.

Does this sound as though we were all amateur psychoanalysts? Perhaps we are. Analytic theory and practice, which has influenced our daily lives, has also affected our response as readers. The average reader today is more sensitive to submerged conflict, more accustomed to looking below the surface.

The first-person story is marvelously suited to the exploration of the reality which is hidden, ignored, disavowed. This is, to my mind, its greatest advantage, its greatest interest.

But what if your character is, to put it bluntly, a bore? Then you must determine what makes him interesting to *you,* and present him so that his very tiresomeness becomes a revealing character trait.

How? That's *your* problem.

47

THE RHYTHM OF A STORY

By Mary Augusta Rodgers

THE quality of rhythm in fiction writing is as difficult to discuss as the quality of charm in people. In the first place, both elements are nearly invisible when used most successfully; they are employed to enhance the complete product, not to draw attention to themselves. Secondly, their success is often a subject for argument. (What is charming to me may be irritating to you, and one man's beat is another's *bête noir*.) They turn foggy under examination, and they resist definition. Any discussion is likely to be vague, contradictory, and frequently interrupted by cries of "No! No!," or, "What do you mean by *that?*" from the gallery.

So we are already off to a bad start, and it will do no harm to get off the subject slightly. Consider the common experience of hearing two people tell the same story. One tells the story and his audience rocks with laughter. The same story is repeated by someone else, at another time, and the result is a sullen silence. What makes the difference? A sense of rhythm, usually.

Speech has its own rhythms, in some ways very different from the written word. What strikes our ears as an unusual accent is often as much a matter of different cadence as it is pronunciation. A line which is unobjectionable—perhaps even effective—on paper may turn out to be impossible when read aloud. On the other hand, a verbal punch line of great impact may dissolve into a blob of nothing on the printed page. The conversational style of writing is effective only when it is *not* an authentic reproduction of informal speech, but an artful mimicry serving the writer's own purposes. In all this, it is the rhythmic differences between the spoken and written word that are involved. Each writer must decide for himself what these differences are, remembering that the points of similarity are important, too.

A writer can learn a lot from watching a good storyteller in action. Storytellers think about the rhythm each story requires, whether they realize it or not. When shock or surprise is the crucial factor, they will tend to keep the story short; in a situation story, they will stretch things out, piling on detail, speeding up here, slowing down there, picking up the pace in part from the mood of their audience. They shrug, laugh, look solemn, make gestures, imitate other voices.

A writer can translate some of these effects, and the questions of *which* to use and *how* are worth thinking about. How would you write a shrug? Well, sometimes space will do it—a new paragraph, a one-line sentence, a pause indicated by a line of dots. And what about the audience's contribution? A writer does have to imagine an enthusiastic response (never difficult), but he is not without his own mute but faithful audience—himself. As writer, he proposes a story idea; as audience, he enters a prompt objection: "I've heard *that* before!" We all know how this works. We know in what limited but important sense we are our own best readers. And it is this reader who can help the most in establishing the tempo of a story.

There is no point in considering the tempo of a story before the story exists. The time to decide this is *after* the story has been blocked out in the first draft and the rough proportions are clear. One trick is trying to imagine how the story would sound if read aloud. Would it sound best read in a dramatic voice, full of theatrical pauses, or in a conversational murmur? In a narrator's even, detached tone, or a conspiratorial whisper? Given the basic beat of the story, is the danger likely to lie in its moving too slowly or too fast? When the story is considered in this way, the rhythm of the writing will inevitably be affected.

A sense of proportion is a vital part of the rhythmic sense. The length of a story will obviously have something to say about its pace. In essence, a *short-short* is one quick, illuminated scene, as clear and confined as a photograph: something that can be remembered like the candid pictures of Cartier-Bresson, which are so full of what used to be called "human interest." (A good exercise to develop your plot-making muscles might be devised from taking a collection of such photographs and seeing how many of them can be matched with simple, but promising, story ideas.)

A *short story* of regulation length—whatever that is—is usually described by a wave-like line. The story starts, develops, reaches a crest (crisis) and then gradually sinks into the shore (resolution, or end).

A *novelette* is long enough to have a series of crises, or points of intensity, but it is also short enough so that the ending must be reflected from the first page on. I don't know how to describe this except, perhaps, as an ominous electrocardiogram. It makes a difference, too, whether the writer thinks of the novelette as a longer short story, or a shorter novel.

Somerset Maugham once wrote that when he was working on *Of Human Bondage,* he pictured it as an immensely long telegram, in which everything was omitted but the essential message. It is doubtful that any reader ever thought of the book in exactly those terms, but the effect is still there. It seems to help many writers if they have some idea of a basic structure in mind. They can compare themselves to the sculptor preparing to carve an elephant from a huge block of marble. (Such a simple job, the sculptor said cheerfully; all he had to do was to chip away everything that wasn't elephant!)

Inexperienced writers often make mistakes that can be seen as a matter of physical proportion on paper. They will spend eight pages setting the stage for a particular scene, for example, and then give a scant two pages to the actual action. Here is the room—great detail on the wallpaper, rug, lighting, choice of magazines, pictures, weather as seen from the window, etc. Now here comes the action—bang-bang, the character falls dead, leaves home, declares his love, or whatever. (There are reasons to do a scene that way, occasionally. But, in most cases, the reason is a bad one—because it's easier to set the stage than to get on with the story—and the result is terrible.)

Detail can be used to slow a story down; its elimination can speed things up; but the choice is not that simple. The greatest bores in the world are those unfortunates to whom every detail is equally significant and interesting. Someone of this breed, writing about a trip to California, will relentlessly include every day's mileage and menus, gas station, service stops, and the full name of the cousin in Osage. In cutting detail, however, the writer must be careful not to cut too

close to the bone; the story could die during the surgery. Detail—
significant detail—makes the difference between a story and a synopsis. It's so simple, really. Just keep chipping away at everything
that isn't elephant.

There are times when actors in rehearsal complain about another
actor "stepping on a good line," and it's easy to understand what
they mean. This mistake can translate itself into writing, where it's
harder to see. With reason, writers are afraid of being dull, of boring
their readers by too slow a pace, and so they are inclined to go too
fast—to step on their own best lines, and rush their most important
scenes. Those with a good rhythmic sense usually avoid doing this.
There is a natural ebb and flow, a swing back and forth—*something*
—which will not allow a good prose style to move too fast or become
too crowded. The moment the writing feels jerky to the writer, something is wrong.

There is also such a thing as being too careful. This is one of the
hazards in too much revision. All the mistakes are corrected; every
line is gone over and polished up and brushed off; and, in the process, the natural rhythm of the story has been lost. So the writer is left
with a splendid story, full of intricate workings and technical improvements, and the only trouble with it is that it won't stand up.

Writing meant to be funny falls apart completely when the writer
rushes his effects. There is nothing more disastrous than a writer
harboring the notion that "if one joke is good, ten will be that much
better." Any kind of comic writing depends heavily on subtle rhythmic effects which give the reader an impression of spontaneity and
ease. Trying too hard—a sense of strain—is deadly. Unfortunately,
some writers seem to feel that humorous writing is like bonus bingo,
and that some sort of pay-off for the reader—in the shape of a funny-
sounding word, a pun, a joke, an outlandish simile, or a wisecrack—
must be embedded in every sentence. The result is not funny, but
hysterical.

In thinking about the rhythm of a story, there are many factors to
consider and then forget. (None of us would write a line if we developed the habit of weighing every word.) Punctuation is obviously
important; so are the length of paragraphs and sentence structure.
Even the look of a typed page can suggest something. I remember an

editor saying, "Shorten those paragraphs! Shorten those sentences! Set some *space* in those pages!" There is the use of time, verb tenses, the flashback technique. (Nobody ever handled the flashback with more skill than John Marquand. His technique is worth some study.) There is something involving a skipping ahead in time, which might be called a flash-forward. There is repetition, omission. The most useful list is the one each writer makes for himself.

For anyone wanting to sharpen his own feeling for rhythm, the benefits in reading poetry are plain. Those who say they dislike poetry simply haven't read enough; there are as many choices in poetry as there are in prose.

Writers learn best from other writers, of all kinds. A woman who writes cookbooks claims that she picked up a good idea, which led to a new way of presenting recipes, from the wild paragraphing of an article in a far-out literary journal. One never knows from what source some seeds may blow. The earlier works of James Joyce and Gertrude Stein are fascinating to anyone interested in rhythmic effects in prose. So are the prose poems in John Dos Passos' trilogy of novels, *U.S.A.*, and the novels of Charles Dickens. It is instructive to remember that Dickens was enormously successful on the lecture circuit, reading dramatic chapters aloud. He had a marked tendency to break into iambic pentameter when writing sad scenes, like the death of Little Nell in *The Old Curiosity Shop*—such a scene is particularly interesting when compared with scenes of revolutionary violence in *A Tale of Two Cities,* where the rhythm of the writing suggests the fierce frenzy of a mob.

There are the famous staccato, machine-gun bursts in much of Ernest Hemingway's writing . . . the swamp murmurs of Faulkner . . . the nervous, urban style of Norman Mailer, something like the symphony of a traffic jam . . . the marching-band style of much of Kipling . . . the subdued, intricate harmonies of Henry James . . . the torrent of Thomas Wolfe's novels. (This is the *You Can't Go Home Again* Thomas Wolfe, not the current Tom Wolfe who does those Zam! Pow! Zowie! articles on stock-car racing and Baby Jane Holtzer and other "thoughty" subjects. Speaking of this current Tom Wolfe, how *does* he manage to work so many sound effects into the printed page?)

The famous names suggested by this subject are many. In the end, your favorite writers will make the best teachers. Read them with close attention.

And one final note on developing a sense of rhythm: Know when to stop. So . . .

48

YOUR PLOT IS CONTRIVED

By Charlotte Armstrong

"The plot is contrived," says your reviewer. You, who always pay attention to criticism, of course, in order to learn, may confidently conclude that he finds something wrong with your story. But you should realize that he isn't saying what he means.

I could argue that all fiction is, and must be, contrived. When the story writer sits to his desk, opens his notes and begins to ponder, I'd like to ask what in the world *else* he is doing! Even the reporter, the historian, the biographer must select, omit, and arrange. It is his art to do this to some facts. The story writer must do all of this and, furthermore, do it to facts he was never given. To invent the "facts" and arrange them, at the same time, is his *art*.

Or, to get away from that word with its hovering capital A (since I am about to discuss the suspense story), let's call it his craft. Which *is* to contrive. And what your critic meant to say, you see, was that you didn't contrive very well.

Of all kinds of fiction, perhaps suspense fiction must have the most plot, plenty of happenings, confrontations, actions and reactions. It cannot be a mood piece that moons along, being ever so sensitive and all that, but almost exclusively the dialogue of one brooding mind with itself. It had better not be written in a style so obscure that the reader has to guess what happens, either. The suspense story must *be* a tale and it must be *told*.

This being so, the first thing the writer of these yarns does is to settle his wits to the cooking up of his plot. How is this done?

The germ of a suspense story may come to you in several ways. You may have taken notice of a certain kind of person, of an interesting complexity, and you would like to "create" him on paper. Or you may find yourself excited by a theme. There is a point you'd like to make, if you can only figure out how to embody it in fiction. Or you may be intrigued by a certain setting.

But most often, the event comes first (or soon, in any case). You must say to yourself, "O.K., now what happens?" And immediately you must add, "to whom?" Even when the germ has come to you in the first place in the guise of an event, you must at once consider the kind of person to whom you will make it happen, because upon his character depends his reaction, and upon that reaction depends what happens next.

Here is a crude example. Suppose a car breaks down at night on a lonely road. What will the occupants do? It depends on who they are, surely. If they are a couple of elderly widows, ignorant of machinery and afraid of the dark, that's one thing. If they are a frolicsome pair of courting young people, that's another.

When the event is an act by a person, first he must be the kind of person who *would* act so, and then the consequence of what he does will depend upon the characters to whom, or before whom, he does it.

So the whole problem of contriving well lies in the matching of events with characters.

It seems to me that the very definition of character is what a given individual will or will not do. Some people wouldn't tell a lie. Some people *will* snoop at your mail. Some people wouldn't think of such a thing!

Why will or won't a person do what? Well, he has his share of the culture, his training, his degree of sophistication, his ignorance or knowledge, his status, values, prejudices, maybe even principles. He also has a state of health, physical or mental, peculiar to him, and his private relationships with, and attitudes toward, all the other characters.

I don't know whether it is better to say that he is what he does, or that he does what he is. But you, his creator, had better be sure what this character *would* naturally do, according to the lights you've given him. Or vice versa.

I say vice versa because, during the part of the work that is the contriving (the composition of the text comes much later) you should hold both characters and events in a fluid suspension, until you succeed in adjusting them to each other.

For instance, you may, and often do, come to a place in your tentative chain of happenings and discover one of your characters simply digging in his heels and refusing to do what you wanted him to do. You have your reasons for pushing him around, but he'll have none of it. He just wouldn't *do* that! He's not that kind of person. It's absurd to pretend that he *ever* would, and worse, impossible to make anybody believe it. Why, you can't believe it, yourself!

When you hit this impasse, there are two ways around it. You can give up that particular plot element, and sometimes you must, even when doing so really messes up the sequence. Or, you can change the character and make him over into the kind who *would* act as you need him to act. This means going all the way back to his roots, not only to the point where you plan to introduce him to the reader, but as far as you yourself have needed to go back into his life, which is always farther than the text goes.

Now, I am by no means saying that a character must be static. Not at all. The most fascinating characters are those who change under the pressures of happenings. But in order to create one of these "growing" characters, you must know *from* what he is changing, *to* what, and also *why*.

Therefore, if you are going to have the miser give the beggar a thousand dollars, or the coward jump the chasm, or the meek rise and fiercely dominate the meeting, you must take care to work this up, as slyly as you like, but nevertheless clearly and soundly, so that the "surprise" turns out to be "Well, of course!" or even "Hooray!" Otherwise, some critic will say that your plot is contrived. But the truth will be that you just didn't work long enough, or hard enough, or well enough at your contriving.

Nobody sits down and spins an excellent plot for a suspense yarn (or any other, I suspect) right off the bat. He works at it. And the work does grow under his hand.

Sometimes, when you are imagining-in-detail, or trying to put a bit of flesh on the next projected happening to check it out and see that it will work, suddenly there comes to you a truth, something that one of your characters *would* do here. But of course he would! It's not what you had been planning for him, but it's better. It gives the story a bonus of excitement. Many of your best so-called "devices," marvelous "twists," the kind that carry both surprise and recognition (the best kind) are found in just this way. You couldn't have dreamed that up in a million years—not from scratch. It comes out of work already done. It appears. And who says this kind of work can't be fun?

Into the weaving of a plot come many other threads, of course. Some may have to do not only with this story, but with stories in general. Let us say that you are in possession of a promising "what-if," an event. What if a housewife, walking down her own residential block, finds a note on the sidewalk that purports to be from somebody who is imprisoned, nearby? Sounds pretty fair, for a thriller. O.K., what does she do? Well, what kind of housewife is she? If she is timidly respectable and doesn't want to get involved, end of story as far as she's concerned. (That won't do.) Yet if she is a conscience-ridden, brother's-keeper, you may have the dickens of a time making anybody *like* her, and you'd better remember that. If she goes overboard in involvement for a stranger's sake, the reader is going to begin to say to himself, "Aw, come on." If you are expecting to get her into any wild trouble, you'll just about have to make her stupid. If she's sensible and turns the note over to the cops, *she* falls out of the story. But if she turns out to be related in any way to the prisoner, ah, ah . . . coincidence. Mustn't touch!

So, unless you can change either the event (there was no prisoner) or the character (she isn't a housewife)—or both, you had better put this one deep into the drawer.

Many things, you see, must be considered and all at once, and they modify each other.

There is, besides, the over-all tone. You do not take the same tone with every story. If, for instance, you are working within some stern realistic mode, your characters had better not react with light-hearted pranks, out of tune with the prevailing effect, *unless* you are using this very incongruity to make a stern realistic point. By the same token, if you are working on a yarn that you intend to make a romp, an entertainment, in semi-frothy or even semi-satirical style, you must be content to let any profound observations of the human scene clothe themselves in the same style. You cannot, for instance, have your gay young protagonist preached at by some grim moralist and *therefore* change his spots. Not out of left field, you can't.

Not only every thread, you see, but the sheen of the finished cloth must be carefully contrived, and, preferably, before you put down a single sentence.

It's possible that only he who sits down and does this sort of thing knows how it's done, and then, perhaps, he knows only how *he* does it. But it is not as simple as some may think, to do it well, and not the least challenging task in the world, and *definitely* not the dullest.

Your plot is contrived, eh? Well, I should hope so!

49

WITH A LITTLE WAND

By Andrina Iverson

HUMAN nature may not change, but human beings do. In the short story, characters change in less than five thousand words. With only black symbols on white paper to show how the girl at the end of the story is not the same (though she wears the same dress and face) as the girl at the beginning, a writer must have sympathy, empathy, a long memory, and a magic wand. To transport an editor from the nondescript here to the thrilling over there where fiction characters live requires wisdom and skill. First, choose the dramatic and different, for though fiction is true to life, it is life compressed and heightened. It is swift. The seven years Jacob served for Rachel are recorded in exactly seven words. The story of an affair—once passionate, now spent—is recalled by a rebellious old lady in a few moments.

The short story is a brief, brilliant insight into a situation and the people involved in it. Its quality and value come from the quality of the central figure, and this hero or heroine comes from the author. The uniqueness of the writer gives him a point of view, a way of looking at life different from other people's. Out of his uniqueness he creates a common denominator—his characters—to speak in sympathy and understanding to the loneliness of all the other unique people who read his story. Unhappily, the law of the silk purse and the sow's ear applies here as everywhere in life. It is not possible to conceive a character more intelligent, more sensitive, more interesting than you yourself are. Water can't rise above its own level. But—happily—levels are temporarily, sometimes permanently, heightened by the impact of experience or emotion. It is also true that we are lazy and seldom write to the full measure of our powers.

The playwright has one distinct advantage over the fiction writer —the printed program. The playgoer willingly accepts such flat facts as "Scene: Living room of Charles D'Arcy's summer home on a morning in August, 1912" because at any moment the curtain will go up and he will see the D'Arcys' summer home with wicker furniture, cretonne cushions, and Tiffany lamp. He has read the "characters in order of their appearance" and knows who they are and their relationships to each other. He knows if the play is modern or a period piece. He has probably read a review of it.

The short story writer does not have these props. With only words and his wits, he must set the stage and introduce his characters at the same time. For this, the best technique seems to be that of the chalk-talk artist: a few bold strokes to give the general impression which can be filled in and sharpened later. The writer, like the sidewalk artist, must catch the reader's interest at the very moment of his passing by.

Since people are always more engaging (to readers) than scenery, begin your story with only enough details to give your central figure a skeleton milieu. Do it at once and do it accurately. I remember how dismayed I was many years ago when I read the opening sentence of a story in class and everyone laughed. It wasn't intended to be funny. A young woman was moving, giving up her first, dearly loved apartment. I had written: "Pat sat on her trunk." The class laughed because it thought Pat was an elephant doing tricks. This, of course, is precisely the kind of mistake you can't afford. I find it helpful to read just the opening sentence of a story—my own or someone else's —and then summarize what it says. This is a harder-than-you-think exercise because if the sentence is well written, you forget to stop. You go on reading. For example, what do you know about the characters here:

Beth Morgan and her friend Katie Stephens were down on the beach building a raft out of the old lumber from the boat house.

Just as if tonight was any ordinary Friday night, Mary pulled her little chair up to the fire between Dad and Louise and opened *Heidi* to page 37.

It was late and they were already a little drunk, but Mrs. Gilbert and Mr. Jordan ordered another "for the road."

As quickly as possible give the physical background. Is it winter, summer, day, night? Give the social setting. Is the hero rich, poor,

refined, boorish? What is the intellectual climate? Is the emotional
tone gay, grim, old, young; realistic or romantic, idealistic or disillusioned? Is the heroine sophisticated or homespun, avant-garde or
bourgeoise? Give enough identifying tags so the reader knows—almost as quickly as the audience at the theater—that the characters
are skiing in the Alps or hiding out from revenue officers, that a
mother is worried about a teen-age marriage, a business man is chart-
ing his son's life, a college girl is deciding about a man.

Now, how do you make your character step out of the page across
the barbed wire of words into your reader's heart and mind? The
secret is the selection of significant details. Be specific. It won't do to
say "Ellen always wore cute shoes." Better say "Only Ellen could—
and would—wear red, white and blue shoes. On her they looked
chic; on her twin, Eloise, bad. Something from the rummage sale or
an old musical comedy."

Robert Frost said we "guess at each other." Certainly it is very
hard to be honest with one's self and almost impossible to be honest
about ourselves with other people. We are hedged about by memories of past pains and fears of future ones. We suppress our guilt and
deny our meannesses. Honest writing is often painful because to create real people—so real the reader will know them better than he
knows his best friends—takes time and soul-searching. Young artists
learning to draw do so from live models. The writer, too, should use
live models, and bring before his mind's eye how the milkman walks,
how the child looks who doesn't believe what you are saying. What
are the telltale mannerisms of the scheming woman? What happens
to the face of a pretty girl when she complains?

There is a painting by Ghirlandaio, *An Old Man and His Grand-
son* (1480). The boy's face is in profile, fresh and beautiful, lifted
trustingly toward the old man's. Our eyes, too, go to the old man's
face. He has strange, almond eyelids, a wart on his temple, a great
bulbous nose, a gentle, patient mouth. It is the old man's face that
makes the painting a masterpiece. The artist knew his sitter did not
elect to go through life with the curse of Cyrano, and he shows us
that by a thousand kindly decisions the old man fashioned the expression his face would wear.

It is precisely this selection of contrasts that makes a character
memorable. People are often not what they seem; they are always

complex compounds the writer sets out to explain and understand, but not make simple. What is the story behind the woman with a patrician nose and peasant legs married to a little dumpling of a man with a baby face? *Poor Richard's Almanac* says, "Why does Susan smile so much? Because she has fine teeth." Does this explain why Martha seldom smiles? What happens to the woman whose nature is refined and whose features are coarse? What about the boy in a family of athletes who is built like a football player but shrinks from the brutality of the game? If you say, "Helen has curly hair and beautiful teeth," I have little more than a vague impression of a thousand girls benefited by permanent waves and orthodontia. If you say, "Helen has brown curly hair, beautiful teeth, and the long nose of all the Hutchins," the focus is getting sharper. If you add "the long nose of the Hutchins that she looked down with the cold disdain of all the Hutchins," I begin to see a person instead of a paper doll. The thing is to know not only *how* your people look, but what their appearance has done to their characters.

Our interest in people is so fundamental it is almost instinct. Modesty inhibits most of us from exposing ourselves emotionally or intellectually, but our need to know people is strong, and so we read. We give ourselves—heart and mind—to those authors who let us know people more intimately than life lets us. We read and make friends across oceans, across centuries, with Russian peasants and Southern belles, British aristocrats and Yankee prisoners, without stirring from the sofa except to get an apple or throw more wood on the fire.

We are all familiar with Chekhov's advice to writers—the gun which hangs on the wall on the first page must go off before the last or there was no need for it to be there. This same economy is essential in first presenting a character because in the short story first impressions cannot be false or misleading. Every detail must be a true and telling one, and it must be used. The chance to reverse an erroneous first feeling, retract a too-hasty judgment may come in life but not in fiction. There is not the leisure in print that life allows for doing things over, because fiction is not life, it is a distillation of it. The character may get a second chance, the writer—never. He has to be right the first time and every time. An obvious illustration of this is our impatience with the man who muffs a joke in the telling. Let him forget the punch line or garble the situation, and nobody laughs or even stays to hear the ending come limping home.

When John Galsworthy's character, Soames Forsyte, died, the *London Times* printed his obituary. So real had this frustrated man become to English readers, they swore they saw him crossing Picadilly, recognized him on his way to the art galleries he loved. The curious thing is that Galsworthy intended Soames to be a heel. He presented him as colorless and stubborn. Soames, inside his well-tailored gray suit, under his correct gray fedora, lived his painful, passionately real life, and readers understood and sympathized with him. Galsworthy, intending the opposite, had created a national hero. How did this happen? It is impossible to say, exactly, because there is magic in writing, and however much an author may wish to tell how he did it, he can't—quite. We can be sure, however, that Galsworthy had enough sense to portray Soames honestly, as he saw him. That the people who read the novel saw not a villain, but a very real, frustrated man is something that happened in spite of the author's intention.

Shakespeare, who did more than any other dramatist to change stock characters into real people, says "the web of our life is of a mingled yarn, good and ill together." People, too, are of mingled yarn. The gangster is often kind to his old mother; the minister may be cruel to his. People are stupidly consistent or dangerously unpredictable. We are brave and we are cowardly—at different times; we are truthful until fear or love or tragedy makes liars of us. We are gentle and cruel by turns, generous or mean depending on who crosses our path that day. We are innocent or evil, merciful or malicious, loyal and false—to ourselves, to others. We think this today, something else tomorrow. Small wonder if we are sometimes accused of being "crazy mixed up." No wonder that we are so fascinating—to ourselves, to each other. We know people, or think we know them, and then they do startling things: our little neighbor in the blue serge suit robs the bank; jolly Joe commits suicide. Why? The reasons lie in the ball of yarn which the writer carefully unwinds and induces his reader to follow into the deep cave of another man's experience, the dark recesses of his mind.

The fiction writer has an advantage denied the conventional playwright whose characters can only be shown by what they say and what other people say to or about them. By stream-of-consciousness writing, characters in stories may reveal their thoughts to the reader without unnaturalness. This device—carefully used—shows people in their complexity: good enough to be admirable, bad enough to be understandable; varied enough to be interesting, enough like the rest of us to be believable. Your hero or heroine must be ordinary and extraordinary, beautiful and mean, in body or spirit, or both. Then readers will come to know the habit of his mind so well they will identify with him. They will see the streets he crosses, the curve of his hand on a child's head, how quickly he hides the pain his wife's sharp criticism provokes. Your hero may be brave though humiliated, honorable though cheated, wise in the ways of the unworldly, a lamb among the lions in the streets, but he may not be perfect. He may wish to be; he may struggle to be; but you, the writer, must never forget the great gap between the ideal and the real, the way we wish life were and the way it is.

I do not know how characters are drawn, but I think it is done by watching and remembering, by thinking and rethinking, by writing and rewriting and rewriting and rewriting. There are many practical suggestions offered in books and articles: writers are told to watch the faces of the people in the bus, listen to the conversation at cocktail parties, keep a notebook, jot things down. I think the best assets for any writer are a thin skin, a long memory, and a love of words. Impressions, like rain, fall on the just and the unjust, those who write stories and those who read them. The writer blest with a receptive consciousness need not go into the highways for impressions, nor stagger around trying to hold a mirror up to life. If he lives with his head and his heart, eyes and ears open, his ragbag mind will be stuffed with impressions. They will sift down over the years, get colored by association with other impressions, sharpened by rubbing against new ideas, mellowed by old convictions, refreshed by being held up to the light of truth. There is no formula, no map to guide you in creating character. You are the paper, and life—casual, erratic, indifferent—is the doodler drawing a line here, a cross there, a curve in the lower corner. It is aimless, mindless, meaningless scribbling, except to you to whom it happened.

Pamela Frankau says, "In life, people make things happen; things don't make people happen." This is also true of the story and its action, but people are what they are precisely because of the things life has done to them. It is the writer's first obligation to his reader to present his characters clearly and sharply, show what life is doing to them. He must make sure the girl is not mistaken for an elephant, the lady for her maid, the hero for a thief. The writer must portray his characters as he knows people to be, not as he wishes they were. This honest reporting comes from grubbing about in the ash heaps of the past to bring out of painful recollection an unflinching acknowledgment of things as they were and are. It is not a retelling of old scandals, the exhuming of old skeletons. Truth is not on the surface nor buried with the dead. It is buried with the past, inside people. The artist brings it to light and to life. The well-drawn character who lives away from the printed page is real, and he is free. If he is made of flesh and feeling with a backbone of his own, he will not let you squash him down into a cube like some wire and calico jack-in-the-box. Do not be troubled by the old generalization that truth is stranger than fiction. Fiction worth reading or writing is nothing but truth as the author sees it. E. B. White has said it all in one small sentence: "Don't write about Man, write about a man."

50

THE CATEGORY NOVEL

By Isabel Moore

WITH the demise of the pulps in the thirties and early forties, the young writer had a hard time finding a training ground, especially for fiction. Now, however, all young writers should be encouraged to know that the pendulum has swung all the way back, and a brand-new—and very hungry—market has emerged. This market is known in the trade as "the category novel," and it provides a solid stepping-stone to good novel writing just as the pulps were a proving ground for the future writer of slick fiction.

First, let me tell you what the category novel is: It is formula writing, by which I mean it has fairly stock characters, a beginning, a middle, a black moment, and a happy ending—*plus* a special category. For instance, we do not sit down just to write a "nurse novel," but to write a novel about a certain kind, or category, of nurse. Thus, you will see among the paperbacks on the newsstand, "Resort Nurse," "Psychiatric Nurse," "Surgical Nurse," "Student Nurse," and so on.

I am going to use the nurse-category novel as my chief example of the category novel because, first of all, it is among the easiest for an unknown writer to sell; secondly, I actually sat down with an unpublished author and helped her work out the writing of one of these, having my greatest reward when she looked up from her typewriter toward the end of our story and said triumphantly, "*I* see how it's done—"

I hope, by the time you have finished reading this article, you, too, will see how it is done. Before we finish, I will offer three possible themes of the "category" novel for the young, inexperienced writer and show, briefly, how each novel would be begun, developed and ended. First, however, let me digress for just a minute to show you the scope of the category novel and point out how, by deepening the characterization and polishing the writing—after you've had a little success with the simpler forms—you can carry your experience into the better paperback and even hardcover novel.

Three novels which, during the past few years, have achieved hardcover publication and have earned a great deal of money are "category" novels: *The Best of Everything,* by Rona Jaffe; *The Group,* by a fine writer named Mary McCarthy; and *Everything But A Husband,* by Jeannette Kamins. They are "category" novels because, had they been written by lesser talents, a paperback editor, sending a résumé to his superior, would have slugged them like this:

The Group—Four Vassar graduates go to the Big City in search of fame, love, husbands.

The Best of Everything—Four young girls in a big New York publishing company invade the Big City in search of fame, careers, love and husbands.

Everything But A Husband—Four girls at a summer resort in search of a husband.

The whole idea of the "category" novel grew out of the need of the paperback publishers—swamped with manuscripts as well as ready outlets for their merchandise—to establish certain categories, and then to determine how many of each category they would publish each month. But, as you can see, if the writer streamlines his thinking by placing his novel in a "category," he need not limit himself to the simple kind of "category novel" I am going to describe in detail here. Many, many young writers, now under contract to hardcover publishers, won their literary spurs by laboring long and hard in the vineyard of the simpler, pulp-paper, category novel. It is well to bear in mind that nothing limits a writer but his own ability, but, faced with a story to tell and a blank sheet of paper in the machine, the novice will be able to get off dead center and get started if he confines himself, first, to a category novel.

I find, for instance, that most beginners have trouble bringing more than two people on stage at the same time. But if you start with your four girls in a typing pool, or at a summer resort, or at the wedding of a classmate, why, lo and behold, there they are, all on stage at once with practically ready-made dialogue as they explain to one another how they got there, and why.

The category novel is also of enormous help in getting a story started. For example: Take the paperback novel with which I helped my young friend, a professional writer of nonfiction, who, when she tackled a novel, did what so many young writers do—put in enough plot for five novels. Her time sequence was all off, moving first forward and then back. Her story sat down and wagged its tail, while she gave the reader a mass of detail unrelated to the story in hand. And, finally, she got trapped, as what beginner does not, in that familiar swampland—the flashback.

The first thing to do when you embark on a category novel is to choose a background with which you are familiar. I know there is a whole school of thought—and I respect it for its beliefs—that says you can find plenty of novel material in the morning newspaper. Maybe you can. I never have, nor have I known many successful examples of this technique. For one thing, you automatically limit yourself and make your writing job doubly difficult, if you write about something you know little or nothing about. Even the simplest story must be embroidered with detail about how your characters earn a living, the kind of home to which they return at night, whether they eat a meager stand-up lunch or a lavish, charge-account, sit-down lunch. Job conflicts, family conflicts, and love conflicts must be felt by the writer to be believed by the reader. The talented professional, or the genius, can just take off into outer space, perhaps, but the beginner is wise, I think, to stick to things he knows about.

FIRST STEP: Choosing the category. My young writer friend had worked for two years as a "lab assistant" in a small-town hospital. She understood the career, love and loyalty problems of doctors and nurses, as well as their conflicts with patients, rich and poor. So we chose as our category, "Small Town Nurse."

SECOND STEP: Theme. Since this novel was slanted at a primarily teen-age audience, we chose that timeworn theme—*love-versus-duty*. Our heroine, Melanie Woods, was a dedicated student nurse who was to become a problem to the man who loved her, her superiors in the hospital and the other student nurses, all of whom saw nursing as primarily a means of earning a living until the right man came along.

THIRD STEP: Conflict. It is to be Edith Rogers, superintendent of nurses—whom Melanie worships because Miss Rogers saved the life of Melanie's father long ago—who becomes Melanie's remorseless foe. This comes about when Melanie realizes that Miss Rogers, in her own cold dedication to duty, puts rules and regulations above patient welfare. As the two lock horns, conflict deepens: Melanie will either be Miss Roger's kind of "by the book" nurse or no nurse at all.

Fourth Step: Background—a small hospital in upper New York State.

Fifth Step: Draw up a list of additional characters on a sheet of paper. *Decide the part each character will play in helping resolve your protagonist's basic conflict.* No matter how tempted you may be to dally along the way by indulging yourself in whimsey, you must be ruthless about cutting out every character who does not advance your plot! And don't tell me—as many young student writers in my courses have told me—about all the great writers who allowed their story to roam all over the lot. Of course they did. But you're not a great writer yet, or you wouldn't be reading this article. Master your technique first, then embellish your story!

Sixth Step: From your own background, I assume you have now decided on the category you wish to choose. In place of a student nurse, you have mentally substituted your own protagonist. You have chosen a theme, set up the basic conflict. (I will give you a few possible examples of these in a minute.) On a piece of paper you have drawn up a list of characters who will play a part in the working out of your protagonist's problem. So, now, let's get started with that terrifying, "Page One, Chapter One."

Its terrors will diminish if you will stick to this category novel, I promise you. You have already, mercifully, limited yourself as to time and background. Now, I will ask that you limit yourself once more; the more limitations you put on yourself at this stage, the simpler your job will be. Take another sheet of paper, and make subheads for each chapter. When you start to write, you will, of course, ignore these subheads, but they are wonderful guidelines. I told my young friend to make every other chapter take place in the hospital—with career-patient conflicts—and every other chapter out of the hospital, with love-family conflicts. You see how smoothly a mass of material begins to be codified? And since people are more interested in people than in jobs, we start Page One, Chapter One by showing Melanie on her way to the hospital with a friend, another young student nurse. (Always open a chapter with two people in conversation. Their dialogue is the simplest way to explain to the reader who the main character is and what problem is facing her.)

Since we know our theme is *love* versus *duty,* our dialogue is, again, as in the case of the more complicated category novels I mentioned earlier, practically ready-made. Melanie's friend asks her when she and her beau are going to be married; Melanie answers, not until she receives her cap, and her friend says, "Suppose he won't wait?"—and we learn why Melanie is such a dedicated nurse when she explains to her friend (thereby to the reader) why she feels she must repay the profession that saved her father's life by becoming one of nursing's most shining lights.

On their way to the hospital, the girls see the town drunk, Jerry Oakes, lying in the gutter outside a cheap saloon. Melanie's friend is all for hurrying on, but Melanie's sharp eye perceives that the man who seems to be dead drunk is, actually, turning blue because he is suffocating. Melanie, forgetting that "nurses nurse and doctors doctor," realizing there isn't a moment to spare, has the man brought inside the beery tavern and laid on an oilcloth-covered table, where, using a kitchen knife, she swiftly performs a tracheotomy which saves the man's life.

We have set our dual conflict in motion at the end of the first chapter (ten pages) when Melanie's friend, Cookie, says, "It was wonderful and brave of you to do it, Melanie, but you broke the rules, and Miss Rogers might even throw you out of nursing school." This career conflict, plus the love conflict revealed in the girls' early dialogue, sets the stage. Will Melanie lose her career? Can compassion finally triumph over duty? Will Melanie lose her beau as well?

Chapter Two takes place in the hospital in Miss Roger's office. And here I am going to let you in on another secret in trying to simplify the writing of your first novel. Open every chapter with a different character. For example, at the end of the first chapter just summarized, as the girls head back up the hill to the hospital, their last exchange of dialogue is about Miss Rogers. Open Chapter Two, therefore, with Miss Rogers. She has heard about the incident and has dispatched an ambulance. She reviews her own duty-dedicated life that included losing the man she loved (now head of the hospital), and unless she upholds that dedication to duty, she will, in a sense, make her own sacrifice meaningless. So we know Melanie is in for trouble. She gets a bawling-out, a warning that if a rule is broken again she will be dismissed from the nursing school. In tears, Melanie, feeling let down by the woman she has worshiped all these years, runs blindly out into the corridor where she collides with the young doctor who is going to be the man she finally marries—but not until she's practically saved the whole town by once more refusing to follow rules blindly.

Chapter Three, then, swings back to Melanie's personal life, her encounter with the small-town boy whose family feels that what Melanie did was shocking, and he indicates they'd better break the engagement.

Chapter Four—We're back in the hospital for further love-duty complications among the patients. And so on. As you can see, it is as regular as a Shakespearean sonnet—and a lot easier to compose! One by one, those characters you listed on a slip of paper are dropped into the hopper of your story, broadening the base of conflict. All this while, of course, tension mounts as Melanie gets closer and closer to her black moment: She loses the small-town beau; the young doctor she's come to love leaves to marry a rich New York debutante; the older doctor who was once her friend sides with Miss Rogers in deciding Melanie has to leave nursing school, and so on. The black moment comes when Melanie allows a dying man to have the sip of bourbon which, with morphine, helps lessen his pain. The bottle is discovered, Melanie is dismissed in disgrace. The small-town beau is off with a beautiful young artist from New York. Then a fire breaks out in the ancient hospital and that ex-drunk, Jerry Oakes, now a worker in the hospital laundry (and cold sober) is, along with Melanie, the hero of the day. Among the patients they save is the richest man in town, who promptly orders that a new hospital be built, and that Melanie be put back in uniform.

So, begin with personal-plus-hint-of-career conflict.

Plan that every other chapter will take place within the office, school, hospital where your career conflict will be developed and, finally, resolved.

Save your emotional resolution till last—girl never gets boy until almost the last page.

Save yourself a lot of heartache and hard work by making a list of chapters, giving each a subhead: a) Melanie; b) Miss Rogers; c) Melanie's wild sister who wants Melanie to help her not to have a baby; d) the young doctor torn between marrying the rich girl in New York and Melanie, whom he has learned to love. You will see that just by giving each chapter a name, you are checking on whether your story is moving forward toward the moment of decision, followed by the black moment, and finally by the ending.

Now, I said I'd mention three possible categories that might fit into the life of any young writer who is toiling at work he may hate during the day, in order to write at night. In other words, I'll mention three possible plots that engage your protagonist in a business-career as well as in a love-duty conflict.

Category A: Ambitious young man, rich older woman, with *ideals* versus *economic pressure* at stake. An ambitious young man, weary of working at menial labor to buy time to write his big novel, paint his picture, is tempted to marry a rich older woman. No sooner has he married her than he a) sells the novel that's been rejected by ten publishers; b) meets a beautiful young girl with whom he falls in love. He is ready to ask the older woman to free him, when her doctor tells him the older woman is dying of an incurable disease. Does he, out of loyalty, stay with the older woman or does he, feeling that he has a right to his own life, that he has given this older woman two years of marvelous companionship, leave her? It is easy to see the other characters who come into play: the woman's grown children; the young girl's fiancé; a greedy lawyer; perhaps another young man this older woman married years ago and who has since debauched himself, convincing our young hero that the older woman is basically cruel, selfish and greedy.

Category B: Nurse-Doctor. Young girl receptionist in office of a doctor she has fallen in love with, finds he has become a drug addict. Does she expose him for the sake of the patients who might die at his unsteady surgeon's hands, or does she try to save him by devoting her own life to at least temporary exile with him? Complications: Patients who have come to mean a lot to her, especially one young man due for serious surgery. She saves the young man, exposes the doctor, marries the young man, receives grateful thanks of patients.

Category C: Young girl has devoted most of her life caring for invalid mother. Story opens six months after mother's death. At dinner with the young man whom her meager savings have put through law school, she expects him to say, "Now we can be married." Instead, he says, "I'm married—I never thought you'd be free." She turns to an older man, marries him. The young man's marriage breaks up. We have that hardy perennial, *love* versus *loyalty* again. To whom do we owe a duty? Ourselves or the people who love us? Complications: The young man's deserted wife who is pregnant; an older woman who loved our heroine's successful husband before he married her; the business itself (does it fail, making it more urgent than ever that our heroine not leave him now?).

A few brief words of advice to the overly ambitious beginner: Don't scorn the category novel. It's a great teacher, just as the pulps were. Don't put roadblocks in your path by introducing characters or situations so unique they have to be explained (and probably won't be believed). Whenever possible, add interesting details of the business in which your characters are involved. This is known in the trade as a "plus-value" and also helps round out your novel by giving your characters a place to go to in the morning; a luncheon dialogue; an office (or factory) conflict; a train to catch at night (more dialogue and neighbor-conflict). My own way of working this out is always to think, "morning, noon and night; morning, noon and night." Get your characters out of bed, have them welcome or dread the day ahead; take them to luncheon with a boss, wife, rival; send them home to a pleasant or unpleasant meeting with wife, children, friends and tuck them into bed again.

The category novel can be science fiction; life on a college campus; athletic director at a resort—there's no end to the ramifications of this simple, formula-type novel. It requires no skill in handling flashback. The story moves steadily forward. Use stock characters and warm them with your own interpretation of their conflict—let your background be unique, keep your characters familiar, placed in unfamiliar situations but always struggling for things any reader can understand and sympathize with: love, honor, success, companionship.

And now I hope that you, like my young friend, will look up from your typewriter halfway through *your* category novel and cry, triumphantly, "*I* see how you do it!"

51

"YOU-ARE-THERENESS" IN FICTION

By Joan Williams

It is my inclination to write as if the reader were standing beside me. I want the reader to feel drawn into my setting and to receive a mood from it. It is my hope that he will see and feel and taste and smell as the character does. But I had not thought much about this being my method until recently when I was asked how to go about trying to achieve a feeling of "you-are-thereness" in fiction. And I had not realized exactly what influenced me toward this way of writing until last summer when I visited in Memphis the professor who had taught me freshman English in college. We had not seen each other in the twenty years since. He had been ill and after a pleasant conversation I was about to leave, thinking he must be tired. Instead he drew from a table beside him an old Manila folder and said, "Wait, I've been saving something to show you." He had followed my career with interest, he said, because from the beginning of his class I had expressed interest in being a writer. But the whole first semester I had showed no promise. However, in the second half of the year a turning point had come. He smiled and asked if I recalled all the paragraphs we had had to write on topics he assigned. And he asked if I remembered that he had stressed vividness, one element of writing he believed could be taught. Until he reminded me of the paragraphs, I had remembered freshman English mainly as the time I first struggled over writing an autobiography. He went on to say that for twenty years he had been saving paragraphs he thought were good examples to show incoming classes. Did I remember a particular assignment called, "How Joe Studies"? I had to admit that I did not. Well, he said, opening the folder, he thought that paragraph had been my breakthrough. After almost a year of reading unimpressive papers from me, he read this one and felt that at last I had understood what he had meant about vivid writing. Then with an odd feeling, I was holding in my hands the paragraph I had written when I was eighteen years old:

Joe slumped down on his spine, sprawled his feet on another chair, and turned the radio a little louder. He took another bite of chocolate cake, afterwards carefully wiping his fingers on the margin of the book he was holding. With a pencil he added a moustache and more eyebrows to the stately gentleman adorning page 781 and then turned to the next page and adorned that margin with B–29's and grinning cats in bow ties. He stuck a piece of bubble gum into his mouth, got up, went to the phone, and held a lengthy conversation, then returned to his chair and radio program. He looked at a few more pages in the book, ate the rest of his cake, sighed deeply, closed his book, turned off the radio and went to bed. Joe had studied.

I think for the first time I must have said to myself that the professor doesn't mean he merely wants to know how Joe studies, he wants to *see* Joe studying. It would not be enough to say that Joe sat in a chair and studied. He had to study in some particular way that was different and that would impress him on the professor's mind. The word "particular" is important. I believe that to write vividly the author has to deal in particulars. It would be easy to write a vivid sentence saying that while studying Joe stood on one foot and balanced a glass of water on his head. But, to me, this is cheating because it is not logically what a person would do. It is much harder to think of logical particulars to bring Joe alive; and that is the aim: to make the reader feel he sees and knows places and people which exist really only in the writer's mind. My own old schoolbooks have margins adorned with drawings and so now do those my children bring home, though their airplanes are a long way from B–29's. It gives a reader a pleasant shock of recognition if a character does something the reader knows he would do in the same situation. And who has not scribbled in his schoolbooks? It is a characteristic almost universally true of students. Even so, the reader does not see anything if the writer says only that Joe drew in his schoolbooks. But the reader will have a visual image if the writer mentions particulars like coats, bow ties, grins and airplanes. Again, Joe did not merely eat cake but a particular kind of cake—chocolate. Do you see, as I did, his mouth closing over a piece of dark brown cake with a shiny fudge icing?

If I were writing the paragraph today, I would give a description of Joe himself, though what is called for is only how he studies. I wonder if I avoided a description back in freshman English because I did not know how to make him memorable when he was also ordinary. This is still a difficult thing for me to do. It is easy to assign to a character a wart on his nose or to make him six feet eight inches tall; but it is difficult to impress on a reader a character he would not ordinarily notice in a crowd. In a book I am writing now, I want to make the reader well acquainted with a pretty girl. But to say she is pretty gives no picture to the reader's mind. A writer has to go to every length to avoid using clichés; I cannot say she has curly hair, blue eyes and rosy cheeks and let the description go at that. My girl so far has long blonde hair but that is by no means a description that is good enough. I wrote a scene in which the fact that she owns a beige cashmere coat with a mink collar becomes important. Now, at least, the reader sees her as a girl with long blonde hair in a beige coat with a mink collar. Throughout the book, more identifying characteristics will have to be added. Hopefully, the pretty girl will become a distinct personality.

If the setting is given in vivid detail, the reader is more apt to feel that he is there. A character can't be set down only in a room or house or in the country or the city. Even if a character is put into a well-described room, the reader will feel more that he is present if he is told about the room in particulars and not in generalities. Beneath a beautiful blue sofa against one wall there is a dog's bone; there is dust on the grand piano in the corner. These settings, with these particulars, can be clues also to a character's personality. He is a kindly person who loves his dog or a lazy housekeeper who never runs a broom under his sofa. To convey a sense of agitation the writer might describe a room minutely and say that the character in the room saw none of it. But how much more vivid for the reader to have seen it and to know just how agitated the character must have been to have missed all the details. Is agitation the reason a character has not seen dust on the piano? Perhaps the character does not notice jonquils poking up in a flower bed outside the room. Now the reader knows also that it is spring; but he has learned it through his own senses, which is more effective than if the writer had merely put down the words, "It is spring." The words could be digested without giving the reader any visual image. Instead, he has stood in a room where a dog's bone is under a blue sofa and dust is on the piano and looking out the window he has seen that spring is coming; in a flowerbed the earth is erupting; the green tips of leaves are appearing, as he has seen them every spring in real life.

Beginning writers are troubled sometimes by wanting to write about places they have never been. But it is easy to borrow particulars from around you and transfer them to other settings. Perhaps you are writing about New York and have said everything you know. There are tall buildings and crowded sidewalks and busy streets. Then go outdoors in your own town and see how the sunlight falls across a building or your own house at five o'clock in the afternoon. Why can't it slant across a New York building in the same way? Looking up from a busy street, your character sees late afternoon sunlight glancing off the Empire State Building. What does it matter if the reflection on the windows is really the way sunlight looks against your own bedroom windows some place else? Go to your local bar or restaurant. Particulars you see there can be transferred to a sidewalk café in Paris.

Repetition is valuable in impressing a mood, a place, a character on the reader's mind. In my second novel, I wanted to convey a man's long struggle to succeed. He is a dynamite salesman traveling the rural South, and over and over I touched on how tired he was when he came home, and many times I described the hot Southern summers and the dusty, inadequate roads and the difficulties he had getting his car into and out of places where there were no roads at all. By these repetitions I wanted not only to impress on the reader's mind the sense of struggle but also the sense of time. It was at the end of each week that he struggled home tired, and it was summer after summer that he fought dusty roads. Eventually he traveled modern superhighways, and this, I hope, conveyed a sense of how many years had passed. I hoped that the reader would think back to the beginning of the book when the roads were tire tracks through weeds and have the feeling that he had experienced many years of the character's life.

In a scene in *To the Lighthouse,* Virginia Woolf lingers over what was eaten for dinner. Very particularly her characters ate Boeuf en Daube, served in a huge brown pot. The meat in the dish is described as being yellow and brown and the reader is told that the stew contains bay leaves and wine. The servant girl removes the lid "with a flourish" and we learn that the pot gave off an "exquisite scent of olives and oil and juice." These particulars give a sense of reality to a book where the main focus is on what the characters are thinking. We identify with sitting at the table because we do it often. We, too, have waited for a lid to be whipped off a pot to see what we are going to have for dinner. If it smells good, we are glad. In any kind of novel, then, particulars can be used to make the reader feel he is present wherever the writer wants him to be and that he has grasped what the writer wants to convey.

52

PER ARDUA AD ASTRA

By Joyce Porter

I STARTED writing at the age of thirty-six. Up till then I had been a perfectly contented regular officer in the Royal Air Force, with every intention of remaining just that until they put me out to grass. In 1960, however, for various reasons I got fed up with service life and applied for premature retirement. This left me with three years to serve and I thought this would be ample time to look around for some more congenial employment. It had always struck me that writing would be a nice cushy job, a pleasant way of earning money without actually working for it—but I must stress that I had no burning ambition to be an author. It was just one of those vague daydreams which nobody has any intention of doing anything about. I would equally well have liked to be a millionairess, or the first woman to win the Victoria Cross, or even a prima ballerina.

Still, being a writer looked a slightly less potty idea than any of the others so, in my spare time, I wrote a book. It was a detective story because that was practically the only type of fiction I ever read. My favorite writer was (and still is) Georges Simenon and my first fifty pages were devoted to a vain effort to produce an English Maigret. On the fifty-first page two lights dawned. I wasn't any Simenon and my detective wasn't a bit like any of the coppers I actually knew. Eventually, I don't quite know how, I found myself landed with a detective who couldn't detect and I felt much happier with him. Personally, I wouldn't read a funny detective story if you paid me and I just don't understand how it is that I've come to write the dratted things. I'd really like to write those huge complicated novels about the achievement and exercise of power, but I can't.

Well, when the first book was finished I started posting it off to various publishers and got down to my second novel while I waited for the rejection slips to come in. Which they did. One publisher (who will surely get his reward in heaven) was generous enough to send me a two-page letter of criticism and encouragement. Rightly or wrongly, it made me feel that I might possibly have a chance and I flogged on. The second novel turned out to be a near miss and the third was accepted for publication about a fortnight after I had finally left the Air Force.

In the years since that momentous day I have had six books published in about ten different languages. The seventh is currently in the pipeline and I am nearing the end of yet another. And, if some good fairy would give me enough money to live on in reasonable comfort, I wouldn't write another word.

Yes, I quite agree! Luck like that shouldn't happen to anybody and, if I could tell you exactly why it happened to me, I would. I am the last person to withhold help from any aspiring writer. The honest truth is, though, that I just don't *know* how to write a book which somebody will publish. If there is a sure-fire formula I'm as greedy to have it as anybody else. People talk happily about plot construction and character motivation and God knows what. It's all Greek to me. I just get an idea for a book, sit down and write it. The only thing I can think of that I do deliberately is to reduce description to the bare minimum. This is simply because, whenever I encounter two-page word pictures of the view from the study window or three hundred lines on the beauty of the heroine, I skip. In big jumps.

This inability to analyze bothers me at times. I consider that a really professional writer should know why he does things in a particular way. Judged by this standard I must rank myself as a fumbling amateur, relying purely on instinct.

About the actual mechanics of writing, though, I'm very fussy. I write by hand with a very sharp pencil (the Simenon influence again) and I always buy folio-sized books which are meant to be used with carbons and have very thin, crackly paper. I like thin paper and find these books with their numbered pages ideal for my purpose. I reckon that a chapter is about fourteen pages in my handwriting so I always mark the page, round about which the chapter should end. I also know now that the complete novel should be one whole foolscap book in length plus an extra forty pages or so. I am usually pretty near these targets.

I write the whole book straight off. I always start with working notes listing the names and ages of the characters, their family relationships if these are important, and plans of rooms or streets when I have to be careful about the geography. I'd like these preliminary notes to be very clear and concise, but they rarely are. As I have gained more experience I find that these notes get sketchier and sketchier. Nowadays I prefer not to have every last detail planned in advance as this tends to make the actual writing rather boring. Much to my amazement, boredom has proved to be my main occupational hazard and so it is important to me to have to think up something new once the book is under way.

When I've finished the manuscript I type it out, with two copies, and these are the typescripts which actually go to my publishers. Sometimes I read the manuscript through first before typing it, sometimes I don't bother. I correct spelling and grammatical mistakes as I type and generally polish up. The final appearance of the typescript is very important to me and I make it as attractive as I can, using very thin onion paper and binding it as professionally as possible. I am more than a bit of a fanatic about this although, in my saner moments, I know it is of minimal importance. I find that making three copies is a tremendous chore and I could easily have it done by a typing agency—but I never do. It would hurt me far more if my agent said the typescript was messy than if she said that the book was bad. You can make of that what you will!

I will, grudgingly and under pressure from my publisher, make minor alterations but large-scale revision is technically and temperamentally beyond me. Rather than even think of rewriting a book I would, and have, thrown it away and written another completely different one.

I have, however, one virtue as a writer and one claim to some sort of professionalism. Once I've started a book, I finish it. Always. No matter how fed up and dissatisfied I get, I struggle on to the bitter end. I think this is something that some would-be writers might do well to emulate. It is, in my opinion, what separates the men from the dabblers. Half a novel is a sheer waste of good paper and anybody who's got one gathering dust on his desk ought to take up stamp collecting or color photography or something.

In fact, now I come to think of it, this is the only advice I can give anybody. The only way to become a writer is to write. I dare say there's a lot to be said for taking courses in creative writing or joining a circle of amateur authors or reading books on how-to-do-it. They just happen to be proceedings that make me cringe with horror. Not that I'm not the complete sucker where other subjects are concerned. Give me a geranium for Christmas and I'll be out at crack of dawn the next day buying an illustrated encyclopedia on the care of house plants. By the end of the week I'll know as much about pot-bound azaleas and the incidence of leaf mould in dwarf petunias as anybody in the country. The geranium will be dead, of course. I just won't have had time to water it. Still, I'm not aiming to make my living as a gardener, am I?

Writing for publication isn't a hobby. It's a job, and very few people are lucky enough to enjoy their jobs. I've never heard a writer yet say that he actually enjoyed writing. I certainly don't. That's why I think it is so essential that the would-be writer doesn't let himself get sidetracked by correspondence courses and evening classes from knuckling down to the sheer grind. I'd sooner read a book about how to write a novel than sit there and write one. I'd sooner do almost anything than shut myself up all alone every day and get on with it. The only pleasure I get out of it is the excitement of thinking about the next novel and the blessed relief of finishing the current one. The part in between is hell and nobody and nothing can help you with that.

When you get right down to it, whether or not you can write anything worthwhile is a matter strictly between you and the publisher. Everything else is totally extraneous to the issue. And the publisher can't do a thing until he has your effort, whatever it is, in front of him. With the best will in the world he can only judge on what you have actually written—not on what you've thought about writing or learned about writing.

Rejection slips are depressing. Dog-eared manuscripts thudding home to roost on the door mat are depressing. But, by the time the tenth rebuff of your little masterpiece smacks you in the teeth, you ought to be past caring. You'll be halfway through your next novel by then, won't you? If you've that much self-confidence, pig-headedness and simple cheek, you may make it one day. If you haven't, you certainly won't.

The Latin title of this chapter is the motto of the Royal Air Force. It is usually translated as: "Through hardship to the stars."

53

THE IMPENDING EVENT

By Vern Sneider

THERE is a particular type of story that can be extremely difficult to write.

It is the story that deals with the revelation of Character or the revelation of Relationship. Chekhov was one of the leading exponents of this type of fiction. John Updike is a present practitioner. But even in the hands of such a master as Chekhov, it has proved dangerous. Dangerous because the verdict of the reader is frequently: "Nothing happens in the piece."

But suppose your orientation is toward this type of fiction. Suppose, like Chekhov, it is the humanness of people that interests you. Suppose you want to reveal their quirks and foibles. This is the type of story you want to write. Is there some technique that you can employ to overcome the seemingly static quality of such fiction, to escape the damning "nothing happens" tag?

There is. It is a comparatively easy technique, once you know it. It simply involves hanging an impending event over the heads of your story characters.

There are at least three types of impending events, applying to the short story, the novel, and all forms of fiction. And if I use plays and musicals primarily to illustrate them, it is only because nowhere does a vacuum show up so much as on the stage.

The first type of impending event appears in such works as the musical *Oklahoma!*, the stage play *Picnic*, and Chekhov's *Three Sisters*.

The musical *Oklahoma!* consists mainly of two relationship lines. The first is the triangle between Laurey, Curly, and Jud. The second is the triangle between Ado Annie, Will, and Ali Hakim. Something does happen in each of these relationship lines. There is a change of attitude, outlook, and viewpoint on the part of the characters toward each other. But simply to play out these two relationship lines would create a seemingly static situation.

To overcome this, at least to give the appearance of something happening, the authors used the impending event. In this case the impending event was the box social. The box social hung over the whole musical.

To illustrate how it gave a guise of busy-ness—in the first act there were the preparations for the social. People were on stage and off stage (a reason for entrances and exits) in order to pack picnic baskets, to change clothes, to water the horses before starting.

In the second act they were at the social, and it gave them something to do on stage. There was the bidding for the basket packed by Laurey. The actual bidding between Curly and Jud was shown, thus creating conflict and projecting stage action.

The stage play *Picnic* by William Inge uses exactly the same device. Again, this is a play of character and relationships. But to play these out on stage would be simply to show a slice of life, a day in the lives of the characters.

So overhanging the whole play is the picnic that is going to take place that evening. Again, you have the characters making plans, the preparations, the looking forward to and the discussion of the event. All of this adds up to the appearance of something happening.

There are several distinctive features to this first type of impending event. For one thing, both the characters and the audience —reader or viewer—are well aware that the event is going to occur.

A second feature is that the event is of an everyday nature—a box social, a picnic, having dinner with the boss and his wife, or some such. This type of event gives the characters an everyday purpose to pursue. The reader is interested in purpose, and even the pursuit of a mundane purpose will help in holding his attention.

A third feature is that the event can give color and can indicate a social atmosphere. Suppose the impending event is a Formosan Pai-Pai festival. Here you have the native priests in their robes and chanting. You would have the drums banging and incense hanging in the air. All of this, in turn, indicating a certain culture, a certain social atmosphere.

But the impending event need not be as exotic as the Pai-Pai. The important thing is that it indicate the type of occurrence that takes place in the lives of the people you are writing about. It may indicate exoticness, or, in turn, utter drabness, or just everyday living.

So the next time you do a story of relationship or character, try hanging an impending event of this type over it. It may be the impending birth of a child. It may be your daughter's impending freshman year at college. Make it what you will. Whatever it is, it will add a new dimension to your story. It will give the reader the impression that something is happening, even though he may fail fully to appreciate that great changes are actually occurring in the characters and their relationships

The distinctive feature of the second type of impending event is this: the reader or viewer is fully aware that the event is going to occur. But the story characters are completely unaware.

Cavalcade, the movie by Noel Coward, illustrates this type perfectly. The young honeymooners are standing at the rail of a steamship. They obscure a life preserver that is attached to the rail. We see their happiness, joy, and love for each other. Then they move away, and we see the name of the ship painted on the life preserver. It is the *Lusitania.*

This type of impending event can create a powerful effect on the reader, especially if the characters are sympathetic, like the young honeymooners, and if the danger is great, such as the sinking of the ship.

Historical events, since the reader has knowledge of them, lend themselves especially well to this type of treatment. Perhaps we see the men of the Seventh Cavalry under General Custer riding out, with the band playing "The Girl I Left Behind Me." Perhaps we see the women and children watching and waving goodbye. The men are heading for the Little Big Horn. They have no knowledge of what is going to happen there. But the reader knows—it is a historical fact—and this knowledge hits at the reader's feelings and emotions, because disaster looms.

This type of impending event need not, however, be strictly historical. If the author plants in the reader's mind that the event is going to occur, it is equally effective. As an example, if the author has planted the fact that a volcano is going to erupt, it is just as effective as if the reader knows the volcano is Vesuvius and the story is being played out in Pompeii. Planting of information makes the big difference.

Nor is it necessary that this type of impending event be serious in nature and hang over the entire story. It may be comic and hang over just one scene as in the Broadway musical *Henry, Sweet Henry* (based on the movie, *The World of Henry Orient*). In this scene the moment has finally arrived when Henry has maneuvered the matron from Scarsdale into his bedroom. He has been working toward this for weeks.

But the audience knows one thing that Henry does not. The audience knows that the police have been tipped off that Henry is pushing dope (although he isn't), and the signal that he has a supply on hand is for Henry to pull down the window shade. This is one of the funniest scenes ever to appear in a musical comedy, a large part of the humor coming from having the audience anticipate the pulling down of that window shade. For the minute Henry pulls it for privacy, all hell is going to break loose. The police are going to come dashing in, raiding Henry on the verge of the intimate moment he has been building up to for weeks.

A similar non-serious, single-scene impending event occurs in many of the old Laurel and Hardy movies. Laurel and Hardy drive their car into one end of a railroad tunnel. By cutting, the camera shows a train entering the other end. There is going to be a confrontation, and the audience howls in anticipation.

Thus, having the reader know of an impending event which the story characters are unaware of is an excellent way to get an effect across on the reader. And it has an added bonus of holding the reader by making him anticipate. Here, again, the reader is made to feel that something is happening, or at least that it is about to happen.

The third type of impending event is one in which both the story characters and the reader know that the event may occur. But neither the story characters nor the readers are sure that it will occur.

The *Sound of Music* is a good example of this. In this case, it is the Anschluss movement—Germany taking over Austria. It is a historical fact, of course, that Germany did take over Austria, yet it is not a well-known fact. Few people are fully conscious that the Anschluss occurred.

Thus, in *Sound of Music* there is a progressive buildup. There is a step-by-step development as Germany comes closer to taking control of Austria. As in the impending event of the second type, this third type adds an element of menace. If Germany takes over, the Trapp family must give up their beliefs or their homeland, one or the other.

Here, again, if the story characters are likable, you can build up a powerful effect. Your reader will be hoping against hope that the event will not occur. He will be pulling for your characters. And while your characters may be playing out a simple love story, this great menace hanging over them will give the reader the feeling of something truly momentous happening.

Another example of this type of impending event is to be found in the musical *Fiddler on the Roof*. Here Tevye, the eternal milkman, is trying to marry off his five daughters. Much of the musical is concerned with three love story lines. Certainly, they are not unusual.

But hanging over Tevye, his daughters, and the whole little Jewish village in Russia is the threat of a Czarist pogrom. There is possible trouble. We see it develop step by step. There is a possibility that these people will be driven from their home village and even from Russia itself.

We hope it doesn't happen, so the story pulls us in emotionally. Yet we fear—then we realize—that it is going to happen. And by the time it does happen—well, I have seen the audience leave this show with tears in their eyes.

So the impending event is a most useful technique. To summarize, it will do the following for your story, either singularly or in combination:

1. Give a static character-relationship story the appearance of something happening.

2. Draw the reader into the story by making him anticipate the event.

3. Give social atmosphere or color.

4. Catch the reader's attention by getting him interested in a character's purpose, even though it may be an everyday purpose.

5. Create a menace to your characters, thereby, if they are likable, gaining reader sympathy.

6. Create a humorous situation.

7. Create reader interest by allowing the reader to see the impending event unfold step by step.

8. Create doubt as to outcome, hence suspense.

54

WHAT MAKES A SALABLE
CONFESSION?

By Jean Jackson

One of the least discouraging and best-paying places for a writer to
begin to sell is the confession field. The confession market is tremendous, and confession editors seem to need capable writers today more
than ever before. New confession magazines are always appearing on
the stands, and the old ones continue on and on. There are currently,
I believe, more than twenty-five confession magazines. Each one
uses six to ten regular-length stories and one or two double-length
stories. This means that around two million words go into print every
thirty days. At three to five cents a word, approximately $720,000 to
$1,200,000 is paid into the bank accounts of confession writers every
year. Some of it might as well go into yours.

But before you are going to get your share of that enticing sum,
you're going to have to learn what makes a salable confession.

I like to think of the writer as a sort of middleman between *Life*,
the manufacturer, and *Editors*, the retailers. The editor in turn sells
to the individual customer, the reading public—and what the public
demands and buys are solutions to its problems. The difference between the writer and the wholesaler in ordinary business is that the
writer must also act as a kind of purifier or filter. A manufacturer
offers a nice, clean-cut, shapely product to his distributor. Life
doesn't. The problems Life gives you glimpses of, very often remain
unsolved, or at least get whisked away out of sight before you can
see how they work out. The writer, therefore, must supply, from his
imagination, the solution to Life's problems. It is, when you stop to
consider it, a tremendous and somewhat alarming responsibility to
be expected to be all-knowing and all-wise. But, in the confession
field particularly, the answers are very simple. The reader must be
firmly guided along the paths of righteousness.

Now let's see if we can find out what makes a salable confession. You must find out first what the confession reader needs. Your best clue to this is in the advertisements. If you have never studied the confession magazines, you may be surprised to find that the same products are ballyhooed in them as in the slick women's magazines. The higher-paying confessions, such as *True Story, Modern Romances,* and *True Confessions,* contain ads not only about the same products, but, month by month, exact duplicates in layout and copy of the ads in *McCall's, Good Housekeeping,* and *Redbook.* Toothpaste, hand lotion, soap, shampoo, baby powder, clothes, deodorants and antiseptics, silverware, cosmetics, rugs, furniture, medicine— all products dealing with phases of the average woman's main interests—love and romance, marriage, a happy home, and healthy, well-adjusted children.

What, then, is the difference between the confession reader and the slick reader?

The first difference is in the amount of education she has. Graduation from high school is about as far as the confession reader ever gets, and many of them don't get that far, though one of the policies of the magazines is to urge them to finish school and not marry too young. Once in a while you will find a story with a college background, but that is the exception rather than the rule, and some editors will not even read such stories, much less print them.

The second difference is a matter of income. The confession reader is a typist, dressmaker, salesgirl or housewife, in love with or married to a hotel clerk, factory worker, or small-pay white collar worker or someone of this sort. She wants to read about people she knows and understands, not about those who move on the society pages of her local paper. She simply cannot visualize fifteen-room mansions, diamond bracelets, and half a dozen cars in the garage. One of her major problems in life is making both ends meet from payday to payday, and she has a hard time understanding why anyone who doesn't have to worry about money should have any problems at all. You and I know this isn't true—that just because you have money in the bank, it doesn't follow that you get into no emotional tangles. But the confession reader, stretching dollars from day to day, is an inveterate bargain hunter, because she has to be. She shops where she'll get the most for her money, even among the magazines. That's why she buys the confession magazines, which offer her eight or ten longer-than-average stories in each issue, instead of the three or four per issue of the slick magazines.

A point I want to bring out here—and I cannot emphasize it too strongly—is that you cannot write down to a confession reader. Not and get away with it. All of you who are reading this are probably better educated than the average confession reader. If you weren't, you wouldn't be writing. You probably are much better off financially than she is. But if you feel a cut above the confession reader; if you believe, even without saying it aloud, that you're "better" than she is, you won't write a passable confession. You will not be able to get inside a confession heroine, reason as she would reason, muddle your way through problems as she would, and I would strongly advise you to forget the confession market and concentrate on the slicks.

The age level of the confession audience is from about thirteen to thirty-five years. Older women do read them, but when they do, they're generally reliving the problems they encountered during those twenty-two years. Confession readers consider eighteen, the age of consent and the approximate age of graduation from high school, as mature enough for marriage. Before that time, the confession heroine is emotionally a child. At eighteen, she suddenly springs, full-blown, into womanly wisdom. Frankly, this reasoning of confession editors has always baffled me, but that's the way it is, and you might as well keep it in mind. I think you'll find the marrying age of slick story heroines is somewhat higher.

Let's get away from generalities and down to particulars. For example, do you really know what a "formula" is?

A formula is a simple, basic pattern upon which a story is built. It has nothing to do with plot or conflict or flashback or complication or any other of those confusing terms you may have had thrown at you. It can be expressed in one or two sentences at the most, and it never varies. There are, in all, only about twenty-five story formulas in existence. One is the confession formula; three or four, I believe, are Western formulas; the rest can be classified as belonging to the slick field. I'm not going into formulas in general here, but will try to explain the confession formula to you.

The confession formula is very hard to find by reading confession stories in print, because it is so overlaid by unbridled emotions, by weeping and wailing, tearing of the hair and beating of the breast that it gets buried beneath all the lamentation. Then, too, unlike a slick story, the action of a confession can be stretched out over weeks or months or even years. I found the confession formula right in my own manuscripts. I wrote dozens of confessions without having any idea what I was doing. Suddenly, they began to sell with some regularity, but I didn't have the faintest idea why. I looked over all my carbon copies and found that, in the scripts that had sold, the story had invariably followed a pattern that was clear enough to see on the typewritten pages. It was then that the Great Light dawned!

You may have heard that the confession story formula is "Sin, Suffer and Repent." That is not exactly true. The protagonist does sin, she does suffer, and she does repent—but not necessarily in that order. Sometimes she sins and suffers anyway, in spite of repenting for pages in between.

There is, I think, a clearer way of expressing the confession formula: "The protagonist persists in making a mistake, and by so doing brings down tragedy either on herself or on those she loves. She realizes she has been wrong and sets about rectifying the mistake as far as possible."

I want you to notice that word "persists." I used it with a purpose which I'll take up with you in a minute. Right now I know what is going through your heads. You're saying, "Why, that's nothing but sin, suffer, and repent, and she said they didn't have to come in that order." They don't. You'll have a better story *if they don't!* If you can arrange your plot so that the heroine sees the light first, but has already, by her actions, set the wheels of tragedy in motion and cannot stop them, your story will probably be bought at a higher rate, or, at least, be featured on the front of the magazine that buys it.

Let me try to illustrate what I mean from a story of my own, which I called "The Middle One" because the heroine, Nora, is the middle child in a family of three. (*Intimate Story* subsequently changed the title to "I Accused Him for Thrills," which is, I admit, a title with much more come-on.) This is a story of a high school girl who has never had much attention. After being overlooked, one way or another, in desperation she blurts out what she thinks is just a mild exaggeration or a meaningless pass made at her by a moronic dishwasher in the high school hangout across the street. Things move along. She brushes off a "wild" boy, accepts a date with a nice one, justifies herself by believing that the nice boy has noticed her because of the fib she's told, and that the talk will die down of its own accord. What she doesn't know is that she has already started the wheels of tragedy moving, and no matter what she does, they are not going to stop. The story runs twenty-six pages. On page 16 she finds out—well, let me quote a bit:

> The uneasiness I'd been feeling rushed over me in a great, engulfing wave, setting the blood to pounding in my ears, as I realized what must have happened. Somehow, the story had got twisted as it ran like wildfire through the school! People thought Uncle Willie—dear, sweet old Uncle Willie—had tried to— Even in my mind, I couldn't quite say the ugly words! [Uncle Willie is a sweet old man who owns a confectionery and all the students love him.]

So you see, she realizes long before the story ends that she's made a mistake, and is terribly sorry about it. The rest of the story deals with the tragedy over which she has no control—in this case a mob scene in which the students, believing Uncle Willie is an old lecher, descend on his shop and wreck it and send him to the hospital with a bashed-in skull. I managed to work out a reasonably happy ending for this one, too, though you can't always do it.

There is one major difference between a slick story and a confession story besides that of formula. In both, the protagonist is faced with a problem he must solve. You know how a slick story is put together. I like to visualize it as a flight of steps going up, with a short and steep slide at the end. The slick heroine keeps going along the wrong way almost to the end; then, when she simply can't get in any deeper and has to decide between right and wrong, she chooses right—with a capital R—and in one or two paragraphs slides down to the solution and splashes into a pool of happiness. The turning point of a slick story, in other words, is almost at the end.

The confession heroine doesn't have such an easy time. The turning point in the confession story comes just halfway through the action—and at the high point, the protagonist *always* makes, not the right, but the *wrong* decision. Because of this decision, tragedy inevitably follows. She then bumbles her way back through more complications to a logical conclusion, with at least a "glimmer of hope" for the future.

Now let's get back to that word "persists" which I used in stating the confession formula. I used it because, all the time that the confession heroine is heading the wrong way, she has a sneaking suspicion of exactly what she's doing. She knows the difference between right and wrong, yet she "persists" in going the wrong way toward an inevitable wrong decision. Here is where you begin to get into difficulties in writing—that delicate matter of reader sympathy for the heroine. Even you, the writer, are going to have trouble sympathizing with your own character when you know she is heading the wrong way, for the wrong reasons. How, then, can you make the far more critical reader like her?

You turn the screws! You make the pressure on her so great that she is pushed, almost against her will, along the path of "sin," to the wrong turning, into the woods where she is lost. Disheartening incidents, people's reactions to her—everything piles up on her, and at the decision point, when she stands hesitating, the signs pointing in the wrong direction are so much bigger and easier to read than the others that she *apparently* has no choice. If you can do this successfully, the reader, while he may not *like* the heroine, can understand why she goes astray. That is what reader sympathy in a confession story is—not necessarily liking for a character, but understanding of her reasoning processes. In a slick story, your central character is almost always a lovable critter underneath. In a confession story, she may not be. She just has to be motivated by circumstances strong enough for the reader to think, "I'd probably do the same thing myself."

Yet, you can't let your heroine gallop gaily down the wrong road, without any thought at all for others or for what is the right thing to do. You have to give her little twinges of conscience now and then, followed by an event that seems to outweigh, by far, what her conscience is telling her. She teeters back and forth in her thoughts, as people do in real life. Confession stories are much closer to real life than slick stories, as you'll realize when you start being "I" in one of them.

This matter of reader sympathy may sound hazy and difficult, but it isn't hard to do once you get into the swing of it. Let's go back to my story, "The Middle One," to show you with specific examples how I handled reader sympathy. Nora is an average girl, not brilliant like her younger brother or beautiful like her older sister, and as a result she's always been sort of taken for granted, though, like everyone else, she'd just love to be important. Not much of a situation, is it? Nothing very novel or out of the way. She's dissatisfied and wants things to be different. Now let's begin turning the screws.

I started the action on the morning of her sixteenth birthday. She wakes up with that beautiful feeling that things are going to be better now. The problem, as it stands, comes in the first three paragraphs:

> I woke very early the morning of my birthday, smiling to myself even before I was fully awake. On the ceiling overhead, the naked branches of the maple tree outside made flickering shadows. The autumn air from my window was cold and crisp and clean, and from the kitchen downstairs came the appetizing smell of bacon frying.
>
> I yawned and stretched, savoring the day and all the days ahead. Life is wonderful when you've reached sixteen at last, and can catch glimpses of all the enchanting vistas that being an adult will open up. The Junior Prom next month —surely someone would ask me to go. Maybe even Tim Hartford! A little thrill shot through me at the thought.
>
> I saw in my mirror that I had changed in the last few months, rounded out and matured even while I grew tall and slender. My blonde hair had taken on a new sheen from constant brushing, and now that Mom allowed me to use lipstick, anyone who looked could see my lips were full and soft and tantalizing. Oh, I'd never be beautiful enough to be a model like Angie, my older sister, or too smart for my own good like Dink, my ten-year-old brother. But maybe now someone would notice me.

You know at once that she wants attention from her world in general and from a certain boy in particular. At the bottom of page 2, the pressure begins. Her folks have forgotten it's her birthday and hustle off about their various businesses without even a birthday greeting:

> I just stood there, listening to the clatter of her heels on the porch and the snap of grease sputtering in the skillet. They were gone, all of them! I was sixteen today, and nobody'd even said Happy Birthday!

There's the first incident.

She goes to school feeling pretty let down. Tim, the boy she likes, can't even remember her name:

I sat the whole hour staring at the back of Tim's head, willing him to turn around and look at me. He didn't, of course. Later, I met him in the hall between classes. He looked toward me and smiled, as you would do at a familiar face you'd seen someplace. "Hi, Tim!" I sang out with bright, forced gaiety.

He looked vaguely puzzled. "Oh, hello there—uh—Nora," he answered after a minute, walking on. What was the use? I thought dejectedly. All the old hurt of this morning came back with a rush. Great stuff, wasn't I? My family forgot all about my birthday, and the fellow I was crazy about could hardly remember my name!

There's incident number two.

She keeps hoping against hope that a birthday celebration is in store, but her busy family has actually forgotten. They remember at the last minute and try to make it up to her:

The kitchen door came open slowly, and they all sang "Happy birthday to you!" Dink headed the parade, carrying the pound cake. He'd stuck sixteen toothpicks in the cake and lighted them like candles. I didn't know whether to laugh or cry.

Dink set the cake down in front of me. "Blow, quick!" he cried. Automatically, I did, and the blackened toothpicks scattered all over the tablecloth. "Happy Birthday, Nora!" Angie said, thrusting her best blue formal in my arms. "I know you've been wanting this for a long time. Now it's yours!" Mom leaned over and kissed me gently on the cheek. "Oh, honey, we're all so sorry! Such a terrible thing, to forget all about your birthday! It's just that we've been so busy—" She stopped, then went on, her voice breaking a little. "You're such a good, steady, thoughtful girl— Oh, I'm sorrier than I can ever say!"

"It's all right," I said shakily. But it wasn't. Deep inside, I ached with unhappiness.

Well, you see how it goes—right up to page 13, *the exact middle of the story,* where she's given a final chance to retract her lie, which has brought her the attention she desires. What does she do? The formula says she must make the wrong decisions, so:

And yet wasn't it because of that very hubbub that Tim was here beside me, his jaw square and firm, looking as if he'd willingly tangle with anybody who bothered me? I knew it was. If Tim hadn't got wind of what I'd told Jane, he never would have noticed me. It was too late now to deny the story. If I wanted to keep Tim's interest, I'd have to play along now and hope the story would die out of its own accord.

And then tragedy follows.

On the surface, it may seem that confession stories begin anywhere, but if you will study them carefully you'll find that they really begin at the beginning of the problem. Sometimes the problem actually starts way back in the heroine's childhood. If it does, begin your story there, and tell it straight. Confession editors don't like cumbersome flashbacks. In this story, for instance, the only real flashback is worked into these two sentences, which are hidden in the presentation of the problem:

I saw in my mirror that I had changed in the last few months, rounded out and matured even while I grew tall and slender. My blonde hair had taken on a new sheen from constant brushing, and now that Mom allowed me to use lipstick, anyone who looked could see my lips were full and soft and tantalizing.

There are only a few other minor points that I think may help you in writing your confession story. It will be, of course, written in the first person, although a few editors are now experimenting with third-person stories. The central character will preferably be a female. Confession editors run about one out of ten or twelve stories with a male protagonist, so your chances of selling are much greater if you stick to the feminine viewpoint.

Emotion in a slick story goes deep, but it flows beneath the surface, like an underground stream. In the confession story, on the other hand, emotion is visible, audible and tangible, as exciting to the eye and ear as a turbulent stream rushing noisily along its rocky bed. The reason for this takes us back again to that matter of education, which leads us to suppress our emotions, to keep them under control. It also teaches us to look beneath the surface in other people for subtleties and innuendoes. Many confession readers, lacking the refinements of education, give vent to their emotions in real life and want the characters they read about to do so, too.

At first, you may feel very silly when you try to write in this highly emotional style. You'll feel that if anyone should happen to read what you are writing, you'd blush and shrivel with shame. After a while, however, you'll realize that being allowed to write this way is fun. You can be as primitive as you like, say the things you don't dare say aloud in real life, scream at the neighbors you hate, kick the dog, snarl at your husband for not hanging up his clothes, rise to ecstatic heights when your dream prince kisses you, plummet to the depths of despair and wallow gloriously in misery. Really, confession story writing is a wonderful way to express, via the typewriter, all those instinctive emotions that civilization forces you to control.

Remember to work in, somewhere in your story, a physical description of your characters, not forgetting that of the protagonist "I." Just as the confession reader wants emotion laid out where she can see it clearly, she wants to be able to visualize the people in her story without being forced to exercise her imagination.

The most salable length for a confession story is between five thousand and six thousand words, about a thousand words longer than a slick short story. This does not, however, mean that you can write sloppily just because you are allowed more leeway in wordage. A confession story must be as tightly knit as a slick story. Actually, when you start setting down all those thoughts that flit through your heroine's head, as well as the action, you'll find you don't have as many words as you thought you had, and every one has to count.

There are no abrupt transitions in a confession, no definite breaks where you pull your heroine out of one scene and plunk her down in the middle of another. The action flows along smoothly, and even if there is a gap of years between incidents, you have to build a bridge of words upon which the reader can cross without jumping and skipping around. The action in my story about Nora begins Monday and Tuesday. Nothing more happens until Friday, but I have to get Nora through the week somehow:

That night I went to sleep smiling happily, and for two days I walked around with my head wrapped in rosy clouds. Maybe it was the clouds that kept me from seeing what was going on at school. Maybe if I hadn't been so excited about dating Tim, I wouldn't have pushed aside the remembrance of the awful lies I had told. As far as I could see, it hadn't made any difference anyway, though. Wednesday and Thursday the kids flocked across the street into Uncle Willie's store after school as usual, though I went straight home. I'd been right, I thought. A story like that is like a headline in a newspaper, causing a lot of uproar today, and tomorrow completely forgotten. . . . Friday afternoon I was the first one home.

To sell, you must watch the trends in confession magazines as closely as in any group of magazines. Sometimes the confessions lean heavily on youth, specifically delinquency and sex problems. They like drama and excitement, leading up to sex scenes, treated naturally, not clinically but emotionally; or they may want stories dealing with teen-age problems caused by dating, dropping out of school, or too-early marriage, which they discourage. For a time, they were all going light on sex, but then the trend shifted, and sex reared its ugly head on page after page.

If, bearing all these minor points in mind, you can dream up a confused teen-age heroine torn by an emotional problem, have her solve it the wrong way, thereby bringing about some kind of tragedy, go through emotional hell, and see at least a faint light of hope for the future—I can practically guarantee you a letter beginning, "I am happy to inform you . . ." and a beautiful, beautiful check enclosed therein.

55

WRITING THE POLICE-ROUTINE NOVEL

By Dell Shannon

THE police-routine novel, which we are seeing more of these days than formerly, makes an emotional connection between the reader and the police, those overworked and much-hampered and harassed guardians of our public and private safety. When the evil forces of conspiracy, encouragement of lawlessness, are today making the police officer's job a thousand percent more difficult, it is salutary that somewhere, in some fashion, the upright forces of law and order should be shown as "the good guys"—which they largely are. I do not mean to say that we writers in this field should show police officers as winged and haloed, but as they really are—and these days the vast majority of police forces have quite high standards and requirements, and attract most excellent men and women.

The detective novel is the morality play of the twentieth century, and a really good detective novel is possibly the most difficult form of fiction to write. It is also the most challenging form. Most detective novels are somewhat shorter than the average "straight" novel, and it is always more difficult (and challenging) to compress adequate characterization, description, and plot-themes into, say, 65,000 words or so, whereas a novel of another kind may run to 100,000 words with no editorial demur. Moreover, of course, the average detective novel has a much more intricate plot than the average novel.

I say the detective novel is our new morality play because about 99% of them (all of them by implication) are on the side of the angels: the good guys, the law officers, always come out on top. In this amoral century, the detective novel fills a great need and serves a great purpose, humble though its form may be, looked down on often by our so-called Great Writers; detective novelists may regard themselves as the plebes among the genus scribblers, but they may turn out to have been the most influential spokesmen. For, while these days the detective novel is no longer crude black versus white, or content to deal in intricate plots minus any attempt at characterization—indeed, some of the most polished and stylistic writing is being done today by detective novelists—still, it deals primarily with basics: with truth versus lie, law and order versus anarchy, a moral code versus amorality.

I don't remember who first said that "everything has the defects of its advantages," but that is particularly applicable to the police-routine novel. But if the writer is handicapped in some ways—e.g., most of the time he must stay with his police officers, writing from their point of view—he also has a great many advantages of much practical help to him in working out the "mystery" part of the story. In the natural course of events, lab reports take time in arriving; witnesses may be difficult to locate or hostile to questioning (this kind of thing is often of great help in marking time, or skipping passages of time plausibly). In most police stations there is always apt to be something going on, so that in the process of constructing the story, perhaps creating interest even in a very simple plot, the writer has a choice of all sorts of "reader distractions"—other police cases besides the major one around which your book takes place; the brief intrusion of some amusing or eccentric or tragic character whom you come across on routine police business; incidents in the detectives' personal lives. These are among such reader distractions, and all offer the writer a useful amount of leeway in constructing a police-routine novel.

Obviously, the detective's personal life—which is not really a "distraction" at all, of course—is the most important. Even in such a relatively narrow field as the police-routine novel, there are many different kinds of novels—all the way from Ed McBain's *The Con Man,* for example, to Hillary Waugh's *Born Victim;* from the Gideon series by J. J. Marric, and Josephine Tey's *The Man in the Queue,* to Ngaio Marsh's urbane tales and Richard Lockridge's Captain Heimrich series. All of these writers have many devoted fans, and I doubt very much whether any of them eagerly reaches for the new McBain or the new Lockridge solely from interest in the plot. They're interested in what new is happening to their favorite sleuth —in seeing him in action once again. Here, of course, we find an overlapping of the "series" field and "police-routine"—but the latter is usually also the former.

Perhaps the greatest amount of reader interest is always in the detectives, not the plots (although the most fascinating police sleuth imaginable will not survive dull plots!). Thus the writer who uses the same detective for several novels has some solid part of the book already created (or sketched out in his mind), ready to be set down. Because of the carry-over reader interest in the detective as a person and the consequent necessity of introducing a certain amount of new material about him in each succeeding book, the writer automatically allots a certain amount of manuscript space to the detective—his foibles and interests and family and his life outside his professional job.

I am lucky that the particular police force I am writing about really happens to be the top force anywhere—the Los Angeles Police Department. I am always being asked, Is there a real counterpart of Lieutenant Mendoza down there at Central H.Q., or Sgt. Hackett, or any of the rest of the boys? I'm afraid I don't know. And I really don't know how these books get written, either. All I did, back there some while ago, was start to write a little suspense novel, and Lieutenant Mendoza rose up off the page, captured me alive, and refused to let me stop writing about him—egoist that he is. I try (always with the exception of the extraordinary Mendoza!) to show these men *as* ordinary men—with all the problems and domestic backgrounds of ordinary men. But also—writing these modern morality plays—I try to involve the reader *from the police viewpoint*. For I believe that this is no more than the duty of those of us who have taken sides, as it were, in the never-ending struggle between good and evil.

I cannot speak for other writers, but in getting involved as I am with four "sets" of series detectives, I have found that the series characters, once evolved and set in motion, tend to develop themselves in logical and sometimes surprising directions.

If it is no longer a convention in detective fiction that the detective must be a good deal larger than life—an eccentric and nearly-omniscient Holmes, or as full of personal foibles as Lord Peter Wimsey—still, he or they must be *enough* larger than life, enough distinctive as persons of definite and interesting individuality, to capture and retain the reader's continuing interest.

Perhaps the popular police sleuth of fiction can never be a *completely* accurate portrait of the police officer, for if the real police detective is—as in most cases he is—an honest, intelligent, trained, and hard-working officer, we are still not apt to find a real Lieutenant Mendoza or Roderick Alleyn or Charles Luke or Stephen Carella sitting at a desk at our local precinct house. It is the job of the writer in this field to convince the reader that he *might*.

Obviously, of course, the writer of police-routine novels must know a good deal about police routine. If he is writing about a real police force, or even a compositely-imagined one based upon real police forces in his county or city, he should know something about how the real forces work: police terms and locally used radio call-numbers for various offenses, criminal slang (which is commonly used also by police officers, of course), and something about police laboratory work. Almost any good library will offer various texts on these subjects. Offhand I might recommend *Crime Lab* by David Loth (Messner), *The Investigator's Handbook* by Arthur Liebers and Capt. Carl Vollmer of the New York City Police Department (Arco), *The Art of Detection* by Jacob Fisher (Sterling), and *Modern Criminal Investigation* by Harry Söderman and John J. O'Connell (Funk & Wagnalls).

Ogden Nash tells us, "If it's trite, it's right"—and up to a point that's so (why else do we call them clichés?). But there are a few rather tired old gimmicks in the field which the tyro should be warned about, as somewhat too hackneyed for warming over. The detective's-wife-who-wants-him-to-quit-the-cops-because-it's-dangerous has been met a bit too often; likewise the bright young modern sleuth resented by the less efficient superior; and (despite my own inadvertent possession of one, or vice versa) the independently wealthy officer dedicated to the job. And in thinking up plots for the boys in blue to grapple with, the ambitious writer need not, in fact *must* not, attempt to outdo John Dickson Carr. Few police cases in real life are very complex, and the aim in writing a police novel is (or should be) plausibility, above all else. There are many ways to inject some element of mystery into the fictional police case without either reaching into outer space or devising interesting but unlikely complexities. Ed McBain has set a good example here, as I like to think I may have done too, in a few books (perhaps notably *The Ace of Spades* and *Detective's Due*).

One of my own (admittedly this is a personal foible and maybe quibbling) objections to some police-routine novels set in large cities, is that the fictional action seems to imply that the sleuths are happily handed only one case at a time to solve. A husband is shot, a wife is strangled, a teen-ager is stabbed, and for the next two hundred pages the plainclothes sleuths concentrate on that alone—just as if, in a city of any size, all the drunk drivers, holdup experts, juvenile delinquents, belligerent brawlers, suicides and other murderers considerately postponed their own moments of truth until the central case of the story is wound up. This is scarcely plausible, if we are trying to give a reasonably accurate picture of real-life police routine. It is perfectly permissible and plausible, on the other hand, when the setting in question (as for instance in Waugh's *Born Victim*) is a small town where the "big case" is very rare; but it is a factor to keep in mind. The locale has a good deal to do with how a police-routine story unfolds.

Much of the creating I do—the sometimes agonized search for plots, for characters, for clue-gimmicks, and the like—is done while I sit staring vaguely into space thinking: "Suppose the corpse looked like one type of person and turned out to be another. . . ." Or, "If you had that kind of witness, then it would follow. . . ." And, "Of course that clue would mislead the cop to think. . . . But what about the wife? Surely she'd realize. . . ." Painfully, some vague notion of a central plot takes shape. I find that I must know just enough about a plot—*and not too much*—when I start to write the book, in order to leave plenty of room for the surprises. The surprises occur when quite unexpectedly some character comes alive—asserts himself, demanding a page or two more space than I had thought would be needed—and when sudden inspirations descend out of the blue, sometimes changing a major part of the story.

If the story is there, get to it and write it! For one thing, I feel that in completing a manuscript in the shortest possible time, the writer necessarily stays closer to the material. I have no quarrel with being methodical; once I have finally committed myself to a plot (however vague), I'm methodical, all right. I start each chapter, writing in longhand, at a quarter to ten each succeeding night, finish the chapter by about half-past twelve, and then type it out with a carbon next morning; so when I finish the thing I have a nice top copy. I evolved this method because typing is the hardest work I do. And from long experience, I have to get the thing written right the first time around; I seldom go back to change anything.

This is a very personal, individual sort of job, and every writer has his own peculiar way of going about it (some of them can be *very* peculiar). If the root of the matter is in you, you will find out how to write in your own way.

As with the writing of any other kind of fiction—or anything at all—only practice and experience will enable the writer to produce top manuscripts in the police-novel field. But suppose you do—you learn all the rules (some of which can conveniently be broken), you write a lot of unpublishable stuff, begin to find your own style, begin to sell, and suddenly one day, lo, you're in business with a beginning-to-be-popular series of police-routine novels. There's another important rule to keep in mind—and to practice, if you can.

One day after that you'll likely find yourself saying, "Oh, dear Lord, it's time I wrote another one to make that deadline. . . ." And the prospect is infinitely boring, you are sick and tired of this preposterous sleuth's mannerisms and attitudes, and try as you will, no vestige of an idea for a plot comes to you.

Right there you had better consciously recover enthusiasm! For if *you* are not interested in your sleuths, no one else will be. But if you are caught up in the fascinating police world as it exists today and really want to please your reader, once you've laboriously worked out a plot and have actually started writing (with many groans), all of a sudden the urgency and excitement flood back and the old fire blazes up again: "This is going to be fun, seeing how it works out in black and white. . . ."

Sergeant Lake thrust his head in the door and said tersely, "It's an APB, Lieutenant!"

—And you're off on another adventure.

Come to think, I'd better start thinking about the next Mendoza, and that's not too bad a beginning, just off the top of my mind. Only what's the All-Points-Bulletin *about?* And what kind of corpse will turn up? And where in the city jungle is it going to happen? And what kind of clues are we going to find? And—I'll have to start thinking about it!

56

ARTICLE WRITING TODAY

By William B. Hartley

When I left the executive editorship of *Redbook* to write, there was a strong suspicion among some of my friends that I had flipped my lid. Why would an editor with some nine magazines behind him suddenly decide to climb across the desk and occupy the visitors' chair?

Apparently everyone had forgotten that I had been writing professionally since I was a kid in prep school. I knew it could be done successfully. I had spent years studying the magazine field, analyzing markets, reading critically. I had produced literally thousands of ideas for magazine articles since 1936; and it seemed to me that I could develop a few for myself instead of feeding them to other writers.

So far, the record has been adequate. My wife and writing partner, Ellen Raphael Hartley, has helped me develop and sell more than four hundred major magazine articles in a period of twelve years. We also have six books to our credit—all sold out, thank goodness. I think we may have learned a good deal in the process.

One of the first things we learned was to concentrate on non-fiction. I have written a good deal of fiction, some good and much that I thought was bad, but my partner and I realize that most of our income depends on magazine article writing.

There are sound reasons for this. Some years ago, *Time* reported that seventy-five percent of all material in magazines was non-fiction. I'd be inclined to raise the figure a trifle. I suspect it is now closer to eighty percent.

It seems logical to go along with the odds. I'm no gambler—professional writers don't gamble—but I'd rather aim for eighty percent of a market instead of dreaming about the twenty percent. Moreover, non-fiction is often assigned. On the basis of a response to your query, you know that the editor is interested in your idea. Fiction, humor and poetry are never assigned—not unless you have a reputation so tremendous that money doesn't matter to begin with.

I've been teaching a series of courses in advanced writing at Miami-Dade College. Some forty percent of the students have sold articles to such magazines as *Good Housekeeping, Redbook, Pageant, Coronet, Saturday Review, Saga,* and perhaps a score of others. In one incredible semester, fifty-five percent of a class of seventeen sold at least one article to a major magazine. Four students have received non-fiction book contracts. On the basis of this statistical background, it's hard to duck the fact that non-fiction is the best area for the novice writer—or the professional writer.

We have found four areas in which most writers are weak. (Oddly enough, writing itself isn't one of them. Given a reasonable degree of intelligence and an ability to read published material, writing itself doesn't represent much of a problem.)

But one difficulty is finding ideas. Another is preparation of the query—something many writers don't understand. A third is interviewing techniques. The final one is irritating but essential—keeping good files.

Let's take ideas first. They exist by the hundreds; and with some seventy-five major magazines around, the ideas can be placed. First, however, the writer must read and analyze his magazines. *There is no way to avoid this—no convenient tip sheet that tells the writer exactly what a magazine wants.* We receive some sixty magazines a month, not counting loads of pamphlets, publicity releases, brochures, specialized publications, and so forth—and we read them all analytically.

It's important to read newspapers carefully. A buried, undeveloped item can lead to a major magazine article. My wife is an expert in spotting these items, sometimes with amusing results. I came back from our Miami, Florida, post office one morning with a puzzling letter from an editor. It said, in part, "Glad you're going out in the Everglades with the game warden to chase alligator poachers. But be careful. I understand they shoot back. I'd like to have the article in two weeks."

I said to Ellen, "Just what in the devil do you make out of this? I never told Dick I was going out to hunt alligator poachers!"

"I did," she said calmly. She had spotted a newspaper item on alligator poaching, and elected me to spend several nights racing around the Everglades in an airboat. So I did. The story turned out well.

The next best source is your public library. Many throughout the country have open stacks of specialized magazines. You can find ideas there, and you can also find them in the so-called vertical files of libraries that bother to maintain clip files.

Ten or twelve years ago, we never read publicity releases. As residents of Miami, Florida, we felt that anything from a release would damage our reputation. This was wrong. In recent years, we have produced ideas from university and civic sources that provide material from the entire country. Public information sources can be invaluable for ideas.

A further source of ideas is simply your own alertness. When we go out on assignment for *Redbook* or *Good Housekeeping* or some other major magazine, we watch for ideas. I don't necessarily recommend our way of doing things, but when we check into a motel or hotel one of us mixes a drink while the other gets every available regional newspaper and brochure. (We also get city maps.)

Then we sit down and study the material. There has been no time during countless assignments when we didn't emerge with a second or third idea (and assignment). I recall one coverage (among many) at Cape Kennedy when we magnified one idea into six sound articles.

One was a social study. Another was a report on the children of persons in the space program. Another was a story on risk workers who had been putting up the support towers from which missiles are fired. One other was just a fun story on entertainment in the Cape area. We also did two profiles—one on Dr. Kurt Debus, Director at the Cape, and another for *Cosmopolitan* on his wife as hostess for celebrities.

Ideas are not much of a problem if you take the time to think.

But the writer, beginner or professional, can't afford to read or think as other people do. He must develop a built-in awareness of story potential and then move the idea toward an appropriate publication.

We don't specialize. Many article writers have crippled themselves by specializing in health, education, science, or some other field. We learned long ago, for example, that you can do only so many articles in the education field. Since you're bound to run out of markets for education articles, it's wise to be able to move into many other fields—travel, the sciences, medicine, social affairs, entertainment, and so forth.

Let's assume that you have your idea. It's valid—most ideas are valid for *some* magazine—and now you're going to write a query. Let's also assume that you've done your homework up to the point of knowing where the idea might sell.

O.K. The first thing a competent writer does is to be sure he has sound preliminary research. This doesn't have to be a big deal; but he has to know what he's talking about. You can't kid good editors—most have been around for a long time and can spot incompetent research within the first five lines of a query.

The second job is to check on the use of the idea. Has another magazine covered the subject within the past five years? How was it handled? Who wrote the piece?

Your best source is the *Readers' Guide to Periodical Literature.* We maintain an index to magazines not listed in the *Guide,* but that becomes one devil of a job. You're safe enough with the *Guide.* You can say, at least, that you have checked.

It happens that there are times when a valid story has been covered before. There may be a new angle to support your story. But never conceal earlier coverage when you write a query to an editor. He has his own facilities for checking up; and if you fib or conceal information on past coverage, you've had it. For all time.

With preliminary research and a check on past use out of the way, write your query. Address it to a specific editor—usually the articles editor. Use his name. That means, at least, that you have read his magazine. About the worst thing you can do is to write: "The Editors."

Your query should be short and absolutely clear. We try to keep them down to a page. In a classic query, we once wrote Claire Safran of *Coronet* a one-line letter in which I said: "Dear Claire: How about "Sex and the Single Skier?" Claire, one of America's most beautiful and perceptive editors, wrote back to say: "Dear Bill: Yes."

I don't suggest that kind of brevity unless you know the editor well—and unless the editor knows you well. My wife, who is a master at query writing, has a very valuable trick. She'll write a query, perhaps on a complex subject, and simply say at the end: "If you wish additional information, we'll be glad to provide an expanded outline." Ray Robinson, formerly at *Good Housekeeping* and now editor of *Seventeen,* has asked for them, and so have editors at *The Reader's Digest.* Many others like this procedure. *But keep your original query short.*

Assuming that you have a favorable response to your query with a go-ahead from an editor, you'll probably have to do some interviewing for an article. This is what separates the men from the boys. Many novice writers, and even many professionals, don't know how to interview. Only the other day my wife (and collaborator) had to interview a prominent business figure during a convention. She knew how; and she suddenly discovered that fourteen reporters from all over the nation were busily and quietly reporting her interview. While they scribbled, she did the work.

We never go into an interview without many hours of preparation. If we can avoid it, we never go in blind. On a celebrity, or on almost anyone, we check out everything in the individual's background. We know when and where he was born, where he grew up, everything about him. We sometimes even know what he eats for breakfast.

Two illustrations. My wife phoned me in Boston one day to ask me to interview the late Senator Bartlett of Alaska in Washington, D. C. By the time I reached my hotel in Washington, I had a complete rundown on the senator waiting for me. The senator, a charming man, was astonished by how much I knew about him. My writing partner had given me the results of the homework she had done.

In another instance, I interviewed Julian Bond in Atlanta, Georgia. Before seeing him, I read everything on Bond that I could find. I even checked out Bond's father in *Who's Who*. Bond's secretary, a lovely girl, sent me an updated biography. By the time I flew into Atlanta, I may have known as much about Bond as he knew about himself.

We may use some tricks in preparation for interviews. I'll check where a man grew up, and then study the town guides. Thus we can say, "Weren't you just down the street from the old Civil War monument?"

The guy says, "My God, how did you know!" Or he says, "No, it was two blocks away." In any case, he's flattered, and you have your interview rolling along on the basis of strong identification.

And that's the real trick in getting the interview moving. Know your man, know as much as possible about his work, and try to be emphatic.

The only other basic rules for interviewing are to be on time and *to get out on time*. With most persons, you can usually arrange to come back later for additional material. We have had to do this only once in twelve years—a complex scientific piece—but we always suggest the possibility.

The writing of the article is straightforward enough. We use the old format of lead, statement of theme, body with abundant illustrations, and a wrap-up conclusion. There isn't anything very mysterious about this. It works today just as well as it always has; and there really isn't any other successful method.

I would, in addition, emphasize the need for keeping good files. We maintain files on perhaps one hundred subjects; the total number is probably far greater. If someone called us the day after an article of ours on widgets was published and asked the name of the chief widgetmaker in Idaho, we could probably have the answer in two minutes.

Files are invaluable to the working writer. About once a month, we spread out some forty feet of table in our home. Then, while my wife mutters a somewhat profane threnody of protest, we sort clippings for filing. We have a sign in the filing room (our garage) that reads: "Look here first."

It's good advice. The writer who doesn't maintain files isn't much of a writer. When you can reach into a file and find exactly the point you need to support an article, you've saved yourself hours of time. You may even produce better copy.

The non-fiction field is a worthwhile one. It isn't easier than fiction. In some respects, it probably is harder to master. But we feel, after much experience, that it's the best bet for a writer.

57

ARTICLES FROM EXPERIENCE

By Rollie Hochstein

When I began writing magazine humor—it cannot be more than eight years ago!—I had a miniature ax that wanted grinding. I was, at the time, the mother of two very young children and had recently taken up residence in the suburbs. I think I was having an Identity Crisis. In those days it was not enough to live impromptu: I felt somehow that I needed to know exactly who and what I was. Experience in both areas has taught me that labeling is utterly irrelevant; but at that raw, unsettled time of my life, it seemed crucial for me to decide whether I was a housewife who wrote or a writer who kept house.

The chief antagonists in my battle for identity were The Sociologists, who continually showed up in mass media authoritatively lumping The American Housewife into one great, sticky glob. The glob was oppressed by a male-dominated culture. The glob emasculated its husbands. The glob was spoiled, child-centered, over-educated, under-emancipated. There I was, having an Identity Crisis, and there they were—those snide Sociologists—trying to agglutinate my Identity!

My method of protest was to burn them with a searingly satirical article, which was to begin: "The sociologists make me feel about as individual as a stick of spaghetti." I really liked that phrase. I clearly remember the demonic relish with which I typed it. And I also remember the reluctance with which I crossed it out when, after many rereadings of the first draft, I had to admit that it didn't go. It was a "pre-peat" of the second sentence, and the second sentence was more germane to the rest of the piece. The final version—called "I'm a Method Wife"—was published in the old *Coronet*. It began: "Whenever I pick up a magazine or tune

335

in a panel discussion, some sociologist is lecturing me about my role in life."

Publication made me feel much better: with one shot, I'd got something off my chest and something into my bank account. It was a fine feeling, but the spaghetti lead was still a-dangle and I was avid to use it.

About four subsequent articles originated with the spaghetti simile and all four, by the final draft, started some other way. My grouch about the sociologists developed into other more general, less didactic, more amusing, less irritable subjects, and that first lead—for unity's sake—had to go. The spaghetti sentence, until now, never made print. It stopped mattering after a while: having authored several personal essays and other kinds of magazine articles, I no longer felt threatened by sociological de-personification. Nobody could make me feel like a stick of spaghetti, and I was far too busy with writing and housekeeping to ponder over pigeonholes.

That's a personal essay. I wrote it (a) for fun, (b) because the editor asked me for an article about technique, and (c) to use as an example and a basis for discussion.

The personal essay is a most satisfactory way to get published. It requires no research, no interviews, no scholarship, no legwork. All you need is an interesting (marketable) idea and the ability to present it pungently.

Editors like to buy personal essays and, I am told, they have a hard time finding usable ones. Mine fall into the category of "domestic humor," and about twenty of them have been published in half a dozen women's magazines and newspaper supplements. Last time I looked, *Good Housekeeping, McCall's* and *Redbook* were running regular reader-written first-person features. *The Reader's Digest* uses several such features under different names. *Playboy* and *Esquire* use satirical essays. *The Atlantic* and *Harper's* run first-person humor on occasion. Though they are often written by VIP's, personal essays often appear in *Vogue, Harper's Bazaar, Holiday* and *Mademoiselle.*

I've gone through some grand markets here, but I should tell you that my earliest anecdotal articles were published in diaper service giveaways, such as *Baby Talk* and *Baby Time*. I was delighted then, too, to get paid for saying something that I wanted to say. I think it's accurate to say that, while the category is special, the market for personal essays is broad.

What I'm writing here is a *how-to* article in the tone and shape of a personal essay. I'm using certain principles that I practice in my domestic humor pieces. The first two of the following principles are probably most applicable to the women's and family field; the last three, I believe, are compulsory in all personal essays.

1. *Reader identification.* When a reader says, "It sounds just like me," or he writes, "That's exactly the way it happens in my house," the writer has done a good job. In women's magazines, I deal with fairly typical domestic situations—the problems of party-giving, a slant on sibling rivalry—written from the viewpoint of a fairly typical housewife. In the first sentence or two, I set myself up for quick and easy identification. A lead might go something like this:

"When a woman has a six-room house to clean, three choosy children to feed and a hearty husband to keep in step with, she finds it hard to understand that the phrase 'Working Mother' means somebody else."

In all my domestic humor pieces, not one line has ever suggested that I do anything other than keep house, raise children, buy clothes, give parties, attend P.T.A. meetings and whatever else is common to all us housewives. Any clowning must be done gently and always with the implication that, though sometimes harassed, I manage to come out ahead, doing a good job at all these things. "Never make a jackass out of yourself," an editor warned me. That's reader identification.

Now notice, in the first paragraph of this article, how quickly I introduce myself as a writer. Right off it gives you and me something in common. The clause, "it cannot be more than eight years ago!" not only tells you that I'm experienced, but it also humanizes me. Time goes too quickly for me, too. You're interested because I'm a professional writer; perhaps you'll learn something from me. You're interested because I've confessed a human weakness and am less likely, after such a confession, to bore you with a lecture from a posture of distant superiority. I tell you that my ax was miniature: it's an indication that I am laughing at myself and that what I will say might be amusing as well as informative. The next sentence may have cost me some male readers, but I'm pretty sure that all writing mothers kept with it. In that opening, I achieved reader identification.

2. *Intimacy*. If you're going to sit down and share your opinions, observations and/or experiences in a humorous or poignant manner, you need a warm relationship with your reader. Back to my opening anecdote: we are introduced; we find we have something in common. I proceed to talk to you in a frank and friendly way. I even take you into my confidence: "I think I was having an Identity Crisis." I capitalize the fashionable phrase to make it humorous; I append "I think" to make it whimsical; but I am still opening myself up to you when I make that statement. It makes us friends and I continue, as a friend, to tell my story. I can talk about things that interest me on the assumption that they will interest you, too.

Here, we must stop to make a distinction. The *I* of the personal essay is not necessarily the author. The unity required in such an essay makes it almost impossible for the *I* to be completely the author; most of us are multifaceted, far too complex to be single-minded about very much. But once the *I* has set up a relationship with the reader, the author must not interfere with it. At no time should he double-cross his reader by contradicting or questioning himself. To keep his rapport, he should make his points directly. The *I* should say what he means and mean what he says. He should never slip out of his role by turning sarcastic, hostile or obscure to his reader. This is not schizophrenia; it's professionalism.

3. *Unity*. One theme is announced, developed, varied and concluded. One idea is proclaimed, clarified, illustrated, modulated and summed up. The personal essay requires disciplined thought and tight writing: no rambling, no diversions. The truth is that you and I are not really friends. You may have to listen to a friend's boring stories, but you can easily turn me off with a flick of the page. Therefore, every sentence that I write should compel you to read the next one. Every sentence must belong to the total structure; that's why my spaghetti line had to be eliminated.

Writers are not paid for expressing themselves. The personal essay, like all other professional writing, is meant to entertain, inform or influence—any one, two or three of these aims—and it must be interesting. What you want to say is your business. How you say it is the writing business. Where there are neither important facts nor famous figures to hold your reader's interest, your stated ideas have to do all the work. They have to be tightly organized; only in unity will they have the strength to hold readers.

4. *Style.* Style, like personal charm, is an elusive quality, highly individual. Writing style is a combination of language, tone and pace. More than any other kind of writing, except poetry, the personal essay needs to be meticulously worded and phrased, cut and polished. The words are selected by weight and color, as well as meaning. I fool around a lot with my essays, substituting bright words for drab words, trimming flabby sentences, lightening heavy ones, compressing, relaxing. I take pains to find the precisely right word; hardly a piece gets written without consultation of both dictionary and thesaurus.

The tone—droll, irate, bewildered, harassed, nostalgic—should be set in the lead and, with minor variations, sustained throughout the essay. If you are ear-minded, it is not difficult to set and maintain a tone. You hear it as you read over what you have written. If not, I suppose reading aloud will help. The tone of my early paragraphs here is, at least to my ears, one of sophisticated amusement. After the first five paragraphs, it turned earnest.

Pacing is almost impossible to pin down. If it's right, nobody except a professional notices it. Wrong, it's something like cold chicken soup: the fastidious are distressed and reject it; the apathetic suffer through with vague discomfort. Many writers get by without it. Non-paced novelists, I've noticed, are the ones called storytellers. In most nonfiction, pace counts as nothing more than an extra added attraction. I'm not even sure that it's compulsory in all essays, though it is a necessary component of the humorous essay. All this leads up to the fact that I can't tell you how to do it. Me, I've always listened a lot to such stand-up comedians as Alan King and Myron Cohen. While I haven't analyzed their timing, I think I've absorbed some of it. Also, I like to read metrical poetry: sonnets, ballades, rondos and villanelles; the footed works of everybody from Chaucer to Ciardi; the crisp couplets of Pope and the iambic pentameter of Shakespeare.

My own style, in fiction as in articles, is always under the influence of other writers. I'm particularly impressed by elegant English novelists: Jane Austen, Evelyn Waugh, Nancy Mitford; and American black humorists: Joseph Heller, Shirley Jackson, Bruce Jay Friedman. I would suggest that anybody who wants to develop a style should do a lot of selective reading and listening, always open to the tones and timings and words that please him.

5. *Arrogance.* The personal essayist has to be assuming. He has to assume that what he's saying is interesting enough to attract and hold a great many people he's never even met. Modesty and self-doubt have to be set aside as he develops, without reservation or qualification, the theme he arbitrarily chooses to present. Even if, like Leacock in "My Financial Career," you are posing as a bumbler, you can't take a clause to apologize or explain yourself; you must be the complete bumbler, arrogant in your ineptitude. You have to take on an authority that—at least in the beginning of your career—you are hardly likely to feel. What else is there to do? You're the author of the piece, and it's all you—or a projection of you. You have to be authoritative.

It takes a certain amount of arrogance plus ardor to get a first personal essay written and off to the editors. A middle-class, public school-educated American is not ordinarily brought up to believe that he is anything special. On the contrary, he (and particularly if he is a woman) is usually led to believe in the virtues of inconspicuousness, humility and keeping his mouth shut. Writing in the first person is not a humble thing to do. It's rather brash, is it not?, to expect to publish a piece of writing based on nothing more than your opinions, experiences and observations. "Why me?" is the question you may ask yourself.

The answer is: "Why not?" Actually, none of us is a stick of spaghetti, and nobody else in the world sees things, feels things and can express things exactly as you do. Nobody else can write the personal essay that you can write.

58

PLOTTING THE BIOGRAPHY

By Catherine Drinker Bowen

A NOVELIST informed me, with magisterial assurance, that compared to fiction writers, biographers have an easy time. Their plot is ready to hand before they even begin to write. When I asked, what plot, exactly?—the novelist said it was self-evident: "Birth, education, marriage, career, death."

Surely the novelist was mistaken, and his five neat sequential nouns indicated a chronology rather than a plot? Consider Monday, for instance, which has its beginning and ending; the sun rises and sets. One breakfasts, works, lunches, takes a walk, goes out to dinner perhaps, comes home, goes to bed. Yet if a writer wishes to engage a reader's attention concerning Monday, his hero must that day meet with trouble, face an obstacle, a danger, a grief, and conquer it. Or if the writer prefers tragedy, then Monday's obstacle can be conqueror, and draw a reader's tears.

The book trade calls it conflict, suspense. By whatever name, it is a quality vital to biography as to fiction. The difference is that the novelist invents his plot, whereas the biographer finds it in history, in actual fact as indicated by the given material, by events as they unfold, and more particularly by the character of the biographical subject, the hero. Maurois has something to say about this. The biographer, he believes, "has greater difficulty than the novelist in composition. But he has one compensation: to be compelled to take over the form of a work ready-made is almost always a source of power to the artist. It is painful, it makes his task more difficult; but at the same time it is from this struggle between the mind and the matter that resists it that a masterpiece is born."

Graduate students of history, having labored for years on a thesis, often feel ambitious to see their work in print. Approaching some available professional writer they inquire how their production can be fixed up for trade publication. "Popular presentation," they have learned to call it.

The professional writer is wary of such assignments. A biography must be planned *before* it is written, not afterward. Yet as an example, the graduate student's problem can be worth careful inspection because it is actually the same problem the seasoned biographer confronts in the early stages of his books. The material is gathered, now what is to be done with it? These pages—this thesis—dry, correct, with serried footnotes, can be extremely useful as reference on a library shelf. And it covers the ground, certainly. But it moves on mechanized wooden legs, without head or guts, humor or humanity. Yet humor and humanity cannot be stuffed into a book at later convenience but must grow from the narrative as it progresses, springing hot and hearty from the writer's own bias and involvement as he sits and thinks about his subject.

Ask such a graduate student what his thesis, his book, is about. Not merely the name and life schedule of the hero, but what the book is *about*, what is its plot, what carries it along? For answer you will be given a chronology, a train of events. Let us say the biographical subject is an agent for Indian affairs on the American frontier, *circa* 1775. Captain B—— has fought the French, he knows Indians; he is prospering and minding his business, when along comes the Revolution—and he chooses the Tory side!

Divided loyalty! Here is a theme, here is plot enough to carry to the end. For what is biography but the story of a man or woman in conflict with himself? Moreover the subject is fresh; the Tory in our Revolution has not been explored in depth, as the professors say. Yet—take the manuscript in hand and what is presented on the page? Battles, boundary lines, Indian raids, with actual tallies of the scalped and the dead. Footnotes, chapter notes, bibliography. Everything neat, verified—and bloodless even though the scene itself is soaked in blood.

But the man who wrote the thesis is not dry. When he talks about his hero-captain he is entertaining, he is funny; what he says concerning his characters is quick and sharp. One knows of course that such qualities, transferred to the page, are of no help toward graduate honors. Yet this young man has not come to discuss academic degrees. Ask him then, if his hero suffered, if the captain doubted his position and his choice, felt sadness at the loss of old friends among the Americans.

For answer the young man begins to explain what it meant to be a loyalist in the Revolution, and what his captain's soul will lose or gain thereby. Suddenly his very word is gold. Write it down! the professional says. Write it on the back of an envelope, quick before it vanishes. . . .

There is, one assumes, proof of the captain's struggle, quotations available in letters, diaries, if not from the captain's hand then from someone in a like position. Did the captain have a family and did they share his views and loyalties? More legwork, as the reporters call it, was desirable, but legwork with a different end in view. Canadian libraries might yield a harvest. It would be worthwhile to visit repositories in Ottawa, Detroit. . . . The thesis is filled moreover with names of Indian tribes, Indian chiefs with whom the hero had close dealings. Is there some indirect way of repeating what they said? We must not have fictional conversation around the council fire. But treaties were made with the French, the English. The language is available, it is written down.

The young man had been excellently trained in evaluating evidence. He could spot a bad source, a dubious statement across a library room. In short, he had completed one phase of a biographer's training. But if he aimed beyond the classroom, if he wished the world to read about his hero, his Tory captain, he would find the next phase of training equally rigorous. He must move into the realm of feeling, of men and women and their emotions. Through historical evidence, fortified and animated by his own experience of living, he must pick these people up bodily from his dry pages, turn them over in his hand, stare at them long and searchingly.

And there is a further task, a pleasant one to my way of thinking. It concerns scene. What about terrain, one asks the writer—the rivers, the hills? This is an outdoor story. We must see the hero's country; a Tory captain does not float in air. In the thesis as it stands there is no field or forest or blockhouse or cellar that one can remember or describe after reading—let alone a face, a voice the figure of a man. The words on the page should be evocative, call up colors, sounds, sights, smells.

This of course is reckless counsel. Not everybody can write a scene or describe a man's face. Not everyone has eyes to see a field, a tree in life, let alone set it down in writing. There is no sense pretending that technique will take the place of talent. Yet here again, practice counts, in perception as in writing. Moreover, at certain stages heroic measures are called for, strong medicine to clear the writer's vision, turn him about to face another direction. He must free himself from his strict specific training, which for its purpose was excellent. Like the student who has mastered the fundamentals of grammar he is prepared, he is ready. Of what he has learned nothing will be forgotten, neglected or distorted. But the time has come to make the material his own, transform it into words that live, that pulse, communicate.

Once the beginner has his plot in mind—his central animating theme—he will do well to think over the chronology of the hero's life, the big things that happened. These he can note down in scenes, as for a stage play but with the dates, keeping always in mind the direction his work is heading, the climax which by now must surely have declared itself. This exercise might fill three or four pages of 8½″ x 11″ paper. Then he can begin to write his book, working from scene to scene, as the composer of a symphony heads for the next theme, whether a secondary subject or a development.

So simplified a program will not of course make a book. But it is a step taken, a map, a way out of the wilderness of research into a final choice of incident. It leads from the library into life, narration, drama, plot. An outline need not, however, be a rigid plan that must be followed letter for letter. Indeed, I have seen biographical outlines so complete, so detailed and heavy they bade fair to crush the story, deceiving the author into thinking he had written his book. What one advocates is a loose chronology which reads vividly simply because the incidents, the characters or occasional quotations from hero or heroine are themselves vivid. For example, Queen Elizabeth, as a young woman, "told the French Ambassador de Foix that whenever she thought about marriage, she felt as if someone were tearing the heart out of her bosom." Again, to her ladies, on hearing that Mary Stuart had borne a child: "The Queen of Scots is lighter of a fair son, and I am but a barren stock."

When Elizabeth Jenkins [author of *Elizabeth the Great*] came across those words in the records, surely her mind leaped forward, imagining the time and place where she could set them in her book.

It is easier to tell someone how than to do it oneself. E. M. Forster is a master of his material, a master of narrative. Yet even he confesses that "people will not realize how one flounders about."

Floundering about is endemic to writers, a phase we all go through at the outset of a work. Psychiatrists say this initial block is intrinsic to the creative process, a forcing of the writer deeper into himself. The procedure can be called by other names: thinking, brooding, dreaming. I have heard it said that most authors sit down at their typewriters too soon. Before words go on paper the biographer must put his notes away, out of sight, while he sits and thinks, or walks about and thinks—a painful exercise which may consume days or weeks while the paper remains blank in the typewriter.

This thinking may well turn upon the business of what the biography is about: its theme, the axis upon which its wheels may turn. Does the plot concern a happy man, a life fulfilled? It has been said that happiness has no story—which in itself is a challenge and a half. The biographer must write very well indeed to make his happy hero come alive; he has an extra dimension to reach, an eighth hurdle to surmount. Happiness has many definitions. Grief is part of living: *Sturm und Drang* does not necessarily mean unhappiness or unfulfillment.

But how variously lives are arranged! The biographer may choose a hero who began in poverty and climbed, or one born into luxury and place, thence falling or maintaining his position as circumstance and his spirit dictate. And how much objective history will these projected chapters include? It is a vital question. Every biography is of course a "life and times." Yet there are degrees and proportions. The life of a statesman is three-quarters "times"; the life of a painter or composer of music may show a very different mixture and balance. A biographer of Justice Holmes told me solemnly that his ambition was to "show Holmes's influence on the stream of American intellectual consciousness." But how could one aim at such an effort or be sure this intellectual stream existed? Will such a plot carry, is it feasible? A biographer can be too high-toned for his own good.

In the biographies I most admire, the story moves forward implacably, inevitably. The reader *believes* in Mary Tudor, Elizabeth the Great, Lord Melbourne, George Sand (*Lélia*), Balzac (*Prometheus*). The reader cannot but believe. There are no awkward hurdles, no holes to fall through. Nothing is stretched too far or condensed to the point of collapse. The narrative—the plot—contains us, we know where we are going.

59

THE MAGIC SENTENCE

By Barbara Lang

CREATIVE writing is not simple. It never was, and there is no reason to expect it to become so in an increasingly complex world with increasingly complex ideas to convey. Perspectives are widening, outlooks are more sophisticated. In the face of all this, the challenge to gain and hold the reader's attention increases to seemingly forbidding proportions. Yet there is a helpful element in writing technique that is so simple it may be overlooked. For me, this is "the magic sentence."

The whole point of the magic sentence is to lead the reader onward. In practice, this may take the form of a tantalizing suggestion that useful information is forthcoming or that a provocative insight will be revealed; or that, through the writer's individuality of approach and style, a truly new reading adventure lies ahead. These magic sentences are *promises,* and the good writer keeps them.

In a short, straightforward article, there may be only one such sentence. It usually appears near the beginning of the manuscript and frequently relates to the focus or "hook" of the article. Take for example a piece I wrote for the *Ladies' Home Journal* on theater tickets. Title: "Tickets, Tickets—Who's Got the Tickets?" Opening paragraph:

A hit show, by definition, is something you can't get tickets for. Or can you?

Then followed a description of how theater tickets are distributed, how some are sold before they are even printed, of the roles played by owners of house seats, theater parties, theater clubs and agents, and of the box-office and mail-order procedures. My goal was to arrive at sound advice for the guidance of the individual playgoer. But at the start, the reader kept going, led onward (I trust) by the promise of those three magic words, "Or can you?"

Another guise in which the magic sentence appears is that of one or more deliberately provocative questions, again with the implied promise of—and the writer's sacred obligation to provide—answers.

An article I wrote on tipping, also for the *Ladies' Home Journal*, held some automatic albeit far from joyful interest for most women facing Christmas tipping decisions. The problem was to make the reader aware that there was human interest in the subject and to dramatize the point that this article wasn't merely a dry listing of "to whom and how much at Christmas." Since tipping is not the best-loved of our social customs, I felt the article would gain if it opened in a sympathetic and hopefully entertaining manner. Here are the first two paragraphs of "Jingle All the Way," with the key magic questions asked at the end of the second paragraph:

> The greeting card is signed, *With Love and Kisses from your Newsboys Louis, Tony, Petey, Benny, Sammy and Mike.* It is a small card, the missive from these mystery children who materialize annually in early December; but it commands your attention because it clearly signifies the start of the Season—the Tipping Season.
>
> While most people dislike tipping, they recognize it as part of "the system." And whether they give out of social pressure, holiday cheer, to reward good service or because they are aware that many of the people who serve them count on Christmas tips as part of their income, tip they do. And while tipping is a highly personal matter, one often ponders this twilight zone of payment with curious thoughts of what is really expected. What are other people tipping? When, if ever, are presents more appropriate than cash? And is there, anywhere, the individual with courage to deny a tip to someone who has roundly not earned it?

I have always been especially interested in that last question and felt that it in particular might excite the reader's curiosity.

In longer, more complex articles, every time there is a change of direction or a change of pace, every time a new subject is introduced, the writer may profitably invoke another magic sentence to lead the reader still farther onward. These sentences are an integral part of the structure of a piece. As the writer builds his article with major blocks of material, these sentences cement the blocks together. Each one is virtually saying: "Go on; there's more to come and it's fascinating and/or important."

In an article I did some time ago for the *Ladies' Home Journal*'s "How America Lives" series (the subject was teen-age marriage), one can find those interlocking sentences, often at the beginning of paragraphs and sections. Here are three:

And yet Dee Dee Floyd . . . was not the type whose friends thought she would marry young.

All the time, without realizing it, the couple was working to break the ties that still bound them to their parents.

What if Dee Dee had to live the last two years over again?

Each carries the reader and the article onward for a bit; thus when impetus threatens to wane, fresh energy is added.

This type of magic sentence involves the matter of pace, which is, I think, knowing when to change the subject. After the change, interest must be renewed. These are, in that sense, *subordinate* magic sentences.

Let us return to the *primary* magic sentence. Even—and possibly especially—in a lengthy, complex article, there is a need to compel, then direct the reader's interest. This demands the writer's best efforts to produce a beautifully turned, provocative magic sentence. It must say something about the *whole* subject and make the reader take the first firm step into the article. It is wider in scope than the ones quoted immediately above; it arises from the writer's being absolutely sure of (and articulate about) his focus and granting his reader a glimpse of its fascination; it creates suspense and it promises revelations; and above all, it beckons invitingly near the beginning of the manuscript. Needless to say, it therefore benefits directly from a strong, dramatic opening that will capture the reader's attention and hold it until this sentence (or two) wings him on his way.

For an example, I'll go back to the beginning of the article mentioned above. The title was "The Teen-Age Marriage: Love Finds a Way." A kind of romance-fraught-with-problems feeling, plus a dash of happy-ending promise. All in all, a subject of potential interest to *Journal* readers, although hardly unique or necessarily dramatic. Here are the first two paragraphs:

Dee Dee Floyd, a vivacious, petite brunette, was 17 and a senior at Headland High School in an Atlanta suburb. John Kortes, tall, blond and reserved, was 19 and a sophomore at the University of Georgia. Both looked even younger, and they had been dating for only two months. But they were in love, and on January 3, 1964, they eloped. Their friends were surprised. Their parents were shocked. Dee Dee and John were ecstatic. They still are.

"We just couldn't wait," says Dee Dee with the excitement of a small girl.

The Korteses' best friends, the Greens, agree that Dee Dee and John did the right thing. Randy Green, who is also a teen-age husband, puts it like this: "You always think when someone quits school to get married it must be because of pregnancy. But sometimes it's just because they really want to be together, the way it was with Dee Dee and John."

Now the first part of the title tells the reader that this article will have relevance to the general subject of teen-age marriage. The first paragraph develops an immediate focus on Dee Dee and John in a compact, almost fictional narrative style. The second paragraph expands on their excitement and hopes; it also reassures the reader (consider the market) that this was not a "marriage of necessity."

And now it's high time to tell the reader just what it is that's going to keep him (or, in that magazine, her) interested in those two particular young people. Here it comes:

And John is, perhaps, the most pleased of all. "From our first date we knew we were going to get married," he says. It is one of many beliefs that John finds hard to explain and adults will find hard to understand. And yet it is no mystery. *Like most teen-age couples, John and Dee Dee decided, in effect, to do much of their growing up while they are married, not before. And so it is really not surprising that their thoughts and actions keep ranging from the remarkably innocent to the model of maturity.*

The last two sentences (italics added), promising the surprises and contrasts that were already written into the article, are the pivotal ones—and they were my editor's addition. I only had the good sense to recognize what they did and the good fortune to mumble something about their being magic sentences, thereby giving a name to an element of technique I had sometimes employed instinctively and have since benefited from using consciously in the articles I write.

I have, of course, used the magic-sentence approach in writing this piece. You might be interested to seek it out. You might even want to borrow it. You're more than welcome!

60

THE HISTORIAN AS ARTIST

By Barbara W. Tuchman

I would like to share some good news with you. I recently came
back from skiing at Aspen in a party of three, which means that one
was always odd man when riding in the double-chair ski lift. On one
such occasion I rode with an advertising man from Chicago, who told
me he was in charge of all copy for his firm in all media: TV, radio,
and the printed word. On the strength of this he assured me—and I
quote—that "Writing is coming back. *Books* are coming back." I
cannot tell you how pleased I was, and I knew you would be too.

Now that we know the future is safe for writing, I want to talk
about a particular kind of writer—the Historian—not just as historian but as artist, that is, as a creative writer on the same level as the
poet or novelist. What follows will sound less immodest if you will
take the word "artist" in the way I think of it, not as a form of praise
but as a category, like clerk or laborer or actor.

Why is it generally assumed that in writing, the creative process is
the exclusive property of poets and novelists? I would like to suggest
that the thought applied by the historian to his subject matter can be
no less creative than the imagination applied by the novelist to his.
And when it comes to writing as an art, is Gibbon necessarily less of
an artist in words than, let us say, Dickens? Or Winston Churchill
less so than William Faulkner or Sinclair Lewis?

George Macaulay Trevelyan, the late professor of modern history
at Cambridge and the great champion of literary as opposed to scientific history, said in a famous essay on his muse that ideally history
should be the exposition of facts about the past, "in their full emotional and intellectual value to a wide public by the difficult art of
literature." Notice "wide public." Trevelyan always stressed writing

for the general reader as opposed to writing just for fellow scholars because he knew that when you write for the public you have to be *clear* and you have to be *interesting* and these are the two criteria which make for good writing. He had no patience with the idea that only imaginative writing is literature. Novels, he pointed out, if they are bad enough, are *not* literature, while even pamphlets, if they are good enough, and he cites those of Milton, Swift and Burke, are.

"The difficult art of literature" is well said. Trevelyan was a dirt farmer in that field and he knew. I may as well admit now that I have always *felt* like an artist when I work on a book but I did not think I ought to say so until someone else said it first (it's like waiting to be proposed to). Now that an occasional reviewer here and there has made the observation, I feel I can talk about it. I see no reason why the word should always be confined to writers of fiction and poetry while the rest of us are lumped together under that despicable term, Non-Fiction—as if we were some sort of remainder. I do not feel like a Non-something; I feel quite specific. I wish I could think of a name in place of Non-Fiction. In the hope of finding an antonym I looked up "Fiction" in Webster and found it defined as opposed to "Fact, Truth and Reality." I thought for a while of adopting FTR, standing for Fact, Truth and Reality, as my new term but it is awkward to use. "Writers of Reality" is the nearest I can come to what I want, but I cannot very well call us Realtors because that has been pre-empted—although as a matter of fact I would like to. "Real Estate," when you come to think of it, is a very fine phrase and it is exactly the sphere that writers of Non-Fiction deal in: the real estate of man, of human conduct. I wish we could get it back from the dealers in land. Then the categories could be poets, novelists and realtors.

I should add that I do not entirely go along with Webster's statement that fiction is what is distinct from Fact, Truth, and Reality because good fiction (as opposed to junk), even if it has nothing to do with fact, is usually *founded* on reality and *perceives* truth— often more truly than some historians. It is exactly this quality of perceiving truth, extracting it from irrelevant surroundings and conveying it to the reader or the viewer of a picture, which distinguishes the artist. What the artist has is an *extra* vision and an *inner* vision plus the ability to express it. He supplies a view or an understanding that the viewer or reader would not have gained without the aid of the artist's creative vision. This is what Monet does in one of those shimmering rivers reflecting poplars or El Greco in the stormy sky over Toledo or Jane Austen compressing a whole society into Mr. and Mrs. Bennet, Lady Catherine and Mr. Darcy. We realtors, at least those of us who aspire to write literature, do the same thing. Lytton Strachey perceived a truth about Queen Victoria and the Eminent Victorians and the style and form which he created to portray what he saw have changed the whole approach to biography since his time. Rachel Carson perceived truth about the seashore or the silent spring, Thoreau about Walden Pond, De Tocqueville and James Bryce about America, Gibbon about Rome, Karl Marx about Capital, Carlyle about the French Revolution. Their work is based on study, observation and accumulation of fact, but does anyone suppose that these realtors did not make use of their imagination? Certainly they did; that is what gave them their extra vision.

Art Buchwald, by the way who started out as a comedian but now frequently produces genuinely creative political satire, is a realtor who has made himself a creative writer by exercising his imagination upon observed fact. It may not be satire in the grand manner on the human condition like *Candide* or *Gulliver's Travels,* but it has that quality of being both perceptive and suggestive which seems to me the mark of the artist.

Trevelyan wrote that the best historian was he who combined knowledge of the evidence with "the largest intellect, the warmest human sympathy and the highest imaginative powers." The last two qualities are no different from those necessary to a great novelist. They are a necessary part of the historian's equipment because they are what enable him to *understand* the evidence he has accumulated. Imagination stretches the available facts—extrapolates from them, so to speak, thus often supplying an otherwise missing answer to the "Why" of what happened. Sympathy is essential to the understanding of motive. Without sympathy and imagination the historian can copy figures from a tax roll forever—or count them by computer as they do nowadays—but he will never know or be able to portray the people who paid the taxes.

When I say that I felt like an artist, I mean that I constantly found myself perceiving a historical truth (at least, what *I* believe to be truth) by seizing upon a suggestion; then, after careful gathering of the evidence, conveying it in turn to the reader, not by piling up a list of all the facts I have collected, which is the way of the Ph.D., but by exercising the artist's privilege of selection.

Actually the idea for my book *The Proud Tower* evolved in that way from a number of such perceptions. The initial impulse was a line I quoted in *The Guns of August* from Belgian Socialist poet Émile Verhaeren. After a lifetime as a pacifist dedicated to the social and humanitarian ideals which were then believed to erase national lines, he found himself filled with hatred of the German invader and disillusioned in all he had formerly believed in. And yet, as he wrote, "Since it seems to me that in this state of hatred my conscience becomes diminished, I dedicate these pages, with emotion, to the man I used to be."

I was deeply moved by this. His confession seemed to me so poignant, so evocative of a time and mood that it decided me to try to retrieve that vanished era. It led to the last chapter in *The Proud Tower* on the Socialists, to Jaures as the authentic Socialist, to his prophetic lines, "I summon the living, I mourn the dead," and to his assassination as the perfect and dramatically right ending for the book, both chronologically and symbolically.

Then there was Lord Ribblesdale. I owe this to *American Heritage* which, back in October, 1961, published a piece on Sargent and Whistler with a handsome reproduction of the Ribblesdale portrait. In Sargent's painting Ribblesdale stared out upon the world, as I later wrote in *The Proud Tower,* "in an attitude of such natural arrogance, elegance and self-confidence as no man of a later day would ever achieve." Here too was a vanished era which came together in my mind with Verhaeren's line, "the man I used to be"—like two globules of mercury making a single mass. From that came the idea for the book. Ribblesdale, of course, was the suggestion that ultimately became the opening chapter on The Patricians. This is the reward of the artist's eye: it always leads you to the right thing.

There are, I think, three parts to the artist's creative process: the extra vision with which he perceives a truth and conveys it by suggestion. Second, medium of expression: language for writers, paint for painters, clay or stone for sculptors, sound expressed in musical notes for composers. Third, design or structure.

When it comes to language, nothing is more satisfying than to write a good sentence. It is no fun to write lumpishly, dully, in prose the reader must plod through like wet sand. But it is a pleasure to achieve, if one can, a clear running prose that is simple yet full of surprises. This does not just happen. It requires skill, hard work, a good ear and continued practice, as much as it takes Heifetz to play the violin. The goals, as I have said, are clarity, interest and aesthetic pleasure. On the first of these I would like to quote Macaulay, a great historian and great writer, who once wrote to a friend, "How little the all-important art of making meaning pellucid is studied now! Hardly any popular writer except myself thinks of it."

As to structure, my own form is narrative, which is not every historian's, I may say—indeed it is rather looked down on now by the advanced academics, but I don't mind because no one could possibly persuade me that telling a story is not the most desirable thing a writer can do. Narrative history is neither as simple nor as straightforward as it might seem. It requires arrangement, composition, planning just like a painting—Rembrandt's "Night Watch," for example. He did not fit in all those figures with certain ones in the foreground and others in back and the light falling on them just so, without much trial and error and innumerable preliminary sketches. It is the same with writing history. Although the finished result may look to the reader natural and inevitable, as if the author had only to follow the sequence of events, it is not that easy. Sometimes events at different places are simultaneous in time—as in the case of the battles on the Eastern and Western fronts and at sea in *The Guns of August*. This presents a problem in sequence.

In *The Proud Tower*, for instance, the two English chapters were originally conceived as one. I divided them and placed them well apart in order to give a feeling of progression, of forward chronological movement to the book. The story of the Anarchists with their ideas and deeds set in counterpoint to each other was a problem in arrangement. The middle section of The Hague chapter on the Paris Exposition of 1900 was originally planned as a separate short centerpiece, marking the turn of the century, until I saw it as a bridge linking the two Hague Conferences, where it now seems to belong.

Structure is chiefly a problem of selection, an agonizing business because there is always more material than one can use or fit into a story. The problem is how and what to select out of all that happened without, by the very process of selection, giving an over- or under-emphasis which violates truth. One cannot put in everything: the result would be a shapeless mass. The job is to achieve a narrative line without straying from the essential facts or leaving out any essential facts and without twisting the material to suit one's convenience. To do so is a temptation but if you do it with history you invariably get tripped up by later events. I have been tempted once or twice and I know.

The most difficult task of selection I had was in the Dreyfus chapter. To try to skip over the facts about the *bordereau* and the handwriting and the forgeries—all the elements of the Case as distinct from the Affair—in order to focus instead on what happened to France and yet at the same time give the reader enough background information to enable him to understand what was going on, nearly drove me to despair. My writing slowed down to a trickle until one dreadful day when I went to my study at 9 and stayed there all day in a blank coma until 5 when I emerged without having written a single word. Anyone who is a writer will know how frightening that was. You feel you have come to the end of your powers; you will not finish the book; you may never write again.

There are other problems of structure peculiar to writing history: how to explain background and yet keep the story moving; how to create suspense and sustain interest in a narrative of which the outcome (like who won the war) is, to put it mildly, known. If anyone thinks this does not take creative writing, I can only say, try it.

61

SKELETON AT THE FEAST

By Evelyn Hawes

The phrase "skeleton at the feast" is in the dictionary. The meaning is given as "something that serves to bring unpleasant memories or prospects to the minds of pleasure-seekers."

"Skeleton" is further defined as "supporting structure."

The skeleton for me is research, and I am haunted by it. I should enjoy being a pure pleasure-seeker; I want to write what I like, as I like. In a fashion, I do. Writing what I like is the feast. But there is always the skeleton, and I often wish when I read the manuscript of a beginning writer that he would see the skeleton as I do. Actually, both non-fiction and fiction must be true. Non-fiction is true to what actually happened; fiction is true to life. In either case, the supporting structure, its padding limited by the desires and talents of the author, had better be properly formed or a collapse is inevitable.

I once saw a taxidermist re-create a raccoon. Pulling gently, he stretched the hide over the armature, and presently I could see the wire and *papier-mâché* and pelt and bones were developing into a reasonable facsimile of an animal. I shall always remember the process of pulling and tugging until the framework was concealed.

Furthermore, I remember my skeleton-haunt so well that I checked just now with a friend at the Museum of Natural Science to be sure I had used the proper terms in telling about mounting (not stuffing!) an animal. It is not necessary to use technical terms, but there should be no error in recounting a well-known process.

Most writers see at once that non-fiction requires research. One begins with facts and hopes to weave the words into an attractive fabric that will catch the reader's eye and hold his interest. Conclusions are a logical outcome of the basic premise. We realize that the conclusion, like the body of the structure, should build on or fill out the skeletal foundation. We must resist mixing fact with fiction in non-fiction writing, although one is severely tempted, at times.

For example, I wrote a documentary book *Proud Vision, The History of The Buffalo General Hospital: The First Hundred Years.* Chapter Two begins:

A strong gale swept across Buffalo on Wednesday evening, November 21, 1855, rattling the shutters of the houses, tearing at the street signs. The yellow glow of the gas street lights on Main Street was diminished, obscured at times, by the driving sleet and rain.

Two sentences. In order to write the first sentence (1) I looked up what *day* of the week it was on November 21, 1855. (2) I wrote the local weather bureau to find out what the weather was. The reply stated there were no records for the year 1855. (3) Sent a letter to the United States Weather Bureau in Washington, D. C. I was told that there had been a report to the Surgeon-General's office of the United States Army, which indicated the weather during a few months in that year. The weather reporter, Elias O. Salisbury, was then (in 1855) at the Poinsett Barracks in Buffalo. (4) I requested a transcript of Mr. Salisbury's report from the United States Department of Commerce, National Weather Records Center, Arcade Building, Asheville, North Carolina.

After studying Mr. Salisbury's report (what was he like, I wonder?), I was able to write one sentence. "A strong gale swept across Buffalo, etc."

What about the second sentence? I went to the Iroquois Gas Company offices in Buffalo. The records of an earlier company were available there. Yes, there were gas street lights on Main Street near Number 7 South Division, where a meeting was held concerning the founding of The Buffalo General Hospital in November, 1855.

I had written two sentences and had spent hours in research, as well as days of waiting for replies to my letters.

Is fiction as demanding as non-fiction in so far as research is concerned? Yes, it is. That is, the facts must be correct. Heaven help the writer who makes a mistake in geography, medicine, law or other fields where exactness is required, even though the work is fictional. Heaven will have to help the writer. The reader and critic certainly will not. Careful checking is preferable by far to indignant letters received by an author when he makes a mistake about the well-known, well-established facts of a situation. And when an author writes a story that is patently impossible, the reader will dismiss the story. He will not believe it. Good fiction must seem true. To err may be human, but it is small comfort to the author to recall the maxim when faced with the waspish reactions of irritated readers.

There are writers who live in the hope that the editor will correct an error. Usually the editor does so, but he is not infallible. It is a mark of a professional writer, moreover, to leave as little as possible to chance. He does his research as he writes, or before he begins writing. Only the amateur attempts to move a lake, a road, or a city in order to "fit the story." I know a bacteriologist who walked out of a motion picture because the microscope of the filmed bacteriologist was so improperly adjusted that the actor could not possibly have examined the slide. I have seen lawyers stalk out of poorly researched courtroom plays or, worse, burst into laughter at a tender moment in the drama on stage. I heard a hospital physician-administrator declare furiously that he would like to get his hands on a certain TV doctor-personality.

"He'd never last in *this* hospital," the director stormed, "nor in any other good hospital. Just one of his tricks, and OUT!"

I once used the term "War Department" in a short story. The editor wrote on the galley proof, "Is this extant?" I called a Navy friend and not satisfied with his answer, checked with several libraries. Of course, I should have made those phone calls initially. I had been referring to the Department of Defense.

There is no virtue in *hoping* to get by. Editors are intelligent; so are the readers. One cannot trust memory. Better pace off the distance, check the word, get the facts. An Ozark boy in a recent novel of mine, *The Happy Land* (Harcourt, Brace and World, Inc.), threw a rock a considerable distance and hit the squirrel target. I consulted a man who could gauge distance, who had been raised in the Ozark Mountains, and who had thrown rocks at squirrels. In the same novel, there were a number of courtroom scenes and some legal language. I asked a lawyer and a judge to read those sections with great care. The *time* of the novel was the 1920's, and I discovered again that one cannot take liberties with events that actually occurred. I reluctantly removed Queen Marie of Romania from one scene. I had liked having her there, and the mention of her name set the era, the flavor of the era, and the color of that particular scene. Alas! She had arrived in the United States for her famous tour on October 18, 1926. My year was 1926, but my scene took place prior to October 18. (I have checked this once more for the purpose of this article.) I could not describe a powerful style of swimming by calling it "the Gertrude Ederle stroke." My year was then 1925. Miss Ederle conquered the English Channel in 1926. Costumes and time run parallel. It isn't good sense to have a character use a zipper before it was invented, or to include a Merry Widow hat before it was designed.

The list for research is endless. One must count the children, figure time, distance, geography. Details are boring, and especially when the feast in writing—the fun, the main reward—is in following the creative urge.

Not only must the author be sure he has done sufficient research, he must be prepared to prove it. I wrote an article about Lord Chesterfield. Before I put down a word, I read every book, article, pamphlet on my subject that I could find, with the aid of those wonderful friends, the librarians. Then I went back to original sources, beginning with Lord Chesterfield's statements, documents, letters, as well as the comments of contemporaries of the eighteenth century. When I submitted the manuscript, I sent a bibliography, but I did not footnote each sentence with exact reference. The editor returned the article and asked that I footnote it. I complied, of course. The second effort was almost as difficult as the initial research. I knew what I knew, but I had to look up again the page, the paragraph, the sentence. How much time could have been saved by proper notation in the first place! One must be able to prove a statement. It is not enough to know it.

Is there danger in too much precision? Yes. There is ever-present danger of loss of spontaneity, of the loss of the easy flow of words, of the loss of that inspiration which is vital in writing. Nonetheless, the facts must be marshaled.

I do not suggest that one has to be on a spot in order to give an adequate description. A writer's imagination is a delicate instrument and almost miraculous, at times. It must be used strongly. However, the effectiveness of a story can be destroyed by misplacing the

Statue of Liberty. Proper research will locate the statue. *Then* let the imagination roam.

It is too bad a skeleton attends the feast.

Look well. It is there. And in order not to distract the guests with gaping grin and rattling bones, we must clothe it. Above all, we must recognize the unwelcome apparition for what it is: our supporting structure.

62

AN EDITOR'S ADVICE
ON ARTICLE SALES

BY CHESTER PETERSON, JR.

EDITORS are human—well, at least I think so. I was a departmental editor with a magazine of a million-plus circulation for four years. It's a bit difficult to judge yourself, but I'm sure most of my fellow editors were at least half human, maybe even 70–80% or so. The point I want to make is that editors are people just like you and me, and should be treated as such.

For example, they make mistakes, too. Here's how a mistake can occur: An editor may have been out of town working fourteen hours a day checking out leads, gathering information, and perhaps directing some photography. His plane is late arriving home, so he walks in the door at midnight. The wife's sanity has been strained by the month-old baby's colic attack. Daddy editor spends most of the rest of the short night parading around the bedroom cuddling Junior.

Back at the office the next day, the editor finds he has a revised deadline on copy needed in the composing room by 10 a.m., the Editor-in-Chief has scheduled a planning meeting at 2 p.m., and four page proofs must be checked within the hour, or the press will start running blank pages. Then his secretary walks in with two stacks of mail divided into "Rush" and "Immediate Attention."

The above is meant to show that editors are people, with the problems of rushed, responsible persons—and with the potential to make an occasional wrong decision. I'm not saying that every manuscript you've had returned was due to an editor's error. All free-lancers (and I'm one now, too) have brain-children returned more or less frequently. In most cases there's a good reason why a manuscript comes back home—a reason you can identify.

My point: There's a lot you can do to insure that even the most harassed editor will be receptive to your manuscript. You might call this a lesson in psychology for the free-lancer. Take advantage of every factor in your power to control! Here are some pointers.

Remember that almost every editor keeps this in mind: To make his particular department and his magazine the best in the business. That's why he gets a kick from "discovering" a timely, top-quality article or new writer.

A young editor who is lucky enough to find several excellent articles in a short time may soon get a reputation as a good man to work with free-lancers, and be marked as a comer by his boss. So, it's to his advantage—both directly and indirectly—for you to send him an article he can buy.

Perhaps you don't realize it, but magazine editors are always hopefully looking for the mail to bring them a story that's unusual, that has a new approach or some news peg.

Except for the giants of the magazine world, most of the thousands of small and medium-sized magazines are always hungry for one- and two-column material. On magazines where the editor is responsible for writing most of the major space articles, he doesn't also have time to prepare "back-of-book" articles. Payment is high for such short pieces—and if you're new to writing, this is an excellent place to break in.

This you've read a hundred times: "Read the magazine before you send in a manuscript." If you're reading this, chances are you're a notch or two above the average free lance. This is the type who uses the shotgun approach. He doesn't bother to read the magazines to which he fires off articles. He figures it's a waste of time and that someone is bound to buy a story sooner or later. (You know this person—he's always complaining about the high cost of postage.)

Editors will often buy a manuscript just for the idea it contains. Perhaps you've described how an old problem can be solved with a fresh approach. Maybe one or two other writers have also found "answers." By buying the idea, the editor can combine the best parts of each manuscript into a harder-hitting article. Payment for use of the idea is usually good, but you'll get no by-line.

Did you know your precious copy *must* usually be changed in order to make it "fit" the page layout? Most medium to large magazines have artists produce page layouts that indicate size and location of visuals, headlines, subheads, and body copy. Although they try to leave as much space as possible for the story and still have visual impact, usually the copy must be "condensed" (rewritten) to fit the space available.

This is one reason you shouldn't make drastic changes in the copy if an editor sends you a galley proof or a copy of the revised manuscript. He's probably spent quite a few hours getting it to "fit." And, he wouldn't take kindly to your adding eight additional paragraphs. Never hesitate, however, to update material in the proof or to clarify any point that might be misunderstood by a reader.

Find out when the magazines you usually write for plan their issues. In other words, do they make plans and set schedules for the December issue in November, September, or May? Many quality publications "work" at least six months ahead. If you send in a Christmas-oriented article in late October it couldn't possibly be used that year. And, it's a tossup whether an article would be purchased and carried on the inventory for a year—unless it was an exceptional article.

So, write an editor or two asking when you should send in material that's slanted toward a certain season. The editor might give you some other hints, too, especially since you've branded yourself as a person who knows something about his business.

Have you noticed how most magazines follow a cycle of fat and lean periods? For example, most magazines you buy at the newsstand are thick in the fall, thin in winter, fat again in the spring, and on a diet again in mid-summer. This doesn't have too much effect on buying habits because a good story will be purchased regardless. But fewer articles of a specific seasonal nature will be bought by editors for use in the thin issues. It's something to keep in mind.

Query before tackling an article if you'll have a large hunk of time and money invested by completion. Don't bother sending a query if you know the article you're planning is the type which can be sold to more than one or two magazines.

Or, you can write an editor you've worked for before to tell him you're checking an idea and will send a manuscript soon. This alerts the editor to the story possibility so he can make some plans.

It's good psychology, too, because the manuscript doesn't hit the editor's desk as a completely unknown quantity. The editor might write or call to inform you of questions he'd like asked of your source, or to tell you what would be required in the way of photographs.

But, don't overdo the query letter. All query and no manuscript makes an extremely irritable and unresponsive editor. One free-lancer used to send me at least a letter a week. But he averaged a manuscript only every three or four months. Conclusion: Must have liked to write letters—or was frightfully lonely.

If possible, address your letter directly to the departmental editor involved when you send a query letter or manuscript. Don't waste time sending it to the editor-in-chief. Editors of publications often receive almost as much mail as Liz Taylor.

If your letter isn't sorted out by a secretary, it might wait a long time to be read by the editor-in-chief, especially if the boss is out of town for two weeks. Then, if the departmental editor to whom it's forwarded is busy, another week or two may flutter by.

In any event, allow three or four weeks to pass before you write inquiring why your manuscript was lost.

You might want to state your qualifications in your initial letter to an editor. This is almost a must if your article concerns a technical subject. Point out that you have a B.S. from the University of Illinois in mechanical engineering or that you have a B.S. from Cornell in hotel management, with seven years' experience in large hotels in Dallas, Denver, and Kansas City.

Always protect your photographs with a layer or two of cardboard. But don't attach photographs to cardboard with paper clips. If you use a rubber band, don't stretch it around the middle of the photographs. Instead, use two rubber bands for maximum security and minimum bending and curling. Hook one rubber band over the corner of the photographs and cardboard, then stretch it over the corner diagonally across. Repeat with a second rubber band on the other two corners, but on the other side of the stack of photographs.

If you're mailing a large number of photographs, send them in a cardboard box of the type used to hold photographic printing paper. Don't write on the back of any photograph. Put your name and address, plus information about the photograph, in a legend that's taped to the bottom margin and folded upward. Many free-lancers use a rubber stamp and an ink of light shade to put their name, address, and negative number on the back side.

Always protect your slides or transparencies with plastic slip-on sleeves. You'd be surprised at the number of slides sent to publications with no protection from scratches or big thumbs. Don't, however, use glass protectors. They often break, ruining the transparency.

A big league magazine will usually use your photographs only for reference and as guides for the professional photographer who shoots the finished visual. Nevertheless, your photographs should be good —and not two-by-three-inch snapshots the photofinisher has blurred, scratched, and darkened.

Take various shots, shooting around the idea. Show various angles and the lay of the land. If the subject is suitable for color, mention in an accompanying description the true colors, directions buildings face, and what you think is the best angle. Also tell who is shown, what's being done, and if the model would be available for later posing by a professional photographer.

Legally, a photograph model release signed by the person pictured and the photographer aren't required if the photograph is to be used solely in editorial material. But some major magazines, such as *Better Homes and Gardens,* require releases regardless. If there's any possibility that a photograph will be used in promotion or advertising, you need a release, but needed or not, it's a professional touch to send releases with your photographs. The editor will appreciate it, and will remember you as a responsible free-lancer.

Give your manuscripts every opportunity to be salesmen for you. It's not enough to have done a good job researching, writing, and rewriting. The little extra touches you add will mark you as a professional—a no-nonsense writer who follows through 100%. Believe me, it works in making an editor more receptive to your work. Some things to keep in mind:

1. Be neat! I've seen hundreds of manuscripts with words crudely crossed out and others substituted or added. It's not unusual to see an entire paragraph X'ed out. The person doing such a thing might have saved a minute by making a needed correction in a messy way, but this is more than offset by the resulting sad appearance. Would you wear your newest suit to a job interview, or your paint-spattered "relaxing clothes"?

I don't mean you can't erase a typing error or make a minor correction—just do it neatly. The editor wants you to correct all errors. He doesn't want to read an article written by an obvious slob.

2. Read your final copy carefully. It must be accurate, especially if you're dealing with a technical field. If you send it in with even a simple transposition error or a misspelled word, the editor begins to wonder if you've also made a mistake in the pertinent facts and figures. His question: Are you slipshod, or can you be trusted?

3. Be consistent in your style, whether it concerns abbreviations, hyphenated words, or use of numbers. Don't start with one style, then switch to another, halfway through your manuscript. An editor leads a confusing enough life without additional complexities.

4. Many schools and books advise putting your name and address, plus article title, on a covering sheet of paper, then starting the manuscript partway down the second sheet. To save minor costs of paper and postage—and additional work by an editor—do this: Start your manuscript on the same sheet on which you've listed title, name, and address.

Then always put a key phrase from the title and your last name in the upper left corner of every following sheet. Basic, to be sure, but a point that's often neglected. Some writers are taught to put "Add 1" on the second page. I've always thought this creates confusion, so would advise just putting a simple "Page 2" under your name and the title identification, and so on, after page 1.

5. As an editor, I saw manuscripts come into my "In" box in half a dozen sizes and several paper colors. Paper quality ranged from expensive bond stationery to little better than tissue paper.

The thinking behind some of this "being different" is that a distinctive paper size and color will be more readily recognized by an editor. I don't believe this is a good idea. An editor is going to read all manuscripts sent his way, and an odd paper color can make your typing harder to read. No efficiency expert has measured this yet, but I think paper different from the standard business sheet takes extra time for the editor. Anyway, you'd be taking a chance on making the editor slightly grouchy, whether he realizes it or not.

6. Don't staple the sheets of your manuscript together. You should have carbon copies anyhow, so loss isn't too important. In reading a stapled manuscript, the editor has to bend the pages back. This means your material can get dog-eared and bedraggled at its

first reading. If you have to send it out three or four times before it's purchased, you might have several retyping jobs just to keep it fresh looking. Use a paper clip.

7. Whatever you do, don't use a script typewriter! And, if you have a choice of pica or elite type, use the pica typewriter. Why? It has larger, more easily read type. Some writers might think the apparent additional length of an article typed on a pica machine will fool an editor into paying more. That doesn't happen often. Most editors were writers at some time, and they already know most of the tricks.

8. Adopt a standard line length of 60 or 70 characters. I've received manuscripts utilizing a 40-space line, but that's overdoing it. This is like asking the editor to make numerous marks in the over-adequate margins.

When an editor knows you use a certain character count line, and so many lines per page, he'll be able to estimate more quickly word counts and article length. This dependability may pay off.

9. Leave approximately an inch to an inch and a half of space at the top and bottom of each page. Double-space. Triple-spacing is harder to read. Double-spacing leaves enough room for minor editing and comments by the editor.

10. If possible, have your source of information or an authority in the field read your article before you send it to a magazine. Then have this person sign a dated statement saying he's read it, and that the article is technically and factually accurate. Attach it to your manuscript.

11. If you receive a revised copy of the manuscript before it is set in type, find out if the editor is also sending a copy to the person quoted in the article or to your source of information. If not, you should again have the source read it and give an O.K. Tell the editor you've rechecked the rewritten article. This should raise your professional stock with the editor at least ten points—another little thing that sets a professional slightly above other writers, not counting writing ability.

12. You must include a stamped, addressed envelope. Tip: To save time in going to the post office to get material weighed, buy your own small postal scale. You can then see weights and rates at a glance. Cost of the least expensive scale is close to $2.50. If you're

continually guessing at postage, the scale will save you the embarrassment of having material arrive postage due.

13. Type addresses and your return address on gummed labels—a small thing, to be sure, but it looks better—especially if your scrawl isn't too readable.

14. Along the same line, if you send material in large Manila envelopes, use gummed labels to indicate first class or air mail. The labels cost 15¢ per box, and certainly help appearances.

63

THE ROUTE TO MAGAZINE
ARTICLE SALES

By Hal D. Steward

If you asked me how to write non-fiction magazine articles that sell, I would give you this general advice:

> Develop your idea, do your research, study published examples of the type of article you plan to write, and then *write*.

That, I believe, is good advice—as far as it goes. It just doesn't go far enough. You need more specific road signs to take you the shortest route to magazine article sales.

My own experience as a full-time writer has taught me a successful magazine piece must have these six major elements:

1. The lead (or hook)
2. Anecdotes (or scenes)
3. Quotes (or dialogue)
4. Description
5. Transitions between anecdotes or scenes to move the article along smoothly and rapidly
6. The conclusion

These elements are indispensable. You cannot drop even one from your article. If you do, the editor will return it in the stamped, self-addressed envelope you enclose. Editors want these elements in all the articles they buy.

So, to state the obvious, if we want to write magazine articles that editors will buy, we must give them what they want. I know no other way to do it.

You have heard that editors nowadays like to have fiction techniques used in the non-fiction they buy. This is true, and nowhere is it more apparent than in the lead paragraph (Element #1) which contains the "hook" that captures your reader's attention and holds him. If you can manage to get an element of suspense into the lead, it helps. This is how I did it in "Escape or Die in Red Laos," published in *Male* Magazine:

> Navy Lieutenant Charles F. Klusmann sat in the pilots' briefing room on the morning of Saturday, June 6, 1964, and listened to the usual pre-mission instructions. He and his wingman, Lieutenant J. S. Kuechmann, would fly the same type of photo reconnaissance that had been flown before over Laos' Communist territory.
>
> The briefing over, Klusmann and Kuechmann walked to the flight deck of the aircraft carrier Kitty Hawk, steaming off the coast of South Viet Nam. The fliers climbed into their F–8 crusader jets and prepared for launch.
>
> Klusmann had no premonition that, in less than two hours, he would start to live the most amazing adventure to come out of the war in Southeast Asia. His main concern was for the success of his unarmed photo reconnaissance flight over Communist-held territory. Klusmann expected the Commies to hurl flak at him.

The idea, as you can see from this example, is to whet the reader's interest—promise him something foreboding or interesting to come; and then keep your promise to him.

Before we move to the second element, here are two more examples of leads which attempted to capture the reader's attention and hold him. This one is from my "Violent Death of A Beautiful Navy Wife," in *True Detective Magazine:*

> The milkman knew something was wrong. [The reader is supposed to say to himself, "Oh, I had better read on and find out what!"] He was new on the milk route, but the few times he had made deliveries to the small house in the quiet residential district not far from San Diego State College, Mrs. Constance E. Dunn was usually busy around the home. Her two young children, Donnie, 3, and Mary Louise, 7 months, would be playing with their Boston bull terrier or watching television in the living room.

If that lead compelled the reader to read on, it was a success. If he turned to another story in the magazine, after reading the lead, it failed.

In my third example of a lead, you will see I have tried to work three of the six major elements into it—the hook, description and dialogue. This is not always possible, but if you can do it I believe you have a stronger lead. The lead is from my "A Man with Murder in His Heart," in *Official Detective Magazine:*

The desk sergeant's telephone cut through the lazy early evening quiet with an ear-piercing sound. As he reached for it with a quick hand he noticed the clock over his desk and saw it was 7:31 on the evening of Thursday, January 7, 1965. He picked up the receiver.

"Sergeant, this is Fred Sayers. I live at 640 North Palm Drive. My daughter, Brenda Sue, has been missing more than three and a half hours now and she is nowhere to be found," the voice on the telephone told the police sergeant.

You can see that lead is crammed with facts. In those two paragraphs are a description of the initial scene, the time, the date, introduction of the two key persons in the article, and a statement of the problem.

In cramming your leads with facts, remember editors and readers want information told them simply and concisely in declarative sentences. So, leads should not be cluttered with adjectives, loose construction and words that fail to contribute to the story's forward movement.

The third paragraph of the lead to "A Man with Murder in His Heart" plunged directly into the story. It read this way:

The desk sergeant, unaware at this moment that the stage was being set for the greatest manhunt in the history of California's Imperial Valley, listened patiently as Sayers continued, "Brenda Sue left the house about 4 p.m. to go roller skating in front of her school and she hasn't been seen since. For more than three hours all the members of my family have been checking with friends she might have visited. No one has seen her. I need police help."

If you have brought the reader along this far, he is "hooked"— you have him into the heart of your story.

Once you have your lead, "the hook," you continue the use of fictional techniques by telling as much of the story as possible in narrative style. As Morton Sontheimer said in the introduction to *A Guide to Successful Magazine Writing,* "The fuel that keeps this narrative style running smoothly is anecdotes."

Now for major Element #2. This is how I used narrative for the next three paragraphs after the lead in "Escape or Die in Red Laos":

"I didn't expect them to throw rose petals at us," he was to say later. Navy intelligence officers have permitted Klusmann to tell the story of his capture by Laotian Reds in his own words. In authorizing the release, the Navy also gave him a clean bill of health on the question of a pro-Communist "letter" which the Pathet Lao has claimed he signed as a prisoner.

It was about 11 A.M. when Klusmann and Kuechmann lifted their jet fighters from the deck of the Kitty Hawk. There was a slight weather condition which limited visibility to half a mile as the two Navy aircraft headed up into the clouds.

The fliers were on their way to the target area—the Plaines des Jarres in southern Laos.

Now before I take up the third major element (quotation), let me digress and discuss professionalism in free-lance writing. Up to this point, I have rapidly moved along about the actual writing of a magazine article. There are, however, three essential truths a writer must learn before he begins to sell regularly.

First, he needs to develop a certain sense of article values—how to find article ideas and then feel reasonably sure they will appeal to an editor. He develops this sense by studying the articles in the magazines for which he wants to write, by carefully reading his daily newspapers for article ideas that fit into the categories covered in those magazines, and by sending a constant flow of queries to magazine editors on the ideas he has for articles. If he does this, he will find that before long he has developed a sense for subjects that appeal to editors.

Second, he must become a thorough researcher and an accurate reporter. There can be, in my opinion, no substitute in a non-fiction piece for complete and accurate facts. Once you begin to sell you will discover editors agree with this premise.

Third, it is important to develop a specialty as a non-fiction writer. My specialties are military affairs articles and true adventure and true detective stories. I have found these specialties have brought me more assignments from editors and a steadier flow of ideas. This does not mean, however, that I restrict myself to these subjects. It simply means I have wider contacts in these areas and can produce articles more quickly on these subjects than others I undertake. These specialties are my bread-and-butter base. Each professional writer decides for himself the areas in which he wants to specialize, based on his own personal interests and opportunities.

We have now arrived at major Element #3 in a non-fiction article —direct quotation or dialogue. This is how a paragraph of direct quotation was interjected into the Klusmann story:

"We proceeded on dead reckoning all the way—no radio navigation aids," Klusmann said. "Cloud cover was such that we could not pick up our ground reference, which was a bend in the Mekong River about twenty miles east of Paksane in central Laos. We began letting down east of that point but the cloud cover was still heavy and we could see nothing, even after we got into the hills."

Quotation or dialogue is used to move a story along. If it does not do this, it cannot contribute to the article's pace—it will read dull and phony.

The point, then, is this: Use quotation or dialogue which contributes movement, description and information.

Description is our major Element #4. This is how both narration and quotation added description to "Escape or Die in Red Laos":

Klusmann tried to regain his visual reference and get out of the hills. In his attempt he flew south and began letting down again in an area 15 miles south of Paksane, where the terrain was flatter.

"We picked up the Mekong River again and flew toward the Plaines des Jarres but again the weather was bad," the pilot said. "We flew at tree-top level and it wasn't until we reached Muong Soui, where the clouds were about 4,000 feet, that we picked up the Plaines visually."

You can see from these paragraphs that they give the reader specific information, which is what he wants in the articles he reads. A writer can learn much about how to be specific by a study of journalistic writing. In his book, *The Professional Journalist*, John Hohenberg provides invaluable advice on this. He points out the importance of one idea to a sentence; and he warns that the tense of a story must be consistent:

News writing [and I add, magazine non-fiction] must be specific. It is often a waste of time to string generalities together.

Instead of writing that a man is tall, it is better to describe him as six feet four. Instead of calling a girl pretty, she should be described briefly. Instead of reporting that a speaker was nervous and upset, it would be more effective to write that he shouted and banged on the table.

Hohenberg emphasizes you must give meaning to what you write.

If statistics are to be used, they must be given some meaning. To say that New York City's subways have only one-candle power confuses the readers. It is more informative to write that the average New York subway rider sometimes reads his paper by less light than Abe Lincoln had when he studied by firelight.

Specific words are used as the keys to make transitions (Element #5) from one anecdote or scene to the next in an article. These transitions are essential to move the story along smoothly and give it continuity. This is an example:

Klusmann was at 10,000 feet altitude and flying at better than 550 miles an hour when he made his decision to eject over Communist territory.
"I called Kuechmann and told him I was ejecting," Klusmann said.

You can see the transition was made with the key word "eject." It also can be done with time, or with time and place, with emotion, or with movement as I did it. The idea is to repeat an exact word or phrase to make the transition. This is how T. H. Huxley did it in his "The Method of Scientific Investigation." I have italicized the key words:

You mean to say exactly what you know; but in reality you are giving expression to what is, in all essential particulars, an hypothesis. You do not know it all; it is nothing but an hypothesis rapidly framed in your own mind. And it is an *hypothesis* founded on a long train of *inductions* and *deductions*.
What are those inductions and deductions, and how have you got at this *hypothesis?* You have observed in the first place. . . .

Transitions are vital to make your article read smoothly.

Major Element #6 in writing a magazine article is the conclusion. In this connection, I recall the words of a successful non-fiction writer:

Whenever I am stuck for a terse line that will chop the thing off clean, I repeat the introductory (lead) line. And if the lead doesn't happen to fit the purpose, I rewrite it so that it does.

That's good advice. It will work more often than not. But in the case of "Escape or Die in Red Laos" it wouldn't. So, I had to wind up my yarn by reporting Klusmann's present physical condition—he was injured and became ill while a prisoner of the Communists—and tell the reader what he was currently doing. I handled it this way:

Klusmann has regained his health and is now a student at the Naval Post Graduate School in Monterey, California. On his return to the United States, he was promoted to the rank of Lieutenant Commander and awarded the Distinguished Flying Cross.

There is nothing wrong with a happy ending in a magazine article
—any more than in a fiction story.

If you have come along with me in the development of "Escape or
Die in Red Laos," you can see it was simply a job of reporting with
fiction techniques as the added ingredient.

64

TITLES THAT TANTALIZE

By Kathryn M. Wilson

HAVING title trouble, especially with articles? Best you can do is "Schools Face Trouble," or "Snakes Are Interesting," or "Honesty Is the Best Policy"? Don't turn the page! Here are some available sources for titles that tantalize.

Look through the Bible. You'll find many expressions, warnings, proverbs, and phrases that will dress up your article instantly. Some can be changed effectively to blend with the subject matter. The familiar "Am I my brother's keeper?" changed to "Am I My Mother's Keeper?" would make an ideal title for an article on the problem of care for aged parents, so much in demand now. Also, either the first half or the last half of "Many are called but few are chosen" would aptly fit a career preparation article. Other possibilities to consider: "Heed your own heart's counsel," "A time of calamity," or "Train a boy in the way he would go."

Keep on hand a copy of the complete works of Shakespeare. Almost every page contains at least one phrase which would make a good title for an article. From Portia's "quality of mercy" speech alone, in *The Merchant of Venice,* have come many inspirations for titles. Titles have come from the "Tomorrow, and tomorrow, and tomorrow" speech in *Macbeth,* and "To be, or not to be," in *Hamlet.* You can find hundreds of less well-known phrases for titles in other Shakespearean plays: "mortal instruments" (*Julius Caesar*); "the worst of words" (*Othello*); "mechanic slaves" (*Antony and Cleopatra*); "bounds of modesty" (*Romeo and Juliet*).

Of course you have a copy of Bartlett's *Familiar Quotations.* It is a gold mine for the non-fiction writer, not only for quotes but also for title ideas. You can search the index under subject matter or key words and find excellent quotations which can be cut in half, turned around, or changed to fit the article. As you go through the book, you'll come across many familiar phrases that have already been used as titles of articles; therefore, try to choose an original arrangement for your own use.

More sources? Nursery rhymes and fairy tales are studded with good titles. Examples: "Ten O'Clock Scholar" (I used that one myself for a school article); "Sleeping Beauty," "Little Boys in Blue," "Pocketful of Rye" (this has been used frequently, as in, "Pocketful of Money," "Pocketful of Herbs," etc.).

Alliteration, which means the repeating of the same sounds or letters in several words, is an excellent way to form a title. For example: "Barbie's Baubles" (about Barbara Hutton's famous jewels); "Kids, Kisses, and Kindergarten" (my own, covering a get-ready-for-school article). And "Tears, Teens, and Trouble," or "A Whiz at Wisdom," etc. Try your own!

Still stumped? Song titles are full of suggestions, too. Change a word or two, and come up with a catchy title. "My Old Unlucky Home" (nostalgia piece). "Hello, Trolley!" (history of trolley cars). "Tiptoe Through Your Own Tulips" (simple article on raising lovely tulips). "Whittle While You Work" (exercising while doing housework).

Now for some quickies: Proverbs and axioms have been done to death, but you still can come up with some good ones. "Make Sure Your Policy Is an Honest One" (insurance racket warnings), or "Taste Makes Waist" (dieting advice). See how it works?

Also to consider: slogans, colors, school phrases like "ABC's of . . ."; plays, speeches, advertisements, science, and history. The Declaration of Independence, the Constitution, and Lincoln's Gettysburg Address are full of good ideas for titles. Lately, too, many articles have titles related to outer space, containing words like "countdown," "rockets," etc. Some good titles have been devised from the latest teen-age expressions—"cloud 9," "dig it," "get with it," etc.

Everyday exclamations can be turned into titles. For instance, "sakes alive" turns into "Snakes Alive"; "gosh darn it" can be "It's easy: darn it!" (advice on easy mending); "for Pete's sake" slides into "For Heat's Sake" (proper furnace maintenance). Get the drift?

There you are. If you try these methods, you may sometimes feel it's easier to find a title than to write the article itself. And sometimes the methods will actually trigger ideas for new articles—that is, you'll find a good title and write an article to fit it!

65

HOW TO WRITE GOOD POETRY
AND GET IT PUBLISHED

By L. E. Sissman

CAN you write good poetry? I don't know; not everybody can. But there are ways to test the verse you've written to find out if it's good or not. First, there's the freshness test. Read over a poem you've written. Is there any phrase or image in it that is completely fresh and apt—that doesn't resemble anything else you've read before? Be objective; if you can still answer yes, you may have something as a poet. Second, there's the compression test. Write one of your poems out as a single prose paragraph. Does it read like prose? If it does, it's not a poem in the first place. But if, on the other hand, it's too terse and compact and energetic for prose, perhaps you're really a poet. Third, there's the influence test. Write down the names of the ten poets whose work means the most to you—not just important names, but people whose work holds deep meaning for you and influences what you write and how you think about poetry. O. K. Now get hold of a copy of Mark Strand's recent book, *The Contemporary American Poets,* and see how many of your favorites are included. If it's fewer than four or five, your influences are not contemporary—and your verse is probably not close enough to the mainstream of what's being written now to be good, at least by contemporary standards. There may be a few poets who are exceptions to this rule; there aren't many.

But suppose you've passed these tests. Suppose you feel very deeply that you do have a talent for poetry, and that you want to pursue it. Then, obviously, your object should be to produce a body of poems—and to get them published. I'll deal with these two points in turn, using my own (admittedly very subjective) experience as a rough guide to what you might expect.

Some years ago, I found myself with a suspected poetic talent and, at the age of thirty-five, not much to show for it. I had won a poetry prize in college; I'd published a few poems in little magazines; I had a thin sheaf of verse written ten to fifteen years before. I decided it was then or never; that if I did have talent, I would have to prove it in my thirties or forget it. So I sat down with the very cold-blooded, hard-headed objective of writing as well as I could and as much as I could, beginning right then and there. It wasn't very easy, as you might expect. But I had three invaluable assets to help me get started again. First, time. I could spare two evenings a week to concentrate on writing; every Tuesday and Thursday from eight to ten, I wrote. Second, a helpful wife. She understood what I was doing and made a time and place for me to do it in. Third, a friend. One who had a good knowledge of poetry and was willing to spend a lot of time and effort to read what I had written, to criticize and encourage me.

These three assets got me over the first hurdle: I found myself actually writing poems and slowly building up a file of them. I learned that it was absolutely necessary for me to begin with a firm idea of what the poem was about and what I wanted it to say; in addition, I learned never to set the first line down on paper until I had worked it out to my complete satisfaction in my mind. Having avoided a false start, I found it easier to go on to the next lines with confidence. And as I worked on these lines, I often found a kind of exhilaration coming over me—a feeling of excitement that the poem was beginning to shape itself, to dictate its own form, so to speak, and to carry me along with it until the end, when my own judgment would reassert itself to provide an apt ending.

At first, because the material seemed simpler to work with, I concentrated on nature poems—short quatrains about things I'd observed in the small town where I live. These soon grew into sonnets, then into sequences of sonnets. Then I began writing longer poems in four-line rhyming stanzas—and my subject matter began to expand. I found myself writing poems about my own experiences in school and college and afterward. I found myself developing that very important (and elusive) thing, a tone and style. In my case, this tone was dry, amused, analytical, a little above, in a mocking way, the experiences it described. The style made use of impacted bits of diction—sharp and smooth edges of language thrown together in such a way as to create a fresh impression of sound unlike, I hoped, anything the reader had heard before. To this I added dialogue, mimicry of sounds, parody of and allusion to other poets of every period. And the whole mix began to develop an individuality, a personality, of its own.

At this point I badly needed the outside encouragement of publishing something—somewhere, anywhere. Fortunately, it materialized. An old friend called and asked if a poem I had written years before could be printed in an English magazine of which he was an American editor. I said yes, of course; and this tiny encouragement was enough to keep me going for a while. But eventually, I knew, I would have to publish one or more of my new poems in order to establish the validity of what I was trying to do. This wasn't easy. I had to decide on my markets and besiege them with poems, in the hope that one would eventually yield and publish something. Rather than scatter my poems broadcast over dozens of literary magazines, I determined to aim high and to send them only to a few publications I particularly respected—*The New Yorker, The Atlantic, Harper's, The Kenyon Review, The Hudson Review,* and a couple of others. It was my plan to send each poem to each magazine on this list until the editors would at least become familiar with my name and style. This I did. For six months or more, I sent each new poem off to these magazines—and garnered a desk full of the usual printed rejection slips. But then a subtle change began to happen: one of the editors sent me a scrawled note of rejection instead of a printed slip; another sent me a typewritten letter of regret, with a request to see more poems. Apparently I was beginning to make some sort of impression. Four more months went by. Then, suddenly, *The New Yorker,* a magazine known for its careful reading of manuscripts submitted by unpublished writers, wrote to say that they were taking a short group of three poems; soon after, *The Atlantic* accepted a sequence of four sonnets. Next, an idea for a light, topical poem occurred to me; I wrote it in one afternoon and rushed it off to *The New Yorker.* They took it, too.

All this was more than enough to make me really serious about my writing. I began to turn out verse in quantity; in the year following my first acceptances, I must have written over 2,500 lines of poetry, much of which was, in turn, accepted by the magazines I had set my sights on. At this point, I became increasingly indebted to the poetry editors of these magazines, not only for accepting my work in the first place, but also for their skilled and excellent criticism and editorial comment, which often rescued a poem from failure. In the years since, I have come to value their judgment and to welcome their suggestions on everything I write.

Today, I still write verse (along with articles and book reviews) at a pretty consistent rate. I try to make every poem strong enough and different enough to warrant publication; then I try to get it published in one of the magazines where most of my work appears. So far, I've been most fortunate; about 75% of the poems I've written since 1964 have seen publication, and I still have hopes for some of the others. I have published three books of verse.

That, in a few hundred words, is my story. Now, let's get back to yours. At the beginning of this article, I suggested a few objective tests to determine whether you're capable of writing poetry that can be published in this day and age. Assuming that you're still reading this article because you have passed these tests, I have some more advice for you.

Though no two people, and certainly no two poets, are alike, the experience I've just outlined suggests that I've run across some basic rules that any aspiring poet can profitably follow. Let me list these and comment briefly on them.

1. *Make writing a habit.* Fortunately for all of us, good habits are as easy to get into as bad ones, and just as hard to break. If you make it an ironclad rule to spend a certain number of hours writing on one or two specific days a week—if you treat it as a hard-and-fast schedule—you'll soon find yourself with a good habit on your hands. Even if you don't have a specific writing project in mind each time you sit down, you'll discover that the leisure to think and concentrate will generate new ideas for you—ideas that will soon turn into words on the page. I don't have a lot of advice about time of day; you should just pick a time that will let you work, free of outside distractions, for a minimum of two hours at a sitting. If that's early morning or late at night, so be it. As far as writing materials are concerned, I'd recommend against a typewriter, on the grounds that typewritten copy seems so final and

unchangeable; it's better, I think, to use an ordinary #2 pencil with a good eraser.

2. *Write about what you know.* This is an ancient rule for writers of all kinds. It's still a good one. The material of poetry is not far-flung, exotic, romantic. It's your own life, what's under your nose.

3. *Think it through before you write it down.* Even with a nice, erasable #2 pencil, words have a way of crystallizing on the page once you've put them down. So don't put them down in the first place until you're reasonably sure of the form they're going to take —and the effect they're going to make. Oh, sure, detail changes and revisions are fine. But make sure that the basic structure is sound before you commit it to paper. This will save you many a false start and a dead end, especially as it applies to the beginning of a poem —and the ending. But even in the middle, when everything is (or seems to be) plain sailing, think before you write.

4. *Concentrate on those beginnings and endings.* As I've said before, those are really the parts of the poem where you're on your own; the middle tends to write itself. So labor hard and long to make every opening a model of power, grace, and impact, and to make every close a model of finality and rightness—the only possible ending for that particular poem.

5. *Use form to help you get started.* You may be absolutely dedicated to the idea of yourself as a stunning free-verse poet, but you'll find it a lot easier to start your career if you begin by working in traditional forms—the pentameter line, the couplet, the rhymed quatrain, the sonnet. Why? Because, paradoxically, following these forms makes less work for you, leaves less for you to think about, frees you to concentrate on the content rather than the form. Most free-verse poems are fiendishly difficult to write, precisely because you have to make up both form and content as you go along; conversely, a formal poem does part of the job for you by presenting you with a ready-made jig, so to speak, to assemble the words in. Also, there's this to consider: you wouldn't attempt to be a great abstract artist without first studying the rudiments of perspective, composition, and anatomy; by the same token, you shouldn't attempt to become a free-verse poet without first studying the traditional forms in which nearly all of the great

English poets have written. It's part of your basic training, no matter what kind of poet you may eventually become.

6. *Get expert criticism.* Unless you're far more objective than most of us, you can't hope to evaluate your progress all by yourself. You need some guidance from an expert. If you're lucky, as I was, you'll have a friend who can supply the needed—and continuing —criticism of your developing verse. If not, seek out such a person: perhaps the instructor in a poetry course at a local evening college or school of adult education. Secure his interest; show him your work over a period of time; take his advice and act on it.

7. *Pick your markets and bombard them.* I'll repeat for emphasis: select the places you'd like to be published; send each of them in turn every new poem you write, once you think you've reached a publishable level. Keep bombarding these chosen markets with your work; sooner or later, if you have an individual voice to offer, somebody will start to listen—and start to encourage you. Read *The Writer* to keep up on poetry markets; go to the library and familiarize yourself with the actual magazines, so you'll know whom you're submitting to and what they expect of their contributors.

8. *Keep at it.* Few poets burst into prominence overnight. Nearly all labor in obscurity for years before they find a market and an audience. You will have to do this, too. And it's not easy. But the right combination of hope, self-confidence, doggedness, and humility can keep you going until the day you get your first acceptance. And that time isn't wasted: in those long weeks and months when your work is unknown except to yourself and perhaps one mentor, you're actually dedicating yourself to the task of perfecting your outlook, your viewpoint, your style and technique, the individual voice you're striving for. In the time of obscurity, the real poet is made. It is, as the adage says, always darkest just before the dawn.

66

A POET'S LETTER
TO A BEGINNER

By May Sarton

You have given me a sheaf of your first poems to read. Are they real poems, you would like to know? And if so, where shall you send them, and how does a young poet get published?

You have just discovered the excitement of seeing before you on a page, separated from yourself, and ready to be given to the world as a gift, a piece of your mind and heart. These first poems seem altogether wonderful to you. You are still astonished, perhaps, at how easy it was to write them, once you got started. You have read them aloud to some of your friends, and they have been most encouraging. You have a strong suspicion that you are a genius, and in your heart of hearts what you hope from me is an accolade. You do not really want criticism any more than someone bringing me a bunch of flowers, and saying, "I grew these myself" wants it. You want to be welcomed into the company of poets, *now,* without further ado. And you hope I shall say, "Let me send these wonderful poems to *The Atlantic Monthly*. They will surely be eager to print them."

If I did not take you seriously I might just brush you off with a few words of easy praise. I might not feel that I had either time or energy to put my mind on your work, as if it were my own. Perhaps you have no idea (I did not at your age) how many such requests an established writer gets, and how hard we have to fight for time to do our own work. It would be easy to spend one's life answering letters, alas! I am taking the time to tell you honestly what I think because although these are not poems yet, in my judgment, they are perhaps the seeds of true poems. I hope that you will come to respect them as seeds, yourself, and give them the care such vital life should command.

Let us take a cold hard look at these pages, at what has actually been put down there in black and white. I am struck at once by the fact that you do *think* in *images,* that your instinctive tendency is to move from the abstract to the concrete. If there is one single quality that tells me you may become a poet, it is this. For before words enter in, concepts exist. The philosopher's kind of mind desires the general and the abstract; the poet's mind desires the specific and the concrete: "to see the world in a grain of sand." You say, for instance, "fire engine color" about an autumn leaf. About love you say, "Bells pealed in my head when I saw you walk down the street." (I shall come back to these images later.)

It looks to me as if a few rhymes came rather easily to you, and you have used these, scattered them around among lines that otherwise have no form, at random as it were. When you tried to follow through on a rhyme or to create a stanza, you had the sense that your precious feeling was being distorted, that to use a formal metrical pattern would be to force it to submit to a Procrustean bed. And this seemed to you not only a kind of dishonesty toward your "inspiration," but actually to do it violence.

First, let me say that rhyming is the least important element in English poetry, although the mastery of it is a challenge and a fruitful one, as one proceeds. (Keats has written a superb unrhymed sonnet, for instance.) What is important is the shape and weight of the poem as a whole, to sense this; the rhythm of the idea is important. The tone is important. I do not get the feeling from your poems that you have given much thought or attention to these matters.

You have, I fear, mistaken the signposts for the destination. It is quite true that when we are in a "writing state," lines and phrases float up and demand to be put down. Some of this is flotsam and jetsam; some of it may turn out to be pure gold. And I would go so far as to say that if nothing is "given" in this way, at the beginning, there will be no poem. But these "given" lines and images that come pouring out without your will are signposts. They help you to find the direction of the poem. Sometimes a single "given" line may suggest a metre; it may even groove the movement of the whole poem. But in themselves, these "gifts" are only communications from your subconscious to you, the maker, the fashioner. They are not communications to a reader.

If I have confidence in your talent, it is because as *first drafts,* these poems have real potential. It seems to me that you see the way a poet sees, and feel the way a poet feels. But you have not yet come to grips with the *fashioning* of your vision. At present you are a poet with no, or very little, *craft*.

How does one learn craft? You will perhaps think it a compliment if I tell you that I see no influences on your work; I do not sense its roots from a craft point of view. We learn our craft by studying other poets. The rebel must know very well what he is rebelling against for the rebellion to be meaningful; sometimes our best masters are those with whom we violently disagree, and against whom we sharpen our wits. Influence is not imitation. It is more fertile and subtle than that, and less conscious. It comes about when we are driven to possess another poet, to absorb him or her as if he were a necessary food.

Have you ever gone really deeply into a single poet, living or dead? By "deeply," I mean beyond just reading for pleasure, or even learning by heart . . . I mean studying the way a young baseball pitcher studies the great pitchers. I can't help wondering. My guess is that you have felt an affinity for a few of your immediate contemporaries, poets who have chosen to break away from form. They appear to you to be more "honest" than their immediate elders, such as Richard Wilbur, whom you call, no doubt, "academic." You want, instead, the naked raw stuff of experience itself. But what you forget is that no work of art *is* experience in that sense; it is something else, something that gives us the illusion of "reality." Craft is the means by which we create the illusion of "the naked raw stuff." If you choose to deny yourself all the magic and charms that severe forms release for a reader, you have got to find a substitute for them. At present, the substitute seems to be shock, shouting, violence of language—and the danger is that shock cannot be *renewed*. A poem may shock once at first reading, but it will not shock a second time: we have "had" it. One of the great values of poetry is that it provides an *indefinitely renewable experience*.

The renewal of craft often occurs when a poet reaches back in time to the generation before—or several generations before—his immediate ancestors. So T. S. Eliot, for instance, revitalized English poetry when he rediscovered, as usable for his purposes, the metaphysical poets, and especially John Donne. There is a huge rich past for you to discover for yourself. My advice is, study both poets whom you instinctively like, and also those whom you instinctively hate. Those you dislike will help you to define and recognize what you yourself wish to aim for.

Each poet has to discover his own true *voice*. And he does this not by instinct, as a bird sings, for bird songs are monotonous and repetitive, but by discovering the past that is usable for him, given his nature and his own relation to his times, and by allowing himself to be fertilized by it. If what you are after is a sort of naked honesty, a thrust, a shock, it might be worth looking Wyatt up again. If you are tired of the long iambic line and feel that it sounds musty, it might be worth looking into Skelton—and, at the opposite pole, Gerard Manley Hopkins. You will pour your own "shocking" language into these old bottles, and the mixture, I think, might be rather potent.

What I hope to suggest to you is that analysis precedes synthesis. The time to exercise your powers of analysis is when you are *not* writing poems, not in a state of inspiration. It is no use, for instance, to decide suddenly to write a sonnet, look up the form in a dictionary, and set to work. But if you have at your command the sonnets of Milton, Shakespeare, Donne, Hopkins, you will perhaps recognize a sonnet idea when you *are* in a state of inspiration, and there will be no need to look anything up. The sonnet form will be there in your subconscious ready to be used. Just as a tennis player does not wait to learn the backhand drive when he is in the midst of a tournament. He has practiced it for hours so when he is actually playing he can forget all about "technique."

More than most of us willingly recognize, the art of writing poetry demands thought. If you will look into Gerard Manley Hopkins' letters, or Dylan Thomas' to Vernon Watkins, or John Keats's or T. S. Eliot's essays you will see this kind of thinking at work. In fact, I would go so far as to say that the process of writing a poem is a process by which we think our feelings out, just as it is also a process by which we feel our thoughts out.

But let us get back now to your own work. I would like to see you learn to test these poems. Against what? Against your own feeling, first of all. There is something wrong for me about naming the color of an autumn leaf, "fire engine color." Why? Because "fire engine" is such a powerful image that what I see is not "bright red," as you intended, but a large red *machine*. The luminosity of leaves is not that of a hard reflecting surface like painted metal, but comes from their transparence. So your image, instead of making us see autumn leaves, does not do its "work"; it makes us see a fire engine instead! What looks strong at first sight turns out to be weak.

A good metaphor surprises us into recognition by bringing together two apparently dissimilar things which are exactly alike *in one respect*. Its explosive power has to do with the distance and exactness. Carl Sandburg's "Fish crier, dangling herring before prospective customers, evincing a joy identical with that of Pavlova dancing" is an example of what I mean. Your image of the "peal of bells" comes closer to this explosiveness than the "fire engine" did. The shock of seeing someone you love might be described in terms of a quick loud *sound*. What troubles me is the "peal," which suggests something that goes on for an interval; what you need is a sound that "shocks," on the instant.

You see, the process of revision is exciting because by means of it, we come to understand more and more about the experience itself. It is a process of self-discovery. And we know only when we come to the end of the poem—after perhaps thirty revisions—what it is really about.

Very well, you may say, but how then does one know when a poem is finished? Is there not a danger of killing it, of over-manipulating? The answer is, yes, there is a risk. There is always a risk. But in time you come to recognize when there is nothing more to "discover," when the poem survives all tests you can think up, and stands there, a complex singing *whole*. Far more poems go dead because the writer of them did not know how to push the limits, than because the writer lost his impetus and became a mere manipulator. Technique is never, once and for all, "learned." For as we ourselves grow and change, our craft also changes and grows. It is possible sometimes to master all that is needed for a specific poem, but the next one will require a whole new set of trials and triumphs.

By now, perhaps I have answered your second question. "Where shall I send these poems?" Send them home to yourself. Keep them. Think and feel them through. They are not ready to send out. They are seeds.

But the time will come, in a few years, when you will surely have a sheaf of true poems ready. Then what? You need the sense of achievement and the recognition that only publication can bring. And you are bound to suffer. For you will find that people like me who have been kind to you while you were still an amateur, will suddenly, if they are editors, become quite ruthless. For it is not you in relation to your own poems that is at stake, but your poems in relation to those of every established poet. You have never stopped to ask yourself, I presume, how many poems a day pour into the *Atlantic* offices, and how very few can be published—two or three in each monthly issue. You are preparing to crash into a world beside which the business world is child's play, from a competitive point of view. For every village and town in the country contains consumers of almost every product *except* poetry. In Finland, a literate country compared with ours, a book of poems by a young poet may sell 6,000 copies; here, only the top five, those who have already won major prizes, can hope to sell even half that many.

But fortunately there is a saving grace: the "little" magazines. *Beloit Poetry Journal, The Lyric, Poetry Northwest* and dozens of others—are always on the lookout for new poets. Try to remember that rejection will not mean that your poems are no good, any more than a few acceptances will mean that you are an authentic genius! As a young poet, you will oscillate between arrogance and despair. Both are expensive emotions. But in the end—this I think can be said with assurance—if you are a true poet, you will be published.

What is beautiful about the life of a poet is that it is still gratuitous. No one, not even Robert Frost, is able to earn a living only through publishing poetry. The only reason for writing poetry is because you *have* to, because it is what gives you joy. At best even glory is a by-product. Write because you need to find out what you really mean; write because you want to define your experience and because you want to communicate it to your friends. If they turn out someday to be counted in thousands, then you are lucky. But you are lucky *now* to have the wish, and to begin to learn about the skill, to do what in any age, in any country, very, very few people ever achieve. So let me welcome you, dear young poet, not into the company of the angels, but into the great company of those who work for joy alone, the poets. . . .

67

THE EXPERIENCE OF THE POEM

By Ann Stanford

ONE may think of the ingredients of a good poem as an experience and a fresh perception of that experience. The experience need not be original or new, but the perception should be. Think of Gerard Manley Hopkins' delight in spring, a feeling old as humanity, couched in the freshest of images:

> Nothing is so beautiful as spring—
>> When weeds, in wheels, shoot long and lovely and lush;
>> Thrush's eggs look little low heavens, and thrush
> Through the echoing timber does so rinse and wring
> The ear, it strikes like lightnings to hear him sing;
>> The glassy peartree leaves and blooms, they brush
>> The descending blue; that blue is all in a rush
> With richness; the racing lambs too have fair their fling.

Hopkins' language is vital because his feeling about spring is intense and his own. He has taken the familiar ingredients of a poem about spring and made them into a new vision.

A contemporary example of a poem drawn from everyday experience is May Swenson's "Water Picture,"* which describes the reflection of objects in a pond; it begins:

> In the pond in the park
> all things are doubled:
> Long buildings hang and
> wriggle gently. Chimneys
> are bent legs bouncing
> on clouds below. A flag
> wags like a fishhook
> down there in the sky.

---

*From *To Mix with Time*. Charles Scribner's Sons. Copyright © 1963, by May Swenson.

> The arched stone bridge
> is an eye, with underlid
> in the water. In its lens
> dip crinkled heads with hats
> that don't fall off. Dogs go by,
> barking on their backs.
> A baby, taken to feed the
> ducks, dangles upside-down
> a pink balloon for a buoy.

Seen in detail from a new angle, an ordinary experience becomes extraordinary and the substance of poetry. The fresh perception makes the old experience unique.

And the perception is conveyed through language. The words and combinations we choose must be carefully screened to see that they are not the old stereotypes through which we blind ourselves to the world. In his poems, e. e. cummings tore words apart and put the parts back into new combinations so that his language might reveal a new view of the world. Most of us will not follow his way, but we need to be sure we see what we see as it is, not as we think it is. There is a tree before you. What kind of leaves does it have? Are they alternating on the stem? Do they resemble plumes? Are they flat on the air like lily-pads in the water? Hopkins' journal frequently takes account of such phenomena:

Elm leaves:—they shine much in the sun—bright green when near from underneath but higher up they look olive: their shapelessness in the flat is from their being made . . . to be dimpled and dog's eared: their leaf-growth is in this point more rudimentary than that of oak, ash, beech, etc that the leaves lie in long rows and do not subdivide or have central knots but tooth or cog their woody twigs.

Such careful looking, such precision in visual perception, is a first step in writing poetry. If you cannot see what a tree looks like, it will be hard to tell anyone what a feeling feels like. Because in poetry we are dependent on the concrete manifestations of the world to use as symbols of our feelings and our experiences. This is especially true in lyric poetry. But apt suggestive details give credibility to narrative poems and character sketches as well. A good exercise in poetry is to record exactly what you see before you with no large statements about what is there. Simply describe it as if you are seeing it for the first time. An artist practices by carrying a sketch pad and drawing wherever he may be. In the same way, the result of the poet's sketch may not be a poem, but the practice will help develop a technique for handling a more complex subject when it does appear. Here is an example, a description of a shell done as an exercise:

> Being which is the size of my palm
> almost and fits the upcurled fingers
> flat-cupped the thirty-four fingers
> end in points set close together
> like the prongs of a comb
> sea-combing straining the waters
> they are printed on your back
> brown waves cutting light sand
> waves—merging inward
> lighter and lighter and closer
> whirling
> into the self-turned center
> of yourself.

Just as there are two kinds of perception—what is seen and what is experienced—there are two kinds of possibilities for exact or innovative language. And there are chances also for trite or easy observation on both levels.

A poem will not always die of a single cliché; indeed, a common observation can even be used for a deliberate artistic purpose. Only someone who has really mastered his craft, however, should dare to use a phrase which borders on the trite. Dylan Thomas sometimes uses old phrases but remakes them by small changes, so that they emerge as live word combinations like "once below a time." But I can think of no poetic situation in which a "rippling stream" or "glassy pond" can add anything but tedium. Worse than the cliché at the literal or visual level, is the cliché at the experiential level, the large abstract concept such as:

> Life, like time, moves onward.

The large concept gives the reader a stereotyped experience. Perhaps this is why some very bad poetry appeals to a number of undiscriminating readers: it repeats the stereotype of experience they have in their own minds and gives them nothing new to test it by. A good poem should jolt the reader into a new awareness of his feeling or his sensual apprehension of the world. One of the great mistakes is to make a poem too large and simple.

Poetry is an art which proceeds in a roundabout fashion. Its language is not chosen for directness of communication, for the passing on of facts, like "the plane arrives at five," or "today it is raining," although either of these facts could be a part of a poem. The truth that poetry attempts to communicate is reached by more devious means. Many of the devices thought of as being in the special province of poetry are devices of indirection: the metaphor or symbol, which involves saying one thing and meaning another; paradox, the welding of opposites into a single concept; connotations beyond the direct meaning of a word or phrase, and so on. When we think of the way things are in the world, we find that poetry is not the only area in which the immediate fact is disguised, distorted, or concealed. Poetry does this in order to reach a more complex truth. Other situations involve indirection for other reasons. Purpose determines the directness of statement. Take the guest telling his hostess he enjoyed the party. Did he really? But in saying this he is expressing some other feeling beyond the immediate situation. He may be expressing sympathy or long affection or any number of emotions rather than measuring the quality of his enjoyment of the moment. Take advertising, which often tries to pass along not so much a fact as a feeling about something. Take the art of the magician—the better the more deceiving. For the poet to speak too glibly may be to oversimplify his experience. The poet must constantly ask himself: "Is this the way it really felt? Is this the whole experience? Am I overlooking or suppressing part of it?"

As I write this, a living example has appeared before my eyes. I am looking at the tree just outside the window. If I should give you my visual experience at this moment, I should have to include a lizard that has climbed twenty feet up the trunk and is now looking at me. In my stereotyped picture of trees, birds sometimes come to rest, but not lizards. In my stereotype of the loss of a friend through death, there is sorrow, not anger. But I have felt anger at the death of a friend, and there is a lizard in this tree. The real includes these disparate elements. The poet must think of what he has really experienced. He gives certain real details, certain suggestions. The reader combines these into the experience intended by the poet, the real message of the poem, and so participates in its creation.

The poet uses three types of ingredients in his poem: at the first level is what can be immediately caught by the senses—by sight, by hearing, tasting, feeling, smelling. I call this the literal level: the poet describes what is literally there. This poem of my own is written almost entirely at this level:

THE BLACKBERRY THICKET *

I stand here in the ditch, my feet on a rock in the water,
Head-deep in a coppice of thorns,
Picking wild blackberries,
Watching the juice-dark rivulet run
Over my fingers, marking the lines and the whorls,
Remembering stains—
The blue of mulberry on the tongue
Brown fingers after walnut husking,
And the green smudge of grass—
The earnest part
Of heat and orchards and sweet springing places.
Here I am printed with the earth
Always and always the earth ground into the fingers,
And the arm scratched in thickets of spiders.
Over the marshy water the cicada rustles,
A runner snaps sharp into place.
The dry leaves are a presence,
A companion that follows up under the trees of the orchard
Repeating my footsteps. I stop to listen.
Surely not alone
I stand in this quiet in the shadow
Under a roof of bees.

The sights and sounds caught by immediate sensation are described; the memories are of the same immediate quality. Even the ending of the poem is a literal description, although the reader may find there, if he likes, connotations that go beyond the literal.

Much of modern American poetry is written at this level. If not total poems as here, at least sections of poems. Most readers of modern poetry, many editors, look for this literal quality. Here, as I said earlier, the poet must look carefully and sensitively and report exactly. Notice, next time you read a poem, how much of it contains this literal looking and what details the poet has chosen to give the appearance of reality. Even an imagined experience should have some of this literal quality.

---

* From *The Weathercock,* by Ann Stanford. Copyright © 1955, by Ann Stanford. Reprinted by permission of The Viking Press, Inc.

The next level of poetry is the metaphoric, in which one thing is compared with another. The conventional poetic devices of simile, metaphor, symbol are part of this level. Comparison often mingles with the literal. In Elizabeth Bishop's well-known poem "The Fish," * exact description is aided by comparison:

> I looked into his eyes
> which were far larger than mine
> but shallower, and yellowed,
> the irises backed and packed
> with tarnished tinfoil
> seen through the lenses
> of old scratched isinglass.

The juxtaposing of two things that are not wholly alike but that are alike in some way is one of the ways that poetry creates a new view of the world. Comparisons or analogies can be used thus as part of description, or they can make a total poem. They can be either one-way or two-way comparisons. For example, the fish's eye can be said to resemble isinglass, but isinglass does not remind one of a fish's eye. It is not always necessary or desirable that the comparisons work both ways. Another example, Shakespeare's comparison of true love to a "star to every wandering bark," is effective even though within the poem he is not also comparing a star that guides to love. He is defining love in terms of a star, but not a star in terms of love.

However, often the poet uses a two-way analogy. The doubleness of the analogy is especially effective where the whole poem is in the form of comparison. Here is a poem of mine which satirizes the work of committees.

THE COMMITTEE †
by Ann Stanford

Black and serious, they are dropping down one by one to the top of the walnut
     tree.
It is spring and the bare branches are right for a conversation.
The sap has not risen yet, but those branches will always be bare
Up there, crooked with ebbed life lost now, like a legal argument.
They shift a bit as they settle into place.

---

* From *Poems: North and South*. Houghton Mifflin Company. Copyright © 1955, by Elizabeth Bishop.
    † © 1967 The New Yorker Magazine, Inc.

Once in a while one says something, but the answer is always the same;
The question is, too—it is all *caw* and *caw*.
Do they think they are hidden by the green leaves partway up the branches?
Do they like it up there cocking their heads in the fresh morning?
One by one, they fly off as if to other appointments.
Whatever they did, it must be done all over again.

Here, what is said about the crows can be applied to a committee, but it is also true of crows, at least the ones I have observed in my neighborhood. This, then, is a two-way analogy.

There is another level at which poets sometimes work: the level of statement. Much of Wordsworth's poetry is statement, as:

> This spiritual Love acts not nor can exist
> Without Imagination, which, in truth,
> Is but another name for absolute power
> And clearest insight, amplitude of mind,
> And Reason in her most exalted mood.

This is a hard and dangerous level for most poets. Much poetry, especially amateur poetry, constantly attempts statement without backing it up with the literal or analogic or comparative level. The poem which merely states, except in the hands of a master, falls flat because it does not prove anything to the reader. He is not drawn into the background of the statement. He is merely told. If his own experience backs up the statement, he may like the poem, but he likes it only because of his experience, not because of what the poem has done for him.

Masters of poetry, on the other hand, sometimes make one large statement and spend the rest of the poem illustrating or proving it. Hopkins does this with the statement "Nothing is so beautiful as spring—"; May Swenson does it in a more specific way in "Water Picture." William Carlos Williams in "To Waken an Old Lady" defines old age by describing a flock of birds in winter. His only reference to age at all is the first line, "Old age is." Without the first line to suggest the definition, the poem could be simply a nature description. Emily Dickinson often makes an abstract idea come to life by defining it in visual terms:

> Presentiment is that long shadow on the lawn
> Indicative that suns go down;

The notice to the startled grass
That darkness is about to pass.

It would be a rare poem which could exist on one of these levels—
that of literal description, that of metaphor, or that of statement—
alone. Poems usually combine these in varying proportions. There
are dangers to the poetry, besides triteness, at all levels. Flatness,
dullness, and poor selection of details menace literal description.
Metaphor is endangered by irrelevance; a metaphor which does not
contribute in tone or feeling may turn the reader away from the
poem as a whole. Statement is most dangerous, for it must be proved.

A poem which succeeds may also have a fourth level—the transcendental level, where the connotations of the poem extend on beyond the limits of the poem. But the transcendental may hardly be
striven for. We only recognize it when it shimmers in the exceptional
poem.

Meanwhile the poet works at what he can. He looks for the whole
significance of the experience. He renders it—even more, he understands it—through language built around his own view. His new seeing is what will make the experience of the poem worth telling once
more.

68

VISION AND REVISION

By Doris Holmes

LET'S see, what are my views on writing poetry? Are special traits, training, insights needed? Can one cultivate imagination? Do you grind out a poem and see it through, or does it come to you in a flash?

The questions you have just read are fake. I concocted them to demonstrate how profoundly our most casual speech reflects certain notions about creativity. The notions I refer to all assume an alliance or a resemblance between creative power and vision or seeing.

How many "visual" phrases do you find above? There are six in those four questions. A very little reflection or research would uncover many more words whose roots suggest that imagery is the work of the visionary, the man who sees the light. Imagination, that magical power of the artist, is the ability to see that which is not, which does not exist (yet), to see it in the mind's eye. The reader, listener, viewer, must also have imagination, to enjoy what the artist sees. However, there are usually two differences between the appreciator and the artist: the artist sees it before other people do; he then "makes" it. This second difference is the significant one.

Before considering the making, the practical matters of technique, let us review (!) some traditional concepts about the vision of the poet.

In the first place, poets are supposed to be good at simply seeing physically. They are always observing, noticing concrete details, or over-all atmosphere. They see eternity in a grain of sand, and they also describe the mica, or is it silica? If they don't know, they look it up, and become fascinated with the words of the definition. They see the violet hidden by a mossy stone, but in addition, insist on the violet in the lady's complexion. Outside the window, the tree is a fountain. The tulip has stripes; one brick is missing from the wall. A skate case is lying among the seaweed and beach debris. It's true, they may be less likely to notice that the gasoline gauge is down, the liquor bill up. They may, though, be alert to the similarity in atomic and stellar arrangements. At any rate, *vision as observation* is certainly an essential poetic power as well as practice, trait as well as training, the poet's gift, in both senses, from life and to life.

Perhaps it is a modern symptom to treat physical vision first. Surely the most central kind of vision associated with the poet over the centuries was what we may call *prophecy*. The poets of the Old Testament were seers (!) who sang forth. As we were taught, the prophets were not foretellers, or fortunetellers, but forth-tellers. Sometimes they predicted—doom if their listeners didn't reform, paradise if they did—but the prognosticating was done with rhetoric rather than sorcery. They saw the handwriting on the wall and told their people to "behold." Sometimes their zealous conjurings were fulfilled in actual later events, and that, combined with their effective verbal performance, brought awe and admiration for ancient bards. Isaiah's prophecy and the coming of Christ need no comment, but it is still eerie to think of Tennyson in the 1840's writing (in "Locksley Hall"):

> For I dipt into the future, far as human
> eye could see,
> Saw the Vision of the world, and all the
> wonder that would be;
>
> Saw the heavens fill with commerce, argosies
> of magic sails,
> Pilots of the purple twilight, dropping down
> with costly bales;
>
> Heard the heavens fill with shouting, and
> there rain'd a ghastly dew
> From the nations' airy navies grappling in
> the central blue;
>
> Far along the world-wide whisper of the
> south-wind rushing warm,
> With the standards of the people plunging
> through the thunder-storm;
>
> Till the war-drum throbbed no longer, and
> the battle-flags were furled

In the Parliament of man, the Federation
of the world.

We who live somewhere between the "ghastly dew" of Hiroshima
and the last unrealized international union may pause over the place
of prophecy.

Inspiration is what we all want, and the non-writer often assumes
that it is some magic that descends from above. It is totally capricious and beyond our manipulation according to this theory. The
muses hit some of us and not others. The poet may go into a kind of
trance or frenzy. He is in some abnormal state, excited and heightened above the mundane or even the real. His vision, then, approaches *hallucination*. The madman, the fool and the artist have
always had something in common. It is not necessarily easy to dis-
criminate between the flights of fancy that indicate talent, and the
flight to phantasy that may mean the mental aberration that is illness. In the richest of writing, though, the author is diving, perhaps,
but not drowning. He sees a phantom of delight, is nearly carried
away, but not quite. He celebrates it, the phantom or his experiencing the phantom. Maybe he seems to play with the materials of his
art. The divine inspiration may look like the divine discontent, but
the true artist has a rage for order. He may be big enough to incorporate a lot of chaos but that's what he does: incorporates it, gives it a
body, with shape or form. His hallucination, then, may issue in some
lucidity after all.

Vision also connotes a kind of *intelligence*. In business or government we say "he is a man of vision" if he has foresight, imagination
and faith. That last element of confidence is, in some subtle manner,
part of the poet's vision, too. He may not be a confident person in
other ways, but he believes, maybe even obsessively, that the thing
may be done, the picture painted, the novel written, the music composed. The poet's vision is sharp, smart. Perhaps he has an angle
view of society and reality, but it's a kind of 20/20 look at life. All of
this vision traditionally "flashes upon the inward eye which is the
bliss of solitude" when his vistas are "recollected in tranquillity."

Psychology teaches us how our subconscious mind relates seeing
with sexual potency, and blindness with loss of that power, or castra-
tion. These deep symbolic processes are beyond our fathoming, of

course, but there is something very basic in our assumptions about vision as a primary part of any human power.

"Writing makes it seem clearer," said Strindberg somewhere in his journal. Many writers feel this way. Writing is a way of pulling things together, of seeing your own experience more clearly, of *revising your vision of life*. This re-viewing and re-ordering gives the writer esthetic pleasure whether his creativity is involved in arranging the facts of reality (as in non-fiction) or in making, or making up, the artifacts, the "fictions" of his craft.

So having submitted that poetry is a kind of revision to begin with, let us look at the more conventional meaning of revision. Of course that holy fire of inspiration that we mentioned must be transmitted through the words of the poem. Whether the poet began with an idea, an experience, the sight of something in the natural world, a grief, an ironic understanding, a lyrical phrase that seems to haunt him, a desire to imitate or translate, a fascination with rhyme, or a free passion, he has to put it down. Even the most beatnik primitive has probably been unconsciously and swiftly revising as he translates, transcribes, transmits his initial impulse into words. Responsible poets have always revised. Of course the Homers of the oral tradition chanted out without benefit of eraser, but they repeated lines, changed them slightly if necessary, and kept in composing trim by constant practice. They had various devices to keep the epic going while they revised in their heads. Have you ever told a story three or four times, polished it till it was a well-rounded anecdote? You've probably pruned the unnecessary parts the second time around, changed key words, highlighted the climax, and so on.

Some poets retain their work sheets. It can be intriguing to follow the patterns of such a poet's thought as you read through his additions, subtractions, enlargements, associations. The hunt for a single word, the perfect word, is still the crucial job. He may need something more specific than his first draft produced. The new word may suggest a whole cluster of new, related auxiliary ideas. The poem may take a different turn then. Or he may be hunting for a rhyme. The margin of his manuscript may have a couple of dozen words that will rhyme, from which he must choose one. His original may have been too obtrusive or too flat. The substitution will change a lot more than the sound, hooking him into a new stream of thought. Scratchings in the margin may be a column of synonyms or near-synonyms, or words that he hopes will lead him to something just beyond his consciousness or memory.

Other poets do this associating in their heads, so their work sheets don't reveal the intervening steps. Some compose on the typewriter, retyping and rewriting or revising, at the same time. They thus re-manage the whole with each revision.

When a writer is very "dry," has no idea, no song, and is miserable because he wants to write, one ploy is to scribble out anything, any foolish random thought, phrase, comment, word, that comes to mind. "But suppose nothing comes to mind?" Sit and look at the room and describe it; record your irritation, blankness, frustration. Write down how stupid you are. You may turn up something that's been escaping you. Tune in on your daydream, even if it's cloudy brooding. Allow strands to ooze up from the great marsh where your reason hasn't organized everything. You may be surprised at the flora and fauna of what you called "blank." Don't underrate straight description either. Precision of expression, the fineness, the accuracy if not the beauty of the words may hook you, or re-hook you. And *looking*—that may do miracles.

I do not usually keep work sheets. Some seem to survive—they may have a gem up in the corner, a provocative word or two for future use. But once in a while a poem simply resists conclusion. I believe it was Robert Penn Warren who said you don't finish a poem; you abandon it in despair. I have one here that has been extant in my life and papers for years. I select it because it is small, as well as in the process of revision, and it may illustrate the preceding commentary. I need hardly say that this selection is offered not as an example of the first word in the title of my article, but as a case of the third:

When I die the telephone

Autobiographical details would help but also delay the presentation here, so I'll be brief. The telephone is part of my life. The poem began with the first line. That's all. I was about to dial a number. Smiling, I heard the first line in my head, which is another way of saying I was talking to myself. I imagined the cleaning out of my house after my demise. Early on, the poem was "Doris' Dirge," half comic. (I have always loved "Fidele's Dirge" in *Cymbeline*, which you remember begins "Fear no more the heat o' the sun.") Here is an early version of my "dirge":

TELL AND TELL

When I die the telephone
Will hang still till
The men rip off my black sin,

The wall rest from the dirt,
My love to the round hole in
Its listening heart.

The coiled cord to my ear
Twisted you all
In my hair,

Dear wordy ones
Who rang me and ring me;
Thanks, from my quiet bones.

The New England Telephone and Telegraph Company became New England Telephone, diminishing my pun in the title. Norma Farber thought "black sin" sounded terrible, like bad Anne Sexton. Margoret Smith said "bones" were absolutely out; too hackneyed. A bright young woman in the Boston Winterfest audience where I read the poem asked why I used so much sexual imagery. I pretended it had been intentional and spouted something about oral compulsion. She also questioned my grammatical structure and I immediately realized that "rest" had to be either "rests" or "will rest" paralleling "rip" or "will hang." Maybe the "will" could be understood, but I never felt comfortable about it again.

I thought "sin" was funny, because true. I thought of "dirt" as the chatter, as well as the actual mark on the wall where the phone had been. "Ring" meant the circle of mourners around my grave at the end, as well as telephone ring. And so on.

Then the pattern bothered me. The dirge was so nearly a tight little artifice of half rhymes going aba cac dbd, etc. But criticism had centered around avoiding clichés and making images sharper. I tried not to be rigid, and attempted variations:

When I die the telephone
        Will hang still till
        The men jerk out the black vine

        The wall rests from the dirt,
        My love to the round hole in
        Its listening heart.

        The coiled cord to my ear
        Twisted you all
        In my hair,

        Dear wordy lovers
                merchants
                wielders
                mothers
                lovers
                sellers
                pedlars
                singers

        Dear wordy lovers of harangue
        Wordy mothers of harangue
        Who ring me and rang;
        Thanks, from my settling tongue.

My children knew this piece in its original form, and made bleating noises when I forced them to listen to the new version. Children are conservative anyway, but the truth was, the early lines rang with an inevitability for me, too. Years passed. I left "Dear wordy ones" and a pencil list of phrases after "from" in the last line including "What remains, that dead tongue, the monotones, quiet bones, the silent tone, my quiet tongue, graver tones and my settled tongue." This year I faced "Tell and Tell" again and set about a more formal arrangement, so that the half rhymes came out aba cac dcd ede. My witchlike insistence that I would haunt my friends forever would, I hoped, carry, if not passion, at least eeriness, the spookiness of machines as well as ghosts:

        When I die the telephone
        Will hang still till
        The men jerk out the black line [not vine]

        While the wall rests from the dirt,
        My love to the round hole in
        Its listening heart.

The coiled cord to my hair
Curled your report
Into my ear.

Dear wordy ones
When you ring me no more
I will still sing, in your dial tones.

I cannot rid myself of "Tell and Tell." Perhaps it is only an exercise in revision. I must say, though, that it meant, means more than that to me. I *saw* myself, by composing it, and I laughed. For such vision, microscopic though it may be *sub specie aeternitatis,* I am humbly grateful. Perhaps some day a revision will satisfy me enough to want to see it published.

69

HOW FREE IS FREE VERSE?

By John Ciardi

Robert Frost created something like an academic cliché when he said that "writing free verse is like playing tennis with the net down." Nor do I mean that the remark itself is a cliché. When first made, in fact, it was not only terse and witty but probably barbed with a bit of malice toward Carl Sandburg, whose unmeasured effusions Frost was always happy to scorn. It is the remark as taken, rather than as made, that has become lumpish; for far too many teachers have accepted it blindly, not as a witty and provocative generalization but as an oracular and incontestable pronouncement.

Even on the basis of its own metaphor the remark can be both respected and contested. For most people tennis with the net down is no tennis at all—true. Poetry, on the other hand, is not written by most people, or at least not well enough to count. What is good enough to count is written by the few whose talent and dedication include the disciplines of engaged form.

As far as the tennis metaphor is concerned, I submit that ranking tennis players, finding themselves on a court from which the net happens to be missing, could still play something very like a hard game of tennis. I am suggesting, as a principle at least equal to Frost's in this case, that if you know the game well enough you can always play it, that knowing where the net is supposed to be can be as good as having the net there.

Whether or not anyone can hope to know the conceptual net as certainly as he would know the actual one is not a question I mean to push hard at any tennis club. In art, however, the conceptual is always its own reality. No one has given greater grace to that thought than has Richard Wilbur in his poem "Mind," in which he compares the mind to a bat wheeling through caverns:

> Contriving by a kind of senseless wit
> Not to conclude against a wall of stone.

The poems ends:

> And has this simile a like perfection?
> The mind is like a bat. Precisely.
>   Save
> That in the very happiest intellection
> A graceful error may correct the cave.

Back once more at the tennis club, one may find the members in full scorn of conceptual nets (and hypothetical baselines). Yet even a tennis player might grant—if only as a speculation over the third martini—that tennis as formalized by the rule book is not the only possible tennis, but only the tennis agreed upon.

But let that be enough talk of conceptual nets on actual courts. Suppose, instead, that two good tennis players came onto the court one day and found that someone for some reason had raised the net three feet off the ground and left it there. They could decide to have some fun out of it and to play a variation of the game in which every shot had to go under rather than over the net. The game they played that day would strike the chance observer as a queer one and the religious tennis player as sacrilege, but if the players entered into it with the right whimsy they might just find that their game, though far off the official version, was a demanding one. And since its rules were hard ones, they could, if they were good players, enjoy it.

So carried away, they might even go on to invent new variations. Suppose that one day they found a net with a great rip in the center and that with a few deft improvisations they rigged the rip into a two-foot circle and gave themselves the latitude (and the difficulty) of permitting the ball to be played, at choice, through that center target as well as over the net.

Or suppose again that two whimsical madmen decided to rig the net from a high pole to a low one, so that it stretched aslant from a height of twelve feet on one side to standard height at the other, with the new rules requiring the players, on any shot, to decide whether to play over the net at the low end or under it at the high one.

Once again, the guardians of the rule books would shudder, but certainly the players, if they were as good as they were venturesome, might find these variations demanding and, therefore, satisfying.

In poetry there is not and cannot be a final rule book. Each poem must go by its own rules. All that is necessary is that there be rules of some sort. The poet is free to invent his rules to any measure including madness, but having invented them he must be ruled by them.

For these reasons, there cannot in fact be any such thing as "free" verse. The term "free verse," when first invented, implied no absolute freedom but only freedom (and, in fact, a rebellion) from certain traditional rules and measures the "free verse" poets took to be moribund. Under Ezra Pound the Imagists and under Amy Lowell the Amygists kept themselves busy enough from the first, proclaiming the rules of their rebellion.

The fact is that something *has* to measure. It may be the wave length of the cadence. It may be the breath group of the phrase. It may be a pattern of caesuras. Or the line length. Or as little as the width of the page. Or the play of one rhythm against another. Or an assonantal or a consonantal pattern combined with the cadence. It may be anything but it has to be Something, and that Something must measure. William Carlos Williams and e. e. cummings did not write to the kind of measure that would have satisfied John Keats. Perhaps it is possible to say that at times Williams and e. e. cummings lost track of their own measure. But the man is mad who will argue that these poets at their best wrote to no measure. The teacher of modern poetry who cannot identify these measures is not qualified to enter the classroom.

Curiously, there seem to be as many teachers bent on encouraging their students to write free verse as there are teachers declaring that they can make no sense of it.

What these encouragers of the formless young seem not to recognize is that no student anywhere is competent to attempt free verse. Students write what they call free verse because they find it easy. The fact is that free verse is only easy to write badly. The poet who writes it well takes on the enormous difficulty of inventing his form as he goes, and I shall insist that the demands of such invention are forever beyond the range of student talent. May our teachers forever be an encouragement to the young, but they destroy their own ends if they encourage them to anything but form, and strictest form.

And between Frost and their misinterpretation of Frost, let me remind them that I have uttered no preachment against real nets, and that if I have suggested that ranking players may make a game of it without the net, or with an altered net, I have at no point suggested that one learns the game with anything but a real net, and that firmly in place.

70

LIGHT VERSE: QUESTIONS
AND ANSWERS

By Richard Armour

LIGHT verse is a minor art or craft, but there is a good deal of art and craft to it. In fact there is often more technique involved in light verse than in serious poetry. Phyllis McGinley once said that light verse is (or should be) less emotional and more rational than poetry, though I think she won the Pulitzer Prize not so much for light verse as for what I would call light poetry. At any rate I agree with her that light verse is not to be taken too lightly by the writer. Quite aside from talent, and a special way with words and ideas, one must know the fundamentals, and more than the fundamentals, of versification: meter, rhyme, and all the rest.

The best modern light verse writers, such as Phyllis McGinley, Ogden Nash, David McCord, Morris Bishop, Arthur Guiterman, Samuel Hoffenstein, Dorothy Parker, Margaret Fishback, and Ethel Jacobson, have also been poets or mock poets. Having read and absorbed the writings of poets and light verse writers who went before them (and light verse is as old as Chaucer), they sharpened their skills and eventually developed styles of their own.

Some of these poets are still with us and still writing, but not quite so much and not quite so lightly. It is about time for a whole new generation. Magazine markets are fewer and book publishers more wary, but there is still a substantial readership for light verse if it is original and skillful and has something to say. I thought it might be helpful to give some basic pointers and to put them in question and answer form. These, at any rate, are the questions I am most often asked and the answers I most often give:

Q. *What is the difference between light verse and poetry?*

A. Light verse is a kind of poetry. It is poetry written in the spirit of play. Since it may not have the high thoughts or the imagery of poetry, it makes up for lack of these by emphasis on technique. The first requirement of a light verse writer is sure command of meter and rhyme. But along with technique, as in any writing, there must be something new to say, or a new way of saying something old.

Q. *What are the best subjects for light verse?*

A. Since you are writing for people, you should write about what people are most interested in. And people are most interested in people. In other words, the best subjects are those that have to do with the foibles of the human race, such as the relations of man to wife and of parents to children; the effort to get along with one's neighbors and one's colleagues and one's boss (unless one *is* the boss); the struggle with waistline and hairline; bank accounts, charge accounts, and no accounts; hosts and guests; passing fads in food and clothing and cars and sports; buying a house or building a house or running a house or being run by a house; vacations and travel and luggage and tips; pets; youth and age and the in-between adolescent; illness and doctors and remedies and recuperation and exercise; automation and the computerized society in relation to the bewildered individual; people who are meddlesome or pompous or stupid or inconsistent— in short, all aspects of the human comedy. Here is an example of a piece of light verse on a subject of universal interest:

> MONEY
> Workers earn it,
> Spendthrifts burn it,
> Bankers lend it,
> Women spend it,
> Forgers fake it,
> Taxes take it,
> Dying leave it,
> Heirs receive it,
> Thrifty save it,
> Misers crave it,
> Robbers seize it,
> Rich increase it,
> Gamblers lose it . . .
> I could use it.

Q. *Where does one look for ideas?*

A. You not only look but listen. You keep your ears open as well as your eyes. Sometimes a chance phrase or a cliché will trigger a piece of verse. In addition to looking at and listening to people, you read, read, read. You read books and magazines and newspapers. Now and then, if you are on the alert, an idea will pop up. Newspapers, especially, are mirrors reflecting the absurdities of mankind—and womankind. Light verse should concern subjects that concern people. It should strike common chords, be human, be universal.

Q. *What is the best length for a piece of light verse?*

A. Brevity is a requisite of all forms of humor. Recently a critic writing in *Esquire* made the wise observation: "Humor is like guerrilla warfare. Success depends on traveling light . . . striking unexpectedly . . . and getting away fast." This applies especially to light verse, which is a condensed, almost telegraphic, form of humor —verse being more compressed than prose anyhow. Light verse is briefer today than it was in the more leisurely nineteenth century, and less intricate than in those days of the ballade and the villanelle. Usually it runs from two lines to eight or ten or twelve. Only rarely to sixteen or more. That is, if you want to sell it. By the way, this is the shortest piece I ever sold (to the *Saturday Review*):

MAID'S DAY OUT
Thurs.
Hers.

Q. *What are the best verse forms to use?*

A. Simple iambic and anapestic meter, rather short lines (trimeter or tetrameter), couplets and quatrains. If you don't know what these are, go to your local library and get Clement Wood's *Poets' Handbook* or look at the back part of Clement Wood's *The Complete Rhyming Dictionary*. You can't expect to enter a highly competitive field, in which technique plays such a large part, without knowing the fundamentals of versification.

Light verse should be technically correct in rhymes and meters, and, if possible, not only correct but fresh and original. I have mentioned short lines. You may also use the longer pentameter (five stress) line, which has been the most popular form in English poetry ever since Chaucer, but it usually leads to somewhat more serious treatment, and the rhymes (much more important in light verse than in serious poetry) are a bit far apart.

Q. *Are there any other suggestions for writing salable light verse?*

A. It should, usually, have an element of surprise or some sort of clincher at the end. (See "Money" quoted above.) But it should not rely too much on the last line, in that case spoken of slightingly as "terminal humor." Good light verse should be amusing all the way through, with maybe something a little special at the close. And it should be given the additional help of a good title—one that is original and appropriate.

Q. *How do you find markets for light verse?*

A. You can look at the market lists that appear from time to time in issues of *The Writer* (or write in for the back issue containing light verse markets). But you should also examine the magazines themselves, to see whether they are using light verse and, if so, what type. I take a good many magazines, but in addition I spend many hours on my haunches at newsstands, checking the magazines I don't take. (Forgive me, managers of drug stores and supermarkets. I still buy enough from you.)

As for knowing markets—submitting light verse to the right place at the right time—this is as important today as ever. It is perhaps more important now than it was thirty years ago, because the markets are fewer and the competition is keener. But, again, when I started out I knew my markets, *The Saturday Evening Post* and *The New Yorker,* as a long-time reader of both.

Markets change and you have to keep up with them. *The Saturday Evening Post,* now that the "Post Scripts" page is all cartoons and there are no poems scattered through the back pages, is no longer a market for light verse. And *The New Yorker* uses less verse, and such verse as it uses is less light than in what I think of as the Good Old Days, when Harold Ross was editor.

Today, the nearest thing to the old "Post Scripts" page is "Look on the Light Side," in *Look,* a highly competitive but gratifying market for light verse and short prose humor. And there is "Light Housekeeping" in *Good Housekeeping,* and "Parting Shots" in *The American Legion Magazine.* In addition to these well-edited pages, where you have to fight off a multitude of free-lancers, there are magazines that occasionally use short humor. But these you will find in market lists or discover for yourself by reading the magazines.

Q. *How do you submit light verse?*

A. Type it, double-spaced, one poem to a page, with your name and return address in the upper corner (it makes no difference whether left or right) of the page. Submit one to three poems at a time. You may be able to get in four, along with a stamped self-addressed envelope, for the same postage, if the paper is not heavier than sixteen-pound weight, a good weight for all manuscripts. No letter is necessary or desirable. What could you say? Editors have enough to read anyhow. Another thing—there is no need to say anything about protecting your manuscript. Editors are honest and the U.S. mails are safe. If something is bought, what is usually bought is first North American serial rights, which means the first run in a North American newspaper or magazine.

Q. *Do you need an agent?*

A. An agent might be helpful, but most agents won't bother with light verse. And most don't know the markets as well as you will know them if you study the magazines as I have suggested. It's a do-it-yourself field.

Q. *When do you do your writing?*

A. Whenever I get a chance, which isn't often enough. I long ago gave up "waiting for an inspiration"—else I would still be waiting. I also gave up trying to set aside regular hours for writing, though I would do this if I could. Since I have several other time-consuming activities, I write when I can. But my conscience or compulsion or whatever it is weighs so heavily on me that I feel frustrated and remorseful if I do not write a little something—prose or verse—each day, seven days a week. (I am writing this on a Sunday morning—

after having gone to church.) Some days I write for ten minutes; some days I write for ten hours. One advantage of light verse is that it can be written during short periods. With a schedule such as mine, I am glad I am not a novelist.

Q. *Do you still get things back?*

A. Yes, indeed. I use returned verses as scratch paper on which to write new verses. My method with editors is erosion. After a while, I wear them down. But it takes patience and postage. The difference between the professional and the amateur, in this business, is that the professional becomes discouraged less easily.

Q. *Do you get printed rejection slips or letters?*

A. Both. And sometimes I get neither—just the poem back, in the return envelope, which is really very sensible. I think rejection slips are a waste of paper. If I get a poem back, I know, without any printed explanation, that it has been rejected. Of course I am grateful for a letter, or even a brief note. One editor with whom I dealt for many years used to grade my poems, as if I were a student in Freshman Composition. Though he might buy a poem that he graded "B minus" or even "C plus," only once did he ever give me an "A." It was for this piece, which is included in my collection, *Nights With Armour:*

THE LOVE LIFE (AND DEATH) OF A MOOSE

Up in Newfoundland some 20 moose, mistaking Diesel train horns for mating calls, have been lured to death on the tracks.—*News item.*

> Imagine this beast of the frozen Northeast
> With its annual amorous craze on,
> Seduced by the toot of a choo-choo en route
> Into making a fatal liaison.
>
> Conceive of its sighs as it straddles the ties,
> Unaware of the killer it's dating.
> The honk of the train has gone straight to its brain,
> And its mind is completely on mating.
>
> Appalling? Of course, but just think how much worse
> It would be, and no words shall we weasel,

Should an engine tear loose from its tracks when a moose
Makes what sounds like the call of a Diesel.

This, by the way, is a pretty good example of playfulness, zany point of view, exaggeration, out-of-the-ordinary rhyming, and fancy footwork (with metrical feet)—some of the ingredients of light verse.

Q. *Of the light verse you have written, what is your own personal favorite?*

A. This is almost impossible to answer. Sometimes, in a depressed mood (that is, daily), I like nothing I have ever written. Other times I run onto something I wrote years ago, and had forgotten, and wonder that I had ever written anything so good. This, instead of making me happy, depresses me further, because it convinces me that I am on the downgrade and shall never do so well again. But usually I like best whatever I have written most recently. This goes not only for my light verse but for my books. Perhaps I can dodge the question by quoting a piece of light verse that seems to be a favorite of others and is fairly typical.

MY MATTRESS AND I
Night after night, for years on end,
My mattress has been my closest friend.

My mattress and I are cozy and pally;
There are hills on the sides—I sleep in the valley.

It clearly reveals the shape I'm in:
Where I'm thin it's thick, where it's thick I'm thin.

Its contours reflect the first and the last of me.
It's very nearly a plaster cast of me.

I miss my mattress when I am gone;
It's one thing I've made an impression on.

This is about all there is to it. Everything depends on your sense of humor, your original way of looking at things (including yourself), your handling of rhyme and meter and words, and your ability to be critical of what you write and to compare it honestly with what is being published.

Now I have to get back to work, because light verse, no matter how easy it looks (and it should be made to look easy) is work, hard work. And when a piece of light verse comes off right—when it is original in concept, and funny, and nicely turned—the light verse writer gets, in his way, as much of a feeling of accomplishment, even creativeness, as a serious poet.

71

WRITING CHILDREN'S VERSE

By Aileen Fisher

You like children—the frankness of their reactions, the nonsense of their humor, the verve of their imagination. You remember your own childhood and recall in flashes of detail how you felt about this or that, and what you thought and wondered about. And you have always liked rhymes—from the time your mother read Mother Goose aloud until you started to jot down some verses of your own. You have, in fact, quite a collection of "poems" hidden away in your desk drawer. Now, looking at the booming market for children's books, you wonder how it would be to try your hand at writing children's verse as a free lance. What are your chances?

One writing friend advises you: "Don't waste your energy on verses. So many of the good children's magazines have fallen by the wayside. And those that are left are flooded with manuscripts. *Everyone* thinks he can write children's verse."

Another friend, who works in the adult field, says, "I'll ask my agent."

The agent's reply is anything but encouraging. "There's so little money in children's verse, most agents can't afford to handle it. And many publishers won't even look at a book of verse. It takes years for a writer in the field to build up a name. I should think your friend would be wiser to stick to fiction or non-fiction or plays."

Are they right?

Yes and no.

I should say the first question you should answer in your own mind is: What is my aim in writing? Is it to make money? Is it to be published? Is it for the satisfaction and fun of putting ideas down on paper on the chance that someone else may sometime get pleasure or inspiration from them?

If you want to make money (and for some reason people have an idea that a great deal of money is to be made at any kind of writing), the children's verse field offers few lures. Only the exceptional writer makes a living at it, whereas a number of writers of children's fiction and non-fiction are able to support themselves year after year.

Of course, there are exceptions to the rule of small financial returns. But I don't believe that the handful of writers who have done well in the children's verse field ever expected to. Certainly it was not with a bank account in mind that A. A. Milne wrote his Christopher Robin poems, and probably no one was more surprised than he that they became so famous. He wrote because, as he watched his son grow up, his own recollections of childhood were rekindled and illumined, and whimsy and humor bubbled forth. I think it is safe to say that Milne had as much fun writing *When We Were Very Young* as anyone ever had reading it.

But it is one thing to try to make a living at writing children's verse and quite another to supplement income from other writing or from a job. The incidental income becomes more and more substantial as one's name becomes better known. After you have been in the field for twenty or twenty-five years, your earnings from verse may really amount to something.

There is the original (usually small) check for first publication in a magazine or newspaper. Then, after a lag of time, perhaps a reprint fee or two for republication in an anthology or textbook. Besides, if you are careful about reserving book rights, you can use published verses in a collection of your own, and royalties will start coming in. After book publication, more requests may come along for permission to reprint. And these fees add up over the years. Recently, for instance, I received a check for $25 for the use of a poem that sold to *Story Parade* years before for $9. And a firm putting out a combination "picture-board" and recording recently offered $30 each for the use of five verses for which I had received a total of $27.50 (for the five) for first serial rights. A reprint fee of $10 or $15 for a verse of twelve lines or so is common enough.

Now, what about the market?

Your best bet as a beginner is to try to get verses published first in one of the juvenile magazines or school papers, or even in your hometown newspaper. Dorothy Aldis caught attention and applause years ago by having some of her verses appear in the column "A

Line o' Type or Two" in the *Chicago Tribune*. I tried it, too, somewhat later. The first verse I sent to "The Line" was published; then
my luck stopped. Obviously I was no Dorothy Aldis!

Although it is true, and regrettably so, that some of the outstanding children's magazines have gone out of business, there are still
plenty left. Just turn to the annual market list of *The Writer* covering the juvenile and teen-age field, and you will find dozens of publications that print verse. Many of them pay very little, it is true, but
just getting published when you are starting out is more important
than making money. Keep verses going in the mails, four or five in a
group, and don't be discouraged by rejection slips.

We all get those slips that are guaranteed to keep a writer humble!
It's part of the free-lance picture. Always remember, though, that
the editor feels no personal malice toward you or your work. She has
problems of her own, plenty of them. I remember reading an article
in *The Writer* some years ago by the editor of *Child Life*. She
pointed out that at least 18,000 manuscripts a year were submitted
to *Child Life*, and only about fifty stories and one hundred poems
could be published. That's less than one acceptance in a hundred
submissions. Somebody, a lot of somebodies, are bound to be
rejected. That's the way the free-lance market operates. For every
need there are dozens of writers offering their wares. But success
waits at the top of the hill for the persevering climbers who have
something worthwhile to offer.

After serving an apprenticeship by having verses published in the
"first serial" market, you come face-to-face with the flourishing business of children's books. Your goal will be book publication, of
course. And what are your chances here?

The field is a big one, and the children's book business is booming.
Each year several thousand new children's books are published. A
score or more of these will be books of verse, new collections of individual poems, or anthologies of both old and new material. Add to
that several hundred other books of children's verse in print, and
you have an impressive total. And that is not all. More and more
picture books are being written in verse, and, as everyone knows,
picture books are perennially popular.

What this adds up to is that the writer of children's verse today
has a wider market than he had a generation ago. Of course, he prob-

ably also has more competition. But openings are there! And a writer's investment in trying to attain publication is negligible. You can write verses anywhere, with little equipment—no months of painstaking research, no doctor's degrees, no electric typewriters. You automatically have the background you need, since you were once a child yourself. And it costs little to keep verse manuscripts in the mail.

Some people have an idea that verses are written only in an ivory tower. "If," they say, "I had a set-up like yours, with such a view from my study window and such peace and quiet all around, I could write, too." But surroundings really aren't the important thing. It's having something to say that counts, and taking joy in saying it— something to open a child's eyes, to make him laugh, or wonder, or venture through a door ajar.

The most reprinted lines I have ever written were jotted down in the most "un-ivory-tower" imaginable. I was working in Chicago at the time, saving every cent I could "to escape to the country." One of my economies was to live in a cheap, dark, first-floor room in a third-rate hotel on Chicago's South Side. The one window opened onto a cement areaway leading to an alley, and there were bars across the panes to keep out prowlers! The room had a steel cot, a wardrobe badly in need of varnish, two straight-backed chairs, and a kitchen table I used for a desk.

I remember coming home from work one winter evening and jotting down some lines I had thought of on the brisk walk from the station. Then I went out for dinner at a little restaurant around the corner where I could get a meal for sixty cents. When I got back to my room, I was amused by the nine lines I had hurriedly written, and I sent them off, with several verses, to the editor of *Child Life*. I have lost track of how many times "Otherwise," written in those stark surroundings, has been reprinted. Here are the nine lines:

> There must be magic,
> otherwise,
> how could day turn to night,
>
> And how could sailboats,
> otherwise,
> go sailing out of sight,

> And how could peanuts,
> otherwise,
> be covered up so tight?

Another verse I wrote during that hectic Chicago interlude has been reprinted time and time again. I was on an elevated train, on my way home from Evanston after a busy day as reporter on a neighborhood newspaper. The train was noisy and crowded, clattering along past rickety back porches and grime-stained apartment buildings. Grayness hung heavy over the city. I yearned for the clean openness of the countryside in northern Michigan where I had spent my childhood. The country! In a flash I was there. Eight short and simple lines wrote themselves on the back of an envelope:

DOWN IN THE HOLLOW

> Down in the hollow,
> not so far away,
> I saw a little ladybug
> when I went to play,
>
> Swinging on a clover
> high in the air . . .
> I wonder if the ladybug
> knew that I was there.

If you are interested in writing children's verse, it is a good idea to keep looking, listening, and wondering about things. How can an apple tree hang all those apples around? What's inside of me making me grow? Where do woodchucks get enough dreams to last them all winter? How is an egg made . . .

> You'd think the yolk
> and white would run
> before the shell
> was ever done . . .
>
> But hens don't lay
> a scrambled one!

But to get back to the ivory tower—it is, of course, far easier as a steady routine to write in pleasant surroundings. After five years in Chicago, I "escaped" to Colorado, and my production curve went up. But even so, few of my later verses have been reprinted as often as some of those early Chicago ones.

Here are a few bits of advice I can give you, gleaned from experience. Write. Keep on writing. But don't "write down." An adult should be able to read children's verse with pleasure. Keep accurate records of submissions and sales. Put down all the flashes about your childhood that come to you. If a poem doesn't work out, or doesn't sell, don't throw it away with a gesture of impatience. Keep it on file. You never know when lines written years before may generate a spark that will light more than one fire. Many times I have gone back over old verses, filed away alphabetically by title, and have come up with something unexpected.

A few years ago I was caught up short on rereading an old verse of mine about birds: How clever they were to balance themselves on wires, to jerk themselves up trees like a woodpecker, to grow webbed feet and swim like a duck. The last four lines struck the spark:

> Oh, birds are clever,
> but where would they be
> if they ever, ever, ever
> wore shoes like me?

"Wore shoes like me." That set me to thinking about going barefoot. How eagerly my brother and I used to wait for warm weather so we could throw off our shoes and stockings and be like the rabbits and birds—barefot! I began to think of all the ones who went barefoot the year 'round—raccoons with their footprints looking like the tracks of a child, deer with their patent-leather hoofs making sharp marks, mice embroidering the snow with dainty stitches. Before I knew it, I was writing stanza after stanza about going barefoot. Some days later, I had nine or ten pages, more or less unified. I sent the manuscript to Thomas Y. Crowell Company, where I was not entirely unknown, since they had published a number of my verses in an anthology the year before. In eighteen months, for the wheels of publishing often turn slowly, *Going Barefoot,* with illustrations by Adrienne Adams, came out as a picture book.

That was only the first fire lit by the spark of a forgotten verse. The editor suggested that I do a series of nature picture books in verse. So I wrote a piece on hibernation (*Where Does Everyone*

Go?), without featuring the perennial woodchuck. Then, remembering how often I had been surprised in the woods and fields by a creature so well camouflaged that I had almost stepped on him, I wrote a little book on protective coloring—*Like Nothing at All*. Leonard Weisgard illustrated it.

Then followed *I Like Weather*. I wrote it from the heart because I do decidedly like weather . . .

> days and days and days
> with different kinds
> of smells and sounds
> and looks and feels
> and ways.

A boy yearning to have a wild rabbit for a pet (*Listen, Rabbit*), a girl taking a birthday-present walk with her father (*In the Middle of the Night*), a lonely child finding all kinds of unexpected "houses" near his own (*Best Little House*)—the subject-matter for children's verse is endless because children's interests and enthusiasm are endless. They rise to the quiet and familiar as well as to the exciting and strange.

Like most writers in the field, I started from scratch and served a long apprenticeship. I knew no editors, had no contacts, and never went to New York to see publishers. Because I loved to do it, I just kept writing children's verse as one string to my fiddle. You can, too. And remember, there are more children than ever these days who are reading, in school and out. There are more books being published. And editors are always on the lookout for something refreshing and original.

72

WRITING FOR CHILDREN

By Irene Hunt

Any writer, whether he writes for children or adults, must face and
answer the questions posed by Goethe to would-be writers:

> Do I have something to say?
> Is what I have to say worth saying?
> How best can I go about saying this thing
>   which I consider to be worth the saying?

Any fictional writing if it lays claim to being literature must leave
the reader with a clearer picture, a deeper understanding of some
aspect of human behavior, of human needs, a more profound knowledge of the human heart, if you will.

Thus the writer must find his answer to the question "Do I have
something worthwhile to say?" by discovering what aspects of human behavior he wishes to explore.

Will it be the courage of a child in overcoming his inner fears,
in overcoming a hostile environment, in overcoming physical or
emotional handicaps? Will it be a child's perceptions of the adult
world around him? Will it be the insights of a young person into
his own behavior? Will it be the interplay between environment
and human needs?

There are an infinite number of problems which beset the family
of man, and they lie waiting for us to present them in a new light
—to clarify and illuminate them through our own originality.

When the question of what one is going to say has been resolved,
the writer must decide how best he can say it—what characters,
what situations he can create which will provide the best setting for
the ideas which are the core of his writing.

Armstrong Sperry, in writing of courage which overcame a terrible fear, chose the terrors of the sea, of storms, of primitive savages to illuminate his theme in *Call it Courage.*

Scott O'Dell pointed up another kind of courage, the courage to live, to survive, in his Robinson Crusoe-like story, *Island of the Blue Dolphins.*

E. B. White and Kenneth Grahame chose fantasy—a fantasy accurately reflecting human values—and where is the child who can miss the dignity and compassion of some of their characters, the bumbling foolishness of others?

Now, a look at the qualifications of the writer himself—the man or woman who aspires to write for that vast crowd of young readers and who aspires to write wisely and well for the audience he has chosen. First, his ability to write for children involves a close affinity with his own childhood, and if he has this, it follows that he will have that same affinity for childhood in general. He must remember! He must remember the anxieties and uncertainties, he must remember the loneliness of being teased or misunderstood. He must remember the dreams, the perplexities, the sudden flashes of joy over something that seemed trivial to adults. He must remember his reaction to tastes, to smells, to colors; his love of a kind hand, his fear of a harsh mouth. He must remember the imaginary companions, the wonderful secret places where he could be alone, the hoarding of nondescript material in an old box— guarding it, rearranging it, caring greatly for it without quite knowing why.

This affinity for our own childhood and for that of others is something that not all of us possess; it is, I sometimes think, as final an attribute as the color of our eyes or the shape of our ears. If we don't have blue eyes or brown, we don't, and there isn't much we can do about it. If we don't understand childhood, we don't, and I doubt if we can ever develop that understanding. This quality is not correlated with either age or intelligence; some great scholars have it, some don't. Some people of twenty have it, some have already lost it at that early age. Some people of sixty or eighty have it; others of the same age do not.

Writers of adult literature are sometimes dismayed when they have turned from their own field to that of children's literature. They often find that they do not know how to speak to children, that they are unable to establish the bond of sympathy which they had believed would be so easy to do. They have found they long since have left their childhood behind them and that they are aliens in a community of readers who sense their kinship with one writer without ever quite realizing that it is present, and who sense equally well the lack of kinship with another writer.

People who have forgotten their own youth tend to carry with them a picture of rosy childhood, protected from all evil, bathed in love and security and winsome innocence. Those of us who remember the anxieties, the anger, the fear—sometimes the cruelties which we perpetrated and have never been able to forget—we are the ones who know that childhood is not always a period suffused in a rosy glow. And those of us who remember the delight at a word of praise, or the sound of a birdsong; the sweet comfort of being understood, the heady excitement of running against the wind, the sense of security in hearing a mother singing at her work —we are the ones who know that childhood delight is not all a matter of camping trips or toys, parties or the approval of peer groups.

Another point which the writer for children must keep in mind is that he must have respect for his audience. Can he lend dignity to a child of seven or nine—or is he one who would say, "No child of such an age can possibly have felt grief or fear or anxiety with such intensity?"

And again, is the writer in tune with that bittersweet period of life which we call adolescence, or does he believe that adolescents are concerned with nothing more than getting a date or getting on the football team or romping around camp for the summer? Worse still, is he one of those writers who have great fun in depicting adolescents as callow, silly, uproariously funny to the "sophisticated" adult? How naïve can such writers be? Have they completely forgotten the sensitivity, the bewilderment, the groping for beauty and truth that are so often characteristic of these years —the years which, I often think, may be described by the words which Dickens used to describe the closing years of the eighteenth century—"It was the best of times and the worst of times; it was an age of foolishness, an age of wisdom."

Children have dignity—they appreciate respect for that dignity.

Children perceive and evaluate, they feel intensely and they look for answers to the many questions with which a capricious society often baffles them. If the writer for children does not remember this, he will soon need to turn to another field.

Closely associated with respect for childhood is the ability to write without preaching. This is difficult. As parents, we are inclined to preach. As teachers, we are very much inclined to preach. And as writers, we still feel the urge. We want to spell the idea out. We're afraid the immature mind may not be aware of the pearls we are offering it. We want to say, "And so you see, boys and girls, if children do this or that, then these or those results are going to ensue." Paul Hazard in his great book, *Books, Children and Men,* has this to say on the subject: "A glance of the eyes, a thrust of the thumb is all they need. They sense the coming of a sermon and they skip it with dexterity."

Preaching is not the only cardinal sin either. There is the matter of the author feeling that he must be instructive. We like to say—implicitly, of course—"I know that you selected this book because you thought it was fiction, but you're going to get a little lesson in science or history or anthropology on the side."

There is nothing wrong with children learning something of science or history or anthropology in a book of fiction. BUT—and this is a very important BUT—it is up to the author to make this kind of information so much a part of the story, to endow it with so much of human interest, that it is an integral part of the story. When a child picks up a book from the shelves devoted to fiction, he has a right to expect a story. He heartily resents the intrusion of what he perceives as a "classroom bit" interfering with that story. He doesn't mind if it's a part of the story; *Johnny Tremain,* for example, contains a wealth of history concerning the American Revolution, but that history *is* the story of Johnny Tremain—it *is* the story, and not a fringe benefit.

Again I quote Paul Hazard when he writes of some of the early works of what was whimsically called children's literature: "To admire an oak for its beauty was considered time wasted; children needed to be able to calculate what the oak might yield in board feet when it was cut into planks."

Next, an author must be true to himself. If he has a story to tell, he must tell it without worrying whether it will appeal to children of seven or ten or sixteen. Incidentally, if it is a good story for a child of seven, it is in all probability a good story for any age. Take Rebecca Caudill's *A Certain Small Shepherd*, for example—take *Winnie, the Pooh*, take *Charlotte's Web*—what age group will like these stories? Any age from seven to ninety, provided the reader has learned to love excellent literature.

I feel that the writer who has a story lurking around in his mind and heart should present it as *he* sees fit. He should be allowed to forget vocabulary and taboo subjects, he should close his ears to the chorus of "children are no longer interested in this or that." One educator told me with a finality that left little room for doubt that children would never read a story of the Civil War: "They are fed up with it," she said firmly. Of course, what she meant was that *she* was fed up with it. I have more than a hundred letters from children all over the country who have read and have told me that they loved my book, *Across Five Aprils*.

Other members of this free-advice chorus have told me, "If your book is written in the first person, you had just as well throw it away right now. Children simply *won't* read books written in the first person." Oh, won't they? Have a look at *Huckleberry Finn*, at *Treasure Island*, at *Island of the Blue Dolphins*, at *Onion John*, at *It's Like This, Cat*. And my own *Up a Road Slowly* is doing pretty well. My advice to writers is: Ignore the chorus, and write as you please. Children are interested in almost any subject, written in either first or third person, if it is presented in an interesting context, if it is written honestly and well.

There is no need to be upset if we feel that we are dealing with a subject that has often been dealt with before. Some authors strain very hard to be original, confusing novelty with originality, forgetting that it is what you as an author bring to the subject which constitutes originality. Flaubert, Tolstoy and Thackeray used the same, time-worn theme: woman's self-destruction. And yet, Emma Bovary, Anna Karenina and Becky Sharp stand out as different, as unique, as sharply drawn as if each had participated in a situation never described before—products of their specific creator's originality.

I feel that originality is that special blend of color and contrast, that quality of vigor or poetic mood, that depth of characterization with which the writer presents his story. Novelty is only an arresting factor; originality is the quality which gives a book endurance. In children's literature, *Alice in Wonderland* is a shining example of novelty. But it is not novelty that makes this book great. It is not Alice's unusual acquaintances or her experiences with changing size or her encounters with frightening incidents which make the book a great one. It is the satire, the wry wisdom, the impish lashing out at certain stupidities of society which give the book greatness—it is the quality which only Lewis Carroll could give that situation—that very personal and private attribute of a writer which is his originality.

Young writers are often concerned with style—they wonder how they can develop that concept which is so elusive, which does not easily lend itself to definition. Style, it seems to me, is an outpouring of the writer's self—his perceptions of life, his grace or lack of grace, his courage or his whining self-pity, his humility and compassion or his cynicism and arrogance.

Think of the delicacy of Katherine Mansfield, the robust humor of Mark Twain, the gentle wistfulness of Kenneth Grahame, the sweet, prim morality and great warmth of Louisa M. Alcott. Each one has a style all his own because each one has poured out a part of himself, the kind of person he was or is, into his writing.

The young or beginning writer cannot copy a style authentically any more than he can *be* the person whose style he admires. He may be influenced by another's style in that he has read and admired the writings of an author until he has come to accept that person's viewpoint. But if he is wise, he will not seek to emulate another writer's work; he will set himself to the task of telling his own story as clearly, as honestly, as gracefully as he possibly can. When he has worked for a while, he may suddenly discover that he, too, has expressed some inner feelings in a way that people will speak of as a particular style.

In conclusion, I would say that our concern over children's books is justifiable and understandable. There is a great need for excellence in children's literature just as there is a need for excellence in all other aspects of education. To train a nation of readers, of people who have at an early age commenced to deal with ideas, who have come to recognize a system of values which includes such concepts as insight, compassion and understanding of human behavior—to do this carries a responsibility which is of towering importance.· For whether a child becomes a scientist or a housewife, a mathematician or a mechanic, a teacher, a businessman, a statesman, a factory worker, a farmer, these values are basic to his fulfillment as a human being.

We must remember that children are not born with these values. Their understanding and appreciation of literature and of life do not suddenly appear full-blown like Athene from the forehead of Zeus. It comes from reading and discussing and learning to love good books; it comes from guidance in discovering wisdom and beauty, it comes because authors and teachers, librarians and parents are providing the books of wisdom, of beauty and joy, for these young learners. The good books, the gay, the sad, the wise ones are providing a basis for a nation of readers, a nation of people who understand themselves and those around them a little better. We do not learn courage, humility, compassion, honor or human decency from penny lectures or from a special unit in the classroom. We learn these things through the people around us—we learn them largely from the behavior of those characters who march through the pages of our books.

73

WRITING BIOGRAPHIES FOR YOUNG READERS

By Olive W. Burt

One of the most popular, and for many writers most rewarding, types of writing for young people is the biography. This seems to be a field in which there are never too many books for the eager youngster, or (what is more important to the writer) never too many for the publishers.

There are several things to be decided before one pitches into such a project. First, of course, is the choice of subject. If by chance you are one of those fortunate people who have publishers sending you frantic telegrams for a book, you may not be free to choose your subject. The publisher may have told you what he needs—subject, age level, and treatment. But let's suppose you are on your own and can decide for yourself what you want to do.

About whom shall you write? Hasn't everyone important been covered in a biography? A glance through several publishers' lists will almost convince you that there is no one left for you to write about. Messner's "High School Shelf of Biographies" now numbers more than two hundred subjects, chiefly Americans. Bobbs-Merrill's "Childhood of Famous Americans" series has over one hundred and fifty titles. Franklin Watts' "Immortals of Science" lists more than thirty books. Watts also publishes other series of "Immortals" in literature, science, engineering, etc.

All this needn't scare you. Your book about any individual will be different from any other book that has been written. If you have something new, some hitherto little-known facts, or just a different approach to your subject, you can write—and sell—biographies even about such perennial favorites as Lincoln and Washington. The spate of books about John F. Kennedy—many just rehashes of newspaper articles—shows that publishers bring out books on subjects that have appeared on competitors' lists.

There are, however, plenty of less well-known persons who are worthy of treatment. It gives an author a peculiar sense of achievement to produce a book about some person children should know, but have, so far, had no opportunity to meet in a biography. A few years ago, *Publishers' Weekly* printed a list of twenty new biographies for young readers and asked how many adults could identify the subjects and their accomplishments. On the list were Anne Neville, Bartholome de las Casas, Francisco de Orellana, William Dampier, Fridtjof Nansen and Kateri Tekakwitha. Some astute writers had performed a real service in presenting these people to children.

Writing for children, you will not want to do an exposé of the sins and foibles of some person, however fascinating these may be. Your purpose should be to present a character whom the young reader may wish to emulate. To do this successfully, you must honestly admire the person you choose to write about. Insincerity is quickly detected by the sharp perception of youngsters. If they once mark you as a hypocrite, your value in this field is lost.

You will, of course, choose a subject you already know something about. Your knowledge may, however, be vague and inaccurate. So you begin to read, swiftly—and without much note-taking —the best biography on your subject that you can find. This will help you to decide whether you have made a wise choice, what age group will be interested, and how you wish to handle the material.

Biographies written for young people fall into the same age-level classifications as do other books. The pre-school child will probably have little interest in biography, but the 9-12-year-olds, the teens and the young adults love it. For the younger readers, the preferred length is around 20,000 to 25,000 words, and it's growing shorter every year. Teen-agers can handle a book of 40,000 or even 50,000 words. Books for young adults may be any length, though many publishers prefer to keep them under 60,000 words.

Biographies for young readers, as, indeed, for adults, may be written either factually or fictionally. The factual treatment is a straightforward account of an individual's life and the events which shaped it. It is completely accurate as to dates and events, but should not have footnotes. It is generally permissible for the writer to invent some dialogue of which there is no record, provided there is evidence that such conversations took place. In using the *factual* treatment, the author is all-knowing. He can present facts and incidents of which the hero is unaware, provided these facts are important in shaping the individual's actions. In writing a factual biography of John Charles Frémont, for example, the author might tell of the cabinet meeting in Washington and of the debates that led up to Frémont's court-martial—events which Frémont, out in California, could not have known.

Fictional treatment is a bit more complicated. Here the author disappears entirely—he tries to get "right into the skin" of his main character, to think and feel as this person must have thought and felt. Nothing can be told that the subject does not know for himself. If events occur beyond the hero's ken, the reader may know of them only when, as and how the subject, himself, learns of them. This point of view must be maintained throughout the book. The author has an advantage, however, in that he may introduce characters and events that are entirely imaginary. But these imagined events and characters must be true to the time and place of the story and *must* be necessary to the development of the character.

Personally, I prefer to write the fictional type of biography. I used it in doing a biography of Frémont for Messner, and in that book, Frémont knew nothing of what was going on in Washington until a messenger brought the news.

Sometimes a combination of the factual and the fictional treatment is attempted, but in such cases the result generally falls short of the ideal. Either history or fiction suffers.

By now you will have read enough about your chosen subject and thought enough about it to be able to write an intelligent letter to a publisher. It is wise to find a publisher before you spend months in research and writing. You are not likely to find one who will say right off, "Yes! I'll take that!" But you may find one who will agree to look at a chapter or two "on speculation." Then it is up to you to produce something the publisher can accept. But how to find a publisher? Visit the library and examine books brought out by various publishers. Or consult the special seasonal issues of *Publishers' Weekly* at your library, and study publishers' lists there.

It is often easier, especially for a person breaking into the field, to get a start via one of the series. The field is large. In addition to those already mentioned, Nelson has "Picture Biographies" for the 9-to-12-year-olds; Putnam publishes "Lives to Remember" and "Westerners." Sheed and Ward's "Patron Saints" deals with the lives of Catholic saints, and Bruce's "Catholic Treasure Books" present the lives of noteworthy Catholics.

Select the publisher you think, from your investigation, will be most receptive to your idea, and write a query letter to the editor of books for young people. It is more effective if you address this editor by name, which you can find in *Literary Market Place* at the library. In your letter, you state clearly, simply, and briefly the name of your subject, a little about him or her, and how you would like to handle the biography. Also, ask the editor if he is interested in seeing two or three chapters and an outline of the whole book. If the answer is yes, get right to work and do those chapters before the editor forgets about you—or takes another book on your subject from an author who is more prompt.

If you write to several editors and do not find one who is interested in your project, you may drop the idea as unfeasible; you may put it aside for the time being and go to work on something else; or you may go ahead and write it anyway, trusting that your fine work will sell the book, once it is written.

The selling of a finished book is difficult, and grows more so every year. Today, the publisher likes to decide on his forthcoming list and then approach writers he knows can fill his requirements. Also, at the risk of ruffling the feathers of some fine editors, it seems that a few feel that to take a book as sent in by an unknown author indicates that the editor has been outguessed. If consulted before the book is written, he can be not only the "chooser," but also the director of the project.

Let's assume that whether you have a go-ahead from a publisher or not, you decide to go on with writing your book. Now you begin *intensive* research, which is far different from the preliminary work you have done. First, you will read all the published biographies you can find about your subject, especially scholarly, accurate works. Read also magazine articles, biographies of your subject's contemporaries, and the history of the period. If possible, study original documents, letters, newspapers, journals—anything written during the period in which your subject lived. These will give you an intimate glimpse of life and language, dress and foods, which you will find nowhere else. Try to visit the locale where your subject lived. If you can see his home, handle his books, touch the doorknobs he turned, you'll find yourself better able to think and feel as he did.

All this time take careful and accurate notes. And always, without fail, make a record of the source of every note, listing the title of the book, author, publisher, date and place of publication, and the page on which your material was found. This may sound like needless work, but I can assure you that if you fail even once to make a complete record, that very item will be one you later wish to check, and you will never, never be able to find it again. Moreover, if the publisher wants a bibliography, as some do, you will have the information handy and will not have to redo your work.

When your research is completed and you feel you are ready to begin writing, you will need an outline of some kind. An effective chart-outline can be drawn on a large sheet of paper. Rule it into columns. In the first, put the dates of your subject's life, chronologically from birth to death. In the second, write the names of family members and their ages at particular years. In the third column, list the names of friends and relations, especially any special or close friend. In the fourth, note where the subject was living in that particular year. In the fifth column set down local events; and in the sixth, national affairs. You may want to add other columns for other information.

A glance at such a chart will show you some years that were especially significant to your subject—highlight years. These will make dramatic chapters. Insignificant years can be passed over with a few phrases of transition. Select the highlight years and arrange them as chapters. Set the scene, as if you were writing a one-act play: set the stage, bring on the characters, give the dialogue, making sure that every word, every action advances the story. Make the whole chapter a unit in itself. Think of it as a one-act play.

These scenes can be linked together by links of transitional material which should be just long enough and detailed enough to bridge the gaps—but they must do that, to bring the characters smoothly into the next act.

Now you can begin writing. The first page is important. Select one of the highlights you have marked as your first scene. This should come from early enough in the character's life to make a good starting point, but it needn't be his birth nor his fifth birthday party. It can be the first significant event—the one that started his career. In *Frémont*, I began with the boy's first job, in a lawyer's office. I started *Jedediah Smith* with Jed's joining Ashley's party of trappers. For my Brigham Young biography, I chose the boy's first camp meeting. Each of these events started a chain that led inevitably to the accomplishments of later years.

Write as fast as you can. Guided by your outline, let your mind and feelings race ahead. If you come to a word, or a date, or a name you can't recall immediately, just draw a line there and go on. Don't stop your flow of thought to look up details. This speed will give your book the accelerated pace young people like.

When you have finished it, put it aside for a while—a week or more. Then read it over carefully. Supply the facts you missed. Correct grammar and punctuation. But more important than these technical jobs is the task of improving your style. Have you used the same word too often? Almost everyone has a favorite word that pops up everywhere. Do you begin several sentences the same way—with a participle, an infinitive phrase, a question? Have you kept the point of view consistent? If your treatment is factual, have you editorialized too much? If fictional, have you slipped up at some point and let the hero know something he could not have known?

Maintaining the viewpoint is sometimes really tricky. It might seem all right for the author to say of his hero, "His eyes blazed." But this immediately puts the author *outside* his subject through whose eyes he is supposed to be viewing the world. The character himself would not know that his eyes "blazed." When in doubt, put the sentence in the first person, and you'll see how ridiculous this is: "My eyes blazed."

Be alert for anachronisms. Clothing, food, furniture, language—all are traps for the unwary. Slang is treacherous. If your subject is a lively child—as are many in the "Childhood of Famous Americans" series—he will probably use some innocent slang expression. But if you do not know what expression children actually used at that time and place, it is safer to make up a word that sounds true to the character, the time and the place.

Watch for spots where you can use senses other than sight and hearing; appealing also to the sense of smell, taste, and touch will help make your book more vivid. In reading the manuscript of my book, *I Challenge the Dark Sea* (John Day), an editor observed that my description of Tangiers was "peculiarly non-smelling for the odoriferous tropics." I corrected that lack with some noisome dogs, horse manure, and rotting fish.

After you have done everything you can think of, and have a clean copy from which to type your final version, set this aside for a week or two and then go over it as carefully as you did before, still correcting, smoothing, polishing. Then, at last, make a final copy for the editor, with at least one carbon, preferably two in case one is needed for the illustrator.

One thing that will help sell your book is humor. It is a help if the subject, himself, is bright and cheerful. But all too often, alas, a great person has little sense of humor. Jed Smith is an example. In his journals, in all contemporary accounts, there is no indication that he ever cracked a smile, let alone a joke. But his biographer is saved by Jed's companions, among whom were the biggest liars in the mountains. Their tall tales, their antics offer the happy element that children delight in.

Needless to say, don't write down to children. Writers for young people who break this rule should not—probably will not—see their books in print. Straightforward, simple, direct language, with vivid phrasing, is needed to give distinction to a writer's style.

Writing biographies for young people is work, but it has its own rewards. Of course, there is the money: A good biography for children may sell far more copies than an adult best seller. Augusta Stevenson, who wrote *Abraham Lincoln,* the first of the "Childhood of Famous Americans" series, in 1935, is said to have sold more than 150,000 copies of that one book alone. After more than thirty-five years, it is still a big seller, and Mrs. Stevenson has produced twenty-five more books for this series, with total sales of more than a million and a half copies.

But money is not the only reward—nor even the most attractive. A person writes because he wishes to communicate with others, and there is no one more ready for communication than a child. A writer feels well repaid when he gets an enthusiastic letter from a young reader, even though it may be as terse as one I received from a little girl: "Madam, next time you write a book, notify me." Such things make the time and effort worthwhile.

74

LET'S BUILD A SKYSCRAPER,
BUT LET'S FIND A GOOD BOOK FIRST

By Roald Dahl

Approximately five out of seven of all children's books being produced today are a cheat. They have glossy King-Size cardboard covers, and if you tear off the covers of one of them and hold only the paper pages between your fingers, you will find that you are holding something that is slightly thinner than a slice of modern, mass-produced, vitamin-enriched, steam-baked bread—and just about as worthless.

If you count the words in this "King-Size" book (the thing is usually too tall to fit into a bookshelf), you will discover that they add up to anywhere between 150 and 1,500, averaging perhaps midway between the two. You can read the whole text to your child in about fifteen minutes, which includes looking at the pictures, and that, almost invariably, is the end of that. When you have done, you lay the book aside with a distinct feeling that somebody has made a fool out of you and that you have been robbed; so you apologize to your child and turn out the light and slink downstairs to wash away the memory with a glass of whisky and water.

For this masterpiece of bookmaking, you have paid perhaps as much as $3.95, which is another way of saying $4, and the profits, if any, from that dismal transaction have been split, albeit unequally, among the bookseller, the publisher and the writer. For them, it is strictly a business, the business of conning parents into buying junk for their children—although I must say that one out of the three profiteers, the poor bookseller, can hardly be blamed for the quality of the product, or indeed for selling it.

I have been buying these books for my children for a number of years now, and I suppose I shall go on buying them for several years to come. Don't ask me why, although I imagine it is for the love of betting on a long shot and for the thrill I experience when I happen to pick a winner. But the winners are very few and very far between. I am sure I have paid $1.95, $2.95 and $3.95 many hundreds of times for a book that takes ten minutes to read, is read only once, and is then, quite probably, never looked at again.

Perhaps it is my own fault. I should examine them more closely in the bookshops, and should spend four or five minutes skimming through the text before buying. But somehow I cannot bring myself to do that. Instead, I foolishly keep insisting that every book that a publisher has taken the trouble to publish must surely possess a modicum of merit. The publisher, with his experienced and discerning Juvenile Department, has accepted the text and commissioned the illustrations and put the thing together, and therefore he, and he alone, must take the blame.

And up to a point, so he should. Unfortunately though, the children do not see it that way. They blame me because I was the one who bought it. At least, they *used* to blame me, but I have recently started to instruct them—all parents should do this—to point their criticism in the proper direction, and now, whenever we read a real stinker, the first thing they say is, "Good heavens, who published *that?*" To which I reply loud and clear, "The house of so and so published it, my darlings. Let us try to remember that name, shall we, when we go to the bookshop next time?"

I know very well that this evil propaganda is only partly deserved, and that the writer is the original culprit; but the notion that writers can be fools is a very dangerous one to instill in the minds of a writer's children, and I refuse to do it. The publisher, though, with all his wealth and power, is fair game, and nothing but good can come of teaching the young that this man, if not always a fool, is anyway a sly and rapacious fellow. All of them are—all except my own.

My own publisher is neither sly nor especially rapacious. Instead, he is a terrible wrathful man with a slow fuse burning in one end of his belly and a stick of dynamite in the other. This is nice, because explosions are exciting. Lovely explosions can be set off inside him by any of one of the following: bureaucracy, circumlocution, bad prose, Irving Wallace, indifferent wine, other publishers, *The New Yorker* magazine and children's books with restricted vocabularies.

The last item will always cause an extra large explosion, and it is only a pity that it isn't big enough to blow all those restricted vocabulary books to smithereens. They are a device of morons and they do a grave disservice to children. More and more, modern scholars are finding that the child who does best in school is the one who has acquired a large vocabulary in the home, both from his parents and from the books that are put in his way. So what in heaven's name do these people think can be gained by depriving the child of the opportunity of learning new words? Nothing. Beatrix Potter could have told them that years ago. (I wrote a restricted-word story once, and I am very sorry that I did so.)

The heads of great publishing houses do not themselves write the books that are published by their Juvenile Departments (there is one notable exception to this rule), and therefore, to be perfectly fair, practically all the blame for the scarcity of good new children's books in these days must obviously fall upon the writers. It seems to me that most writers in this field have become thoroughly lazy. If they can persuade their publishers to accept a manuscript of 750 words of absolute rubbish about a pony or a rabbit or a day at the zoo, they will happily do so. The more threadbare the text, the more illustrations the publisher will have to put in as padding.

The writers know this, and it pleases them very much. It pleases them firstly because it means that the hard work will have to be done by the illustrator, and secondly because they believe that a book containing lots of pictures and few words sells better than its opposite. Well, maybe it does, but for children of six and over, there is no doubt that too many pictures in a book is a bad thing. It teaches *them* to be lazy also. It makes it unnecessary for them to use their imaginations and to visualize a scene in detail in their own minds. Television, in a more vicious way, has the same effect.

How many writers of children's books will take the trouble to sit down and construct a story or a fantasy of twenty-five or thirty thousand words? Precious few. That sort of thing is hard work and it takes a long time. But it is in this category that the good ones come up, books like *The Lion, the Witch and the Wardrobe,* by C. S.

Lewis; *Charlotte's Web,* by E. B. White; *Pippi Longstocking,* by Astrid Lindgren; *The Secret Garden,* by F. Hodgson Burnett; *The Railway Children,* by E. Nesbit; *My Naughty Little Sister,* by Dorothy Edwards; and *Mary Poppins,* by P. L. Travers.

These are all long, wonderful books, written with care and skill and patience, and were you to take these seven, and only these, and were you to read from them one after the other to your 6- or 7- or 8-year-old child for ten or fifteen minutes every single night, they would still last you for half a year. Each of them possesses that rare quality—the mark of a first-class children's book—which makes it just as acceptable to the adult who reads it aloud as to the child who listens. What is more, the books mentioned are nearly all available in paperback (in England, anyway), and one is therefore getting an astonishing quantity of good reading for very little money.

To me it is incomprehensible that anyone should go out and buy a single copy of one of those ten-minute, one-night, coy "King-Size," copiously illustrated, almost textless, completely pointless, $2.95 or $3.95 books *until* they have bought and read all the lovely long ones that have real stories in them and that last for a month on the first reading, a month on the second, and a month on the third. It makes no sense at all. All it makes is money for the three profiteers. The reason I buy the silly ones myself is simply that we have read and reread all the good long ones we can think of, and we can find no more.

It is more difficult, I think, to write a long book for children than it is to write an adult novel of comparable quality. I have written only two long children's books myself, and for all I know, they may be completely worthless. But I did make the effort. Each of them took somewhere between eight and nine months to complete, with no time off for other work, and eight or nine months is a big slice out of the life of any writer, and a big drain on his batteries. For one who is used to writing for adults only, it is also an uneconomic diversion.

These days, original works of fantasy and imagination are becoming scarcer and scarcer. Forty years ago, we had almost nothing else, and it was wonderful. Today they hardly ever appear. Instead, we are being showered with those horrible things that are called educational books—*The Life of the Guppy, Your Wonderful Body and How It Works,* and *Let's Build a Skyscraper.* The emphasis, right from the start, in this increasingly practical and materialistic world we live in, is upon practical things and upon cramming the head of the child with facts. Ten years from now, there will probably be a spate of children's books with titles such as *How to Sell Insurance, The Thrills of Being an Advertising Man* and *The Stock Exchange Is Fun.*

There is nothing wrong with facts, and there is nothing wrong with learning about the body or the guppy or the stockbroker, but don't forget that the poor child is going to have to concentrate upon almost nothing but the assimilation of facts all the way through from the age of ten to twenty-three, and it would seem not only wise, therefore, but also kind, to give him a break during his early years. The nicest small children, without the slightest doubt, are those who have been fed upon fantasy, and the nastiest are the ones who know all the facts.

75

THE HOLE IN THE LIBRARY SHELF

By Elizabeth Allen

EVERY time I go into the branch library nearest us I glance covertly toward the shelf marked "books for young people," hoping to see my novel *The In Between* on the shelf. It's never there. Occasionally I inquire. "It's out," the librarian tells me. "As soon as it comes back, someone is waiting for it."

What I should do now is stop right here and let the reader suppose that my book is "out" because it is so beautifully written, appealing, and generally marvelous. Honesty (or is it stupidity?) compels me to repeat what the librarian also tells me:

"There are simply not enough books of this type. An eleven-year-old, a fourteen-year-old, or sometimes a 'young adult' who is discouraged by the convolutions of modern fiction, comes in here for something to read. We know what they want. They are looking for a book that holds their interest, characters they can identify with, and a story that gives them some insight into the lives they lead. It's hard to find."

She sighs, and then adds, "There are holes in our library shelves."

Why should this be true? Why, with so many people trying desperately to get into print, with courses in creative writing jammed and with several magazines devoted to the needs of writers, are there holes in our library shelves?

Perhaps too many writers are trying to produce that mythical Great American Novel. That's fine; but working on a short narrative for the young reader might provide a useful apprenticeship. Well, you may ask, *how* young are these readers? I can only go back to the librarian's words: *an eleven-year-old, perhaps a fourteen-year-old sometimes a young adult*. The book jackets for both of my novels for young people indicate "for twelve-year-olds and up." Most of my mail comes from fourteen-year-olds, but I've had letters from ten-

and eleven-year-olds, from twenty- and thirty-year-olds, from professionals in the field of child psychology, and from librarians.

The average "over twelve" reader is looking for exactly what my librarian friend describes, and I should add another qualification: This group is extremely sensitive to what they call "anything fakey." They do not want to be talked down to, dislike sermons, and they need no insults.

Your material? If you have young people growing up in your own home your material is underfoot and on top of you. You also have your own memories and scar tissue. In my own case I have too much material, simply from listening and remembering. I have never found it necessary to do "research," although this works very well for some writers. My difficulty is to cut the film in the right places, cart out the worst of the junk, dim the sound.

Do I get it "right"? You will never get it exactly right. Even the very young writer cannot catch the delight and pain of growing up. The young are too close to it; the rest of us can only try, with an eager pen and a tin ear, to get as close as we can.

It may be helpful to those of you interested in writing "for twelve and up" for me to describe some of the difficulties I encountered in writing my second book for this age group.

I called this story *The Loser,* and it appeared first as a two-part novelette in *Seventeen* Magazine. Originally, it was told in a flashback. A word of warning. The flashback technique works well in a short story or novelette, but I got hopelessly tangled up when I tried to use it in a longer narrative. Unless you can handle the flashback with great skill it is best to abandon it when writing for this age group. You might get tangled and your young reader will stop turning the pages. I also used the first person in telling the story of *The Loser,* and I'm not sure I'll do this again. The first person viewpoint is limiting. You must portray your heroine by inference, rather than description. My other main problem with this book (which I found pleasantly challenging) lay in the fact that I departed from the usual "Cinderella" motif. Most books for girls use as their protagonist someone who feels inferior and "out of it." But Deirdre, of *The Loser,* is definitely "in." She is so "in" that the very smoothness of her life, the lack of obstacles, is in itself a problem. Yet Deirdre has enough intelligence and insight to be aware of this.

We first meet her in a Little Theater as she watches some of her friends try out for a teenage part in a play. Deidre evaluates them, and herself, as follows:

> The boys were all wearing Ivy League shirts and a certain pale sort of jeans popular right now, and the girls were in short tight skirts and piled-up hairdos, which has been the way to look, this winter. To tell the truth, I was wearing a tight skirt and a piled-up hairdo.

Deirdre rather wryly puts herself into the general category of those around her, and in so doing gives us a glimpse of her own conformity—and of her own candor and basic good sense.

But, you may ask, will your reader really get any idea of what Deirdre is like? Will description by inference *work* with a young reader? I think it will. You are not writing for a stupid audience. These young people haunt the libraries because they are dissatisfied with the movies aimed at them and the TV programs directed toward them. Their contemporaries are discussing such books as *Lord Of The Flies* or *A Separate Peace,* or the short stories of Hemingway. They are not yet ready for this type of fiction—but they're reaching.

To get on with *The Loser* and Deirdre, sitting as a spectator in the theater:

> Suddenly I noticed a boy who was different. He was wearing cowboy boots, which no one our age wears, in spite of the fact that this is the southwest. He had on a torn shirt and he needed a haircut . . . His features were fine, and yet strong.
> "There's a loser," someone behind me muttered, and I knew they meant the boy in the cowboy boots.

These words introduce Denny, the other main character in the book. In *The Loser,* theme and story intermingle as I tell of Deirdre, who finds her life changed by meeting "this strange new boy," and who does some growing up along the way.

I tried to leaven this story with as much humor as possible. I used some slang, more as seasoning than straight speech; the use of slang is difficult. All young people use it, but slang, alas, "dates," and expressions current in one part of the country are unknown in another.

If you have the gift of the light touch, you are ahead of the game the minute you sit down to write for a youthful audience. Beverly Cleary, who delights the very young with her *Henry* stories, does equally well with a high school audience. I would advise anyone who is interested in writing successful fiction for the "over twelve" group to pore over *Fifteen* and *The Luckiest Girl*. Mrs. Cleary fulfills the "reader identification" requirement beautifully.

And then, it might be wise to re-read two other books that break this "reader identification" requirement: Mark Twain's *Huckleberry Finn* and Salinger's *Catcher in the Rye*. (Am I confusing you?) And I must add my own favorite book-for-any-age: Jane Austen's beautiful love story, *Persuasion*.

Of course, sooner or later you must stop reading, and stop thinking about "requirements" and "technique," and *write*. Write about someone who interests you. I stuck with Deidre, despite her conformity and initial inertia, because she interested *me*. This girl, I told myself, is not as complacent and confident as she appears. What will happen when she starts asking a few questions? What will happen when she is thrown with a boy who questions everything? I wanted to find out. I hoped some sparks would fly. I, the writer, was "grabbed" by my heroine; and I hoped that she might "grab" somebody else.

If you start a book for young people, be sure that you yourself are concerned about those characters on your page. If you are curious to find out what will happen to them, your readers—you can at least hope!—will want to find out about them, too.

And you'll have the satisfaction of filling up one of those holes in the library shelf.

76

WRITING FOR YOUNG CHILDREN

BY CHARLOTTE ZOLOTOW

CHILDREN'S book writing includes fiction for children from picture books on up to the young adults, non-fiction—biography, autobiography and factual books—and of course poetry. In short, it includes every category of adult writing that exists, and everything that is true of distinctive writing for adults is also true of fine literature for children.

But there is in writing for children an additional skill required. It is easier to address our peers than those who are different from ourselves. And children are different from adults because they live on a more intense level. Whatever is true of adults is true of children, only more so. They laugh, they cry, they love, they hate, they give, they take as adults do—only more so. And this is what makes writing for children different from writing for adults.

One must first of all, over and above everything, take children seriously and take writing children's books seriously. Over and over I have met people who feel that writing for children is a first step to doing "something really good." A fairly successful, but undistinguished author of many children's books said to me one night, "Some day I'm going to do something really good. I'm going to write a novel or a play."

What this gentleman's abilities as an adult writer will be, I don't know. His children's books, however, lack something. There is nothing in them that would make a child put one down and say, "What else has this person written?" (A question children have asked many times after first reading a book by Ruth Krauss, Maurice Sendak, Else H. Minarik, Laura Ingalls Wilder, Margaret Wise Brown, E. B. White, Marie Hall Ets, E. Nesbit, P. L. Travers, Beatrix Potter— the great writers of children's literature.)

This remark of his made me understand why. *He doesn't respect what he is doing.* If he ever gets to his serious play or novel, it won't be that he came via children's books, but that he finally did take seriously what he was doing. I don't think writers of this sort should be writing for children at all. Children's books are an art in themselves and must be taken seriously. Anyone who regards them simply as a step along the way to "real" writing is in the wrong field.

I should make clear here that when I use the word *seriously* I don't mean *pompously.* I don't mean that every word is holy or that it should be heavy-handed. Some of the most delightful humor in books today is in the books for children. Some of the wildest kind of nonsense is there, too. But the writers are saying something seriously in their humor and in their nonsense—something that is real to them and meaningful to them—and they are saying it the best way they can without writing down to an audience whose keenness and perception they must completely respect.

There is a popular misconception about children's books that exists even among literate people. And it exists most particularly in the area of the picture book. A television writer once told me, "I never read my children what's in a picture book. I make up my own story to go with the pictures." He was quite pleased with himself—had no idea of the absurdity his smug assumption "that anyone can write a children's book" contained. He didn't realize that though his stories might amuse his own kids, delighted with the sound of his voice, the expression of his face, and the feeling of well-being his spending time with them gave them, a *published* story must be a finished, well-rounded work of art. In cold print, a story has to be good. The wandering, sketchy bedtime stories we tell our children have to be formed and shaped and sharpened before they can be printed, illustrated, bound in a book to be read over and over again to thousands of children who are strangers to the author's face and voice.

Some of my own books have indeed come out of stories I originally told my children, but years later, and after much thought, much reforming, reshaping, pruning, and in a voice or style that was a writer's, not a mother's. There is an immense difference.

In some picture books there are just a few words on a page. Certain immortal lyrics are four lines long. A sonnet has only fourteen lines. But the brevity doesn't mean they are "easy" to write. There is a special gift to making something good with a few words. The ability to conjure up a great deal just from the sound of a word and its relation to the other words in the sentence, the gift of evocation and denotation, is not only special to the poet but to children themselves. To say that he has had a good time at school that morning, a child may simply tell you, "The teacher wore a purple skirt." The recipient of this confidence would have to be close enough to the particular child to know that purple is her favorite color; that summing up a whole morning's events by that color is equivalent to having an adult say, "excellent wine"; that, in fact, in this child's vocabulary "purple" is a value judgment and the sign of a happy morning. And since children themselves so often use this oblique, connotative language, the writer who is fortunate enough to have retained his own childlike vision can speak to them in this special poetic shorthand that evokes worlds in a word.

A picture book writer must have this gift of using words carefully, of identifying with, understanding, projecting himself into the child's world. He must know and feel what they know and feel with some of the freshness of their senses, not his experienced adult ones. He must know what children care about a given situation. This is usually quite different from what an adult in a similar situation is thinking, wanting, seeing, tasting, feeling; and sympathy and empathy (and memory) are necessary, not condescension, not smugness, not superiority, not serious observation from an adult point of view.

And while the brevity of a picture book makes the author's use of words particularly selective, the rest of what I've said applies not only to picture books but to books going up in age group to the young adults. It is a question of experiencing at that particular level how the small or "middle-aged" child feels.

The best children's book writers are those who look at the world around them with a childlike vision—not childish, which is an adult acting like a child—but with that innocent, open vision of the world that belongs to the various stages of growing up, a clearer, more immediate, more specific, more honest, less judging vision than the adult one.

Children come fresher, with less cant, less hypocrisy, less guilt, to the world around them than even the most honest adults are apt to. Children smell good and bad things without inhibition. They taste, they hear, they see, they feel with all their senses and not so much interfering intellect as the adult, who will label things by applied standards, preconceived standards of good or bad—a good smell or a bad smell, a good taste or a bad taste. Children are realists of the first order. They have fewer preconceived ideas than adults. To them, flowers may smell bad. Manure may smell good. They have no fixed judgments yet. Most things are still happening to them for the first time. The first time water comes from a faucet, heat from a radiator, snow falls, the *real* itself is *magic*.

Because of this, children are open to belief in fantasy—fairies can exist if snow can fall, magic can happen if there are cold and heat, moon and stars and sun. Nothing is routine yet. They live more immediate lives than adults, not so much of yesterday or tomorrow. They are open to the moment completely. They respond to every detail around them completely. (That is why they are so often tiring to be with.)

I remember once the poet, Edwin Honig, came to visit us. He had never met our daughter Ellen, who was then four. They liked each other immediately. And when she offered to show him the house, he left his drink on the front porch and went off into the house with her. When I came in a few minutes later, he was holding her in his arms, and she was pointing into the living room.

"That is the fireplace where we have fires in winter.

That is the rubber plant where one leaf died.

That is the radio where we had the tube fixed.

That is the best chair but our dog sits in it." She might have invited him to see if he could smell the dog in the chair if I hadn't come in.

"You know," Honig said to me, "she's living everything here for me."

A poet could understand this. And in this sense that is what everyone who writes for children must be.

Always remember that the field of children's books is exciting and specialized. It is full of pitfalls that adult writing is free from, not the least of which is that a child's point of view is so different from that of an adult—more different at three than at six, and more so at six than at nine. And even when the child and adult reaction is identical—at any age level—in being hurt, in wanting, in hating, in loving, it is more intense. Adults are like a body of water that has been dammed up, or channeled. Children haven't these constrictions yet on their emotions. They abandon themselves to emotion, and therefore everything from a cake crumb to an oak tree means more to them.

If you are to write for children, you must be absolutely honest with yourself and with them. Willa Cather once advised a young writer never to hold back on any idea or phrase when it fitted something he was writing, in the hope of using it later in something better. Never hold back on what fits the book you are writing for children either. Remember how you felt about things when you were a child; remember, remember that adults might laugh and say, "tomorrow he'll forget," but right then, at the moment, the child feels and believes in his pain or his joy with his whole being.

Ursula Nordstrom, director of children's books at Harper and Row, has, I think, discovered more wonderful children's writers than anyone. "Young people can and will accept the very best truly creative people will give them," she says. And in a recent *New Yorker* article about Maurice Sendak, one of the finest children's book artists and writers today, she said, "Too many of us . . . keep forgetting that children are new and we are not. But somehow Maurice has retained a direct line to his own childhood."

This is what anyone who wants to write for children must do.

77

WRITING THE PICTURE BOOK STORY

By Mary Calhoun

You want to write for children. Picture books. You tell stories to your children or the neighbor's children, and they just love your stories. *And this is good.* If you're telling stories, you already have the first qualification for writing picture books: You are a storyteller. The person who can spin a yarn is the golden one who will fascinate the four-to-eight-year-olds.

Then why aren't the publishers snapping up your stories and publishing them in beautiful four-color editions? Just what I wanted to know when I first started writing down the stories I'd told my boys. Rejection notes from editors commented:

"Too slight."

"Not original."

"We've used this theme several times."

"Too old for the age group."

I can't tell you all the reasons editors reject picture book scripts—such as "might encourage kids to make mess in the kitchen," "might encourage kids to try this and kill themselves." You'll just have to experience some of the rejections yourself. However, these are the general heart of why picture books are rejected:

"Not enough body and plot."

"Idea not big enough."

"Not ready to be a book."

"Things happen to the hero rather than he making things happen."

"Action too passive."

"Basic situation not convincing."

And over and over, "Too slight."

Sound familiar? Use the rejection list to check your stories—my compliments. The thing is, there's a lot more to writing for children than reeling off a story.

Now about picture books.

First, definitions: A picture book is one with pictures and a story to be read to or by a child between the ages of three and eight. (Publishers usually say four-eight, but many a "mature" three-year-old can enjoy having a picture book read aloud to him.)

Of course, there are other picture books for young children. For the two- and three-year-old there are the counting books, the ABC books, the "see-the-cat" books. There are picture books with a very slim text line, books conceived by the artists mainly for the sake of the art work. (No, you don't have to supply the artist for your story; the editor will do that.) There are the "idea" books: non-fiction—exploring "what is night?", "what is time?"—and such books as *A Hole Is to Dig* and *Mud Pies and Other Recipes,* charming ramblings on an idea, but not stories.

Here let's concern ourselves with the traditional picture book, one with a story from which the artist gains his inspiration for the pictures.

What goes into a picture book story?

As I see it, the elements are four: idea, story movement, style and awareness of audience.

First of all, the *idea.* Without a good idea, the writer is dead. Most often, I'd guess, a picture book script is rejected because the idea isn't good enough. What's a good idea? Make your own definition; I suppose each writer and editor does. I'd say, though, that basically the hero is vivid, the basic situation and the things that happen in the story are fascinating to a child. And generally there is a theme, some truth you believe, such as "you can master fear." Not a moral tacked onto the story, but the essence of the story, the hero and events acting out the theme.

How do you come by good ideas? Perhaps in the long run only heaven can help you, but it seems to me that primary is rapport with children—and a strong memory of your own childhood feelings and reactions.

"Tell me a story" many times a day keeps the old idea-mill grinding. Many of my picture book and magazine stories grew directly from contact with my children.

One day I hugged Greg, saying, "You're an old sweet patootie doll." "What's a patootie doll?" asked Greg, so I launched on a spur-of-the-moment tale. The theme was (I discovered after I'd written down the story) "know who you are and be glad for it." *The Sweet Patootie Doll* was first published in *Humpty Dumpty's Magazine* and later became my first published picture book.

A magazine story, "Cat's Whiskers", came into being because Greg was always climbing into things and getting stuck—in buckets, under the porch, even in the washing machine. I coupled this with the idea that cats use their whiskers to measure whether they can get through openings; in the story the boy sticks broomstraws on his face for whiskers, and the story goes on.

However, here was a story idea too slight for a picture book. Not enough happened, really, and there was no real theme in the sense of a universal truth.

This brings us to a point valuable to beginning writers: If your story is rejected by book editors, try it on the children's magazines. The magazines have high standards, too, of course, but they can be your training ground and means of being published while you learn. It was my lucky day when a book editor said, "Not ready to be a book. Have you thought of sending it to a magazine?" My story, "Lone Elizabeth," went through many rewritings, but finally was published in *Humpty Dumpty's Magazine*. "Bumbershoot Wind" was termed "too slight" by a book editor but appeared in *Child Life*.

Actually, all of the elements of a story are tied into the idea, but let's go on to consider them in detail.

Story movement. I choose to call it this, rather than plot, for this suggests just what a story for children must do: move. Children like a story that trots right along, with no prolonged station-stops for cute conversation or description. Keep asking yourself (as the child does), "What happened next?"

In picture books there needs to be enough change of action or scenery to afford the artist a chance to make different pictures. Some stories are very good for telling aloud, but when you look at them on paper, you see that the scene hasn't changed much.

A book editor pointed this out for me on my "Sammy and the Something Machine." In this fantasy, Sammy makes a machine out of which come in turn mice, monkeys, mudpies, pirates and hot dogs. (It grew from my Mike's chant at play, "I'm making, I'm making!") This story went down on paper perfectly well in *Humpty*

Dumpty's Magazine, where there are fewer illustrations than in a picture book. But the scene doesn't change; there's that machine, over and over, turning out different things.

When your story is moving along vigorously, the scene changes will follow naturally—*if* the idea is storybook material. If the story moves but there's not much possibility for picture change (better let the book editors decide this), it may still be a fine story for some magazine.

Style. Of course, your style will be your own, and only you can develop it through writing and trying out and thinking about it and forgetting about it as you plunge ahead in the heat of telling a story.

The story content to some extent will indicate the style, that is, choice of words, length and rhythm of sentences. The story may hop joyously, laugh along, move dreamily, or march matter-of-factly. For study, you might read aloud folk tales and attune your ears to varieties in cadence: the robust, boisterous swing of a western folk tale; the rolling, measured mysticism of an Indian folk tale; the straightforward modern "shaggy dog" story; the drawling wry humor of the southern Negro folk tale.

If you already are telling stories to children, you're on your way to developing your style. However, "telling" on paper is slightly different from telling aloud, where the *effect* is achieved by a few judiciously chosen words and the swing of sentences.

I've had some success with one approach to the written story, and I've seen examples of it in other picture books. I call it "vividry." To me it's more vivid and succinct to say that than "vivid effect," and this explains what "vividry" is: words chosen with economy for their punch. For example, in a certain book I choose to say "little mummy mice." "Mummified mice" might be more proper, but to me it sounds textbookish. "Mummy mice" rolls off the tongue and seems a more direct idea-tickler for the child.

In college journalism courses, our bible was Rudolf Flesch's *The Art of Plain Talk.* From it we learned the value, in newspaper writing, of using sentences of short or varied length; strong verbs; short, strong nouns and many personal pronouns. Flesch might have been writing a style book for children's picture books.

We all know the delight in finding "the exact word" for a spot in a story. Never is this more effective than in children's books. Maga-

zines for children generally have word-length requirements. Try putting a full-bodied story into 800 to 1,000 words. Every word counts.
Writing for the magazines can be excellent training in choosing
words and cutting out the lifeless ones.

I'm not saying, however, that big words have no place in a picture
book script. Writing "controlled vocabulary" books for the young is
a specialized art, and those books are used mostly by teachers and
parents to stimulate a child's desire to read. Several book publishers
now put out series of "easy-to-read" books. If you are interested in
this field, read some of the books and query the editors on requirements. In the general picture book, though, I think children like to
come upon an occasional delightfully new and big word. Haven't you
seen a four-year-old trotting around, happily rolling out "unconditionally" or some other mouthful he's just heard? It's the *idea* of the
story that the writer suits to the age group, not every given word in
the story.

And this brings us to *awareness of audience*. I've mentioned rapport with children. If you're around them you know what they're
thinking and wishing, what their problems are. And you'll know if a
story idea is too old for the three-to-eight-year-olds or just plain
wouldn't interest them.

With a small child underfoot or in tow, you see the details of the
world that fascinate him: how a spot of sunlight moves on the floor;
a cat's relationship with his tail (I used this one in "Tabbycat's Telltale Tail"); or the child's own shadow. (I haven't been able to make
a good story of this; maybe you can.)

A child will watch a hummingbird moth at work in a petunia bed
and report wisely, "He only goes to the red ones. White petunia must
not taste good."

All of this, *plus awareness of the child's emotions, plus turning
your mind back to remember how it was with you as a child,* tells you
what to put into a picture book.

And then there's the other way to be aware of your audience:
reading, reading all the good books and stories written for that age.
Then you begin to see what has pleased children. You get the feel of
what is suitable for that age group. You also see what has already
been done, so that your own ideas can be fresh, not trite. You read
"The Three Pigs," and the books about the Melops and you say to

yourself, "Very well, but a story about a pig has never been told just in *this* way," and you start off on your own particular pig story. As you read (perhaps to a child to catch his reactions, too), you may begin to draw your conclusions of what is good in children's literature, what is slightly sickening, how the stories are put together, what has worked.

It has interested me, for instance, to notice how many of the traditional stories are built on what I call a "core of three." Three brothers, three mistakes, three attempts at a solution. "The Three Pigs" makes me wonder if the composer weren't slyly trying to see just how many times he could use three. Three pigs, three encounters with men carrying building materials, three houses visited by the wolf, "chinny-chin-chin," etc. In so many of the stories, the use of three attempts to solve the problem is effective in building intensity to the climax.

So there you have it: idea, story movement, style and awareness of audience. Study them, use them in your rewrites, let them sink into your subconscious.

And then don't worry about techniques as you tell the story. For the first, last and most important thing is: you must *like* the story! You're having a ball telling it. Right at this moment, it's the most wonderful story ever told to man or child.

That, finally, is what gives the story sparkle and makes editors say, "This will make a wonderful picture book!"

78

THOUGHTS ON PLAYWRITING

BY ROBERT ANDERSON

I AM AT a period in my life (52) when I would much rather be getting wisdom from someone else than trying to give it to others. I have just finished a new play, which means that I have spent over a year wrestling with what I know, what I don't know, shapes, forms, the new modes, the old modes. I have ended up with an imperfect piece of work, as we all do. Every writer knows better than he can manage to do. (I am reminded of the story of the government agriculture advisor who watched a farmer for a week and then sat him down to give him some advice. The farmer cut him short by saying, "Hell, I'm not farming as well as I know how to farm right now.") In the same way, no writer ever writes as well as he knows how to write because material just never presents itself to us that neatly. Someone said that the act of writing is the act of undoing a dream. We never end up with the near-perfect piece of work we dreamed of writing. I never read over anything I have written on a play until I have finished the whole play. If I knew day by day how far short of my "dream" I was falling, I probably wouldn't go on.

These, then, will be some rather tentative, disorganized thoughts on playwriting. They may inform and encourage the right people and inform and discourage others.

This is a really fine time for the young playwright. Never before has there been so much opportunity for him to see his work done: colleges, cafés, Off-Off-Broadway, barns, parking lots, lofts, street corners, churches. This is all to the good. But I keep worrying about these young playwrights ten years from now. Things were never worse for the "established" playwright with a family who must make his living from his work. By and large there is very little money for the young playwright in the colleges, churches, Off-Off-Broadway, etc. This is all right. He is learning, enjoying himself and entertaining others. But this can go on only so long, especially if he is a family man. I have been quoted a number of times as saying, "You can make a killing in the theatre, but not a living." (Incidentally, the killing usually goes for taxes.)

The playwright generally has to be a moonlighter in one way or another. Before *Tea and Sympathy*, I worked on my plays in the morning, wrote for radio and TV in the afternoons, and four nights a week taught from eight to eleven. My second play was an artistic success but earned me almost zero, and I started writing movies to supply me with the money for the two to three years it takes to write a play and get it produced. Very few playwrights I know make their living solely from the theatre.

Very often young playwrights say to me, "Oh, but you're established. You have it easy." This is not true. My first successful play, *Tea and Sympathy*, was turned down by almost every producer, and my agent, Audrey Wood, told me that it was still being read by one producer, but it would probably be returned and I should get on to my next play. It was not returned, and my career was started. Thirteen years later my plays, *You Know I Can't Hear You When the Water's Running*, were turned down by almost everyone, and they were on their way into my files when two young producers rescued them. The same was true of my next play, *I Never Sang for My Father*, which waited five years to be produced. In short, it never gets easier. It would be unthinkable if novelists like William Styron, Philip Roth, or John Updike couldn't get their novels published. But there are many established and successful playwrights who cannot find producers for their new plays. The cost of production is enormous now, and few people have a continuing interest in a playwright and his work. (I will pass along a terrible story. I attended a preview of Tennessee Williams' play, *The Seven Descents of Myrtle*. I was alone, as my wife was acting in one of my plays. Before the curtain went up, Tennessee appeared in one of the boxes, and some people recognized him and started to applaud. Most of the audience joined in. The lady next to me said, "Why are they applauding?" I said, "That's Tennessee Williams." She said, "Why are they applauding when they don't know whether or not they will like the play?" My blood ran cold. But I know this is the prevailing attitude. The years of great plays Williams had given us meant nothing. The lady would applaud only if *this* one pleased her.)

It is generally conceded that playwriting is the most difficult form of writing. Add to this the difficulty of getting a play produced (depending on availability of the actors, director, theatre, *and* money). Add to this the deplorable situation now prevailing in New York where a bad review from the critic on *The New York Times* can finish off your play, and one wonders why anyone wants to be a playwright.

For a playwright there is the "What?" and the "How?" *What* he feels, thinks, believes, loves, fears, hopes, and *how* to express these in terms of theatre. Very often a young playwright is first attracted by the *how's* of the theatre, the theatricality, just as a girl might be drawn to being an actress because of a striking entrance she saw some great actress make one evening. To be thus stagestruck is a good thing. Infatuation of this sort often will see a person through the inevitable doldrums to follow. But the playwright soon learns that the theatricality must convey drama, and the aspiring actress learns that there was more to the entrance than show.

Right now the theatre seems to be very much concerned with the *how*, the manner, the outward show. The Emperor's clothes. I am often inclined to think that the clothes have no Emperor, that the matter with the theatre is that the manner is the matter. But in the end this is probably healthy, fun and stimulating, to call attention to the stage as stage, the theatre as theatre. A friend of mine who teaches in a college theatre department tells me that the students come to work in the theatre full of ideas of how they want to do something on the stage—projections, soundover, turntables, lights—but they rarely have any idea of *what* they want to do, what they want to convey by all these devices.

And the *what,* of course, is what finally makes the writer. Perhaps I am old-fashioned, but I finally tire of an endless barrage of stage effects signifying little or nothing. The playwright, of course, must learn to communicate in terms of any and all techniques available to him or congenial to him, but there must be something there to communicate, a strong feeling expressed as drama or comedy. (Comedy is just as serious as drama.)

Granted that a writer knows how to write, the most important asset for him is strong feelings. I once was encouraging a young writer of short stories. I sent him to Edward Weeks, then Editor of *The Atlantic Monthly*. Mr. Weeks read his story and then said to him, "You want to be a writer, but you didn't really want to write *this* story." There is great wisdom for all writers in this sentence.

Someone has said that art gives form to feeling. There must be the feeling first. Like all writers, I am offered a number of stories or ideas by friends, acquaintances and passers-by. I hardly ever listen to such stories, first, because of a certain pride in dreaming things up for myself, but secondly because they rarely make a connection with any reservoir of feeling inside me. I think it was Tennessee Williams who said in an interview that he writes about what's bugging him at the moment. Centuries ago, Sir Philip Sidney said, "Look in thy heart and write."

One word of warning and contradiction. Often the thing that is bugging the writer most is his life as a writer. This is of little interest to anyone except another writer. I think an audience asks of a writer, "Were you there, Charlie?" This does not mean that they want a writer to write nothing but autobiography, but they want to sense the author's involvement with his story, his knowledge of the truth of whatever he is writing about. With television documentaries and movies, we are able to know so much more about the factual truth of everything that faking on this level is hardly possible any longer. But faking on the psychological level is hardly possible either. I do not want to read someone who knows no more about a situation than I know or than I could pick up from the papers and magazines and television. I want to know what it's really like. I want a letter from the front. I do not want to seem to imply by this that I just want something strange and bizarre beyond my ken. As a matter of fact, while this is sometimes fascinating, the great works usually deal with areas of life known to us all, but I want to know that the author knows that area, has suffered or laughed in that area, that he is, in short, authentic.

When I taught playwriting, I used to have a great deal to say about technique, concepts which were dramatic or not dramatic, shape and form. The more I see, the more I read, I think a great deal of the problem comes down to one word, PROGRESSION. It is the nature of an audience, any audience, to bore quickly. People in groups become restless much more quickly than they do when alone. The majority of plays I read or see which do not "work" are static. They are mood pieces, brilliant in their observation of human nature, but they start nowhere and get nowhere. Much has been said about the vanishing need for plot. It's presumably a dirty word. But whenever I start getting bored in the theatre, a voice keeps murmuring inside me, "Get on with it! Move!" And plot, no matter how slight, is what moves a play forward and holds our interest. I hate it. I fight it. It is Hell sometimes to try to wrestle with your "marvelous material" so that you can get some movement into it. I have written plays without progression and suffered the consequences. Forward-moving action is the most difficult thing to come by. But it is what holds our interest while we are absorbing the richer texture of the characters and the relationships. The developing action sometimes is relatively unimportant, but it keeps us in a frame of mind to enjoy the rest.

For example, in *Life with Father*, what we remember are the charming family scenes and the characters truly and humorously drawn, but what holds our attention though we may not know it at the time, is the simple plot of Mother trying to get Father baptized. In *Mister Roberts*, the texture is the characterizations, the humor, but the story is hung on a simple progression, Mr. Roberts' efforts to get transferred. In *The Glass Menagerie*, the story moves forward with the efforts of the family to find a gentleman caller for Laura. I have seen more beautifully written, deeply felt plays bog down after thirty minutes simply because they were going nowhere. I have often thought it would be good training for us all to write farce and melodrama, which are all forward-moving action, progression.

To give you some idea of the principle of progression . . . I was once involved in a summer theatre production of *The Emperor Jones*. You will remember that a feature of this play is the drum which starts early in the play and keeps going to the end. I remember at one rehearsal the director stopped the actors late in the play and called back to the drummer, "I can't hear you. I can't hear the drum." The drummer came forward, haggard and frazzled, and said, "I'm hitting it so hard I'm almost breaking it." The point is that we had been· listening to the drum for twenty minutes or so, and in order for us still to be conscious of it, the drummer had to beat it almost beyond the point of possibility. Progression. Lines which get laughs in the First Act will not get laughs in the Second Act. A situation which will alert an audience in the First Act will leave them nodding in the Second Act. The demand for progression is basic in human nature. Think of the sex act.

For the rest, my words of wisdom are the same as always. Work. Write, act, direct. See and read as many plays as possible. It's a long haul, depending as much on your rate of personal growth as on your acquisition of dramatic technique. And at the end of the haul, there is one man who determines whether it was worth it or in vain . . . whoever may be the critic on *The New York Times*. Madness, right? . . . I must end this now so that I can start on my next play.

79

SCIENCE FICTION: SHORT STORY AND NOVEL

By Harry Harrison

THE western novel is about the west, the historical novel is about history, the crime novel is about crime. The science fiction novel is *not* about science.

There are people who like to list all of the inventions that were written about first in science fiction, but this is thinking after the act. There is so much gadgetry proposed in science fiction by writers who know their technology, that it would be strange if some of it did not prove workable at some time. This is completely incidental. Science fiction is about the impact of science upon people, and upon our environment and society.

It is very hard to give a single definition that will adequately describe *all* science fiction, so I shall not attempt it. It is enough if we realize what science fiction does. First, and most important, science fiction deals with today and tomorrow. All other fiction is about yesterday. Take almost any mainstream short story or novel. With a simple change of props, horses instead of autos, it could have taken place at any time during the last hundred years— because these writers are most interested in the eternal verities of interpersonal relationships. Even if "today" is mentioned in the book, or if this concept is in the author's mind, it is "yesterday" by the time the book is published.

Science fiction holds the opposite view. If the story takes place "today," it is the real today, even by the time it sees print, because it is about the existing world that has been changed in every way by the arrival of science on the world scene. If the story is about tomorrow, it is about the continued alterations and results of these changes. Science is the inescapable bedrock of science fiction.

In the paleolithic science fiction days, the hard sciences dominated the field: chemistry, physics, biology, and the like. The wonders of the new things that could be invented and discovered were of the utmost importance. The rocket story was about how the ship was put together in the cellar, and the story ended when ("with a licking tongue of lambent flame . . .") it blasted off. If you read about a rocket today, it will probably be treated as just another vehicle, as prosaic as the Boeing 707 is now, and the story will concern itself with the passengers aboard it. The softer sciences are being admitted to science fiction, and you will find stories based upon sociology, psychology, anthropology, political science —anything and everything.

The basic attitude of the science fiction author must be humanistic. He must feel that man is perfectible, that human nature can be changed, that this will not come about through wishing or praying, but by the application of intelligence, using the tools that the scientific method has given us. Once this is thoroughly understood, there will be no question about how science *fact* blends into science *fiction*.

The facts of science are there, all around us, inescapable. The science fiction author buys all of the scientific magazines and books that he can afford because he is fascinated by the ceaseless discoveries and the endless permutations of nature. There is even material galore in the daily press. I have a clipping on my wall with the headline "DIRTY AIR MAY CAUSE ICE AGE": EXPERT. Isn't that a plot for a story? A few months ago, there was an article about how the Marines in Vietnam use dowsing rods to locate mines. This story plots itself: the contrast between the old soldier who doesn't believe this and the rookie who does.

Or take the announcement that flatworms fed on their intelligent and chopped up brothers became smarter themselves. Curt Siodmak read that and wrote *Hauser's Memory*.

And how about the frightening overpopulation and overconsumption figures? I read them and applied them to New York City in the year 2000, and wrote "Make Room! Make Room!"

The list of extrapolations from new knowledge could be extended. (Science fiction has borrowed the term *extrapolation* from mathematics and made it its own: using present knowledge to extend a trend or possibility into the future.) Of equal importance is the "what if" type of plotting that can be traced right back to H. G. Wells. and his, "What if pigs had wings?" Brian Aldiss said, "What if no more children were born into the world?" then he wrote *Greybeard*. Robert Heinlein said, "What if we used the moon as a penal colony?" then he wrote *The Moon Is a Harsh Mistress*. Daniel Keyes said, "What if we could raise a moron's I.Q. by chemical methods?" then he wrote *Flowers for Algernon* (*Charly* in the movie version).

In order to write science fiction, one must not only like science fiction but must like science as well—some one science, any science, all science; the science fiction author must be a *fan* of science. He must realize that there are no monster brains lurking in computers, ready to destroy us all, just as there are no secrets that mankind "should not know." The scientific method is mankind's crowning achievement. It is the only really new thing in the entire universe. With it our race of hairless apes can talk around the world in the fraction of a second—or can refine a few pounds of a particularly heavy kind of rock and blow up that world. If you don't think this is the most fascinating thing to ever come down the pike—then you should not consider writing science fiction.

Science fiction is idea-oriented. The idea comes first—and is many times the hero—and the story follows. The complexity of the idea is what determines the length of the story. A single concept produces a short story. It might be argued that most science fiction short stories are back-plotted, *i.e.,* the ending is known in advance, then the story is filled in to reach the desired ending. Or the sequence is reversed and they are front-plotted, with a "what-if" statement, then a solution. There is little or no character development, because the characters are there to illuminate the concept. The basic story is not about the characters as people. The story is *concept*-oriented, not person-oriented. One, or at most two, of the characters will be fleshed out with personalities. The rest will be cardboard props with labels (laboratory assistant, soldier, second pilot) who do their bit and vanish.

Only in the science fiction novel, and in the longer intermediate lengths, can character be developed to any degree. Even then, rounded and real as the people may be, the concept is king. John Wyndham had real people in *The Day of the Triffids*, yet their names are forgotten while his strange plants lurk in memory. Can you remember the name of a character in any science fiction story or novel you have read recently? Now try this with *Gone with the Wind,* or *Crime and Punishment,* or any other general novel that you recall with warmth.

There are exceptions, of course, to all these rules and statements, as well as an entire school of science fiction writers, often referred to as the "New Wave," who would deny everything I have said. But these new writers would all admit that they write science fiction because they first read and enjoyed the basic stuff. You have to learn the rules before you can break them.

As an editor, I can truthfully say that there is very little good science fiction around in any length, old or new wave. As a writer, I can say that good science fiction is not easy to write. Of course the bad stuff is just about as simple to do as hack westerns—and is just about as important.

Where the science fiction short story is a vehicle for a single idea or concept, the novel, when it is not just a short story written long, can not only explore more complex concepts, but can show interrelationships. Ecology has far more interconnections than are possible between all of the characters in *War and Peace.* An ecological concept would have to be handled in the form of a novel. All of the "earth destroyed" novels are ecological, as are the multi-generation starship novels.

The "world created" is also a novel-length concept. This is rarely found outside of science fiction—*Islandia* and the Tolkien books are the only examples that come to mind—yet this label could be applied to at least 9 out of 10 novels inside the field. (Or more. I just went to my unsorted-science fiction-novels shelf, and the first twenty out of twenty books are "world created" novels.) In the science fiction field, this concept is as old as H. G. Wells, the man who invented modern science fiction books such as *The Sleeper Awakes* and *The Shape of Things to Come.* A first-class science fiction writer can invent a world, down to the smallest detail—or generate the illusion that the smallest detail has been revealed—then populate it and set a story in it that could take place in no other possible world. This, I believe, is one of the reasons for the continuing, and expanding, interest in science fiction. The western is in the west, and the murder mystery has a corpse, and we have been there many times before. But, from time to time, in the best science fiction novels, the reader will have a chance to enter a wholly new and logical world and to watch an interesting story take place there. No other form of fiction can make this statement!

I wish there were an easy formula that I could give to tell just how to write the science fiction novel, or the short story. There is none. As a first step, the prospective science fiction writer must seriously *like* the stuff. Then he must accept the idea that we live in a changing world, not a repetitive, generation-unto-generation feudalistic one. Change in itself—like science—is neither good nor bad. It is just there. Then he must accept the concept that we can change change, that all things are possible. (Whether probable or not is another matter.) Then he must read a great deal of science fiction, both old and new, to see what has been done and what is being done. Then he must read a lot of *non*-science fiction to understand what good writing is, because so much of science fiction is so terribly written. Then he must apply seat to chair and fingers to typewriter and create something that never existed before.

Then, and only then, he may have written a salable piece of science fiction. Maybe.

Still, there is very little competition at the top. Or at the bottom either, for that matter. It is certainly worth the try.

80

TRAVEL WRITING TODAY

By Arthur R. Pastore, Jr.

TIME was when you could frequently sell a travel article based on the Edmund Hillary principle for climbing Mount Everest—simply "because it was there."

However, that was in the prehistoric days of travel writing, over twenty-five years ago when global postwar travel began to mushroom, and airplanes made everywhere in the world only hours away. It was easy then for a travel writer to go anyplace, tell how to go, how much it cost, what modes of transportation were available, briefly mention hotels and other tourist facilities, and in a paragraph or two lump in the main sightseeing attractions—and *voilá*, in a thousand words or so, you had a nice, light travel article, neatly packaged like a travel agent's all-expense tour which included everything but the cost of postcards. And travel writers then never bothered, for the most part, to travel much farther than their local public libraries, merely rewriting the guidebooks and scanning an Atlas. All they added was an occasional, "Gee, whiz, what grandeur!" or "the breathtaking, panoramic view," etc.

Basic research of this type is still important for background, but the situation has changed. Today's travel writer not only has to go there—whether around the block or around the world—but has to see and feel the place and the people and be able to record his impressions accurately in readable, entertaining style.

Washington Post Travel Editor Morris David Rosenberg describes travel as "an experience—a personal approach." Like many of today's travel editors, he seeks honest, offbeat, *personalized* reactions in depth. To potential contributors to his travel pages, he advises: "I'd like my reader to be able to experience a little of what's going on, to react to people, not places." What he means is that the people

of a country, the atmosphere of a city or a place, the overall sociological aspect are far more important than a dull inventory of
museums, landmarks and other points of tourist interest, which any
traveler can cull from a guidebook, a bus tour or a travel brochure.
For example, Paris has many memorable historic and cultural attractions, yet for most people, watching the passing parade of people
from the vantage point of a sidewalk café table is one of the alluring
travel adventures in that wonderful city.

The Washington Post's requirements are essentially no different
from those of the *East Cupcake (Ohio) Gazette's* travel pages. Now,
all travel editors want a new look, a new approach, a rethinking on
the writer's part as to what all this means to him on a subjective
rather than objective basis. And what all this will mean to the
average tourist reading it, whether he is a first-tripper, or a seasoned
world traveler always looking for something "different," something
"unique."

As a result, travel articles today have adopted fiction techniques,
heavily interlarded with anecdotes, quotes, and human interest material to lighten the mixture. You have to use magazine feature treatment now, rather than the simple "service" travel article which was
common ten years ago. Also, travel articles are much harder to
write because of length restrictions. With space limits in today's
publications, the requirements are for much shorter pieces; the
2,000-word travel article is pretty much *passé* nowadays. Most
newspaper travel pieces run about 700–800 words compared with
1,000 or more of even five years ago, and some are as little as 500
words in print, which means severe blue-penciling, careful cutting
and tight organization. There are still a few markets, like *The New
York Times* Travel Section, which will run a double-spread article
of nearly 2,000 words, but this length is rare today.

Because today's travel article markets have radically changed,
you must have an original angle, an attention-getting gimmick, plus
a fresh approach in planning your travel piece. Perhaps its angle
is camping out in a trailer, or, it may have a special focus—a garden
tour, a music festival trip, or anything to induce a reader to make
another trip to a familiar tourist mecca like London, Paris, Rome,
or even San Francisco. Or you may look for a different method of
transportation—traveling by pogo-stick, hitchhiking, bicycling, or as

one family recently traveled to Washington, D. C., in an old-fashioned covered wagon drawn by horses! They plan to travel around the country this way, and I'm sure they will have ample material for original travel articles. I recently read an article in *The Washington Post* on traveling on ocean liners as a stowaway, which, you must admit, is a bit unusual.

A beginning travel writer has more of a chance in both newspaper and magazine travel markets with domestic or, more particularly, *localized* topics, such as an old blacksmith shop, a Civil War battlefield in your town, or local historic houses, places or regions. For in travel writing, the tried-and-true writing principle, "write what you know," also applies, because, like Dorothy in *The Wizard of Oz*, you can find everything you want right at home, without traveling "the yellow-brick road to Oz"—or to Europe or the Far East. In fact, I saw America first, all 50 states, before I made my first overseas trip—good advice for *any* travel writer.

Perhaps the best way to get started in travel writing is via the newspaper market, which offers small pay, frequently on publication, but the competition is less here than in the magazine markets which are supplied by higher paid professionals, most of whom belong to the Society of American Travel Writers (SATW). In addition, in the lower and slower pay fields, you will get a chance to learn the travel writing craft with a friendlier editor. Start by checking the large metropolitan newspapers in the region where you live, since few local, small dailies or weeklies can afford the luxury of a travel section or even a page. However, a number of large newspapers which blanket a state-wide area, particularly on Sundays, have travel sections. Look them over carefully, reading even the ads, to gain some insight into the readership; see what places they feature—foreign, domestic, local and regional, etc.—and what style the writers use.

Most of the travel articles in these publications are by-lined by the travel editor; others may be provided free by transportation companies and municipal and state tourist offices, and some may be syndicated features which the paper buys for a certain fee depending on circulation. A brief letter or query, or even a phone call, to the travel editor, may get you a few nibbles, or at least a cautious "send some material in, and we'll look it over," particularly if you can offer a few credits from other papers. Or you can offer to do a travel piece on speculation, always submitting manuscripts with stamped, self-addressed, return envelopes. You always have a much better chance if you query before leaving on your trip, mentioning that you plan to visit such-and-such a place and can send copy while en route. If what you suggest appeals to him, it gives him a chance to plan tentatively (there is always a chance he may not like the finished piece) for his seasonal needs for the travel pages.

A catchy or attention-getting title or headline can often swing the balance of a so-so travel article, so try to provide one. Avoid "label" heads, which are dull and lifeless, and give an indication that the writing style is likely to be the same. For example, a few years ago, I wrote a humorous, light travel piece for the *Los Angeles Times* about a small hotel in France's Burgundy wine region which furnished free white and red wine on tap in the bathroom for guests, and used the title: "Bacchus in the Bathroom" which seemed to hit the editor just right.

For the travel writer, a camera is as essential as a notebook and pencil. Often, a travel article may sell on the strength of a good picture or two, and extra payment is made for each published picture (even if the photo has been acquired free by the writer from a public relations source or office of a large company or professional association).

I make no claims of being the world's best photographer and use a simple-to-operate, inexpensive, Yashica-D Reflex camera (twin-lens), which provides me with negatives $2\frac{1}{4}$ by $2\frac{1}{4}$ inches, large enough to see what I have. These negatives can be reasonably blown up to the 5 x 7 or 8 x 10 glossy-type picture most editors require. Besides basic composition, I try to get pictures of *people*, either in colorful, native dress, or riding in a pedicab, or working at native handcrafts. If I take a picture of a monument or landmark, I always try to get people in the picture looking on, and try to avoid the stiff, posed typical tourist shot which is as phony as a three-dollar bill. Also, my pictures are captioned for easy identification, and my name and address is attached to the caption or back of the picture, and a suitable credit line provided.

Each year in one of its issues *The Writer* lists travel markets, giving a checklist of what travel editors are currently looking for, length, payment, and special emphasis. You may find it helpful to consult the recently published *Around the World with the Experts*, edited by Richard Joseph (Doubleday), which contains seventy articles by members of the Society of American Travel Writers. The rest is up to you. Good traveling and good luck!

81

REALITIES OF THE GREETING CARD MARKET

By Carl Goeller

What is the outlook for the greeting card free-lance writer in the seventies? On the negative side, there have been some discouraging developments for free-lancers during the past year. The economic slump has not spared the greeting card industry, and there has been a good deal of belt-tightening on the part of editors of major companies as well as smaller ones. There are fewer purchases of border-line material—material that has merit but will take working over before it is publishable. This naturally hurts greeting card writers who specialize in ideas rather than in finished, craftsmanlike writing.

But, on the positive side, this is the most exciting period in greeting card history. Editors are competing for new ideas, new gimmicks, new products, and they're paying more than ever for what they buy. And they are buying ideas as well as words. To succeed in the greeting card field during the seventies, you have to be an idea man as well as a writer.

Who is going to make it in the next decade—and who isn't—and why? Here is my appraisal of what's in store for various kinds of greeting card writers in the seventies:

The conventional writer, who writes only conventional 4- and 8-line verse for serious occasions, is in trouble. In the sixties there were as many as ten rather good markets for straight verse; today there are fewer than five, and some of these are buying only a fraction of what they once did. One reason for this is that conventional verse is a reusable commodity—a popular verse can be modified and used with a dozen or more different designs throughout a card line, and these can last for years. Greeting card editors, therefore, don't need much new conventional verse, no matter how well written it may be. The writer who is convinced that conventional verse is the only type he can do will have to content himself with a limited income from his free-lancing.

Small greeting card publishers, as well as the large ones, are insisting on fresh, new approaches which will help get their wares into stores handling more than one line. They are stressing originality, especially in their studio card lines.

The ostrich sits behind the typewriter day and night, writing card ideas by the dozens—conventional, humorous, juvenile and studio ideas. He's been at it quite a few years and has been pretty successful because he knows what the editors want. Or so he thinks!

But he hasn't been out into the greeting card departments recently; he hasn't been reading the trade magazines to see just what's been happening in the industry. He's neglected the research end of his job to the point that he doesn't even realize that there have been more changes in the greeting card business in the last three years alone than there were in the preceding twenty. As a result, he's showing editors only a fraction of the kinds of material they really want to see. Unless he removes his head from the sand—quickly— the ostrich will find his hits becoming fewer and his misses becoming commonplace.

The in-tune writer does what the ostrich fails to do—he keeps in tune with what's happening in the industry, and he slants his efforts accordingly. He notices, for example, that the major publishers are coming out every year now with many new groups of "promotions" —series of cards with some unifying theme, either design or sentiment oriented. So, instead of simply sending one batch after another of individual card ideas, he includes some interesting promotional idea groups. One enterprising writer last year sold six promotional ideas to several different companies, and each brought him a handsome check. He notices, too, the trends in copy which appeal most to the consumer. For example, American Greetings' "Soft Touch" cards—cards using mood photography and simple, meaningful copy, all in prose—found immediate acceptance with the youth market, and they sold over ten million cards in less than a year. Other companies rushed into print with their imitations of Soft Touch . . . and a writing market was born.

The creative idea person asks himself, "Why should my creative efforts be limited to writing? Why not sell ideas as well as words?"

and he begins approaching the card companies in a new way. He begins selling them ideas for new products and new twists to existing products. Look at what the "card" industry is making and selling these days—books, puzzles, games, party items, toys, calendars, posters, badges, candles, candy, writing instruments, gift items . . . the list is endless. The idea person is aware of these, studies them, and then comes up with fresh new ideas for them. Only recently an idea man came up with an idea for a series of books which he presented and sold to a major card company for several thousand dollars. Another sold a series of games to one of the publishers and was well paid for them. The *very* creative idea person goes one step further. He researches a product before the card companies go into it, then gets in on the ground floor. How? By reading and shopping to see what's on the market and what isn't; by talking to clerks and store managers about what is in demand that they can't supply; and by creating something to meet that demand. The method by which he sells the idea to a manufacturer may well tax his creative ability more than coming up with it—but the results can be well worth it.

The analyst takes his writing and creating seriously enough to analyze his successes and failures. Someone once defined a professional as a person who doesn't make the same mistake twice. The analyst is a professional. He periodically reviews the cards he's sold to see what slant is hitting, and, perhaps as important, he reviews his rejections to see why he missed. Further, he is willing to ask the help of others—fellow professionals or even an editor—in determining *why*. If the editor likes his work in general and feels that he has something to contribute, he will be glad to comment and suggest improvements.

Which of the five different greeting card writers we've looked at are you? If you are *the conventional writer* or *the ostrich*, the seventies are going to be rough sledding, and you had better start now to enlarge your markets by trying other types of writing. If you are *the in-tune writer, the creative idea person,* or *the analyst,* you will find the greeting card market a real challenge, and an exciting and profitable one as well.

Five years ago, the greeting card market consisted of verse for conventional, humorous, and juvenile cards, and studio card gags—

period. Today, as we have already noted, it includes new products and new twists for old categories. Let's see what new twists are in demand.

Conventional cards: There is a great interest in simplified conversational verse which avoids the clichés which have been so reliable in past years. Forget about lines like "this card has come to say," "today and all year through," and "every thought prompts wishes." Every word and every line must count. Use ideas in your verses—design, sentiment tie-ins, fresh and interesting thoughts, and unusual verse formats. Don't always use verse. If you can put your thoughts into rhythmic, readable prose, do it. Keep your verse as brief as possible but have something to say.

Humorous cards: There's more emphasis now on cleverness and less on gimmick in humorous cards. This is a matter of economics as much as anything. All the companies are finding a real cost squeeze which makes mechanical gimmicks almost prohibitive except in the highest-priced cards. Separate pieces, too, which need to be attached, are costly because of the hand labor required. This means that words and art work are practically all an editor can use at 50¢ and under. Paper is still reasonably inexpensive, so many editors are receptive to novelty folds and unusual stock ideas (paper bags, etc.). There's a definite trend away from the old cornball type of humor and toward the more youthful, sophisticated approaches. Card ideas that were considered strictly for studio cards a few years back are now used on humorous cards with pictures of bunnies, dogs, cats, etc. A word of advice—you'll sell more humorous ideas if you think design as well as words. If your gag is accompanied by some clever designing, you're saving the editor and the art director some extra work, and they will appreciate it.

Juvenile cards: There is very little demand for straight juvenile verse. Most companies are interested in "idea cards"—things to do and play with, semi-educational, and easily designed. Don't talk down to the kids with your copy—they see lots of television and their vocabularies are much broader than ours were at that age. Some greeting card companies are buying stories, both for cards and for hardback books they are now publishing.

Studio cards: As previously noted, gags that used to appear only in studio lines have now spread to the humorous lines, and studio card editors are looking for more originality and youth-oriented copy. This doesn't mean hippie-type ideas, "cool" talk, drug-culture bits, and the like; it means humor that doesn't rely on slamming the recipient (today's kids are a sentimental bunch, no matter what they say), or getting drunk, or growing old (age gags just aren't cutting it in the studio card racks these days). Love is big—and so is sex—and little digs at the Establishment—and ecology, pollution, and the like. Not every company is moving its studio line in this direction, so don't rush out and throw away your pile of straight humor. There are some editors who still want that type. But be forewarned: most major greeting card publishers are heading in this direction (upon the advice of their research people).

Books: One of the hottest items to hit the card departments in the past three years has been the little hardback book. It was pioneered by American Greetings, and now more and more companies are building sizable book lines. There are several approaches which will bring checks from editors who find they have no backlog at all of this type of material. Here are a few:

Cute stuff—Girl-to-girl or girl-to-boy messages done in a cute, almost juvenile-sounding simplicity. These are especially strong in such subjects as love, friendship, "missing you," and in birthday messages. Some are in verse; most in very simple prose.

Humorous—Often these are collections of ideas that are taken from the studio card files, but on "missing you" compliments, love, birthdays, and get-well. Items must be short and quick. Long, involved humor goes nowhere.

Studio—These have been the weakest books, and consequently bring the greatest number of rejection slips. And yet, editors need them. The material should be timely, youth-oriented humor, usually girl-to-boy stuff.

Conventional—Many of these are similar to the old *Ideals* magazine—collections of very traditional, conventional verse and poetry. This is a very small market, but it's there if you have the right idea.

This is just the start of the book business for the major greeting card publishers. The next obvious step will be larger, high-priced books, and the ideas for them could just as well come from you as from their staff writers. Here's a prediction: By 1975, at least two of the card companies will be considered major book publishers. If you get in on the ground floor now . . . who knows—you may have some published books to your credit five years from now.

Novelties: Ceramic figures are big with a dozen publishers— the little characters that say, "I wuv you," "The devil made me do it," and so on. Watch the stores to see which companies are selling figurines, then send them ideas for new approaches—not just more of the same.

Calendars are a big item with many of the major companies. They have plenty of ideas for designed calendars, but they can use you for novelty approaches.

Posters are hot. The big companies wrote them off as a fad when they were introduced about five years ago (they did that with studio cards, too), but now they realize posters are here to stay, so they're going into the business. Submit some original ideas, and they'll sell.

Puzzles and games are relatively new to most card publishers, but destined to be big items. If you have the kind of complicated mind it takes to do puzzles, etc., send them to major companies —they're interested now.

The card companies are in the business of helping people communicate with one another—and who says that cards are the only way to do this? When you're thinking of items, products, gadgets, and copy for the greeting card field, keep that in mind. If you yourself use an unusual method of communicating with your friends or relatives, you may have the makings of a new product that will be of interest to the card companies.

To return, then, to the basic question posed in this piece, does the free-lance greeting card writer stand a chance in the seventies?

Yes, but he'll have to think of himself as more than just a greeting card writer. A better title might be creative communicator.

Yes, but he'll have to remember he's living in the seventies, and writing for the future decade, not the past.

Yes, but he's going to have to stay alert to the changing times and attitudes of the people. You're in for some exciting days, months, and years ahead as you become the complete creative communicator.

82

THAT CERTAIN SMILE

By Lesley Conger

WHEN I was young and gay, unencumbered by children and debts, sans crow's-feet and gray hairs, and thought that middle age began in the mid-thirties, I began my writing career—with stark and relentless tales of hopeless invalids, murdered innocents, miserable homosexuals, suicides, funerals, hatred, spite, and bitterness, and with a novel which centered about a grisly infanticide, with mental illness and a dash of incest thrown in for good measure.

Now I am older, in debt, harassed by a half-dozen hungry children who have razor blades set in their knees and elbows; I have crow's-feet, a few gray hairs, and have learned that middle age always begins in the next decade—and, sadder and wiser, I write humor.

Some of my early work sold. It wasn't bad, just sad. But I had to get used to rejection slips which read, "Too macabre for us" . . . "This is too unrelievedly grim" . . . "gloomy" . . . "morose" . . . and the whole thing was summed up nicely in a creative writing seminar when an older classmate broke out in despair after a reading of one of my harrowing little pieces, "How can such a nice girl as you write such *nasty* stories?"

Just how the metamorphosis took place I couldn't say. I must assume that the constant hammering of those rejection slips beat my malleable metal into a different and more amiable shape; at any rate, I woke up one day to find that I was being funny on the radio, that I was anthologized in *The Family Book of Humor,* that my short stories were more often amusing than tragic, and that I had written a book which was billed as being by a "humorist." Nobody was more surprised than I, except perhaps my husband and children, who still find me unrelievedly grim, gloomy, and morose—a classic state of mind with humorists.

Humor is easier to sell than tragedy, by a long shot. Among those of my stories remaining stubbornly unsold, half again as many deal with tragic or unpleasant themes as deal with light or humorous themes. But humor is also harder to write than tragedy—also by a long shot. Only the most inept writers create unintentional giggles in the middle of a tragic scene, while even a skilled writer can often bungle humor so that it just isn't funny.

If you haven't a natural funny bone, no one can teach you to write humor—no one, not Thurber, not Benchley, not Mark Twain, certainly not I. Your account of your sister named Eileen would produce a prodigious, public, cross-country yawn that would rival the Grand Canyon; you could buy a chicken farm on the Olympic Peninsula and never raise a cackle. Furthermore, I may be billed as a humorist but I am not a comic and very little of what I write is really comedy. Although occasionally I write a story with an ironic twist, the plots of my stories are rarely inherently funny; if you haven't the insane, priceless gift of creating wacky plots, I cannot pass it on to you, for I don't have it myself.

What I do have, and hope to pass on, is not the socko punch straight to the source of the belly laugh, but rather the gentle touch that lifts the spirit—and the corners of the mouth.

I'm going to talk, then, not about the comic story but about the story (a romance, a problem story, whatever it may be) which can profit from that certain smile, that lighter-than-air touch. Profit? I am sure of it; I am convinced that many a story of mine made it across the finish line with the editor-in-chief not because of plot, not because of drama, not because of some great truth or magnificent platitude it proclaimed, but because it floated across with the lightness of a cluster of balloons. As a case in point, let us contrast the fate of the story of Deborah with the fate of the story of Jenny:

The story of Deborah, which I called "The Unready Heart," dealt soberly with the theme of a young wife not ready for the responsibilities of motherhood. Soberly, soberly—all the way through. We first meet Deborah lying in bed, shamming sleep to avoid her husband; when she wakes in the morning, she wakes guiltily, and thus she goes through the day, guiltily and full of fear. The story was full of phrases such as these: *Her second cup of coffee was as tasteless as the first, and she let it grow cold . . . she swallowed at nothing with her stiff and aching throat . . . felt the same cold shrinking . . .*

all her own fear gathered into a cold agony in her stomach . . . and so on, to within a hair's breadth of the end. And even then, when Deborah suffers a change of heart, she does so without the least glimmer of a smile. Looking back at Deborah, I see her now as a pretty humorless sort, and I suspect she'll make a rotten mother, even if I did think I had written a happily-ever-after ending for my story. Nevertheless, the story was not completely without merit; it sold in England and was later translated into Swedish. But it never made the grade with an American magazine.

Still, the theme continued to interest me, and several years later I decided to take the same theme and try again. This time I wrote the story of Jenny. Jenny, like Deborah, is not without self-pity and misery, but when we first meet Jenny she is knitting, *working a magic transformation, turning the fluffy, butter-yellow wool into a lumpy, bulging, grubby mass which only an expert and tolerant eye could recognize as Baby Sweater, Pattern No. 348.* Jenny looks at it. Her heart sinks, surely, but it does not drag the reader down too far, for what Jenny concludes is *All right, Mama, said the baby moth, I'll eat it, but I won't like it.*

Deborah had compared herself, rather unpleasantly, with her capable and blithely pregnant neighbor; Jenny compares herself with her mother-in-law, thinking, *If you gave Mrs. Cartwright a few balls of steel wool, she could knit you an armored tank.* This bit of fancy arrived naturally—I cannot knit at all, and regard knitting as akin to sleight-of-hand—and I decided to expand it into a running gag. A few paragraphs later, therefore, Jenny muses, *If you gave Mrs. Cartwright a bunch of old cobwebs, she could knit you a moonbeam,* and finally, when her despair grows deepest, *Maybe if I gave her a lot of nothing, thought Jenny, she could knit me a hole in the ground to crawl into.* Oh, Jenny had miseries enough, but as I wrote, I tried to leaven every misery with a grin. Jenny wept over her knitting— but *she wept loudly into her ten-thumbed hands;* Jenny, enormously pregnant, had trouble getting out of the car—but she managed it *as deftly as a hippopotamus emerging from a three-inch drainpipe;* and when Jenny wanted to die, she didn't merely want to die—she told herself *I'll commit hara-kiri with my knitting needles!*

The story of Deborah brought me about seventy dollars, all told. The story of Jenny became "Secret of the Attic" (*Redbook*) and has, so far, brought me fifteen times as much. (I mention this for the benefit of those low characters who must measure everything in crude, monetary terms.)

Still, the theme of these two stories, though not humorous in itself, was not dead serious either. But what about a story of a young father and his small son, suddenly bereaved, facing life together alone? Violet Wood began her story, "Colors of the Morning" (*Redbook*), "The day of his mother's funeral Mike awoke slowly, vaguely conscious of something waiting to hurt him." This clearly is a story that could be unrelievedly grim, gloomy, and morose—and I assure you that if *I* had written it in my early days as a writer, that is precisely the manner in which I would have written it; and *Redbook* would never have printed it, that you can be sure of. There are tears in the story, and loneliness, and even nausea, but there is something else as well—the gentle touch, even in this story of grief. How? Small Mike, who is only four, crawls into the bed that now holds only his father and says, soberly, "We can't make a Mike-sandwich today. We need Mama next to me in bed with us to make a Mike-sandwich, and Mama isn't here." To which his father replies, "No, we can't make a Mike-sandwich any more. But we can make something, you and I. We can make an open-face Daddy-and-boy sandwich—just like this," and the crucial scene that could be merely doleful, dogged bravery is instead brightened for the reader with a smile of pleasure and recognition.

I think the most tragic script I have ever written was my radio play *Bruno,* broadcast by the Canadian Broadcasting Corporation on Good Friday, a few years back. I wept tears over *Bruno* and wrote sore-throated and blurry-eyed for many hours of the month it took me. Giordano Bruno was burned at the stake on February 17, 1600, and his ashes cast to the winds, and my play dealt with his last week in the civil prison in Rome. You could not ask for a theme less likely to make an audience smile. There is, nevertheless, humor in the play. It is not zany and lighthearted humor, to be sure, but rather sardonic, caustic, and doomed. But it is still humor and serves the purpose of humor. The official sentence of death upon Bruno contains the phrase "with our request that there be no shedding of blood nor mutilation of bodily members." (Actual translation.) Bruno comments: "No shedding of blood—what a dainty phrase

that is! I wonder what is so much more agreeable about *burning?*"
When the jailor complains that he doesn't like the prisoners the In-
quisition sends to him, preferring thieves and common murderers,
Bruno replies, "Lean closer, I shall empty your pocket and enter
their preferable company. Or lend me a knife—and your throat." He
remarks what a distinction it will be to die in front of so many distinguished visitors, cardinals and what-not, it being a Jubilee Year;
served his last supper, he asks, "Since when does breast of peacock
look like this?" None of this made *Bruno* into a comedy; but, paradoxical as it may seem, it may have made the play a better tragedy.

One last example: More than a decade ago, a women's magazine
bought a story of mine called "Kingdom's Child," which they published under the title "Forever Young." Subsequent radio and television productions—it was produced by two different TV networks,
one Canadian and one American, within the same month—reverted
to my original title. Here was a theme most difficult to handle, the
story of a young girl whose father is a preacher, a leader of a Dooms-
day sect. True, the story itself was partly a romance, but the religious aspect of it made it a questionable entry in the taboo-ridden
market of the slicks, and religion loomed large in the story and was
crucial. But I tried to treat the contrast between the doom-oriented
religion of the father and the life-oriented natural faith of the girl
with—well, with that certain smile.

"Are you ready to be judged at the Throne?" her father asked Kingdom's
Child. "Is your soul clean and uplifted this morning, Child?'
She didn't know. The times she felt clean and uplifted most never came when
she was shelling peas, even if work was a form of prayer. And most of all, those
times never came when her father confronted her with the Imminence of Doom.
Her soul crawled away then, like a small, anxious worm seeking cover under a
leaf.
"Yes, Pa," she answered him. She lifted at least a clean and shining face to him,
no matter what the condition of her soul.

And when at last Kingdom's Child is kissed by the young geologist, Johnny, she cries. He admonishes her not to be ashamed, for he
would hate himself if she were ashamed.

She groped for some support, argument, answer, something to begin with.
Would Pa be ashamed of her? She knew that one. Would *He?* It occurred to her
that her father and God might have a difference of opinion.

No, this is not humor to make you burst out laughing; but it leavens the serious loaf of the story, and it helped to make a successful story and play out of what might otherwise never have seen print.

Of course I still write serious stories. There are places where even the unrelievedly grim, gloomy, and morose story can be published, if it's good enough. My long experience with letters of rejection, however, inclines me to quote the old saw, *Laugh and the editor laughs with you; cry and you cry alone.* If you want to reach a wide audience and if you want to cash a four-figure check, give careful thought to the leaven of humor. Perhaps you can use it.

After fifteen years of writing in bedrooms, kitchens, and living rooms, I at last have a room in which nothing goes on but writing, a room devoted to writing, a room all my own. Admittedly, it is a *closet*—but it is a large closet, and it has a nice little window out of which I can see mainly sky, which is a very good thing. One of the boys donated the closet, and the girls donated their kindergarten table and a kindergarten chair (which I find a very comfortable combination, requiring a certain amount of alertness, since a 39-year-old woman can't really slump in a kindergarten chair unless she wants to land on the back of her neck). There is nothing in this room but the chair, the table, the typewriter, and blank paper. All my files, memoranda, bills to pay, budget books, notebooks, old manuscripts, correspondence, etc., are remaining downstairs at my battered desk, where I have an aged Underwood to use for less concentrated work. Up here, not even a dictionary. I bring up here only one thing at a time, and there is nothing to distract me. It is marvelous.

On the wall above the table where I work is tacked one of those ubiquitous little cards with red printing, advising me to SMILE! I'm smiling now; and, remembering my success with the turning of dolorous Deborah into jaunty Jenny, I think I shall go back into my files and see if I can salvage another of those unsold, sadly-told tales.

Crow's-feet? Heck no, those are *laugh lines!*

83

CHECKLIST FOR HUMOR WRITERS

By Peggy Cameron King

If you aspire to success as a humor writer you will need more than a ready wit and a clean typewriter ribbon. Any one of four basic mistakes can rob the most amusing material of humor:

Lack of theme
Wrong narrator
Unsuitable subject matter
Unsuitable style

Your hilarious essay hasn't sold? Check it again with these points in mind.

The commonest flaw in a humor piece is likely to be the same one that spoils many articles or short stories, namely, lack of theme. If you know where you're going, you should be able to define your theme in one sentence. A beginner is likely to string together a lot of jokes, funny incidents and observations about an experience like losing weight, but unless these hilarious comments are related to one another and say something definite, the whole piece lacks impact. The message may be, "I lost thirty pounds and my husband," or "Count your calories." Then you must discipline yourself to omit anything irrelevant to that theme, however funny. In writing "It'll Come in Handy Some Day" for *The American Home,* I found myself digressing from the subject of the junk stored in the basement to how to make pot holders from scrap fabrics. It was just as hard for me to drop the digression as to throw out the junk, but I had to eliminate the pot holders.

You are more likely to stick to your theme if you work from an outline. The outline may be on paper or just in your head but, if your piece is going to be coherent, it must be well organized. I belong to the school that achieves order by attacking the first draft with scissors and stapler. You may function best with a step-by-step outline.

It doesn't matter, as long as you don't emulate Stephen Leacock's hero who "flung himself upon his horse and rode madly off in all directions."

The most popular written humor today is the first-person essay with which the reader can identify. The "I" of the essay, the narrator, must be a personality who resembles the prospective reader. So in the interests of his craft, the humorist will assume the role that allows the greatest reader identification. Who wants to identify with a senior citizen? (Only a senior citizen.)

A study of the leading women's magazines will show that they are directed at the career girl or the young housewife. Elderly readers (over 35) don't mind identifying with younger women, but a young woman can't with much enthusiasm imagine herself so ancient. Hence, you will increase the salability of your material if you juggle your own age, your children's, and even your husband's. If you are sufficiently versatile to write for the men's markets also, be prepared to assume the role of a male narrator. Looking over my recent sales, I find I've played more roles than Elizabeth Taylor. I've spoken as a 16-year-old boy in *Boys' Life,* as a young girl in *Hi Way,* as a bride for the *Toronto Star Weekly* (now called *SW Magazine*), as a grandmother for *Baby Talk* (a *young* grandmother), and as a middle-aged matron several times for *Family Digest.* (I hope you're completely mystified!)

Many times your material can be presented from several viewpoints. Study the possible markets to see if by changing the narrator you can get more than one salable piece from the same material. Suppose you attend a limbo contest and are inspired to do a humorous presentation. As narrator, you could be an uninhibited teen-ager, a middle-aged participant, even an unsympathetic spectator who thinks the whole performance degrading. Assuming you are skillful enough to handle all of these roles, decide which viewpoint will appeal most to your potential reader. You may even do more than one. Five years ago I sold a piece entitled "I Wear My Daughter's Hand-me-downs," but the article was never printed. Finally, I decided that by updating the material and changing the narrator from mother to daughter I could again market the basic idea. It appeared as "What's Hers Is Mine," in *Ingenue.*

See that your by-line fits the identity of your narrator. A thirteen-year-old reader wrote me that she assumed from my by-line that I was married, although the story in *American Girl* was written in the first-person from the point of view of a teen-ager. I learned my lesson, and now I am Patty Sue King for teen publications, and Cameron King or P. C. King for male markets. As long as I can cash the check, I don't care what I'm called.

Where do you get your subject matter? You adapt it. If you keep your eyes open and your ears attuned, you'll find material all around you. Use all your senses to observe and record the little things that are of general and universal appeal. Wherever you go, jot down observations or phrases that you may be able to use later. However, if the appeal is too narrow or limited, the idea won't be suitable for a general article. My articles on roughing it at a summer cottage without modern plumbing probably wouldn't interest young urbanites, but *The Northern Sportsman of Canada* buys regularly. If you write about the trials of being a teacher, your presentation may interest only teachers, but if you talk about the trials of being a parent you'll reach a much larger audience.

You must also consider the timeliness of your material. It mustn't be dated in subject or references. Don't refer to an astronaut by name; by the time your piece gets in print, your man will have yielded his place in the cosmos to another (or even to a woman!). I did several versions of "Operation Hairdo" before it was published in the *Philadelphia Inquirer* because I had to change the hair styles more often than my typewriter ribbon.

In deciding on suitable subject matter you need to be aware of editorial taboos. I once remarked to my family, "What I write is pure humor," and my husband commented, "If it's pure, it'll never sell." But this isn't true in the family markets where the domestic piece is most popular. Here you must soak every word in a mental detergent or it will be deleted. Denominational markets have specialized taboos of which you need to be aware. In Sunday school publications your teen-agers must not smoke; some editors even object if the young people chew gum, drink pop, or go steady.

Be careful about making fun of household appliances, cars, etc., since editors have to consider the risks of offending their advertisers. Religion, alcoholism, race, physical handicaps, and politics are all risky subjects for levity. Likewise sex. I have been unable to place one of my favorite pieces entitled, "Double Bedlam." Apparently, the subject of the double bed versus the single bed is not acceptable, although my piece is as clean as the washings on television. One editor wrote that he thought it hilarious, but "we have to stay out of the bedroom." There *are* publications that have no prejudices against bedrooms, but I'll have to give the piece a much more bawdy (body?) treatment.

If you write only humor, you will probably have to market it yourself because magazines don't pay as much for laughs as for tears, alas, and agents like clients who make money. Obviously it's important that the humorist study the markets and offer them suitable subject matter.

Many beginners make the mistake of overdoing their funniness. It's a temptation to explain or amplify your joke to be sure the reader gets it. He would prefer to have you assume he's smart enough to get it all by himself. In my clubwoman satire for *Family Circle* ("As Amended"), many of the punch lines would have been spoiled if elaborated, *e.g.,* "The ladies claimed they hadn't read *Lady Chatterley's Lover* except in parts. . . ." "Dolores Snodgrass pointed out that dishcloths are responsible for dishpan hands, and Henrietta Hoppensniggle departed in a huff." Need I say more?

Humor can't be forced; it must have a quality of spontaneity. Producing in quantity to gain fluency is more profitable than reworking, revising and polishing until your work loses its sparkle.

Try to develop an informal, conversational style, and avoid long involved sentences. You may use slang expressions provided their popularity is not temporary. If your material sounds stilted, see where you can substitute a contraction. In a travel-with-a-teen piece for the *Chicago Tribune,* my conclusion reads, "Your young companion will point out that you can sleep when you get home, so let's not miss anything. 'Can't we save some of it for next year?' you plead. Your teen-ager will point out heartlessly that next year you may be dead. All right, kid, you win. *Marchons!*"

Many amusing commentaries on contemporary society and its foibles have failed because the writer could not hide his scholarly background. Save your big words and pedantic observations for academic papers. People read humor for entertainment, and they don't want to work too hard. Keep it short. (My articles seldom exceed a thousand words.)

In writing humor, your style must flow as smoothly as a stream; it must sparkle and twist unexpectedly like the current and course of a stream. Above all, the stream of humor must lead someplace and by the shortest possible route.

Now you know how to succeed in being funny. Write your humor piece with a definite theme, an acceptable narrator, subject matter with wide appeal, and an informal style. Then get it in the mail.

84

THE ABC'S OF BOOK REVIEWING

By Anne Pence Davis

A WRITER'S first by-line is an unforgettable thrill. If you have yet to experience it, a book review for your local or regional book page is a promising path to print.

Ask the local book editor for a chance to prove your ability. Know about book reviewing in general and about the newspaper review in particular. Discuss current best sellers with him. Be familiar with *The Book Review Digest, Publishers' Weekly,* and with other magazines dedicated to your field. Know the names and the styles of reviewers most often quoted. This should convince the editor that you could please his readers.

And you can. If you love books and read them intelligently, with practice you can write acceptable reviews.

If your paper does not have a book page or a column, ask the managing editor to let you start one. Suppose he says no? Then suggest book notes for special occasions: graduation or Christmas, vacation reading, a recommended list for Children's Book Week, celebrated each fall. Anything for a toehold.

Most editors want a book page and agree with Stanton Peckham, book editor of The Denver (Colo.) *Post,* that a book section builds the reading habits of a community and increases interest in reading.

The whole purpose of book reviewing is to further reading. In choosing your first book to review ask yourself where your own reading interests lie. Do you like historical novels, biography, travelogues, stories of the sea, or technical treatises? Are you an authority in any field: Indian lore, the American Revolution, landscaping, contemporary music or poetry, coin collecting? Have you lived in a foreign country? What geographical area are you from or where do you dream of going on your next vacation? Do you lose yourself in psychological novels or would you rather swing out into space?

Since the whole idea of a book page is to *interest more people in reading more books,* most of your remarks should be constructive. Margaret Walraven Reid, book editor of The Wichita Falls (Texas) *Times,* tells her reviewers: "If a book is wholly unworthy, do not attempt to review it. Exchange it for another. Our space is limited and we want to recommend books, not pan them. However, if a book is both good and bad (as many are), be free to say so, but be specific as to limitations."

If you are weary of prostitutes with hearts of gold, studies in moral degeneration, and flagrant filth, have the courage to express your opinion. In long years of reviewing, I have refused only three books. Two I exchanged. One I wrapped with the garbage and sent to the incinerator, not because it was vile (and it was) but because it was dishonest.

In the light of the foregoing, let's work on your review.

Read the book thoughtfully. Bracket paragraphs you may wish to quote. Jot down the numbers of pages you may wish to re-read. Let your reaction simmer a few days.

In part one, trap your reader's interest. Also give the essence of the subject matter. You may arrest the reader's attention with "a narrative hook," with a provocative one-sentence paragraph, with some startling fact about the book, the author, or the subject. Perhaps timeless is a good lead. Did the author's last book win a Pulitzer prize and have you been eagerly awaiting his latest? Well, here it is!

"Never, never," I have been cautioned many times, "begin with: This book is about so-and-so."

Let us assume you have chosen a novel to review. Tell the reader when and where the action takes place. Who is the protagonist? What is his problem? What obstacles block the hero's way? State the theme interestingly and concisely. Give the mood and atmosphere. You should have about three paragraphs by now, two of them long.

Part two, *your evaluation,* is most important. It answers the simple question: What do you think of the book? What did you like, and why? What discrepancies annoyed you? Did the characters come alive and grow? Did each undergo a change before the ending? Were any threads of the plot left dangling? Was the solution so inconclusive that you felt cheated? What of the author's style? Is it vigorous and dynamic, or poetic? A quotation demonstrates style better than you can describe it. (Check permission to quote.) What about the pace? Did the story race along or did it drag?

Always be fair to the author. Try to see his purpose. Ask yourself: What was his goal? Did he attain it? Measure in terms of what he was striving for, not by what you would have done with the same material. Be objective. Do not lambaste his book because it is about cats and you hate cats. Be wary with negatives. Be encouraging if you can honestly. Pass up minor flaws. After all, you are not his teacher; you are his liaison with the reading public. To evaluate the creative work of another is a grave responsibility. Glib, clever comments are poor taste and cruel.

If you are thoroughly confused by now, do this:

The novel you have read is exactly what your best friend likes. Relax and share your enthusiasm with him. Pique his curiosity without giving away the ending. In so doing, you will have answered many of the questions above. (Also, you will have learned much about style and structure.)

In part three of your review, add information about the author not used in the introduction. If he is from your region, be sure to say so. Compare this novel to his other work. Perhaps it is the second of a trilogy. Is it as well-written as the first? Are you impatient for the third? List prizes, awards, grants, or book club selections. Have the movie rights been sold? Strive to make your last sentence the best.

To maintain my integrity as a reviewer, I seldom read the publisher's publicity or other reviews until I have written my own. I've learned much from analyzing other writers' books. So will you.

Now your review is finished. It is terse, unbiased, and interesting to the average reader. Every word is pertinent. Here are instructions for the final typing. Unless you are otherwise instructed the following form is generally acceptable.

Leave one inch left-hand margin. Begin two inches from the top of the page. Type three double-spaced copies: one copy for your own file, one for your editor's, and one for the composing room.

Your first line is the title in capitals, the author's name, the publisher, and the price. Double space. The second line is the reviewer's name. Yes, there it is. Your name in print! Now triple space. Type your review.

A reviewer is a guide to reading and to book buying. Be an informed, enthusiastic one. Satisfaction in a job honestly done is the most of your pay, that and the book. Occasionally, a publisher, pleased with previous reviews I have written of books published by his house, asks for me by name. Some authors write notes of appreciation. I treasure one such from Jesse Stuart written from Egypt. Recently at a writers' conference where those attending wore "name badges," I was greeted several times with: "Oh, I know you. I read your reviews."

Just as books are friends, so are the people who read your reviews of books.

85

SIX RULES FOR SELLING
TO THE TRADE JOURNALS

By Fred Hamlin

There is a broad and hospitable market for free-lance material in today's business and professional magazines—the so-called trade journals—but in my opinion too few free-lancers are approaching these magazines in a sensible, businesslike manner. They are therefore short-changing themselves.

Some months back, one of the big publishing houses ran a series of ads with the headline, "It pays to wear a business suit when you call on a businessman." That goes for selling the trade market, too, and what I want to do here is talk about putting a "business suit" on the next manuscript you send out.

I write the rejection slips—and buy what's bought—for a trade magazine, and it's a rare month when I spend as much money as is budgeted for top-flight free-lance editorial material. Every month of the year, I write more thanks-but-no-thanks notes than I should have to, if more free-lancers would consider my type of magazine carefully and then use a bit of common sense before trying to sell material.

The market I'm talking about is made up of those magazines which serve specific and specialized groups of people with business, general, and technical information about their jobs, about themselves, and about the business they are in. Most of these magazines, like *Modern Veterinary Practice,* the one I edit, are partly technical and partly non-technical. I'm not talking about the *technical* material here. What I *am* talking about is the news and non-technical feature material: the kind of article that's headlined "How a Hardware Store Cut Inventory in Half—And Doubled Income"; or, "The Window Display the Ladies Couldn't Resist." These headlines are imaginary—what comes next is plain and simple fact.

499

What I'd like to do here is list half a dozen common-sense rules that could turn most of the rejections I have to send into good green checks. If what follows seems elementary to you, bear in mind that this is an editor's viewpoint—I'm talking about rules that I see broken over and over again. I'm talking about the sort of thing that can give your manuscript a polished, professional, salable touch— the difference between "instant rejection slips" and that happy time when most of your manuscripts are accepted for publication.

I promised six rules—and here they are:

First—and I think this is most important of all—read the magazine you plan to submit articles to, before you write your article or send in your outline or before you even query. This rule won't guarantee you a sale, but if you violate it, I don't see how you can hope to avoid a rejection. A single afternoon in a good library should give you enough time to read at least the past half-dozen issues of any magazine, and to read them carefully. You should probably read the back issues of one or two publications in the same field. If your library doesn't have the magazine you're looking for, check with some firms in the business you want to write about. They may subscribe to the magazine, and even if they don't, the contact you've made will prove valuable later on, as we'll see in a moment.

By reading the magazine, you'll get a good idea of what's current in the trade you plan to write for, and you'll pick up a good idea of what editors in the field are likely to look for in the articles they buy. You'll also pick up a feel for the language of the people you want to write for, and believe me, they all have their own language and ta-boos. (For example, do medical magazines speak of John Smith, M.D., or Dr. John Smith? Having it right is a point in your favor.)

Also, you will see what the magazine or magazines use in the way of story length or photographs. I know of one magazine that buys no photographs at all; it hires models and poses exactly what it wants, to be shot by a staff photographer. Think of the film you could save by checking this first. And if 1,500 words is the maximum article length they've used in the past two years, why write 5,000?

Second rule: If you're going to write for a trade magazine, you will be dealing with a *specialized audience.* For example, take a magazine for consulting engineers. The people who read it have spent at least four years of tough college work learning their profession, and many more practicing it. They know their job inside and out, and they take it seriously. So don't try to bluff them. If you don't know what you're talking about—and by that I mean understanding your subject matter thoroughly—these readers will spot it before they get past who, what and when.

Certainly you don't have the time—or probably the inclination—to become a full-fledged expert in the field. But there's a shortcut to knowledgeability that's open to every free-lancer in the country. What's more, depending upon where you got your back issues of the magazine, you may already be set up for it.

The shortcut is this: Take your article, or outline, or idea, or all of them in reverse order, to the best salesman, traffic engineer, baker or whoever is in the field you are writing about, and ask him what he thinks of it. Odds are he'll be pleased to help you out, and his advice can go a long way toward giving your manuscript the professional and knowledgeable touch that editors must always look for.

Rule number three: If you want to get paid, contribute something. Don't ask the editor to feed you ideas and money, too. Not too long ago, I received a query from a free-lancer saying he wanted to do an article for our magazine. He'd attached the briefest of all possible newspaper clippings, announcing the opening of, let's say, a new variety store in his home town. Just let me know the angle you want, he said, and I'll do it.

The problem here was that I had no way at all of knowing that there even *was* an angle—there may have been nothing new or different or interesting at all. What I look for in a query is this: Is there anything different about the store? Is it the cheapest store that's ever been built? Does it take fewer people to run the store? Unless I see a "yes" answer to at least one question of this nature, I couldn't care less—because the readers won't.

How do you find the angle? Check with the owner or manager of the store, or somebody else who's in the field or knows about it. One of these people can probably give you a fair slant on what's new and different—or if there really isn't a story there, he can probably tell you that, too. Particularly in a query (and I believe in querying), it's important to have a strong slant on "what's new" if you want any encouragement at all.

Like most editors, I simply don't have the time to write half a dozen letters to dig for a story idea that may not be there in the first place. On the other hand, if your query convinces me that you really have a story there, I'll write that many letters and more, and do whatever I can to help you make the article materialize.

Fourth rule—and this applies to magazines other than the trades, but to the trades in particular—do eight times the research that you think you will need, begin writing with six times the notes that you will use in your final article, and spend four times as much time interviewing as you do writing. If you try to pad your article out, we'll cut it, and it doesn't take too much padding to stop us from buying it in the first place. The real plus factor about extensive research, incidentally, is that it will allow you to write from a foundation of knowledge, and make you that much more of an expert in the field you're writing about.

Fifth, don't cut corners in your writing. There seems to be a real tendency for free-lancers to say something like, "It's not for *The New Yorker*, so I won't worry about the prose." The other side of that coin is "This free-lancer doesn't write carefully, so we won't buy it."

I don't really care if you split an infinitive, or if you now and then dangle a phrase, but please, please try to interest me. Our readers are all busy men. They read our magazine to get information, to get it fast, and to get it without being bored. If you're writing about people, make them human. If you're writing about a building, let's see what it looks like. If you're writing about industrial air pollution, readers will want to know how it smells. I'd rather edit out a few marginal items of information if a major point can be made stronger, or more graphic, with a little bit of life, and color, and good lively description.

Sixth and last is the Rule of Common Sense. No, I don't want that underexposed snapshot with the thumbprint in the corner. It may even make me wonder how many other "thumbprints" there are in the package you so kindly sent along. (Incidentally, on photographs, it's hard to have the cover story without a cover photograph.) To save postage, check a market listing for free-lancers to be sure the magazine you plan to submit to is actually buying. What looks like free-lance work may actually be staff written. As a rule of thumb, hold your covering letter to half a page. Most magazines *do* prefer queries. My own preference is a headline, plus lead paragraph, plus outline. Clean copy, please, and until I know you better, a return stamped envelope.

Summing all this up, notice that my first four rules have nothing to do with writing. That was deliberate on my part, and I believe it says a lot about the trade magazines. Not that we don't value good writing because we certainly do. But knowing your material, and the magazine you are writing for is, as in these rules, two-thirds of the battle. Don't spend less time writing, but *do* spend more time getting ready to write.

Finally, remember this about the trade journals—a lot of free-lancers eat by writing for them. Rates don't compare with *Playboy* perhaps, but some of these magazines will go to three and even four figures for really outstanding material. It's not *easy* to sell the trade journals, but it's not *easy* to sell any other magazines these days either. On the other hand, I'm confident that careful and competent writing will bring you results faster and more regularly in the trade journals than practically any other market going. Why not give it a try?

86

WRITING FOR THE
DENOMINATIONAL PUBLICATIONS

By Louise Berthold

THE old prospector who said "There's gold in them thar hills" might be compared to the struggling writer who climbs down from the lofty peaks of the top magazines, where he has tried unsuccessfully to peddle his wares, and wakes up to the potentialities in the less lucrative but still rewarding "hills" of the denominational publications.

During the time I have been writing for these magazines,I have made around two hundred sales, most of them in this field—fiction, articles, bits of verse, fillers and quizzes, mainly because there are approximately three hundred markets to aim for, and they need so much material. This reason alone should present a challenge, but there are three other reasons that might tempt a writer to try these markets. First, there is not so much competition here as in the general publications; second, the rate of payment is better than writers not familiar with this field may think; and third, the editors of these magazines are unusually friendly and cooperative. They rarely reject a manuscript without saying why, and they often include an encouraging note with either an acceptance or a rejection. Two editors to whom I had sold before wrote and asked me for seasonal stories, another worked with me through two revisions to make a story right for his magazine, and still another editor sent me his readers' comments on an article I submitted about Christmas carols. One of the readers wrote: "I'm not too enthusiastic about this article, but if we have to print a seasonal piece it will suffice. However, I'd like to see a Christmas story by this writer. I think she could write a good one." The editor wrote at the end of this reader's comments: "Would you like to take this on from here?" Of course I *did* like and they bought my short story called "A Very Special Christmas Tree."

With all the varied denominational markets and with all these cooperative editors, surely something *you* have written will fit in some-where. Consult the lists of denominational markets with their editorial requirements, select one into which your work might fit, and write for a sample copy—then study the contents thoroughly.

It is important to keep up with the markets because, as with the general magazines, a few fold each year. Furthermore, new magazines appear every year; a magazine may change its name or address or there may be a change of editors. If possible, address editors by name when you mail manuscripts because it is more personal. Letters accompanying your manuscripts are not necessary unless you have something special to say about your qualifications or research of an article. But some of the editors in this field like to know if you have sold and to what magazines.

Denominational publications are divided into age groups, and there are many in each group. If you like to write for children, why not try the kindergarten, the primary or the junior publications? There are also a good many teen-age magazines in this field but the adult markets far outnumber the others.

In writing for denominational publications you do not necessarily have to be of an editor's faith. Sincerity, smooth writing and something to say are the important essentials. But of course he will not accept any material that is offensive to his religious beliefs. Each magazine has its own slant and word length and some of them have taboos, such as divorce and birth control in the Catholic magazines (lately the scope of acceptable writing in this group has broadened to a certain extent), illness or infirmity in the Christian Science or the Unity magazines; dancing or smoking in a few Protestant publica-tions; and sex or drinking (unless a constructive article) in all of them. But, on the whole, the editors of denominational publications are broad in their concept, and most of them welcome any whole-some story or article that would be acceptable to a general magazine.

Of course this does not mean that denominational editors will buy just any old manuscript dragged out of moth balls. All of them want careful writing, good plots for fiction, and articles about interesting people, places or things, and most of them want fillers, quizzes, good poetry and light verse. Only a few ask that submitted material be didactic—in fact they stress that they do not want Pollyanna stories or those which are resolved by a miracle. This is not to say that editors in this field do not want inspirational material—they do and lots of it, when it is written in a colorful, helpful way without obvious preaching. If you *show* how someone you know (of course no names) courageously adjusted to the loss of a loved one or to a serious handicap, or if you know someone who lives his faith by service to others, you will have a ready market here for such an article.

Several of the larger denominational publications pay up to ten cents a word.

In the Jewish group, *Dimensions in American Judaism* pays up to $150 for short fiction and articles, and the *National Jewish Monthly* pays up to five cents a word.

In the Catholic field (which has more magazines than any other church), *The Sign* pays up to $300 for an article or story, and *Extension, The Catholic Digest, St. Joseph Magazine, Catholic Home, Ave Maria, Sacred Heart Messenger, The Lamp* and *St. Anthony Messenger* pay very good rates. I have sold *The Catholic Digest* a short article, *Ave Maria* a short story and a fiction serial on which I collaborated with my husband, *The Lamp* two articles and a short story, *Catholic Home* a travel article, a nostalgic essay, and an historical piece, and *St. Anthony Messenger* some light verse.

Among the better paying Protestant markets are *Christian Herald, Together* and *The Christian Home* (both Methodist), *Guideposts, This Day* (Lutheran), *The War Cry* (Salvation Army), *The Sunday Digest, Presbyterian Life, Presbyterian Survey, The Lutheran* and *The Lutheran Standard*. Of these magazines I have sold *The Christian Home* two short stories and four pieces of light verse; *This Day* an article and a story, *The War Cry* an article; *The Lutheran Standard* a short story and *The Sunday Digest* some fillers. The checks you receive from these magazines may not seem like a fortune, but when you sell fairly consistently to both Protestant and Catholic publications, it not only provides the jam for your bread and butter but gives a writer a wonderful lift.

A few of the smaller denominational publications may be a trifle slow about reporting because they are often understaffed, but you *will* hear from them, and the larger magazines are prompt. The editors in this field as a rule prefer that the material sent them be short. Some will accept from 800 to 3,500 words, others will buy longer material and divide it into serial lengths. All seasonal material (and they use a lot of it) must be submitted from six to eight months in advance, except for weeklies.

In creating fiction, plotting is a bugaboo to some writers, but it need not be if you base your story on a germ of truth. There are people who like to write about strange lands and strange people they have never seen or known. But I've never sold a story that was not founded on something that happened to me or to someone with whom I am familiar, an overheard bit of conversation, an unforgettable character, an unusual setting I know well, or even a newspaper story that struck me forcibly. These are the germs of truth around which you can easily plot a story. Perhaps when you finish the story, it will have changed considerably, but the germ of truth will remain to make it plausible and real.

However, no matter how authentic your material may be, don't let it strain the reader's credulity. How many times have you heard a writer say when challenged, "But that really *did* happen to me!" Well, it may have, but probably it was something that could happen only once in a lifetime, and readers want to identify with the main character—they want the story to be about something that *might* have happened to them.

Before you put a word on paper, *think* about your plot and your characters, get to know these characters and the problems they face. How would *you* work out their problems? Unless it is humor, before the climax the main character should face what is called his "dark moment" to sustain suspense and make the reader wonder if the problem can be solved. Throw obstacles in his way, make him *do* something about them, but be sure to make *him* do it—don't let the problem be solved by coincidence. Of course you may have read stories where the problem was never solved but you won't sell that type to the denominational magazines—they like happy endings.

In writing nonfiction for the denominational publications, there is almost as wide a range of subjects as in the general magazines. But these editors particularly like articles about family life, personality pieces, travel, seasonal, inspirational and historical articles, how-to pieces, success stories and articles about people's hobbies, such as collecting milk glass or old coins, wood carving or flower arranging. If you can show in a dramatic way how a family or a community solved their problems, you'll have a sure-fire sale.

Travel articles are a little more difficult to sell because, though some years ago people sat in easy chairs and *read* about strange and interesting places, now so many people *visit* these fascinating places that competition is keen. But the travel article of today for most magazines must be detailed. Not only should one write about the sights he sees but the best way to travel to that place, the cost, the best hotels or motels and interesting sidelights. Among others I have sold a travel article about Mexico's Floating Gardens at Xochimilco to *Catholic Home* and one about the pyramids at San Juan Teotihuacan to *Classmate*. Pictures are essential in travel articles and will enhance the salability of any article.

Articles about community projects are popular with the denominational publications. Not long ago in my home city vandals cut down thirty-five beautiful young trees from the grounds of Mt. Carmel High School. The trees had been set out a year earlier at a cost of $500. A 17-year-old girl and her younger brother read about the vandals in the newspapers and were so incensed they decided to do something about it. They called on other teen-age volunteers to help collect donations to replace the trees and solicited the aid of a nursery man who sold them the trees at cost. One morning soon after, a hundred teen-agers gathered at the school. There were a few college students among them, a Jewish boys' group, a youth group from an Episcopal church, Catholic boys and girls, Negroes, Latin Americans and a boys' group from the YMCA. By noon the volunteers had dug up all the old tree stumps and replaced them with new trees. I sold this story to *Catholic Digest*.

I have sold a number of hobby articles to the denominational magazines, ranging from a man who collected antique clocks to a young radio commentator who, while serving with the Armed Forces overseas, vowed that if he ever returned home safely, he would devote the rest of his time to sculpture—this, in spite of the fact that he'd never had an art lesson. Today he is an outstanding sculptor, specializing in religious art for churches.

Fillers are used in most magazines to fill up the space left at the end of an article or short story. They may be brief items from various newspapers or other publications for which the source must be given, or they may be seasonal shorts (always in demand) original human interest or humorous items, poetry, light verse or bright sayings of children. The market is varied and some of the denominational magazines pay quite well for fillers. For instance, *Catholic Digest* has several departments that pay from $20 to $50 for short contributions. Among them are "Hearts Are Trumps" (true cases where a kindness is rendered with no hope of reward) "The Perfect Assist" (reports of tactful remarks or actions), and "People Are Like That" (true incidents that illustrate the instinctive goodness of human nature). It would be wise to study these departments before sending fillers.

Quizzes are also popular, but this market is flooded with Bible quizzes so try to make yours different. Many of these magazines accept light verse, as well as serious poetry. The rate is usually from $3 to $10 for either poetry or verse, but some magazines pay more.

You may be surprised to know that many famous writers started their careers with the denominational publications; this is proof enough that they offer unlimited opportunities to the young writer today.

87

THE PRACTICE OF PLAYWRITING

By Mary C. Chase

You have asked me—what are the most important techniques for the beginning playwright to master? Well! Well! Well! First of all, is the beginner a playwright?

If so, he was born a playwright, with an instinct for the theater. If not, he cannot learn playwriting, as he could not learn to sing without a voice or to dance without an innate sense of rhythm.

He may have a desire and talent to spin stories and a need to communicate to others his sense of the wonder and beauty and terror of life; he may have understanding of character, a feel for narrative and style. He may have all of these qualities and yet not be a playwright. He may be a great artist, a superb intellect, a Titan of literature. He may be much, much more talented than a playwright and yet not be a playwright.

What then is a playwright? First, he is one who has a heightened awareness of the living presence of other human beings in the same room—a room seating five people or a theater seating five hundred. He has an awareness of creatures, animal creatures, a love and a fear of them; a knowledge of the banked fires of conflict between them and an almost guilty excitement in the desire to stir these fires into blaze; above all, he has a need to attract these animals, to please them, to entertain them, satisfy them and even uplift them. It is a social act, theater. And the playwright is closer to the actor than he is to the novelist; closer to the clown than to the professor; closer to the evangelist and the minister in the pulpit than he is to the scholar in the library.

If the writer has this extra dimension of sensitivity to the presence of others listening in the same room, he should fortify his instinct by studying the proven rules of dramaturgy. He should begin with Aristotle's *Poetics* and then go to William Archer's *Playmaking*. This is old-fashioned here and there but very, very sound. Then he should study the Greek plays, Shakespeare, Molière, Ibsen and O'Neill. Then he should study melodramas and perhaps try imitating one for practice.

The melodrama, while considered superficial in substance, is so dependent upon mounting suspense that it is an excellent form to study for construction. Several prize-winning modern plays are actually souped-up melodramas—even drawing on the past for the use of musical interludes. And whatever else melodrama may lack in the way of embellishments, it is always—theater.

The playwright should read Fielding's essay on comedy, Victor Hugo's essay on the art of preparation in the drama and Tolstoy's discussion of the drama in *What Is Art?*

Is he going to write comedies or dramas? He should learn that the main difference here is one of attitude: his own attitude toward a plot and characters; the attitude of the characters toward the plot and each other. If Hamlet, for instance, had been a milquetoast in the opening scene, and if the specter had tried to persuade him to forget about his father's murder and go back to sleep, the play would have had to zoom off into farce comedy.

At some point early, the playwright should decide that he is a playwright and get out of the library and into the theater—right where he is. He should begin to practice the techniques of the play form first with those around him—his friends, his family, his acquaintances.

When he tells a joke, a personal experience, an anecdote, he should observe the uses of the beginning, the middle, the end; how to arouse interest and hold it; how to satisfy the listener in concluding the story. He should watch carefully the change which comes in the telling of a story, say, to one person and then, as others join to listen; how the tempo accelerates, how he now condenses here or expands there, elaborates or cuts depending on the attention of the listeners. Telling stories aloud to children provides a superb laboratory in which the beginning playwright may practice theater techniques and learn to provoke interest—to hold it, make it rise, and then sum up. This audience is perfect for him, because children are even more impatient than adults and have not yet learned to conceal boredom. This is a primitive thing the playwright is doing while he is learning, and it fits the case. The theater itself is a primitive animal, a wonderful, wonderful thing.

When a writer writes a story, he is addressing a letter that is to be read and absorbed quietly by one person. The playwright is always addressing a group. He is interesting, rabble-rousing, clowning or inspiring—for the ear. He is doing this actually or in his imagination—always. Because even in the latter case he must be aware of others—listening!

The playwright must *wright* and not merely *write*. He must "wright" plays and scenes because he is primarily a builder and his job is to build scenes to play before a living audience.

When, after some practice in the telling of anecdotes, etc., he begins to feel a little more sure of himself with the rules, he must begin cautiously here and there to inject into these little shows and "tryouts" a bit of himself—certain of his own personal idylls, ideas, memories and dreams. These personal trial balloons may now and then excite, interest or bore his listeners. This will throw him into despair and shame. And it should. It must. But he must go on.

If something does strike fire from his audience—maybe it was an anecdote about an old aunt in Peoria—he must tell it again to another group. If it strikes fire again and still again, he will know he has something which interests people. Should he make a play out of this? Wait. Test it first with these questions. Ask—not if it will make a good play, or a bad play, a short play or a full-length play, but first—is it a play at all? Maybe it's a story or a novel. Think of the word play here as a verb, not as a noun. What would be "playing" against what? What forces against what other forces? For what stakes? What moments of change and crisis would be there to watch?

And be careful about using philosophical conclusions as the germ of a play. These can enrich a play but may not have enough vitality to initiate one. It has been my personal experience that plays which came into my mind as completed pieces of stage business always pleased an audience more than those written from a philosophical conclusion I had reached and then found a plot to illustrate.

A play is not a narrative in dialogue, like the talking picture which is acted out on a sound stage, filmed and shown later, coming across like scenes in memory. A play is an imitation of an action being performed in public, before other people sitting out there watching it happen—*now!*

Suppose the playwright decides he has a play. Where does he begin? At what point does he open the play? Stalk the game very carefully here. This is the only real choice the playwright has. After that he is bound by the laws of growth and the rules of dramatic progression. His choice here must be determined by his own instinct. He is on his own. And he trembles—rightly.

With his choice of the opening made, his chart of scenes set down, his acquaintance with his characters increased, he waits for the moment when his inner excitement propels him to the workroom to put down the dialogue in whatever scene he is now impelled to get moving. With every word he writes, he must hold in his consciousness the feeling of the actors on the stage and the presence of a living audience in the room with him. This inspires him to effects he had never calculated. He is amazed, awed, suspended in time, at one with the dramatists of the past. Have the shades of the past great playwrights come to stand behind his chair? Don't move. This is the theater—not Broadway. It is happening here—now. It is *playing!*

What happens to the play itself later will be determined at this point. If the writer's own heart does not pound—no one else's ever will. If he is not amused—nobody else will be—ever.

Eugene O'Neill was able to hold in his mind at the same time scenes and characters and background on a stage, and an audience watching these characters; he did this with such intensity that his plays can transcend bad acting and shabby productions. Once I saw a group of high school amateurs attempting one of his sea plays in the dingy auditorium of a women's club in Denver. Bad as the actors were—as the play went on, I felt the spray in my face. O'Neill had transcended the production and had brought me into his workroom where *he* was feeling the spray as he wrote.

When the playwright has a draft of his play which pleases him, he should not put it into an envelope and mail it to a producer—yet. He should try it out, reading it aloud to a group of three or more people in his home. He doesn't need to invite experts to these readings—just people. He should notice when, during the reading, the chairs scrape, the bracelets rattle, and the bodies shift positions; when there is a blessed stillness or wholehearted laughter. But he should never,

never, never listen to the friends who expound to him afterward on where the play went off and why. The friends don't know. The critics won't know. He must know. His audience has reacted or not reacted. The playwright watches, suffers, and learns why.

The late Frank Fay once told a young beginning comic who had met with a lukewarm reception, "Kid, you learn your trade through flop sweat. That means when you're doing it and you're dying and you know they don't like you and the sweat comes out on your brow. In that split second you learn more than in all the beforehand planning or theories. There's no other way."

What you learn from a fiasco in your living room or from a flop before an audience of a thousand in a theater—and the difference is only one of degree—you will make good use of.

Go back to your chart, your sequence of scenes, re-wright, re-build. Then read the play to another group. If you now hold them, try to form a contact with an acting company, amateur or professional, through a producer.

And don't ever let anybody tell you this is impossible for the beginner. It is not—not if he has a play that plays.

There is so little real theater in the true sense of the word: excitement, mounting interest, breathless waiting, a sense of fate and eternity outside the window or the joy of the comedy whisking the audience up and away from care. The world hungers for such experiences and goes patiently to the theater, time after time—waiting.

The theater is a mysterious, mystical place. And just as each play, no matter how much craft you learn, has within it a special secret which you alone must solve (perhaps in outright defiance of one of the rules of the craft you've learned), so each play has its own vitality and its own fate and will find its way somehow to the stage. Play your hunches about your work.

The theater is like war. The audience is your enemy to be overcome. At first it is ill-natured and skeptical and "show me." Your play is your plan of attack. You must meet your audience at the point where they are at this moment in time, interest them, hold them and try to lift them.

If your play fails and the audience wins, leaving the theater intact —unmoved, unamused—pay no attention to the notices explaining why. And don't pore over Sunday newspaper articles about your work or any other playwright's, measuring yourself and your plays against the weighty edicts handed down by journalists. These are the armchair generals leaning back to give opinions after the battle. They are around the theater but not "of" it. Nobody really understands the theater until he has risked everything for it. Until he himself has known "flop sweat."

If your play succeeds and the articles are full of raves explaining the victory—pay no attention. Take what you've learned here, too, sharpen your tools, and go back to work.

88

Rx FOR COMEDY

By Neil Simon

THE idea of a prescription for comedy is obviously ridiculous. What works for one playwright rarely works for another, and even the fact that a certain approach succeeded for a writer before does not mean that it will surely produce an amusing play for that same scribe a second time. The knowledge of this grisly reality gives me a healthy insecurity, which I consider a great asset. Insecurity encourages a writer to be open to criticism by competent professionals; it allows him to face up to the need to revise or rewrite. Of course, *everybody* cheerily tells a playwright how to repair his script and it takes cool courage and wondrous manners to endure the amateurs' well-meant advice. In Boston during the tryout of *The Odd Couple*, I had been up till four o'clock in the morning rewriting the third act—for the fifth time. Exhausted, I finally fell asleep on my typewriter. At seven A.M. a dentist from Salem, Mass., phoned to tell me how *he* would fix the third act. I thanked him and promised myself I would call him at five the next morning to tell him how I would fix his bridgework.

I happen to like rewriting, a good deal of which is often necessary after one sees how a scene actually "plays" on stage in rehearsal or tryout. Each chance to fix, polish and tighten is a glorious reprieve— something I never had in the urgent world of weekly television. I suppose the greatest problem the writer in the theater has is to face "those ferocious critics." My problem is even greater. I write my own critics' reviews as I'm writing my play. I place Walter Kerr just behind my right shoulder holding in his hand a big stick—with rusty nails. If I get verbose or careless or stretch for jokes, Mr. Kerr lets me have it right across the knuckles.

This article originally appeared in *Playbill* Magazine, January 1966. Reprinted courtesy of Playbill, Inc.

The jokes are a special hazard. In the first of 112 versions of *Come Blow Your Horn,* the opening five minutes of the play were crammed with good jokes—in fact, some of the best I had ever written—and the scene was terrible. The audience, knowing nothing of the characters or the situation, could not have cared less. Now I know enough to start with the characters. Where do they come from? In the case of *The Odd Couple,* from a party I attended in California. All the men there were divorced, all their dates were their new girl friends. Most of these men were sharing apartments with other divorced men because alimony payments forced them to save money. In *Barefoot* and *Come Blow Your Horn,* at least one or two characters in each play resembled, perhaps in speech patterns, mannerisms or personal outlook, someone I've actually known.

Looking back at what and how I write, I seem to begin a play with two people of completely opposite nature and temperament, put them in an intolerable situation, and let the sparks fly. The extra ingredient, and very important, is that they must both emphatically believe that their way of life is the right one. Then it's the playwright's job to support *both* those beliefs. As for form, I prefer my comedies in three acts. When I start, I write extensive notes for the first act, a sketchy outline for the second and nothing for the third. I'm rather curious myself as to what will happen in the third act. Sometimes I don't find out for certain until a week before we open on Broadway.

If there is anything remotely resembling a key to comedy in theater, I'd guess that it is for the writer, director and actors to apply one simple rule. Never treat it as a comedy. The actors and characters must treat their predicament as though their lives depended on it. Not an easy achievement, I admit. Play it too seriously and the laughs are gone. Play just the comedy and ditto. In casting, my preference is not to go with the "established comic" but with a good actor who understands comedy. Walter Matthau, Robert Redford and Mildred Natwick are among the best.

One question I'm asked quite often is if I consider myself funny. I suppose I apply my own personal humor to life in the same manner as I would in a play. I need a situation. Put me around a table with real funny men like Buddy Hackett or Jonathan Winters or Mel

Brooks and I fade like a shrinking violet. No fast repartee for me. I shine trapped in an elevator with six people and a German Shepherd licking my ear.

To me, the first ten minutes of a comedy are critical. The writer must (1) set up the rules and the situation, (2) catch the audience almost immediately. Once the rules are announced, farce, satire, straight comedy or whatever game you're playing, the audience will believe you so long as you stick to those rules and that game. I believe in starting the conflict in the opening minutes (e.g., the poker game in *Odd Couple*) and to be as theatrically arresting as possible. The idea of opening on an empty stage in *Barefoot* intrigued me. Then I begin with some new event in the life of our hero, something that has never happened to him before.

My writing routines are actually rather prosaic. No midnight oil burns in my lamp. I type in an office or at home, and put in a ten to five day with a short lunch break. I may do a complete draft of a play, use it as an outline and then set to work on a more finished version. I like to get into the writing quickly to "hear how the characters speak," for once I hear the speech patterns it is easier going. I ought to point out that my insecurity is such that even as I'm writing one play, I'm beginning to think ahead to the next. So if this one doesn't quite pan out, well. . . .

Once a play goes into rehearsal, my "normal" routine ceases and the midnight oil begins to burn. There seems to be less time for social obligations, children and—horror of horrors—the Giants' football games.

Do I need quiet when I'm working? It depends. If there are no problems in the script, they could be digging the new subway under my typewriter. But one day recently my two little girls were on the other side of the house playing jacks. And as the ball bounced softly on the thick rug, I ran from the study screaming at my wife, "Can't you keep those kids quiet?"

She looked at me with knowing affection and pity.

"I'm sorry the scene's not going well, Doc," she answered with ancient female wisdom.

If there's anything I can't stand, it's a smart aleck wife—who happens to be right.

89

TELEVISION WRITING TODAY

By Edward Barry Roberts

In this electronic age, it well may be that the ability to write is the last thing expected of a television writer. For instance, in a recent Red Skelton show, in a skit called "Baby's First Birthday," there appeared this stage direction:

> In comes an attractive nurse in a short dress—she's carrying a birthday cake. NOTE (says the script): A split screen pre-taped—or Chromo-key her in and double hands to put cake on high chair tray.

The writer of the script wrote in that stage direction. My point is, before the writer could do his job, that is, use his writing talent to its expected value, he had to know what a split-screen pre-taped is, or what it means to Chromo-key the nurse in and double the hands that put the cake on the high chair tray. He had to know that he could solve a problem he faced by using the devices those two technical terms describe.

The writer's problem was this: Red Skelton, in baby clothes, was sitting in an out-sized highchair in order to put him in the right proportions for a proper baby. The nurse had to bring in his birthday cake. If she appeared in the same shot with Red, he'd be gigantic in relation to her, and the illusion of his being a proper baby would be destroyed. So, the writer suggested two possible methods: one, the split screen, which everyone has seen on televsion many times; the other, the Chromo-key method, which is much like the old motion picture "process shot," by which action can be superimposed on a background previously photographed through a color masking process which I'll not stick my neck out to describe.

In other words, writing for television today takes something more than being able to put words together. While all aspiring television playwrights need not expect to be faced with a split screen pre-taped, they should be aware of its technical possibilities, and, most important, they must be familiar with its writing rules and format requirements which the technical devices impose on the medium.

Early television scripts intended for live production (and for production live on tape) were written only on the left-hand side of the page, double-spaced, and only halfway across the page, leaving the right half blank.

The vacant half of the page was a notepad used by the technicians responsible for producing the script. The director used this space for stage business (note how the old terms survive—*stage* business), for his camera position, for cues, for any other memoranda he might wish to record. If that blank half page had not been available, there would have had to be *another* blank page adjoining the script to record the directors' and technicians' handwritten notes.

Dialogue is upper and lower case, and the names of the characters capitalized and centered above their speeches. The writer's stage directions and camera terms are capitalized in this format, merely to distinguish them from the dialogue. Also, regarding the double-spacing, sometimes the writer himself forgot that he had to keep in mind his transition scenes in live television production—those scenes which allowed the camera, the microphones, and the actors themselves to move from position to position without interfering with the flow of the drama on the viewer's TV screen.

In short, the generous spacing was to allow ease in reading and room for corrections when corrections might be needed—as well as for the actors to make those mysterious doodlings to themselves which are their own way of recording the instructions the director has given them.

After "live" production, there came "live on tape." I understand "live on tape" to mean that the play was recorded on magnetic tape, with the actual performance being continuous, as if it were on the air. The format does not look any different from that of a "live" script. However, there is one very important—even crucial—difference in a script written for tape production in this half-page format. The need for the writer to devise those all-important transition scenes—the cover scenes—was gone. The taping process, with the incredible machines doing the recording, could simply be stopped while the actors moved to the next set, changed costume or makeup, or had a coffee break. With magnetic tape recording, an actor could appear in swimming shorts on the beach, and a second later, could be in evening clothes in the ballroom, dancing with his lady love.

When magnetic tape recording came in, the playwright had to learn his technique all over again (actually, the technique was a lot easier) and such a change in technique inevitably changed the construction of his drama, allowing total freedom from internal time, as contrasted with *external* time—the allover length of his allowed time on the air. I have said many times, and it is not original with me, in television, *Time* is the overlord of everything—and I don't mean the magazine.

In my opinion, there is an enormous benefit to be gained by the television playwright from his mastering the technique of writing for live production. This benefit is the ability so to condense his material within the bed of Procrustes that establishes his time limits that he learns to tell a story better, more cleanly, more sparsely, with no excess words—assuming that he has a suitable story in the first place. By that I mean, I'd hate to see Proust's *Remembrance of Things Past* or one of Scott's Kenilworth novels reduced to the 54-minute length of an hour live program—or an hour filmed program, for that matter.

For television plays written for "live" production or in the "live" format for taping, the following table of *maximum* number of pages for dramatic scripts is generally accepted by television producers. This table is based on typing halfway across standard 8½″ × 11″ paper, using a typewriter with pica (12-point) type. If your typewriter has elite (much smaller) type, scale down the number of pages by roughly one-third, since with elite type you get much more on each page. (Should you wonder why an hour script is not twice the 40 pages of a half-hour script, but is instead 100 pages *maximum*, it's because of the difference in the handling of commercials and station identification time.)

15-minute script	20 pages
Half-hour script	40 pages
Hour script	100 pages
Hour-and-a-half script	150 pages

At the current stage of television production, I think that the playwright can safely assume that his play will be filmed, and write accordingly. Always I urge my television playwriting classes to "write with the camera" (that is, for dramatic visual effects), as well as with the typewriter.

A motion picture is a longitudinal mosaic of strips of film, in varying lengths, literally glued together—I believe the correct word is cemented—to form the complete motion picture. Each strip of film represents one scene of the writer's screenplay. Television plays for motion picture filming are written entirely across the page (the standard $8\frac{1}{2}'' \times 11''$). For half-hour filmed plays, the average *maximum* number of shots—*every single shot described*—is 90. For hour-long filmed plays, the average number of shots—*every single shot described*—is 200. For motion pictures of indeterminate length —a movie that's "as long as it's long"—there is no numerical limit, although one surely will be set as filmed television plays come under television's severe over-all time limitations.

Ideally, each scene in the script describes the following: the size of the shot (medium shot, close up, follow shot, and so forth); the physical location of the shot (interior—the kitchen, exterior—the south forty acres, etc.); the lighting effect desired (day, night, twilight, gloom, sunrise); any possible movement of the camera (zoom in for a close-up); the actors in the shot—and any unusual business the writer dreams up—and any sound effects to be recorded directly or to be added.

Please notice that for convenience sake and for no other reason, *all directions concerning the camera are capitalized,* so that the cameraman and his assistants may pick out easily what the camera is required to do on a specified shot. Also, the *first time* they're mentioned in each shot, the names of all the actors involved in that scene are capitalized, so that the assistant director can round them up and have them ready.

And sound effects are capitalized so that the sound man can pick out his responsibilities in the shot. Any department of production, any technician in any department, certainly would be justified in thinking that his services are not required in a given scene if he fails to see his duties spelled out in capitals. And to prepare these duties— in capitals—is the playwright's responsibility. I repeat: all this capitalization is done for convenience, for utility, so that the technician involved in the scene can easily select what he's supposed to do.

It should be remembered that each specified *shot* requires a new and different *camera setup*. Inside a studio, that means balancing the lights so that there will be no different light values in closely connected scenes, unless such a difference is desired, and, if it is, it's the job of the playwright to indicate it; it means physically moving the *camera* around to a new place.

Tedious? Yes, but it's indispensable knowledge for the writer of scripts to be filmed. The first time I worked in a Hollywood studio, I was told by my supervisor that if I wrote ten shots a day, I was doing what was expected of me.

It is the screen playwright's duty to prepare all these scenes which, cemented together, end to end, make the complete motion picture. It's called, first, a rough cut. The editors—the cutters—have to keep track of the proper sequence. So at the start of each shot, a clapstick is used—an ordinary slate on which are written in chalk the scene number (supplied by the script), the name of the production, the director's name, usually; and the number of the "take," that is, the number of the time that the scene is being photographed.

The "slate" is called a "clapstick" because there's a hinged stick or clapper on top which is banged smartly at the beginning, producing a sharp knock which is a cue to the cutter—the editor—that the sound is functioning from that point on. And we get the familiar direction, "Lights! Camera! Speed! Action!" and the actors act.

You see, then, that the first process of putting a motion picture together, after it's been photographed, is an arithmetical process. And that's why you, the screen playwright, must number the shots as you write the drama and advance the story. I believe it's the practice in Hollywood nowadays among some producers not to number the shots until the final version of a script has been approved, to avoid messing up the sequence with divisions and subdivisions of numbers. You might like to know, too, that different rewrites are written on different colored paper, to show what's new.

I started with the writing of the finished script, because that's what most new writers think of, and dream of. Behind it in practice, however, lie several steps: first, usually, a synopsis of the proposed story which the writer must prepare. Most writers hate like the devil to write synopses; it's difficult to do and it's hard to keep a synopsis from being dull and sounding like a bunch of nothing. "And then she murders him, and then he kisses her"—the bold statement can so often produce the glazed look. It's also an art to read a synopsis and to detect the values and uniqueness of a story.

There's another kind of—well, synopsis—which is more than a synopsis. This more elaborate prose writing, which may include some dialogue, is a *treatment*. A producer may call on the writer to give him a treatment, which is a sort of road map of the planned production. The treatment shows how the story will be handled, will be developed. Say there is a ski sequence. Shall it be photographed in the Swiss Alps or in Aspen, Colorado? Shall the heroine wear a mink coat or a good cloth coat? Shall the lovers be shown reclining in the Waldorf Towers or in a hideaway on East 22nd Street? A treatment, then, is a detailed master scene arrangement in sequence showing the nature of the production and its handling. A friend wrote the screenplay of the original *Mutiny on the Bounty*. For several years, treatments of this story had been written, none of them satisfactory. Another friend tried to write the screenplay of the Kipling novel, *Kim*. She was never able to produce a satisfactory treatment which convinced the producer that a successful picture would result. *Kim* was not produced until years later and only when another writer did a successful treatment and screenplay.

A treatment can run to ten pages or a hundred, depending on the detail which the producer demands. Once upon a time I sold one which ran about eighty-five pages. This was the only form in which the producer saw the story. It was never done, but that's still another story.

I've mentioned master scenes—that a treatment can consist of a collection of master scenes in the proper sequence. A master scene is a scene which is a hunk of related action explained in narrative, stage directions, and/or in dialogue—or all three—which does not break down the content of the action into final detail—into camera shots, in the case of a movie. Many of the television playwrights adapting their own work into screenplays for the first time wrote master scenes because they did not know how to write separate camera shots which would make up the mosaic of a motion picture.

Sometimes a treatment is called a final script before dialogue.

And some really tough producers may insist on a scene-by-scene breakdown, before dialogue. This is real torture for the screen playwright, because it forces him to work out his story in the minutest detail without the help, the lift, the inspiration of the moment which comes from writing dialogue and which gives life and interest to the script.

Closely related to the scene-by-scene breakdown is the line-by-line breakdown. I once had to do it for a fiend of a producer. Here you describe in one declarative sentence after another the progression of the action of the complete picture.

Some brilliant and clever writers will prepare the complete shooting script—shots, dialogue, action all described—and hide it. Then they write the required scene-by-scene breakdown, based on the completed script. This is, I think, legitimate cheating, if you can get away with it, and if you hate, loathe and despise the task of writing any form of scene-by-scene breakdown.

Perhaps you know that sometimes when two writers are put on a script, one is the renowned author of the best-selling novel and the other is a skilled screenplay technician who knows nothing beyond how to write camera shots in acceptable terminology. If you are now, or plan to be, a renowned author, I urge you to learn how to write camera shots—continuity, as it's called—as soon as possible, for otherwise not only do you share the credit of the screen play with the technician, you also share the money.

Production of television drama has largely been concentrated in Hollywood, so much so that in New York, in the spring of 1967, the only assignment a high official of the Writers Guild with impressive credits could get was to write a documentary film for a fund-raising foundation combating a serious disease. Accordingly, he moved himself and his family to Hollywood, since he wished to continue writing for television. The much-touted "drama revivals" announced variously by the networks have not materialized; it is a matter of common knowledge that sponsors (who pay the bills) for drama are not easy to find; the costs of sponsorship have become astronomical; potential sponsors demand the prospect of the highest rating. Original dramas have not in the past always commanded such ratings.

In my opinion the "ratings" control more and more what will be telecast and what will not. "Spot" sponsorship—the numerous commercial interruptions of a program by perhaps as many as a dozen different sponsors, in the case of a full-length motion picture—has been created by economic necessity. These are the present facts of life which the television playwright must live with as long as he's writing for commercial television.

But—television is show business! It could change overnight. The agitation for change, which might come through Educational Television or "Public Television," is very great. The important thing for the individual beginning television playwright is to be ready with the indispensable knowledge of *how* to write a television play when his opportunity comes. (It might not be out of line to remark that the Broadway Theatre also is formidable in its difficulties for the unknown, unestablished playwright.) The best route to television (and Broadway) seems to lie through making a name, large or small, in some other medium—a paperback or hardcover novel; a play done off Broadway or off off Broadway, by a little theatre, a regional theatre, a university theatre, as a summer theatre tryout; or a television play on a local station; that is, any form of production of a writer's work which will set that writer apart.

In my opinion, the most reliable Market List for the television playwright is the Monthly Talent & Script Report issued by Television Index, Inc., 150 Fifth Avenue, New York, New York 10011. This costs $1.25 plus 16¢ postage per issue (plus New York City 6% sales tax where it applies), and will be sent on request. This monthly report is as up-to-date as it is humanly possible to be in the world of television. It identifies markets and market conditions in all possible detail. It locates agents by name, address, kind of agent and telephone number. It is still highly desirable that you have an accredited agent; the report usually tells which agent will consider new material and new playwrights and which won't. To get a free list of the literary agents who are members of The Society of Authors' Representatives, write to the Society at 101 Park Avenue, New York, New York 10017. Enclose a self-addressed, stamped envelope.

With all its abrupt changes, through its vicissitudes, upheavals and contradictions, television, of course, is here to stay; and someone must write it. To write for television, you must know and be able to implement its fundamental principles.

90

WRITING FOR TELEVISION

By Barbara Schultz

ONE of the most persistent (and plaintive) questions asked by the young writer today is: how do I get a foothold in television?

It is a reasonable question, since television presents such an inviting target for the writer: it is seen by more people more frequently than any other medium of communication; it consumes more creative material in a week than most media consume in a year; and, generally speaking, it pays more for this material.

Moreover, television is a vast market, embracing three major television networks and more than eight hundred individual television stations, all of which are broadcasting the writer's product on an average of fifteen hours a day.

Given these circumstances, the opportunities for a young writer to get into television would seem to be golden. Yet his own experience clearly denies this. What, then, is the answer?

One answer which may not be immediately apparent to him is the great number of *established* writers who are currently producing material for television. To this output must be added the enormous stream of material that pours into the offices of television story editors from young and inexperienced writers like himself.

During the course of a single year some five thousand unsolicited manuscripts are submitted to the CBS Television Network alone. They come from all kinds of people in all kinds of occupations in all sections of the country. And they come in all shapes and sizes—from a two-paragraph synopsis of a plot, to a five-page outline for a comedy series, to a complete dramatic script. With only rare exceptions they are imitations or adaptations of programs that are already on the air. And, if the blunt truth is stated, they are, with rare exceptions, not very good.

For anyone involved in screening material for television production, it is difficult to escape the impression that virtually every citizen of voting age is trying to write for television.

Like any other field of creative activity, writing for television imposes heavy demands on talent, skill and experience—attributes that are notoriously in short supply. For the most part the programs appearing on the television screen today are written by people possessing these qualities. They are the work of writers who began their careers in undergraduate dramatic activities, and who have gone on to drama schools to learn the specialized techniques of writing for the stage, the screenplay, and the still different forms required by television. Upon leaving school they have continued to write for amateur theatrical groups in their local communities and have digested the process by which a dramatic script takes on the dimensions of flesh and blood in performance.

With this experience behind them, and hopefully, a production which has come to the attention of a producer, director or literary agent, they have finally succeeded in breaking into the professional world of television, the theater or the movies. But it has only been after a long and searing period of trial, error—and rejection slips. Frankly, I know of no short cut to this process, and I can think of many examples confirming it.

A case in point is the recent premiere of CBS PLAYHOUSE, the project established by the CBS Television Network to revive original drama on television. The initial presentation, a drama entitled "The Final War of Olly Winter," was the work of Ronald Ribman, a relatively unknown 34-year-old New Yorker. It was the author's first television play.

Mr. Ribman's interest in dramatic writing started as an undergraduate at the University of Pittsburgh. Following his graduation he entered military service and continued writing while in the army, subsequently returning to the university to get his Ph.D. in English Literature. This was followed by a year of college teaching during which he began writing professionally for the theater. He then gave up teaching to devote himself exclusively to playwriting.

After he spent two years of concentrated effort, one of his plays was given an off Broadway production at the American Place Theater. This was followed by another off Broadway production which won the 1966 Obie Award.

These initial successes brought Mr. Ribman to the attention of story editors, producers, and directors. Since we were on the lookout for promising young writers whose work might be suitable for CBS PLAYHOUSE, I arranged through Mr. Ribman's literary agent to read several of his plays. They were extremely impressive. I then got in touch with him directly and in due course he submitted "The Final War of Olly Winter." Although it needed a great deal of work, it seemed to me an exceptional play. It had something important and dramatic to say, and its development of character was remarkable. We were naturally delighted to find our judgment confirmed by the critical acclaim which the broadcast received.

To be sure, this was not a case of receiving a manuscript in the mail and accepting it. The chances of this happening, frankly, are one in a thousand. Indeed, before approaching Mr. Ribman, we had read more than eight hundred unsolicited manuscripts for CBS PLAY-HOUSE. Professionally, they simply were not in the same league as Mr. Ribman's.

One of the difficulties facing young dramatists who want to write for television is the absence of a familiar frame of reference. Unfortunately, the things they see on television for the most part are not of much help in writing an original drama. Actually this is what such dramatic series as CBS PLAYHOUSE and REPERTOIRE WORKSHOP, which is presented by the five CBS-owned stations, hope to provide. The latter program is a weekly show more experimental in nature and has as its main emphasis the work of new writers and performers, whereas CBS PLAYHOUSE is a series of dramatic specials done at irregular intervals during the year and concentrating on the work of both established authors and lesser known ones.

What should be remembered, however, is that every unsolicited manuscript that is submitted to CBS is read. In several instances where we have not been able to use the material on the network, we have passed it along to our stations for consideration, or to one of the various educational stations that are now presenting drama. On rare occasions the script is bought and produced.

The point is, we are constantly searching for new talent and new ideas. We are eager to encourage young writers. Specifically, we are looking for plays that concentrate on human drama and character rather than plays dealing with social or political issues.

If I were asked to advise the young writer who is interested in breaking into television drama, I would urge him to write about something that is personally meaningful to him. Naturally it should have relevance to contemporary life. However, he should not be too concerned with writing about "important contemporary themes." The primary requirement is the writer's personal commitment to his subject.

As to the chances of getting his play produced on television, I can offer no magical solutions. The road to recognition is inevitably long and painful. I would suggest that he first learn the techniques of dramatic writing either in the various schools established for this purpose or through direct association with local amateur or professional theatrical groups such as the off-Broadway movement in New York, and the various theater groups that are springing up all over the country.

I would further suggest that he submit his work to a local television station, where the economics of production are on a much smaller scale than at a network.

I would strongly recommend that he try to work through a literary agent who not only can offer editorial guidance, but is familiar with the market and can send a manuscript where it is most likely to be considered sympathetically.

Finally, I would urge the young writer to keep trying in the face of discouragement. Genuine talent is bound to be recognized sooner or later, and if he can outwait the intervening setbacks, he will some day have the rewarding experience of seeing his work produced on television.

PART III

THE EDITORIAL AND BUSINESS SIDE

91

THE MAN ACROSS THE DESK

By Samuel S. Vaughan

IF you write at book length, you could find yourself one day facing a man (or woman) across a desk who announces himself as your editor. A certain amount of confusion arises at times about what one's editor is supposed to do for the writer, or do to the written work.

If we confuse authors and, on occasion, our employers, perhaps it is because your editor can turn out to be anything from a slightly helpful acquaintance to a valuable friend to, at times, a deeply involved collaborator.

The thoroughly professional author, or the singular and striking writer whose book is a work of art, may require little editing—that is, little penciling on paper. The beginner, or the writer with ideas but stylistic problems, or the stylist who lacks ideas, needs more help. In every case, each book requires handling in the publishing process.

One of the shocks ahead is that you might overhear the editor, or someone around him, referring to what you have written as "his" book—i.e., the editor's. *Whose* book? Good question. For if an editor accepts your manuscript for publication, it becomes, to an extent, his book, no matter how little work he does on it.

A unique pleasure of authorship is that a book, unlike a magazine article or a play or a motion picture script, is first and last the author's. It belongs to him; it is his, an individual creation in an age of the collaborative arts and merger. But the editor's proprietary interest, his assumption that it is "his" book, too, can work in your best interest.

It is his book in the publishing house only. It is his judgment that is on the line, his recommendation that the house take the risk.

This means that your editor will identify himself—and be identified personally—with your work in the small world of book publishing.

In practice, the process is more beneficent and less heavy-handed than it sounds. On a magazine, the editor seldom thinks of an article or story as his. He may, instead, think of it as the magazine's. Magazine editing is much rougher and more arbitrary (and sometimes better) than book editing. It is frequently done with little or no consultation with the original writer. A piece for *Time* becomes *Time's*. A story for *The New Yorker* or *Commentary*, especially after their skillful editing (and sometimes cutting and rewriting), can take on the tone and feel of a *New Yorker* or a *Commentary* piece.

But the book remains yours. It can be lightly edited, not edited, or extensively edited. The only tone and content it should have are whatever you finally agree to. In the center is your friendly neighborhood middleman, the editor, and while he is in the process of trying to bring you together with your readers out there somewhere he will tend to think of what you have written as, at least in part, his.

A great many words have been written in behalf of the writer. These few are in behalf of the editor, in the interests of peaceful coexistence.

Having disposed of any silly notion that it is only your fate which is hitched to your manuscript, let us see what to expect from the man or woman across the desk. The more you understand him, the more you are able to form a useful mutual assistance pact.

Your editor is usually an anonymous figure, a curious combination of ego and self-effacement. His job is somewhat akin to that of the director in the theater or in movies, but his hand is invisible and he is even less well known. His job, to begin with, is to represent the reader to you; to represent you in the publishing house; and to represent that publishing house to you. Eventually you will learn that any book has many people working for it and that even the quietest publication is the sum of a thousand separate actions and efforts.

It is reasonable to suggest that the job of the book editor is to edit books. Most of us understand that the editor also must seek out people with talent or intelligence or information, with special experience or celebrity or, now and then, genius (or with any combination of the above) who want to or can be persuaded to write at book length. If we can agree on those reasonable assumptions, we can give up reason for the next hour. Obviously, one would expect the editor to spend his day looking for writers and in reading and editing their works.

He does not. He spends his day in editorial meetings, discussing what was in the Sunday *Times,* filling out forms to accompany the transmission of manuscripts to production departments, badgering his colleagues in sales and advertising and publicity and art departments. An editor often spends his morning drinking coffee, his lunch time drinking seriously, and his afternoon repenting the lunch hour. Before becoming an editor, he assumed that his day would be taken up with writers, people with patches on their elbows who write books. Instead, he finds much of his day given over to lawyers, agents, PR men, people with patches on their eyes who negotiate contracts. Once in a while a good writer makes his way through the lines and into the office; the editor is usually so glad to see him that the writer mistakes enthusiastic noises of welcome for blanket approval of his manuscript.

Manuscript? The editor does work on manuscripts. But he spends much of his time in trying to take delivery of books contracted for before there was a manuscript.

Why isn't the manuscript ready? The main reason is that every book is more work than anyone intended. If authors and editors knew how much work was ahead, fewer contracts would be signed. Every book is beautiful before the contract. Every book, for the author, becomes a hate object in the middle of the writing. For the editor, it becomes a concrete necklace in the middle of editing. Both author and editor will recover the gleam in their eyes, will see it as the masterwork it is, when the manuscript is ready.

What else does your editor do with his day? He concerns himself with The List. Publishers spend countless hours worrying about the group of books they plan to release on a suspicious world. Endlessly we discuss the spring list, the fall list, the winter list. . . .

Everyone, perhaps especially you, knows that the fall is the best time to publish your book. After all, nobody reads in the summer. And the book will be out in time for the Christmas trade. No matter that the facts show January and June to be excellent months for book sales or August a good time to launch a best seller. Let's not let facts get in the way of launch or lunch. No matter that you delivered your manuscript in April, almost complete, that your editor didn't get to edit it for six weeks, and then spent most of three weeks doing so—leaving three months to make the fall. (Most books require about nine months from finished manuscript to publication day.) No matter—because you and your editor are not likely to make the publishing date decision anyhow. Other sensitive minds are at work on the problem.

They'll probably agree that fall is the best time for your book. ("*Fall?* You'd have to be out of your mind to release her fragile little book after September!") I mean spring. ("You some kind of guru, you want to do that kid's novel in May? Who reads in May?") Or do I mean winter? ("Come *on*, Sam—you don't do a political book in February. Everybody's going to the Bahamas in February; who cares for politics then?") Okay, how about shortly before Christmas? ("Now you're talking. Put that nice fat package on the list in time for Christmas, and we'll be swimming in money.") A publisher's Christmas is properly celebrated just after Labor Day; his idea of Christmas Eve is July 20. Any expensive volume must be published in time for the Christmas trade, we all know, or it will die. This is absolutely true. Except for the expensive volumes that are published in other seasons and sell nicely, while all those expensive, unsold volumes from the previous Christmas are still swimming back to the warehouse.

At any rate, the purpose of these glimpses into the philosophical life of your publishing house is to show something of what editors do when they're not actually editing.

Do editors edit? Yes, some editors do. At times we over-edit; some are lazy; some become virtual co-authors and now and then ghost writers.

What is editing? What should you expect your editor to do for, or to, your manuscript? He is, to start with, your first reader, a sympathetic but objective one. Make your mistakes in front of this reader; he will help you not to make them in public.

He should offer you comment, general and detailed, on style, structure, and substance. He should offer suggestions for improvement where appropriate. For a novel, he ought to respond to the characterizations, plotting, plausibility, length, pace, the title, and, if he understands it, your theme.

For a non-fiction work, many of the same comments apply, including characterization, oddly enough. People in books, all books, are important.

Behind every editor is, like the legendary woman behind every successful man, a copy editor. A first-rate copy editor is a godsend to the author and helps to make an honest man of the editor. The copy editor is responsible for your spelling, punctuation, grammar, and—though you should discuss this in advance—house style. (This includes such matters as rules for capitalization, the use of commas in series, which dictionary should be relied on as final authority, etc.) If you have special stylistic wishes, declare them in advance, before type is set. The copy editor will be on the lookout for inconsistencies, repetitions, and may do a certain amount of spot fact-checking. But neither the editor nor the copy editor is the researcher or the expert on your book: you are. If you have written a history of the Battle of Bourbon Station, don't expect your editors to check every fact. You, or they, should arrange for outside readings (sometimes called "vettings," although this also applies to legal check-readings, too) by experts, if required.

Why is your editor so slow? Because he has manuscripts to read that arrived before yours did. Because his fellow editors ask him to do second readings for them. Because he conducts an elaborate correspondence, his phone list is twenty-four names long at the moment, and an English publisher's cable is fighting it out with a California agent's telegram on top of a stack of memoranda, each headed URGENT, *Do Now,* or "Pass Quickly—by Hand." (At times, your editor would like to Pass Quickly—out.)

The time problem is not a matter of reading your manuscript—it is getting to read it. Your editor is slow because he needs time to think, because he cannot know positively things he has to assert flatly. ("Your Bill Breadloaf is brilliantly original. He will go on to become one of the titans." "Murray, people will be *breaking* into book stores to grab this book—how often do you get a rabbi who knows this much about the sex life of the Apostles?")

Your editor travels, seems to run around a good deal, may leave you feeling out of touch. Be of good cheer. Some of that traveling is in your behalf; he could be off to sales conferences, selling your book or talking to friends who are reviewers, agents, reprint or book club or movie people, advancing your reputation. As with agents, the editor with time on his hands to talk with you, to answer every letter and phone call promptly and at length, can be reassuring. But the one who is busy because he is successful may do something for your success, too, even if he does nothing for your ego by his glacial response to letters, manuscripts, or phone calls. Whatever the case, there are no perfect editors, agents, or publishing houses.

When does your editor edit? At night. When he is supposed to be buying a friend veal piccata, with a good, sensible, inexpensive wine. ("What a day I've had. Postponed my whole list from spring to fall.") Or when he is supposed to be helping his children with their homework ("New math? Is this kid in school or in an IBM branch office?")

Some editors read and edit in the office. But the more active your editor is, the less likely he is to spend the day editing. His is not simply an agreeable job, full of fun and excitement and gambles; publishing is a vocation—commanding, compelling, demanding. Editing itself is hard work, not the least of which is finding time and residual energy beyond publishing duties to edit.

There are other problems. Unless he has a surgeon's streak of sadism, the editor will be reluctant to put pencil to somebody else's paper unless he can see clearly that it can be, and how much it should be, improved. He may know what is wrong but not quite how to tell you. He may want to fix it himself but be unable to; some editors can write; others cannot. Either person can be an excellent editor.

He is often tempted to take more time with a manuscript than it is likely to be worth. And yet the least likely books are frequently among the ones that most intrigue him.

There is always the danger lurking out there of an alert reviewer. That reviewer can lay into the book when it is published, attacking its author and its editor. Once, years ago, I stuck my head into the office of Kenneth D. McCormick, Doubleday's editor-in-chief.

A book he had handled, on its way to best sellerdom, had been greeted in some quarters by questions rich in human charity. ("Why wasn't this miserable mess edited?" "What has happened to American editorial standards?" etc.)

"Ken," I said, a cub seeking enlightenment from a lion, "how do you feel when a book you've handled is one that a reviewer says needs editing?"

"I say to myself," Ken remarked, without looking up, "that he should have seen the book *before* I got it."

What about the relationship between you? Is your editor required to be your friend? Not always. Forced friendships work no better here than anywhere else. An editor and author can work together smoothly if they remain a little distant. In fact, a certain distance may be an asset. Relationships have broken down where the author and editor have become too close. When genuine friendship occurs, fine. It had better be genuine; it is certain to be tested.

Authors suspect that their editor has the best of both worlds. He works with words; he earns a regular salary, has an expense account, a secretary, and all that. In part, the author is correct. But (a) the words the editor works with belong to somebody else; (b) the salary is supplemented by an expense account because there are laws against malnutrition; (c) the secretary belongs to somebody else. (She vacations in Majorca and has promised her boss an introduction to Robert Graves if the editor ever goes abroad.)

Most people interested in books think that the editor lives with wooly-headed literary superstars, who are difficult to handle but are really lovable—underneath. Most of us live in wooly-headed perplexity, handling difficult problems, but we are really lovable—on the surface. We have the privilege of serving as the writer's friend, flack, devil's advocate, drinking buddy, financial adviser, lay analyst, sensor, and censor. Increasingly, we are asked to counsel him on and to invest in words he wishes to put on paper but has not. The editorial job has become, unlike the ancient age when one judged what one read, a job of making judgments on outlines, ideas, reputations, previous books, scenarios, "treatments," talk, and promises.

For every first novelist of promise there is an editor who has made fifty promises—about writers' futures. We are also trying to appraise not only the manuscript in question but what sort of books lie ahead. Serious publishers undertake to publish an author, not a book. We want to contract with a writer who will go on writing, not a man who is momentarily with book.

Is your editor well read? Once he was. He used to read a great deal, the good stuff. That was one of the reasons he got into the trade. Now he doesn't read a lot, he reads all the time. And everything is a modern classic in manuscript. His voluntary reading is drastically curtailed, and he suspects semi-literacy is creeping up on him.

One of the chief sacrifices he has made is the privilege of reading what he feels like reading. Does this have anything to do with you? Yes. He wants to like your book. Remember, if the going gets rough between you: *he wants to like your book*. Your success is, to a certain extent, his success.

You and the publishing house are linked by the royalty system; if the book sells, both the author and the house make out. Your editor, the man in the middle, does not profit as directly. But a publishing house, Mr. Alfred Knopf once wrote, is known by the company it keeps. An editor is known by the authors he gets and keeps. If he is critical of your work, try not to take it personally. There is a wrong time to eliminate the middle man.

In some respects, he will disappoint you. He deals with the intangible—with glimmers of talent and flashes of hope and with changing tastes. You want him to produce the concrete—sales and readers and dollars and advertisements full of praise for your name.

He has a limited amount of power, easily diffused, and little glamour, except the gilt by association with well-known authors. His power is arbitrary. He cannot command his colleagues or reviewers or the reader to react as you and he want them to. He can only try to present your work with intelligence and flair and conviction, to be persistent in your behalf, and yet to temper your expectations with his realism. He relies on a deep well of optimism that must spring eternal.

Daily, your editor faces fear and failure and frustration. His is a job of visions, some demented; of ideals, frequently compromised; of high standards, not always met. He has a chance to do some good in this world—and an equal opportunity to add to the meretricious trash that threatens to swamp the continent.

Why, then, is your editor apt to be a fairly cheerful man, younger than his years? Because his job allows him to, in fact requires him to, indulge his taste. He not only has opinions, he lives by them. His work permits him, a grown man, to tell other men or women that he likes their work, and (often, if not always) that he likes *them*. In a society where many people are too embarrassed or inhibited or sophisticated to admire openly someone else, where everyone is a critic, his job is to be positive, to pass on praise, and to appreciate.

There is another reason why your editor, dour as he may seem at times, is apt to be reasonably happy. A year or so ago I was working one evening, deep in a pile of manuscripts, when my oldest son stopped at the desk, regarded me evenly, and said: "What are you doing?"

It was a fair question. I'd asked Jeff as much twenty or thirty thousand times. I was pleased to be asked.

"I'm working on a translation, a marvelous book, a biography of Tolstoy," I said. Then I told him something of the riches of Leo Tolstoy's life and of Henri Troyat's book and explained a few of the niceties of editing translations.

After we talked, Jeff turned to go, to return to his own homework. But before he went up the stairs, he said simply: "You must learn a lot."

He was right and I was grateful to him for becoming one of my teachers, too. For a parade of people come into my life, and each one of them has something on his mind, something to say. If everything goes right, for a year or two I'll have the privilege of learning what they are so excited about or interested in, of becoming a temporary semi-expert in their field, and of helping them get it said. As anyone who buys a house becomes, for a time, a real estate specialist, I have been, once removed, an explorer, a novelist, an historian, a musician, a magician who can make other people laugh or stir them.

That is why, I suppose, when you come to face the man across the desk, he will—even if he has spent the morning arguing about ad budgets, reprint rights, civil rights, or whether the Extreme Left is more extreme than the Extreme Right—be very glad to see you sitting on the other side of the desk. The man or woman who can transform a box of typing paper into a living document is the most valuable visitor to the man who will help transform that manuscript into a book.

92

EDITING THE MYSTERY AND SUSPENSE NOVEL

By Joan Kahn

Being a mystery book editor (which is what I am primarily, though I've edited a variety of books, including an etiquette book, biographies, poetry, art books and non-mystery fiction) is like being any old kind of an editor, except that it may be a little more fun, partly because the manuscripts one gets to read are usually above the general average and usually the author seems to have rather liked writing his book.

Though I have edited non-fiction happily, I am especially interested in fiction, in the novel, and I think that the best mystery/ suspense fiction these days has many (or more) of the same qualities that make the good non-mystery novel good.

The novel, for me, is a piece of writing with a definite form, a form which has infinite variations, and gives the experimenter as much room as he needs. But a novel is a novel—it isn't a short story, or a prose poem, or an essay, or a form of biography or even a purge. In a novel the things an author saw or experienced, the emotions he felt, the information he acquired, and the ideas that came to him have been absorbed and digested and reproduced in a particular, if elastic, form—that of a novel.

A mystery novel is a novel. Once the mystery novel was fairly rigid in format, and the emphasis was primarily on detection and a puzzle. In the introduction to a 1932 book, *The Floating Admiral*, Dorothy L. Sayers (who, whether she knew it or not, widened the horizon of the detective mystery so successfully that her novels read as well today as they did when she wrote them—and Lord knows that seems to me to be no longer true of many of her contemporaries) said while talking about The Detection Club: "Its membership is confined to those who have written genuine detective stories (not adventure tales or 'thrillers')."

Genuine detective stories that are original and good are not readily available today, and Miss Sayers (who ultimately turned scornfully from all detective story writing, including her own, as her main interest became the field of religious writing), if she were still interested in the mystery novel today, might have agreed to widen the membership of The Detection Club and make it less restrictive.

The suspense novel label came into being to cover much of the widening mystery field (actually it is too generally used and often on some books not worthy of it). The suspense novel isn't limited to deductive mysteries and, in fact, some books under its free-wheeling label don't even have a detective (police or private) in them, and, though this is rare, sometimes don't include a murder.

But some of Miss Sayers' rules for Detection Club members could still be of use to today's suspense novelists: "Detectives must detect by their wits, without the help of accident or coincidence; the author must not invent impossible death rays and poison to produce solutions which no living person could expect; he must write as good English as he can, to keep the detective story up to the highest standard that its nature permits, and to free it from the bad legacy of sensationalism, claptrap and jargon."

At its best the present-day mystery novel often reaches, it seems to me, very high standards of writing, and it also is trying to explore a variety of new approaches to its story. But—and this time I quote Howard Haycraft quoting Somerset Maugham—"The reason that so many modern readers have turned to mystery fiction is that here, and here alone, they can be sure of a novel which tells a story."

The suspense novel tells a story, on many levels. We know that some of the levels appeal to Presidents of the United States, professors and provosts of colleges, lawyers and scientists. I think the average steady mystery reader is a lot brighter than the average man. The mystery is like caviar or a very good dry martini. At its best, only intelligent readers appreciate it. Today the mystery market is a vast one, reaching people who may not ordinarily be interested in book reading. Some of this vast market is the result of television and films which pluck characters out of books and return them in other mediums enticingly embodied in attractive actors and actresses.

I've been lucky, as an editor, in that I've been able to edit and publish what seem to me the best books I can find. I've never had to worry first about where or how big the market for the books will be, and I think Harper books have sold well enough to keep our authors fairly happy and to keep Harper's fairly happy, too, but how they would sell isn't what I thought about first. I feel that no writer or painter or musician should choose to enter his field primarily because he wants to make money. There are other fields in which one can make money faster and more easily and with far more certainty, though on the whole a writer has an easier time supporting himself than other creative people (there are more book buyers than there are concert goers or art collectors, and a book is easier to reproduce and to get to its audience).

To be a writer is hard work, but exciting work, even if one isn't sure one can make a living from it. To be an editor is hard work, too, and exciting work (and one does get a pay check), but publishing is a gambling game. We never *really* know what books are going to sell well—or sometimes even why a given book is selling.

I would like, as I'm sure every editor would, to find on my desk of a morning a manuscript that, when read, would have me saying, "Oh boy, is this a book!" And then I could dash around the House yelling, "Hey, you should see what *I* just found!" and the salesmen would all agree with me, and we'd turn the manuscript as fast as possible into a handsome book, and when the bookstores heard about the book, they'd take a lot of copies, and when the critics read the book they'd give it rave reviews, and when the public read the reviews, it would buy the book like mad. And then the book clubs and the reprint houses and the motion picture people would come storming in. Sometimes that does really happen. But not absolutely all the time, alas.

When it doesn't, then there is the need for an editor. An editor's job, as you probably know, is a lot of different things, Once he has decided to publish the book, he or she has to try to figure out (sort of guess) how many copies to print and what price to put on the book, and he has to consult the designer, and to worry about the jacket and the jacket copy, and the advertising and promotion, along with the various departments who watch over all these things.

But the most important thing an editor does, I think, is to help the author get his book into its best possible shape. To do this the editor has to be very gentle in part and very firm in part—and he must try to get into the author's mind and to understand what the author's intentions were as fully as he can. This is often especially hard if the editor and the author have never met (the author often lives far away) and the editor knows the author only through his manuscript and correspondence. Usually an author who has just finished a book is in a very touchy state: he's proud but defensive. The book was a part of him—for a long time his energies and his mind were devoted almost entirely to it. He must have loved it (or at least admired it) while he was working on it, or he couldn't have gone on working, and now that he's brought it into being he not only still loves it—but he's hoping it will go out and support him— and that it may also make him respected—or even famous.

An author who has just finished a book is often still infatuated with it; he hasn't the judgment he would have if he could put the book aside until time could take the rosiness out of his vision. Usually a writer can't afford to (or won't) wait for time. So he needs an editor, one who seems to understand him and to make sense to him. And the editor has to be able to respond with sensitivity, and sense, to the particular book of the particular author. To guide the author through the revision—sometimes minor, sometimes major—of the book he has written is a delicate (and often sometimes absolutely exhausting) job.

In fiction, the editor's hand must be as light and as accurate and knowledgeable as the hand of a very good surgeon as he probes the intricate network of veins and tissues, cutting away what should come out without cutting anything vital and making sure the patient will live, in a healthier condition. An author who needs the help of an editor to guide him through revisions must find the editor encouraging and reassuring as well as firm, because hard as writing often is, revision is often harder. And after the long hours at the typewriter, an author probably wants to lie down or to go dancing, or, if he's going to write, to start a completely new book.

One of the hardest things, I think, that an editor has to do (its not exactly easy on the author, either) is to turn down a book that seems to the editor so far below the author's level that publishing it won't do him any good. It's especially hard if one admires the author's work—and if the author has a reputation—because one knows that another publisher may very well take the book just to get the author and won't be concerned whether the publication of an inferior work a) will make the author sloppy and willing to do other inferior works later and b) will make the critics, bookstores and readers wonder if the author is really so hot. This is unlike the situation in other creative fields: a musician doesn't expect everything he writes to be heard, a playwright doesn't expect all his plays to be backed, a painter doesn't expect all his paintings to be hung and to be sold. Some manuscripts—even those of a good writer—*don't* work out, and, *very* hard though it is, these should be put aside. There's no easy sledding in writing or any of the arts. For artists in any field to depend upon their work to support them is a dangerous thing; it's much better to give the work a chance by doing something else for bread and butter—even if it means a double job.

I am a demanding editor—but I'm also a painstaking editor. I care about fiction and the mystery/suspense field. And I think *care* and *caring* pay off. I still, after a long time in it, find the field very exciting. I have made the usual, or perhaps more than usual, mistakes along the way; it would be a great help to be clairvoyant but I'm not. Sometimes I fail to reach an author I admire, and the author goes away and I'm saddened.

But the author-editor relationship is, I feel, a very close one, and it has to be an honest one. An author who doesn't trust my judgment and thinks I'm foolish would be even more foolish to keep on working with me. And I cannot fight wholeheartedly for a book I don't think is any good.

I've been very lucky in getting a good many good manuscripts from good authors. And I've never felt that suspense fiction was second-class fiction or should be so treated.

More and more readers are beginning to discover the quality and pleasure of today's suspense fiction, though I'm sorry to say it is still too often reviewed in little boxes and given short shrift. Too many people say simply that they never read suspense fiction. What, I wonder, if they like fiction, are they reading instead? Not too many general novels are superior to the better suspense novels as far as writing or general reading pleasure goes.

Occasionally a novel (or a non-fiction book) in the crime field shoots up on the best seller list and is wildly heralded, and I consider how much the readers of those books would enjoy other good —and sometimes better—books in the mystery field that they haven't bothered to notice the existence of, and I think, "Oh, hell, the idiots." But the situation is getting better all the time (I'm an optimist). I do believe that books, good books, in the suspense field are not only here to stay, but here to be noticed a lot more in time to come.

93

LEGAL RIGHTS FOR WRITERS

By Jeanne Pollett

Josh Billings once remarked that man's problem isn't so much the things he doesn't know, as the things he knows that aren't so.

Writers and photographers are no exception. Some of the most widely held beliefs about their legal rights and responsibilities have no foundation in law. Often the writer or the cameraman is on firmer legal ground than he thinks. He may worry about restrictions that simply don't exist. But sometimes he acts with false confidence, risking liability without realizing it.

Let's look at some of the legal principles important to those who write or take photographs for publication.

Use of the word "allegedly" or the naming of a source gives no legal protection to the writer.

There are perfectly valid reasons for a newsman to qualify a statement this way. The practice alerts the reader to the source and probable reliability of information. But it's no defense in a legal action.

"John Smith is alleged to have shot the victim" or "Police said John Smith fired the fatal shot" may literally be true, even though Smith was innocent and five hundred miles away at the time. But so far as the law of defamation is concerned, the words are the precise equivalent of the flat statement, "John Smith shot the victim." If John is innocent, he may bring a successful action for libel.

Inconsistently enough (and who ever said the law was consistent?), a retraction, to be legally effective, must be put forth as the writer's own statement. In the case of that shooting, it's not enough to say by way of retraction, "Police stated further investigation showed

John Smith had no connection with the shooting." The retraction must be a flat denial that Smith shot the victim.

Even reporting and denying a rumor may get the writer into a legal jam. An editorial stating, "This newspaper does not believe the report that Councilman Jones accepted any favor in return for changing his vote," may be treated as furthering a rumor that Jones did take a bribe. Courts say, perhaps somewhat unrealistically, that one may not escape liability for repeating a defamatory statement by adding that the writer does not believe it.

Recent court rulings regarding public figures have not abrogated the basic principles of libel law.

The cases of *New York Times* v. *Sullivan* and *Associated Press* v. *Walker,* and later pronouncements of the courts, do give writers considerably more leeway where public figures are concerned. But on the whole, the old concept of libel still stands:

> Libel is a malicious publication, expressed either in printing, writing, type-writing, or by signs and pictures, tending either to blacken the memory of one who is dead, or the reputation of one who is alive, and expose him to public hatred, contempt, or ridicule.

Truth is a defense to an action for libel. Under the more recent decisions, it doesn't have to be an absolute, every-i-dotted-and-every-t-crossed truth. But substantial accuracy is required. One cannot imagine a twentieth-century court holding it libelous to say a man had stolen two pigs when in truth he had stolen only one (although that rule used to be the law in England).

Mere name-calling is not actionable.

A writer isn't likely to become involved in this one except perhaps indirectly, in reporting a quarrel at a meeting, for example.

William L. Prosser, former dean of the University of California School of Law, puts it this way:

"The courts have held that mere words of abuse, indicating that the defendant dislikes the plaintiff and has a low opinion of him, but without suggesting any specific charge against him, are not to be treated as defamatory. A certain amount of vulgar name-calling is tolerated, on the theory that it will necessarily be understood to amount to nothing more."

Use of a person's name without his consent is not actionable.

Any working newsman has had the experience of watching an irate individual pound his desk, red-faced, and shout, "If you use my name again without my permission—I'll sue!"

The law doesn't give that kind of protection to even the most publicity-shy. So long as an event is newsworthy (and that's a broad definition indeed), the name of even a reluctant participant may appear in print. (A few states do prohibit publishing the identities of juvenile offenders or of victims of sex crimes.)

A newspaper or magazine may not be restrained from publishing— or required to publish—anything.

A surprisingly large number of otherwise well-informed persons will speculate whether a publication "should have been allowed" to print a controversial piece.

The First (freedom of the press) Amendment is construed as allowing no prior restraint on publication. After publication, writer and publisher are accountable for libel, invasion of privacy, or other actionable injury.

As to the reverse—the question whether a publication may be required to print a particular item or advertisement—the answer is a resounding "no." The question has in fact seldom even been raised. A publisher may reject anything (even crucial legal advertising) for any reason or for no reason but pure caprice.

A writer can get into trouble even if he sticks to facts which can be proved.

As we have seen, truth is ordinarily a complete defense to a civil action for libel. But a writer may risk suit on another ground— invasion of privacy—if he goes too far in exposing another's private life.

A typical example would be bringing up the fact that Joe Blow, who has for years lived a blameless life in the community, once was prosecuted for embezzlement. If Joe is running for county treasurer, his record is very much a matter of legitimate public concern. If he's simply going his own quiet way as a private citizen, digging into and publicizing his past may well be held to be actionable. Authors of factual police and detective yarns need be particularly aware of this problem.

The person who owns a photographic negative doesn't necessarily have the right to reproduce it.

There's a persistent belief among even professional photographers that ownership of a negative carries with it the right to reproduce the picture. The rule is neat, easily applied—and completely without legal foundation.

The test isn't who owns or holds the negative, but for whom the work was done. When a customer pays a commercial photographer to take a picture, it's the patron, not the cameraman, who owns the right to reproduce it. Conversely, an amateur or a professional photographer who takes a picture at his own expense owns the rights to it.

The same general rules govern publication of children's pictures as those of adults.

Another bit of photographic folklore has it that a minor child may not be photographed, or his picture printed, without his parents' consent.

The same rules govern the photographing of children as the portraying of adults. In general, any non-embarrassing picture taken in a public place can safely be used in the editorial pages of a magazine or newspaper. It's O.K. to photograph that schoolyard full of children without making the rounds of their parents with model release forms. (Commercial use of a picture, of either child or adult, in an advertisement or on a product is another matter entirely.)

A writer is not free to quote from letters and diaries that have come into his possession.

Just as ownership of a photographic negative does not carry with it a right to reproduce a picture, ownership of another person's letters or diaries does not imply the right to copy their contents.

A letter, once written, mailed, and delivered, belongs to the recipient. He may save it, destroy it, sell it, frame it and hang it on the wall. He is owner of the physical object—the paper and the ink. But literary property remains with the letter writer. The latter has what is called a common-law copyright, the same right an author has in his own unpublished manuscript.

An author who wants to quote from letters (even family letters) or diaries should first obtain permission. If the letter writer or the diarist has died, approval should be obtained from his heirs.

A writer may make limited use of copyrighted material.

Facts cannot be copyrighted. Otherwise research, writing, knowledge itself would come to a grinding halt. The *form of expression* of those facts is subject to copyright.

Even so, a writer may make fair use of material which has been copyrighted by others. Fair use has been described by Melville B. Nimmer, professor of law at the University of California at Los Angeles and authority on copyright law, as "copying by others which does not materially impair the marketability of the work which is copied."

The law does not specify a particular amount of copyrighted material that may be used.

Many persons in the book and music publishing industries firmly believe that up to eight bars of music (or lyrics) may be duplicated without risk.

Some countries do define fair use in mathematical terms, specifying for example that not more than eight bars may be taken from a piece of music, and not more than 1,000 words from a scientific or a literary work. There's no such specific rule in the United States.

A writer may use the title from another copyrighted work without infringement.

Titles are not subject to copyright. An author needn't search to see whether the one he has in mind has been used before.

But he shouldn't on that account dash off something under the name of *Everything You Always Wanted to Know About Sex but Were Afraid to Ask*. A title may be protected under another theory of law, unfair competition. If it's become identified with one writer's product in the public mind, the title may not be appropriated and used in such a way as to make a buyer think he's getting the first writer's work rather than another's.

There's no surefire way to avoid a lawsuit.

A writer or a photographer may be on firm legal ground, and still be sued.

Unfortunately, "Can they sue?" is an utterly meaningless question. Anybody can sue anyone, however groundlessly, if he can persuade a lawyer to take the case or if he follows the proper court procedure and files the action himself without benefit of counsel. He can sue, but he may be thrown out of court long before the action gets to the trial stage.

The sorting-out process occurs after the action has been brought. In the federal courts and in some states, the person being sued files a "motion to dismiss." Other states call the pleading a "demurrer." What it says in effect is, "Even though everything alleged in the complaint is true—and we're not admitting it except for purposes of argument—you still don't have a case."

Going back to the man who didn't want his name used without his permission: If he were to bring a lawsuit against the writer or the publisher, the defendant would demur and the court would say in effect: "Plaintiff has not suffered any wrong the law recognizes. Case dismissed."

94

RESEARCH AT UNCLE SAM'S BOOKSTORE

By Dee Stuart

Someone once said that successful writing is 80% research and 20% rewriting. But what if you are tied to home or office and can't get away to do research? Or, if you are free to go, suppose there are no resources available?

As a beginning writer with two pre-schoolers, I hit these problems head-on while trying to research an article suggested by a friend.

"I'd love to grow gourds to make into decorative arrangements," she said. "But I've no idea how to grow them, much less preserve them."

Challenged, I, too, searched for information—with little success. Our garden book didn't cover gourds. My only other resource was the high school library. Encyclopedias were too general. The *Readers' Guide* turned up nothing. In my ignorance, I was pleased to find that nothing had been published on gourds. This would mean a plus value for my article. I soon learned there was a reason nothing had been written: No information was available.

Discouraged, I told a fellow writer I'd have to abandon the idea. Then she told me about "Uncle Sam's Bookstore."

This vast storehouse boasts approximately 27,000 different publications currently available for sale by the Superintendent of Documents, U. S. Government Printing Office, Washington, D. C. They range in price from 10¢ to $10.00 and up. Uncle Sam's Bookstore was as near as my mailbox.

We consulted my friend's list of publications and to my delight found two booklets on gourds. I promptly sent for them. A few weeks later I had more information about gourds than I could ever use.

Result? Two articles, two sales: "Gourds—Pretty and Practical," to *Popular Gardening,* and "Gourds Are for the Birds" to *Flower Grower.*

From then on, I resolved that Uncle Sam's Bookstore would be my first resource rather than a last resort.

A leaflet, "How to Keep in Touch with U. S. Government Publications," describes what's available. For the sake of convenience, Uncle Sam has broken down the listings into 47 subjects or areas of interest. For each subject there is a free list of titles and prices, revised approximately once a year to include newly-issued or still-popular publications for sale.

Among the free price lists are: *Home Economics, Geology, Fish and Wildlife, Occupations, National Parks, Forestry, American History, Plants, Weather, Astronomy and Meteorology,* and *Space, Missiles, the Moon, NASA,* and *Satellites.*

One list, *Consumer Information,* includes family finances, appliances, recreation, gardening, health and safety, food, house and home, child care, and clothing and fabrics. All of these subjects are gold mines of information for writers of home, garden and women's magazine features.

Government publications are a prime source of information from many points of view. Not only will you find material on ordinary subjects, such as gourds, but you can learn all about the newest discoveries in the fields of science, space, homemaking, and other areas that you may not be able to learn about anywhere else. The data is current, valid, authoritative, and the price is low.

These publications are ideal for supplementing previous research and for double-checking facts and accuracy. A woman I know who is working on a Civil War novel supplements her research by culling facts from the vast selection of National Park Service Civil War Historical Handbooks. Another friend who writes Indian stories for juvenile readers visited Bandelier National Monument in New Mexico. She absorbed the feel of the place and developed a story plot. But when she started writing, she found she needed more specific information. Since she lives on a ranch in Montana, miles from the nearest library, additional research could have been an unsolvable problem.

She scanned the Government Printing Office price list titled *Smithsonian Institution National Museum and Indians* and found

"Bandelier National Monument," 25¢. She ordered the booklet and from it gleaned information on the origins and life of the Indians who lived there. She added authenticity to later Indian stories with the aid of booklets on various tribes—without ever leaving home!

Our family camping trips from coast to coast have provided raw material for many travel stories. And GPO publications have served many times to jog my memory of sites we've seen and to add "nuts-and-bolts" to the articles that followed.

Recently we camped at Sylvan Lake, South Dakota. I took detailed notes on scenery and what to see and do. Later when I began writing a roundup piece on the Black Hills, I discovered I needed a few concrete facts to give the story depth and substance. I trekked down to the Government branch bookstore in Kansas City and found all the information I needed in brochures on Wind Cave National Park and Mount Rushmore. Result? A sale to *Midwest Motorist*.

The Government Printing Office operates branch bookstores across the country. In addition to the Kansas City branch there are stores in Boston, Chicago, Los Angeles, and San Francisco. Washington, D. C. alone boasts five. According to E. J. Brink, Bookstores Manager, branches are scheduled to open in Dallas and Atlanta. If you are lucky enough to live near one of Uncle Sam's bookstores, you may find that just browsing through the hundreds of publications on display will spark ideas for articles and stories. Some stores stock as many as 1400 publications.

But you don't have to live near a store. Merely perusing price list titles can turn you on. For example, a 10¢ pamphlet on John Muir, noted 19th-century scientist, author and conservationist, could be the inspiration for an article, short story or even a juvenile biography.

Writers of how-to articles find that the home economics publications offer a wealth of material. For instance, *Consumer Guides in Buying* includes "Be a Good Shopper" and "Money-saving Main Dishes."

Moneymaking ideas for young people—topics such as "Catfish Farming," "Raising Rabbits," "Mushroom Growing" and "Bee-Keeping for Beginners" could all be developed into salable articles.

If you need a few appropriate phrases for the American Field

Service student in your story to speak, send for a foreign phrase book. Uncle Sam has them—from Arabic to Tagalog.

Although U. S. Government publications are primarily a source of information, you are free to quote from them without asking permission—to give your article validity. U. S. Government publications are in the public domain. Be sure, however, that the government publication is *not a reprint* of copyrighted material; if it is, the copyright remains in force, and you will have to write for permission to the copyright owner to quote from it. A booklet of special interest to writers is "Copyright Laws of the U. S. of America," 45¢. Another helpful one is "The Seven Keys to Better Faster Typing," 50¢.

New titles appear monthly. A popular new release, "Search for Solitude," a 36-page color brochure, describes wilderness areas for the use and enjoyment and spiritual enrichment of the American people.

A recent GPO best seller, "Questions about the Oceans," 55¢, is designed to answer questions about oceanography and marine sciences. This 120-page book also answers such questions as, "Why is the ocean salty?" "Where do waves come from?" "How deep has man gone in the ocean?" It lists colleges and universities which offer oceanographic courses and tells who hires oceanographers. An imaginative writer could transform this material into a juvenile picture book, a science article for a children's magazine or a career article for young people.

Answers to the above questions and others in the 47 subject areas are yours for the asking. The first step is to send for the leaflet "How to Keep in Touch with U. S. Government Publications," describing the 47 categories or price lists. Then send for the price lists that interest you. From them choose the publications you want to buy. Fill in the order blank on the last page of the price list booklet and mail with your check or money order. Or you can use Special Documents Coupons sold in sets of 20 for $1 and good until used. Address all requests to: Superintendent of Documents, U. S. Government Printing Office, Washington, D. C. 20402.

The quickest way to order is to call or mail your request to the bookstore nearest you. If they stock what you want, they will ship it direct. If not, they will order it for you from Washington.

Thirty to forty thousand orders a day flood the Superintendent's office. Service is remarkable in the face of such a logistics nightmare. "In one section," Mr. Brink reports, "all the employees do is open mail, working sixteen hours a day in two shifts." A priority desk handles *bookstore* orders, all of which are shipped within forty-eight hours. If possible, place your order through a branch store to take advantage of this high-speed service.

The best way to keep informed about the avalanche of new and popular Government publications is to send for the free biweekly list of *Selected U. S. Government Publications.* The lists furnish a brief description of contents, price and an order blank. Take advantage of this service even if you think you don't need it. You'll be surprised at how many topics will interest you. Call the nearest bookstore and ask to be placed on the mailing list or send your request direct to Washington. Or, you may subscribe to the *Monthly Catalog,* a comprehensive listing of all publications issued by the departments and agencies of the U. S. Government each month, costing $6.oo a year.

Writers today need not be discouraged or put off by lack of opportunity for doing research. If you don't drive, if you are tied down with children or otherwise housebound, if you work eight hours a day and have no time to seek out information, if you live in the boondocks and no library is near you, or if you merely want to explore untapped resources, you will find Uncle Sam's bookstore a rich storehouse of knowledge just waiting for you to open the door.

95

LITERARY AGENTS

By James Oliver Brown

I speak on occasion to writers and aspiring writers, and the assumption is that I have a special knowledge of the questions such audiences ask. A few questions have been singled out as most recurring and this piece is devoted to them.

There is a lack of understanding on the part of inexperienced writers, and some experienced, of the functions of the East Coast literary agent who, while handling all rights and forms of writing, concentrates on the selling of rights to books and magazine stories and articles. The image of these agents is of rather grasping, ill-mannered, ill-bred parasites, who resist seeing and handling the works of writers, and who make the rounds of publishing houses, manuscripts in hand, persuading publishers to publish books. If females, they probably wear large flowered hats, and if males, they probably smoke cigars. I know of no such East Coast "book" literary agents.

A writer doesn't need an agent to sell a book for him here in this country. On the other hand his book will get closer attention if it has on it the imprint of a good agent. It might even sell bearing the agent's imprint where it would not have sold without such imprint, but such a sale would be rare, because manuscripts get read, regardless of who submits them. Reactions to writing are emotional, and the endorsement of an agent who is known for his taste and success might push the emotional scales in favor of the work. If I started telling an editor why he should like and buy a book, the editor would assume I was trying to get rid of a dud. The editor knows the James Brown imprint and for what it stands. He pays attention, in relation to that standing, whatever it might be in the mind of that particular editor.

The agent for "talent" (performers) and for all phases of the performance side of our business (stage, motion pictures, television) has a job of presentation different from that of the "book" agent, and the image of this kind of agent has had greater presentation by playwrights and novelists to the general public. Partly as a result of this exposure, the public has a wrong image of the "book" agent. In the performance side of the business, the buyer more than often has to be told. He has to be made to see how to blend everything together, the writing being only a part of the whole. The added factors are things such as casting, directing, stage designing. The "book" agent, on the other hand, usually presents the finished product. Ordinarily it doesn't need to be spoken about; it speaks for itself. I don't know of any of the literary agents on the performance side who wear hats and smoke cigars.

The literary agent performs a complex and varied function, which can't be too well defined. His function depends upon the kinds of writers he represents. I can speak only for my own operation. I'm a business manager-adviser, coordinator, protector of rights, exploiter of all rights to all writings of the writers I represent, such rights including book, magazine, dramatic, motion picture, radio, television, recording, translation. My important function as an agent is bringing in money for the writer, getting the most money possible in the interests of the writer, from every possible source. When an agent starts to work on a piece of writing, a story, an article, a book, whatever, he thinks of it in terms of all rights and gets it to the people who buy the rights, here and abroad. He is an expert in knowing the markets and having the organization to get to them.

The practices of the members of our agents' professional society, the Society of Authors' Representatives, are prescribed by reasonable and rigid rules. We don't advertise, and we don't live on reader's fees and editorial fees. We get clients from recommendations of people who know us, writers, editors, and others, and we live on a percentage take of the amount we take in from a sale. Theoretically, at least, if we don't sell we don't eat. Many, and I suspect, most "book" literary agents have independent incomes or some other subsidy such as rich or working spouses. A few of us actually live on 10% of our writers' earnings. This is not enough for much more than just modest, non-caviar, non-Rolls-Royce living.

I feel that if a written contract with one of my clients is necessary, I probably shouldn't have him for a client. On the other hand, if a simple letter agreement is signed stating what the relationship is anyway, I think it is in everyone's interests. I usually send such a document (if I happen to remember to do it) to a new client and leave it up to the client. They usually sign. Except in some situations where the interests of the writer were to be protected by doing it, I advise against the signing of an agency contract which goes beyond stating what the agent-client relationship is. An agency contract, for example, may provide that the agent will continue to handle the unsold rights to a property the agent has handled, should a writer leave the agent. This is not what would happen without the contract, and a writer should know this. Except in extraordinary cases, an agent should cease being the agent when the agency relationship ends. Rarely, if ever, is it in the writer's interests to have two agents working for him on different properties. The deserted agent is a deserted agent, alas, and has left only the right to receive monies and be paid under contracts with book publishers, etc., that he negotiated before the desertion. (Who cares about a deserted parasite?)

We members of the Society of Authors' Representatives feel that a writer does well to limit his search for an agent, to fit his particular needs, to the Society's membership of almost forty agents of the eighty-seven listed in the Manhattan Telephone Directory. There are at least one or two, and perhaps more, perfectly good agents, not members of the Society. One can consult a nationally known book publisher or magazine or The Authors Guild. By correspondence the author and agent can proceed to get together. I like to meet the people I take on, but not until I have read what they write to see whether they can write.

I consider it not in the writer's interest to be handled by different agents for different rights, but this is because in the operation of my office we handle everything and every right for our clients. We are represented abroad and on the West Coast by agents who carry on our work in these areas for us. We do not take on writers who divide their representation. Some perfectly reputable agents do, I am told. This is a matter of policy, having nothing to do with ethics; rather with efficiency. Commissions are 10% on U.S.A. rights and 15% on British and 15% and 20% on translation rights.

I have been asked whether a writer should pay his agent a commission on something the writer happens to place himself. If a writer questions the payment of a commission, but the agent feels he should receive this commission, I suggest a termination of the agency relationship at once since the agent should have his commission regardless of who makes the sale. A dispute of this sort sets up bad feeling not in the interests of the writer. A writer who questions the value of his agent by wanting to withhold his commission obviously is with the wrong agent. I cannot conceive of representing someone who thought I was not earning every commission on every sale. We are underpaid for the services we perform as it is. We can exist only by taking the low and high commissions on everything. Asking about *obligation* to pay a commission indicates a bad agency relationship or a misunderstanding of the agent's function. Agents often have little to do, for example, with the conferences which result in assignments to their writers of non-fiction articles by editors. Sometimes they don't know until a check arrives that there has been a conference. The agent earns his commission even here by the over-all services he performs in the over-all writing career of the writers on his list. The agent even earns it in the case of the arrived check by being sure that the pay is what it should be and that the contract of purchase is proper.

Most experienced professional writers indoctrinated in this country have a good relationship with their agents. Occasionally one runs into a writer who feels that he must be with an agent with whom he has no social life and, in fact, has an arm's length, challenging relationship. I'm sure these are fine relationships for the parties concerned. There's nothing wrong with them, ethically. The interesting thing is that the best agents, the most successful, those with the best reputations, seem not to have this kind of relationship with their clients.

Most agents of all kinds like writers and like to see manuscripts. A writer does not have to be published to get a hearing from most of the very best agents. Some of the largest successes I have had on my list have been first novels by previously unpublished writers, and an important part of my list is made up of successful writers with whom I have worked from the beginning of their published careers. A professional writer can be unpublished. He must know how to write and have that dedication which compels him to write and to consider writing as a primary function, even if, until he gets underway, he has to have a job to eat. We agents have a special sense of who is and who is not a "pro." One lady agent (and I'm told she is not being facetious, although I hope she is) claims that she can spot a writer by observing his wrists and ankles!

I'm looking now as I write this at a list of the members of the Society of Authors' Representatives. I know most of them, some better than others. Most of us are close friends. I once was an editor with a publisher, as several of us were, and got to know most of the members then. We also meet together regularly to discuss mutual problems. You can't go wrong with any of them as far as their qualifications and ability are concerned. You can go wrong as to personality. We all are pretty much alike in our attitudes toward the business, but we differ very much as people. It would be good if every writer deciding on an agent could meet several before making a decision. It saves a lot of trouble for both parties.

Good hunting to all of you. When you find the agent who inspires the best work from you, let him or her carry the ball. They will do it better than any writer can for himself. The agent knows his area of operation. And he can take the blame for any difficulties with a buyer of the writer's product. The agent is better equipped to get the buyer (publisher, producer, whatever) to do more for his client. One of the great functions of the agent is to act as a buffer and to see that love is maintained between the principals. Most people function better when they feel they are loved and that what they are doing is being appreciated. The wise writer will let his agent be the nonloved.

When I get to the end of my talks to writers, I get the questions. Down in one of the first few rows is a young man who asks the questions, "If I can place my novel myself, why do I need an agent?"

My reply, "As long as you ask that question, you don't. It's when you don't ask it that you will need an agent."

What do I mean? When this young man, I hope not too much later in his career, discovers that his career isn't as far along as it should be and realizes what a good agent can do for him, he's ready for an agent. The writer is alone in the world without an agent. He may be the kind of person incapable of working with an agent. There are some of those, and, alas, they usually don't get as far in the commercial world as they could if they were working with the experts in the competitive market place. The young man, now older, in trouble with contracts he has signed, checks with unread endorsements he has signed, out on too many tangents and limbs, without direction and proper counseling, without anyone to fight the battle for money, respect, proper promotion, proper printings and advertising, acceptable salable titles to his work, feeling alone and unwanted, realizes why placement of his work is a minor part of the function of the agent.

96

WRITING AS BUSINESS

By Nannine Joseph

WRITING is an art but it is also a business, and the two are not mutually exclusive, but rather inclusive. Writers may be only craftsmen, but often are artists as well.

Because those often called trade writers—professionals—think of themselves as businessmen, they usually know about and appreciate agents. Agents are middlemen with the same relation to writers and their markets as commission men have to farmers, and the retailers or the wholesalers to manufacturers. This is true because agents are primarily marketing experts, but they can be and often are much more.

Writers who think of themselves purely as artists, and believe they do not need an agent are often the ones who could profit most from an agent. An agent can be a buffer between a shy writer and the businessmen—editors and publishers—with whom they must deal. Many an author soon becomes discouraged when manuscripts are refused, and instead of sending them further, he drops them into the bottom of a trunk and gives up writing, when all that was wrong was that the manuscripts went to the wrong market. A slight change in emphasis or just picking the right spot might have made an immediate sale.

An agent can often not only nurse and protect an author but also serve as a catalyst, suggest subjects, and follow up myriad details, free the author for creative effort, and so save him valuable time.

A good agent is often a good editor and can help to orient writing toward a special market. Many busy agents do no editing but suggest markets at which to aim and methods of handling material.

An agent also relieves an author's money problems. It is difficult for most authors to haggle with an editor, but the agent knows what the work is worth and can often demand and get better terms than originally offered, and these will more than offset the agency commission.

Editors, especially book editors, like to work through agents, for they can express themselves more bluntly to the agent than they could to the naturally sensitive author, and the agent will pass on criticism in terms suited to the particular author, understanding the problems on both sides.

An agent should have some legal knowledge and be sure that contracts offered are as fair to the author as to the publisher who may have more than one printed form or be prepared to shade terms on request. This is especially true of the so-called subsidiary rights. The Authors League has sent its members suggestions about the best possible terms and their inherent rights, but few individual authors can bring as much pressure on the editor as an agent who may have other authors the publisher would like to add to his lists.

There are a few writers who do not need an agent. Writers of purely technical material seldom do. If a writer is a good tough businessman, has no sensitivity in money matters, has good foreign connections, he may need no go-between.

Beginners, though they often seem to think that the chance of sale is very small unless they work through an agent, should get the benefit of direct editorial response and send out their own manuscripts until some at least have been published. After all, agents are business people, and they can't afford to work with the very small markets. But it is essential for beginners to see their work in print. Things in print often look quite different from typed material, and it is a salutary experience to see just what print does to one's own work. There are hundreds of small magazines scattered through the country, trade papers and small newspapers that buy at low figures, figures so low that the agency commission wouldn't pay for the office overhead. If authors will watch these markets carefully, they can often make a fair amount of money out of them, and get the full value of the experience of working with these editors. In fact, beginning writers should work directly instead of trying to have their stories handled by an agent. When they have sold a few stories then a good agent will be interested. Few author's representatives can afford the luxury of working with beginners.

However, beginners, as well as writers who have been at it some time, should learn to read carefully the magazines at which they are aiming. Articles especially need to be slanted for a particular market. Many writers are too set in their way of writing and lack the adaptability that makes for good work.

Many beginners do not realize that if they have seen articles on a given subject in other magazines, it is probable that they will be unable to sell the same subjects elsewhere. Even if they know more about it than the writer whose article has already appeared, by the time another can get into print, it will be old stuff. Few beginners take into account the time-lag between acceptance of a manuscript and the publication date. It is necessary to think ahead so that articles will be of current interest at the time the magazine is published.

Fiction writers, of course, haven't this problem. In fact, the best fiction is written exactly as the particular story requires; but even there it is necessary, if writing for the slick paper field, to watch the current pattern to a greater or lesser extent, depending upon how good the craftsman is. Too many beginning writers say, "Well, it seems curious that I can't sell to so-and-so. I write a good deal better than most of the stories they print." My mental answer is always, "Oh, yeah?" Writers should learn not to look down on what appears in print, not to keep thinking how much better they could do. Instead they should try to figure out *why* the editor bought that particular story. They might then see that even if they have a better story (and I say that "if" with a mental question, too), there was some extra something in the published story that was lacking in their own. Remember that a magazine editor has to know what his readers like —if he doesn't, he'll soon be out of a job.

Too many writers forget that they have a reader, and write without visualizing that reader. While the writer must know all about the characters so that they will come alive on paper, the reader needs to know only what is essential to the particular story or article being written at the moment.

The difference between a $75.00 article and a $750.00 article is exactly how much research has been done and how much the author really knows about the subject, and how much authority shows through.

No writer can do a good job unless his approach to his file is an honest one. Writing, as has been said often before, is a craft as well

as a profession, and it is necessary always to learn a craft. Of course
if you are a genius, that may not hold. If you are a born storyteller,
you can be a bad writer. There are very few geniuses—very few born
storytellers; and a good master of technique can sometimes get even
further than some who try to get by on native ability alone. It takes
a combination of ability and a great deal of steady, hard work to
make a living out of the profession. No agent is interested in handling people who do one story and then wait a year until the inspiration strikes again before writing the next. Steady production is what
gets one ahead, whether it be in writing or any other profession.

Good-looking manuscripts, clearly typed on the right kind of
paper so that the purely physical appearance is good, help to sell an
agent. Pick the right agent, accept valid criticism, trust your agent,
or find another one you do trust.

An agent should be chosen as carefully as a doctor or lawyer. Any
of the following will supply a list of reputable agents:

1. The Authors Guild of America, 234 West 44th Street, New
   York, N.Y. 10036.
2. Any nationally known book publisher
3. Any national magazine.

In 1928 a group of literary agents organized the Society of Authors'
Representatives, the address of which is 101 Park Avenue, New
York, N.Y. 10017. This is a voluntary group of agents who subscribe
to the following ethical practices:

1. The agents takes ten per cent commission on domestic sales and
   up to twenty per cent on foregn sales.
2. He pays out the author's share of monies promptly after receipt.
3. He charges the author with no expense incurred by the normal
   operation of his office, such as postage or local phone calls. He
   does charge the author for such things as copyright fees, manuscript typing fees incurred at the author's request, copies of
   books for submission overseas.
4. He does not advertise his services.
5. Some agents may charge a reading fee for unsolicited material
   but refund this in the event of acceptance of the material.

An agent is not a miracle worker. He cannot sell an unsalable
manuscript—he can only find the best markets and the best terms
for a salable one.

An agent is not an instructor in writing. He cannot afford the time to give detailed critical help to authors whose work has not reached a professional level.

An agent is not a rewrite man. He may direct an author to reputable people when he thinks the material warrants it, but he cannot be expected to do more than minor editing of manuscripts himself.

A literary agent is an author's business representative. He is responsible for all business and many other matters relative to the writer's total literary output.

97

WRITERS, AGENTS, AND
MANUSCRIPT SALES

By Paul R. Reynolds

Why does the beginning author want an agent?

After collecting a certain number of rejection slips, the beginning writer is apt to wonder whether an agent can help him.

The beginning author hopes that the agent will sell a manuscript which the author himself could not sell. There is little if any basis for such a hope. Also the beginning writer wants someone to do the work of writing letters of submission to editors, to do the work of wrapping and mailing manuscripts. Finally, the beginner wants to avoid the unpleasantness of personally receiving a rejection slip.

However, once an author has attained a certain proficiency with the written word, there are areas where an agent can help him. Usually, but not always, the author at this stage in his career has made some sales through his own efforts.

What agent is the beginning writer likely to choose?

The beginning writer chooses someone he has heard about, namely a man or firm who advertises, a pseudo-agent. Off goes his manuscript to such pseudo-agent, one who "lunches with editors" or one whose clients "have made in some cases fabulous sales and in some cases modest ones" or one whose advertisements display testimonials of sales. By return mail comes a letter from the pseudo-agent asking the author for a check, sometimes for a large one, sometimes for a quite modest one. The beginning writer usually sends his check. Back comes a letter full of praise for the manuscript and with a request for more manuscripts accompanied by more checks. This process continues until the author runs out of money or out of patience. The author has made no sales.

The pseudo-agent makes his money by cashing checks from authors, not from commissions on sales of manuscripts. Some of these advertising sharks seldom if ever offer manuscripts to magazines or publishers for publication. If they do offer a manuscript to an editor, it is under a cloud. Editors, knowing that these pseudo-agents rarely have a publishable manuscript, start with a prejudice against their wares. Have some of these pseudo-agents made sales? Yes, but very infrequently. An author's chance of a sale is enhanced if he offers his manuscript himself and avoids the sponsorship of one of these literary spongers.

What about the legitimate agent?

The legitimate agent does not advertise. He makes his living from commissions on sales. This means that he must represent selling writers. There are several literary agents who sell more than two million dollars worth of literary property a year; a larger number whose sales are between one million and two million and many whose gross is a quarter of a million dollars up. These agents will have a staff of from three to twenty. Since a secretary in New York City receives at least $100 a week, successful authors are essential just for the agent to pay his overhead.

Most article writers should and do start writing pieces for the minor markets, for newspapers, trade magazines, regional publications, etc. Payment for an acceptable manuscript is usually small, but the number of markets is very large. No agent follows these markets or can make a living selling to them, and an author can do as well or better in this area on his own.

After one or more years writing for the very numerous minor markets, writers try to graduate to the high-paying, mass circulation magazines, and many are successful. Once a writer has made one or more sales to the mass circulation magazines such as *The Reader's Digest,* the *Post, McCall's,* etc., some of the legitimate literary agents will take the writer on as a client. The author will be helped some but still must do much of the selling work. Many writers at this stage continue to handle their own work. Authors who attain the steady success in the article field of a Richard Gehman, Joseph Wechsberg, or Geoffrey Hellman, can have any agent in the country. The above three writers do use agents.

What about the agent for short stories?

No agent will handle a writer whose short stories are published exclusively in the "little" magazines or in the small-paying markets. When a writer graduates to the high-paying, mass circulation magazines, some agents will take him on; some will not. The short story market has been continually contracting during the last ten years so that few writers seem to be able to make a living in this field.

What about the agent for television?

It is almost impossible to sell an original television script except through an agent of standing. Most of the buyers, partly for fear of lawsuits over alleged plagiarism, partly because of a lack of a staff of readers, will not consider scripts submitted by an unknown writer. Television script buying is more and more being done out on the Coast, and a Hollywood agent should be sought. This is a very technical field, very difficult to break into.

What about the agent and the play?

The newcomer in this field should try to get a play-broker, an agent who specializes in plays. Success in this field requires unusual skill and proficiency. Breaking into the amateur play market is difficult; surmounting Broadway is overwhelmingly difficult and here an agent is almost obligatory.

What about the agent in connection with sales of poetry?

No agent will handle poetry with the possible exception of the very big names. Ogden Nash or Richard Armour can certainly be helped with their books, but in the case of their magazine sales, it is doubtful if any agent can do any better than they can do themselves. Ogden Nash and Richard Armour both use agents.

What about the agent and writers of books?

Here perhaps is where the agent can be most helpful. A successful book, fiction or non-fiction, has so many rights to be promoted, publishers so differ in their ability to sell a particular type of book, the contracts they will proffer and the contracts that they can be induced to sign are at such variance that a good agent, although never essential, can be very helpful. The author of a specialized book such as a cookbook or a garden book has far less need for an agent. Here there are generally no rights of value involved other than American book publication rights. In the case of the general interest book, hard-cover or paperback or both, a good agent will make the author money over and above his commissions. One manuscript may involve many individual contracts. The above is true of the author's second or tenth or fortieth book; it is also true of a first book which is really good. All of the large agents have had one or more first novels or first non-fiction books which have been very successful.

Is it difficult for the new writer with a really good manuscript to obtain a good agent?

The answer is yes. It is sometimes said that it is easier to find a publisher than it is to find a good agent. Unless the agent believes or hopes that an author will make at least $5,000 a year, the agent is not interested. A book may earn a minimum of $500 to a maximum of $500,000 in the case of an enormous number one best seller. Will an agent read a first novel? The author can only write and ask. An agent is busy. He has only one pair of eyes. He knows that nine out of ten writers submit manuscripts before they have learned their trade, and hence submit second-rate manuscripts. With every new writer an agent is from Missouri. However, if there is any reason to believe that a first manuscript may be good, such as previous publi-cation of the author's short pieces in minor markets, or such as a recommendation from one or more people who seem qualified to rec-ognize a good manuscript, or perhaps just from the author's back-ground, many of the agents will read it. The good agents are always looking for new talent. Of course an agent makes mistakes (just as publishers do) and may miss the good qualities of a manuscript, or the agent may like it and may be wrong, but if the agent reads the manuscript, likes it, and is right in his judgment, the author is off to the races. All kinds of interesting and profitable things will occur.

How should an author select an agent?

We have already spoken about the fee chargers, the advertising sharks, the literary spongers. Do not waste your money on them. The Society of Authors' Representatives, all of whose members are believed to be competent and reputable, publishes a short pamphlet which lists the members of the Society and their addresses. This pamphlet will be mailed by *The Writer*, 8 Arlington St., Boston, Mass. 02116, if you will ask for it and enclose a stamped, self-addressed envelope.

Really, how important is an agent?

No agent can sell any manuscript that an author cannot sell if the author is sufficiently persevering. If someone wants to buy, the agent may obtain more money; he has no magic, no influence in producing a sale. No writing career was ever made by an agent or blasted by the lack of an agent. Success in writing depends upon what is between the first and the last page of a manuscript. Learning to get the right material and to use it with the right words, learning the trade of a writer involves very hard work over a long period of time. The agent looms far larger in the minds of many writers than is justified. The agent cannot solve the writer's problems; continuous intensive work and the refusal to be beaten by discouragement usually can solve them.

98

A CONCISE GUIDE TO COPYRIGHT

A COPYRIGHT is a form of protection given by the law of the United States, to the authors of literary, dramatic, musical, artistic, and other intellectual works. The owner of a copyright is granted by law certain exclusive rights in his work. In addition to the exclusive right to copy his work, there are rights such as:

a. The right to sell or distribute copies of the work.

b. The right to transform or revise the work by means of dramatization, translation, musical arrangement, or the like.

c. The right to perform and record the work.

Not all of the rights granted by the copyright law are without limitation. For example, in the case of musical compositions, the performance right is limited to public performances for profit. Likewise, recording rights in musical works are limited by the so-called "compulsory license" provision, which permits recordings upon payment of certain royalties, after the initial recording has been authorized by the copyright owner.

Writers often ask if they should copyright a manuscript before submitting it to a publisher for possible publication.

As outlined below under "Unpublished Works," such manuscripts as novels, short stories, poems, narrative outlines, etc. *cannot* be copyrighted before publication, but are protected by common law until publication. Plays, lectures, musical compositions, etc., may be copyrighted before they have been published, but here again it is not *necessary* to copyright such manuscripts before submitting them for publication, since they are also protected by common law.

WHAT CAN BE COPYRIGHTED

The Copyright Law (Title 17, United States Code) lists thirteen broad classes of works in which copyright may be claimed, with the provision that these are not to be held to limit the subject matter of copyright. Within the classes are the following kinds of works:

Books (Class A)—Works of fiction and non-fiction, poems, compilations, composite works, directions, catalogs, annual publications, information in tabular form, and similar text matter, with or without illustrations, published as a book, pamphlet, leaflet, card, single page, or the like.

Periodicals (Class B)—Such publications as newspapers, magazines, reviews, newsletters, bulletins, and serial publications, which appear at intervals of less than a year; also, contributions to periodicals, such as stories, cartoons, or columns published in magazines or newspapers.

Lectures or similar productions prepared for oral delivery (Class C) —Unpublished works such as lectures, sermons, addresses, monologs, recording scripts, and certain forms of television and radio scripts.

Dramatic and dramatico-musical compositions (Class D)—Dramatic works such as the acting versions of plays for the stage, for filming, radio, television, and the like, pantomimes, ballets, operas, operettas, etc.

Musical compositions (Class E)—Musical compositions (other than dramatico-musical compositions), in the form of visible notation, with or without words, as well as new versions of musical compositions, such as adaptations, arrangements, and editing when such editing is the writing of an author. The words of a song, unaccompanied by music, are not registrable in Class E.

Maps (Class F)—Published cartographic representations of area, such as terrestrial maps and atlases, marine charts, celestial maps, and such three-dimensional works as globes and relief models.

Works of art: models or designs for works of art (Class G)—Works of artistic craftmanship, insofar as their form but not their mechanical or utilitarian aspects are concerned, such as artistic jewelry, enamels, glassware, and tapestries, as well as works belonging to the fine arts, such as paintings, drawings, and sculpture.

Reproductions of works of art (Class H)—Published reproductions of existing works of art in the same or a different medium, such as a lithograph, photoengraving, etching, or drawing of a painting, sculpture, or other work of art.

Drawings or plastic works of a scientific or technical character (Class I)—Diagrams or models illustrating scientific or technical works, or formulating scientific or technical information in linear or sculptural form, such as an architect's or an engineer's blueprint, plan, or design, a mechanical drawing, an astronomical chart, or an anatomical model.

Photographs (Class J)—Photographic prints and filmstrips, slide films, and individual slides. Photoengravings and other photomechanical reproductions of photographs are registered in Class K.

Prints, pictorial illustrations, and commercial prints or labels (Class K)—Prints or pictorial illustrations, greeting cards, picture postcards, and similar prints, produced by means of lithography, photoengraving, or other methods of reproduction. A print or label, not a trademark, published in connection with the sale or advertisement of an article or articles of merchandise, also is registered in this class.

Motion-picture photoplays (Class L)—Motion pictures, dramatic in character, such as feature films, filmed television plays, short subjects and animated cartoons, musical plays, and similar productions having a plot.

Motion pictures other than photoplays (Class M)—Nondramatic motion pictures, such as newsreels, travelogs, training or promotional films, nature studies, and filmed television programs having no plot.

WHAT CANNOT BE COPYRIGHTED

The fact that a work does not fit conveniently into one of the thirteen classes does not necessarily mean that it is not copyrightable. However, there are several categories of material which are generally not eligible for statutory copyright protection. These include, among others:

a. Words and short phrases such as names, titles, and slogans;

familiar symbols or designs; mere variations of typographic orna-
mentation, lettering, or coloring; mere listings of ingredients or
contents.

b. Works designed for recording information which do not in themselves convey information, such as time cards, graph paper, account books, diaries, bank checks, score cards, address books,
   report forms, order forms, and the like.

c. Works consisting entirely of information that is common property containing no original authorship, such as for example:
   standard calendars, height and weight charts, tape measures and
   rulers, schedules of sporting events, and lists or tables taken from
   public documents or other common sources.

d. Sound recordings, and the performances recorded on them.

e. Ideas, plans, methods, systems or devices, as distinguished from a
   description or illustration.

WHO CAN CLAIM COPYRIGHT

Only the author or those deriving their rights through him can
rightfully claim copyright. Mere possession of a work does not give
the possessor the right to copyright. There is no provision for securing a blanket copyright to cover all works of an author. Each work
must be copyrighted separately if protection is desired. In the case of
works made for hire, it is the employer, and not the employee, who is
regarded as the author.

UNPUBLISHED WORKS

An unpublished work (that is, generally, a work of which copies
have not been made available to the public) may be eligible for one
of two types of protection:

a. *Common Law Literary Property*. This type of protection is a matter of state law, and arises automatically when the work is created; it requires no action in the Copyright Office. It may last as
   long as the work is unpublished, but it ends when the work is
   published or copyright is secured.

b. *Statutory Copyright*. This is the protection afforded by the federal law upon compliance with certain requirements. Only the following types of work are eligible for statutory copyright before
   they have been published: musical compositions, dramas, works

of art, drawings and plastic works of a scientific or technical character, photographs, motion pictures, and works prepared for oral delivery. While there is no requirement that any of these works be registered for statutory copyright, there may be advantages in such registration. However, if they are registered in their unpublished form, the law requires that another registration be made after publication with the copyright notice affixed to the copies.

The following types of material *cannot* be registered as unpublished works: books (including short stories, poems, and narrative outlines), prints, maps, reproductions of works of art, periodicals, and commercial prints and labels. Such works secure copyright by the act of publication with notice of copyright.

HOW TO SECURE STATUTORY COPYRIGHT FOR AN UNPUBLISHED WORK

Procedure to follow. Statutory copyright for unpublished works is secured by registering a claim in the Copyright Office. For this purpose, it is necessary to forward the following material:

a. *Application Form.* The appropriate form may be ordered from the Copyright Office. Forms are supplied without charge.

b. *Copy.* In the case of manuscripts of music, dramas, lectures, etc., one complete copy should accompany the application. It will be retained by the Copyright Office. For photographs deposit one photographic print. Special requirements concerning motion pictures, and certain graphic and artistic works, are stated on the application forms.

c. *Fee.* The registration fee for unpublished works is $6.00.

PUBLISHED WORKS

Published works are those which have been made available to the public in some way, usually by the sale or public distribution of copies. The copyright law defines the "date of publication" as "the earliest date when copies of the first authorized edition were placed on sale, sold, or publicly distributed by the proprietor of the copyright or under his authority, . . ." The dividing line between limited distribution and general publication is sometimes difficult to determine. No specific number of copies or method of distribution is required for a general publication. If you are in doubt about publication in a particular case, it may be advisable to consult an attorney.

It is essential that all published copies of a work for which statutory protection is desired or claimed bear a notice of copyright in the form and position described below or the rights may be permanently lost. After a work has become public property by reason of publication without notice of copyright, adding a notice to copies serves no purpose and may be illegal.

In the case of works which cannot be registered in advance of publication, it is the act of publication with notice of copyright, rather than registration in the Copyright Office, that secures copyright. While the Copyright Office registers *claims* to copyright, it does not grant copyright.

How to secure statutory copyright for a published work

Procedure to follow. Three steps should be taken to secure and maintain statutory copyright in a published work:

a. *Produce copies with copyright notice.* First, produce the work in copies by printing or other means of reproduction. It is essential that all copies bear a copyright notice in the required form and position.

b. *Publish the work.*

c. *Register your claim in the Copyright Office.* Promptly *after* publication, you should forward the following material:

1. *Application Form.* The appropriate form may be requested from the Copyright Office from the list printed below.

2. *Copies.* Send two copies of the best edition of the work as published.

3. *Fee.* The registration fee for published works is $6.00.

The law requires that after a work is published with the prescribed notice, two copies "shall be promptly deposited," accompanied by a claim of copyright.

The copyright notice

Form of the Notice. As a general rule, the copyright notice should consist of three elements:

a. *The word "Copyright," the abbreviation "Copr.," or the symbol* ©. Use of the symbol © may result in securing copyright in countries which are members of the Universal Copyright Convention.

b. *The name of the copyright owner.*

c. *The year date of publication.* If the work has previously been registered as unpublished, the year date of such registration should be given, since the copyright term began on that date.

These three elements should appear together on the copies; for example:

© John Doe 1968

Optional Form of Notice. For works registrable in Classes F through K (namely, maps, works of art, models or designs for works of art, reproductions of works of art, drawings or plastic works of a scientific or technical character, photographs, prints and pictorial illustrations, and prints or labels used for articles of merchandise) a special form of notice is permissible. This may consist of the symbol ©, accompanied by the initials, monogram, mark, or symbol of the copyright owner, if the owner's name appears upon some accessible portion of the work. A tag bearing a copyright notice attached to the work is not acceptable in lieu of a notice on the work itself.

Position of the Notice. For a book or other publication printed in book form, the copyright notice should appear upon the title page or page immediately following. The "page immediately following" is normally the reverse side of the page bearing the title. For a periodical, the notice should appear upon the title page, upon the first page of text, or under the title heading. For a musical work, the notice may appear either upon the title page or upon the first page of music.

Unpublished Works. The law does not specify a notice for unpublished works. However, to avoid the danger of inadvertent publication without notice, it may be advisable for an author to affix notices to any copies that leave his control.

DURATION OF COPYRIGHT

The first term of statutory copyright runs for twenty-eight years. The term begins on the date the work is published with the notice of copyright, or, in the case of unpublished works registered in the Copyright Office, on the date of such registration. A copyright may be renewed for a second term of twenty-eight years, provided an application for renewal is made to the Copyright Office and duly registered during the last year of the original twenty-eight-year term, which is measured from the exact date on which the original copyright began. For information concerning renewal, request Circulars 15 and 15X. Pending possible changes in the copyright laws currently under consideration by Congress, certain renewal copyrights about to expire have been extended until December 31, 1968.

APPLICATION FORMS

The following forms are provided by the Copyright Office, and may be obtained free of charge upon request:

Class A   Form A—Published book manufactured in the United States of America

Class A or B

- Form A–B Foreign—Book or periodical manufactured and first published outside the United States of America (except works subject to the *ad interim* provisions of the copyright law of the United States of America; see Form A–B Ad Interim)
- Form A–B Ad Interim—Book or periodical in the English language manufactured and first published outside the United States of America and subject to the *ad interim* provisions of the copyright law of the United States of America

Class B

- Form B—Periodical manufactured in the United States of America
- Form BB—Contribution to a periodical manufactured in the United States of America

Class C   Form C—Lecture, sermon, or address, prepared for oral delivery

Class D   Form D—Dramatic or dramatico-musical composition

Class E

- Form E—Musical composition by an author who is a citizen or domiciliary of the United States of America or which is first published in the United States of America
- Form E Foreign—Musical composition by an author who is not a citizen or domiciliary of the United States of America and which is not first published in the United States of America

Class F   Form F—Map

Class G   Form G—Work of art; model or design for work of art

Class H   Form H—Reproduction of a work of art

Class I Form I—Drawing or plastic work of a scientific or technical character

Class J Form J—Photograph

Class K { Form K—Print or pictorial illustration
{ Form KK—Print or label used for article of merchandise

Class L { Form L-M—Motion Picture
or M {

Form R—Renewal copyright

Form U—Notice of use of musical composition on mechanical instruments

Transfer or assignment of statutory copyright

A copyright may be transferred or assigned by an instrument in
writing, signed by the proprietor of the copyright. The law provides
for the recordation in the Copyright Office of transfers of copyright.
The original signed instrument should be submitted for the purpose
of recording. It will be returned following recordation. For effective
protection, an assignment executed in the United States should be
recorded within three months from the date of execution. Assignments executed abroad should be recorded within six months.

Mailing instructions

Address. All communications should be addressed to the Register
of Copyrights, Library of Congress, Washington, D. C. 20540.

Fees. Do not send cash. Fees sent to the Copyright Office should
be in the form of a money order, check, or bank draft, payable to the
Register of Copyrights.

Fee Schedule

All registrations (except renewals)	$6.00
All renewals	4.00
Additional certificates	2.00
Other certifications	3.00
Assignments, etc. (containing not more than 6 pages and not more than 1 title)	5.00
—Each additional page or title	0.50
Searches (hourly fee)	5.00

Mailing. Processing of the material will be more prompt if the application, copies, and fee are all mailed at the same time and in the same package.

FOREIGN WORKS

If a work is by an author who is neither a citizen nor a domiciliary of the United States and the work is first published outside the United States, special instructions should be requested.

LEGAL ADVICE

The Copyright Office does not give legal advice. If you need information or guidance on matters such as disputes over the ownership of a copyright, it may be necessary to consult an attorney. Specific questions relating to copyright problems not dealt with here should be addressed to the Register of Copyrights, Library of Congress, Washington, D. C. 20540.

99

WHAT'S IN A PEN NAME?

By Deborah N. Kassman

When Queen Victoria told Charles Dodgson, author of *Alice's Adventures in Wonderland,* how much she liked his book and how eagerly she looked forward to reading something else he had written, he promptly sent her his *Syllabus of Plane Algebraical Geometry.* We do not know if the Queen was amused.

Dodgson would undoubtedly be amused, however, to learn that today, more than one hundred years after the publication of *Alice,* his pen name, Lewis Carroll, is famous throughout the English-speaking world. In fact, it is said that, with the exception of Shakespeare and the Bible, the most quoted works in the English language are *Alice* and its sequel, *Through the Looking Glass.*

Dodgson limited himself to one pen name. But most authors using pseudonyms generally find themselves in the position of William Sydney Porter, who had several pen names although he signed most of his stories O. Henry. Today, many authors erupt in a veritable rash of pen names: Don Ross, who abandoned the stage at the age of forty-nine to take up novel writing and has been described by *The New York Times* as "what must be one of the most formidable writing factories in this or any other hemisphere," uses Marilyn Ross (for Gothic novels), Rose Dana (for nurse books), Don Roberts (for Westerns), and Alice Gilmer, Ellen Randolph, and Jane Rossiter (for modern novels).

Sometimes, pen names are so well known that a reviewer could write, " 'Jeremy York' rises above his usual level and suggests one of John Creasey's better pseudonyms (perhaps 'Kyle Hunt') in *The Man I Killed.*" This pen name dropper knew, of course, about Mr. Creasey's twelve other pseudonyms, which include Gordon Ashe, J. J. Marric, Anthony Morton, Richard Martin, Robert Caine Frazer, etc. (Perhaps bowing to the inevitable in the case of Mr. Creasey, his publishers noted on the cover of one of his recent books, "A Mystery Novel by John Creasey as Anthony Morton." Another well-known pen name was acknowledged by the publishers in an advertisement of a new Ellery Queen mystery, giving the names of Manfred B. Lee and Fredric Dannay as the writing team behind this pseudonym.)

Often, however, even the critics are surprised by a pen name. "Some years ago I swore off reading all detective stories except those by Michael Innes," began *New York Times* critic Orville Prescott in a review. "Only the other day did I discover that Michael Innes is the pseudonym of J. I. M. Stewart, a distinguished scholar (author of *Character in Shakespeare's Plays* and a volume of the formidable *Oxford History of English Literature*) and also the author of six non-detective novels," continued the dumbfounded Mr. Prescott.

Why all these pen names? Is a pen name a good idea for a new author? There are many valid reasons why pen names are used.

1. Prolific authors sometimes use pen names simply because publishers do not want to flood the book market with many books by the same author in one year. Mr. Creasey, who completes about a dozen books a year, has three hardcover and many paperback publishers sharing his output in the United States. John Dickson Carr uses three names for his books: One publisher brings out his books under the name of John Dickson Carr; another publisher issues his books by "Carter Dickson," a pen name, and occasionally Mr. Carr has used Carr Dickson as another pseudonym. Erle Stanley Gardner writes mysteries for his publisher both under his own name and under his pen name, A. A. Fair. (Pen names are, obviously, especially widely used in the mystery and detective field, where a bonus mystery is sometimes offered to the reader: what is the *real* name of the author?)

2. Authors who have several different specialties sometimes want to use different names for each specialty. Leo C. Rosten uses his real name for serious work, the pen name Leonard Q. Ross for humor (*The Education of H*Y*M*A*N K*A*P*L*A*N*, etc.) and Leonard Ross, without the "Q," for his "melodramas" (he wrote the original story and screenplay for *Walk East on Beacon*). Bernard DeVoto wrote novels, history, and criticism under his own name, light

fiction under the name of John August, and light essays under the name of Cady Hewes. Willard Huntington Wright, who as S. S. Van Dine created the famous detective Philo Vance, noted, when he decided to leave literary criticism and become a writer of detective stories, "I rather feared ostracism if I boldly switched from esthetics and philologic research to fictional sleuthing, and so I hid behind an old family name (Van Dyne) and the Steam-Ship initials." Historical novelist Norah Lofts occasionally uses the pseudonym of Peter Curtis for suspense fiction (*No Question of Murder, The Devil's Own,* etc.).

3. Personal confessions and revelations are sometimes published under pseudonyms. *A Grief Observed,* reflections on the death of the author's wife, was signed N. W. Clerk. This name was a pseudonym for C. S. Lewis (*The Screwtape Letters,* etc.), who felt the book was so personal he should use another name. (The real name of the author was revealed by the newspapers only after Mr. Lewis died.) *The House of Tomorrow,* the diary of an unwed mother, was published under a pen name, as was *American Woman and Alcohol* by a now happily-married member of Alcoholics Anonymous.

4. Sometimes, an assumed name has already been used for other purposes. Rebecca West (author of *The Meaning of Treason,* etc.) was born Cicily Isabel Fairfield; when she began a brief stage career, she took as a stage name Rebecca West, the name of a woman in Ibsen's play *Rosmersholm,* and then used it as a pen name when she turned to writing.

5. A doctor, lawyer, or other professional person might use a pen name for non-professional writing to keep his two spheres of activity separate. Michigan Supreme Court Justice John Donaldson Voelker, especially well known for his bestselling *Anatomy of a Murder,* writes his novels under the pseudonym of Robert Traver. Sir Anthony Hope Hawkins wrote all of his books, including the famed *Prisoner of Zenda,* using his first and middle names as a pen name, Anthony Hope. Although he later regretted the pen name, he had decided to use it when he was a successful barrister and expected to continue his career as a lawyer. When *New York Times* art critic John Caraday was teaching art at the University of Virginia some

years ago, he wrote seven mystery novels under the pseudonym of Matthew Head because he wanted to use his own name solely for his art criticism.

6. Authors of non-fiction dealing with shocking or confidential material often do not use their real names because it might be unpleasant or even dangerous for them to do so. (Books by former members of secret organizations, ex-spies, etc., come in this category.) A recently published first novel about college professors and their wives—*Tell the Time to None* by Helen Hudson (a pen name) —might also be mentioned here. Declaring that the use of a pen name in this case "was clearly motivated by prudence," *Time* Magazine explained, " 'Helen Hudson' displays such knowledge of faculty politics . . . that it is obvious she occupies, or once occupied, her own glade in the groves of academe."

7. An author who has a name similar to another author's might use a pen name simply to avoid confusion. John P. Marquand's son decided to write under the name of John Phillips, rather than as John P. Marquand, Jr. Another "Jr." using a pen name is David E. Lilienthal, Jr., son of the former Atomic Energy Commissioner, who as "David Ely" has written two well-reviewed novels: *Seconds* and *The Tour*.

8. Sometimes the sex of an author is concealed by a pseudonym. Charlotte Brontë's *Jane Eyre* first appeared under the pseudonym Currer Bell, and Emily Brontë's *Wuthering Heights* originally was printed under the name Ellis Bell. George Eliot was the famous pen name of Mary Ann Evans, and George Sand the well-known pseudonym of Amandine Aurore Lucie Dupin. These women took pen names primarily because "female authors" were unpopular. Today, many women take pen names (or use initials plus last names) because they are writing sport, western or adventure fiction—and many men will not read such books or stories if they know the authors are women. Mary Grace Chute's popular Sheriff Olsen stories were therefore published under the by-line of M. G. Chute.

9. Pen names are widely used in television today. Sometimes a television playwright will be unhappy about the changes made in his script by other writers, producers, etc., and will therefore ask that

his name be dropped from the credits. But in these days of tapes and films, if a show is repeated and there is no writing credit, the producer does not have to pay a residual fee to the writer. Therefore, for his own protection, the playwright has a pen name registered with the Writers Guild of America. When he takes his real name off the script, his pen name is substituted—and when checks arrive at the Writers Guild office, made out to his pen name, they are forwarded to him. Ernest Kinoy, a former president of the Writers Guild, used B. Chweig on scripts that had been changed; another former Guild president, David Davidson, made use of his middle names, Albert Sanders. As one television playwright put it, "I use a pseudonym to protect my scripts. My name, to me, has value. It's all I've got."

(The Writers Guild of America—East and West—represents professional writers in the fields of radio, television and motion pictures.)

10. Throughout history, pen names have been used for political reasons, and the practice continues today, of course. Baroness Blixen of Rungstedlund, better known as world-famous fiction writer Isak Dinesen, wrote what the Germans considered a harmless Gothic romance during the time that the Nazis occupied Denmark. The book, which actually made use of quite subtle symbolism in presenting a parallel between the fictional villain and the Nazis, was published under the pen name Pierre Andrézel; after the war, the real name of the author was revealed. Frank O'Connor, the Irish short story writer, was born Michael John O'Donovan, and for political reasons assumed his mother's maiden name for his writing.

11. Sometimes, a pen name will be selected because several authors are involved in a collaborative effort, and listing all the names might prove cumbersome. The recent best-seller *Hurry, Sundown,* signed K. B. Gilden, was written by the husband-wife team, Katya and Burt Gilden. Other famous writing teams include Richard Wilson Webb and H. C. Wheeler (who use the names Q. Patrick, Patrick Quentin and Jonathan Stagge for their mystery novels).

12. Some business firms and government organizations do not permit employees to use their own names for writing *not* connected with their work. David Cornwell, who wrote best-selling spy novels

(*The Spy Who Came in From the Cold, The Looking-Glass War*) under the pen name John le Carré, had to use a pseudonym because he served in the British Foreign Office and thus came under Civil Service rules and restrictions. But the air of mystery surrounding Cornwell's experiences was considerably helped by the use of the pen name; even headlines in *The New York Times* after *The Spy* reached the best-seller list announced: SPY AUTHOR SHEDS UNDER-COVER POSE . . . Cornwell (Alias le Carré) Submits to Interrogation.

13. Many writers of juvenile books use pseudonyms (some authors of books for adults want to keep their writing for children quite separate). An astonishing number of pen names in the juvenile field are controlled by The Stratemeyer Syndicate, an organization founded by Edward Stratemeyer when dime novels were being replaced by the pulp magazines. Stratemeyer, who was writing The Rover Boys series under the pen name Arthur M. Winfield, contracted with various writers to turn out books on assignment, under specified pen names, for such popular juvenile series as The Bobbsey Twins, Tom Swift, The Hardy Boys, Nancy Drew, Honey Bunch, etc. In *My Father Was Uncle Wiggily*, Roger Garis describes how his mother and father worked for Stratemeyer: The titles, the pen name, and a sketchy outline were provided by Stratemeyer, and the author did the rest, receiving a flat payment of one hundred dollars for each book. Notes Mr. Garis (who also wrote for Stratemeyer):

There was, in fact, a practical reason for writing a series under a fictitious name. If the writer died while the series was still continuing, it might be possible to find some other writer to carry it on. But if the author's own name were used, this would be impossible.

The Stratemeyer Syndicate still operates today—impressive evidence of the soundness of this particular use of pen names.

Should a new author use a pen name? In general, it is not advisable, but if a writer has a valid reason for wishing to write under a pen name, he should indicate this to an editor. However, the new author who wants to use a pen name must have excellent reasons for doing so; there are many disadvantages connected with pen names, and these may prove especially troublesome to him.

A major disadvantage is the attitude of editors toward pen names.

Simply put, editors are suspicious of writers who use pen names, and they have good reason for their distrust. Generally, editors feel an author should be proud to have his real name connected with his writing; if he is not, then perhaps the writing should not be published. This same editorial attitude extends even to letters published in a newspaper. Most newspapers will not publish any "Letter to the Editor" unless they know the real name of the author, and, in most instances, they dislike printing letters where the name of the writer must be witheld unless there is a very good reason for this. (Sometimes, the letters as published are *anonymous*—which the new *Random House Dictionary* defines as "without any name acknowledged as that of author. . . ." and sometimes the letters are *pseudonymous,* "bearing a false or fictious name.") A new writer who decides to use a pen name must be prepared to encounter editorial suspicions—and it may prove harder for him to have manuscripts accepted if editors are not in sympathy with his reasons.

Also, the writer using a pen name faces many complications, legal and otherwise. He may run into trouble trying to cash a check made out to his pen name (usually, the procedure here is for the author to endorse the check with his pen name and then his real name, and then deposit the check at a bank where he is known). Since many bankers question whether it is legally possible for an account to be opened for two names for one person, a writer might open an account only under his pen name. However, banks report that often legal troubles arise when an author dies, leaving a bank account under a pen name, and therefore they generally require full disclosure—a written document and means of verification—to be filed with the bank when an account under a pen name is opened.

If an author will be receiving correspondence addressed to him under his pen name, he should either arrange to have his real name appear on envelopes also (pen name, *in care of* real name), or else he should make sure his local post office and his mailman know about the pen name. The Post Office generally follows the rule that name has preference over address, *e.g.* an order addressed to R. H. Macy Company at Times Square in New York City will not be left at Times Square but will be delivered to Macy's at the correct address, Herald Square, New York City. The result may be that if the postal authorities do not know about a pen name, they may not leave a letter at the street address given but may simply return it to the sender.

Pen name complications may occur if an author uses a pseudonym only for writing, and has no bank account, etc., under that name. Certainly an author using a pen name should arrange to have his editor state in writing that his real name and his pen name belong to the same person.

If an author has decided to use a pen name, and his editor has agreed to cooperate, does this mean that the author's real name will remain a secret, known only to the author and the publishing firm? Not at all!

Of course, a copyright may be taken out under a pen name since the current Copyright Act does not forbid it. (The Copyright Office recognizes the common use of pseudonyms, and the standard application form even provides space for their insertion.) A married woman may take out a copyright under her maiden name, and, if proper legal arrangements are made, the copyright may also be taken out by someone designated by the author—for instance, the publisher.

However, many people are interested in bringing to light the real name of an author using a pen name. Reporters will often unearth an author's real name if a book has news value. (For many years the real identity of Mark Epernay, pseudonymous author of *The Mac-Landress Dimension* was not revealed by the publishers, although magazines and newspapers speculated and stated that Epernay was really John Kenneth Galbraith, Harvard economist and former United States Ambassador to India. Confirmation of this was definitely made by *The New York Times,* which explained that Galbraith had made up this pen name from Mark Twain and Epernay, Napoleon III's headquarters during the Franco-Prussian war.) Librarians make an effort find out the real name of an author so that they can assemble all material written by an author in one place in their catalogues, and they will indicate cross-references for the various names. This library practice is, of course, important to any researcher who may not know all the books written by the same author if a pen name has been used. Generally, courts have not considered it a violation of privacy when the real name of an author writing under a pen name is made known.

Is there any procedure an author must take before selecting and using a pen name? Most states do not require any legal steps. However, it would be advisable for the author to make a check of the names of other authors before selecting a name, so that he does not choose a pen name that is similar to the name of another writer. (The easiest way to do this is to check through the card catalogue of a fairly large library.)

Pen names are not protected by copyright. However, the laws relating to unfair competition may often provide protection for pseudonyms.

If an author decides that he must use a pen name, the name he has selected should appear on his manuscript under the story title as a by-line. The author's real name should appear in the upper left-hand corner of the first page of the manuscript, above the address; the pen name might be put in parentheses after the author's real name.

Though the use of a pen name can often cause unpleasant or troublesome complications for an author, there are some pleasant developments that may follow, also. A famous science-fiction writer reports that recently he was given a pile of science-fiction books to review. He was most interested when he discovered that one of the titles he was asked to appraise bore a familiar by-line: his own pen name!

100

MANUSCRIPT PREPARATION
AND SUBMISSION

By Joyce T. Smith

A MANUSCRIPT submitted for publication competes with hundreds of others which cross the editor's desk. It follows that the manuscript which is professional in appearance, easy to read, and is free of careless mistakes is more likely to receive better attention than those which do not meet these requirements. The rules of manuscript preparation are simple, but the writer who wishes to have his manuscript considered seriously by editors should follow them carefully. For the most part, the mechanical requirements for manuscripts are the same for all publishing houses and magazines. Publications which have special style requirements will usually send such information on request.

The basic and most important rule of manuscript preparation is: *The manuscript must be typed, double-spaced, on standard 8½ × 11 white paper, on one side of the page only.* Handwritten manuscripts, however legible, are not welcome.

TYPING

Any type face which is clear and easy to read is acceptable, and the typewriter may be standard or portable, manual or electric. The size of the type is also a matter of preference; either pica type or the smaller elite type is commonly used. Some of the unusual type faces now available on typewriters, while suitable for personal use, tend to become illegible on manuscripts. The type should always be clean, and the ribbon (black) should be in good condition, producing clear, legible type. Margins of one inch to an inch and a half should be left on both sides and at the top and bottom of the page.

Manuscripts should be typed on good white bond paper (8½ × 11).

Weights of 14 lbs., 16 lbs., or even 20 lbs. for short manuscripts, are acceptable. Avoid too thin a paper (onionskin, for example) or a very heavy weight (such as parchment), which are difficult to handle and to read. Remember, too, that paper especially treated for easy erasing is also easily smudged. For making carbon copies, inexpensive "second sheet" paper is available. But whatever paper is used, a writer should always make and keep a carbon copy of every manuscript, since occasionally a manuscript is lost. Copies made by Xerox or similar duplicating processes should not be submitted to an editor, though a writer may make such copies of the original for his own use.

The name and address of the author should be typed in the upper left- or right-hand corner of the first manuscript page. About one-third down the page, the title is typed in capital letters, followed a line or two below by the author's name. Leave a three-line space and begin the text.

Pages should be numbered consecutively in the upper right- or left-hand corner, followed by the author's surname or the title of the manuscript in full or abbreviated form. This helps identify a page that may become separated from the whole manuscript. The first page does not have to be numbered.

Although not essential, the approximate number of words in the manuscript may be typed in the corner of the first page opposite the author's name and address. The figure should be *only approximate*, and may be estimated to the nearest round number by multiplying the average number of words in a line by the average number of lines on a page, and then by multiplying that answer by the number of manuscript pages.

After the manuscript has been typed, the author should read it over carefully, not only for sense and factual errors, but also for typing, spelling, and grammatical errors. If a page has only one or two errors, the corrections may be made neatly in ink by crossing out the whole word and writing it correctly in the space immediately above. Or an omitted word or short phrase may be inserted in the space above, with a slant line or caret to indicate the exact place for the insertion. If lengthy insertions are necessary, the entire page (or sometimes several pages) should be retyped.

Since editors assume factual accuracy as well as correct spelling, punctuation, capitalization, and word usage, a final check of these "mechanics" of writing is essential before you send out your manuscript. Here are a few check points:

Enclose all direct quotations in quotation marks. Quotations within quoted material are indicated by single quotes. All quoted material must appear exactly as originally printed. Whether you are quoting the Bible, Shakespeare, a few lines from a poem that you remember (song lyrics, however brief, *always* require permission for quotation), recheck these before you send your manuscript out; do not rely on your memory.

When quoting material of more than three lines, indent the passage quoted, omit quotation marks except to indicate quoted dialogue, and type it single space. (If you wish to quote copyright material of more than a few words, it is advisable to obtain permission of the copyright owner.)

Dialogue is enclosed in quotation marks, with the words of each new speaker beginning a new paragraph.

Italics to indicate emphasis should be used sparingly for maximum effect, but there are some "rules" for italicizing. Book and play titles names of magazines and newspapers, and foreign words are generally italicized. (Titles of short stories, essays, poems, and other parts of books or longer works are enclosed in quotation marks.)

The pages of short manuscripts should be fastened with a paper clip. Do not pin, tie, bind, or staple the pages together in any other way. The pages of a book manuscript should be left loose and mailed in a box.

Book manuscripts

Follow general rules for manuscript preparation, and also include a title page (not required for short manuscripts) on which the title is typed in capital letters about half-way down the page. On the line immediately below type the word "By" and your name. The entire manuscript should be numbered consecutively from the first page to the last. (Do not number the pages of the individual chapters separately.) Begin each new chapter on a new page, typing the chapter number and chapter title (if any) about three inches from the top. Leave two or three spaces and then proceed with the text.

Sometimes the question of illustrations arises, especially in writing children's books. Most publishers assign artists after the manuscript is accepted. If the author has collaborated with an artist, then, of course, the text and sample illustrations may be submitted together. Similarly, if the author is also the artist, it is not advisable to submit *complete,* original illustrations, unless the publishers request you to do so.

SHORT ITEMS

Type poetry double-spaced, leaving three or four spaces between stanzas. Begin each new poem—no matter what its length—on a separate page, putting your name and address at the top right of each.

Fillers are also typed double-spaced, one to a page, with your name and address on each, and for fact fillers the source should be indicated. Because of the volume of manuscripts received, many magazines do not acknowledge or return fillers, but the author may assume that if he has not heard in three months, he may offer it for sale again.

Greeting card publishers sometimes have special specifications for the submission of verses or ideas, i.e., ideas should be submitted on 3 × 5 cards, one idea to a card, etc. Requirements for art work also vary greatly, and prospective contributors should check directly with the companies and should study manuscript market lists.

PLAY AND TELEVISION SCRIPTS

In typing dramatic material for the stage or for television, you must follow a special format. Specifications and illustrations for television scripts may be found in Chapter 93, "Television Writing Today." There are two commonly used styles in typing plays: (a) Type the names of the characters in capital letters at the left margin, followed by the dialogue in upper and lower case; (b) Type names of characters in capital letters at center of page. On next line, begin the speech at the left margin, in upper and lower case.

FOOTNOTES

Research publications and other scholarly works may require footnotes and bibliographies, and in typing these manuscripts, writers should follow standard accepted forms as given in the widely accepted reference manual, *A Manual of Style* (University of Chicago Press).

If the manuscript requires footnotes, type these in the body of the manuscript, immediately after the line to which the note refers, using a raised number or a symbol such as an asterisk in the text and correspondingly at the beginning of the footnote. Footnotes more than one line long should be typed single-space and set off from the text by a rule above and below it.

QUERY LETTERS

Before you submit a complete nonfiction manuscript—either article or book length—it is advisable to send a brief query letter to the editor describing the proposed article or book. The letter should also include information about the author's special qualifications for dealing with the particular subject, and for a book-length manuscript, an outline of the book and a sample chapter may be included. Otherwise, no covering letter is necessary when submitting a manuscript, though the writer may include a brief note simply indicating that the manuscript is submitted for possible publication. No amount of self-praise will bring about a sale if the manuscript is unsuitable, nor will the absence of a letter discourage an editor from accepting it. If you are submitting a manuscript following a positive response to your query letter, you may indicate this fact in a brief note accompanying it. For book manuscripts, a letter is often sent separately, stating that the manuscript has been mailed under separate cover.

REPORTS ON MANUSCRIPTS

Monthly or weekly magazines, as well as large publishing houses, may take several weeks—and often longer—to read and report on manuscripts. For bi-monthlies, quarterlies, some literary magazines, and small publishing houses with limited editorial staffs, two or more months may elapse before reports are made to authors.

If you have had no report on a manuscript after a reasonable time —six to eight weeks for a large company—you may write a brief, courteous letter inquiring about the status of your manuscript.

To save time and postage—and to approach the business of marketing manuscripts in a professional way—it is essential for free-lance writers to study editorial requirements of various publications as described in market lists and by examining the publications themselves. Read several issues of any magazine to which you may wish to submit material. Familiarize yourself with the types of books published by various publishers by browsing in a library or bookshop, and by watching their advertising.

It is common practice to submit a manuscript to only one publisher at a time. Although this may seem unfair and time-consuming, it is the only way to avoid the difficulties that may arise if, for example, two editors wish to buy the same manuscript. The same practice also applies to writing query letters—send only *one at a time*.

When submitting a manuscript, address it to the editor by name, if you know it, or to the editor of the particular part of the magazine— Fiction Editor, Articles Editor, Features Editor, etc., also by name, if possible, otherwise by title. The same is true for book publishers: Address your manuscript to the editor in charge of the particular division for which your book is suited: Juvenile Editor, Religious Editor, etc.

RIGHTS

As a rule, a writer submitting a manuscript to a magazine should not stipulate on his manuscript or in an accompanying letter what rights he is offering. Although most magazines buy only "First North American Serial Rights," some publications buy *all* rights as a matter of policy. It is therefore best to discuss what rights the magazine is interested in—and what limitations the writer may wish to set— *after* a manuscript is accepted.

First North American serial rights means that a magazine is buying the exclusive right to publish the material for the first time and only once. Purchase of *second serial rights* gives the magazine the right to reprint the material once after its original publication— twice in all. Some magazines buy *all periodical rights,* that is, the exclusive right to print and reprint the material here and abroad in magazine form. Generally, magazines buy only periodical rights, and all further rights—for television, motion pictures, book use, etc., belong to the author.

Books are handled quite differently, and if your book manuscript is accepted, you will receive a contract from the publishers outlining carefully the rights they are buying and those the author retains. These contracts are fairly standard throughout the industry, and writers may have confidence in the good faith of any reputable publishing company. When a writer has established an important reputation and achieved prestige and success, he may (directly or through his agent) be justified in negotiating with the publishers for higher royalties and other more liberal terms which he may want (and will often be able to arrange with the book or magazine publishers).

MAILING

Short manuscripts should be mailed flat in Manila envelopes. If the manuscript is only 3 or 4 pages in length, it may be folded twice, and sent in an ordinary long (#10) envelope. Book manuscripts should be sent loose, in a cardboard box, such as the kind typing paper comes in.

Under present postal regulations, manuscripts for books and periodicals may be mailed at the regular first-class mail rate, or, less expensively, by the Special Fourth Class Rate for Manuscripts; ask at your Post Office for this rate. Manuscripts or boxes sent by this rate must be marked Special Fourth Class Rate—Manuscript. If you wish to include a letter with a manuscript sent via the Special Fourth Class Rate, you may do so, provided you note on the outside of the box or envelope that first-class material is enclosed, and that you place additional first-class postage on the package.

Manuscripts sent at the Special Fourth Class Rate may also be insured at the post office.

A stamped self-addressed return envelope should always be enclosed when a manuscript is submitted to a publisher, in case the manuscript is rejected. If you are using the Special Fourth Class Rate, be sure that the return envelope is marked Special Fourth Class Rate—Manuscript.

PART IV

THE WRITER'S MARKETS

Where to Sell

This section of THE WRITER'S HANDBOOK is devoted to manuscript market information that will help writers sell their manuscripts. All information concerning the needs and requirements of markets comes directly from the editors of the periodicals, publishing companies, and television programs listed.

Although we have taken every precaution to have the information accurate, there will undoubtedly be some changes in the requirements listed as the needs of editors change from time to time. Therefore writers are advised to study recent issues of a publication before submitting any manuscripts to it. New magazines and television programs should always be checked carefully, since frequent changes occur in these markets.

FICTION MARKETS

The following list is divided into three categories: general magazines; college, literary, and little magazines; and religious and denominational magazines. Markets for popular or pulp fiction (men's adventure fiction, romance and confession stories, science fiction, true detective, mysteries, etc.) are listed under *The Popular Market*. Juvenile fiction markets are listed under *Juvenile, Teen-Age and Young Adult Magazines,* and markets for book-length juvenile and adult fiction are listed under *Book Publishers.*

GENERAL MAGAZINES

ADAM—8060 Melrose Ave., Los Angeles, Calif. 90046.
Fiction with male-female relationships, and modern slice-of-life stories. Also well-written science fiction, westerns, horror stories, satire. Length, 1,000 to 5,000 words. Pays from $50 for short-shorts to $250 for longer material. Reports in three to six weeks.

ALFRED HITCHCOCK'S MYSTERY MAGAZINE—784 U.S. 1, Suite 6, North Palm Beach, Fla. 33408. Ernest M. Hutter, Editor.
Uses original, well-written, well-plotted and plausible mystery, crime and suspense stories of from 1,000 to 10,000 words, including some foreign intrigue and supernaturalism. No cheap sensationalism of any sort or actual crimes. Pays 3¢ to 5¢ a word, on acceptance.

ALL OUTDOORS MAGAZINE—601 West Chestnut St., Denison, Tex. 75020.
Fiction, 1,500 to 2,500 words, on outdoor activities and adventures. Payment varies, is after publication. Enclose stamped, self-addressed envelope with all manuscripts.

THE AMERICAN-SCANDINAVIAN REVIEW—127 East 73rd St., New York, N. Y. 10021. Erik J. Friis, Editor.
Short stories, 2,000 to 3,000 words, about Scandinavia. Photos and drawings. Pays $20 to $50.

ARGOSY—420 Lexington Ave., New York, N. Y. 10017.
No short fiction; book condensations through publishers only.

THE ATLANTIC—8 Arlington St., Boston, Mass. 02116. Robert Manning, Editor.
One or two short stories an issue. High literary standard, considerable variety. Occasional stories up to 14,000 words. Pays on acceptance.

AUSTIN—Austin Chamber of Commerce, Box 1967, Austin, Tex. 78767. George Seagert, Editor.
Occasionally uses fiction, 800 to 1,000 words on business or community oriented subjects. Negotiable rates.

BEST FOR MEN—Kimtex Corp., 1133 Broadway, New York, N. Y. 10010.
Entertaining fiction, to 2,500 words; also short-shorts to 800 words. Man-woman interest. Pays $20 to $100 for original fiction. Same address and requirements for *Rascal* and *Men's Digest*.

BLACK WORLD—820 South Michigan Ave., Chicago, Ill. 60616. Hoyt W. Fuller, Managing Editor.
Short stories, up to 3,900 words, dealing with black life. Humorous stories particularly welcome. Pays $75 to $100, on publication.

BOYS' LIFE—North Brunswick, N. J. 08902. Stan Pashko, Fiction Editor.
Short stories and novellas aimed at boys, aged 10-17. Preferred length is 3,500 to 4,500 words. Pays $400 and up.

BROADSIDE—21322 Lassen St., Chatsworth, Calif. 91311. Arthur S. Long, Editor.
Strongly plotted fiction, appealing to men, revolving around sharp male-female relationships, eroticism and physical conflict, with either adventurous action or sophisticated story line. Preferred length: 2,000 to 3,000 words. Pays $75 minimum. Also welcomes short humor, to 2,000 words. Reports in two weeks.

CAT FANCY—11760 Sorrento Valley Rd., San Diego, Calif. 92121. Leslie S. Smith, Editor.
Uses fiction, not necessarily about cats, though a cat should have some part in the story. "Avoid 'cute' stories told by a cat." Length: to 1,500 words. Pays 3¢ a word, on publication.

CATS MAGAZINE—P.O. Box 4106, Pittsburgh, Pa. 15202. Jean Laux, Editor.
Occasionally uses fiction dealing with cats and cat owners, to 1,500 words. "No fiction by feline writers." Pays 2¢ a word, on publication.

CAVALIER—236 East 46th St., New York, N. Y. 10017.
Quality fiction to 4,000 words, for young male readership with sophisticated and informed tastes. Pays up to $300. Query first.

CHARLIE CHAN MYSTERY MAGAZINE—See *Mike Shayne Mystery Magazine*.

CHATELAINE—481 University Ave., Toronto 2, Ont., Canada. Doris Anderson, Editor; Almeda Glassey, Fiction Editor.
Fiction with women interest—love, adventure, mystery. Short stories up to 5,000 words. Pays $400 and up for short stories.

CO-ED—Scholastic Magazines, 50 West 44th St., New York, N. Y. 10036.
Stories up to 5,000 words for girls 14 to 18, dealing with realistic problems of contemporary teen-agers: home, family, love, personal relationships, boy-girl relationships. Humor is welcome. Prefers fall, winter, and spring rather than summer settings. Pays good rates, on acceptance. Address Editor, Manuscript Dept.

COMMENTARY—165 East 56th St., New York, N. Y. 10022. Norman Podhoretz, Editor.
Occasional fiction of literary excellence; may have concrete social reference or Jewish interest. Pays about 3½¢ a word.

THE COMPASS—Mobil Sales and Supply Corp., 150 East 42nd St., New York, N. Y. 10017. K. V. W. Lawrence, Editor.
Short stories and articles on the sea and deep sea trade, to 3,500 words. Pays up to $250. Overstocked until mid-1974. Query.

COSMOPOLITAN—224 West 57th St., New York, N. Y. 10020. Helen Gurley Brown, Editor; Junius Adams, Fiction Editor.
Magazine aimed at sophisticated young career women. Uses well-plotted, brightly entertaining stories, 3,000 to 6,000 words, and mystery or suspense novels, 25,000 words. Pays $600 and up for short stories, by arrangement for longer fiction.

DELL CROSSWORD PUZZLES—1 Dag Hammarskjold Plaza, New York, N. Y. 10017. Kathleen Rafferty, Editor.

Short mysteries, 500 words, with clues given so that solver can figure out the solution through general knowledge. Pays $25, on acceptance. Logic problems with solutions; pays $20 each.

DOG FANCY—11760 Sorrento Valley Rd., San Diego, Calif. 92121.
Welcomes fiction, but does not want "cute" stories told by dogs. Pays 3¢ per printed word, upon publication.

THE ELKS MAGAZINE—425 West Diversey Parkway, Chicago, Ill. 60614.
Occasional short, humorous fiction.

ELLERY QUEEN'S MYSTERY MAGAZINE—229 Park Ave. South, New York, N. Y. 10003. Ellery Queen, Editor; Eleanor Sullivan, Managing Editor.
Detective, crime, and mystery stories of all types, preferably between 4,000 and 6,000 words. Quality of writing and originality stressed. Pays 3¢ to 8¢ a word.

ESQUIRE—488 Madison Ave., New York, N. Y. 10022. Gordon Lish, Fiction Editor.
Fiction, any length. Literary excellence only criterion. Unsolicited fiction to Julie Schwartz, Assistant Fiction Editor. Pays from $750 up.

EXPLORING—Boy Scouts of America, North Brunswick, N. J. 08902. Jack Haring, Editor.
For ages 15 to 20. Short stories, up to 2,500 words. Pays $300 to $500 on acceptance. Query.

FAMILY CIRCLE—488 Madison Ave., New York, N. Y. 10022.
Short stories of interest to women, 2,500 to 4,000 words, and short-shorts. Pays on acceptance.

FIELD & STREAM—383 Madison Ave., New York, N. Y. 10017.
Rarely uses fiction, but it should be related to outdoor topics. Pays 20¢ a word and up, on acceptance.

FLING—161 East Erie St., Chicago Ill. 60611. Arv Miller, Editor and Publisher.
Uses two types of fiction directed to adult male readers: Serious stories examining off-beat and far-out relationships between the sexes, from 3,000 to 4,000 words; up-beat, humorous or satirical stories, 2,000 to 3,000 words. Sharp, contemporary dialogue important. Pays from $100 to $250. Read magazine before submitting.

FOR MEN ONLY—575 Madison Ave., New York, N. Y. 10022. Ivan Prasker, Editorial Director.
Fiction appealing to men—humor, adventure, rugged action, etc.—with strong sex angle preferred, 3,000 to 5,000 words. Pays up to $300, on acceptance.

GIRLTALK—380 Madison Ave., New York, N. Y. 10017.
In the market for fiction, of interest to women, 2,000 words or less. Pays varying rates.

GLAMOUR—350 Madison Ave., New York, N. Y. 10017.
Occasional quality fiction. Pays $750.

GOLF DIGEST—297 Westport Ave., Norwalk, Conn. 06856. Nick Seitz, Editor.
Occasionally uses unusual or humorous stories about golf, up to 2,000 words. Also golf "fables," 750 to 1,000 words. Pays from 15¢ per published word.

GOOD HOUSEKEEPING—595 Eighth Ave., New York, N. Y. 10019. Wade H. Nichols, Editor; Naome Lewis, Fiction Editor.
Short stories, 2,000 to 5,000 words, on any modern theme, with clear element of identification for women; novelettes to 30,000 words; two- and three-part serials, usually condensed from forthcoming books. Pays top rates, on acceptance.

KNIGHT—8060 Melrose Ave., Los Angeles, Calif. 90046.
Needs fiction for adult males; humorous and controversial pieces also used. Pays $75 to $175 for short stories, 1,500 to 4,500 words only.

LADIES' HOME JOURNAL—641 Lexington Ave., New York, N. Y. 10022.
Limited market. "We publish only first-rate fiction with which our readers can identify. Books, articles, and short stories are usually bought through recognized literary agents."

McCALL'S—230 Park Ave., New York, N. Y. 10017. Helen DelMonte, Fiction Editor.
Strong, memorable fiction that has depth, will make reader think, feel and respond. Length is flexible; short stories average 3,000 words, novel excerpts 10,000 words, novel condensations 15,000 words. Pays top rates.

MADEMOISELLE—350 Madison Ave., New York, N. Y. 10017. Ellen A. Stoianoff, Fiction and Poetry Editor.
Non-formula short stories; accent on literary quality, 2,500 to 6,500 words. Pays $300, on acceptance.

MAN TO MAN—280 Madison Ave., New York, N. Y. 10016. Everett Meyers, Editor.
Strong, imaginative stories, 1,500 to 5,000 words, in a modern mood, including man-woman relationships. No hackneyed, dull writing. Pays $75 and up, on publication. Same address and requirements for *Mr. Magazine* and *Sir!*

MEN'S DIGEST—See *Best for Men.*

MIDSTREAM: A MONTHLY JEWISH REVIEW—515 Park Ave., New York, N. Y. 10022. Shlomo Katz, Editor.
Fiction of Jewish or general social and political interest, up to 8,000 words. Pays 4¢ a word, on acceptance.

MIKE SHAYNE MYSTERY MAGAZINE—8230 Beverly Blvd., Los Angeles, Calif. 90048. Cylvia Kleinman, Editor.
Good detective and mystery stories of all types: 1,500-word short stories to 12,000-word novelettes. Pays 1¢ a word and up, on acceptance. Same address and requirements for *Charlie Chan Mystery Magazine.*

MR. MAGAZINE—See *Man to Man.*

MODERN MATURITY—215 Long Beach Blvd., Long Beach, Calif. 90802. Hubert Pryor, Editor.
Occasionally uses short stories that will appeal to older readers. Pays from $50 to $500, on acceptance.

MS. MAGAZINE—370 Lexington Ave., New York, N. Y. 10017. Suzanne Levine, Managing Editor.
Wants fiction and poetry for a general audience, including men and women who are curious about the women's liberation movement. Payment rates are competitive.

THE NEW INGENUE—635 Madison Ave., New York, N. Y. 10022.
Adult fiction for teen-agers, dealing with their problems and interests. Pays $175 to $500, on acceptance.

THE NEW YORKER—25 West 43rd St., New York, N. Y. 10036.
Short stories, 1,000 to 6,000 words. Humor and satire. Pays on acceptance.

OUI—919 North Michigan Ave., Chicago, Ill. 60611.
Short stories, 2,500 to 3,000 words. Pays $500 and up.

THE PTA MAGAZINE—700 North Rush St., Chicago, Ill. 60611. Donal Mahoney, Editor.
Quality fiction, to interest parents. No tales with a "moral." Length: 1,800 words. Pays $100 to $150.

PEN—444 Sherman St., Denver, Colo. 80203. Jean Blair Ryan, Editor.

Short, general, family-type fiction to 2,000 words. Payment 3¢ per word, on acceptance.

PENTHOUSE—909 Third Ave., New York, N. Y. 10036.
Wants good, sophisticated and sexy fiction, from 4,000 to 6,000 words. Reports in about a month on unsolicited manuscripts. Payment is 10¢ a word.

PLAYBOY—HMH Publishing Co., 919 North Michigan, Chicago, Ill. 60611. Hugh M. Hefner, Editor and Publisher, Robie MacCauley, Fiction Editor.
Sophisticated, well-constructed fiction, 1,000 to 10,000 words. Strong plots and colorful writing important. Humorous fiction always welcome. Payment: $3,000 for lead stories; $2,000 standard; $1,000 for short-shorts; also $1,000 bonus for the best story of the year. All payment on acceptance.

PLAYERS—8060 Melrose Ave., Los Angeles, Calif. 90046.
Fiction, 2,000 to 6,000 words, humor, satire, for black men. Pays 5¢ to 6¢ a word, on publication.

PLAYGIRL—1801 Century Park East, Suite 2300, Century City, Los Angeles, Calif. 90067. Marin Scott Milam, Editor.
Fiction for aware, contemporary female audience, 1,000 to 7,500 words. Pays from $300, after acceptance.

RASCAL—See *Best for Men.*

REDBOOK—230 Park Ave., New York, N. Y. 10017. Mrs. Neal G. Thorpe, Fiction Editor.
Fiction directed to young adults: basic themes of love, marriage, young parenthood preferred, but buys some high quality off-beat stories. Pays on acceptance from $850 for short-shorts (1,500 to 1,800 words), $1,000 for short stories (6,000 words), and $6,000 for novels. Takes up to six weeks to read and report on manuscripts.

ROGUE—Captain Publishing Co., Inc., 95 Madison Ave., New York, N. Y. 10016. Christopher Watson, Editor.
Fiction: 1,500 to 2,500 words; tastefully erotic. Cartoons always in demand; sexy.

THE SATURDAY EVENING POST—1100 Waterway Blvd., Indianapolis, Ind. 46202. Frederic A. Birmingham, Managing Editor.
Interested in structured stories—short-shorts of 1,000 words, as well as longer stories of 2,500 words. Looking for pure narration at its dramatic best; no stream-of-consciousness writing. Payment will be determined by quality and length.

SCHOLASTIC SCOPE—Scholastic Magazines, 50 West 44th St., New York, N. Y. 10036.
For ages 15 to 18, with 4th to 6th grade reading level. Stories of 500 to 1,000 words and plays up to 3,000 words, dealing with the interests of today's students, relationships between people (interracial, adult-teen-age, employer-employee, etc.) in family, job, school situations. Strive for honesty, directness, realism, and action. Pays good rates, on acceptance.

SCHOLASTIC VOICE—Scholastic Magazines, 50 West 44th St., New York, N. Y. 10036.
For ages 14 to 17. Uses stories and plays, 1,500 to 3,000 words, strong on plot and characterization and dealing with problems of interest to teen-agers. Authors should steer clear of teen-age stereotypes. Good subjects are boy-girl situations (avoid formula stories about puppy love), school situations, adventure, mystery, science fiction, family situations, sports. Problems that confront teen-agers, like finding one's own identity, setting standards of conduct, reconciling ideals and reality, bridging the generation gap, etc., are good. Pays good rates, on acceptance. Addess Editor of Manuscript Dept.

SEVENTEEN—320 Park Ave., New York, N. Y. 10022. Babette Rosmond, Fiction Editor.
Well-written fiction, adult in its techniques and conception, but limited to situations involving adolescent experiences. Pays good rates, on acceptance.

SIR!—See *Man to Man.*

STAG—575 Madison Ave., New York, N. Y. 10022. Noah Sarlat, Editor.
Fiction appealing to men, up to 5,000 words. Emphasis on adventure, crime. Strong sex element. Pays up to $300, on acceptance.

SUNSHINE MAGAZINE—Litchfield, Ill. 62506.
Wants wholesome, well-written, short stories with clearly defined plots, 1,250 word maximum. Each story should have a purpose but the "moral" or lesson should be well-concealed in the plot development. Payment varies and is on acceptance.

SURFER MAGAZINE—Box 1028, Dana Point, Calif. 92629. Drew Kampion, Editor.
Fiction, 1,000 to 2,500 words, on anything with a surfing theme. Good, light, well-plotted stories are needed. Pays 4¢ a word and up, on publication.

SWANK—1560 Broadway, New York, N. Y. 10036.
Fiction, about 2,500 words, on any theme, but sex, science fiction and man-woman relationships preferred. Pays $100 to $200.

'TEEN—8490 Sunset Blvd., Los Angeles, Calif. 90069.
Short fiction, 2,000 to 4,000 words, or 6,000-word two-part serials. Mysteries, travel or adventure, humor, romance, contemporary teen life, social problems, drama are all possible subjects. Pays $150 and up, on acceptance.

TODAYS FAMILY MAGAZINE—P.O. Box 31467, Dallas, Tex. 75231. Sherry Gish, Editor.
Short stories, to 3,000 words, aimed at family fun. Pays up to $50, on publication. Query, enclosing stamped self-addressed envelope.

TODAY'S SECRETARY—1221 Ave. of the Americas, New York, N. Y. 10020.
Short lively fiction, 500 to 1,300 words, dealing with a secretary's business or private life. Wholesome subjects and settings. Pays $25, on acceptance.

VERTEX—8060 Melrose Ave., Los Angeles, Calif. 90046.
Quality science fiction, 3,000 to 6,500 words. Pays $125 to $600, after acceptance. Overstocked at present.

VOGUE—420 Lexington Ave., New York, N. Y. 10017. Grace Mirabella, Editor.
Rarely uses fiction and then only of high literary quality. Preferred length: about 2,000 words. Pays on acceptance. Send manuscripts to Kate Lloyd.

WEIGHT WATCHERS MAGAZINE—635 Madison Ave., New York, N. Y. 10022.
Matty Simmons, Editor; Edythe Tomkinson, Features Editor.
Uses family-oriented fiction, from short-shorts to longer stories, 2,500 words maximum, appealing to both men and women. Also occasional mysteries and sci-fi. Pays $75 to $300, on acceptance.

WOMAN'S DAY—1515 Broadway, New York, N. Y. 10036.
Quality fiction, both humorous and serious, to interest women. Length, 1,500 to 3,000 words. Pays top rates, on acceptance.

WOODMEN OF THE WORLD MAGAZINE—1700 Farnam St., Omaha, Nebr. 68102.
Leland A. Larson, Editor.
Fiction slanted for a family magazine. Pays 2¢ a word, on acceptance.

YANKEE—Dublin, N. H. 03444. Judson Hale, Editor.
Fiction about New England characters or locale, not over 2,500 words. Pays $300
to $500.

ZANE GREY WESTERN MAGAZINE—8230 Beverly Blvd., Los Angeles, Calif.
90048. Cylvia Kleinman, Editor.
Short stories, 2,000 words. Pays 1¢ a word and up, on acceptance.

COLLEGE, LITERARY AND LITTLE MAGAZINES

THE AMERICAN REVIEW (formerly *New American Review*)—Bantam Books,
666 Fifth Ave., New York, N. Y. 10019. Theodore Solotaroff, Editor.
Looking for contemporary fiction with fresh, articulate writing and thought. High
quality is the only restriction. Buys first rights only. Manuscripts must be accompanied by stamped return envelope.

THE ANTIGONISH REVIEW—Dept. of English, St. Francis Xavier University,
Antigonish, N. S., Canada. R. J. MacSween, Editor.
Wants short stories, 1,800 to 2,500 words.

ANTIOCH REVIEW—The Antioch Press, Yellow Springs, Ohio 45387. Lawrence
Grauman, Jr., Editor; Nolan Miller, Fiction Editor.
Uses one or two short stories per issue, 2,000 to 10,000 words in length. Pays $8
per published page, on publication.

ARIZONA QUARTERLY—University of Arizona, Tucson, Ariz. 85721. Albert F.
Gegenheimer, Editor.
Fiction up to 3,500 words. No payment. Annual awards.

ARTS IN SOCIETY—University Extension, University of Wisconsin, 610 Langdon
St., Madison, Wis. 53706.
Fiction, 2,500 to 3,500 words, in the following categories: teaching and learning
of the arts; aesthetics and philosophy; social analysis; and examples of creative
expression in media. Pays honorarium at publication. Query before submitting
manuscripts.

ASIA CALLING—Pan Pacific Centers, Inc., 845 Via de la Paz, Pacific Palisades, Calif.
90272. Mary Ellen Hawk Saunders, Editor.
Adult fiction, 500 to 3,000 words, from and about the Orient—especially China,
Korea, India and Japan. No payment.

BALL STATE UNIVERSITY FORUM—Ball State University, Muncie, Ind. 47306.
Merrill Rippy and Frances Mayhew Rippy, Editors.
Short stories, 500 to 3,000 words. Pays in copies.

BEYOND BAROQUE—1639 West Washington Blvd., Venice, Calif. 90291.
Experimental fiction, to 5,000 words.

THE BLACK COLLEGIAN—3217 Melpomene Ave., New Orleans, La. 70125. N. R.
Davidson, Editor.
Uses some fiction and poetry, relating to the conditions or experiences of black
students. Pays on publication.

BLACK CREATION—Institute of Afro-American Affairs, 10 Washington Pl., Fifth
Floor, New York University, New York, N. Y. 10003.
Short stories, up to 5,000 words. No payment.

BLACK MARIA: WOMEN SPEAK—Box 230, River Forest, Ill. 60305.
Pro-women short stories, any length. Pays in copies.

BOSTON UNIVERSITY JOURNAL—P.O. Box 357, B.U. Station, Boston, Mass.
02115.
Short stories, 2,500 to 6,000 words. Pays in copies.

THE CARLETON MISCELLANY—Carleton College, Northfield, Minn. 55057. Wayne
Carver, Editor.
Literary short stories. Pays on publication.

THE CAROLINA QUARTERLY—Box 1117, Chapel Hill, N. C. 27514. Bruce M.
Firestone, Editor.
Looking for young writers doing controlled experimental writing. Fiction limited
to about 6,000 to 7,000 words. Pays $5 per printed page. Enclose stamped self-
addressed envelope.

THE CHICAGO REVIEW—University of Chicago, Chicago, Ill. 60637. Alexander
Besher, Editor.
Interested in well-written fiction. No length limit.

CIMARRON REVIEW—Oklahoma State University, Stillwater, Okla. 74074. Jeanne
Adams Wray, Managing Editor.
Fiction of high quality dealing with contemporary life. Sample copy on request
for $1. No payment.

THE COLORADO QUARTERLY—Hellems 124, University of Colorado, Boulder,
Colo. 80302. Paul Carter, Editor.
Quality fiction, 2,000 to 4,000 words. Pays up to $20, on acceptance.

CONFRONTATION—English Dept., Long Island University, Brooklyn, N.Y., 11201.
Martin Tucker, Editor.
High-quality fiction of all types, 5 to 20 pages in length. Pays on publication. Re-
ports in six weeks.

CONTEMPORA—P.O. Box 673, Atlanta, Ga. 30301. Paula G. Putney, Editor.
Fiction, up to 3,500 words. Payment made on publication.

DASEIN—G.P.O. Box 2121, New York, N. Y. 10001. Percy Johnston, Editor.
Fiction of high quality, 2,000 to 3,000 words. No payment.

THE DEKALB LITERARY ARTS JOURNAL—DeKalb College, 555 Indian Creek
Dr., Clarkston, Ga. 30021.
Fiction of any length. Pays in copies.

DESCANT—Texas Christian University, T. C. U. Sta., Fort Worth, Tex. 76129. Betsy
Colquitt, Editor.
Fiction, to 7,000 words, of literary quality. No payment.

EPOCH—245 Goldwin Smith Hall, Cornell University, Ithaca, N. Y. 14850.
High literary standards. Payment in copies.

EVENT—Dept. of English, Douglas College, 426 Columbia St., New Westminster, B.C.,
Canada. David Evanier, Editor.
Novellas, short stories and excerpts from novels. Pays in copies.

EVERGREEN REVIEW—53 East 11th St., New York, N. Y. 10003. Barney Rosset,
Editor.
Contemporary high-quality fiction and nonfiction of varying lengths. Pays $45 a
page, on publication. Query.

THE FALCON—Belknap Hall, Mansfield State College, Mansfield, Pa. 16933.
Uses four or five short stories or portions of novels per issue, 2,000 to 6,000 words.
Payment is in contributors' copies, on publication.

FICTION—193 Beacon St., Boston, Mass. 02116. Vincent McCaffrey, Editor.
Fiction, drama, poetry, any length. Payment varies.

FICTION—Box 112, Stuyvesant St., New York, N. Y. 10009. Mark J. Mirsky, Editor.
Wants high-quality, serious fiction.

FICTION INTERNATIONAL—Dept. of English, St. Lawrence University, Canton,
N. Y. 13617. Joe David Bellamy, Editor-in-Chief.
Especially receptive to innovative forms or rich personal styles, originality and
the ability to create living characters. No length limitations. Pays $5 to $100.

THE FIDDLEHEAD—Dept. of English, University of New Brunswick, Fredericton,
N. B., Canada.
High quality fiction, 2,500 words, verse, drama. Pays about $5 per published page,
upon publication.

FORUM—University of Houston, Houston, Tex. 77004.
Occasional literary short stories of moderate length. No payment.

FOUR QUARTERS—LaSalle College, Philadelphia, Pa. 19141. John Keenan, Editor.
Character-centered stories that offer some revelation. No slicks. Pays up to $25.

THE GEORGIA REVIEW—University of Georgia, Athens, Ga. 30601. James B. Colvert, Editor.
Short fiction. Pays on publication.

GREEN RIVER REVIEW—Box 812, Owensboro, Ky. 42301. Raymond Tyner and
Emil Ahnell, Editors.
Wants to see short stories about 3,000 words in length. Payment is in copies.

THE GREENFIELD REVIEW—Greenfield Centre, N. Y. 12833. Joseph Bruchac III,
Editor.
A new literary quarterly which uses some very short fiction. Payment is in copies.

HUDSON REVIEW—65 East 55th St., New York, N. Y. 10022. Frederick Morgan,
Editor.
Quality fiction up to 10,000 words. Pays 2½¢ a word.

THE IOWA REVIEW—EPB 453, The University of Iowa, Iowa City, Ia. 52240.
Short stories, poems, prose poems. Pays $1 a line for poetry, $10 per page for
fiction on publication.

KANSAS QUARTERLY—Dept. of English, Kansas State University, Manhattan, Kansas 66502.
Fiction. No payment.

KARAMU—English Dept., Eastern Illinois University, Charleston, Ill. 61920.
Interested in quality stories using traditional or experimental forms. Pays in copies.

THE LITERARY REVIEW—Fairleigh Dickinson University, Rutherford, N. J.
07070. Charles Angoff, Editor.
Fiction of outstanding literary quality. Pays in copies.

LITTLE MAGAZINE—P. O. Box 207, Cathedral Station, New York, N. Y. 10025.
Fiction to 5,000 words. Pays in copies.

MACABRE—26 Fowler St., New Haven, Conn. 06515. Joseph Payne Brennan, Editor.
Short-shorts and short stories up to 3,500 words. Weird, supernatural, and horror
stories. No science fiction or humor. Pays in copies.

THE MALAHAT REVIEW—University of Victoria, Victoria, B. C., Canada. Robin Skelton and John Peter, Editors.
High quality stories, 2,000 to 5,000 words. Interested in first English translations of work from Latin America, Continental Europe, and Asia. Pays $25 per 1,000 words. Also uses photos or drawings in groups of 12 to 16. Pays $10 each.

THE MASSACHUSETTS REVIEW—Memorial Hall, University of Massachusetts, Amherst, Mass. 01002. Robert G. Tucker, and John H. Hicks, Editors.
Short fiction. Modest payment.

MICHIGAN QUARTERLY REVIEW—3032 Rackham, University of Mich., Ann Arbor, Mich. 48104. Radcliffe Squires, Editor.
Fiction, to 5,000 words, of lively intellectual interest. Pays 2¢ a word, after acceptance.

MISSISSIPPI REVIEW—Southern Station, Box 37, Hattiesburg, Miss. 39401. Gordon Weaver, Editor.
High quality fiction, 5,000 words. Pays $3 per printed page, on publication.

MUNDUS ARTIUM: A JOURNAL FOR INTERNATIONAL LITERATURE AND THE ARTS—Department of English, Ellis Hall, Box 89, Ohio University, Athens, Ohio 45701. Rainer Schulte, Editor-in-Chief.
Fiction.

NEW ENGLAND REVIEW: A JOURNAL OF OPINION & CURRENT LITERATURE—P. O. Box 127, Cheshire, Conn. 06410. John DeStefano, Editor.
Fiction up to 3,000 words, emphasizing characterization rather than plot. Payment is in copies.

NEW LETTERS (formerly *The University Review*)—University of Missouri-Kansas City, Kansas City, Mo. 64110.
Extremely high quality; modest payment. No unsolicited manuscripts. Query, and include a self-addressed return postcard.

NEW ORLEANS REVIEW—Loyola University, New Orleans, La. 70118.
Short stories, poetry. Pays $50 for fiction, $10 for poems.

THE NEW RENAISSANCE—9 Heath Rd., Arlington, Mass. 02174.
Short stories, excerpts from novels. Pays up to $25 for fiction after publication. Manuscripts will not be returned unless accompanied by a stamped, self-addressed envelope.

THE NORTH AMERICAN REVIEW—University of Northern Iowa, Cedar Falls, Iowa 50613. Loree Rackstraw, Fiction Editor.
No length, content, or style limitations, but only highest quality fiction considered. Pays minimum of $10 per published page.

NORTHWEST REVIEW—University of Oregon, Eugene, Ore. 97403. Patrica L. Brooks, Managing Editor.
Highest quality literary fiction. Query first.

OCCIDENT—Eshleman Hall, University of California, Berkeley, Calif. 94720.
Fiction. Manuscripts without stamped return envelopes are not returned. Pays in copies.

THE OHIO REVIEW: A JOURNAL OF THE HUMANITIES—Ellis Hall, Ohio University, Athens, Ohio 45701.
Short stories (average length; 5,000 words). Pays in reprints and copies.

OYEZ!—Roosevelt University, 430 South Michigan Ave., Chicago, Ill. 60605.
Fiction to 20,000 words. Pays in copies.

PARIS REVIEW—45-39 171 Pl., Flushing, N. Y. 11358.
Quality fiction. Address manuscripts to Fiction Editor and enclose stamped, self-addressed envelope. Pays on publication.

PARTISAN REVIEW—Rutgers, 1 Richardson St., New Brunswick, N. J. 08903.
Fiction. Manuscripts held at least 3 months. Pays 1½¢ a word, on publication.

PERSPECTIVE—Washington University P. O., St. Louis, Mo. 63130. Jarvis Thurston and Mona Van Duyn, Editors.
Serious fiction, up to 10,000 words. No payment.

PRAIRIE SCHOONER—201 Andrews Hall, University of Nebraska, Lincoln, Nebr. 68508. Bernice Slote, Editor.
Short stories up to 5,000 words. Not confined to regional themes. Pays in copies.

PRISM INTERNATIONAL—c/o Creative Writing, Univ. of British Columbia, Vancouver 8, B. C., Canada.
Fiction, up to 5,000 words. Payment varies, is on publication.

PSYCHOLOGICAL PERSPECTIVES—595 East Colorado Blvd., Suite 503, Pasadena, Calif. 91101.
Fiction, 5,000 to 7,000 words, with a psychological framework. Pays in copies.

PYRAMID—32 Waverly St., Belmont, Mass. 02178, Ottone Riccio, Editor.
Experimental fiction. Pays in copies.

QUARTERLY REVIEW OF LITERATURE—26 Haslet Ave., Princeton, N. J. 08540. T. Weiss, Editor.
Short stories, 1,500 to 4,000 words, which may be either experimental or conventional, but must be of high literary quality. Study magazine before submitting manuscripts.

QUARTET—1119 Neal Pickett Dr., College Sta., Tex. 77840. Richard Hauer Costa, Editor.
Quality short stories, under 4,000 words. Both well-made and coherent experimental stories welcomed. Pays in copies.

RED CEDAR REVIEW—325 Morrill Hall, Michigan State University, East Lansing, Michigan 48823. Alan
Uses fiction, especially experimental fiction, and portions of novels, from 4,000 to 8,000 words. Pays in copies.

ROANOKE REVIEW—English Dept., Roanoke College, Salem, Va. 24153. Robert R. Walter, Editor.
Quality short stories, and poetry. Pays in copies.

THE SATIRE NEWSLETTER—State University of New York, Oneonta, N.Y. 13820.
Short fiction, up to 15 pages, either satirical or on satire. Pays in copies.

THE SECOND WAVE—Box 344, Cambridge A, Cambridge, Mass. 02139.
Fiction, to 10,000 words, with feminist slant. Pays in copies.

THE SENECA REVIEW—Box 115, Hobart and William Smith Colleges, Geneva, N. Y. 14456. James Crenner and Ira Sadoff, Editors.
Quality short stories. Pay is $25 per story, upon publication.

SEWANEE REVIEW—Sewanee, Tenn. 37375. Andrew Lytle, Editor.
Stories of highest literary quality, up to 8,000 words. Pays $10 to $12 a printed page.

SHANTIH—P.O. Box 125, Bay Ridge Station, Brooklyn, N. Y. 11220.
All types of fiction, especially experimental, to 3,000 words. Possible payment.

THE SMITH—5 Beekman St., New York, N. Y. 10038. Harry Smith, General Editor; Sidney Bernard, Roving Editor.
Fiction from 500 words to novella length. Tries to encourage new writers, but has very high standards. Modest payment, plus contributors' copies.

SNOWY EGRET—220 East College Ave., Westerville, Ohio 43081. William T. Hamilton, Fiction Editor.
Short stories or self-contained portions of novels, up to 10,000 words, dealing with man and nature. Pays $2 a page, on publication.

SOUTH CAROLINA REVIEW—c/o English Dept., Clemson University, Clemson, S. C. 29631.
Short stories of 3,000 to 5,000 words. Pays in copies.

SOUTH DAKOTA REVIEW—Box 111, University Exchange, Vermillion, S. D. 57069. John R. Milton, Editor.
Wants to see fiction, any length, with a regional emphasis (Western setting). Open to experimental fiction, as well. Payment is in copies.

SOUTHERN HUMANITIES REVIEW—Auburn Univ., Auburn, Ala. 36830.
Short stories, 3,500 to 5,000 words. Pays in copies.

SOUTHERN REVIEW—Drawer D, University Sta., Baton Rouge, La. 70803. Lewis P. Simpson and Donald E. Stanford, Co-Editors.
Fiction, 4,000 to 8,000 words, of lasting literary merit. Pays minimum of 3¢ a word, on acceptance. Stamped, self-addressed envelope required with all submissions. Allow 2 to 3 months for editorial decisions.

SOUTHWEST REVIEW—Southern Methodist University, Dallas, Texas 75222. Margaret L. Hartley, Editor.
Stories, 3,000 to 5,000 words, emphasizing characterization. Pays on publication.

STONECLOUD—Associated Students, Stanford University, Stanford, Calif. 94305.
Uses stories, up to eighteen pages. Pays in copies.

THE STUDENT—127 Ninth Ave. North, Nashville, Tenn. 37203. Norman Bowman, Editor.
Light features and short stories with collegiate flavor. Pays 2½¢ a word, on acceptance.

THE SUNSTONE REVIEW—P.O. Box 2321, Santa Fe, New Mexico 87501. Jody Ellis, Editor.
Short stories, not more than 1,500 words. Pays in copies.

TAMARACK REVIEW—Box 159, Postal Sta. K, Toronto 12, Ont., Canada.
Literary fiction, to 7,500 words, mainly by Canadian authors. Pays $10 per printed page on publication.

THREE SISTERS—Box 969, Georgetown University, Washington, D.C. 20007.
Fiction, any length. Pays in copies.

TRANSATLANTIC REVIEW—Box 3348, Grand Central Sta., New York, N. Y. 10017. Joseph McCrindle, Editor.
Short stories of literary quality, 2,000 to 5,000 words. Payment is arranged.

TRIQUARTERLY—University Hall 101, Northwestern Univ., Evanston, Ill. 60201.
Fiction for an international audience. No length or subject limits. Payment varies, is on publication.

THE UNIVERSITY OF DENVER QUARTERLY—University of Denver, Denver, Colo. 80210. Burton Feldman, Editor.
Literary fiction. Also considers book reviews. No length limit; queries welcome. Pays $5 per printed page for prose.

THE UNIVERSITY OF PORTLAND REVIEW—University of Portland, Portland, Oregon 97203. Thompson M. Faller, Editor.
Occasional fiction which makes a significant statement about the contemporary scene, 500 to 2,500 words. No payment.

THE UNIVERSITY OF WINDSOR REVIEW—Dept. of English, University of Windsor, Ontario, Canada. Eugene McNamara, Editor.
Uses a limited amount of fiction; preferred length is 10 to 15 pages. Payment is in copies and offprints. Send manuscripts with international reply coupons to The Editor.

UP FROM UNDER—339 Lafayette St., New York, N. Y. 10012.
Feminist magazine aimed at working-class women. Fiction, 1,000 to 10,000 words, about women's experiences, problems. No payment.

VERSUS—Box 4416, Station B, Vanderbilt University, Nashville, Tenn. 37235.
Quality short fiction. No payment.

THE VILLAGER—135 Midland Ave., Bronxville, N. Y. 10408.
Fiction, up to 2,000 words. No payment.

VIRGINIA QUARTERLY REVIEW—1 West Range, Charlottesville, Va. 22903.
Fiction of a high literary standard, 3,000 to 7,000 words.

WASCANA REVIEW—Wascana Parkway, c/o Regina Campus, Regina, Saskatchewan, Canada.
Short stories, 2,000 to 6,000 words. Pays $3 per page for fiction, after publication.

WEST COAST REVIEW—Simon Fraser University, Burnaby 2, B. C., Canada.
Fiction, especially experimental writing, from 1,000 to 3,000 words. Pays from $5 to $25, on acceptance.

WESTERN HUMANITIES REVIEW—OSH 316, University of Utah, Salt Lake City, Utah, 84112. Jack Garlington, Editor.
High-quality fiction of any length. Pays in copies and reprints.

YALE REVIEW—28 Hillhouse Ave., New Haven, Conn. 06507. Mary Price, Managing Editor.
Limited market for highest grade short stories.

RELIGIOUS AND DENOMINATIONAL MAGAZINES

BRIGADE LEADER—Christian Service Brigade, P. O. Box 150, Wheaton, Ill. 60187. Daniel C. Jessen, Editor.
Short stories to 1,200 words, with definite Christian (Protestant) emphasis, for men guiding boys in Brigade. Pays 3¢ a word and up.

CAMPUS LIFE—Box 419, Wheaton, Ill. 60187. Harold Myra, Editor.
For Christian teen-agers. Fiction, to 1,500 words. Pays 2¢ a word and up, on acceptance.

THE CANADIAN MESSENGER—833 Broadway Ave., Toronto M4K 2P9, Ont., Canada. Rev. F. J. Power, S. J., Editor.
Stories of 1,800 to 2,000 words, about daily life and problems of men and women. Catholic tone and humorous treatment preferred. Pays 2¢ a word, on acceptance. Address manuscripts to Mrs. M. Pujolas.

CATHOLIC RURAL LIFE—3801 Grand Ave., Des Moines, Iowa 50312. Msgr. J. G. Weber, Editor.
Short fiction with a spiritual emphasis and rural background. Pays $20 to $30 shortly after acceptance.

CATHOLIC WORLD—1865 Broadway, New York, N. Y. 10023.
Uses some short stories, 2,800 words, reflecting a religious concern about modern problems. Payment is $75, on publication. Query first.

THE CHRISTIAN HOME—201 Eighth Ave. South, Nashville, Tenn. 37203.
Methodist. Adult fiction, 2,000 to 3,500 words, with parent-family themes. Payment is on acceptance.

CHRISTIAN LIFE MAGAZINE—Gundersen Dr. and Schmale Rd., Wheaton, Ill. 60187. Robert Walker, Editor.
Fiction, 2,000 to 3,000 words, on significant problems faced by Christians today, solved by character action. Pays up to $150, on publication.

THE CHURCH HERALD—146 Division Ave. North, Grand Rapids, Mich. 49502.
Official magazine of the Reformed Church in America. Uses children's stories, 500 to 800 words, on themes of present-day interest with practical, moral, and religious teaching. Pays 2¢ a word.

COLUMBIA—Box 1670, New Haven, Conn. 06507. Elmer Von Feldt, Editor.
Fiction to 3,000 words, of general interest or Catholic interest, written from a thoroughly Christian viewpoint. Pays up to $300, on acceptance.

COMMENTARY—165 East 56th St., New York, N. Y. 10022. Norman Podhoretz, Editor.
Fiction of high intellectual quality, of Jewish interest. Pays on publication.

THE COMPANION—15 Chestnut Park Rd., Toronto M4W 1W5, Ont., Canada.
Fiction, 1,200 to 1,500 words. Pays about 2¢ a word, on acceptance.

CONQUEST—6401 The Paseo, Kansas City, Mo. 64131. Paul Miller, Editor.
Church of the Nazarene. Short stories of interest to young people in late teens and early twenties, up to 2,500 words. Dominant moral tone preferred. Payment is 1½¢ a word, on acceptance.

CONTACT—302 United Brethren Building, Huntington, Ind. 46750. Stanley Peters, Editor.
United Brethren in Christ. Christ-centered fiction for teens and adults, 1,200 to 1,500 words. Pays ⅔¢ a word, on acceptance.

THE EVANGEL (formerly *Light and Life Evangel*)—999 College Ave., Winona Lake, Ind. 46590. Vera Bethel, Editor.
Free Methodist. Fiction, 1,500 to 2,000 words. Pays 2¢ a word.

EVENT MAGAZINE—American Lutheran Church Men, 422 South Fifth St., Minneapolis, Minn. 55415. James Solheim, Editor.
Accepts short stories, up to 2,000 words, but these must avoid the sentimental or "preachy" viewpoint. Pays 2¢ a word and up, on acceptance.

FACE-TO-FACE—201 Eighth Ave. South, Nashville, Tenn. 37203. Kenneth Winston, Editor.
Methodist. Fiction, 2,500 to 3,000 words, on problems and concerns of older teens. No straight moral fiction. Pays 2¢ a word and up, on acceptance. Query first.

FRIAR: THE MAGAZINE OF CATHOLIC OPTIMISM—Butler, N. J. 07405. Rev. Rudolf Harvey, O.F.M., Editor.
Light and humorous fiction, up to 2,500 words, preferably on Catholic or Franciscan themes. Payment varies, is on acceptance.

HOME LIFE—127 Ninth Ave. North, Nashville, Tenn. 37203. Dr. Joe W. Burton, Editor.
Southern Baptist. Fiction of interest to parents, to 3,000 words, on the growth of children, family interrelationships, etc. "Professional in depth but popular in style." Also uses human-interest short-shorts, 200 to 500 words. Pays 2½¢ a word, on acceptance.

JEWISH FRONTIER—45 East 17th St., New York, N. Y. 10003. Marie Syrkin, Editor.
Fiction, 2,500 to 4,000 words, related to Judaism. Payment is 2¢ a word, on publication.

THE LINK—122 Maryland Ave., N. E., Washington, D. C. 20002. Lawrence P. Fitzgerald, Editor.
Interdenominational. Fiction, to 2,000 words, for young Christian men and women in military service. Pays 1¢ to 1½¢ a word, on acceptance.

LIVE—1445 Boonville Ave., Springfield, Mo. 65802. Dorothy Morris, Editor.
A Sunday School paper for adults. Fiction, 1,500 to 2,000 words, with evangelical emphasis.

THE LOOKOUT—8121 Hamilton Ave., Cincinnati, Ohio 45231. Jay Sheffield, Editor.
Good, clean fiction with a punch, 1,000 to 1,400 words. Pays monthly; usual rate is $35.

LUTHERAN STANDARD—426 South Fifth St., Minneapolis, Minn. 55415. Dr. George H. Muedeking, Editor.
Occasional fiction, to 1,300 words, related to the church or to the Christian life. Payment is 2¢ a word, on acceptance.

MATURE YEARS—201 Eighth Ave. South, Nashville, Tenn. 37203. Daisy D. Warren, Editor.
Methodist. Fiction appealing to older adults. Length: 1,200 to 1,500 words. Pays 3¢ a word, on acceptance.

MIDSTREAM: A MONTHLY JEWISH REVIEW—515 Park Ave., New York, N. Y. 10022. Shlomo Katz, Editor.
Fiction of Jewish or general social and political interest, up to 8,000 words. Payment is 3¢ a word, on acceptance.

THE MIRACULOUS MEDAL—475 East Chelten Ave., Philadelphia, Pa. 19144. Rev. Donald L. Doyle, C. M., Editorial Director.
Stories to 3,000 words, within framework of Catholic teaching, but not necessarily religious. Payment is 2¢ a word, on acceptance.

THE ORPHAN'S MESSENGER—81 York St., Jersey City, N. J. 07302. Sister Eleanor Quin, C. S. J., Editor.
Fiction, 1,000 to 1,500 words, Catholic in content. Pays 1¢ to 3¢ a word.

OUR FAMILY—Box 249, Battleford, Sask., Canada. Rev. A. J. Materi, OMI, Editor.
Fiction, 1,500 to 3,000 words. Pays up to 2¢ a word, on acceptance.

THE PENTECOSTAL EVANGEL—Gospel Publishing House, 1445 Boonville, Springfield, Mo. 65802.
Religious material only, conforming to doctrines of Assemblies of God churches. Uses Christmas fiction, 1,500 to 1,800 words. Pays 1¢ a word and up, on publication.

PEOPLE—1312 Massachusetts Ave. N. W., Washington, D.C. 20005.
Uses some fiction. Pays various rates.

PURPOSE—610 Walnut Ave., Scottdale, Pa. 15683. David E. Hostetler, Editor.
Short stories, 1,000 to 2,000 words; serials, from two parts to book length, to help readers find meaning in life through Christian faith. Pays up to 2¢ a word for manuscripts. Free sample copies on request.

QUEEN—40 South Saxon Ave., Bay Shore, N. Y. 11706. Rev. James McMillan, S.M.M., Editor.
Fiction, 1,000 to 2,000 words, preferably with a Marian theme. Payment on acceptance.

THE RECONSTRUCTIONIST—15 West 86th St., New York, N. Y. 10024. Dr. Ira Eisenstein, Editor.
Fiction, 2,000 to 3,000 words, dedicated to the advancement of Judaism. Payment is $20 to $25, on publication.

REVIEW FOR RELIGIOUS—612 Humboldt Bldg., 539 North Grand Blvd., St. Louis, Mo. 63103.
Fiction of interest to religious men and women; any length. Pays $5 per printed page at time of publication.

ST. ANTHONY MESSENGER—1615 Republic St., Cincinnati, Ohio 45210. Rev. Jeremy Harrington, O.F.M., Editor.
Catholic. Fiction for adults written out of a totally Christian background, illuminating truths of human nature. Should not be preachy or overly sentimental. Pays 5¢ a word and up.

THE SIGN—Monastery Place, Union City, N. J. 07087. Rev. Augustine P. Hennessy, C.P., Editor.
Catholic. Short stories of general or religious interest, to 4,000 words. Pays $200 to $300, on acceptance.

VISTA—Box 2000, Marion, Ind. 46952.
Needs fiction showing the implication of following Christ in today's world, 2,000 to 2,500 words. Serials of 6 to 8 chapters. Pays 2¢ per word, on acceptance.

THE WAR CRY—860 North Dearborn St., Chicago, Ill. 60610.
The Salvation Army. Fiction, 1,200 to 1,800 words, with evangelical slant; pays $25 to $40.

WORKING FOR BOYS—601 Winchester St., Newton Highlands, Mass. 02161. Send mss. to Brother Jason, CFX, Assoc. Editor, 800 Clapboardtree St., Westwood, Mass. 02090.
Fiction to 1,000 words. Material should appeal to early teenagers and parents. Sample copy available on request.

THE POPULAR MARKET

The popular market includes the magazines which used to be called the "pulps": men's magazines, detective and mystery, science fiction, confession and romance magazines. Both fiction and nonfiction needs of these magazines are listed here. Most of the popular magazines use fiction primarily, although a number of the detective and adventure magazines want only factual material. Publishers of paperback books also have a continuing need for western, mystery, science fiction, love and adventure novels, and writers should consult the list of *Paperback Book Publishers* for their requirements.

MEN'S MAGAZINES

ADAM—8060 Melrose Ave., Los Angeles. Calif. 90046.
Will consider any well-written fiction, particularly stories with male-female relationships. Sexy humor and satire needed. Articles on personalities, human sexuality and social themes. Length: 1,000 to 5,000 words. Pays from $50 to $250, on publication.

AMERICAN ART ENTERPRISES, INC.—21322 Lassen St., Chatsworth, Calif. 91311.
Publishers of quarterly men's magazines. Uses fiction and fact articles, 2,000 to 3,000 words, of general interest to men. Articles: observations and commentary on

some aspect of today's mixed-up society, done in a witty, provocative manner and designed to be accompanied by stimulating photos and illustrations. Fiction: action-packed short stories with strong male-female relationships, eroticism and physical conflict. Also uses photos with articles, cartoons, jokes. Pays $75 minimum for articles and fiction; $10 for cartoons; $5 for jokes. Address: George Bemos, Manuscript Editor.

ARGOSY—420 Lexington Ave., New York, N. Y. 10017.
No short fiction; book condensations through publishers only.

ARMY TIMES—475 School St., S.W., Washington, D. C. 20024. Anthony March, Editor.
Cartoons, puzzles, pin-ups; features purchased outright. Material should be connected with military service, if possible. Payment varies. Query first.

BEST FOR MEN—Kimtex Corp., 1133 Broadway, New York, N. Y. 10010.
Entertaining fiction, preferably with man-woman interest and surprise ending, from 2,000 to 5,000 words. Also nonfiction articles on subjects of male interest, up to 2,000 words. Contributors should study recent issues for specific editorial requirements before submitting material. Pays from $20 to $100, on acceptance. Same requirements for *Men's Digest* and *Rascal*.

BLUEBOOK—235 Park Ave. South, New York, N. Y. 10003.
Entertaining and well-written adventure articles, to 5,000 words. Payment is on acceptance. Query first. No fiction, fillers, or poetry. Same address and requirements for *Man's Conquest* and *Man's Illustrated*.

BROADSIDE—21322 Lassen St., Chatsworth, Calif. 91311. Arthur S. Long, Editor.
Witty, provocative fact articles of interest to men: sex, drinking, gambling, trends; odd-ball aspects of well-known people. Action-packed fiction involving scenes with beautiful women, eroticism, and physical conflict. Fact and fiction must be suitable for photo illustration. Length, 2,000 to 3,000 words. Pays $75 minimum.

CAVALIER—236 East 46th St., New York, N. Y. 10017. Douglas Allen, Editor.
Articles, 2,500 to 4,000 words, and quality fiction, 3,000 to 4,000 words, of interest to young men with informed and sophisticated tastes. Especially likes off-beat articles. Pays up to $300.

CHARGER—See *Wildcat*.

DARING—See *Wildcat*.

ESQUIRE—488 Madison Ave., New York, N.Y. 10022. Harold Hayes, Editor. Don Erickson, Managing Editor.
Articles, 1,500 to 5,000 words, to interest sophisticated masculine audience. Literary fiction, 3,000 words and up, and short-shorts, to 1,500 words. Strong need for humor. Pays top rates, on acceptance.

FLING MAGAZINE—161 East Erie St., Chicago, Ill. 60611. Arv Miller, Editor.
Fiction: serious stories with off-beat, man-woman themes, from 3,000 to 4,000 words; humor or satire, from 2,000 to 3,000 words. No science fiction, Westerns, mysteries, plotless vignettes, stories involving children, animals or ghosts, period pieces, or ribald classics. Nonfiction: controversial and off-beat themes that reflect the adult viewpoint of today and tomorrow. No sports, food-drink pieces, puzzles, travel, or general interest fillers. Pays from $100 to $250 for fiction; from $125 to $300 for articles.

FOR MEN ONLY—575 Madison Ave., New York, N. Y. 10022. Ivan Prasker, Editorial Director.
True adventure stories with rugged action, current articles of interest to men, exposés, etc., up to 6,000 words. Payment is $275 to $400 for articles, on acceptance; $10 to $25 for single photos; up to $50 per page for picture stories.

FRONTIER TIMES—See *True West*.

GEM—303 West 42nd St., New York, N. Y. 10036. Will Martin, Editor.
Articles and short stories on any contemporary theme, preferably sex-oriented, from 500 to 1,500 words. Payment depends on length, and is made after assignment to a specific issue.

GENTLEMEN'S QUARTERLY (GQ)—488 Madison Ave., New York, N. Y. 10022. Jack Haber, Editor.
Queries only; no fiction, poems, or cartoons. Unsolicited manuscripts returned unread.

GOURMET—777 Third Ave., New York, N. Y. 10017.
Articles, 2,500 to 3,000 words, on travel, adventure, hunting, fishing, and other facets of good living for sophisticated male reading audience interested in fine foods and fine wines. Purchases recipes only in connection with articles. No short features or fillers. Payment on acceptance.

HUGHES RIGWAY—Hughes Tool Co., Box 2539, Houston, Tex. 77001.
Oilfield and drilling stories, appealing to unsophisticated male audience, up to 2,500 words. Pays 10¢ a word. Queries preferred.

KNIGHT—8060 Melrose Ave., Los Angeles, Calif. 90046. Jared Rutter, Editor.
Sophisticated fiction of interest to men; stories with male-female relationships. Topical articles and social comment pieces. Length: 1,000 to 5,000 words. Pays from $75 to $300, on publication (usually three months following acceptance.).

MALE—575 Madison Ave., New York, N. Y. 10022. Carl Sifakis, Editor.
Authentic true adventures, set in exotic backgrounds; World War II and contemporary cold war stories. No historicals or westerns. Powerful, dramatic articles; contemporary exposés; profiles of unusual men: 4,000 to 6,000 words. Query first. No fillers. Pays up to $600 for lead articles, on acceptance. Same address and requirements for *Men*.

MAN TO MAN—280 Madison Ave., New York, N. Y. 10016. Everett Meyers, Editor.
Strong, imaginative stories in a modern mood, including man-woman relationships, from 1,500 to 5,000 words. Sharply-angled articles: travel, sex, new art forms, unusual entertainment, etc., from 2,000 to 5,000 words. Uses photos with articles. Pays $75 and up for fiction; $100 minimum for articles, on or before publication. Same requirements for *Mr. Magazine* and *Sir!*

MAN'S CONQUEST MAGAZINE—See *Bluebook*.

MAN'S ILLUSTRATED—See *Bluebook*.

MAN'S WORLD—625 Madison Ave., New York, N. Y. 10022.
Powerful, dramatic articles, profiles of unusual men, authentic true adventures, 4,000 to 5,000 words. Exposés, crime and other standard male magazine subjects are welcomed. Pays up to $400, on acceptance. Query first.

MEN—See *Male.*

THE MEN'S DIGEST—See *Best for Men.*

MR. MAGAZINE—See *Man to Man.*

MODERN MAN—8150 North Central Park Ave., Skokie, Ill. 60076.
New format covers all areas of sexual exploration, in a dramatic, humorous, or documentary style. No subject is taboo. Articles must lend themselves to pictorial illustrations. Maximum length: 2,500 words. Payment to $200. No fiction.

OLD WEST—See *True West.*

OUI—919 North Michigan Ave., Chicago, Ill. 60611.
Aimed at a young audience. Articles and short stories, from 2,500 to 3,000 words. Pays from $500.

PENTHOUSE—909 Third Ave., New York, N. Y. 10036.
Good, sophisticated, sexy fiction, 3,000 to 5,000 words; general-interest or hard-hitting controversial articles, to 6,000 words. Pays to 25¢ a word, after acceptance.

PLAYBOY—919 North Michigan, Chicago, Ill. 60611. Hugh M. Hefner, Editor and Publisher. Jack J. Kessie, Managing Editor.
Sophisticated, well-plotted fiction of all kinds, 1,000 to 10,000 words (average length, 4,000). Articles on topics of interest to urban men, up to 5,000 words. Humor and satire especially welcome. Pays $3,000 for lead material; $2,000 standard; $1,000 for short-shorts, on acceptance; also three $1,000 bonuses for best story, article and humor/satire of the year.

PLAYERS—8060 Melrose Ave., Los Angeles, Calif. 90046.
For black men. Articles, 1,000 to 4,000 words; fiction, 2,000 to 6,000 words; reviews to 500 words; humor, satire. Pays 5¢ to 6¢ a word, on publication.

RAILROAD MAGAZINE—420 Lexington Ave., New York, N. Y. 10017. Freeman Hubbard, Editor.
Articles on railroad topics. Authors must query first.

RASCAL—See *Best for Men.*

ROGUE—Captain Publishing, 95 Madison Ave., New York, N. Y. 10016.
Fiction: sophisticated sex, avant-garde and contemporary male-female situations, 1,500 to 2,500 words. Articles of interest to the male reader and sophisticated humor, to 3,000 words. Pays various rates. Query first.

SAGA—333 Johnson Ave., Brooklyn, N. Y. 11206. Martin M. Singer, Editor.
Nonfiction only, 4,500 to 5,500 words, on subjects of interest to men: adventure, interviews and profiles of newsworthy figures, humor, travel; articles on hunting, fishing, sports, war (World War II or later); also picture and text stories on action sports, dangerous pastimes. See issues before submitting. Rates begin at $250.

SIR!—See *Man to Man.*

STAG—625 Madison Ave., New York, N. Y. 10022. Noah Sarlat, Editor.
Articles, up to 7,000 words, on personalities, true adventure, exposés, etc. Pay-

ment is up to $500 for articles, on acceptance; $10 to $25 for single photos, up to $50 per page for picture stories.

SWANK—1560 Broadway, New York, N. Y. 10019.
Good-quality fiction, 2,500 words; sex, man-woman relationships, science fiction preferred subjects. Articles to 2,500 words on politics, social trends, profiles, how-to information. Query first. Pays $125 to $300.

THE SWINGER—Kenden Publications, Inc., 303 West 42nd St., New York, N. Y. 10036. Will Martin, Editor.
Articles on contemporary themes with which vital young people can identify, sophisticated fiction, and satire. Length is 750 to 1,500 words.

TRUE—1515 Broadway, New York, N. Y. 10036. Clare Conley, Editor.
Publishes articles on subjects of peculiar interest to men: personal adventures, outdoor participant sports and recreation, contemporary crime, science, spectator sports, automobiles, environment. Also 1,000-word columns on health, money management, travel; pays $500. Pays $1,000 and up for main articles, to 3,000 words. Send outline first.

TRUE WEST—Western Publications, Inc., P. O. Box 3338, Austin, Texas 78704. Joe A. Small, Publisher. Pat Wagner, Editor.
Publishes articles dealing with true incidents of the Old West (1830–1910), 750 to 8,000 words. Good photos help greatly. Pays 2¢ a word on acceptance. Same address and requirements for *Frontier Times* and *Old West*. Source list required unless first-hand account.

WILDCAT—235 Park Ave. South, New York, N. Y. 10003. Dan Sontup, Editor.
Fast-moving fiction and articles, serious or humorous, about modern relationships or encounters between young men and women, with an element of sex, presented in a credible manner. Quality and originality are most important. Length: 2,000 to 3,000 words. Pays up to $125, on acceptance. Same address and requirements for *Charger* and *Daring*.

ZANE GREY WESTERN MAGAZINE—8230 Beverly Blvd., Los Angeles, Calif. 90048. Cylvia Kleinman, Editor.
Short stories, 2,000 words, and 3,000-word articles. Pays 1¢ a word and up, on acceptance.

DETECTIVE AND MYSTERY MAGAZINES

(Fact and Fiction)

ALFRED HITCHCOCK'S MYSTERY MAGAZINE—784 U.S. 1, Suite 6, North Palm Beach, Fla. 33408. Ernest M. Hutter, Editor.
Uses original, well-written, and well-plotted mystery and suspense stories, including spy and foreign intrigue, the supernatural, and science fiction in the mystery/suspense vein, all with an emphasis on plausibility. No cheap sensationalism or actual crimes. Length: 1,000 to 10,000 words. Pays from 3¢ to 5¢ per word, on acceptance. Prompt replies.

ARMCHAIR DETECTIVE—3656 Midland, White Bear Lake, Minn. 55110. Allen J. Hubin, Editor.
Will consider all types of nonfiction relevant to the mystery and detective fiction field: biographical sketches, critiques, book reviews, etc. No payment.

CHARLIE CHAN MYSTERY MAGAZINE—See *Mike Shayne Mystery Magazine*.

CONFIDENTIAL DETECTIVE CASES—235 Park Ave. South, New York, N. Y. 10003. B. R. Ampolsk, Editor.
True fact detective cases, 3,500 words. Must have a woman as a principal charac-

ter. Good photos must be available. Plenty of action and emotion are essential. Payment on acceptance. Query first. Same address and requirements for *Crime Detective*.

CRIME DETECTIVE—See *Confidential Detective Cases*.

ELLERY QUEEN'S MYSTERY MAGAZINE—229 Park Ave. South, New York, N. Y. 10003. Ellery Queen, Editor. Clayton Rawson, Managing Editor.
Detective, crime, mystery and spy fiction. Needs suspense stories of straight detection. Preferred length, under 10,000 words. Pays 3¢ to 8¢ a word, slightly less for reprints, on acceptance.

FRONT PAGE DETECTIVE—See *Inside Detective*.

INSIDE DETECTIVE—245 East 47th St., New York, N. Y. 10017. James W. Bowser, Editor.
Fact detective stories, stressing suspense and detective work, characterization and emotion. Timeliness and pictures are important, and it is best to query first. Length, 3,500 to 4,500 words. Pays $200 and up, on acceptance. Also pays $25 and $50, on acceptance, for current crime shorts of 1,500 words or less. No fiction. Same address and requirements for *Front Page Detective*.

MASTER DETECTIVE—235 Park Ave. South, New York, N.Y. 10003. Edward Gibbons, Managing Editor.
Factual detective and police cases, with authentic photos, told in detail and with a strong human-interest angle, 5,000 to 6,000 words. Pays $200; extra for photos. Same address and requirements for *Official Detective* and *True Detective*.

MIKE SHAYNE MYSTERY MAGAZINE—8230 Beverly Blvd., Los Angeles, Calif. 90048. Leo Margulies, Publisher. Cylvia Kleinman, Editor.
Good detective and mystery stories, ranging from 1,500-word short-shorts to 12,000-word novelettes. Payment is 1¢ a word, and up, on acceptance. Same address and requirements for *Charlie Chan Mystery Magazine*.

OFFICIAL DETECTIVE STORIES—See *Master Detective*.

STARTLING DETECTIVE—1440 St. Catherine St. West, Montreal 107, Canada.
Photos necessary. True stories, up to 6,000 words, detailing police work on current murder cases upon indictment or solid evidence of guilt. Payment is 5¢ a word for stories, on acceptance. Query first. No fiction.

TRUE DETECTIVE—See *Master Detective*.

TRUE POLICE CASES—1440 St. Catherine St. West, Montreal 107, Canada.
Fact detective stories, by-lined articles of law-enforcement officers, and articles about personalities in the world of crime, 4,000 to 6,000 words. Most interested in current cases. No fiction. Payment is 5¢ a word, on acceptance. Query first.

SCIENCE FICTION AND FANTASY MAGAZINES

ANALOG: SCIENCE FACT & FICTION—350 Madison Ave., New York, N. Y. 10017. Ben Bova, Editor.
Science fiction, with human characters against a background of a believable future or environment. Short stories, 3,500 to 7,500 words; novelettes, 10,000 to 20,000; serials, up to 100,000 words. Short fact articles, giving modern facts with probable future developments, 3,500 to 5,000 words. Pays up to 5¢ a word, on acceptance for short stories. Query first on novels and fact articles.

FANTASY & SCIENCE FICTION—347 East 53rd St., New York, N. Y. 10022. Edward Ferman, Editor.
Imaginative fiction, supernatural or scientific, from short-shorts to (very rarely) serialized novels. Payment is 2¢ a word, on acceptance. Pays 1¢ a word for one use only of reprints that are not from science fiction magazines. At present chiefly

needs *real science* fiction and well-plotted fantasy. Light material in either category always welcome.

GALAXY MAGAZINE—235 East 45th St., New York, N. Y. 10017. Ejler Jakobsson, Editor.
Adult science fiction, which must be based on human problems and conflicts arising from situations or environments that are extensions of present scientific knowledge or hypotheses. No fantasy. Lengths: short stories, up to 5,000 words; novelettes, up to 10,000 words; novellas, 17,000 to 20,000 words, usually, but not always, by arrangement. Pays 3¢ a word, on acceptance.

IF SCIENCE FICTION—235 East 45th St., New York, N. Y. 10017. Ejler Jakobsson, Editor.
Science fiction stories, in all lengths up to 20,000 words. Does not buy fantasy. Starting rate is 1¢ a word, higher thereafter by arrangement, on acceptance.

WEIRDBOOK—Box 35, Amherst Branch, Buffalo, N. Y. 14226. W. Paul Ganley, Editor.
Wants weird, supernatural fiction, up to 6,000 words (occasionally up to 8,000 words); poetry, up to 15 lines, occasionally longer. Black-and-white drawings or photographs on weird subjects only. Pays $1.00 per printed page, on publication. Authors should be familiar with specialized material—a good background would include Poe, Bierce, Lovecraft, Lord Dunsany, Robert E. Howard, etc.

ROMANCE AND CONFESSION MAGAZINES

BRONZE THRILLS—Good Publishing Co., 1220 Harding St., Fort Worth, Tex. 76102. Mrs. Edna K. Turner, Editor.
Confession stories, 5,000-8,000 words, with black interest. Also 8 x 10 black-and-white glossy prints. Pays on acceptance. Same address and requirements for *Hep* and *Jive*.

CONFIDENTIAL CONFESSIONS—1120 Ave. of the Americas, New York, N. Y. 10036. Jean Sharbel, Editorial Director.
First-person confession stories: shorts, 2,000 to 6,500 words; novelettes, up to 8,500 words. Payment is 3¢ a word, on acceptance.

DARING ROMANCES—17 West 44th St., New York, N. Y. 10036. Jean Sharbel, Editorial Director.
Dramatic first-person marriage and courtship stories based on hit-home problems, with strong realism and emotional tone. Short stories, 2,000 to 6,500 words; novelettes, up to 8,500 words. Payment is 3¢ a word, on acceptance.

EXCITING CONFESSIONS—17 West 44th St., New York, N. Y. 10036. Jean Sharbel, Editor.
Confession stories on marriage and courtship problems with strong emphasis on excitement, 2,000 to 8,500 words. Pays 3¢ a word, on acceptance.

HEP—See *Bronze Thrills.*

HERS—IPC Magazines, Ltd., 205 East 42nd St., New York, N. Y. 10017. (New York Office)
British romance magazine. First-person story magazine for women of an emotional, romantic, realistic nature. Preferred length is 5,000 to 8,000 words. Pays good rates, on acceptance.

INTIMATE ROMANCES—See *True Secrets.*

INTIMATE SECRETS—See *True Secrets.*

INTIMATE STORY—295 Madison Ave., New York, N. Y. 10017.
First-person stories from 2,000 to 6,500 words stressing love, courtship, marriage, family problems. Also stories based on exciting current happenings in the news today. Reader must be able to identify with narrator, and feel sympathy for her

even if she is mixed-up or sinful. Stories should end with a ray of hope for the future. Teen-age problems especially needed. Pays 3¢ a word.

JIVE—See *Bronze Thrills.*

MODERN LOVE—See *Real Confessions.*

MODERN ROMANCES—245 East 47th St., New York, N. Y. 10017. Rita Brenig, Editor.
Good first-person stories for wives and daughters of blue-collar class, with emphasis on plot and characterization. Length: 5,000 to 7,000 words. Payment is 4¢ a word for the first two stories bought; thereafter, 5¢ a word.

MY LOVE SECRET CONFESSION—21 West 26th St., New York, N. Y. 10010. Ardis Sandel, Editor.
Confession stories, to 7,000 words, dealing with problems of teen-agers and young marrieds. Pays $100 to $150, depending on length, 30 days after acceptance.

PERSONAL ROMANCES—Ideal Publishing Corp., 295 Madison Ave., New York, N.Y. 10017.
First-person romance stories, preferably from woman's point of view. Story must have a moral. Length: 1,500 to 6,500 words. Pays 3¢ a word, on acceptance.

REAL CONFESSIONS—75 Rockefeller Plaza, New York, N. Y. 10019. Ruth Beck, Editor.
First-person confession stories told by female narrators involved in romantic, unique, exciting, tragic or frightening situations, growing out of basic human relationships to parents, lovers, husbands, children. Upbeat endings preferred. Background must be authentic. Length: 4,000 to 7,000 words. Also looking for very short stories, 2,000 to 3,000 words. Pays on acceptance. Same address and requirements for *Modern Love.*

REAL ROMANCES—21 West 26th St., New York, N. Y. 10010. Ardis Sandel, Editor.
Stories about problems of courtship, young marrieds, 1,500 to 7,500 words. Prefers uncontrived slice-of-life or one-incident stories that deal with the modern woman. Pays $100 to $150, 30 days after acceptance.

REAL STORY—21 West 26th St., New York, N. Y. 10010. Ardis Sandel, Editor.
Confession stories dealing with problems of young marrieds, to about 7,000 words. Male viewpoint and older viewpoint used occasionally. Pays $100 to $150 for manuscripts, 30 days after acceptance.

REVEALING ROMANCES—See *Secrets.*

SECRET ROMANCES—1120 Ave of the Americas, New York, N. Y. 10036. Jean Sharbel, Editorial Director.
Uses dramatic first-person stories, 2,000 to 6,500 words (novelettes up to 8,500 words), on marriage and courtship, based on hit-home problems, with strong realism. Pays 3¢ a word, on acceptance.

SECRETS—1120 Ave. of the Americas, New York, N. Y. 10036. Jean Sharbel, Editorial Director.
First-person courtship and marriage stories with strong reader identification and hit-home situations. Lengths: short stories, 2,000 to 6,500 words; novelettes to 8,500 words. Pays 3¢ and 4¢ a word, on acceptance. Same address and requirements for *Revealing Romances.*

TRUE—IPC Magazines Ltd., 205 East 42nd St., New York, N. Y. 10017. (New York office).
British romance magazine. First-person stories of interest to British women, with strong drama, emotion, and credibility. Preferred length is 3,000 to 8,000 words. Pays good rates, on acceptance.

TRUE CONFESSIONS—205 East 42nd St., New York, N. Y. 10017. Florence J. Moriarty, Editor.
Woman-told confessions with strong emotional conflict and intriguing, suspenseful situations involving man-woman relationships. Stories of 2,500 to 7,000 words most needed, but good stories of any length, up to 18,000 words, considered. Pays top rates, on acceptance. Special nonfiction feature each month, which must be well-researched or written by an expert. Query Helen Vincent about feature ideas. Pays good rates.

TRUE EXPERIENCE—205 East 42nd St., New York, N. Y. 10017. Bruce Elliott, Editor.
Good fresh stories, with realism, insight, lively characters, a genuine feeling of adventure in living. Stories should be in the first person; deal with family life, love, courtship, health, religion, inspiration, behind-the-headlines topics, suspense. Pays a top price of $250. Length: 4,000 to 8,000 words.

TRUE LOVE—205 East 42nd St., New York, N. Y. 10017. Bruce Elliott, Editor.
Realistic stories, 5,000 to 7,000 words, with sympathetic heroine (generally first-person), of interest to women 18 to 34. Avoid conventional type of confession story. Payment usually 3¢ a word, on acceptance.

TRUE SECRETS—Magazine Management Co., 625 Madison Ave., New York, N. Y. 10022. Cara Sherman, Editorial Director.
First-person confession stories, 5,000 words, reflecting present-day sexual attitudes, behavior, and mystery, baby and teen-age stories. Emotional conflict without "sin, suffer, repent" syndrome. Pays 4¢ a word to $125 maximum. Same address and requirements for *My Romance, Secret Story, Intimate Romances, Intimate Secrets,* and *My Confession.*

TRUE STORY—205 East 42nd St., New York, N. Y. 10017. Suzanne Hilliard, Editor.
First-person stories, 1,500 to 10,000 words, mirroring the hopes, fears, drama and humor of life as it is lived today. Also articles of interest to women, 1,500 to 8,000 words. Pays 5¢ a word and up, on acceptance.

UNCENSORED CONFESSIONS—21 West 26th St., New York, N. Y. 10010. Ardis Sandel, Editor.
Stories, 1,500 to 7,500 words, dealing with current problems faced by teen-agers and young marrieds today. Prefers slice-of-life stories. Pays $100 to $150, 30 days after acceptance.

ARTICLE MARKETS

The magazines in this list are in the market for free-lance articles. The list is divided into the following categories: general magazines; college, literary and "little" magazines; religious and denominational magazines; magazines devoted to sports, outdoors, travel, cars, etc.; home and garden or women's magazines; trade and business magazines; and specialized magazines.

Only the largest trade and business publications which particularly want to see free-lance material are listed, and a selected list is given of highly specialized magazines in such fields as education, agriculture, science, etc. Writers who are able to write articles in a particular technical or business field can find the names of thousands of other specialized magazines in N. W. Ayer and Son's *Directory of Newspapers and Periodicals,* which is available in most libraries and contains an index according to classification. Since Ayer's *Directory* does not list editorial requirements, writers should query these magazines before submitting manuscripts.

Juvenile article markets are listed under *Juvenile, Teen-Age and Young Adult Magazines,* and markets for popular or pulp articles (men's true adventure stories, true detective stories, etc.) are listed under *The Popular Market.*

GENERAL MAGAZINES

ADAM—8060 Melrose Ave., Los Angeles, Calif. 90046.
Humorous, satirical and serious articles dealing with entertainment, travel, sports, and celebrity profiles. Needs articles about erotic aspects of life in history or in exotic locations. Length: 2,000 to 5,000 words. Pays $50 to $400. Reports in three weeks.

ADAM FILM WORLD—8060 Melrose Ave., Los Angeles, Calif. 90046. Lee Jensen, Editor.
Articles dealing with entertainment, films, film personalities, film erotica.

ALLIED PUBLICATIONS, INC.—P. O. Box 23505, Fort Lauderdale, Fla. 33307.
Articles on home and family interests, travel; articles on secretaries to famous personalities; articles slanted toward beauticians, business executives, secretaries; articles on art. Pays 5¢ a word, on acceptance; $5 for photos or cartoons.

AMERICAN ASTROLOGY—2505 North Alvernon Way, Tucson, Arizona 85712.
Popular, astrology-slanted articles, no longer than 3,000 words. Also publishes American Astrology Digest (yearbook). Payment upon publication.

AMERICAN BAR ASSOCIATION JOURNAL—1155 East 60th St., Chicago, Ill. 60637. Richard B. Allen, Editor.
Nonfiction, 3,000 to 3,500 words, dealing with the law or legal history, public affairs, political science. No payment. Query.

AMERICAN HERITAGE—1221 Ave. of the Americas, New York, N. Y. 10020. Oliver Jensen, Editor.
Limited amount of free-lance material dealing with American history and historical figures, 3,000 to 6,000 words. No rewrites or purely local history. Authors should check index of back issues before submission. Pays $400 to $600 on acceptance.

THE AMERICAN HOME—641 Lexington Ave., New York, N.Y. 10022. Fred R. Smith, Editor.
General interest articles on home subjects, to appeal to young families. Home improvement articles on remodeling, redecorating, landscaping, etc. Before-and-after stories and how-to stories, with illustrations. Articles on conservation, education, travel, living trends. Payment is on acceptance.

AMERICAN LEGION MAGAZINE—1345 Ave. of the Americas, New York, N. Y. 10019. Robert B. Pitkin, Editor.
Articles on national and international affairs, American and military history. Query first.

THE AMERICAN-SCANDINAVIAN REVIEW—127 East 73rd St., New York, N. Y. 10021. Erik J. Friis, Editor.
Articles, 2,000 to 3,000 words, about Scandinavia and Scandinavians in America. Pays about $50, on acceptance. Uses photos and drawings.

THE AMERICAN SCHOLAR—1811 Q St., N.W., Washington, D. C. 20009. Hiram Haydn, Editor.
Nontechnical articles and essays on current affairs, the American cultural scene, politics, the arts, religion and science, 3,000 to 4,500 words. Pays $150, on acceptance.

AMERICAN WEST—599 College Ave., Palo Alto, Calif. 94306. Donald E. Bower, Editor.
Solid well-illustrated articles on the history of the American West, 3,000 to 5,000 words. Pays $100 to $250, on acceptance. Query first.

AMERICAS—General Secretariat of the Organization of American States, Washington, D. C. 20006.
English, Spanish and Portuguese editions. Illustrated articles, 3,000 words, with "hemisphere-wide appeal." Pays from $60 to $75, on acceptance. Query first.

ANIMALS—180 Longwood Ave., Boston, Mass. 02115. William A. Mallard, Editor.
Articles about animals, 300 to 600 words, with black-and-white photos. Taboo subjects are animal training, commercial use of animals for entertainment, domesticated wild animals and birds, animals in captivity, hunting, etc. Pays ½¢ a word and $1 and up for photos, on acceptance.

ARGOSY—420 Lexington Ave., New York, N. Y. 10017
Articles about actual experiences, up to 3,000 words. Pays $400 to $750.

ATLANTA JOURNAL-CONSTITUTION SUNDAY MAGAZINE—Box 4689, Atlanta, Ga. 30302. George Hatcher, Editor.
Feature material, 800 to 1,500 words, on subjects of regional interest. Prefers advance query. Pays 5¢ a word and up, on publication.

THE ATLANTIC—8 Arlington St., Boston, Mass. 02116. Robert Manning, Editor.
Articles on various topics, with emphasis on public issues, politics, the social sciences, education, business, criticism, literature, and the arts. Prose should be of highest quality. Pays about $100 per *Atlantic* page.

THE ATLANTIC ADVOCATE—Gleaner Bldg., Phoenix Sq., Fredericton, N. B., Canada. John Braddock, Managing Editor.
Prefers regional articles about Eastern Canada, but also considers general-interest articles, especially unusual, well-researched pieces. Photos. Pays by negotiation.

B. C. OUTDOORS—Box 900, Postal Sta., A, Surrey, B. C., Canada. Art Downs, Editor.
Articles, 2,500 to 3000 words of topical, historical, outdoor and general interest, about the people, places, and industries of British Columbia and the Yukon. Also hunting, fishing, travel, and boating pieces on the same region. Pays $50 to $100 for articles with black-and-white photos.

BETTER HOMES & GARDENS—1716 Locust St., Des Moines, Iowa 50303. James A. Autry, Editor.
"While our material is over 75% staff-produced, well-aimed free-lance contributions are used in areas of travel, health, cars, money management, and family entertainment. We are also interested in do-it-yourself projects, which should be accompanied by 'before' and 'after' snapshots. Articles should run from 250 to 1,000 words. We prefer a query first with an outline. We pay top rates, based on estimated space of the published article. Payment is on acceptance. Direct the manuscript to the department where the story line is strongest."

BLACK WORLD—820 South Michigan Ave., Chicago, Ill. 60616. Hoyt W. Fuller, Managing Editor.
Articles, up to 3,500 words, dealing with blacks or black life. Think pieces, controversy, figures out of black history, essays on black literature and black literary figures, dissent.

BLUEBOOK—235 Park Ave. South, New York, N. Y. 10003.
Articles for men, to 5,000 words. Photos. Pays various rates. Query first with detailed outline. Same address and requirements for *Man's Conquest* and *Man's Illustrated*.

BON VOYAGE—4700 Belleview, Kansas City, Mo. 64112. Jane Rosenthal, Managing Editor.
Articles on all aspects of world travel for the sophisticated and discerning traveler. Content 75% foreign, 25% U.S.A. Color transparencies, if possible. In addition to feature length articles of 1,200 to 1,500 words, needs short pieces of 400 to 600 words with one color transparency and black-and-white glossy.

BOSTON GLOBE MAGAZINE—*Boston Globe,* Boston, Mass. 02107. Robert Levey, Editor.
General-interest articles, 1,000–5,000 words, photo essays. Pays $150–$200 for articles, $150 for photo-layouts, $100–$150 for covers on publication. Query first.

CALIFORNIA HIGHWAY PATROLMAN—1225—8th St., Sacramento, Calif. 95814. Joseph L. Richardson, Editor.
2¢ per word and $2.50 per accompanying photo or illustration. Queries desirable. Write for a free sample copy.

CALIFORNIA TODAY—750 Ridder Park Drive, San Jose, Calif. 95131. Fred Dickey, Editor.
Distributed with San Jose *Mercury-News.* Wants fact, history and humorous articles with strong tie-in with California, particularly Northern California and the West. Reflects the "good life" with a strong emphasis on spectator and partici-pant sports, outdoors, leisure home. Pays $35 and up for short humor and history articles; 5¢ a word and up for fact articles, to 2,500 words; $20 each or $50 per page for color or black-and-white photos; $50 and up for cover photos, on accep-tance.

CAMPING JOURNAL—229 Park Ave. South, New York, N. Y. 10003. Kenneth G. Grant, Managing Editor.
Wants articles on hunting, fishing, climbing or other outdoor sports that require skill. Also camping skills articles that are well-researched. Feature articles, 2,500 to 3,000 words, with at least ten 8 x 10 glossy black-and-white photos. Payment is $100 and up, on acceptance; $25 and up for short, how-to articles. Query first. Include social security number and self-addressed, stamped return envelope with manuscript.

THE CANADIAN MAGAZINE—The Canadian Star Weekly, Simpson Tower, 401 Bay St., Toronto 1, Ont., Canada.
Controversial, thought-provoking articles on timely topics with Canadian appeal, up to 2,000 words. Profiles, sports, human-interest, adventure, entertainment page articles. Pays 10¢ a word and up, on acceptance. Address manuscripts to Michael Hanlon, Editor.

CARTE BLANCHE MAGAZINE—3460 Wilshire Blvd., Suite 1200, Los Angeles, Calif. 90054. J. Walter Flynn, Publisher and Editor.
Limited amount of nonfiction for magazine of travel, entertainment, dining out. Query first.

CAT FANCY—11760 Sorrento Valley Rd., San Diego, Calif. 92121.
Well-written and accurate articles appealing to owners of cats: pieces on health, grooming, and care of cats, etc. Length, 1,500 words and up. Uses color transpar-encies and black-and-white glossy prints. Pays 3¢ a word, on publication.

CATS—P.O. Box 4106, Pittsburgh, Pa. 15202.
Unusual-experience articles about cats; factual articles on veterinary medicine ad-

vances, cats in art, literature, or science, 1,000 to 2,000 words. Needs cover and Picture of the Month contest photos. Some photo articles. Pays 2¢ a word; extra for photos.

CAVALIER—236 East 46th St., New York, N. Y. 10017.
Articles, 2,500 to 4,000 words, appealing to a young male readership with informed and sophisticated tastes. Especially likes off-beat articles. Pays up to $300. Query first.

CHATELAINE—481 University Ave., Toronto, Ont., Canada. Doris Anderson, Editor.
Canadian articles, 3,500 words, of interest to women, on arresting controversial subjects, outstanding and colorful personalities, and on "you" interest topics in medical, psychological and emotional fields. Pays $300 and up per article, on acceptance.

THE CHICAGOAN—645 North Michigan Ave., Suite 540, Chicago, Ill. 60611. Richard Christiansen, Editor.
Articles on the Chicago area, 1,500 to 5,000 words. Query first. Pays $200 to $500.

THE CHRISTIAN SCIENCE MONITOR—One Norway St., Boston, Mass. 02115. John Hughes, Editor.
Free-lance material for travel pages, Family Features, education, homemaking pages, Home Forum page, etc. Articles for Family Features should be humorous or human-interest. The Home Forum accepts literary essays of up to 1,200 words. Articles for the editorial page should deal in some respect with news events. Pays various rates.

CIRCLE K MAGAZINE—101 East Erie Street, Chicago, Ill. 60611.
Will consider articles of interest to college students, especially those about social action, political issues, leadership, group dynamics. Length: 800 to 2,000 words. Pays on acceptance. Pays extra for photos.

CIVIL SERVICE LABOR DIRECTORY—Editorial Dept., 216 West Jackson Blvd., Chicago, Ill. 60606.
Uses 800- to 1000-word articles on U.S. and foreign travel, health care, women's interests, interior decorating, sports, and other subjects. Also longer articles of interest to civil service employees. Pays from 3¢ a word. Sample copies available for 60¢. Query with letter.

COLORADO—7190 West 14th Ave., Denver, Colo. 80215. Davis Dutton, Executive Editor.
Exciting adventures, both current and historical, about people in the Rocky Mountain West, from 2,500 to 3,000 words. Photos should accompany all articles. Pays 10¢ a word, on acceptance.

COLUMBIA—Box 1670, New Haven, Conn. 06507. Elmer Von Feldt, Editor.
Official journal of the Knights of Columbus. Articles, 1,000 to 3,000 words, on science, history, sports, current events, religion, education and art. Short humorous pieces to 1,000 words. Pays $100 to $300, on acceptance.

COLUMBUS DISPATCH SUNDAY MAGAZINE—Columbus, Ohio 43216. Clyde C. Long, Editor.
Sunday magazine section. Articles to 1,800 words, with a local or Ohio slant. Pays 2¢ a word minimum, $3 for photos, 10th of month after publication.

COMMENTARY—165 East 56th St., New York, N. Y. 10022. Norman Podhoretz, Editor.
Articles, 5,000 to 7,000 words, on the contemporary scene, here and abroad: politics, Jewish affairs, social sciences, community life, religious thought, cultural activities. Pays about 3½¢ a word.

COMMONWEAL—232 Madison Ave., New York, N. Y. 10016. James O'Gara, Editor.
Catholic. Articles on political, social and literary subjects, up to 3,000 words. Pays 2¢ a word, on acceptance.

CONTEMPORARY—The Denver *Post*, Denver, Colo. 80201. Lois Cress, Editor.
Sunday supplement. Magazine-style news features, 500 to 1,500 words, with photos and drawings, keyed to the Rocky Mountain area preferably. Submissions must be exclusive to *Contemporary* in the Colorado-Wyoming-New Mexico area. Pays $20 and up, $7.50 for photos used, on publication. Query.

THE CONTINENTAL MAGAZINE—Rom 950, World Headquarters, Ford Motor Co., Dearborn, Mich. 48121. Robert M. Hodesh, Editorial Director.
Sophisticated service articles, 1,300 to 1,700 words, on travel, entertainment, shopping, collecting, cuisine, for the well-to-do. Pays on acceptance. Query essential.

CORONET—7950 Deering Ave., Canoga Park, Calif. 91304.
Brief outlines of ideas for general-interest articles or picture spreads. Query first.

COSMOPOLITAN—224 West 57th St., New York, N. Y. 10020. Helen Gurley Brown, Editor; Roberta Ashley, Articles Editor.
Magazine aimed at young career women, women who want to do things. Uses articles, to 3,500 words, and shorter features, 1,000 to 2,000 words, which tell readers how to improve and enjoy their lives. Pays roughly $1,000 and up for full-length articles, less for short features. Other payment by arrangement.

THE DALLAS TIMES HERALD SUNDAY MAGAZINE—Pacific & Griffin Sts., Dallas, Tex. 75202. Paul Rosenfield, Editor.
Features of general interest in Texas and the Southwest, 500 to 1,000 words, with photos or drawings. Payment varies, is on publication. Query first.

THE DES MOINES SUNDAY REGISTER PICTURE—*Des Moines Register and Tribune,* 715 Locust St., Des Moines, Iowa 50304.
Articles and photos about Iowa and Iowans, to 1,000 words. Pays on publication; $5 for black-and-white photos and $25 for color transparencies.

THE DESERT MAGAZINE—Palm Desert, Calif. 92260.
Illustrated features about the Southwestern desert, on history, natural science, lost mines, ghost towns, travel, etc., 500 to 2,000 words. Pays 2¢ a word, on publication.

DIXIE-ROTO—*The Times-Picayune,* 3800 Howard Ave., New Orleans, La. 70140. Terence P. Smith, Editor.
Sunday supplement. Factual feature articles, with a Louisiana-Mississippi background. Pays $40 and up for articles. Pays $20 for Deep South anecdotal stories, 750 to 1,000 words, that are completely true but have dramatic interest—these stories usually laid in past. Sample copies on request. Query essential.

DOWN EAST—Camden, Maine 04843. Duane Doolittle, Editor.
Articles, 1,500 to 3,000 words, on subjects related to Maine. Photos (black-and-white and 4 × 5 color transparencies). Pays 2¢ a word, on acceptance.

EARLY AMERICAN LIFE—Box 1831, Harrisburg, Pa. 17105.
Illustrated articles, 1,000 to 4,000 words, on early American life: arts, crafts, furnishings and architecture. Pays $25 to $200, on acceptance. Query.

EBONY—820 South Michigan Ave., Chicago, Ill. 60605. Herbert Nipson, Managing Editor.
Photo-feature material on the Negro, with emphasis on achievement, civil rights, human interest. Pays $100 and up, on acceptance.

ELKS MAGAZINE—425 West Diversey Parkway, Chicago, Ill. 60614.
Works with professional writers on assignment or speculation basis. Query on article ideas preferred. Pays good rates, on acceptance.

EMPIRE MAGAZINE—The Denver *Post*, Denver, Colo. 80202. Bill Hosokawa, Editor.
Weekly supplement. Regional features up to 3,000 words, on personalities, history, oddities. Also true adventures with strong regional peg. Photographs, if possible. Pays about 3¢ a word, on acceptance; buys first magazine rights only. Query first.

ENTHUSIAST—Harley-Davidson Motor Co., Inc., P.O. Box 653, Milwaukee, Wis. 53201. T. C. Bolfert, Editor.
Articles on motorcycling subjects, racing, tours, etc., featuring Harley-Davidson cycles. Also photos. Pays 5¢ a word and $7.50 to $15 per photo, on acceptance.

ENVIRONMENT—438 North Skinker Blvd., St. Louis, Mo. 63130. Sheldon Novick, Editor.
Factual articles, 5,000 to 7,000 words, presenting technical information in layman's terms on environment pollution, effects of technology. Pays $100. Submit brief proposal first.

ESQUIRE—488 Madison Ave., New York, N. Y. 10022.
Articles, 1,500 to 3,000 words, with depth of insight and strong impact, to interest intelligent adult audience. Particular interest is "revelatory, newsworthy lead pieces" and 1,000-word one-pagers about a major problem or a dramatic piece of news. Pays $350 to $1,000, on acceptance.

FAMILY CIRCLE—488 Madison Ave., New York, N. Y. 10022. Babette Ashley, Articles Editor.
Women's interests. Buys articles on all "service" subjects. Also interested in human interest stories that have personal significance for readers. Top-level quality a must.

FAMILY HEALTH—1271 Ave. of the Americas, New York, N. Y. 10020.
Articles, about 3,000 words, and photo-essays, on health, beauty, physical fitness, marriage, child care, nutrition, etc. Submit outline first. Pays on acceptance.

FAMILY MAGAZINE—Army Times Publishing Co., 475 School St., S.W., Washington, D. C. 20024.
A twice-monthly rotogravure supplement to *Army Times, Air Force Times, Navy Times*. Articles from 800 to 3,000 words with black-and-white or color photos when possible. Articles can cover any subject so long as they relate directly to military men and families. Payment on publication.

FAMILY WEEKLY—641 Lexington Ave., New York, N. Y. 10022. Mort Persky, Editor-in-Chief.
Sunday supplement. Short, lively articles and picture features with emphasis on prominent individuals. Most women's service features staff-prepared. Pays on acceptance.

FLING—161 East Erie St., Chicago, Ill. 60611. Arv Miller, Editor.
Articles directed to adult male readers, 2,500 to 6,000 words. Controversial and off-beat themes should reflect an adult viewpoint. Careful research, authenticated case histories, strong point of view required. No self-help, sports, travel used. Pays up to $350, on acceptance. Authors must query first and should see copies of the magazine before submitting material.

FOCUS/MIDWEST—Box 3086, St. Louis, Mo. 63130. Charles L. Klotzer, Editor.
Controversial regional and national articles of concern to readers in the Midwest, on political, social and cultural issues, especially urban problems in Chicago, St. Louis, and Kansas City, about 900 to 3,000 words. No taboos. Pays on publication.

FORD TIMES—Ford Motor Company, The American Road, Dearborn, Mich. 48121. Hal Butler, Managing Editor.
Articles, 1,200 to 1,500 words on all phases of motor travel and recreation—places, planning, etc.; especially wants articles about participation sports, "swinging" places to go, with a travel tie-in, for 25 to 35 age group. Pays $250 and up for full-length articles. Query preferred.

FOREIGN SERVICE JOURNAL—2101 E St., N.W., Washington, D. C. 20037. Shirley Newhall, Executive Editor.
Professional journal of foreign affairs. Articles dealing with American diplomacy and foreign affairs, or material of particular interest to Americans representing the United States abroad. Uses few travel articles, generally of experiences of foreign affairs officers. Pays on publication.

THE FREEMAN—Foundation for Economic Education, Irvington-on-Hudson, N. Y. 10533. Paul L. Poirot, Editor.
Nonfiction explanations of the economic, political, and moral philosophy behind the concepts of private property, limited government, competitive bargaining, and voluntary exchange, 3,000 words or less. Pays 5¢ a word, on publication.

FRIENDS—17390 West Eight Mile Rd., Southfield, Mich. 48075.
Photo-articles on travel, recreation, sports, personalities, etc. Photos must tell story. Writers' guide available on request. Pays $75 to $150, depending on photos, on acceptance. Query.

FRONTIER TIMES—Western Publications, Box 3338, Austin, Texas 78704. Pat Wagner, Editor.
Accurate, entertaining histories of the Old West. Source list should accompany manuscripts. Accompanying photos welcome. Preferred length: 1,500 to 5,000 words. Query first. Pays 2¢ a word, on acceptance. Same address and requirements for *True West* and *Old West*.

GEM—L & L Publications, Inc., 303 West 42nd St., New York, N. Y. 10036. Will Martin, Editor.
Articles on any contemporary theme, preferably sex-oriented, from 500 to 1,500 words. Payment depends on length, generally made after assignment to a specific issue. Same address and requirements for *The Swinger*.

GENTLEMEN'S QUARTERLY—488 Madison Ave., New York, N. Y. 10022. George Mazzei, Managing Editor.
Hip, sophisticated, male-oriented features about personalities, travel, good living, sports, etc. No fiction; no poetry. Query letter *must* precede unsolicited manuscripts; otherwise they are returned unread. Pays shortly after acceptance.

GEORGIA MAGAZINE—Box 1047, Decatur, Ga. 30031. William Stubbs, Editorial
   Director.
   Articles on Georgia, past and present, under 2,000 words. Interested in people,
   history, scenic beauty, industries, vacation opportunities, and folklore. Pays up to
   $25, on publication.

GLAMOUR—350 Madison Ave., New York, N. Y. 10017. Ruth Whitney, Editor-in-
   Chief; Phyllis Starr, Managing Editor.
   Lively, well-written articles of varying lengths; good humorous pieces, serious
   pieces on all aspects of life today. Pays $50 to $500.

GOOD HOUSEKEEPING—959 Eighth Ave., New York, N. Y. 10019. Wade H. Nichols, Editor. John B. Danby, Executive Editor. Betty Frank, Articles Editor.
   Informative, exemplary articles for women. Articles are usually written on assignment, but queries are considered. Especially interested in dramatic first-person experiences in the fields of human relations, individual achievement, practical living,
   romance, and social techniques. "Better Way" occasionally buys research reports
   on news of practical interest about women's activities, jobs, etc. Pays top rates,
   on acceptance.

GOURMET—777 Third Ave., New York, N. Y. 10017.
   Articles of 2,500 to 3,000 words—reminiscences, adventure, hunting and other
   facets of good living—for sophisticated audience interested in fine food and wines.
   Recipes purchased only as part of articles. No short features, profiles of living persons, reports on festivals or wine tastings. Gourmet Holidays feature is written
   by staff writers only. Send manuscripts to Mrs. Justine Valenti, Managing Editor.
   Pays on acceptance.

GRIT—Williamsport, Pa. 17701. Kenneth D. Loss, Feature Editor.
   Illustrated articles, 300 to 800 words, on wide variety of timely subjects; also
   articles, photos on personalities and small towns for News, Family and Women's
   sections, Men's Interests, and Teen pages. Pays on acceptance.

HARPER'S BAZAAR—717 Fifth Ave., New York, N. Y. 10022.
   Articles on ideas of advanced interest to women. Very few unsolicited manuscripts
   accepted.

HARPER'S MAGAZINE—2 Park Ave., New York, N. Y. 10016. Robert B Shnayerson, Editor.
   Timely articles, 2,000 to 7,000 words, on social, political, economic, cultural
   aspects of American life. Also foreign reporting. Pays on acceptance. Queries
   necessary.

HARVEST YEARS/RETIREMENT LIVING—See *Retirement Living*.

HOLIDAY MAGAZINE—1100 Waterway Blvd., Indianapolis, Ind. 46202. Corey Ser-
   Vaas, Executive Editor; John J. Rea, Senior Editor.
   Articles on travel and leisure subjects, 2,500 to 3,000 words. Pays on acceptance.

HORIZON—551 Fifth Ave., New York, N. Y. 10017. Charles L. Mee, Jr., Managing
   Editor.
   Articles on the arts and cultural subjects. Pays on acceptance. Query first.

HUMAN BEHAVIOR MAGAZINE—12031 Wilshire Blvd., Los Angeles, Calif. 90025.
Articles relating to new developments in social sciences field and human behavior
research, 1,500 to 3,000 words. Pays $150 to $300. Query first.

THE HUMANIST—923 Kensington Ave., Buffalo, N. Y. 14215. Paul Kurtz, Editor.
Journal of humanist and ethical concern. Articles, 2,000 to 4,500 words, dealing
with social and moral issues. Query first.

INFANTRY—Box 2005, Fort Benning, Ga. 31905.
Articles on military organization, weapons, equipment, tactics, techniques and
leadership. Published by U.S. Army Infantry School, but welcomes civilian contributions. Length, 2,000 to 5,000 words. Writers' guide sent on request. Pays
various rates, on publication. Query first.

JURIS DOCTOR, MAGAZINE FOR THE NEW LAWYER—555 Madison Ave.,
New York, N. Y. 10022. Wendy Lyon Moonan, Editor.
Feature articles, to 1,500 words, on new developments in the legal profession;
profiles of outstanding young lawyers. "Muckraking" pieces, 2,000 words, on conflicts of interest, legal fees, the organized bar. Pays $300 for investigative articles,
$100 for profiles, 60 days after acceptance or upon publication. Query with out-
line and three previously published articles.

KEYNOTER—101 East Erie St., Chicago, Ill. 60611. Andrew A. Leckey, Executive
Editor.
Will consider articles of interest to high school students, particularly those pertaining to ecology, human relations and community action. Length: 800 to 2,000
words. Pays on acceptance. Pays extra for photos.

KIRKLEY PRESS, INC. (formerly *The Drumcliff Company*)—Box 300, Timonium,
Md. 21093. Walter Kirkley, Editor.
Publishes material aimed to motivate employees on such topics as: ambition,
initiative, honesty, cooperation, etc. Pays $35 for manuscripts of 350 to 400
words. Also buys booklets of 2,000 to 2,400 words, for which payment is $200 to
$250. Samples sent on request.

THE KIWANIS MAGAZINE—101 East Erie, Chicago, Ill. 60611. Dennis K. Moore,
Executive Editor.
Illustrated articles on domestic problems of the United States and Canada, and
on topics of social, economic, and educational interest, up to 3,500 words. Also
historical articles and humor. Picture stories. Pays up to $500 on acceptance, for
full-length articles.

KNIGHT—8060 Melrose Ave., Los Angeles, Calif. 90046. Jared Rutter, Editor.
Articles for young adult men on personalities, sports, travel; humorous and controversial pieces. Pays $25 to $75 for short-shorts, 350 to 1,250 words, and $100
to $300 for articles, 1,250 to 4,500 words. Query first.

LADIES' HOME JOURNAL—641 Lexington Ave., New York, N. Y. 10022. Dick
Kaplan, Managing Editor.
Exciting, accurate, tightly-written articles of interest to contemporary women.
At present, most articles are staff-written or assigned through recognized literary
agents. Authors must submit queries and outlines.

LADY'S CIRCLE—21 West 26th St., New York, N. Y. 10010. Betty Etter, Editor.
Articles of interest to housewives on health, child care, how to make money,
travel in the U.S., etc., from 2,500 to 3,000 words. Pays $125 and up, on publica-
tion.

LEATHERNECK—P.O. Box 1918, Quantico, Va. 22134. Ronald D. Lyons, Managing
Editor.
Current articles, with photos, about U.S. Marines. Length: 1,500 to 3,000 words.
Query first. Pays $150 to $300, on acceptance.

THE LION—York and Cermak Rds., Oak Brook, Ill. 60521. Dennis Brennan, Senior
Editor.
Factual, informative articles to interest North American readership of business and
professional men, 1,500 to 2,000 words. Pays 10¢ a word. Also cartoons, photo
features, and short humor.

LISTEN—6840 Eastern Ave., N.W., Washington, D. C. 20016. Francis A. Soper, Editor.
Illustrated articles on all phases of the narcotics problem, including alcohol problems and their prevention; emotional balance and mental health, 500 to 1,500
words. Especially interested in youth-slanted features with a positive approach.
Pays 2¢ to 4¢ a word, on acceptance.

THE LOS ANGELES MAGAZINE—342 North Rodeo Drive, Beverly Hills, Calif.
90210. David R. Brown, Editor.
Urbane articles for Southern California readers, 1,000 to 2,500 words. Some photo
stories on interesting California events, locales, and people, directed at a sophisticated metropolitan readership. Humor, satire. Contributors should be familiar with
area and current interests of its inhabitants. Pays 5¢ a word, on publication.

McCALL'S—230 Park Ave., New York, N. Y. 10017.
Timely, major features and articles on all subjects. Average length: 2,500 to 4,000
words. All service articles are staff-written. Also, regional material with wide appeal. Pays top rates, on acceptance.

MACLEAN'S MAGAZINE—481 University Ave., Toronto, Ont., Canada.
Canadian-slanted articles (entertainment, sports, politics, business, etc.), 2,000 to
3,000 words. Submit full outline first.

MADEMOISELLE—350 Madison Ave., New York, N. Y. 10017. Mary Cantwell,
Managing Editor.
Articles of general interest to literate young women, often on controversial or
timely subjects, 1,500 to 4,000 words. Pays on acceptance.

MALE—575 Madison Ave., New York, N. Y. 10022. Carl Sifakis, Editor.
Powerful, dramatic articles, appealing to men; exposés; profiles of adventurous
men, both contemporary and historical; stories of survival, escape, heroic deeds
set in exotic backgrounds. Pays up to $500 for articles of 5,000 to 6,000 words, on
acceptance; considerably more for 15,000-word book-lengths of particular appeal.
Queries preferred. Same address and requirements for *Men* and *Man's World*.

MAN TO MAN—See *Mr. Magazine*.

MAN'S CONQUEST—See *Bluebook*.

MAN'S ILLUSTRATED—See *Bluebook*.

MAN'S WORLD—See *Male*.

MARRIAGE: THE MAGAZINE FOR HUSBAND AND WIFE—St. Meinrad, Ind.
47577.
Articles, to 2,500 words, slanted to married adults, their problems, aspirations, etc.
Pays 5¢ a word.

MEN—See *Male.*

MIDWEST MAGAZINE—*Chicago Sun-Times,* Chicago, Ill. 60611.
Articles up to 1,500 words. Regional Chicago-related material of topical interest.
Pays $35 to $175, on publication. Query first.

MILITARY LIFE— W. B. Bradbury Co., 6 East 43rd St., New York, N. Y. 10017.
Will Lieberson, Editor.
Family-type articles, 500 to 700 words, with a military slant, for monthly
military newspaper supplement. Photos or drawings to accompany manuscripts.
Query first. Pays $75, on acceptance.

MINNESOTA AAA MOTORIST—Minnesota State Automobile Assoc., 7 Traveler's
Trail, Burnsville, Minn. 55378. Ron Johnson, Managing Editor.
Articles, 800 to 1,500 words, on travel, motoring, car care and related subjects.
Also buys 8 × 10 black-and-white photos of travel scenes, usually with articles
submitted. Pays $125 and up for articles; $15 per photo, on acceptance.

MR. MAGAZINE—21 West 26th St., New York, N. Y. 10010. Everett Meyers, Editor.
Sharply-angled articles that reflect contemporary trends in such subjects as travel,
music, sex, new art forms, unusual entertainment, sports, and other activities of
interest to men. Length: 2,000 to 5,000 words. Good 8 × 10 glossy photos will
help sell articles. Pays $75 and up, on publication. Same address and requirements
for *Man to Man* and *Sir!*

MODERN MAN—Publisher's Development Corp., 8150 North Central Park Blvd.,
Skokie, Ill. 60076.
All areas of sexual exploration, approached in a dramatic, humorous, or documentary style. Emphasis should be on the human side of sex. No taboos. Length:
2,500 words maximum. Payment to $200.

MODERN MATURITY—215 Long Beach Blvd., Long Beach, Calif. 90802. Hubert
Pryor, Editor.
Service articles on housing, food, health, employment, for persons over 55 years.
Also nostalgia, inspirational articles, personality pieces, Americana, interpretations
of the current scene, to 2,000 words. Some short stories. Pays from $50 to $500 for
articles and fiction, on acceptance; from $15 up for black-and-white photos, and
from $50 up for color photos.

MONEY—Time & Life Bldg., Rockefeller Center, New York, N. Y. 10020. William
Simon Rukeyser, Managing Editor.
Articles queries on subjects such as investments, taxes, market trends, budgets, etc.
Pay various rates.

MONTANA: THE MAGAZINE OF WESTERN HISTORY—Montana Historical
Society, Roberts at 6th Ave., Helena, Mont. 59601. Vivian A. Paladin, Editor.
Documented nonfiction, 3,500 to 6,000 words about the old West or frontier West.
Pays 1½¢ a word and up, on acceptance. Query first.

MS.—370 Lexington Ave., New York, N. Y. 10017. Gloria Steinem, Editor.
Articles on women's liberation movement. Query first.

THE NATION—333 Sixth Ave., New York, N. Y. 10014. Carey McWilliams, Editor.
Articles on matters of current interest, 2,000 to 2,500 words. Pays 2¢ a word, on
publication. Query first.

NATIONAL ENQUIRER—600 South East Coast Ave., Lantana, Fla. 33460. Mel Snyder, Executive Editor.
Weekly newspaper. In-depth articles of any length on subjects appealing to a mass audience: fresh slants on topical news stories, medical "firsts," scientific breakthroughs, human drama, personality profiles. Pays $125 and up, on acceptance.

NATIONAL GEOGRAPHIC—17th and M Sts., N.W., Washington, D. C. 20036. Gilbert M. Grosvenor, Editor.
Articles, 2,000 to 4,000 words (8,000 words maximum), on travel and exploration, mountaineering and seafaring, archaeological discoveries, natural history, important or unusual industries, occupations, or commodities, advances in science, and notable festivals and folkways. A manuscript, especially of adventure in a hard-to-reach place, has a better chance of acceptance if it is accompanied by original photographic color transparencies, 35 mm or larger, of high quality and interest. Pays $1,500 to $3,000 and up. Query first.

THE NATIONAL GUARDSMAN—1 Massachusetts Ave., N.W., Washington, D.C. 20001. Allan G. Crist, Editor.
Articles, 2,000 to 4,000 words. Articles exclusively on the military, both air and ground; combat lessons; current developments; also short humorous anecdotes, up to 250 words, for "Tales from the Troops." Pays 3¢ and up per published word, on publication.

THE NATIONAL HUMANE REVIEW—Box 1266, Denver, Colo. 80201. Mrs. Eileen F. Schoen, Editor.
Articles, 1,000 to 2,000 words: human-interest stories demonstrating humane treatment of animals and prevention of cruelty to animals. Photo stories with captions. Pays 1½¢ a word, on publication.

NEVADA HIGHWAYS AND PARKS—State of Nevada Department of Highways, Carson City, Nev. 89701.
Articles with a Nevada slant, 1,000 to 2,500 words, and color transparencies and black-and-white glossies. Pays 5¢ to 8¢ a word, and $10 to $40 for photos, upon scheduling. Query first.

NEW ENGLAND GALAXY—Old Sturbridge Village, Sturbridge, Mass. 01566. Catherine Fennelly, Editor.
Articles, 2,000 to 3,000 words, on New England, particularly episodes of political and social history. Pays $75 to $150, on publication. Query first.

NEW HAMPSHIRE PROFILES—Box 900, Portsmouth, N. H. 03801. Peter E. Randall, Editor.
General interest and historical articles about people, places and events in New Hampshire, 1,500 to 3,000 words. Pays on publication.

THE NEW INGENUE—635 Madison Ave., New York, N. Y. 10022. Joanna Brown, Editor-in-Chief.
Articles: controversial, entertainment, guidance, etc., treated in depth and relating to contemporary teen-agers. No preaching or sensationalism. Query.

NEW MEXICO MAGAZINE—113 Washington Ave., Santa Fe, N. M. 87501. Walter Briggs, Editor.
Fact articles only, on New Mexico subjects, 1,500 to 5,000 words. Pays $25 to $40, on publication.

THE NEW REPUBLIC—1244 19th St., N.W., Washington, D. C. 20006. Gilbert Harrison, Editor-in-Chief. David Sanford, Managing Editor.
Features on political, social, economic, and cultural subjects, 2,000 words or less. Payment is by arrangement. Query first.

THE NEW YORK TIMES MAGAZINE—Times Sq., New York, N. Y. 10036. Max Frankel, Editor.
Sunday supplement. Timely articles, 2,500 to 3,500 words, based on specific news items, forthcoming events, anniversaries, trends. Humor must have news "peg." Also short articles, 1,000 to 2,000 words. Pays $400 for full-length articles, $50 a column (about 400 words) for short articles, on acceptance.

THE NEW YORKER—25 West 43rd St., New York, N. Y. 10036.
Factual, historic, and biographical material in "Profiles," "Reporter at Large," "That Was New York," "Annals of Crime,' "Onward and Upward with the Arts," etc. Query first. Pays good rates, on acceptance. Address all material to The Editors.

OCEANS—125 Independence Dr., Menlo Park, Calif. 94025. Don Greame Kelley, Editor.
Articles up to 5,000 words, with photos, on marine life (biology and ecology), oceanography, etc. Pays 8¢ a word, on publication. Query.

OKLAHOMA TODAY—Will Rogers Memorial Bldg., State Capitol, Oklahoma City, Okla. 73105. Bill Burchardt, Editor.
Articles on Oklahoma. Study several back issues carefully before querying. Pays 3¢ a word, on publication, extra for photos.

OPTIMIST MAGAZINE—4494 Lindell Blvd., St. Louis, Mo. 63108. Gary Adamson, Managing Editor.
Articles, 800 to 1,000 words, or photo stories of interest to business and professional men in the U.S. and Canada, on science, education, industry, travel, economics, government, current events, etc. Particularly interested in stories slanted to Canadian readers. Pays up to $100, on acceptance.

OUTDOOR ARIZONA—1230 East Camelback Rd., Phoenix, Ariz. 85014.
Articles on outdoor activities, especially for family groups; fishing, hunting, camping, in Arizona region. Pays about 1¢ to 2¢ a word. Photos necessary; pays $3 to $4 for 8 × 10 black-and-white glossies. Reports in 2 weeks.

OUTDOOR WORLD—24198 West Bluemound Rd., Waukesha, Wis. 53186. Dorothy Deer, Associate Editor.
Articles with photos on nature and outdoor activities associated with nature. Needs unusual nonfiction, outdoor activity stories and in-depth articles on personal observations of wildlife. No hunting or fishing. Pays $200 to $250 for major articles accompanied with photography; $10 to $90 for short pieces. Query first.

PAGEANT—205 East 42nd St., New York, N. Y. 10017.
Queries only—possible article topics include health, medicine, humor, current social trends, how-to's. Pays about $300. Query with outline.

PANORAMA—Chicago *Daily News,* 401 North Wabash Ave., Chicago, Ill. 60611. Richard Christiansen, Editor.
Articles on the serious and lively arts and other subjects, 500 to 1,500 words: "think" pieces, profiles, humor, reminiscences, by-liners. Some pieces may also be included in the Chicago *Daily News* Service weekly feature packages. Pays 2¢ a word and up, on publication.

PARADE—733 Third Ave., New York, N. Y. 10017. M. David Detweiler, Associate Editor.
National Sunday newspaper magazine. News-related lead articles on important general interest subjects, up to 2,500 words. No spot news. Also shorter stories of interest or service to families. Quizzes considered. Pays well, on acceptance.

PARENTS' MAGAZINE—52 Vanderbilt Ave, New York, N. Y. 10017. Mrs. Genevieve Millet Landau, Editor.
Articles on children's physical and mental growth and development, family and

marriage relationships, community activities, baby care, health, and education, 2,500 to 3,000 words. Prefers warm, anecdotal style, quotes from experts. To query, send one-page outline and one-page introduction. Pays on acceptance.

PEN MAGAZINE—444 Sherman St., Denver, Colo. 80203. Jean Blair Ryan, Editor.
For government employees and public servants. Interesting and informative articles suitable for the family, from 1,500 to 2,500 words. Original ancedotes, fillers. Pays up to 3¢ a word, $7.50 for cartoons and $5.00 for photos (black-and-white glossies only, 8 × 10 preferred), on acceptance.

PENTHOUSE—909 Third Ave., New York, N. Y. 10022. James Goode, Editor.
General-interest or hard-hitting controversial articles to 6,000 words. Pays 25¢ a word, after acceptance.

PETROLEUM TODAY—1801 K. St., N.W., Washington, D. C. 20006. Robert L. Feuquay, Jr., Editor.
Articles of broad general interest related to the oil industry: on oil products, personalities, history, operations, cars, etc. Pays good rates.

PHILADELPHIA INQUIRER TODAY MAGAZINE—Broad and Callowhill Sts., Philadelphia, Pa. 19101. Howard A. Coffin, Editor.
Local interest features, "how-to-cope" articles on contemporary problems, 500 to 2,000 words. Payment varies, is on publication. Query first by letter.

PLAYBOY—HMH Publishing Co., 919 North Michigan, Chicago, Ill. 60611. Hugh M. Hefner, Editor and Publisher.
High-quality entertainment for urban male readers. Timely satire; articles on The Good Life, current events, travel, prominent male personalities, other subjects. Pays up to $3,000, on acceptance. Send articles and queries to David Butler.

POLLUTION CONTROL JOURNAL—144 West 12th St., Denver, Colo. 80204.
Articles, 2,500 to 3,000 words, with glossy prints or color transparencies, on pollution subjects. Pays from $25 to $200, upon publication.

POPULAR PSYCHOLOGY—14018 Ventura Blvd., Sherman Oaks, Calif. 91403. Stephen West, Editor.
Articles, 1,000 to 7,500 words, to interest young, educated adults. All material must be well-researched. Pays $50 to $400, after acceptance. Query.

THE PORTLAND OREGON JOURNAL—Portland, Ore. 97201.
Feature section. Articles of all types, of regional interest, 1,200 words. Pays about $15.

POTOMAC—*The Washington Post*, 1515 L St., N.W., Washington, D. C. 20005. Stephen D. Isaacs, Editor.
Articles on national subjects that have an application in Washington, D. C., or local subjects that have national application. Reportage desired, no fiction or poetry. No word limitation. Pays from $50 to $500.

THE PROGRESSIVE—408 West Gorham St., Madison, Wis. 53703. Morris H. Rubin, Editor.
Articles, 1,000 to 3,500 words, on political, social, economic and international problems. Occasional light features and profiles. Pays $50 to $100, on acceptance.

PSYCHIC—The Bolen Company, 680 Beach St., San Francisco, Calif. 94109.
Accepts articles dealing with psychic phenomena on a sophisticated level. Straightforward, reportorial material only. No fiction, short stories, or personal experiences. Query mandatory. Pays from $75 to $150.

READER'S DIGEST—Pleasantville, N. Y. 10570. DeWitt Wallace and Lila Acheson Wallace, Co-Chairmen.
Condenses material from other publications, but also publishes much original material, especially articles of outstanding merit in the field of personal experience and "Dramas in Real Life." Pays $3,000 for articles in "First Person" category. In all article categories, suggests authors submit query or outline, highlighting especially wide applicability and high readability. Pays top market rates.

REAL WEST—Charlton Publications, Inc., Charlton Bldg., Derby, Conn. 06418.
Articles, 3,000 to 5,000 words, on pioneering experiences in the West during the late 19th and early 20th centuries. Pays 2¢ a word, on acceptance.

REDBOOK—230 Park Ave., New York, N. Y. 10017. Sey Chassler, Editor.
Articles dealing with problems of vital concern to young families. Also dramatic or humorous narrative articles of interest to men as well as women; articles on controversial topics, if well handled. Query Silvia Koner, Assistant Articles Editor with outline. Pays on acceptance.

RELAX—136-138 North Montezuma, Prescott, Ariz. 86301. Travel, hobby, and sports articles, 2,000 to 2,500 words, for doctors. Include names and photos of doctors wherever possible. Pays $250 to $300, on publication.

RETIREMENT LIVING (formerly *Harvest Years/Retirement Living*)—150 East 58th St., New York, N. Y. 10022. Charles Monaghan, Editor.
Articles, 1,000 to 1,500 words, with photos, on needs and activities of recently retired or those planning retirement. Particularly interested in personal-experience articles by experts. Pays 7¢ a word and up, $10 to $50 for photos, on acceptance. Query.

THE RHODE ISLANDER—Providence Sunday *Journal,* Providence, R. I. 02902. Ted Holmberg, Sunday Editor. Garrett D. Byrnes, Special Features Editor.
Articles, up to 2,000 words, about Rhode Island subjects and people, or topics of special interest to the Rhode Island reader. Illustrations are required. Pays up to $225 a week after publication.

ROLL CALL: THE NEWSPAPER OF CAPITOL HILL—636 Pennsylvania Ave., Washington, D. C. 20003.
Factual, breezy articles—history, human-interest pieces, grass-roots political lore, material involving Congress, political changes, good satire or political humor. All material must have strong political or Congressional angle. Slow reports. Prestige high, rates low.

THE ROTARIAN—1600 Ridge Ave., Evanston, Ill. Karl K. Krueger, Editor.
Articles of special interest to business and professional men, featuring international, social and economic problems, ethics of business, community and family better-ment, humor, travel, 1,200 to 2,000 words. Query first. Pays first-class rates, on acceptance.

SAGA—333 Johnson Ave., Brooklyn, N. Y. 11206. Martin M. Singer, Executive Editor.
Nonfiction only, 4,500 to 5,500 words, on subjects of interest to men: first-person adventure, sports, hunting and fishing, war experiences, travel, cars, people in the news, entertainment, etc. Accompanying photos help sale. Authors should read issues of the magazine before submitting material. Rates begin at $300, with peri-odic increases and additional payment for lead articles.

SAN FRANCISCO MAGAZINE—120 Green, San Francisco, Calif. 94111. Geoffrey Link, Editor.
Articles on current and historical personalities, places, and events in the San Fran-cisco Bay area. Articles under 2,500 words with photos preferred.

THE SATURDAY EVENING POST—1100 Waterway Blvd., Indianapolis, Ind. 46202.
Articles, 2,500 to 3,000 words, on topics of contemporary interest in education, the arts, science, politics, etc., for general readers. Advisable to query with brief outline. No opinion pieces or retrospective essays. Pays competitive rates.

SATURDAY NIGHT—52 St. Clair Ave. East, Toronto, Ont., M4T INA, Canada. Robert Fulford, Editor.
Articles of general interest to Canadians, on current affairs, economics, literature, etc., up to 2,000 words. Pays up to $250, on publication.

SCOUTING MAGAZINE—North Brunswick, N. J. 08902. Walter Babson, Editor.
Magazine for adult Scout leaders. Articles of 500 to 1,000 words, on Scouting. Pays from $25 to $75 per magazine page, on acceptance. Query first.

SEA CLASSICS MAGAZINE—7950 Deering Ave., Canoga Park, Calif. 91304.
Historical articles, 1,000 to 3,500 words, with photos, dealing with men and ships at sea. Pays up to $150 on publication.

SEATTLE TIMES SUNDAY MAGAZINE—Box 70, Seattle, Wash. 98111. Richard Johnson, Editor.
Nonfiction only, of regional interest, on topics in the Pacific Northwest, 800 to 1,200 words. Occasional articles on Alaska. Pays $35 if suitable art is furnished; $50 for double spread.

SEPIA—75 East Wacker Dr., Chicago, Ill. 60601. Ben Burns, Editor.
Articles up to 3,000 words, of interest to blacks: personalities, blacks in unusual jobs, news, controversy, entertainment, sports, religion, medicine, education, oddities. First-class picture stories. Needs 2¼ x 2¼ or 4 x 5 transparencies. Pays on acceptance.

SEXOLOGY—200 Park Ave. South, New York, N. Y. 10003. Thetis Powers, Editor.
Queries for articles on all aspects of sexuality. Pays from $125.

SHOWCASE—Chicago *Sun-Times*, 401 No. Wabash Ave., Chicago, Ill. 60611. Herman Kogan, Editor.
Wants articles, profiles and interviews in the field of the serious and lively arts. Maximum article length is 1,500 words and black-and-white photos and drawings are also used. Payment varies and is up to 10¢ a word, on acceptance. Query first.

SIGNATURE—260 Madison Ave., New York, N. Y. 10021.
Diners Club magazine. Articles aimed at young, urban, affluent, well-traveled businessmen. Regular features: travel, impact articles on some issue of social relevance, sports, business, profile of man of national significance, entertainment, good eating and drinking. Query. Pays on acceptance.

SIR!—See *Mr. Magazine.*

SMALL WORLD—Volkswagen of America, Englewood Cliffs, N. J. 07632.
Articles, 600 to 1,400 words, which relate to Volkswagen or Volkswagen owners: personality pieces on well-known VW owners, inspirational or human interest stories with VW tie-in, travel, Volkswagen lore, humor. Color transparencies required. Does not publish poetry. Sample issue and writer's guide on request. Pays $100 per page for text and photos, $250 for covers. Query.

SOUTH CAROLINA MAGAZINE—Box 89, Columbia, S. C. 29202. Sidney L. Wise, Editor.
Features, 1,000 to 2,000 words, about South Carolina and former South Carolinians, past and present. Modest payment, on publication. Replies in two to three weeks. Black-and-white photos should accompany features.

SOUTHLAND MAGAZINE—Long Beach *Independent Press-Telegram,* Sixth and Pine, Long Beach, Calif. 90812. Bob Martin, Editor.
Articles with a Southern California flavor, to 2,500 words, on subjects with mass appeal, including well-known personalities. Suitable photos, if available. Pays about 3¢ a word, following publication. Usually reports in two weeks.

SPORT MAGAZINE—205 East 42nd St., New York, N. Y. 10017. Al Silverman, Editor.
New angles on current controversies and personalities in sports; articles about college athletes. Length: from 750 words for pieces on college athletes, to 6,000 words. Pays from $100 to $750 and up. Query.

SPORTS ILLUSTRATED—Rockefeller Center, New York, N. Y. 10020. Patricia Ryan, Articles Editor.
All material must have some connection with sports, however tenuous. Short, off-the-news features, 600 to 2,000 words; humor, personality, or reminiscence; long pieces, 2,000 to 5,000 words, on major personalities or sporting subjects; fast-breaking news stories for current issue. Pays $250 for short features, $750 and up for long pieces, on acceptance.

STAG—575 Madison Ave., New York, N. Y. 10021. Noah Sarlat, Editor.
Articles to 5,000 words: personality pieces, true adventures, exposés, etc. Pays up to $500 for articles, on acceptance; up to $25 for single photos, up to $50 per page for picture stories.

SUCCESS UNLIMITED—The Arcade Bldg., 6355 North Broadway, Chicago, Ill. 60626. Og Mandino, Executive Editor.
Good market for inspirational and self-help articles stressing positive mental attitude. Also personality pieces on celebrities (entertainment, sports, business) who overcame obstacles and handicaps to reach success. Photos not necessary, but will help sell articles. Pays 5¢ a word for articles, on acceptance; $7.50 for photos, on publication. Reports promptly in three to four weeks.

THE SWINGER—See *Gem.*

TV GUIDE—Radnor, Pa. 19088. Roger J. Youman, Managing Editor.
Articles on television topics. Pays on acceptance. Query first.

TEXAS PARADE—P.O. Box 12037, Austin, Tex. 78711. Kenneth E. Lively, Editor.
Illustrated articles, 1,500 to 2,000 words, on Texas subjects. Pays $25 per printed page, on publication.

TOLEDO BLADE SUNDAY MAGAZINE—Toledo, Ohio 43604. Mike Tressler, Editor.
Sunday newspaper supplement. Occasional local articles of interest to northwestern Ohio readers, with photos. Pays up to $35, on publication; $5 for photos.

TROPIC—*The Miami Herald,* 1 Herald Plaza, Miami, Fla. 33101.
Sunday newspaper supplement. Professional, general-interest articles, 1,000 to 4,000 words, on topics appealing to the more sophisticated reader. Especially interested in personality pieces. Pays up to $250, on acceptance. Query first.

TRUE—1515 Broadway, New York, N. Y. 10036.
Articles on subjects of interest to men, including science, politics, military topics, spectator sports, hunting, fishing, crime, contemporary personalities and true personal adventure. Preferred length: 4,000 words. Also short features, 1,100 words. Pays $1,000 and up for full-length articles. Query first, with outline.

TUESDAY MAGAZINE; TUESDAY AT HOME—437 Madison Ave., New York, N. Y. 10022. Warren Picower, Editor.
Newspaper supplements. Articles, 2,000 words, for black, urban audience. *Tuesday at Home* is aimed primarily at the homemaker. Pays to $350 six weeks after acceptance. Query first.

UNDERSTANDING—Box 206, Merlin, Ore. 97532. Dr. Daniel W. Fry, Editor.
Articles up to 1,000 words on extrasensory perception and related phenomena; new ideas and predictions of things to come; how to create better understanding among peoples of the earth; how to create better understanding of controversial issues. Pays 1¢ a word and up, on publication.

VFW MAGAZINE—Broadway at 34th, Kansas City, Mo. 64111.
Published by Veterans of Foreign Wars of U. S. Timely and factual articles on any subject of national interest, especially features on ways to cope with problems of daily living. How-to features, articles on personalities and sports, and historical pieces are also used. Preferred length: 1,200 to 1,500 words but will consider longer articles. Pays 5¢ to 10¢ a word, on acceptance; extra for photos.

VERMONT LIFE—61 Elm St., Montpelier, Vt. 05602. Walter Hard, Jr., Editor.
Factual articles relating to Vermont, 500 to 2,000 words, especially picture stories. Pays 10¢ a word and up for text, $10 minimum for pictures, shortly after acceptance.

VOGUE—420 Lexington Ave., New York, N. Y. 10017.
Articles of general interest on the arts, music, medicine, travel, original comment on anything that interests the intelligent mind, up to 2,000 words. Pays good rates, on acceptance. Query first.

THE WASHINGTON MONTHLY—1028 Connecticut Ave., N.W., Washington, D. C. 20036. Charles Peters, Editor.
Articles illuminating the processes of government, good and bad. Pays 10¢ a word, on publication. Query essential.

THE WASHINGTONIAN—1218 Connecticut Ave., N.W., Washington, D. C. 20036. Laughlin Phillips, Editor.
Perceptive, non-pompous articles on a variety of subjects for a literate audience, interested in Washington, 1,000 to 4,000 words. Pays 8¢ to 10¢ a word, on acceptance. Query first.

WEEKDAY—20 North Wacker Drive, Chicago, Ill. 60606.
Informative articles, 200 to 1,000 words, on meeting everyday problems—consumer buying, legal problems, community affairs, real estate, education, human relations, etc. Pays $10 to $40, on acceptance.

WEEKEND MAGAZINE—231 St. James St. West, Montreal, Que., Canada. Frank Lowe, Editor.
General interest articles and light fiction from 500 to 2,750 words. No "how-to-get-thin" or dieting pieces. Pays from $15 to $400, on acceptance. Query first.

WEIGHT WATCHERS MAGAZINE—W/W Twenty-first Corp., 635 Madison Ave., New York, N. Y. 10022. Matty Simmons, Editor. Edythe K. Tomkinson, Feature Editor.
General-interest articles and light fiction from 500 to 2,750 words. Include word count with manuscript. No "how-to-get-thin" or dieting pieces. Pays from $15 to $400, on acceptance. Query first.

WESTWAYS—Box 2890, Terminal Annex, Los Angeles, Calif. 90051.
Articles, 1,000 to 3,000 words, and photo essays on western U.S., Canadian and Mexican activities, natural science, travel, contemporary events, history, etc. Pays 10¢ a word and up, on acceptance; $20 and up for black-and-white photos; $25 to $200 for color transparencies. Query preferred.

WOMAN'S DAY—1515 Broadway, New York, N. Y. 10036. Geraldine Rhoads, Editor.
Serious or humorous articles, 1,500 to 3,500 words, on subjects of interest to women: marriage, child care, family health, money management, vacations, education, leisure activities, etc. Short service or inspirational pieces of 400 to 750 words on all subjects. Top rates, on acceptance.

WOODMEN OF THE WORLD MAGAZINE—1700 Farnam St., Omaha, Neb. 68102. Leland A. Larson, Editor.
General-interest articles, on history, travel, outdoor and indoor sports, do-it-yourself, science, television, movies, household tips, etc. Pays 2¢ a word, on acceptance; $5 per photo.

YANKEE—Dublin, N. H. 03444.
Articles with New England locale, not over 2,000 words, preferably with black-and-white photos and/or 4 x 5, 2¼ square, or 35 mm color transparencies. Pays $25 to $400; average $250 to $300.

THE YANKEE GUIDE TO THE NEW ENGLAND COUNTRYSIDE—143 Newbury St., Boston, Mass. 02116. Georgia Orcutt, Editor.
Biannual guidebook. Articles, 500 to 2,000 words, with photos, on family activities in New England. Also, short features two printed pages long. Pays from $50 to $200, on publication. Query a must.

COLLEGE, LITERARY, AND LITTLE MAGAZINES

AMERICAN JOURNAL OF POLITICAL SCIENCE (formerly *Midwest Journal of Political Science*)—Wayne State University Press, Detroit, Mich. 48202. Address John H. Kessel, Editor, Dept of Political Science, Ohio State University, Columbus, Ohio, 43210.
Articles, to 6,000 words, addressed to professional concerns of political scientists. Query. Pays in reprints.

AMERICAN QUARTERLY—Box 1, Logan Hall, University of Pennsylvania, Philadelphia, Pa. 19174. Murray G. Murphey, Editor.
Careful studies of any aspect of U.S. culture from an interdisciplinary point of view. Articles, 3,000 to 5,000 words; notes, 1,000 to 2,000 words; reviews, 200 to 2,000 words. No payment.

THE AMERICAN REVIEW (formerly *New American Review*)—Bantam Books, 666 Fifth Ave., New York, N. Y. 10019. Theodore Solotaroff, Editor.
High-quality essays showing fresh, articulate writing and thought. Send complete manuscript with stamped return envelope. Reports in about four weeks.

ANTIOCH REVIEW—Yellow Springs, Ohio 45387. Lawrence Grauman, Jr., Editor.
Articles of current significance and more than scholarly interest, in the humanities and social sciences, 2,000 to 8,000 words. Pays $8 per published page, on publication.

ARARAT—109 East 40th St., New York, N. Y. 10016.
Publication of the Armenian General Benevolent Union of America. Articles, 1,000 to 5,000 words, on some aspect of Armenian experience in America. Pays $30 to $60, on publication.

ARIZONA QUARTERLY—University of Arizona, Tucson, Ariz. 85721. Albert F. Gegenheimer, Editor.
Literary essays, Southwestern regional material, and articles of general interest. No payment. Annual awards.

ARTS IN SOCIETY—University Exchange, University of Wisconsin, 610 Langdon St., Madison, Wis. 53706.
Articles, 2,500 to 3,500 words, on teaching and learning of the arts; aesthetics and philosophy; social analysis; significant examples of creative expression in media which may be served by printing process. Pays honorarium upon publication.

BALL STATE UNIVERSITY FORUM—Ball State University, Muncie, Ind. 47306.
Merrill Rippy and Frances Mayhew Rippy, Editors.
Articles of general interest in any field, 500 to 4,000 words. Pays in copies.

BOSTON UNIVERSITY JOURNAL—P.O. Box 357, B.U. Station, Boston, Mass.
02115.
Articles, photographs. Pays in copies.

BUCKNELL REVIEW—Bucknell University, Lewisburg, Pa. 17837. Harry R. Garvin,
Editor.
Scholarly articles in letters, arts and sciences. No payment.

THE CANADIAN FORUM—56 Esplanade St. East, Toronto, 1, Ont., Canada.
Abraham Rotstein, Managing Editor.
Articles of interest to Canadians, on current events, politics, art, etc., 1,500 to
2,000 words. No payment.

THE CHICAGO REVIEW—The University of Chicago, Chicago, Ill. 60637. R. A.
McKean, Editor.
Essays, interviews, book reviews, of any length.

CIMARRON REVIEW—Oklahoma State University, Stillwater, Okla. 74074. Jeanne
Adams Wray, Managing Editor.
Nonfiction of opinion, comment, and observation in all humanistic fields: history,
philosophy, sociology, economics, political science, etc. Length: 1,500 to 3,500
words. No payment.

COLORADO QUARTERLY—Hellems 124, University of Colorado, Boulder, Colo.
80302. Paul Carter, Editor.
Non-technical articles, 4,000 words, for the general reader, preferably written by
specialists in humanities, science, economics, politics, Western problems and history. Pays up to $20, on acceptance.

THE CONNECTICUT CRITIC (formerly *New England Review*)—P.O. Box 127,
Cheshire, Conn. 06410. John DeStefano, Editor.
Articles to 3,000 words, on cultural topics appealing to educated readers. Short,
amusing pieces, and informal criticism. All types of fillers. Pays in copies.

DASEIN—G.P.O. Box 2121, New York, N. Y. 10001. Percy Johnston, Editor.
Nonfiction of a serious nature on scholarly subjects. No payment.

THE DEKALB LITERARY ARTS JOURNAL—DeKalb College, 555 Indian Creek
Dr., Clarkston, Ga. 30021.
Personal and expository essays, of any length. Pays in copies.

DESCANT—Texas Christian University, T.C.U. Sta., Fort Worth, Tex. 76129. Betsy
Colquitt, Editor.
Critical articles on modern literary works and literary philosophy, up to 3,000
words. Pays in copies.

EIGHTEENTH-CENTURY STUDIES—Dept. of English, University of California,
Davis, Calif. 95616.
Scholarly and critical essays dealing with aspects of eighteenth-century culture, to
6,500 words. No payment.

EVERGREEN REVIEW—53 East 11th St., New York, N. Y. 10003. Barney Rosset, Editor.
Contemporary, high-quality, nonfiction of varying lengths. Pays $45 a page, on publication.

FORUM—University of Houston, Houston, Tex. 77004.
Articles aimed at the intelligent layman, on topics in letters, science, and the arts. Pays in copies.

FOUR QUARTERS—La Salle College, Philadelphia, Pa. 19141. John Keenan, Editor.
Critical articles on particular authors or individual works. Think pieces on history, politics, the arts. Literate style, free of jargon. Length: 1,500 to 6,000 words. Pays up to $25, on acceptance.

THE FREE LANCE—6005 Grand Ave., Cleveland, Ohio 44104. Casper LeRoy Jordan, Editor.
Short, critical essays. Pays in copies.

THE GEORGIA REVIEW—University of Georgia, Athens, Ga. 30601. James B. Colvert, Editor.
Articles in the general field of the humanities. Pays on publication.

GREEN RIVER REVIEW—Box 812, Owensboro, Ky. 42301. Raymond Tyner and Emil Ahnell, Editors.
Essays, about 3,000 words in length. Pays in copies.

HUDSON REVIEW—65 East 55th St., New York, N. Y. 10022. Frederick Morgan, Editor.
Essays on literature, the arts, and general cultural subjects; criticism and reviews. Pays 2½¢ a word.

INDIAN VOICE—P.O. Box 2033, Santa Clara, Calif. 95051.
Accurate, scholarly articles, to 3,000 words, on Indian history, with black-and-white photos. Pays in copies.

JOURNAL OF THE WEST—1915 South Western Ave., Los Angeles, Calif. 90018. Lorrin L. Morrison and Carroll Spear Morrison, Editors.
Scholarly articles, 2,500 to 7,500 words, on historical, geographical, and archaeological aspects of the western United States. Illustrative photos and maps. Pays in reprints.

KANSAS QUARTERLY—Dept. of English, Kansas State University, Manhattan, Kansas 66502.
General articles and criticism. Articles on history, sociology, art and the folklore of the Midwest or High Plains area used in special issues, but query first. No payment.

THE LITERARY REVIEW—Fairleigh Dickinson University, Rutherford, N. J. 07070. Charles Angoff, Editor.
Sketches and imaginative essays about literature, of any length. Pays in copies.

MACABRE—26 Fowler St., New Haven, Conn. 06515. Joseph Payne Brennan, Editor.
Brief articles; weird, supernatural, eerie, macabre subject matter, including "true experience" accounts. Pays in copies.

THE MALAHAT REVIEW—University of Victoria, Victoria, B. C., Canada. Robin Skelton and John Peter, Editors.
High-quality articles, 2,000 to 5,000 words. Interested in first English translations of work from Latin America, Continental Europe, and Asia. Pays $25 per thousand words for prose. Also uses photos or drawings in groups of 12 to 16. Pays $10 each.

MASSACHUSETTS REVIEW—Memorial Hall, University of Massachusetts, Amherst, Mass. 01002. Robert Tucker and John H. Hicks, Editors.
Literary criticism, articles on public affairs and articles of general interest in the intellectual disciplines. Small payment.

MEDITERRANEAN REVIEW—Orient, N. Y. 11957.
Criticism, commentary, essays, reviews, interviews, and profiles. Pays by arrangement.

MICHIGAN QUARTERLY REVIEW—3032 Rackham Bldg., University of Mich., Ann Arbor, Mich. 48104. Sheridan Baker, Editor.
Articles, 2,000 to 3,000 words, of lively intellectual interest. Pays 2¢ a word, after acceptance.

MIDWEST JOURNAL OF POLITICAL SCIENCE—See *American Journal of Political Science.*

MIDWEST QUARTERLY—Kansas State College, Pittsburg, Kans. 66762. Rebecca Patterson, Editor.
Analytical and speculative articles of a scholarly nature, on any topic of contemporary interest. Best length is 2,000 to 4,000 words, but lengths up to 5,000 words are occasionally acceptable. No payment.

MONTHLY REVIEW—116 West 14th St., New York, N. Y. 10011. Harry Magdoff, and Paul M. Sweezy, Editors.
Serious nonfiction, 2,500 words, on politics and economics from an independent socialist point of view. Pays $25 to $50 on publication.

MOSAIC—Box 2, Administration Bldg., University of Manitoba, Winnipeg, Canada.
Scholarly, lively articles, to 5,000 words, relating to the comparative study of literature and ideas. Query first.

MOVING OUT—Box 26, University Center, Wayne State University, Detroit, Mich. 48202.
Feminist magazine. Essays about women, interviews with prominent women. Pays in copies.

NEW ENGLAND QUARTERLY—Hubbard Hall, Brunswick, Maine 04011. Herbert Brown, Editor.
Historical, biographical and critical articles dealing with New England life and letters; around 20 pages. No payment. Query first.

NEW ENGLAND REVIEW—See *The Connecticut Critic.*

NEW LETTERS (formerly *University Review*)—University of Missouri at Kansas City, Kansas City, Mo. 64110.
High-quality articles and essays, 1,200 to 4,000 words. Modest payment. No unsolicited manuscripts.

NEW ORLEANS REVIEW—Loyola University, New Orleans, La. 70118.
Scholarly, scientific or general-interest nonfiction, up to 24 typed pages, plus book and movie reviews. Pays $50 for articles.

THE NEW RENAISSANCE—9 Heath Rd., Arlington, Mass. 02174.
Provocative or controversial articles, well-researched and written with style. Also, quality essays and criticism (literary, theatre, film). Query first. Pays up to $25, after publication.

NEW UNIVERSITY THOUGHT—Box 7431, Detroit, Mich. 48202. Nicolette Carey, Managing Editor.
Articles on foreign and domestic politics, student problems, academic subjects; literary and film criticism; reviews, 3,000 to 12,000 words. No payment.

THE NEW YORK QUARTERLY—Columbia University Club, 4 West 43rd St., Rm. 603, New York, N. Y. 10036.
Critical essays on craft and technique of poetry, 800 to 2,000 words.

THE NORTH AMERICAN REVIEW—University of Northern Iowa, Cedar Falls, Iowa 50613. Robley Wilson, Jr., Editor.
Articles on contemporary affairs, and regular reports from North American cities; most are commissioned, so query first. Payment arranged, minimum $10 per printed page.

OCCIDENT—Eshleman Hall, University of California, Berkeley, Calif. 94720.
Essays of literary interest. Pays in copies.

THE OHIO REVIEW: A JOURNAL OF THE HUMANITIES—Ellis Hall, Ohio University, Athens, Ohio 45701.
Articles within the general area of the humanities, aimed toward the learned but not specialized reader, especially those articles not limited in interest to a single discipline. No length restrictions; average length, 6,000 words. Pays in reprints and copies.

OYEZ!—Roosevelt University, 430 South Michigan Ave., Chicago, Ill. 60605.
Essays on the arts. No payment.

PARTISAN REVIEW—Rutgers, 191 College Ave., New Brunswick, N. J. 08903.
Nonfiction. Manuscripts held at least 5 months. Pays 1½¢ a word, on publication.

PERSONALIST—School of Philosophy, University of Southern California, Los Angeles, Calif. 90007. John Hospers, Editor.
Articles on philosophy. No word limit. No payment.

PERSPECTIVE—Washington University P. O., St. Louis, Mo. 63130. Jarvis Thurston and Mona Van Duyn, Edtiors.
Articles on contemporary literature, to 10,000 words. No payment.

PLACE: WORKINGMAN'S GUIDE TO THE UNIVERSE—855 High St., Palo Alto, Calif. 94301.
Articles, to 8,000 words, that are place-oriented. Pays 1¢ a word, on publication.

PRAIRIE SCHOONER—219 Andrews Hall, University of Nebraska, Lincoln, Nebr. 68508. Bernice Slote, Editor.
Criticism bearing on contemporary American scene. Pays in copies and reprints.

PRISM INTERNATIONAL—c/o Creative Writing, University of British Columbia, Vancouver 8, B. C., Canada.
Literary essays, to 5,000 words. Payment varies, is on publication.

PYRAMID—32 Waverly St., Belmont, Mass. 02178. Ottone M. Riccio, Editor.
Articles and essays on experimental writing and preferably in that style. Pays in copies.

QUEEN'S QUARTERLY—Queen's University, Kingston, Ont., Canada.
Literary articles, 2,000 to 3,000 words, treated objectively in a style which avoids journalistic and academic jargon. Pays $3 per page, on publication.

THE SATIRE NEWSLETTER—State University of New York College, Oneonta, N. Y. 13820.
Essays, articles, either satirical in nature or relating to satire. Pays in copies.

THE SERIF—Kent State University, Kent, Ohio 44242. Alex Gildzen and Dean H. Keller, Co-editors.
Articles on bibliography, book collecting and rare book librarianship. Preferred length for major articles: 5,000 to 7,000 words. Also checklists of works by and about writers and on special subjects. No payment.

SEWANEE REVIEW—Sewanee, Tenn. 37375. Andrew Lytle, Editor.
Literary articles of high quality. Pays $10 to $12 a printed page.

THE SMITH—5 Beekman Street, New York, N. Y. 10038. Harry Smith, General Editor; Sidney Bernard, Roving Editor.
Nonfiction of almost all kinds except the *Reader's Digest* type of sentimentality. Modest payment on acceptance, plus copies on publication.

SNOWY EGRET—205 South Ninth St., Williamsburg, Ky. 40769. Humphrey A. Olsen, Editor.
Articles up to 10,000 words on naturalists and nature subjects from a literary point of view, including fiction, biography, criticism and essays. Pays $2 per magazine page, on publication.

THE SOUTH ATLANTIC QUARTERLY—Duke University Press, College Station, N. C. 27708. W. B. Hamilton, Editor.
Current-interest, historical and critical articles, not too technical in appeal, about 8 to 12 printed pages. Pays $2 per printed page, shortly after publication.

SOUTH DAKOTA REVIEW—Box 111, University Exchange, Vermillion, S. D. 57069. John R. Milton, Editor.
Articles to about 5,000 words. Regional emphasis. Pays in copies.

SOUTHERN HUMANITIES REVIEW—Auburn University, Auburn, Ala. 36830.
Essays and articles, 3,500 to 5,000 words. Pays in copies.

SOUTHERN REVIEW—Drawer D, University Sta., Baton Rouge, La. 70803. Donald E. Stanford and Lewis P. Simpson, Co-Editors.
Essays, 4,000 to 10,000 words, of lasting literary merit. Pays 3¢ a word, on acceptance.

SOUTHWEST REVIEW—Southern Methodist University, Dallas, Tex. 75222. Margaret Hartley, Editor.
Articles, 1,500 to 4,000 words. Pays on publication.

THE STUDENT—127 Ninth Ave., North, Nashville, Tenn. 37203. Norman Bowman, Editor.
Articles on the spiritual and moral concerns of contemporary college students and on practical aspects of campus life; also lighter feature materials with collegiate flavor. Pays 2½¢ a word, on acceptance.

TAMARACK REVIEW—Box 159, Postal Sta. K, Toronto 12, Ont., Canada.

Literary articles to 7,500 words, mainly by Canadian authors. Pays $10 per printed page, on publication.

THE TEXAS QUARTERLY—Box 7517, University Sta., Austin, Tex. 78712. Harry Ransom, Editor.
Lively essays in the humanities, science and social sciences, written for the literate general reader and preferably crossing academic lines. Pays on publication.

TRIQUARTERLY—University Hall 101, Northwestern University, Evanston, Ill. 60201.
Articles for an international audience. No length or subject limits. Primarily a review of arts, letters, and opinion. Payment varies, is on publication.

THE UNIVERSITY OF DENVER QUARTERLY—University of Denver, Denver, Colo. 80201. Burton Feldman, Editor.
Literary, cultural essays and articles. Also book reviews. No length limit; queries welcome.

THE UNIVERSITY OF PORTLAND REVIEW—University of Portland, Portland, Ore. 97203. Thompson M. Faller, Editor.
Articles and essays, 500 to 2,500 words, of scholarly or academic interest. No payment.

THE UNIVERSITY OF WINDSOR REVIEW—Dept. of English, University of Windsor, Ontario, Canada.
Articles, 15 to 20 typed pages, on arts and sciences, politics, and social sciences. Pays in copies.

THE UNIVERSITY REVIEW—See *New Letters*.

VIRGINIA QUARTERLY REVIEW—1 West Range, Charlottesville, Va. 22903.
Serious essays and articles on literary, scientific, political and economic subjects, 3,000 to 6,000 words. Pays $5 a page (about 350 words), on publication.

WASCANA REVIEW—Wascana Parkway, c/o Regina Campus, Regina, Saskatchewan, Canada.
Nonfiction, 2,000 to 6,000 words. Pays $3 per page, after publication.

WEST COAST REVIEW—Simon Fraser University, Burnaby 2, B. C., Canada.
Nonfiction with a focus on creativity, 1,000 to 3,000 words. Pays from $5 to $25, on acceptance.

WESTERN FOLKLORE—University of California Press, Los Angeles, Calif. 90024.
Folklore material with philological treatment only, 2,000 to 3,000 words. Also fillers. No creative writing. No payment. Address D. K. Wilgus, Editor, Folklore Mythology Group, Univ. of California, Los Angeles, Calif. 90024.

WESTERN HUMANITIES REVIEW—OSH 316, University of Utah, Salt Lake City, Utah 84112. Jack Garlington, Editor.
Nonfiction on art, politics, world affairs, music, and literary criticism. Pays in copies and reprints.

YALE REVIEW—28 Hillhouse Ave., New Haven, Conn. 06507. J. E. Palmer, Editor; Mary Price, Managing Editor.
Limited market for a variety of highest-grade articles, 3,000 to 5,000 words. Pays on publication.

RELIGIOUS AND DENOMINATIONAL MAGAZINES

A.D.—Presbyterian Life Edition and United Church Herald Edition, 1840 Interchurch Center, 475 Riverside Dr., New York, N. Y. 10027.
Articles, to 2,500 words, of interest to members of United Church of Christ and United Presbyterian Church. Pays $35 to $150, on acceptance. Query.

AMERICA—106 West 56th St., New York, N. Y. 10019. Donald R. Campion, S.J., Editor.
Nonfiction from 1,000 to 1,500 words, discussing current events, social criticism, international and domestic problems, family life, and humor. Pays $50 to $75, on acceptance.

AMERICAN BIBLE SOCIETY RECORD—1865 Broadway, New York, N. Y. 10023. Benjamin A. Bankson, Editor.
All material must be related to the purposes and work of American Bible Society. Pays on acceptance.

THE AMERICAN ZIONIST—145 East 32nd St., New York, N. Y. 10016. Elias Cooper, Editor.
Articles on Israel, the Middle East, Jewish issues in the United States or elsewhere, 2,000 words. Pays $50 to $100, on publication.

ANNALS OF GOOD ST. ANNE DE BEAUPRÉ—Basilica of St. Anne, Quebec, Canada. Eugene Lefevre, C.S.S.R., Editor; Jean-Claude Nadeau, Managing Editor.
Articles of general Catholic interest, 1,500 to 1,800 words. Welcomes articles on the devotion to St. Anne. Wants photos and illustrations. Pays 1½¢ to 2¢ a word.

BAPTIST HERALD—Roger Williams Press, 7308 Madison St., Forest Park, Ill. 60130. Dr. R. J. Kerstan, Editor.
Nonfiction 800 to 1,600 words; photos or drawings. Pays about $5 for 800 words, after publication.

BAPTIST LEADER—Valley Forge, Pa. 19481.
Articles about churches, church school work and social issues, 750 to 1,600 words. Photos to illustrate articles, or pictures of special interest. Pays 2¢ a word and up, on acceptance.

BRIGADE LEADER—Christian Service Brigade, Box 150, Wheaton, Ill. 60187. Daniel C. Jessen, Editor.
Articles and talks for men to use in boys' club meetings, to 1,200 words. Must have definite Christian (Protestant) emphasis. Photos. Pays 3¢ per published word, $4 to $8 for photos. Writer's Guide available on request.

CAM—General Council of the Assemblies of God, 1445 Boonville, Springfield, Mo. 65802.
Articles, 1,500 to 2,000 words, of religious significance or practical help to Pentecostal Christians attending secular colleges or universities. Pays 1¢ to 2¢ a word.

CAMPUS LIFE—Box 419, Wheaton, Ill. 60187. Harold Myra, Editor.
For Christian teen-agers. Articles must have evangelical slant but cannot be preachy; non-religious articles on *unique* high school activities, with good action photos. Query. Pays 2¢ a word and up, on acceptance.

THE CANADIAN MESSENGER—833 Broadview Ave., Toronto M4K 2P9, Ont., Canada. Rev. F. J. Power, S. J., Editor.
Articles, 1,800 to 2,000 words, about daily life and problems of men and women. Canadian and Catholic tone preferred. Pays 2¢ a word, on acceptance. Address manuscripts to Mrs. M. Pujolas.

CATHOLIC DIGEST—P.O. Box 3090, St. Paul, Minn. 55165.
Articles, 2,000 to 2,500 words, on Catholic and general subjects but is 95% reprint

in content. Fillers for special departments; see magazine. Pays up to $200 for original articles, $50 and up for reprints; $4 to $50 for fillers. Send manuscripts attention of Articles Editor.

CATHOLIC LIFE—9800 Oakland Ave., Detroit, Mich. 48211. Robert C. Bayer, Editor.
Catholic missionary magazine. Needs articles, 600 to 1,200 words, on Catholic missionary work in Hong Kong, East Pakistan, India, Burma, Japan, Latin America, and underdeveloped nations around the world. Accompanying photos or drawings. Pays 2¢ a word, $2 for photos, on publication.

CATHOLIC RURAL LIFE—3801 Grand Ave., Des Moines, Iowa 50312. Msgr. J. G. Weber, Editor.
Short articles with spiritual emphasis and rural background. Pays $20 to $30, shortly after acceptance. Also cartoons and photos.

CATHOLIC WORLD—1865 Broadway, New York, N. Y. 10023.
Articles, up to 2,800 words, on national and international events, politics, science, literature, etc. Pays $75, on publication. Query first.

THE CHAPLAIN—122 Maryland Ave., N. E., Washington, D. C. 20002. Edward I. Swanson, Editor.
Interdenominational. Articles on chaplaincy, history, biography, and program. Also on preaching, worship, theology, church school, etc., aimed at chaplain-ministers in military service. Length, about 1,500 to 2,000 words. Pays 1½¢ to 2¢ a word, on acceptance.

CHICAGO STUDIES: AN ARCHDIOCESAN REVIEW—Box 665, Mundelein, Ill. 60060.
Scholarly articles, 5,000 to 6,000 words, on the fields of scripture, theology, liturgy, catechetics, canon law, and philosophy. Payment varies. Address The Editors.

CHORAL OVERTONES—See *The Church Musician.*

CHORAL TONES—See *The Church Musician.*

THE CHRISTIAN—See *The Disciple.*

CHRISTIAN ADVOCATE—See *United Methodists Today.*

CHRISTIAN BOOKSELLER—Gundersen Dr. and Schmale Rd., Wheaton, Ill. 60187.
Trade magazine for Christian booksellers, publishers and suppliers. Articles, 800 to 1,000 words, with photos, on various phases of operating religious book and supply stores, management, sales techniques, success stories, trends in the Christian book trade. Pay from $25 up to $50 for articles with photos, on publication. Queries preferred.

THE CHRISTIAN CENTURY—407 South Dearborn St., Chicago, Ill. 60605.
Ecumenical. Articles on education, economics, social problems, current issues, etc., particularly with religious angle, 1,500 to 2,500 words. Pays 2¢ a word, on publication.

CHRISTIAN HERALD—Chappaqua, N. Y. 10514. Kenneth L. Wilson, Editor.
Interdenominational. Articles 2,500 words, on current social problems and solutions or subjects with religious, moral implications. Also, personal experience articles in these areas. Pays $100 and up for full-length nonfiction; $10 and up for short pieces.

THE CHRISTIAN HOME—201 Eighth Ave. South, Nashville, Tenn. 37203.
Methodist. Educationally sound articles, 1,000 to 2,000 words, of interest to parents; may be humorous. Pays on acceptance.

CHRISTIAN LIFE MAGAZINE—Gundersen Dr. and Schmale Rd., Wheaton, Ill. 60187. Robert Walker, Editor.
Articles, 2,500 to 4,000 words, on evangelical Christian devotional subjects, trends in present-day missions, Christian organizations, churches, etc., outstanding spiritual developments in the lives of Christians; inspirational articles on the practical aspects of successful Christian living. Photos. Queries preferred. Pays up to $150, on publication.

CHRISTIAN LIVING—Mennonite Publishing House, Scottdale, Pa. 15683. Daniel Hertzler, Editor.
Articles on the application of Christian faith to personal life, family life, and church-community building. Preference for anecdotal and first-person style over abstract "think-piece" writing. Photos. Aspires to high level of literary excellence for somewhat specialized audience. Queries recommended. Modest payment, on acceptance.

CHRISTIANITY AND CRISIS—537 West 121st St., New York, N. Y. 10027. Wayne H. Cowan, Editor.
Articles on political analysis, theological analysis, social comment from 2,000 to 4,000 words; small cuts and photos used. Payment up to $50 for a full-length article, upon publication.

CHRISTIANITY TODAY—1014 Washington Bldg., Washington, D. C. 20005. Harold Lindsell, Editor.
Doctrinal, devotional and interpretive essays from an evangelical Protestant perspective, 1,500 to 2,500 words, for students of the Bible and ministers and laymen. Pays $75 to $100.

THE CHRONICLE REVIEW—491 Lawrence Ave. West, Suite 400A, Toronto 20, Ont., Canada.
Articles, 1,000 to 5,000 words, on Jewish themes, preferably with Canadian slant, and with photos. Pays from $20 to $50.

CHURCH ADMINISTRATION—127 Ninth Ave. North, Nashville, Tenn. 37203. Lucy R. Hoskins, Editor.
Southern Baptist. Articles, 750 to 1,200 words, in such administrative areas as programming, staffing, organization, financing, facilities, and communication. Pays 2½¢ per usable word, on acceptance.

THE CHURCH HERALD—630 Myrtle St. N. W., Grand Rapids, Mich. 49504.
Official magazine of the Reformed Church in America. Wants articles, 800 to 2,500 words, written from a Christian perspective on: the creative use of leisure, communication between the generations, personal fulfillment, Christian faith and practice, possible solutions to problems of age, divorce, sex, planned parenthood, abortion, race relations, drug and alcohol addiction. Pays 2¢ a word and up.

CHURCH MANAGEMENT: THE CLERGY JOURNAL—115 North Main St., Mt. Holly, N. C. 28120. Norman L. Hersey, Editor.
Articles, 500 to 1,800 words, on Protestant church administration, education, worship, law, building, etc. Pays $10 and up per article.

THE CHURCH MUSICIAN—127 Ninth Ave., North, Nashville, Tenn. 37203.
Published by the Church Music Department. For Southern Baptist music leaders. Articles, 500 to 1,200 words, on church music. Biographical sketches of musicians; fillers, puzzles, cartoons with a musical touch. Pays about 2¢ a word, on acceptance. Same address and requirements for *Choral Tones* and *Choral Overtones* (slanted for adults).

CHURCH SCHOOL BUILDER—See *The Edge.*

THE CHURCHMAN—1074 23rd Ave., North, St. Petersburg, Fla. 33704. Edna Ruth Johnson, Editor.

Independent journal of religion with liberal views. Articles to 1,000 words on the current social scene. No payment.

COLUMBIA—Box 1670, New Haven, Conn. 06507. Elmer Von Feldt, Editor.
Official journal of the Knights of Columbus. Articles, 1,000 to 3,000 words, directed to the Catholic layman and family, and dealing with current events, social problems, Catholic apostolic activities, education and topics of general interest. Pays $100 to $300, on acceptance.

COMMENTARY—165 East 56th St., New York, N. Y. 10022. Norman Podhoretz, Editor.
General articles, and articles of special Jewish interest, of high intellectual quality. Pays on publication.

COMMONWEAL—232 Madison Ave., New York, N. Y. 10016. James O'Gara, Editor.
Catholic. Articles on political, social and literary subjects, up to 3,000 words. Pays 2¢ a word, on acceptance.

THE COMPANION—15 Chestnut Park Rd., Toronto M4W#1W5, Canada. Rev. Leo Linder, O. F. M. Conv., Editor.
Articles, 1,200 to 1,500 words, on up-to-date national and international subjects, moral and social issues, and inspiration toward better Christian living. Accompanying photos and drawings, if possible. Pays 2¢ a word, on acceptance.

THE CONGREGATIONALIST—26275 Northwestern Hwy., Southfield, Mich. 48076.
Articles, 800 to 1,200 words preferred, 2,000 maximum, emphasizing the free church concept and moral and spiritual concepts. Small honoraria.

CONGRESS BI-WEEKLY—15 East 84th St., New York, N. Y. 10028. Herbert Poster, Editor.
Topical articles, factual or opinion, on issues of interest to liberal Jewish readers. Reviews of books, movies, plays of Jewish interest. Length, 1,500 to 2,500 words. Pays $60 to $75 an article, $25 to $50 for reviews, on publication.

CONQUEST—6401 The Paseo, Kansas City, Mo. 64131. Paul Miller, Editor.
Chuch of the Nazarene. Devotional, informational, illustrated articles, up to 1,200 words, of interest to young people of high school and early college age. Moral tone preferred. Pays 1½¢ per word and up.

CONTACT—302 U.B. Building, Huntington, Ind. 46750. Mary Lou Funk, Associate Editor.
United Brethren in Christ. Christ-centered articles for teens and adults. True stories of notable Christians, 1,20 to 1,500 words; devotional articles, 500 to 1,000 words. Pays ⅔¢ a word, on acceptance.

CROSS AND CROWN: A SPIRITUAL QUARTERLY—6851 South Bennett Ave., Chicago. Ill. 60649.
Doctrinal, Biblical, liturgical, ecumenical, and biographical articles dealing with the spiritual life, 3,000 to 4,000 words. Pays 1¢ a word, on publication.

DAILY BLESSING—P. O. Box 2187, Tulsa, Okla. 74102. Oral Roberts, Editor.
Quarterly. Daily devotionals using lively, timely illustrations followed by a link with Scripture truth, summed up to give a guide and blessing for the day. Simple writing style. 300 words. Writers' guide and sample upon request. Pays $5 to $15. No fiction, cartoons or fillers, little verse. Pays $35 to $75 for scenic color photos; $7.50 for black-and-white.

DAILY MEDITATION—Box 2710, San Antonio, Texas 78206. Ruth S. Paterson, Editor.
Inspirational, self-improvement, nonsectarian religious articles, showing the way to

greater spiritual growth, or on God's mysterious ways. Also articles on Mayan archaeological discoveries. Length, 650 to 2,000 words, fillers to 350 words. Pays ½¢ to 1¢ a word, on acceptance.

THE DISCIPLE (combining *The Christian* and *World Call*)—Box 179, St. Louis, Mo. 63166.
Disciples of Christ biweekly. Some articles related to enrichment of Christian life and church's involvement in society. Pays to $15.

THE EDGE (formerly *Church School Builder*)—6401 The Paseo, Kansas City, Mo. 64131.
Church of the Nazarene. Short articles on Christian education. Pays $20 per 1,000 words, on acceptance.

ENGAGE/SOCIAL ACTION—100 Maryland Ave., N. E., Washington, D. C. 20002.
Articles on social issues and problems for an audience of United Methodist local leaders in social concerns; length 2,000 to 2,500 words; uses photographs. Pays $35, upon publication.

THE EPISCOPALIAN—1930 Chestnut St., Philadelphia, Pa. 19103.
Articles of interest to Protestant Episcopal Church members, 500 to 2,000 words. Photos and art work. Payment varies.

ETC.—6401 The Paseo, Kansas City, Mo. 64131. Paul Miller, Editor.
Church of the Nazarene. Devotional, Bible study and Christian guidance articles up to 1,200 words, of interest to young adults. Pays 1½¢ per word and up, on acceptance.

ETERNITY—1716 Spruce St., Philadelphia, Pa. 19103. William J. Peterson, Editor.
Articles with special religious interest, to 2,000 words. Pays from $15 to $65, on acceptance.

EUCHARIST—194 East 76th St., New York, N.Y. 10021. Rev. William J. O'Halloran, S.S.S., Editor.
A magazine that explains the work of the Blessed Sacrament Fathers and Brothers. Articles, 500 to 2,000 words, should instill Eucharistic spirituality, inspire prayer and apostolic activity and explore private devotion in relation to liturgy and Vatican II. No fiction. Pays 2¢ a word and up, on acceptance.

THE EVANGEL (formerly *Light and Life Evangel*)—999 College Ave., Winona Lake, Ind. 46590. Vera Bethel, Editor.
Free Methodist. Nonfiction, 1,000 to 2,000 words, dealing with the Christian answer to contemporary problems. Also human-interest articles, 1,000 to 2,000 words. Pays 2¢ a word for prose, on acceptance.

EVANGELICAL BEACON—1515 East 66th St., Minneapolis, Minn. 55423.
Evangelical Free Church. Articles, 1,200 to 1,500 words, on religious topics. Pays $10 and up, on publication.

EVENT MAGAZINE—American Lutheran Church Men, 422 South Fifth St., Minneapolis, Minn. 55415. James Solheim, Editor.
Looks mainly for issue-oriented nonfiction. Pays 2¢ a word and up, on acceptance. Interested in freelance photography and artwork.

FACE-TO-FACE—201 Eighth Ave. South, Nashville, Tenn. 37203. Kenneth Winston, Editor.
Methodist. For older teens. Illustrated articles, 1,200 to 1,500 words. Pays 2¢ a word and up, on acceptance. Query first.

FAMILY DIGEST—Noll Plaza, Huntington, Ind. 46750. John Laughlin, Editor.
Catholic. Articles for family reading—instructive, entertaining, inspirational. Length, 500 to 1,500 words. Pays 4¢ a word and up.

FRANCISCAN MESSAGE—Franciscan Publishers, Pulaski, Wisc. 54162. Rev. Richard Tulko, O.F.M., Editor.

Articles, 1,500 to 2,000 words, dealing with positive solutions to everyday problems, and current issues affecting the average American Christian. Pays 1¢ to 2¢ a word.

FRIAR: THE MAGAZINE OF CATHOLIC OPTIMISM—Butler, N. J. 07405. Rev. Rudolf Harvey, O.F.M., Editor.
Catholic. Articles, up to 3,000 words, on general and religious topics. Payment varies, is on acceptance.

FRIENDS JOURNAL—152-A North 15th St., Philadelphia, Pa. 19102. Alfred Stefferud, Editor.
Uses articles on religious and social concerns, to 1,500 words. No payment. Query.

GOSPEL HERALD—Scottdale, Pa. 15683. John M. Drescher, Editor.
Mennonite. Articles, up to 1,200 words, on Christian experience and concerns. Pays up to 1½¢ a word, on acceptance.

GUIDEPOSTS—747 Third Ave., New York, N. Y. 10017.
An inspirational monthly magazine for all faiths. Wants articles and features which tell in simple terms how to apply faith to everyday life. Pays $10 to $25 for short features, 250 words; $25 to $50 for short manuscripts, 250 to 500 words; $50 to $100 for full length manuscripts, 500 to 1,500 words. Send manuscripts with stamped, self-addressed envelope.

HIS—5206 Main St., Downers Grove, Ill. 60515.
Magazine for Christian university students, graduates, faculty. Articles on Christian living on campus; relationship of Christianity to current life, culture, and problems; biography and missionary work. All material must be oriented to the Scriptures. Pays 1¢ a word, on acceptance.

HOME LIFE—127 Ninth Ave. North, Nashville, Tenn. 37203. Dr. Joe W. Burton, Editor.
Southern Baptist. Articles of family interest, up to 3,000 words. Pays 2¢ a word and up, on acceptance.

INTERACTION—3558 South Jefferson, St. Louis, Mo. 63118. Earl Gaulke and Paul Pallmayer, Co-Editors.
Popularly written articles, up to 2,000 words, of educational or inspirational nature, to aid part-time and full-time teachers of religion. Pays $20 to $50.

JEWISH FRONTIER—575 Sixth Ave., New York, N. Y. 10011.
Articles dealing with Judaism, Zionism, Israel and labor in the U.S. or abroad. Length, 2,500 to 4,000 words. Pays 2¢ a word, on publication.

THE LAMP—Graymoor, Garrison, N. Y. 10524. Rev. Charles Angell, Editor.
Articles on ecumenical topics, 1,500 to 2,000 words. Pays $75 to $100 per manuscript.

THE LINK—122 Maryland Ave., N.E., Washington, D. C. 20002. Edward I. Swanson, Editor.
Interdenominational. Articles, to 1,500 words, for young Christian men and women in military service. Pays 1¢ to 1½¢ a word, on acceptance.

LIVE—1445 Boonville Ave., Springfield, Mo. 65802. Dorothy Morris, Editor.
Sunday school paper for adults. Articles, 1,000 to 1,500 words. Should show the reader how to put Bible principles into action in everyday living. Pays up to 1¢ a word, on acceptance. "Suggestions for Writers" sheet sent on request.

THE LIVING LIGHT—Our Sunday Visitor, Inc., 1312 Mass. Ave. N. W., Washington, D. C. 20005.
In-depth theoretical and practical articles, 1,500 to 4,000 words, on developments in religious education and related fields, current trends and problems. Pays 5¢ a word; book reviews, 3¢ a word, on acceptance.

THE LOOKOUT—8121 Hamilton Ave., Cincinnati, Ohio 45231. Jay Sheffield, Editor.
News-type articles. Length, 1,000 to 1,400 words. Pays monthly; usual rate is $35.
Sample suggestions to authors sent on request.

THE LUTHERAN—2900 Queen Lane, Philadelphia, Pa. 19129. G. Elson Ruff, Editor.
Articles, up to 2,000 words, on Christian ideology, personal religious experience,
human-interest topics, the church at work. Pays 2¢ to 5¢ a word, on acceptance.

LUTHERAN STANDARD—426 South Fifth St., Minneapolis, Minn. 55415. Dr.
George H. Muedeking, Editor.
Articles, 500 to 1,300 words, on the church or the Christian life: social, economic
or political issues in the light of Christian•principles; human-interest items; personality articles. Illustrations. Pays 2¢ a word and up, on acceptance.

THE MARIAN—4545 West 63rd St., Chicago, Ill. 60629. Rev. A. Miciunas, M.I.C.,
Editor.
Specific questions on religion, morals, Christian culture, and social problems.

MARRIAGE—Abbey Press Publishing Div., St. Meinrad, Indiana 47577. John J.
McHale, Editor.
Primarily nonfiction, dealing with the relationship between husband and wife.
Interviews, personal experiences, humor, etc., 1,200 to 2,000 words. Some photos
and drawings on assignment only. Payment 5¢ per word, on acceptance. Outlines
preferred rather than completed manuscripts.

MARYKNOLL—Maryknoll Fathers, Maryknoll, N. Y. 10545.
Articles, to 1,500 words: profiles of mission people; socio-economic studies of
mission countries, personal experiences on development-mission work abroad.
Photos. Payment for unillustrated articles, up to $150 depending on length and
quality. Photos: $10 and up for singles, $100 and up for black-and-white photo
essays, $150 and up for color. Query required.

MESSAGE—Southern Publishing Association, Box 59, Nashville, Tenn. 37202. W. R.
Robinson, Editor.
Negro family magazine. Articles, to 2,500 words, on moral issues, mental health,
temperance, inspirational and patriotic themes, nature, juvenile delinquency, the
Bible, religious liberty, marriage and the home, slanted for Negro readers. Pays up
to $35, on acceptance.

MIDSTREAM: A MONTHLY JEWISH REVIEW—515 Park Ave., New York, N. Y.
10022. Shlomo Katz, Editor.
Quality articles and book reviews up to 8,000 words. Pays 3¢ a word, on acceptance.

THE MIRACULOUS MEDAL—475 East Chelten Ave., Philadelphia, Pa. 19144. Rev.
Donald L. Doyle, C.M., Editorial Director.
Stories, up to 3,000 words, within framework of Catholic teaching, but not neces-
sarily religious. Pays 2¢ a word and up, on acceptance. No reprints.

MUSART—National Catholic Music Educators Association, Inc., 4637 Eastern Ave.,
N. E., Washington, D. C. 20018. Rt. Rev. Msgr. Sylvester J. Holbel, Chmn.
Editorial Board.
Articles of general musical interest, 1,200 to 2,000 words, with photos. Special
interest at this time: articles dealing with music in the renewed liturgy of the
Catholic Church. Payment on publication.

NATIONAL CATHOLIC EDUCATIONAL ASSOCIATION MOMENTUM—Suite
350, One Dupont Circle, N.W., Washington, D. C. 20036. Carl Balcerak, Editor.
Articles, 1,500 to 3,000 words. Prefers material on outstanding programs, issues,
and research in education. Book reviews, 500 to 1,500 words. 2¢ per word.
Photos $5. Query.

THE NATIONAL JEWISH MONTHLY—B'nai B'rith, 1640 Rhode Island Ave.,
N.W., Washington, D. C. 20036. Bernard Simon, Editor.

Shorts, 200 to 800 words; articles, 1,000 to 2,500, words of contemporary Jewish interest. Pays 5¢ to 10¢ a word, on acceptance. Additional payment for dramatic photographs to illustrate articles.

NEW/WORLD OUTLOOK—475 Riverside Drive, New York, N. Y. 10027. Arthur J. Moore, Jr., Editor.
Articles on Christian missions, home and foreign; world events and Christian activities. Length, 1,500 to 2,500 words, with photos. Occasional poetry, up to 16 lines. Pays 2¢ a word.

OMI MISSIONS—The Oblate Fathers, Box 96, San Antonio, Tex. 78206.
Catholic. Human-interest articles. Mission stories of the Oblate Fathers, 1,000 to 1,600 words. Pays about 1¢ to 2¢ a word.

THE ORPHAN'S MESSENGER—Box 288, Jersey City, N. J. 07303. Sister Eleanor Quin, C.S.J., Editor.
Catholic. Articles, 500 to 1,000 words, on modern and inspirational topics. Pays 1¢ to 3¢ a word, within a month. Also uses fillers.

OUR FAMILY—Box 249, Dept. E, Battleford, Sask., Canada. Rev. A. J. Materi, OMI, Editor.
Articles, 1,500 to 3,000 words, for family readers: Catholic family living—problems of home, youth, marriage, church, community, national and international affairs. Religious and family cartoons. Pays up to 2¢ a word. Buys reprint rights.

OUR SUNDAY VISITOR—Huntington, Ind. 46750.
Four articles—1,200 to 1,500 words—bought every week: personality features, stories of Catholic lay groups, philosophical, theological. Pays 10¢ a word and up, on acceptance, for most material. Pays $10 to $20 for cartoons.

PASTORAL LIFE—Canfield, Ohio 44406. Rev. Victor Viberti, S.S.P., Editor.
Articles for priests and ministers on pastoral activities, needs, trends, problems and contemporary issues, with practical implications. Uses book reviews, of interest to clergymen. Pays 3¢ a word and up. Query.

THE PENTECOSTAL EVANGEL—Gospel Publishing House, 1445 Boonville, Springfield, Mo. 65802. Robert C. Cunningham, Editor.
Religious material only. Must conform to doctrines and practices of the Assemblies of God, a nationwide fellowship of Protestant evangelical Pentecostal churches. Personal experience articles, 500 to 1,000 words; inspirational fillers (each must illustrate a single thought); black-and-white photos; also full-color transparencies. Pays 1¢ per word and up, upon publication. Also buys second rights. Free sample upon request.

PRESENT TENSE: The Magazine of World Jewish Affairs—165 East 56 St., New York, N. Y. 10022. Murray Polner, Editor.
Serious reportage and analysis of international developments that should concern Jews; memoirs; profiles of Jewish life abroad; 3,000 to 5,000 words, with black-and-white photos if available. Pays on acceptance. Query first.

PEOPLE—1312 Massachusetts Ave., N.W., Washington, D. C. 20005. Carolyn Sherman, Editor.
Catholic. Feature articles on current ideas and action programs in community, church, family and international affairs; cartoons. Pays $1 per published inch.

THE PRIEST—1111 North Richmond St., Chicago, Ill. 60622.
Contemporary, well-written articles, not more than 10 pages double-spaced, on life and ministry of priests, current theological developments, liturgy, pastoral theology, Sacred Scripture, etc., for priests and seminarians.

PURPOSE—610 Walnut Ave., Scottdale, Pa. 15683. David E. Hostetler, Editor.
Articles, 350 to 1,500 words; first-person accounts of faith at work; biographical material on Christians, past and present; personalized pieces on the church at work. Also 8 x 10 photos. Pays up to 2¢ a word for manuscripts, and $5 to $10 for photos. Free sample copies.

QUAKER LIFE—Friends United Meeting, 101 Quaker Hill Drive, Richmond, Ind. 47374.
Nonfiction, 600 to 1,500 words.

QUEEN—40 South Saxon Ave., Bay Shore, N. Y. 11706. Rev. James McMillan, S.M.M., Editor.
Published by the Montfort Fathers to foster a sincere devotion to Mary, and thus encourage personal consecration to Jesus. Fact articles, 1,000 to 2,000 words, dealing with any activity that brings out the importance of devotion to Mary. Illustrative photos. No art work or fillers. Pays various rates, on acceptance. Reports in less than one month.

THE RECONSTRUCTIONIST—15 West 86th St., New York, N. Y. 10024. Dr. Ira Eisenstein, Editor.
Articles, 2,000 to 3,000 words, dedicated to the advancement of Judaism. Pays $20 to $25, on publication.

REVIEW FOR RELIGIOUS—612 Humboldt Bldg., 539 N. Grand Blvd., St. Louis, Mo. 63103.
Nonfiction of interest to religious men and women; any length. Pays $5 per printed page at time of publication.

ST. ANTHONY MESSENGER—1615 Republic St., Cincinnati, Ohio 45210. Rev. Jeremy Harrington, O.F.M., Editor.
National Catholic family magazine. Articles, 2,500 to 3,000 words, on outstanding personalities, major movements in the Church, application of Christian life, education, and personal living (labor, leisure, art, psychology, spirituality). Also human-interest and humor articles, photos and picture stories. Queries welcome. Pays 5¢ a word and up.

SCIENCE OF MIND—Science of Mind Publications, 3251 West 6th St., Los Angeles, Calif. 90005.
Inspirational articles, 1,500 to 2,000 words, on the metaphysical aspects of science, philosophy and religion, that will help the reader deal with problems of daily life. Pays varying rates, on publication.

SH'MA—Box 959, Ansonia Station, New York, N. Y. 10023. Eugene B. Borowitz, Editor.
Articles, all lengths, on ethics, Jewish social strategy, legalization of gambling and homosexuality, Zionism and current events. No payment.

THE SIGN—Monastery Place, Union City, N. J. 07087. Rev. Augustine P. Hennessy, C.P., Editor.
Current events articles, religious articles of particular appeal to Catholics, 1,000 to 3,000 words. Pays $200 to $300, on acceptance.

SIGNS OF THE TIMES—Pacific Press Publishing Association, 1350 Villa St., Mountain View, Calif. 94040. Athur S. Maxwell, Editor.
Seventh-day Adventist. Devotional articles, up to 1,800 words.

SOCIAL JUSTICE REVIEW—3835 Westminister Pl., St. Louis, Mo. 63108. Harvey J. Johnson, Editor.
Articles which view social problems in the light of Catholic social teaching and current scientific studies, 2,000 to 4,000 words. Pays 1¢ a word, on publication.

SPIRITUAL LIFE—2131 Lincoln Rd., N.E., Washington, D. C. 20002. Rev. Christopher Latimer, O.C.D., Editor.
A professional religious journal. Religious essays of expository nature about spirituality in contemporary life, from 3,000 to 5,000 words. No first-person accounts. Pays $40 and up, on acceptance. Consult previous issues.

SUNDAY DIGEST—850 North Grove Ave,, Elgin, Ill. 60120.
Articles up to 1,800 words, on the application of the Christian faith to current problems, the Christian home, interpersonal relationships, Christian personalities, and Protestant church work. Accompanying black-and-white photos, if possible. Anecdotes and inspirational fillers, to 300 words. Pays 3¢ per word and up, on acceptance. Send for free samples and editorial requirements booklet.

THEOLOGY TODAY—Box 29, Princeton, N. J. 08540. Hugh T. Kerr, Editor.
Interested in social, religious, and theological articles treating some aspect of contemporary life from a religious perspective, and in literary analysis. Length: to 1,500 words for shorter articles, 5,000 to 7,000 words for full-length. Also uses poetry. Pays $35 to $50 per article, on publication.

THESE TIMES—Southern Publishing Association, Box 59, Nashville, Tenn. 37202. K. J. Holland, Editor.
Family magazine. Articles, up to 2,500 words, on moral issues, mental health, temperance, inspirational and patriotic themes, nature, juvenile delinquency, the Bible, religious liberty, marriage and the home. Pays up to 10¢ a word, on acceptance.

THE THOMIST—987 Michigan Ave., N.E., Washington, D. C. 20017. Rev. Nicholas Halligan, O.P., Editor-in-Chief.
Scholarly articles on philosophy and theology. Book reviews in the field.

THOUGHT—Fordham University, 441 East Fordham Rd., Bronx, N. Y. 10458. Rev. Joseph E. O'Neill, S.J., Editor.
Scholarly articles on the world of culture and ideas from a Catholic point of view, on questions having permanent value and contemporaneous interest. Well stocked at present. No payment.

TODAY'S CHRISTIAN MOTHER—8121 Hamilton Ave., Cincinnati, Ohio 45231. Wilma L. Shaffer, Editor.
Articles, 600 to 1,000 words, about problems and pleasures of mothers and their preschool children, showing Christian principles in action. Also material for fathers' pages, and pages with creative children's activities. Payment varies.

TOGETHER—See *United Methodists Today.*

TRIUMPH—278-280 Broadview Ave., Warrenton, Va. 22186.. Michael Lawrence, Editor.
In-depth articles with historical and theological approaches welcomed; discussions of current affairs, ecclesiastical and secular, as they relate to Catholicism. Book reviews usually by assignment. Uses artwork of high quality. Pays on publication.

UNITED EVANGELICAL ACTION—Box 28, Wheaton, Ill. 60188. Jim O. Jones, Editor.
Articles on religious, social, and political problems in an evangelical context, 1,500 to 2,500 words. Pays 1¢ to 3¢ a word, on publication. Query first.

UNITED METHODIST TODAY (combining *Christian Advocate* and *Together*)—
1661 North Northwest Highway, Park Ridge, Ill. 60068.
Articles, to 2,000 words with photos, that inform, inspire, and encourage people
in their lives as individual Christians and members of the Christian community.
Pays about $100.

UNITED SYNAGOGUE REVIEW—3080 Broadway, New York, N. Y. 10027. Rabbi
Alvin Kass, Editor.
Articles on synagogues, Jewish worship services, ritual, etc. Length, 1,000 to 1,500
words. Pays 2¢ a word, on acceptance.

UNITY MAGAZINE—Unity School of Christianity, Lee's Summit, Mo. 64063. James
A. Decker, Editor.
Inspirational and metaphysical articles, 500 to 2,500 words. Religious poetry to
20 lines; fillers to 500 words; color transparencies for cover. Pays 2¢ a word
and up for articles; 50¢ a line and up for poetry, on acceptance.

THE UPPER ROOM—1908 Grand Ave., Nashville, Tenn. 37203.
Meditations on Bible texts, 250 words, with illustrations, including a prayer and
Thought for the Day. Pays $5, on publication. Leaflet on writing meditations and
list of topics sent on request.

VENTURE/DASH—Box 150, Wheaton, Ill. 60187.
Published in two editions: for boys 8–11 and young men 12–18. Wants articles
on Christian life-style, youth scene, current issues, interpersonal relationships.
Needs photos, photo-essays of boys in action. Cartoons. Pays 3¢ a word and up,
$7.50 per cartoon, varying rates for photos. Address Manuscript Editor or Graphics
Editor for photos, cartoons. Send for author's guideline packet. Query.

VISTA—Box 2000, Marion, Ind. 46952.
Feature articles, nature, travel, historical, science, 500 to 1,000 words, with photos
or other illustrative material. Also devotional and biographical articles. Pays 2¢
per word, on acceptance.

THE WAR CRY—860 North Dearborn St., Chicago, Ill. 60610.
The Salvation Army. Articles, 1,000 to 1,700 words, on evangelical and inspirational topics; pays $20 to $35.

THE WAY—Mennonite Publishing House, Scottdale, Pa. 15683. Paul M. Schrock,
Editor.
Fast-moving, personal-experience articles, 300 to 1,500 words, showing how faith
in God gives meaning and purpose to life. Inspirational poems, 4 to 12 lines.
Pays 2¢ a word for articles and $5 for poems, on acceptance.

WAY: CATHOLIC VIEWPOINTS—109 Golden Gate Ave., San Francisco, Calif.
94102. Rev. Simon Scanlon, O.F.M., Editor.
Articles: 1,700 to 2,200 words on matters of concern to morally mature persons.
Uses personality profiles showing how a single person's efforts can help create a
better world for others; current social, artistic, cultural trends are explored. "No
preachiness or sentimental pieties, please, but hard-hitting, constructive material."
Photos help. Pays $25 to $50, on acceptance. Sample copies on request.

WORKING FOR BOYS—601 Winchester St., Newton Highlands, Mass. 02161.
Uses general articles, 500 to 1,000 words, and seasonal articles. Send mss. to
Brother Jason, CFX, Assoc. Editor, 800 Clapboardtree St., Westwood, Mass. 02090.

WORSHIP—Liturgical Press, St. John's Abbey, Collegeville, Minn. 56321. Rev. Aelred
Tegels, O.S.B., Editor.
Articles treating Christian worship in its theological, historical, psychological and
sociological aspects. Pays 2¢ a word, on publication.

YOUNG ISRAEL VIEWPOINT—3 West 16th St., New York, N. Y. 10011. Joel Saibel,
Editor.
Articles, for Orthodox Jews, of general Jewish or religious interest.

SPORTS, OUTDOORS, TRAVEL, RECREATION AND CONSERVATION

AERO MAGAZINE—P.O. Box 1184, Ramona, Calif. 92065. Wayne Thomas, Editor.
Factual articles of any length, related to aircraft ownership, from single engine to light business jet, general aviation aircraft. Uses photographs and illustrations. Payment is from $25 to $50 per printed page. Query.

AIRFAIR MAGAZINE—5909 Wilshire Blvd., Los Angeles, Calif. 90036. James C. Clark, Editor.
Travel articles, 3,000 words, on cities in the United States, Europe and other parts of the world. Payment is $150, within 30 days of publication. Send queries or manuscripts with self-addressed, stamped envelopes.

ALASKA, MAGAZINE OF LIFE ON THE LAST FRONTIER—Box 4–EEE, Anchorage, Alaska 99503. Robert A. Henning, Editor.
Articles on Alaska by writers familiar with the subject. Length, 1,500 to 3,000 words. Also uses short articles, 100 to 1,000 words. All material must be accompanied by photos. No fiction or verse. Cartoons (Alaska-Yukon subjects only). Pays $10 to $25 for short pieces, $25 to $100 for longer articles, on publication.

ALOFT—4025 Ponce de Leon Blvd., Coral Gables, Fla. 33146. Karl Y. Wickstrom, Editor.
National Airlines' in-flight magazine. Uses articles, about 1,300 words, giving fresh approaches to cities along the National route. Off-beat angles on places to go; sports or show business personality profiles. Pays $150 to $200 for articles. Query first.

AMERICAN AIRCRAFT MODELER—Potomac Aviation Publications, 733 15th St., N.W., Washington, D. C. 20005. Edward C. Sweeney, Jr., Editor.
Articles, at least six double-spaced pages, on construction and new designs in model aviation. Photos accompanying articles; cartoons related to modeling. Pays the month of publication.

THE AMERICAN FIELD—222 West Adams St., Chicago, Ill. 60606. William F. Brown, Editor.
Good yarns about hunting trips and upland bird shooting experiences. Short articles, up to 1,500 words, on breeding and training hunting dogs, and pointer and setter field trials. Features, up to 3,500 words. Conservation of game resources and restoration of game emphasized. Payment varies, is on acceptance.

AMERICAN FORESTS—1319 18th St., N. W., Washington, D. C. 20036. James B. Craig, Editor.
Well-documented factual articles, to 1,800 words, on outdoor subjects, with pictures. Emphasis on how-to-do-it camping, trailer vacations, horseback trips and hiking. Also 4 × 5 transparencies of outdoor subjects for cover use. Pays 3¢ to 5¢ a word, on publication.

THE AMERICAN RIFLEMAN—1600 Rhode Island Ave. N. W., Washington, D. C. 20036. Ashley Halsey, Jr., Editor.
Factual articles, all lengths, on use and enjoyment of sporting firearms. Pays varying rates, competitive in the field.

ANIMALS—180 Longwood Ave., Boston, Mass. 02115. William Mallard, Editor.
Nonfiction to 600 words, about animals, particularly with humane import. Also articles relating to current animal events and natural history. Good illustrations or photos of animal life. Pays ½¢ a word, on acceptance. $1.50 to $3.00 for photos accepted with accompanying story.

ARCHERY—Rt. 2, Box 514, Redlands, Calif. 92373.

Articles, 1,000 to 2,500 words, on bow and arrow hunting and fishing; also interviews with field archery personnel and articles dealing with the fun and appeal of field archery (as opposed to target archery). Will consider fillers, humor, jokes, etc., individually. Uses photographs and drawings to illustrate articles. Pays up to $50 per published page, including photos and illustrations, on publication. Query.

ARCHERY WORLD—534 North Broadway, Milwaukee, Wis. 53202. Glen Helgeland, Editor.

Articles 1,000 to 3,000 words, on all aspects of archery for hunters and competitive shooters, beginners and professionals. Semi-technical stories, how-to, short photofeature tips. Plenty of hunting coverage. Also related archery subjects. B/W photos inside, color cover. Pays $35 and up, $10 for individual photos. Pays on acceptance.

ARGOSY—420 Lexington Ave., New York, N. Y. 10017.

First-person adventures; exploration, domestic travel, recreation. Fiction of male interest, adventure, the outdoors, mystery; with good character development, conflict and action. Pays $400 to $750 for nonfiction, extra for photos, two weeks after acceptance.

AUTO RACING DIGEST—See *Baseball Digest*.

AWAY—ALA Auto and Travel Club, 888 Worcester St., Wellesley, Mass. 02181. Gerard J. Gagnon, Editor.

Articles, from 800 to 1,500 words and short humor, 500 to 800 words, on travel, tourist attractions and history, preferably with a New England slant. Black-and-white accompanying photos. Pays 10¢ a word, on acceptance. Query.

B. C. OUTDOORS—Box 900, Sta. A., Surrey, B. C., Canada. Art Downs, Editor.

Articles, 2,500 to 3,000 words, on hunting, fishing, travel, hiking, nature, and boating in British Columbia and the Yukon. Pays $40 to $60, on acceptance, extra for black-and-white photos.

THE BACKSTRETCH—19363 James Couzens Highway, Detroit, Mich. 48235. Ruth A. LeGrove, Editor.

Published quarterly in January, April, July and October by United Thoroughbred Trainers of America. Feature articles and stories, with accompanying photos, slanted to the interests of thoroughbred horsemen and fans. Payment after publication.

BASEBALL DIGEST—1020 Church St., Evanston, Ill. 60201. John Kuenster, Editor.

Articles, 800 to 1,200 words, pertaining to the game of baseball and its players. Pays on publication. Same address and requirements for *Football Digest, Basketball Digest, Auto Racing Digest* and *Hockey Digest*.

BASKETBALL DIGEST—See *Baseball Digest*.

BETTER CAMPING—500 Hyacinth Pl., Highland Park, Ill. 60035. Paul Foght, Editorial Director.

Illustrated, quality articles, 1,200 to 2,400 words, covering all types of camping: tents, camping trailers, vehicles. Travel stories must include campground information. Pays 5¢ minimum, on acceptance. Query first. Author's information sheet on request.

BICYCLING!—55 Mitchell Blvd., San Rafael, Calif. 94903. Gail Heilman, Editor.

Articles and fiction, 500 to 3,000 words, for cycling enthusiasts, on touring or racing bicycles here and abroad. Humor, photos, drawings. Pays 50¢ per column inch, on publication; $5 for black-and-white photos, $25 for color transparencies.

BLACK BELT—5455 Wilshire Blvd., Los Angeles, Calif. 90036. Steve W. Smyser, Editorial Director.
Monthly magazine uses articles on judo, ju-jitsu, karate, aikido, kendo, and other Oriental arts and sports of self-defense. Length: 200 to 3,000 words. Illustrations and photos. Pays various rates, according to quality and length.

BOATING—One Park Ave., New York, N. Y. 10016. Moulton H. Farnham, Editor.
Articles on all aspects of boating, both fresh and salt water, especially adventure, navigation, and how-to-do-it projects. Little fiction used. Illustrations important. Length: usually 1,000 to 1,500 words, except for exceptional material. Pays good rates, on acceptance.

BOW & ARROW—Box HH, Capistrano Beach, Calif. 92624. Chuck Tyler, Editorial Director.
Articles, 1,500 to 2,500 words, on bowhunting, target archery, historical pieces and do-it-yourself projects. Emphasis is on the practical and specific. Top payment is $125. Query.

BOWLING—5301 South 76th St., Greendale, Wis. 53129. Stephen K. James, Editor.
Articles on almost any bowling subject, emphasizing league or tournament bowling done in ABC male competition. Popular treatment; pictures important. Length, up to 1,000 words. Pays 3¢ to 5¢ a word. Query first.

BRANIFF PLACE—230 N.E. 70th St. Miami, Fla. 33138.
Uses travel articles, 750 to 1,500 words, on airline's destination-cities. See copies in ticket offices for style and trends. Pays $50 to $100 per article. Query first.

CAMPER COACHMAN—23945 Craftsman Rd., Calabasas, Calif. 91302. Bill Estes, Editor.
Wants articles to 1,500 words on camping coaches hauled on light trucks. Uses travel, novelty, human-interest articles and good do-it-yourself articles relating to campers. Photos required. Pays from $50 to $125, on publication.

CAMPING AND TRAILERING GUIDE—Box 1014, Grass Valley, Calif. 95945. George S. Wells, Editor.
Articles on practical aspects of family camping and trailering; general first-person camp-travel stories. Also build-it-yourself articles, technical tips, boating and wilderness trips. Length: 300 to 800 words plus 2-3 photos for short-short travel pieces; 1,200 to 2,000 words for illustrated feature articles. Pays $25 for short-shorts, $40 and up for features, $10 for cartoons, on acceptance. Also includes *Motor Coach Travel* as a special supplement covering motor home travel.

CAMPING JOURNAL—229 Park Avenue South, New York, N. Y. 10003.
Prefers features about family camping trips: recommended routes, recreational, historic attractions, do's and don'ts, campsite locations and facilities, costs and sources of information. No "My First Camping Trip" stories. Short how-to's should include captioned photos or line drawings. 2,500 words accompanied by at least ten 8 x 10 glossy, black-and-white, captioned photos. Payment, $25 to $75 for 'how-tos"; $100 and up for other articles, on acceptance. Submissions should provide author's Social Security number and a self-addressed, stamped return envelope.

CAMPING MAGAZINE—5 Mountain Ave., North Plainfield, N. J. 07060. Howard P. Galloway, Editor and Publisher.
Articles on organized children's camp administration and operation; leadership training; education, guidance, group work; buildings and equipment; food and feeding programs: Length: shorts, 750 words; longer articles, to 1,500 words. Photographs. No payment.

CANADIAN MOTORIST—2 Carlton St., Toronto 102, Ont., Canada. Jerry Tutunjian, Editor.
Uses travel articles on Canada, the U.S. and abroad. Preferred length: 1,000 to 1,500 words. Uses black-and-white and color pictures. Pays 5¢ per word, $7.50 for black-and-white glossies, $35 for color transparencies.

CAR AND DRIVER—One Park Ave., New York, N. Y. 10016. Bob Brown, Editor.
Nonfiction, to 2,500 words, directed to an audience of knowledgeable enthusiasts." Articles on Detroit or foreign car manufacturers, new developments in cars, safety on highways, profiles of outstanding automotive designers, company heads. Pays up to $500.

CAR CRAFT—8490 Sunset Blvd., Los Angeles, Calif. 90069.
Pictorial features on hot rods, drag cars, events such as drag racng, hot rod car shows, etc. Must have many photos, with captions, and story copy must be concise. Needs colored drag race action photos. Pays $50 a page, on acceptance; occasionally special rates. Query first.

CAROLINA SPORTSMAN—P.O. Box 2581, Charlotte, N. C. 28202. Sidney L. Wise, Editor.
Fiction and nonfiction dealing with outdoor sports (hunting, fishing, boating, camping, riding, etc.) in North and South Carolina, 1,000 to 1,500 words Glossy black-and-whites, preferably 8 x 10. Drawings to illustrate stories in black-and-white line. Pays 1¢ to 2¢ per word, on publication.

CHEVRON USA—The H. M. Gousha Co., 2001 The Alemeda, San Jose, Calif. 95114. Robert L. Iacopi, Editor.
Interested in articles on travel in the West, with emphasis on automobile trips. Length, 300 to 2,000 words. Pays 15¢ a word and up, on acceptance. Also uses humorous anecdotes, 100 to 250 words; cartoons; black-and-white and color photos, for which payment is $35 to $200.

COLORADO—7190 West 14th Ave., Denver, Colo. 80215.
Nonfiction and photos about the Rocky Mountain West, particularly Colorado, Wyoming, New Mexico, and Utah. Length: about 3,000 words. Pays up to $300 for full-length articles.

COMPETITION PRESS & AUTOWEEK—Box A, Reno, Nev. 89506. Russell R. Goebel, Publisher.
Weekly newspaper covering news of all motor sports. Automotive news items and features to 1,200 words. Pays $1 per column inch, $5 for photos, $10 for cartoons, on publication. Query.

THE CONTINENTAL MAGAZINE—Room 956, Central Office Bldg., Ford Motor Company, Dearborn, Mich. 48121. Robert M. Hodesh, Editorial Director.
Service articles, 1,300 to 1,700 words, on travel, entertainment, shopping, sport for the well-to-do. Articles of high quality. Pays on acceptance. Query.

COSMOPOLITAN—224 West 57th St., New York, N. Y. 10020. Helen Gurley Brown, Editor.
First-person narratives about vacation spots for single girls within possible price range. Accompanying candid, 35 mm photos. Preferred length—2,000 to 2,500 words. Payment varies. Query Roberta Ashley, Articles Editor.

CYCLE GUIDE—1440 West Walnut St., Compton, Calif. 90220.
Articles, photos, short stories, or miscellany relating to motorcycles. Pays $35 per page, and up, on publication.

CYCLE WORLD—1499 Monrovia Ave., Newport Beach, Calif. 92663. Ivan Wagar, Editor.
Technical and feature articles of general interest to motorcycle enthusiasts, 1,500 to 2,500 words. Humor, fiction and photos. All material must be accurate and reflect favorably on the sport. Pays 5¢ to 10¢ a word, $5 to $50 for photos, on publication. Query.

THE DESERT MAGAZINE—Palm Desert, Calif. 92260.
Illustrated features about the West and travel in this area, 1,000 to 3,000 words. Photos. Pays 2¢ a word, on publication, plus $3 and up for photos.

DIVE MAGAZINE—P.O. Box 7765, Long Beach, Calif. 90807. Bud Smith, Publisher; Mavis Hill, Associate Editor.
Articles of skin and scuba diving interest only. Some fiction. Uses treasure stories, wreck diving, travel, short humor stories, underseas development, equipment. Unique, glamorous, clear, good quality underwater photos used. No shark scare stories. Payment varies, on publication. One-time rights. Send stamped, self-addressed return envelope.

DIVERSION—1271 Ave. of the Americas, New York, N. Y. 10022. Curtiss Anderson, Editor.
Articles, 300 to 3,000 words with color photos, on sports and recreation, for physicians, dentists, veterinarians, and their families. Pays varying rates. Query.

DOG WORLD—10060 West Roosevelt Road, Westchester, Ill. 60153. George Berner, Publisher.
Technical material of interest to professional dog breeders, exhibitors, and judges.

ENTHUSIAST—Harley-Davidson Motor Co., P.O. Box 654, Milwaukee, Wis. 53201. T. C. Bolfert, Editor.
Fiction and articles, to 5,000 words, on motorcycling subjects. Travel stories, particularly about places not readily accessible by car. Pays 5¢ a word, $7.50 to $15 per photo, on publication.

FAMILY HOUSEBOATING—23945 Craftsman Rd., Calabasas, Calif. 91302. Art Rouse, Editor.
Uses all types of material dealing with houseboats, including how-to, personal experience, and articles on waterways suitable for houseboating. Also uses photos. Pays from $50 to $150, including photos, on publication. Length: to 2,000 words.

FIELD & STREAM—383 Madison Ave., New York, N. Y. 10017. Clare Conley, Managing Editor.
Nonfiction, 1,500 to 2,500 words, with good photographs as illustrations. Occasional fiction; no verse. Pays 12¢ a word and up, on acceptance.

FISH AND GAME SPORTSMAN—P.O. Box 1654, Regina, Sask., Canada. Red Wilkinson, Editor.
Articles, to 2,000 words, on fishing, hunting, camping and outdoor trips and experiences in Alberta and Saskatchewan. Also how-to articles on the areas. Photos. Pays from $40 to $100, on publication.

FISHING FUN MAGAZINE—P.O. Box 24024, Speedway, Ind. 46224. William Wood, Editor.
Fiction, articles, to 1,500 words, on unusual places to fish, family fishing trips, camping-fishing trips; also how-to articles, articles for women and children who fish. Uses humor, fish recipes, fillers, and cartoons. Black-and-white 8 x 10 glossies to illustrate articles, with caption sheet. Pays 3¢ per word and up; from $10 per cartoon and $5 per filler; $3 for black-and-white photos, and $40 to $50 for color transparencies for cover, 35mm or larger. Query for long features.

FISHING IN VIRGINIA—P.O. Box 305, Alexandria, Va. 22313.
Articles, to 2,000 words, on the "how, when and where" theme of fishing in Virginia, offshore Virginia or Chesapeake Bay area. 6 to 8 photos to accompany each article. Pays to $150, on publication.

FISHING WORLD—51 Atlantic Ave., Floral Park, N. Y. 11001. Keith Gardner, Editor.
Articles for sports fishermen, told in narrative form, 1,500 to 3,000 words, dealing with outstanding fishing experiences, angling in particular areas, methods and tackle, in both fresh and salt waters. Photos a must. Pays $150 per package with black-and-white photos, to $200 with color, on acceptance, plus $75 for color transparencies used on cover. Few black-and-white articles needed. No verse or cartoons.

FLORIDA SPORTSMAN—4025 Ponce de Leon Blvd., Coral Gables, Fla. 33146.
Articles, 800 to 1,500 words, on outdoor sports in Florida and the Islands. Looking for lively, although informative material. Good solid how-to stories preferred; no "fish stories", please. Takes strong, positive stand on how to conserve. Pays $50 to $100, or negotiated, on publication.

THE FLYFISHER—4500 Beach Dr. S. W., Seattle, Wash. 98116.
Articles, 2,000 words and under, with black-and-white 8 x 10 glossy photos, on fly-fishing—all game fish eligible. Short pieces.

FOOTBALL DIGEST—See *Baseball Digest*.

FOOTBALL FROM THE EDITORS OF SPORTS TODAY—444 Madison Ave., New York, N. Y. 10022.
Articles, 1,500 words, on top pro football stars. Specializes in hard-hitting, controversial stories. Pays $100 within a month of acceptance.

FORD TIMES—Ford Motor Co., The American Rd., Dearborn, Mich. 48121. Hal Butler, Managing, Editor.
Articles of 1,500 words or less, on recreation and travel related to car ownership; humor; unique and little-known places to visit. Pays 10¢ and up a word, on acceptance. Query preferred.

FOUR SEASONS TRAILS—534 North Broadway, Milwaukee, Wisc. 53202. Glenn Helgeland, Managing Editor.
Articles, 750 to 2,500 words, with color and black-and-white photos, on activities for campers: fishing, rockhounding, snorkeling, shell collecting, hunting, photography, etc. Pays $75 for short black-and-white features to $400 for major full-color work; $100 for cover photo. Query.

FRIENDS—4-213 General Motors Bldg., Detroit, Mich. 48202. Alexander Suczek, Editor.
Photo articles and photos with caption material. Uses articles on travel, with route and recreation information, sports, personalities, unusual news or recreation events, human-interest articles. Both color and black-and-white photos used; write for information on submitting. Pays from $75 a page to $150 a page, including photos. Query first with outline and photo situations.

FUR-FISH-GAME—2878 East Main St., Columbus, Ohio 43209.
Illustrated articles, 2,000 to 2,500 words, on hunting, fishing, etc. Pays 1½¢ to 3¢ a word, on acceptance.

GARCIA FISHING ANNUAL—329 Alfred Ave., Teaneck, N. J. 07666. Robert E. Stankus, Editor.
Yearly publication devoted to international rod and reel sport fishing. Interested in articles, 1,000 to 3,000 words, on angling, with photos. Pays from $100 to $300, on acceptance.

GOLF—380 Madison Ave., New York, N. Y. 10017.
Articles of 1,500 words, on topics of national interest to golfers, with photos if possible. Also short articles, to 500 words. Pays up to $350 for long articles; $50 to $150 for short articles; $50 and up for cartoons. Query first.

GOLF DIGEST—297 Westport Ave., Norwalk, Conn. 06856.
Articles, 500 to 3,500 words, on golf; personalities, special events, instruction (especially authorized by a golf professional), remarkable feats, golf sidelights, etc. Also fiction, fillers, photos, and cartoons. Pays up to 25¢ a word, on acceptance; $50 for cartoons.

GOLF USA—P.O. Box 2102, Jackson, Miss. 39205. Paul Tiblier, Editor.
Short articles about golfers and country clubs, with illustrations. Payment varies, is on publication.

GRIT AND STEEL—P.O. Box 280, Gaffney, S. C. 29340.
Material about game (fighting) fowl, only. Payment, upon publication. Does not want any material from anyone not familiar with this sport.

GUN DIGEST AND HANDLOADER'S DIGEST—20604 Collins Road, Marengo, Ill. 60152. John T. Amber, Editor.
Factual, well-researched articles, to 5,000 words, on guns and other shooting equipment. Hunting material acceptable only if it contains considerable information on guns and ammunition. Pays 4¢ to 10¢ a word, on acceptance. Query first.

GUNS—8150 North Central Park Blvd., Skokie, Ill. 60076. J. Rakusan, Managing Editor.
Articles, 1,500 to 2,500 words, on methods of shooting for target, military, self-defense and hunting. Articles on history or design of guns. Gunsmithing tips. Good photos and illustrations. Pays about 5¢ a word, on publication. Query first.

GUNS & AMMO—8490 Sunset Blvd., Los Angeles, Calif. 90069. George Martin, Editor.
Articles, 1,500 to 2,000 words, of a technical nature directly related to guns and ammunition, target shooting, gunsmithing, etc. Also general articles related to guns and accessories. Photos required. Uses some filler material about guns. Pays from $50.

GUNSPORT AND GUN COLLECTOR—Suite 2100, Clark Bldg., Pittsburgh, Pa. 15222.
Authoritative articles on new sports equipment and/or guns, 'scopes and related items. "Factual" fiction, preferably illustrated, with at least one line drawing or glossy; 2,500 to 5,000 words to book-length. Cartoons with gunning, sports, etc. Uses cover and pictorials in four-color Ektacrome. $10.00 for single cartoon to $125.00 for illustrated hunt story, upon publication. Send stamped, self-addressed return envelope with all material.

GYMNAST—410 Broadway, Santa Monica, Calif. 90401. Glen Sundby, Publisher.
Uses gymnast news: competitions, instructions, personalities, with many photos; fillers. No payment.

HANDBALL—U.S. Handball Association, 4101 Dempster St., Skokie, Ill. 60076.
Articles, 200 to 400 words, and fillers, 30 to 50 words, on handball and handball players. No payment.

HOCKEY DIGEST—See *Baseball Digest.*

HOLIDAY—1100 Waterway Blvd., Indianapolis, Ind. 46202. Cory SerVass, Executive Editor; John J. Rea, Senior Editor.
Articles on travel and leisure subjects, 2,500 to 3,000 words. Pays on acceptance.

HORSE, OF COURSE—Temple, N. H. 03084. R. A. Creene, Editor.
Articles, to 2,000 words, on training, management, and travel involving horses. Fiction dealing with horses and horse people, to 1,800 words. Horse cartoons. Pays to $50 for feature articles with photos, $40 to $75 for cover story including full-color photos, on publication.

HORSEMAN—5314 Bingle Rd., Houston, Tex. 77018. Bob Gray, Editor.
Uses articles on techniques of western horsemanship and horse management, only on approval of query. Photos required. Average length from 1,000 to 4,000 words. Pays 4¢ per word, $6 per photo used, on acceptance.

HORSEMEN'S JOURNAL—Suite 1038, 425 13th St., N. W., Washington, D. C. 20004. Tony Chamblin, Editor and Publisher.
Solid, in-depth articles or features, 500 to 3,000 words, reflecting an inside knowledge of thoroughbred (flat) racing. Racing fiction for owners, trainers, and breeders. Payment varies.

HOT ROD—8490 Sunset Blvd., Los Angeles, Calif. 90028.
How-to features pertaining to auto mechanics and hot rods. Photo stories of custom or performance-modified cars. Some pieces on track and drag racing, hill climbing, or other types of hot-rod competition. Glossy photos and cover transparencies. Pays up to $75 per page.

HUNTING DOG—Box 330, Dept. A1, Greenfield, Ohio 45123.
Nonfiction about sporting dogs and the outdoors, about 1,000 words, with art or photos. Pays 1¢ to 2¢ a word, to $5 for black-and-white photos, on acceptance.

INSIDE GOLF—3100 Riverside Drive, Los Angeles, Calif. 90027.
Wants features on famous personalities on or off the golf course. Accepts photos or drawings. Pays $150 for features, on publication.

INSIDE KENTUCKY SPORTS—512 East Main St., Lexington, Ky. 40508. David Reed, Editor.
Feature articles, 1,200 to 1,500 words, on all levels of Kentucky sports, from little league to professional. Also human-interest features on major sporting events involving Kentuckians, and on former Kentuckians in sports in other areas. Black-and-white photos and color transparencies. Pays $30 to $100 for features, $25 to $40 for short items (500 to 600 words), 10 days after publication.

KARATE ILLUSTRATED—5455 Wilshire Blvd., Los Angeles, Calif. 90036.
Monthly magazine, which accepts articles on karate, kung-fu, tae kwon do, kendo and other related arts. Length: 200 to 3,000 words. Illustrations and photos preferred. Looking for stringers all over the U.S. Payment varies.

KENDALL SPORTS TRAIL—The Kendall Sports Division, 20 Walnut St., Wellesley Hills, Mass. 02181. John S. O'Neill, Editor.
Needs articles to 2,500 words on all aspects of athletic department and sports management. Material should be slanted toward high school and college athletic directors, business managers, coaches, trainers, equipment managers, student trainers and team physicians. Especially interested in athletic department organization and management, legal aspects, equipment purchasing, sports medicine, etc. Pays 5¢ per word for articles, plus $5 per photo used. Sample copies on request. Query essential.

LAKELAND BOATING—416 Longshore Dr., Ann Arbor, Mich. 48107. David R. Kitz, Editor.
Articles on all phases of powerboating, sailing, outboarding, in the Great Lakes region. Also illustrated coverage of major boating events and activities in the area.

THE LUFKIN LINE—P.O. Box 849, Lufkin, Tex. 75902. Virginia R. Allen, Editor.
Articles on travel in the United States and Canada, 1,000 to 1,200 words, with 8 X 10 black-and-white photos. Pays $45, on acceptance.

MASSACHUSETTS WILDLIFE—Division of Fisheries and Game, Westboro, Mass. 01581.
Articles on outdoors with Massachusetts focus. No payment.

MINNESOTA AAA MOTORIST—Minnesota State Automobile Assoc., 7 Traveler's Trail, Burnsville, Minn. 55378. Ron Johnson, Managing Editor.
Articles, 800 to 1,500 words, on domestic and foreign travel, motoring, car care safety and related subjects. Pays $150 and up. Photos, $10 and up. Cartoons, $15. All payment on acceptance.

MOBILE LIVING—Box 1418, 1359 Main St., Sarasota, Fla. 33578.
Articles of interest to the owner of a travel trailer, camper or mobile home: travel articles, tips on decorating, landscaping, household hints, etc. Best length, 500 to 1,500 words. Pays 1¢ a word, on publication.

MODERN CYCLE—7950 Deering Ave., Canoga Park, Calif. 91304. Dave Ekins, Editor.
Well-rounded articles, 1,000 to 2,500 words, and photo stories, with broad appeal for every degree of motorcycle enthusiast. Also trail articles, with maps and good scenic photos, illustrating one or more riders operating their machines. How-to articles with photos for Maintenance Tips section. Pays various rates; $5 for photos, on publication. Query first.

MONTANA WEST, MAGAZINE OF THE NORTHERN ROCKIES—Box 894, Helena, Montana 59601.
Nonfiction pertaining to the Northern Rockies (Montana, Idaho, Wyoming). Length: up to 4,000 words. Accepts verse, photographs and drawings. Payment varies and arrangements will be made with the individual writer. Query.

MOTOR—250 West 55th Street, New York, N. Y. 10017. Bill Wolfe, Editor.
Articles, 800 to 1,200 words, telling how garages and service stations are attracting customers and boosting profits. Pays $70 to $100, plus $7.50 per photo used, on acceptance. Query.

MOTOR BOATING AND SAILING—224 West 57th St., New York, N. Y. 10019. Peter R. Smyth, Editor.
Informative and entertaining articles on motor boating, sailing, yachting, cruising, with illustrations. Length, 1,000 to 2,500 words, some one-pagers. Cartoon spots. Occasional verse. Pays on acceptance.

MOTOR COACH TRAVEL—See *Camping Guide.*

MOTORCYCLIST—Petersen Publishing Co., 8490 Sunset Blvd., Los Angeles, Calif. 90069, Bob Greene, Editor.
Articles, with professional quality photos, should be 1,000 to 3,000 words, and are received on speculation only. Payment, at time of acceptance, is based equally on text and photo quality. Also wants good action or creative motorcycle photography in color and black-and-white. Query in advance.

MOTORHOME LIFE—23945 Craftsman Rd., Calabasas, Calif. 91302. Art Rouse, Editor.
Wants articles, to 2,000 words, dealing with motorhomes, self-propelled recreational vehicles, etc. Also uses travel articles involving motorhomes, and how-to articles. Accompanying photos. Pays from $50 to $150, on publication.

MOTOR NEWS—150 Bagley Ave., Detroit, Mich. 48226.
Colorful articles on American tourist objectives, with information on costs, tips

on trip planning, good and bad points; articles for tourists on things to do. Particular interest in pieces with Michigan slant. Photos. Length, 800 to 2,000 words. Pays $100 and up, on acceptance.

MOTOR TREND—8490 Sunset Blvd., Los Angeles, Calif. 90069. Eric Dahlquist, Publisher.
Articles, 1,000 to 2,000 words, on foreign and domestic automobiles, past, present, and future. Also colorful character sketches. Sparkling, authoritative copy essential. Black-and-white photos preferred, but good, dramatic color photos considered. Pays $250 and up for major features, on acceptance.

MOUNTAIN GAZETTE—1801 York St., Denver, Colo. 80206. Mike Moore, Editor.
Articles, generally 1,000 to 2,500 words with 8 x 10 black-and-white photos, on mountaineering, skiing, and other outdoor recreation; also on environment, wilderness preservation. Occasional fiction, 500 to 5,000 words. Pays 75¢ per column inch, $10 per photo.

THE NATIONAL BOWLERS' JOURNAL AND BILLIARD REVUE—Hemingway Professional Building, 1825 North Lincoln Plaza, Chicago, Ill. 60614. Mort Luby, Jr., Editor.
Trade or consumer articles, 1,000 to 1,500 words, on any facet of bowling or billiards having national interest. Photographs should accompany features. Cartoons with a bowling or billiard theme. Pays $40 to $60 for articles; $5 for cartoons, on publication.

NATIONAL GEOGRAPHIC MAGAZINE—17th and M Sts., N. W., Washington, D. C. 20036. Gilbert M. Grosvenor, Editor.
Articles on geography (travel, exploration, natural history, archaeology, etc.). Length, 2,000 to 8,000 words; shorter lengths (2,000 to 4,000 words) are very desirable. First-person narrative style. Pays $1,500 to $3,500 and up, on acceptance; good photos, especially original color transparencies, greatly increase chance of acceptance and amount paid. Query first.

NATIONAL MOTORIST—65 Battery St., San Francisco, Calif. 94111. Jim Donaldson, Editor.
Illustrated articles, around 500 or 1,100 words, for the California motorist, on motoring in the West; car care; motor travel techniques; roads; interesting people and places in the western U. S. and in the history of the western U. S.; outdoor subjects, etc. Pays 10¢ a word, $10 and up per black-and-white photo, on acceptance.

NATIONAL PARKS AND CONSERVATION MAGAZINE—1701 18th St., N.W., Washington, D. C. 20009. Eugenia Horstman Connally, Editor.
Articles (preferably illustrated) about the great environmental problems affecting the world today and plans and programs to solve them; about national and state parks, monuments, forests, and refuges and other open spaces; about outdoors and wildlife appreciation and protection; about natural history—in short, a broad range of conservation and natural resources topics. Photos of park subjects.

NATIONAL POLICE GAZETTE—520 Fifth Ave., New York, N. Y. 10036. Nat K. Perlow, Editor.
Articles, 1,500 to 2,000 words, on sports and theatrical personalities; adventure stories; fishing and hunting experiences; fact detective cases; fraud exposés. Pays 5¢ a word, on publication. Query.

NATIONAL WILDLIFE AND INTERNATIONAL WILDLIFE—534 North Broadway, Milwaukee, Wis. 53202.
Articles related to wildlife, conservation, and recreation that are or can be illustrated; shorts, 1,000-word one-pagers, 2,500-word features, with pictures if possible. Pays $25 to $100 per magazine page; $15 and up for black-and-white photos; $35 and up for color photos; $25 and up for cartoons, on acceptance. Query, with photos.

NATURAL HISTORY MAGAZINE—Central Park West at 79th St., New York, N. Y. 10024. Alfred Meyer, Editor.
Photo articles in natural sciences, geology, astronomy, anthropology, and environment. Text to 4,000 words, preferably by scientists, with basic scientific point. Pays to $600 for full-length articles; $100 for cover photos and $75 per page for color; $50 for black-and-white.

NATURE CANADA (formerly *Canadian Audubon*)—46 Elgin St., Ottawa K1P 5K6, Ont., Canada.
Informational articles, 1,000 to 2,000 words, on natural science, conservation of natural resources. Must be authentic and bear on Canadian conditions, either directly or by comparison. Wants accompanying photos or sketches. No fiction or poetry.

NEVADA OUTDOORS AND WILDLIFE REVIEW—P.O. Box 10678, Reno, Nev. 98510.
Will accept historical material, material on parks, forestry, boating, bottle collecting or any other activity related to the outdoors. No payment.

NEW MEXICO WILDLIFE—State Capitol, Dept. of Game and Fish, Santa Fe, N. M. 87501. R. McKown, Editor.
Outdoor, hunting, fishing, camping, how-to articles that would apply directly to readers in New Mexico. How-to articles may be general but should apply to outdoor activities and not be obviously based on locations other than New Mexico. Length: 1,000 words. Cartoons relating to hunting, fishing, camping used; also photos and drawings on speculation; must be concerned with wildlife related to New Mexico. $5 to $10 for pictures that accompany articles; $7.50 for drawings. No payment for manuscripts other than by-line and copies.

THE NEW YORK TIMES—Times Square, New York, N. Y. 10036. William Honan, Travel Editor.
Appropriate, timely travel articles, 750 to 2,500 words, in lively, anecdotal style, with indepth treatment of area, including positive and negative aspects. Photos. Pays about 10¢ a word, $35 per photo. Query first, indicating subject and approach.

NORTHEAST OUTDOORS—95 North Main St., Waterbury, Conn. 06702. Tom Crider, Editor.
Tabloid newspaper format. Articles, 800 words and up, and photos on camping, hunting, fishing, skiing, conservation, recreation, travel, nature, etc., in northeast U.S. Pays $25 and up, on publication.

NORTHLINER—1999 Shepard Rd., St. Paul, Minn. 55116. Don Picard, Editor.
The inflight magazine for North Central Airlines. Articles, 1,000 to 2,000 words, with 35 mm color transparencies, on travel, business, personalities and humor in Minnesota, Wisconsin and Michigan areas. Also occasional puzzles, jokes and cartoons. Pays $50 to $400, on acceptance. Query.

NORTHWEST SKIER—P.O. Box 29, University Station, Seattle, Washington 98105. Robert B. Hinz, Editor.
Fiction, 250 to 2,500 words; non-fiction, 250 to 3,500 words; verse, 100 to 500 words. The editorial format is "information that is important to the enjoyment of the out-of-doors." It is the voice of skiing in the Pacific Northwest. Pays 50¢ per column inch average, minimum.

OUTDOOR ARIZONA—1230 East Camelback, Phoenix, Ariz. 85014.

Features about outdoor Arizona and the Southwest, with black-and-white photos. Pays on publication.

OUTDOOR INDIANA—Dept. of Natural Resources, Indianapolis, Ind. 46204. Articles to 2,000 words, on Indiana subjects only. Photos. Pays 2¢ per word on publication.

OUTDOOR LIFE—380 Madison Ave., New York, N. Y. 10017. William E. Rae, Editor.
Hunting and fishing magazine using factual material. True-adventure articles, 3,500 to 4,500 words, that blend personal experience with how-to-do-it information. First-person viewpoint is preferred. How-to-do-it articles on hunting, fishing, woodcraft, camping, firearms, motorboats, tackle. Also, controversial and humorous articles are considered. Picture stories, four to six published pages. Brief, dramatic true experiences which can be illustrated for "This Happened to Me" feature. Pays $350 and up for full-length features with good black-and-white photos, on acceptance.

OUTDOOR WORLD—24198 West Bluemound Rd., Waukesha, Wis. 53186.
Uses four to six major features per issue, 1,500 to 2,000 words; also short articles 600 to 1,000 words. Photos preferred with articles. Subjects: environment, camping, hiking, sailing, observations of wildlife and plantlife. Pays $65 to $75 for short articles, $125 for features, including photos. Query.

OUTDOORS—Outdoors Bldg., Columbia, Mo. 65201. Lee Cullimore, Editor.
Illustrated articles, accompanied by 8 x 10 black-and-white photos, on recreational subjects, with emphasis on boating. Manuscripts should be informative and objective. Length: to 1,200 words. Pays $35 to $100, on acceptance.

OUTDOORS IN GEORGIA (formerly *Georgia Game and Fish*)—Dept. of Natural Resources, 270 Washington St., S.W., Atlanta, Ga. 30334. Bob Wilson, Editor.
Nonfiction, 1,200 to 1,800 words, on conservation, hunting and fishing in Georgia, with black-and-white and color photos. Pays $35 up for stories and photos; cover photos (35 mm transparencies), $50 and up, on acceptance. Samples available.

PSA, THE CALIFORNIA MAGAZINE—5900 Wilshire Blvd., Los Angeles, Calif. 90036.
Informative business, sports and travel articles, 1,500 words, geared to the California life-style, to interest Pacific Southwest Airlines passengers in flight. Accompanying photos, if possible. Pays varying rates on publication. Same address and requirements for *Continental Flightime* and *Hughes Airwest Sundancer, Clipper*.

PV4—Bond/Parkhurst Publications, 1499 Monrovia Ave., Newport Beach, Calif. 92663. Granville L. King, Editor.
Wants do-it-yourself articles and nonfiction, 2,500 words, related to off-road driving or camping with pickups, vans or four-wheel-drive vehicles. Also jokes related to off-road driving or camping and travel or racing photographs. Pays $45 per page, on acceptance. Query.

PARACHUTIST—U.S. Parachute Association, Box 109, Monterey, Calif. 93940.
Articles on technical and news subjects pertaining to parachuting. Cartoons; photos, in color or black-and-white. No payment. Query.

PENNSYLVANIA ANGLER—Pennsylvania Fish Commission, Harrisburg, Pa. 17120. D. Thomas Eggler, Editor.
Short features, 300 to 1,200 words, on fresh water fishing, recreational boating, and camping in Pennsylvania. 8 x 10 black-and-white glossy photos should accompany manuscript. Also some cartoons and fillers. Pays $50 to $75 for single-page spreads; $75 to $100 for double-page spreads. Query.

PENNSYLVANIA GAME NEWS—Game Commissions, Harrisburg, Pa.
Articles covering all outdoor subjects except fishing and boating. Must have Pennsylvania locale. 2,500 words maximum. Uses black-and-white pictures; 8 x 10

glossy preferred. Pays 3¢ minimum per word and $5 minimum per picture, on acceptance.

POINTS—465 West Milwaukee, Detroit, Mich. 48202.
Uses articles from 700 to 900 words; "features must involve the 'how' and 'why' of hobbies, sports, and other subjects relating to travel." Color transparencies required. Pays from $100 to $400 for articles and photos. Query essential.

POLLUTION CONTROL JOURNAL—144 West 12th St., Denver, Colo. 80204. Mark Levy, Editor.
Factual news articles on pollution subjects and science fiction incorporating pollution themes. Black-and-white glossy prints or color transparencies (8 x 10) should accompany articles. Preferred length for both fiction and nonfiction, 2,500 to 3,000 words. Pays from $25 to $200, upon publication; sample copies 50¢.

POOL 'N' PATIO—3923 West 6th St., Los Angeles, Calif. 90005. Fay Coupe, Editor.
Articles of interest to owners of residential swimming pools, particularly in California.

POPULAR HOT RODDING—Argus Publishers Corp., 131 South Barrington Pl., Los Angeles, Calif. 90049. Lee Kelley, Editor.
Articles of any length on cars and car mechanics. Photos and drawings welcome. Pays top rates for its field, on acceptance. Query first.

POPULAR SCIENCE MONTHLY—380 Madison Ave., New York, N. Y. 10017.
Authoritative, factual articles focusing on new, ingenious, and useful products which add to men's enjoyment of home, yard, car, boat, workshop, or outdoor activities. Length not to exceed 2,000 words. Black-and-white photos or illustrations a must. Payment on publication. Queries welcome.

POWERBOAT—Powerboat Publishing, Inc., P.O. Box 3842, Van Nuys, Calif. 91407.
Articles, with original photos, for performance-minded power boaters. Emphasis on water-skiing, boat tests, personalities, and in-depth technical articles.

PRIVATE PILOT—11558 Sorrento Valley Rd., San Diego, Calif. 92121. Leslie Smith, Editor.
Articles, 1,000 to 2,500 words, with photos, for light-plane enthusiasts. Extensive flying knowledge a must. Occasional short stories, to 2,500 words. Pays on publication, $50 and up for 2,500 words plus photos.

RAILROAD MAGAZINE—420 Lexington Ave., New York, N. Y. 10017. Freeman Hubbard, Editor.
Feature articles, 2,000 to 3,000 words, on any phase of railroading, combining technical information with human interest and anecdotes. Query first.

ROD AND CUSTOM—8490 Sunset Blvd., Los Angeles, Calif. 90069.
Automotive how-to-do-it articles and photo stories on particular "rods and customs," their owners and specific parts. All manuscripts must be accompanied by return postage. Pays on acceptance.

RUDDER—1515 Broadway, New York, N. Y. 10036. Stuart James, Editor.
Boating articles up to 1,500 words. Photos. Pays on acceptance.

Rx SPORTS AND TRAVEL—447 South Main St., Hillsboro, Ill. 62049. Dick Voelkel, Editor.

A controlled circulation magazine for physicians. Wants how-to articles, 1,500 to 3,000 words, on participation sports and travel, particularly with doctor involved. Also profiles of physicans wth unusual sports achievements; participation sports tips, humorous sports happenings and other filler material, ranging from 250 to 750 words. Uses black-and-white and color photos with articles. Has a candid camera section with photos of physicians in sports and recreational activities. Payment ranges from $25 to $300, on acceptance. Query preferred.

SAGA—333 Johnson Ave., Brooklyn, N. Y. 11206. Martin M. Singer, Editor.
First-person adventure articles from 4,000 to 5,000 words. Also, articles on sports, as long as they present in-depth reporting on personalities or new aspects of the game. Hunting and fishing—particularly big game anywhere in the world—are always welcome. Color or black-and-white photos should accompany manuscript. Pays from $300.

SAIL—38 Commercial Wharf, Boston, Mass. 02110. Murray Davis, Editor.
Wants articles, from 1,500 to 2,000 words, with black-and-white photos, on sailing, sailboats, sailboat equipment and related subjects. Payment is from $75 to $300, upon publication.

SALMON TROUT STEELHEADER—P.O. Box 02112, Portland, Ore. 97202. Frank W. Amato, Editor.
Articles, 750 to 2,500 words, with 5 to 10 black-and-white photos, on salmon, trout, and steelhead fishing in the western states and Great Lakes region. Authors should know area. Also uses cartoons. Payment is $15 to $60 for articles with photos, $2.50 for cartoons, on publication.

SALT WATER SPORTSMAN—10 High St., Boston, Mass. 02110. Frank Woolner, Editor.
How-to articles, 2,500 to 3,000 words, on salt water sport fishing on the Atlantic, Gulf, and Pacific coasts of North America; also Central and South America. Good glossy action photographs of salt water sport fishing. Color transparencies for cover. Pays 4¢ and up a word, on acceptance.

SCOUTING MAGAZINE—North Brunswick, N. J. 08902. Walter Babson, Editor.
For adult leaders of the Boy Scouts of America. Articles on the outdoor activities of Scouting and Exploring; successful unit and council conservation projects; family-type camping based on Boy Scout camping skills. Pays on acceptance. Submit outline or idea first.

SCRUMDOWN—Applied Visual Communications, Inc., 45 West 34th St., New York, N. Y. 10036. A. Jon Prusmack, Editor/Publisher.
Rugby magazine; articles and reports, to 2,500 words, on events and tournaments, and the social and cultural background of the sport. Uses some related fiction, to 1,000 words. Query.

SHOOTING TIMES—News Plaza, Peoria, Ill. 61601. Alex Bartimo, Executive Editor.
Articles, 2,000 to 2,500 words, on guns and pistols, hunting and shooting, black powder, reloading, conservation, gunsmithing. Pictures essential. Pays on acceptance. Query.

SKATING—178 Tremont St., Boston, Mass. 02111. Karen S. MacDonald, Editor.
Fiction and nonfiction, to 2,000 words, on ice figure skating, skating clubs and personalities around the world. Opinion and photos on skating; skating's relation to other sports. Pays 2½¢ a word, $25 minimum; $5 per photo.

SKI MAGAZINE—380 Madison Ave., New York, N. Y. 10017. John Fry, Editor.
Articles on skiing, illustrated with photos or drawings. Query first.

SKIER—22 High St., Brattleboro, Vt. 05301.
Articles dealing with any topic having a direct or indirect bearing on skiing—personality, human interest, ski techniques, ski history, etc. Also photos and cartoons. Pays 2¢ a word and up for articles.

SKIING MAGAZINE—Ziff Davis Publishing Co., One Park Ave., New York, N. Y. 10016. Al Greenberg, Editor.
Travel, personality profiles, humor, history, personal reminiscience, related to skiing. Length 1,000 to 3,000 words; also shorter articles, from 800 words. Pays from $100 to $500.

SKIN DIVER MAGAZINE—8490 Sunset Blvd., Los Angeles, Calif. 90069. Paul J. Tzimoulis, Editor.
Nonfiction stories and articles directly related to skin diving activities, equipment, or personalities. Length, 1,000 to 2,000 words, well-illustrated. Accepts black-and-white photos, 8 x 10 glossies; color, 35mm, 2¼ x 2¼ or 4 x 5 transparencies, line drawings, sketches, charts. Payment is $35 per page for editorial copy, $35 for inside photos, $100 for cover photos, $5 for cartoons, on publication. Enclose stamped, self-addressed envelope with manuscript.

SKY DIVER MAGAZINE—P.O. Box 1024, La Habra, Calif. 90631. Lyle Cameron, Editor.
Uses fiction and nonfiction, photos and drawings, miscellany: fillers, humor, skits, jokes, puzzles. No payment unless exceptional.

SMALL WORLD—Volkswagen of America, Englewood Cliffs, N. J. 07632. Jonathan Fisher, Editor.
Fiction and articles, 600 to 1,800 words, which relate to Volkswagen or Volkswagen owners. Also short humor, photos. Pays $100 per page for text and photos.

SMITHSONIAN—Arts and Industries Bldg., 900 Jefferson Dr., Washington, D. C. 20560.
Articles on wildlife, environment, science (hard and natural), art, handicrafts, for membership magazine of Smithsonian Institute. Query first.

SNOTRACK—534 North Broadway, Milwaukee, Wis. 53202. Glen Helgeland, Editor; Dorothy Deer, Articles Editor.
Published monthly October through March. Wants interesting photo-articles on all types of snowmobiling activities, how-to-do-it material, race events, rallies, trail rides, family activities. Also humor, cartoons. Length, 700 to 2,000 words. Black-and-white photos for the inside; color photos for the covers. Payment for full-length articles, with photos, is $150 or $200; for color cover photos, $100, on acceptance. Query.

SNOWSPORTS—1500 East 79th St., Minneapolis, Minn. 55420. Henry Fiola, Editor.
Articles with black-and-white photos or color transparencies on family snowmobiling, places to go, things to do. Pays within 45 days of acceptance. No recent report. Query.

SPORT—205 East 42nd St., New York, N. Y. 10017. Norman Lewis Smith, Managing Editor.
Human interest, or controversial articles about important figures and events in the spectator sports world. Short gossipy items for Sport Talk column. Pays $250 to $1,000, on acceptance. Query first.

SPORTS AFIELD—250 West 55th St., New York, N. Y. 10019. Lamar Underwood, Editor.
Instructive hunting and fishing articles, how-to-do-its, photo stories, controversial sports pieces, conservation articles, some personal experience, nature, camping, where-to-go pieces, humor, fiction. Preferred length, 500 to 2,000 words. Top-notch color and black-and-white photos. Pays top rates, on acceptance.

SPORTS AFIELD FISHING ANNUAL—250 West 55th St., New York, N. Y. 10019.
Published each year by the staff of *Sports Afield* Magazine. Wants 3,000 word
how-to and personal experience articles on fishing, and one- and two-page how-to
fillers. Photos are essential. Prospective contributors who are not experts have
little chance to be accepted. Payment is $400 and up, on acceptance. Study the
Annual and query the editors. Same address and requirements for *Sports Afield
Hunting Annual*, except that articles are on various aspects of hunting.

SPORTS AFIELD HUNTING ANNUAL—See *Sports Afield Fishing Annual*.

SPORTS DIGEST—P.O. Box 494, North Miami, Fla. 33161. Douglas A. Lang, Executive Editor.
High-quality articles, to 1,500 words, favorable to amateur and pro sports, personalities, events, with 35mm color transparencies, captions. Pays $110 to $140
for package, upon acceptance. Include stamped, self-addressed envelope.

SPORTS ILLUSTRATED—Rockefeller Center, New York, N. Y. 10020. Pat Ryan,
Articles Editor.
All material must have some relation to sports, however tenuous. Buys short off-
the-news features, 600 to 2,000 words; humor, reminiscences, and personality
pieces; long pieces, 2,000 to 5,000 words, on major personalities or sporting subjects; fast-breaking news stories for current issue. Pays $250 for short features,
$750 and up for long pieces; on acceptance.

STREET CHOPPER—731 Melrose Ave., Placentia, Calif. 92670. Charles Welch Editor.
Technical and semi-technical articles, 4,000 words, on motorcycles, with 5 × 7 or
8 × 10 black-and-white glossies. Pays $50 per published page.

SURFER MAGAZINE—Box 1028, Dana Point, Calif. 92629. Steve Pezman, Editor.
Fiction, 1,000 to 2,500 words, and nonfiction, 5,000 words, on anything with a
surfing theme and from the expert's point of view. Good light, well-plotted stories
as well as articles, fillers, short humor, and good black-and-white photos or color
pictures of surfing. Occasional verse. Pays 4¢ a word, on publication.

SWIMMING WORLD—5507 Laurel Canyon Blvd., North Hollywood, Calif. 91607.
Albert Schoenfield, Editor.
Nutrition, body-building, diet and technique articles; competitive swimming; diving; water polo; profiles of swimming-meet winners, for high school, collegiate
and national competitive swimmers. Payment varies, is on acceptance.

TWA AMBASSADOR—1999 Shephard Rd., St. Paul, Minn. 55116. Roy J. Dunlap,
Editor.
Free to TWA passengers. Travel, humor, business, and personality articles, 1,500
to 2,000 words, with sharp 35mm photos related to article. Pays $150 to $500,
upon acceptance. Queries preferred. Editorial requirement sheet upon request.

TRAILER LIFE (incorporating *Mobile Life*)—23945 Craftsman Rd., P.O. Box 500,
Calabasas, Calif. 91302. Arthur J. Rouse, Editor and Publisher.
Articles, up to 1,500 words, amply illustrated, on trailering and related interests,
truck campers, motorhomes, hobbies, etc. Please submit both black-and-white and
four color photos, transparencies preferred. Illustrated "how-to" articles, up to
800 words. Write for Editorial Guide. Pays up to $150, on publication.

TRAVEL—Travel Bldg., Floral Park, N. Y. 11001. Robert H. Rufa, Editor.
Personal-experience travel articles only. Fresh material on places to visit, what to see and do, with costs and prices worked in wherever appropriate. Photos necessary. Length: 1,000 to 3,000 words; preferred length, 2,500 words. Queries welcomed. Currently seeking material on offbeat areas in the United States. Pays $50 to $100, on acceptance, including black-and-white photos.

TRAVEL & LEISURE—61 West 51st St., New York, N. Y. 10019. Caskie Stinnett, Editor-in-Chief.
Goes to holders of American Express Money Cards. Wants sophisticated articles, 2,500 to 3,000 words, on travel and the good life. Articles on assignment. Pays $500 to $1,500 for a 2,500-word article. Query.

TROUT—737 South Sparks St., State College, Pa. 16801.
Nonfiction, 800 to 2,500 words. Photos, with articles, 8 x 10 black-and-white preferred; covers, 8 x 10 black-and-white. Pays $25 to $50 per article, $5 per photo as illustration in article, and $20 to $25 for covers, upon publication.

TRUE—1515 Broadway, New York, N. Y. 10036. Mark Penzer, Editor.
Articles on sports, such as baseball and football, 1,000 to 4,000 words. Also essays and current subjects for profiles. Query with outline. Pays $250 to $1,500.

TRUE'S FISHING YEARBOOK—1515 Broadway, New York, N. Y. 10036. Peter Barrett, Editor.
Articles, 3,000 to 4,000 words, on fishing spots, fishing trips, personal experiences, fishing techniques, etc. Uses photos. Query first. Payment is $300.

TRUE'S HUNTING YEARBOOK—1515 Broadway, New York, N. Y. 10036. Peter Barrett, Editor.
Articles, 3,000 to 4,000 words, on new hunting spots, techniques, and tips, with photos. Payment is $300. Query first, with outline and photos.

TRUE TREASURE—P.O. Drawer L, Conroe, Tex. 77301. John H. Latham, Editor and Publisher.
Articles, 100 to 2,500 words, about specific lost mines or buried or sunken treasures. Pays 2¢ per word and up on acceptance, $5 per picture, $100 for color photos for cover. Query. Reports in four weeks. Same address and requirements for *Treasure World*.

TURF AND SPORT DIGEST—511-13 Oakland Ave., Baltimore, Md. 21212. Louis P. Boer, Editor.
Fiction, 2,500 to 3,500 words; must have a background of Thoroughbred racing and authentic details. Nonfiction, 1,500 to 3,000 words, on careers of nationally known turf figures and playing the races, with human interest and emphasis on racing's color. Pays 3¢ a word and up, on publication. Query.

UNDERWATER MAGAZINE—P.O. Box 216, Gloucester, Mass. 01930. Phil Holt, Editor.
Articles, 2,000 to 4,000 words, on marine biology, underwater photography, oceanography, travel and adventure related to the Scuba diving community. Occasional poetry if related to the ocean, etc. Photos and drawings related to ocean or scuba diving. No payment.

WATER SKIER—7th St. and Ave. G, S.W., Winter Haven, Fla. 33881.
Buys occasional off-beat articles and picture features on water skiing.

WATERSPORT—Boat Owners Council of America, 534 North Broadway, Milwaukee, Wisc. 53202. Glenn Helgeland, Managing Editor.
High-quality articles and photos of outboard motor boating, canoeing, sailing, water skiing, other water based topics such as personalities, boat camping, fishing, shell collecting, etc. No "cruise plan" or mechanical "how-to" pieces. Pays $50 to $400 for stories with photos, depending on quality, length and importance; various rates for photos. Query.

THE WESTERN HORSEMAN—3850 North Nevada Ave., Colorado Springs, Colo. 80901. Chuck King, Editor.
Articles on care and training of stock horses. Historical articles. Photos to illustrate. Length: about 1,500 words. Cartoons. Pays 3¢ a word, on acceptance.

WESTWAYS—Box 2890, Terminal Annex, Los Angeles, Calif. 90051.
Articles, 700 to 2,500 words, on western U.S., Canadian and Mexican activities: natural science, travel, history, etc. Also prints verse, to 45 lines. Pays 10¢ a word on acceptance, for articles; $25 per black-and-white photo, $25 to $200 for color photos; $25 and up for poems. Overstocked. Query.

WHEELS AFIELD—8490 Sunset Blvd., Los Angeles, Calif. 90069. Ken Fermoyle, Editor.
Articles, 2,000 word maximum, with recreational vehicle slant; with emphasis on how-to-do-it projects for camper/trailer owners. Not using travel or where-to-go material. Illustrative material must accompany all articles. Pays about $50 per page ($100 to $200 per feature), on acceptance.

WORLD TENNIS—8100 Westglen, Houston, Tex. 77042. Gladys M. Heldman, Editor.
Features and instruction articles on tennis, with photos; photos of tournament action. Pays varying rates, on publication. Contributors must know tennis, study magazine. Query first.

WRESTLING GUIDE—Jalart House, Inc., P.O. Box 642, Scottsdale, Ariz. 85252. Tommy Kay, Editor.
Profile or dressing-room articles on pro or amateur wrestling stars, 800 to 3,000 words, with black-and-white photos. Also profiles of wrestling fan clubs and picture stories on big matches or top stars. Pays $15 to $35, before publication, $25 for color transparencies used as cover shots. Enclose stamped, self-addressed envelope.

YACHTING—50 West 44th St., New York, N. Y. 10036. William W. Robinson. Editor.
Articles and stories on recreational boating (sail and power). Technical articles on all phases of yachting. Occasional articles dealing with historical subjects. No fiction. Pays 6¢ a word, on acceptance.

HOME AND GARDEN; WOMEN'S MAGAZINES

ALLIED PUBLICATIONS, INC.—P.O. Box 23505, Fort Lauderdale, Fla. 33307. Marie Stilkind, Associate Editor.
General, noncontroversial articles on home and family interests; travel; beauty; decorating; hobbies; art; techniques; methods; new ideas and materials; profiles of noted artists; "how-to-do-it" articles. Black-and-white photos preferred with art articles. Articles and photos slanted toward beauticians. Profiles on secretaries of famous people. Pays 5¢ a word, $5 per photo, on acceptance.

AMERICAN BABY (formerly *Mothers-to-be/American Baby*)—10 East 52nd St., New York, N. Y. 10022. Judith Nolte, Editor.
Articles to help new and expectant parents, and pieces on child care for ages one month to three years, from 400 to 1,500 words. Payment varies.

AMERICAN HOME—641 Lexington Ave., New York, N. Y. 10022.
Wants short, informative articles dealing with home service subjects: decorating, remodeling, entertaining, gardening; environment, recreation. U.S. family travel pieces. No fiction or poetry. Pays on acceptance. Query first.

THE AMERICAN ROSE MAGAZINE—4048 Roselea Place, Columbus, Ohio 43214. Harold S. Goldstein, Editor.
Articles for the average home gardener who has an interest in roses; new products, varieties, experiments that readers can put into practice. Fillers. No payment.

ANTIQUES JOURNAL—P.O. Box 88128, Dunwoody, Ga. 30338. John Mebane, Editor.
Illustrated articles about antiques. Many original photos required. No museum photos. Articles must be factual and well-researched. Query first.

BABY CARE—52 Vanderbilt Ave., New York, N. Y. 10017. Mrs. Maja Bernath, Editor.
Feature articles, to 1,800 words, on basic infant care (bathing, feeeding, common illness, safety), emotional and physical development, "how-to's," husband-wife-baby relationships, seasonal topics (travel, summer or winter care). Short features, to 1,000 words, with a humorous, narrative or reflective approach. No fillers but occasionally accepts cartoons and short poetry. Payment for "Focus on You" (500 words or less) is $25; for "Family Corner" (100 words or less) $10. Payment for feature articles ranges from $50 to $125, on acceptance.

BABY TALK—66 East 34th St., New York, N. Y. 10016. Eve Hammerschmidt, Editor.
Interested primarily in true-experience pieces, 500 to 1,000 words, by mother or father, on baby, baby care, family relations, etc. "Your Opinion" department uses short articles expressing a point of view rather than experience.

BETTER HOMES & GARDENS—1716 Locust St., Des Moines, Iowa 50303. James A. Autry, Editor.
Articles of home and family interest. Uses freelance material in areas of travel, health, cars, money management, and home and family entertainment. Pays top rates on acceptance, based on estimated space of published article. The editors suggest authors examine a current issue before submitting material, and query first with outline.

BRIDES MAGAZINE—420 Lexington Ave., New York, N. Y. 10017. Barbara Donovan, Editor-in-Chief.
Articles of interest to brides-to-be and newlyweds on money handling, marital adjustment, entertaining, keeping romance alive, etc. Length: 1,000 words and up. Pays $75 to $500. Query first. Address material to Ann Diamond, Copy and Features Editor.

CALIFORNIA HOMEOWNER—953 8th Ave., San Diego, Calif. 92101. John Nagy, Editor.
Articles, 250 words, on reform of the property tax, for homeowners and small business. Also interested in how economics affects the property taxpayer. No payment.

CAMPER COACHMAN—23945 Craftsman, Calabasas, Calif. 91602. Bill Estes, Editor.
Articles, 500 to 1,000 words, amply illustrated with both black-and-white photos and color transparencies on all phases of truck campers. How-to-do-it, maintenance of camper and truck, travel, etc. Editor's Guide available. Pays good rates, on publication.

CHATELAINE—481 University Ave., Toronto, Ont., Canada. Doris Anderson, Editor.
Fiction to interest women: love, adventure, mystery themes, about 5,000 words.
Canadian articles, 3,000 words, on arresting, controversial subjects and women's
activities. Humorous fillers and good verse. Payment is $500 for articles; $400 and
up for fiction; $25 to $150 for fillers, on acceptance.

THE CHRISTIAN HOME—201 Eighth Ave. South, Nashville, Tenn. 37203.
Material of interest to parents; must be sound educationally, may be humorous.
Articles, 1,000 to 2,000 words; fiction, 2,500 to 3,500 words. Special articles by
arrangement. Payment, 2¢ a word, on acceptance. Also pays 50¢ a line for poetry.
Query first for articles. Study magazine before submitting.

THE CHRISTIAN SCIENCE MONITOR—One Norway St., Boston, Mass. 02115.
Uses homemaking, foods, and fashion features, articles on new products, and
feature articles on women of achievement. Also buys household hints. Pays various
rates.

CONGRATULATIONS—175 Rock Rd., Glen Rock, N. J. 07452.
Articles, 1,000 to 1,200 words, on medical, post-partum baby care. Payment
varies. Query.

COSMOPOLITAN—224 West 57th St., New York, N. Y. 10020. Helen Gurley Brown,
Editor.
Magazine aimed at young career women, women who want to do things. Uses
articles, to 4,000 words, and shorter features, 1,000 to 2,000 words, which tell
readers how to improve and enjoy their lives. Fiction: short-shorts, 1,500 to 3,000
words; short stories, 5,000 to 6,000 words; mystery or suspense novels, 20,000
words. Must have solid plots, sharp characterization, focus on man-woman relationships. Pays $1,000 to $1,500 for full-length articles, less for short features,
from $300 to $600 for short-shorts, to $1,000 for short stories. Other payment by
arrangement.

THE COUNTRY GUIDE—1760 Ellice Ave., Winnipeg 21, Manitoba, Canada.
Well-illustrated articles of 1,000 to 1,500 words and 450 to 800 words, dealing with
farming and country life in Canada. Short stories of 2,000 to 3,500 words (1st or
2nd rights), preferably in a rural setting. Short, well-illustrated articles on homemaking, handicrafts, child development, health and rural living for Home Department. Also short poems of 4 to 16 lines. Pays on acceptance.

EXPECTING—Parents' Magazine Enterprises, Inc., 52 Vanderbilt Ave., New York,
N. Y. 10017. Maja Bernath, Editor.
Articles for expectant mothers on prenatal development, nursery planning, hus-
band-wife relationships, etc.; medical pieces by R.N.'s and M.D.'s. No fiction.
Pays $50 to $125 for articles from 700 to 2,000 words, on acceptance; slightly
higher for professionals in medical fields.

FAMILY CIRCLE—488 Madison Ave., New York, N. Y. 10022. Arthur M. Hettich,
Editor.
Articles on child care, health, etc., of interest to women. Also short humor. Most
service articles staff-written. Payment arranged.

THE FAMILY HANDYMAN—235 East 45th St., New York, N. Y. 10017.
Non-technical step-by-step articles, to 1,000 words, with black-and-white photos,
on home improvement, repair and maintenance for do-it-yourselfers. Pays $40 to
$100, on acceptance. Shorts, 100 to 300 words, with or without photos and rough
drawings, on expert tips or shortcuts for do-it-yourselfers. Pays $5 to $15, on
acceptance.

FAMILY HOUSEBOATING—23945 Craftsman, Calabasas, Calif. 91602. Art Rouse, Editor.

Articles, 500 to 2,000 words, illustrated with black-and-white photos, color transparencies, maps, on all phases of houseboating. Design features used as well as rental experiences, homebuilt series, travel. Pays good rates, on publication.

FAMILY WEEKLY—641 Lexington Ave., New York, N. Y. 10022. Mort Persky, Editor-in-Chief.

Sunday supplement. Short, lively articles and picture features with emphasis on prominent individuals. Most women's service features staff-prepared. Payment on acceptance.

FLOWER & GARDEN MAGAZINE—4251 Pennsylvania Ave., Kansas City, Mo. 64111. Rachel Snyder, Editor-in-Chief.

Articles, up to 1,500 words, with good photos, on indoor and outdoor gardening; may refer to particular region as magazine is published in three editions: Eastern, Western, Mid-America. Pays 3¢ a word, on acceptance.

GIRLTALK—380 Madison Ave., New York, N. Y. 10017.

Manuscripts—fiction, articles, fillers and poetry—of interest to women. Short stories and articles 2,000 words or less; short poems, only. Only one manuscript per month from the same author. Payment rate varies.

GLAMOUR—350 Madison Ave., New York, N. Y. 10017.

Helpful, informative material, humorous or serious, on all aspects of a woman's life—medicine, mental health, household, travel; social, economic and emotional problems. Unusual career stories; entertainment. Short features, stressing personal viewpoint or experience, 1,500 to 3,000 words. Pays $300 to $700.

GOOD HOUSEKEEPING—959 Eighth Ave., New York, N. Y. 10019. Wade H. Nichols, Editor. Betty Frank, Articles Editor. Robert M. Liles, Features Editor. Naome Lewis, Fiction Editor. Timothy H. Mulligan, "Better Way" Editor.

Short stories, 2,000 to 5,000 words. Novelettes and book condensations to 25,000 words. Occasional two- and three-part serials. Informative, exemplary articles for women. Articles are usually written on assignment, but queries are considered. Especially interested in dramatic first-person experiences in the fields of human relations, individual achievement, practical living, romance and social techniques. "Better Way" buys research reports on news of practical interest about women's activities, jobs, etc. Pays top rates, on acceptance.

GOURMET—777 Third Ave., New York, N. Y. 10017. Mrs. Justine Valenti, Managing Editor.

Articles, 2,500 to 3,000 words, on travel, adventure, hunting, fishing, and other facets of good living for sophisticated male audience interested in fine foods and fine wines; should also appeal to women who are informed on good living. Purchases recipes only in connection with articles. No short features or fillers. Pays on acceptance.

HAIRDO & BEAUTY—245 East 47th St., New York, N. Y. 10017. Dorothea Zack Hanle, Editor.

Predominantly staff-written but occasionally buys articles on hairdo and beauty topics. Query first, with outline.

HORTICULTURE—300 Massachusetts Ave., Boston, Mass. 02115. Edwin F. Steffek, Editor.
Authoritative articles on gardening or some phase of horticulture, 500 to 1,200 words Pays 3¢ a word, on publication.

HOUSE & GARDEN—420 Lexington Ave., New York, N. Y. 10017.
Rarely buys unsolicited articles.

HOUSE BEAUTIFUL—717 Fifth Ave., New York, N. Y. 10022.
Interested in seeing detailed outlines for proposed articles.

LADIES' HOME JOURNAL—641 Lexington Ave., New York, N. Y. 10022.
Limited market. "Most of our articles are staff-written or assigned through recognized literary agents."

LADY'S CIRCLE—21 West 26th St., New York, N. Y. 10010. Betty Etter, Editor.
Articles, 2,500 to 3,500 words, of interest to housewives: health, child care, how to make money, travel (in the U.S.). Also uses 1 story a month, to 2,500 words. Photos to accompany articles. Pays $125 and up, on publication.

McCALL'S—230 Park Ave., New York, N. Y. 10017.
Timely major features and articles on all subjects. Well-written, distinguished fiction. All service articles are staff-prepared. Pays top rates, on acceptance.

MADEMOISELLE—350 Madison Ave., New York, N. Y. 10017.
High-quality short stories and articles appealing to young women from 18 to 25 years of age, 2,500 to 6,500 words. Submit stories to Ellen A. Stoianoff, Fiction Editor; articles to Mary Cantwell, Managing Editor. Pays $300 for fiction, and varying rates for nonfiction, on acceptance.

MOBILE LIVING—Box 1418, 1359 Main St., Sarasota, Fla. 33578. Frances Neel, Editor.
Uses articles of interest to travel trailer and mobile home owners. Needs articles on travel clubs, vacation trips in trailers or campers. Length: 500 to 1,000 words. Payment is 1¢ a word, on publication.

MODERN BRIDE—One Park Ave., New York, N. Y. 10016. Robert W. Houseman, Editor.
Articles on etiquette, marriage, and all phases of home planning and travel, about 1,500 words and up. Payment on acceptance.

MODERN MATURITY—215 Long Beach Blvd., Long Beach, Calif. 90802. Hubert Pryor, Editor.
Service articles on housing, food, health, employment, hobbies, for persons over 55. Also nostalgia, inspirational articles, personality pieces, Americana, interpretations of the current scene, to 2,000 words. Some short stories. Pays from $50 to $500 for articles and fiction, on acceptance; from $15 up for black-and-white photos, and from $50 up for color photos.

MOTHERS MANUAL—420 Lexington Ave., New York, N. Y. 10017. Beth Waterfall, Editor.

Authoritative articles for parents of babies six weeks to five years old, 1,000 to 1,500 words. Pays 2¢ to 5¢ a word, on publication. Address Editor, 176 Cleveland Dr., Croton-on-Hudson, N. Y. 10520.

MOTHERS-TO-BE/AMERICAN BABY—See *American Baby.*

MOTORHOME LIFE—23945 Craftsman, Calabasas, Calif. 91602. Art Rouse, Editor. Articles, 500 to 2,000 words, amply illustrated with both black-and-white photos and color transparencies on all phases of motorhomes, only. Pays good rates, on publication.

MS.—370 Lexington Ave., New York, N. Y. 10017.
Uses articles on topics relevant to women as people, not stereotypes. Query first.

ORGANIC GARDENING AND FARMING—Emmaus, Pa. 18049. M. C. Goldman, Managing Editor.
Articles, 1,000 to 2,500 words, on aspects of organic agriculture: natural home garden methods for growing vegetables, flowers, etc., control of pests, fertilizers, etc. Payment rates are $35 to $70 for full-length articles, $5 to $15 for fillers, on acceptance. Also black-and-white photos, cover transparencies. Author's Handbook, Photographer's Guide and free copy sent on request.

THE PTA MAGAZINE—700 North Rush St., Chicago, Ill. 60611. Mrs. Eva H. Grant, Editor.
Nonfiction on child welfare, parent education, and related fields, human interest stories, 1,800 words.

PARENTS' MAGAZINE—52 Vanderbilt Ave., New York, N. Y. 10017. Genevieve Millet Landau, Editor-in-Chief. Selma G. Lanes, Articles Editor.
Articles on the physical, emotional and mental development of infants, school children, and adolescents. Pieces on family relationships, and adults in the community. Lively, readable articles on important research in medicine, science, education. Prefers warm, colloquial, anecdotal style, with quotes from experts, 2,000 to 3,000 words. Pays on acceptance.

PERFECT HOME—427 6th Ave., S. E., Cedar Rapids, Iowa 52400. Donna Nicholas Hahn, Editor.
Photographic coverage of complete moderate cost homes, remodeling projects, built-in ideas, unusual decorating projects, etc., with brief captions. Also 500-word editorials on "What Home Means to Me," by nationally known figures. Payment $50. Query first to avoid duplication.

REDBOOK—230 Park Ave., New York, N. Y. 10017. Sey Chassler, Editor.
Practical articles on home, health, parent-child relationships, etc., aimed at young married people, 500 to 5,000 words. Home and garden market limited; mainly staff-written. Fiction with basic themes of love, marriage, parenthood, etc.; also on social and moral questions, etc. Pays $1,000 and up for short stories on acceptance; pays $600 to $850 for short-short stories, 1,400 to 1,600 words; pays $5,000 to $10,000 for novels, 25,000 to 35,000 words.

THE SECRETARY—616 East 63rd St., Kansas City, Mo. 64110. Mrs. Shirley S. Englund, Editor and Publishing Manager.
Articles, 800 to 2,000 words, on office procedures, secretarial skills, administrative responsibilities, and human relations. Emphasis is on development of executory qualities beyond stenographic skills. Pays on publication.

SPHERE, THE BETTY CROCKER MAGAZINE—625 North Michigan Ave., Chicago, Ill. 60611. Joan Leonard, Editor.
Imaginative, how-to women's interest articles.

TODAY'S CHRISTIAN MOTHER—8121 Hamilton Ave., Cincinnati, Ohio 45231.
Wilma L. Schaffer, Editor.
Articles, 600 to 1,200 words, showing Christian principles applied in home training
of children. Material for father's page, and ideas for creative children's activities
also used. Payment varies.

TODAY'S SECRETARY—1221 Ave. of the Americas, New York, N. Y. 10020.
1,000 to 1,500-word articles on *young* secretaries, with candid photos. Also articles
on new office techniques and trends; lively fiction, 500 to 1,000 words, of general
interest or dealing with secretaries' business life. Rarely uses romance. Also uses
articles on self-improvement, especially in job preparation and subjects of interest
to young women, ages 16 to 21. Submit outline or query first. Pays $25 for fiction,
$35 to $150 for features.

TRAILER LIFE—23945 Craftsman, Calabasas, Calif. 91602.
Articles, to 2,000 words, amply illustrated, on all phases of trailering, mobile home
beautification, hobbies, how-to-do-it, etc. Writers should request Editor's Guide.
Pays good rates, on publication.

UP FROM UNDER—339 Lafayette St., New York, N. Y. 10012.
Fiction and nonfiction, 1,000 to 10,000 words, aimed at working class women,
about women's experiences, their problems and how they overcame them. Also
poetry, cartoons, photos. No payment.

VOGUE—420 Lexington Ave., New York, N. Y. 10017.
Articles of general interest. Serious or humorous essays on topical matters. Fiction
of unusual quality. Length, up to 2,500 words. Pays good rates, on acceptance.
Buys little unsolicited material. Query first.

WEIGHT WATCHERS MAGAZINE—635 Madison Ave., New York, N. Y. 10022.
Edythe K. Tomkinson, Feature Editor.
General-interest articles, humor, travel pieces, and how-to's, plus fiction. No
health or diet articles. Pays on acceptance.

THE WOMAN—235 Park Ave., South, New York, N. Y. 10003. Diana Lurvey, Editor.
First-person articles dealing with everyday situations and today's world from
the point of view of the married or once-married woman. Pays $50 on acceptance.

WOMAN'S DAY—1515 Broadway, New York, N. Y. 10003.
Serious and humorous articles, 1,500 to 2,500 words. Fillers of one and two col-
umns. Also buys ideas and finished articles on crafts and personal experiences.
Short stories, 3,000 to 3,500 words, with modern settings, humor or satire, romance.
Pays top rates, on acceptance.

WOMAN'S WORLD—261 Fifth Ave., New York, N. Y. 10016. Diana Willis, Editor.
Articles, 500 to 1,500 words, light in tone, of interest to women: how-to articles,
humorous accounts, interviews, profiles, new product information, and articles on
full- or part-time careers and business opportunities involving women. Pays from
$15 to $35, on publication.

THE WORKBASKET—4251 Pennsylvania, Kansas City, Mo. 64111. Mary Ida Sullivan, Editor.
Articles, 500 to 700 words, on how specific women have improved their home
environment. Concise how-to-do-it articles on women's home crafts. Short items,
up to 200 words, on how specific women make extra money, for "Women Who
Make Cents." Payment is 2¢ a word, on acceptance.

THE WORKBENCH—4251 Pennsylvania, Kansas City, Mo. 64111. Jay W. Hedden, Editor.
Do-it-yourself articles with emphasis on home workshop, home improvement and repair projects. Pays from $20 to $50 per published page to new writers, for complete article with photos or drawings; more for articles done on assignment.

TRADE AND BUSINESS MAGAZINES

ADVERTISING AND SALES PROMOTION—708 Third Ave., New York, N. Y. 10017. Louis J. Haugh, Editor.
Articles on topics in the advertising and sales promotion fields.

AERO—Box 1184, Ramona, Calif. 92065. Wayne Thoms, Editor.
Factual articles, any length, with photos, on upgrading skills and technical know-how, for pilots and owners of any aircraft from single engine to light business jet. Pays $25 to $50 per printed page. Query.

AIR FORCE MAGAZINE—1750 Pennsylvania Ave., N.W., Washington, D. C. 20006. John F. Loosbrock, Editor.
Articles 1,500 to 3,000 words, on military aviation and aerospace; current developments, historical and semi-technical reports. Query. Pays 5¢ to 7¢ a word, on acceptance, and $10 for true anecdotes of Air Force life, 250 words.

AMERICAN BICYCLIST AND MOTORCYCLIST—461 Eighth Ave., New York, N. Y. 10001. Stan Gottlieb, Editor.
Articles 1,500 to 2,000 words, on successful bicycle dealers, covering sales and/or service practices useful to dealers intent on improving store management. Pays 3¢ per word, $5 per photo, on publication. Query.

AMERICAN COIN-OP—500 North Dearborn, Chicago, Ill., 60610. Bob Harker, Editor.
Articles, from 250 words, on successful coin-operated laundries and dry-cleaners, with photos; also industry trends, promotion. Cartoons. Pays 3¢ per word, on publication. Query.

AMERICAN DRYCLEANER—500 North Dearborn, Chicago, Ill. 60610.
Well-documented case histories about the development by cleaners of important programs in merchandising, production, etc. Photos. Pays 3¢ and up a word, on publication. Write for guide sheet and sample copy.

AMERICAN PAINTING CONTRACTOR—2911 Washington Ave., St. Louis, Mo. 63103. Erwin L. Below, Editor.
Technical descriptive articles up to 2,500 words, on residential and commercial decorating, industrial maintenance painting, how prominent painting contractors advertise or sell, etc. Illustrated features preferred. For professional painters only; no do-it-yourself. Pays 4¢ and up a word, on publication; extra for usable photos.

AMERICAN ROOFER AND BUILDING IMPROVEMENT CONTRACTOR—221 Lake St., Oak Park, Ill. 60304. J. C. Gudas, Editor.
Timely articles, 600 words, on sales, case histories, manufacturing, estimating of roofing, siding, and building improvement. No stories based on metropolitan newspaper Real Estate Section news. Contractor stories based on neighborhood newspaper items welcomed. Pays 1¢ a word and up.

THE AMERICAN SOFT DRINK JOURNAL—136 Church St., Jonesboro, Ga. 30236. Jim Browne, Editor.
Illustrated articles on advertising, merchandising and selling of carbonated beverages, 1,000 to 2,000 words. Illustrated shorts, 200 to 500 words.

AMUSEMENT BUSINESS—1719 West End Ave., Nashville, Tenn. 37203. Irwin Kirby, Editor.
For owners, operators, managers, and booking agents associated with mass-audience amusement enterprises, including fun parks, fairs, stadiums, tourist attractions, circuses, and carnivals. Query.

AREA DEVELOPMENT—114 East 32nd St., New York, N. Y. 10016. Albert H. Jaeggin, Editor.
Instructive, useful articles directed to leading industrialists and top executives of manufacturing companies on all aspects of industrial facility planning (plant relocation and expansion, etc.). Authors should query first. Pays $32 per printed page including photos and heads.

AUDECIBEL—24261 Grand River, Detroit, Mich. 48219.
Articles, 200 to 2,000 words, about hearing aids, sound, and related topics, for those who work with the hard-of-hearing. Pays 1¢ to 2¢ a word. Write for "Fact Sheet for Writers."

AUTO GLASS JOURNAL—6654 Chestnut, Cincinnati, Ohio 45227. James B. Colborne, Editor.
Interviews on successful auto glass replacement shops, 500 to 1,000 words with photos. Pays 5¢ a word, on acceptance.

AUTO TRIM NEWS—129 Broadway, Lynbrook, N. Y. 11563. Nat W. Danas, Editor.
Success stories, management and merchandising features on auto trim shops, seat cover specialty stores. Also auto trim departments which are part of chain operations, such as Montgomery Ward, Sears-Roebuck, etc. How-to articles on specific aspects of auto trim shop work, and short features, 300 to 400 words. Photos. Pays $25 per published page.

THE BAKER—4308 North Central Hwy., Dallas, Tex. 75206. Donna Scheibe, Editor.
Articles on how a baker solved labor problems, improved his plant, improved profits, etc. Pays 1¢ a word and up. Uses only material concerning bakeries and baking executives in Southern, Southwestern, and Rocky Mountain states.

BAKING INDUSTRY—200 South Prospect Ave., Park Ridge, Ill. 60068. Joe Gregory, Editor.
Articles, 1,000 to 1,500 words, on some feature of wholesale or retail bakery merchandising, expansion, display, automation, or advertising. Pays on publication. Query.

BAR/SERVER (formerly *The Server*)—Jobson Publishing Corp., 488 Madison Ave., New York, N. Y. 10017. Allen Schwartz, Editor.
Merchandising and promotional material to 800 words on bar operation of clubs, hotels, and restaurants. Pays up to $125, on acceptance.

BARRON'S—22 Cortlandt St., New York, N. Y. 10007. Robert M. Bleiberg, Editor.
Business and finance articles of national interest, 1,200 to 2,500 words. Pays on publication.

BIG FARMER—131 Lincoln Highway, Frankfort, Ill. 60423.
Challenging articles for and about high-income commercial farmers, to 1,500 words. Dramatic, top-quality photos essential. Short items on new cost-cutting, money-making ideas for top farmers. Pays on acceptance.

BOATING INDUSTRY—205 East 42nd St., New York, N. Y. 10017. Dave Kendal, Senior Editor.
Business articles about boating dealers. Pays 4¢ to 5¢ a word, $5 for photos, on publication. Query.

BOOT AND SHOE RECORDER—56th and Chestnut Sts., Philadelphia, Pa. 19139.
Short-short picture-caption stories, 100 words, that detail merchandising ideas at the retail level. Also feature stories, 800 to 2,000 words, about successful merchandising ideas of shoe stores and departments, retail problems, new production techniques, industry trends. Shoe lore and history. Must be specific. Also trade news. Pays $50 per page for features. Query first.

BROADCAST ENGINEERING—1014 Wyandotte, Kansas City, Mo. 64105. Ron Merrell, Editor.
Practical, engineering-management oriented articles, 1,000 to 2,800 words, on cable TV, broadcasting, educational radio and TV, and recording studios. Also Engineer's Exchange column for short cuts and equipment modification. Uses interesting photos of unique communications situations. Pays $75 to $200 per article; $10 to $25 for Engineer's Exchange, on acceptance. Query.

BUSINESS AND COMMERCIAL AVIATION—Ziff-Davis Publishing Co., 1 Park Ave., New York, N. Y. 10016.
Articles with photos, on aviation, directed to semi-pros and professional pilots, 2,500 words. Pays $100 to $500.

CAMPGROUND AND RV PARK MANAGEMENT—P.O. Box 1014, Grass Valley, Calif. 95945.
Features, 300 to 1,200 words, describing some phase of a park owner's successful business operation, with black-and-white photos. Pays up to $50, on publication. Specific detail essential.

CAMPGROUND MERCHANDISING—20-21 Wagaraw Rd., Fair Lawn, N. J. 07410. Martin Dowd, Co-Publisher.
Articles quoting managers of campground recreation vehicle parks on what type of equipment and merchandise they sell to RV'ers. Pays up to $1 per published inch, $10 each for high-quality photos.

CANDY AND SNACK INDUSTRY—777 Third Ave., New York, N. Y. 10017.
Illustrated features, 1,000 to 1,250 words, which describe production and promotion activities of national market candy firms and local retail manufacturers. Also short news stories. Pays 5¢ a word, $5 for photos. Query on plant stories.

CANNER-PACKER—Box 664 Barrington, Ill. 60010.
Queries considered for articles to interest canned, glasspacked, frozen and dry processed food industries, on industry problems and news, labor, herbicides and insecticides, etc. Pays 5¢ a word, on publication, $5 for photos used.

CARS & TRUCKS—2000 K St., N.W., Washington, D. C. 20006.
Published by the National Automobile Dealers Association. Management articles, 750 to 2,000 words, covering all phases of automobile retailing. Articles must be dealer case histories. Photos. Pays various rates, on acceptance. Query.

THE CATTLEMAN—410 East Weatherford, Fort Worth, Tex. 76102. Paul W. Horn, Editor.
Articles on cattle-raising topics. Payment varies, is on publication.

CERAMIC SCOPE—6363 Wilshire Blvd., Los Angeles, Calif. 90048. Mel Fiske, Editor.
Articles, 1,000 to 1,500 words, about business operations of ceramic studios: merchandising and promotion, layout and display, inventory systems and recordkeeping, studio management on retail or wholesale level. Photos of studios. Pays 2¢ a word, $5 a photo, on acceptance. Query.

CHAIN SAW AGE—3435 N. E. Broadway, Portland, Ore. 97232.
Merchandising features on dealers and distributors of chain saws; unusual uses for chain saws, etc. Pays 2¢ a word, on publication; extra for photos. Query first.

CHEMICAL WEEK—1221 Ave. of the Americas, New York, N. Y. 10020. Ralph R. Schulte, Editor-in-Chief.
News material of chemical business significance, up to 200 words, usually on assignment. Pays $2 per column inch, minimum of $5 per item. Query first.

THE CHRISTIAN BOOKSELLER—Gundersen Dr. and Schmale Rd., Wheaton, Ill. 60187.
Articles from 1,200 to 1,500 words, on successful advertising programs, sales promotions, remodeling projects, store fronts of religious book stores. Anecdotal approach. Photos. Pays $25 to $50.

CLEANING MANAGEMENT—710 West Wilson Ave., Glendale, Calif. 91209. Charles F. Wheeler, Jr., Publisher.
Articles, 1,000 words, on educational and instructional subjects to assist cleaning and maintenance personnel improve efficiency, increase economy, and upgrade performance. No case histories. Pays 3¢ a word and up, $5 for photos, on publication.

COINAMATIC AGE—60 East 42nd St., New York, N. Y. 10017.
Factual articles, 1,000 to 1,500 words, with 3 to 6 glossy photos, emphasizing ingenuity of store owner in coin laundry, drycleaning, or coin-operated car wash business. Complete list of all trade-named equipment should be included. Pays 3¢ a word and up, $10 for first three photos, $5 per each additional photo used, on publication. Query first.

COLLEGE MANAGEMENT—22 West Putnam Ave., Greenwich, Conn. 06830. Paul Cuneo, Editor.
Feature articles on any subject that concerns college administrators, written from practical approach and documented with actual examples and/or live interviews. Payment on acceptance. Query.

COLLEGE STORE EXECUTIVE—P.O. Box 788, Lynbrook, N. Y. 11563. Pamela Kay Smith, Editor.
Wants articles, 800 to 1,600 words, with black-and-white photos, on news of activities at college stores around the country. Pays varying rates, on acceptance.

COMMERCIAL CAR JOURNAL—201 King of Prussia Rd., Radnor, Pa. 19087. James D. Winsor, Editor.
Feature articles concerning truck and bus fleet operation and maintenance. Knowledge of industry essential. Pays $50 and up, on final acceptance. Queries invited.

COMMERCIAL KITCHENS AND DINING ROOM—209 Dunn Ave., Stamford, Conn. 06905. Ken Jones, Editor.
Articles, 800 to 1,000 words, with photos, on assignment, on restaurant, cafeteria and nursing home equipment. Pays $50 per published page. Query.

COMMUNICATION NEWS—402 West Liberty Drive, Wheaton, Ill. 60187. Bruce Howat, Editor.
Technical articles on developments in voice, signal and data communications, 500 to 1,500 words. Also news, case histories and how-to articles.

COMPUTER DECISIONS MAGAZINE—50 Essex St., Rochelle Park, N. J. 07662. Robert Haavind, Editor.

Wants articles, 800 to 4,000 words, on generic uses of computer systems. Also brief, filler-length computer-games, including a program and explanation of the program. Pays $30 to $50 per published page. Query.

CONCRETE PRODUCTS—300 West Adams St., Chicago, Ill. 60606. William J. Blaha, Editor.
Articles on production methods, processes, distribution, marketing and promotion of ready-mix concrete, concrete block, pipe, and precast and prestress concrete, and all matters of interest to the concrete products industry. Pays 3¢ a word, extra for photos, on acceptance. Query first.

CONTRACTOR—Berkshire Common, Pittsfield, Mass. 01201. Seth Shepard, Editor.
Articles for the larger plumbing, heating and air conditioning contractor; news stories on strikes, legal actions, local associations, etc. Pays 15¢ a line.

COSMETICS FAIR—65 East 55th St., New York, N. Y. 10022. Stephan A. Tuchman, Editor.
Articles, 500 to 2,000 words, dealing with cosmetics departments, special promotions or sales experiences in either drug or department stores. Photo features, profiles of cosmetics industry personalities desired. Pays from $25 to $100.

CRAFT HORIZONS—44 West 53rd St., New York, N. Y. 10019. Rose Slivka, Editor.
Articles on professional handcrafts and craftsmen: weaving, ceramics, metalworking, woodworking. Outlines with photos. Pays up to $75, following publication.

CREDIT AND FINANCIAL MANAGEMENT—475 Park Ave. South, New York, N. Y. 10016. Thomas D. Kenny, Editor.
Articles, 3,000 words, on business credit, financial and business conditions, management policies and techniques in manufacturing, wholesaling, and service companies. Payment varies, is on publication.

CURTAIN, DRAPERY & BEDSPREAD MAGAZINE—Columbia Communications, 370 Lexington Ave., New York, N. Y. 10017. Ruth L. Lyons, Editor.
Articles, to 1,500 words, with 5 to 8 photos, about new operational or promotional techniques; 250-word merchandising tips. Pays 5¢ a word, $5 for each photo with caption, upon publication.

DAIRY HERD MANAGEMENT—P.O. Box 67, Minneapolis, Minn. 55440. Fred Tunks, Editor.
Articles, 50 to 2,000 words with photos, on large dairy operations and innovative techniques and equipment used by major U.S. dairymen. Fillers, clippings. Pays $10 to $150. Query.

DAIRY INDUSTRY NEWS—145 Sixth Ave., New York, N. Y. 10013. Robert W. Hardy, Editor.
News articles about every facet of the dairy industry. Prefers correspondents with newspaper experience. Payment is monthly. Query.

DE/JOURNAL—450 East Ohio St., Chicago, Ill. 60611. Stephen J. Schafer, Editor.
Articles on plumbing, heating, air conditioning, process piping, etc., up to 3,000 words. Photos. No clippings. Pays $20 to $35 per published page, on publication.

DEFENSE TRANSPORTATION—1612 K St., N.W., Washington, D. C. 20006. Jo Anne M. Thompson, Editor.
Articles, 2,500 to 3,000 words, reporting and analyzing concepts, trends and developments in the transportation industry, relating to national defense and emergency planning. Pays up to $150, on publication.

DELI NEWS—Delicatessen Council of Southern California, Inc., Box 706, Hollywood, Calif. 90028.
Uses feature articles, humorous fiction, photos and cartoons relating to the delicatessen department of supermarkets. No jokes, puzzles, fillers or clippings. Pays about $15 to $25 for articles, $2 to $10 for cartoons and photos, on acceptance.

DENTAL MANAGEMENT—Ridgeway Center Bldg., Stamford, Conn. 06905.
Articles, up to 1,500 words, on taxes, insurance, office procedures, etc., of interest to dentists. No technical or clinical material. Pays 5¢ to 10¢ a word, on acceptance.

THE DISCOUNT MERCHANDISER—Macfadden-Bartell Corp., 205 East 42nd St., New York, N. Y. 10017. Nathaniel Schwartz, Editor.
Articles and photos on innovations in mass-merchandising techniques and ideas for discount stores. Pays up to $150 for article and photos, on acceptance.

THE DISPENSING OPTICIAN—1980 Mountain Blvd., Oakland, Calif. 94611. Robert L. Pickering, Editor.
Articles, 750 to 2,000 words, on operation of optical dispensing businesses. Uses nothing on optometrists or retail operations that include eye examination services. Pays 4¢ a word, $7.50 for photos, on acceptance. Queries welcome.

DRIVE-IN FAST SERVICE—757 Third Ave., New York, N. Y. 10017. Lawrence Witchel, Editor.
Uses articles with photos about success stories of drive-in restaurants. Cover only one phase of the operation—no general profiles. Also short fillers with photos on promotional gimmicks. Pays 5¢ a word, $5 to $7 for photos.

DRUG TOPICS—496 Kinderkamack Rd., Oradell, N. J. 07649. Walter Cousins, Jr., Editor.
News stories on retailers and associations in the retail drug field. Also merchandising stories; query first. Photos. Pays 3¢ a word, on publication.

EARNSHAW'S INFANTS' AND CHILDREN'S REVIEW—393 Seventh Ave., New York. N. Y. 10001. Pat Van Olinda, Managing Editor.
Articles on promotions, fashion shows, business-building ideas in infants', children's, boys' and subteen departments. Pays $60 per published article. Query first.

EASTERN AUTOMOBILE JOURNAL—P.O. Box 373, Cedarhurst, N. Y. 11516.
Wants wholesaler-oriented articles, 1,000 to 1,500 words with three to five black-and-white photos, dealing with automotive replacement parts trade from Maine to Virginia. Payment is negotiable, upon publication. Query.

EDITOR & PUBLISHER—850 Third Ave., New York, N. Y. 10022. Jerome H. Walker, Executive Editor.
Articles, up to 1,200 words, relating to newspapers and journalists—news preferred. Photos. Query first.

ELECTRICAL CONTRACTOR—7315 Wisconsin Ave., Washington, D. C. 20014. Larry C. Osius, Editor.
Articles, 1,000 to 1,500 words, with photos, describing electrical construction techniques and/or management techniques, for electrical contractors. Pays $50 per published page, before publication. Query.

ELECTRONIC TECHNICAL DEALER—1 East First St., Duluth, Minn. 55802. Phillip Dahlen, Editor.

Articles on successful TV-radio service dealers, CCTV audio sound systems, MATV, two-way radio, other articles of interest to TV, radio and communications service technicians and dealers. Occasionally uses cartoons. Pays $25 per estimated magazine page; $7.50 per cartoon.

FARM AND POWER EQUIPMENT MAGAZINE—2340 Hampton Ave., St. Louis, Mo. 63139. Glenn S. Hensley, Editor.
Articles on retailers selling light industrial power equipment and farm implements. Photos and photo features. Pays up to $300, on acceptance, for top-quality, well-illustrated pieces written to specifications. Will work with authors. Query first.

FEED INDUSTRY REVIEW—3055 North Brookfield Rd., Brookfield, Wisc. 53005. Bruce Smith, Editorial Director.
Feature articles, with photos, 1,200 to 5,500 words, about full-scale manufacturing of brand-name feeds. Immediate replies to queries naming and describing proposed subjects.

FEEDSTUFFS—2501 Wayzata Blvd., Minneapolis, Minn. 55440. Daryl Natz, Editor.
Illustrated articles on animal and poultry nutrition, feed manufacturing; news feature articles.

FENCE INDUSTRY—307 North Michigan Ave., Chicago, Ill. 60601. Paul Eduard Miller, Editor.
Articles and interviews with dealer-erectors on fence industry topics and on themselves: history, gross volume, etc.; on-the-job articles. Query. Pays $5 to $10 for photos; 4¢ per word if tightly written.

THE FISH BOAT—624 Gravier St., New Orleans, La. 70150. Linwood Davis, Managing Editor.
Articles on commercial fishing, and promotion and merchandising of seafood products. Short items on commercial fishermen and their boats. Must include boat specifications and equipment. Payment varies. Query first.

FISHING GAZETTE—461 Eighth Ave., New York, N. Y. 10001. Robert J. Burns, Editor.
Articles with photos, up to 1,000 words, on commercial fisheries, fish processing plants, freezing plants, new products and plans. Payment varies. Query.

FLORIDA TREND—Box 2350, Tampa, Fla. 33601. Don Teverbaugh, Editor.
For industrial executives. Articles with an industrial significance, personality pieces, and short, factual items. Must have Florida slant. Photos. Payment varies, is on acceptance. Query first.

FLORIST—900 West Lafayette, Detroit, Mich. 48226. Frank J. Baccala, Editor.
Articles to 1,000 words, dealing with retail flower shop business improvements. Uses 8 × 10 glossy photos. Pays 3¢ a word, and $7.50 a photo.

THE FOREMAN'S LETTER—Bureau of Business Practice, 24 Rope Ferry Rd., Waterford, Conn. 06385. Frank L. Berkowitz, Editor.
Interviews, to 750 words, with black-and-white head-and-shoulders photo, describing successful employee leadership practices used on the job by industrial supervisors and foremen. Pays 6¢ to 7¢ per usable word, on acceptance; additional for photos. Similar requirements for newsletters directed to construction and public utilities supervisors.

FURNITURE AND FURNISHINGS—1450 Don Mills Rd., Don Mills, Ontario, Canada. Jane Vale, Editor.
News items and articles with photos of interest to retailers, furniture buyers, decorators, contract salesmen, distributors and manufacturers' representatives concerned with the distribution and sales of furniture, floor coverings, draperies, lamps and decorative accessories. Uses fillers and cartoons. Payment varies, on publication.

GAS APPLIANCE MERCHANDISING—1 E. First St., Duluth, Minn. 55802. James
Couillard, Editor.
Articles with photos, 500 to 1,200 words, on gas utility or gas appliance dealer
operations and promotional activities; display, special projects, etc. Pays 5¢
per word; $5 to $7 per photo, on acceptance.

GASOLINE NEWS—100 North Grant St., Columbus, Ohio 43215.
Monthly trade newspaper for service stations. Pays 50¢ for clippings on subjects
concerning the service station industry.

GIFT AND TABLEWARE REPORTER—1515 Broadway, New York, N. Y. 10036.
Jack McDermott, Editor.
Illustrated merchandising stories and news items for the giftware and tableware
retail buyer. Query.

GIFTS AND DECORATIVE ACCESSORIES—51 Madison Ave., New York, N. Y.
10010.
Articles with 8 x 10 photos, 1,500 to 3,000 words, on quality gift retailers (shops
or departments), social stationery and greeting card retailers, and their business
activities. Only merchandising features are acceptable. Pays up to $50, on publica-
tion; black-and-white or color photos extra.

GLASS DIGEST—15 East 40th St., New York, N. Y. 10016. Oscar S. Glasberg,
Editor.
Case histories of building projects and glass/metal dealers, distributors, and store-
front and glazing contractors, 1,200 to 1,500 words. Pays 3½¢ to 5¢ a word, $5 for
photos, occasionally more, depending on subject and assignment.

GOLF SHOP OPERATIONS—297 Westport Ave., Norwalk, Conn. 06856.
Case histories of successful pro shop operations and new ideas relating to merchandising, display, bookkeeping, etc., in a pro shop, 200 to 800 words, including short
personal items on golf professionals. Pays on publication.

GRAPHIC ARTS MONTHLY—7373 No. Lincoln Ave., Chicago, Ill. 60646. Dr. Paul
J. Hartsuch, Editor.
Technical articles pertaining to the printing industry. Pays 3¢ per word, on accep-
tance. Query.

GROCERY COMMUNICATIONS—436 West Colorado St., Glendale, Calif. 91204.
D. David Dreis, Editor.
Articles on supermarkets and grocery stores in 11 western states (except Cali-
fornia). Pays around $50 to $100.

HANDBAGS AND ACCESSORIES—80 Lincoln Ave., Stamford, Conn. 06904. Renee
Prowitt, Editor.
Articles and features, with photos, of interest to handbag and accessory buyers:
unique store displays, retail promotions, designers and manufacturers of interest.
Pays $50 for short articles, $100 and up for major features with photos, on publi-
cation. Query.

HARDWARE AGE—Chilton Way, Radnor, Pa. 19089.
Fillers with black-and-white photos describing unique merchandising methods for
hardware. Pays $10 to $15 for photos used.

HARDWARE MERCHANDISER—7300 North Cicero Ave., Chicago, Ill. 60646. W. P.
Farrell, Editor.
Articles, to 1,000 words, with black-and-white photos, on hardware marketing;
also general and specific merchandising of lines. Buys few articles.

HEATING/PIPING/AIR CONDITIONING—10 South LaSalle St., Chicago, Ill.
60603. Robert T. Korte, Editor.
Articles up to 5,000 words, on heating, piping and air-conditioning systems in industrial plants and large buildings; engineering information. Pays on publication.

HOME AND AUTO—757 Third Ave., New York, N. Y. 10017.
Articles on merchandising methods of auto supply stores, home and auto stores,

and automotive departments of discount stores. Pays by arrangement. Query first.

HOMESEWING TRADE NEWS—129 Broadway, Lynbrook, N. Y. 11583.
Wants articles, 750 to 1,000 words, with 2 to 4 photos, aimed at shop owners, buyers, in homesewing field. Query Editor for desired focus of piece. Pays $35 to $50, on publication.

HOSPITAL SUPERVISOR'S BULLETIN—681 Fifth Ave., New York, N. Y. 10022. Jill Wechsler, Editor.
For hospital supervisors of nonmedical areas. Wants interview-based articles, 900 to 1,350 words, with emphasis on solving problems, and good methods of "getting things done through others." Pays $25 per 450 words, on acceptance; $7.50 for cartoons. No photos. Query. Send for copy of publication and editorial requirements.

HOTEL & MOTEL MANAGEMENT—845 Chicago Ave., Evanston, Ill. 60202.
Articles, 1,000 to 2,000 words, on management subjects. Query.

HOUSEWARES REVIEW—757 Third Ave., New York, N. Y. 10017. George A. Glenn, Editor.
Articles and picture stories on promotional merchandising by retail houseware outlets. Pays 9¢ per published word. Query first.

THE INLAND PRINTER/AMERICAN LITHOGRAPHER—300 West Adams St., Chicago, Ill. 60606. Jack Homer, Editor.
Articles on plant management and operation, shop technique, sales, design, etc. Payment varies, is on publication. Query first.

THE JEWELERS' CIRCULAR-KEYSTONE—Chilton Way, Radnor, Pa. 19089.
Articles on specific phases of retail jewelry store merchandising or operation, with photos. Needs features on successful ideas in merchandising silverware. Length, 200 to 1,500 words. Pays $25 per published page, on acceptance. Also 200- to 300-word shorts, focusing sharply on some single activity that built traffic and sales or cut costs for a jeweler or jewelry department in a department store. Pays $10, on acceptance.

JOBBER & WAREHOUSE EXECUTIVE—53 West Jackson Blvd., Chicago, Ill. 60604.
Articles, 800 to 1,200 words, with photos, for management personnel in automotive wholesaling firms. Payment varies.

KENTUCKY BUSINESS MAGAZINE—300 West York St., Louisville, Ky. 40203.
Articles, about 2,000 words, keyed to Kentucky business leaders. Most material staff-written. Pays by arrangement, after acceptance.

KIRKLEY PRESS, INC.—Box 200, Lutherville, Md. 21093.
Articles, 700 words and 2,200 to 2,400 words, that promote better on-the-job employee relations, and higher personal efficiency. Query with lead-in material. Pays $35 to $50 for folders, and $200 to $300 for booklets. Address Alan Dugdale.

KITCHEN BUSINESS—1501 Broadway, New York, N. Y. 10036. Patrick Galvin, Editor.
Case histories, 500 to 2,000 words, with photos, on specific management or merchandising procedures of successful dealers in cabinets or built-in products for kitchens. Also covers plastic fabricating plants making plastic-surfaced kitchen cabinets or countertops, and needs good production stories. Stories must be in depth, accompanied by excellent photos. Pays $50 first printed page, $30 per succeeding page. Query first.

KITCHEN PLANNING—757 Third Ave., New York, N. Y. 10017. Lawrence Witchel, Editor.
Trade journal for designers of commercial food facilities. Interested in articles, photographs and blueprints of new commercial and industrial kitchens. Length: 750 to 1,500 words. Pays 5¢ a word, on acceptance, and $5 per photo.

photographs and blueprints of new commercial and industrial kitchens. Length: 750 to 1,500 words. Pays 5¢ a word, on acceptance, and $5 per photo.

KNITTING INDUSTRY—44 East 23rd St., New York, N. Y. 10010. Perry Antoshak, Editor.
Articles, 1,500 to 2,000 words, with photos, on manufacturing processes in knitting industry: outerwear, underwear, hosiery, packaging. Pays 70¢ per inch and $2.00 per photo, after publication.

LP-GAS MAGAZINE—1 East First St., Duluth, Minn. 55802.
Business articles, 1,000 to 1,500 words, with three to five black-and-white photos, on LP-gas/propane gas uses and operations. Pays 5¢ a printed word and $5 to $7 per photo used, on acceptance. Query.

LAW AND ORDER—37 West 38th St., New York, N. Y. 10018. Frank G. Mac-Aloon, Editor.
How-to articles on police work, 1,500 to 2,000 words, with photos, for police chiefs: communications, education, public relations, civil disturbances, traffic, police science, mobile patrol and equipment. Pays 2¢ a word, on publication.

LAWN & GARDEN MARKETING—1014 Wyandotte St., Kansas City, Mo. 64105. Wendall J. Burns, Editor.
Articles and photo-features, 600 to 1,200 words, with 5 x 7 black-and-white glossies, on management, for retailers of landscaping and gardening supplies, outdoor power equipment and outdoor recreational equipment. Pays $75 to $100 for articles, $25 for photo-features, $5 to $10 for photos, on acceptance.

LINENS, DOMESTICS AND BATH—373 Fifth Ave., New York, N. Y. 10016.
Articles, 700 to 900 words, on linens and domestics (blankets, sheets, towels, bedspreads, tablecloths, etc.) in department, specialty and chain stores. Pays $25 per published page, on publication. Query first.

MADISON AVENUE—866 U. N. Plaza, New York, N. Y. 10017.
Business articles, 1,000 to 2,500 words, dealing with advertising, from the agency or client viewpoint. Payment varies, is on publication.

MANAGE—9933 Alliance Rd., Cincinnati, Ohio 45242.
Articles, 1,500 to 2,200 words, on management and/or supervision. Photos, drawings related to story material; also cartoons. Payment 3¢ to 5¢ a word, on acceptance.

MARKING INDUSTRY—18 East Huron St., Chicago, Ill. 60611. A. W. Hachmeister, Editor.
Technical or sales-material on manufacture and distribution of steel stamps, checks, badges, etc., in the U. S. or Latin America. Pays on acceptance.

MILITARY REVIEW—U. S. Army Command and General Staff College, Fort Leavenworth, Kan. 66027. Col. O. W. Martin, Jr., Editor-in-Chief.
Well-written articles, 2,500 to 6,000 words, which will stimulate military thinking on tactics, history, military forces, strategy, logistics, etc. Pays on publication. Query first.

MILK HAULER AND FOOD TRANSPORTER—221 North LaSalle St., Chicago, Ill. 60601. Emil J. Blacky, Editor.
For tank truck haulers who pick up milk from dairy farms and transporters who deliver milk to markets. Particularly interested in success stories, with photos, on transporters who haul cheese and other dairy products, liquid sugar, molasses, citrus juice and other edible foods. Pays about $50 per article, $5 each for sharp black-and-white photos, on acceptance. Reports in 2 to 3 weeks. Queries welcome. Enclose stamped, self-addressed envelope.

MINERALS PROCESSING—645 North Michigan Ave., Chicago, Ill. 60611. A. W. Orloski, Editor.
Articles on heat-processing technology of cement, lime, gypsum, heat-expanded aggregates; new plants and plant expansion. Also features about plants and people in the industry. Photos required. Payment is $35 per printed page plus photos and diagrams, on publication. Query essential.

MODERN PACKAGING—1221 Avenue of the Americas, New York, N. Y. 10020. Illustrated articles for producers of packaged products. Pays $30 per published page. Queries required.

MODERN PLANT MAGAZINE—209 Dunn Ave., Stamford, Conn. 06905. Ken Jones, Editor.
Articles, 800 to 1,000 words, and features, with photos, on assignment, dealing with plant operation and maintenance. Pays $50 per published page. Query.

MODERN RETAILER—50 Hunt St., Watertown, Mass. 02172. Harold S. Larkin, Editor.
Articles, based on interviews, about multi-unit mass merchandising chains (discount, department, drug, variety, supermarket). Uses 10 interviews per month. Pays $60 to $100, $7.50 for photos, on acceptance. Query first.

MODERN TIRE DEALER—P.O. Box 5417, 77 North Miller Rd., Akron, Ohio 44313. Charles Slaybaugh, Editor.
Merchandising, management and service articles about independent tire dealers and retreaders, with photos. Length, 1,000 to 1,500 words. Pays 5¢ a word and up, on publication.

MOTOR—250 West 55th St., New York, N. Y. 10019. Philip Nochlin, Managing Editor.
Articles, 750 to 1,500 words, with glossy photos, describing how one particular repair shop, garage or service station does an outstanding job merchandising automotive accessories (TBA). Each article should deal with only one automotive item. Pays on acceptance. Query.

MOTOR AGE—56th and Chestnut Sts., Philadelphia, Pa. 19139. John P. Kushnerick, Editor.
Merchandising and management articles, 1,500 words, for managers of automotive repair outlets (new car dealers, garages, service stations). Photos needed on case study articles. Pays $50 to $70, on acceptance. Query first.

MOTOR IN CANADA—1077 St. James St., Box 6900, Winnipeg, 21, Manitoba, Canada. Ralf Neuendorff, Editor.
Short merchandising and service articles, 250 to 1,000 words, slanted for the automotive trade in Western Canada. Pays $1 per column inch, on publication. Extra for pictures.

NATIONAL BOWLERS' JOURNAL AND BILLIARD REVUE—1825 North Lincoln Plaza, Chicago, Ill. 60614.
Stories about promotions which increased business for bowling and billiard proprietors. Photos. Pays $40 to $50, on publication.

NATIONAL BUSINESS WOMAN—2012 Massachusetts Ave., N. W., Washington, D. C. 20036. Lola S. Tilden, Editor.
Articles, to 1,200 words, of interest to business and professional women, their personal development, opportunities, responsibilities, etc. Pays 3¢ a word, on acceptance. Manuscripts without postage not returned.

NATIONAL LIVESTOCK PRODUCER—155 North Wacker Dr., Chicago, Ill. 60606. Frank Lessiter, Editor.
Articles of varied lengths of interest to livestock producers all over the country. Payment is usually about $150, on acceptance. Query first.

THE NATIONAL PUBLIC ACCOUNTANT—1717 Pennsylvania Ave., N.W., Washington, D. C. 20006 Stanley S. Stearman, Editor.
Articles of 1,800 to 5,000 words, on accounting, taxation, bookkeeping, data processing and business administration.

OCCUPATIONAL HAZARDS—614 Superior Ave. West, Cleveland, Ohio 44113. Peter J. Sheridan, Editor.
Articles, 500 to 2,000 words, dealing with industrial safety, health, fire prevention, and security. Related cartoons and photos. Pays 3¢ a word and up, on publication; $3 for photos and article illustrations, $5 for cartoons, on acceptance.

OFFICE PRODUCTS—Hitchcock Building, Wheaton, Ill. 60187. Thomas J. Trafals, Editor.
Illustrated merchandising articles for and about office supply, machine and furniture dealers. Pays minimum of $25 per printed page, including pictures, on acceptance. Query.

OFFICE SUPERVISOR'S BULLETIN—681 Fifth Ave., New York, N. Y. 10022. Catherine Contos, Editor.
For first- and second-line office supervisors. Wants interview-based articles, 900 to 1,350 words, with emphasis on solving problems, and good methods of "getting things done through others." Pays $25 per 450 words, on acceptance; $7.50 for cartoons. No photos. Queries preferred. Send for copy of publication and editorial requirements.

THE OPTICAL JOURNAL AND REVIEW OF OPTOMETRY—Chilton Way, Radnor, Pa. 19089. John F. McCarthy, Editor.
Articles, to 1,500 words, on optometric practice and ophthalmic optical work. Pays 60¢ per published inch, on publication.

PACKAGE ENGINEERING—5 South Wabash Ave., Chicago, Ill. 60603.
Feature articles pertinent to the technical and operational packaging field: engineering, production, research and development, testing, purchasing and top management. Illustrations. Pays $25 per published page. Query first.

PACKING AND SHIPPING—437 East 5th St., Plainfield, N. J. 07060. C. M. Bonnell, Jr., Editor.
Illustrated articles of about 1,000 words, on physical distribution, industrial packing, handling, shipping-room practice. Short items. Pays on publication.

PAPER, FILM AND FOIL CONVERTER—200 South Prospect, Park Ridge, Ill. 60068. Robert Heitzman, Editor.
Articles or picture stories on converter processes, production, equipment operation, and product development.

PAPERBOARD PACKAGING—777 Third Ave., New York, N. Y. 10017. Joel L. Shulman, Editor.
Articles on paperboard mill, corrugated container, folding carton fields and related activities. News items. Lengths vary. Pays $50 per 1,000 words, on publication. Query with outline.

PETROLEUM TODAY—1801 K St., N. W., Washington, D. C. 20006.
Articles on topics related to the oil industry, of broad general interest—oil products, personalities, operations. Pays good rates.

PHOTO MARKETING—603 Lansing Ave., Jackson, Mich. 49202. James L. Crawford, Managing Editor.
Articles on how camera stores and finishing plants have been successful in a particular area, such as promotion, advertising, personnel management, etc. Pays 3¢ to 5¢ per printed word; $5 to $7.50 per published photo.

POOL NEWS—Leisure Publications. Ltd., 3923 West Sixth St., Los Angeles, Calif. 90005. Fay Coupe, Editor.
News stories on the swimming pool industry. Pays 5¢ a word, $4 per photo.

POULTRY TRIBUNE—Mt. Morris, Ill. 61054. Milton R. Dunk, Editor.
Business stories on egg production, processing, and marketing, stories related to the egg business, 200 to 1,000 words. Pays 2¢ to 5¢ a word, on acceptance; extra for good photos. Query first.

POWER ENGINEERING—1301 South Grove St., Barrington, Ill. 60010. Ray Schuster, Editor.
Articles pertaining to design, construction, operation and maintenance of large power facilities for big industry and utilities. Pays $30 to $40 per page, on acceptance.

PRINTING MAGAZINE—106 Benton Rd., Paramus, N. J. 07652. Jeremiah E. Flynn, Editor.
Articles, 1,000 to 3,000 words, on management, marketing and technical problems and how they are resolved, for commercial printers with offset and letterpress facilities. Pays from $25 to $35 per page, after publication. All submissions on speculation only. Query.

PRODUCTION MAGAZINE—Bramson Publishing Co., Box 101, Bloomfield Hills, Mich. 48013. Robert F. Huber, Editor.
Articles, 300 to 3,000 words, on improved mass production metalworking operations. Photographs and drawings used. Pays on acceptance.

THE PROFESSIONAL PHOTOGRAPHER—Professional Photographers of America, Inc., 1090 Executive Way, Oak Leaf Commons, Des Plaines, Ill. 60018.
Articles, 1,000 to 2,000 words, about professional photographers. Photos essential. Query first.

PROGRESSIVE GROCER—708 Third Ave., New York, N. Y. 10017. Robert W. Mueller, Editor.
Fact articles, to 2,500 words, on supermarket management, operations, merchandising, and promotion. Shorts, 100 to 200 words, on sales and promotion ideas. Photos. Pays $10 and up per black-and-white photo and caption, $25 for color transparencies, on acceptance. Article rates vary.

PURCHASING—205 East 42nd St., New York, N. Y. 10017.
Articles of 1,500 words dealing with buying techniques and methods used in industrial purchasing departments; also photos, illustrative charts and materials. Cartoons. Pays about $50 per printed page.

RVB (Recreational Vehicle Business)—3000 France Ave. So., Minneapolis, Minn. 55416. Jerry Hoffman, Editor.
Case history articles on snowmobiles, ATV, trail and mini-bike dealers. Pays on acceptance.

RADIO AND TELEVISION WEEKLY—145 Ave. of the Americas, New York, N. Y. 10013. Cy Kneller, Editor.
News concerning the activities of radio, television and electronic wholesale distributors and retail dealers. Brief news items. Payment is monthly.

RADIO-ELECTRONICS—200 Park Ave. South, New York, N. Y. 10003. Larry Steckler, Managing Editor.
Technical articles on electronic equipment and maintenance; servicing TV, hi-fi audio, AM and FM, CB and other forms of communication equipment. Construction projects on electronic devices. State of the art reports and other general interest items. Pays on acceptance. Guide to Writing available on request.

REFRIGERATED TRANSPORTER—1602 Harold St., Houston, Tex. 77006.
News articles on transportation under refrigeration, by both for-hire and private motor carriers, preferably illustrated. Pays from $25 per printed page.

RESORT MANAGEMENT—1509 Madison Ave., P. O. Box 4169, Memphis, Tenn. 38104. Allen J. Fagans, Editor.
Case histories of successful resort programs, described in detail. Subjects include how a resort attracts and entertains guests, saves money, or gives outstanding service in bar, kitchen, dining room, housekeeping and front desk departments. Pays up to $75 for articles, and $5 minimum for black-and-white photos. Reports in two weeks.

ROCK PRODUCTS—300 West Adams St., Chicago, Ill. 60606. Sidney Levine, Editor.
Articles on production methods and processes in the nonmetallic mineral field. Pays on publication.

SCHOOL MANAGEMENT—22 West Putnam Ave., Greenwich, Conn. 06830. Paul K. Cuneo, Editor.
Articles on practical, proven solutions to school management problems; examples of courageous or dynamic school district leadership; unusual or unusually effective school programs. Study magazine and query before submitting. Pays 3¢ a word and up; major articles negotiable.

SKIING TRADE NEWS—One Park Ave., New York, N. Y. 10016. William Grout, Editor.
Brief news items about new developments in ski equipment retailing. Also features of 1,500 words about how to make profits in retail ski shops, with black-and-white photos. Pays 10¢ per word, on publication.

SMALL WORLD MAGAZINE—c/o Earnshaw's Infants' and Children's Review, 393 Seventh Ave., New York, N. Y. 10001. Thomas W. Hudson, Editor.
Wants articles about department stores and large discounters retailing juvenile furniture, 1,000 words. Accepts jokes and photos. Pays $60 per story, including 3 photos, on publication.

SNACK FOOD MAGAZINE—Harcourt Bldg., Duluth, Minn. 55802. Jerry Hess, Editor.
Serving the cookie, cracker, potato chip, pretzel, popcorn and snack food industry with feature articles, profiles, trade news and short articles about promotions and ad campaigns and packaging. Uses photos. Payment on acceptance.

SOUTHERN HARDWARE—1760 Peachtree Rd., Atlanta, Ga. 30309.
Articles on merchandising activities of specific Southern hardware retailers. Pays $40 per printed page and up, on first of month after acceptance. Query first.

SOUVENIRS AND NOVELTIES—20–21 Wagaraw Rd., Fair Lawn, N. J. 07410. Martin Dowd, Editor.
Articles quoting souvenir shop managers on types of items that sell well, display ideas to improve sales, problems in selling souvenirs and novelties, and trends in the industry. Pays up to $1 per published inch, $10 each for photos.

SPECIALTY SALESMAN—307 North Michigan Ave., Chicago, Ill. 60601. Ben Newman, Editorial Director.
Articles, 300 to 1,000 words, for the independent salesman and woman selling to homes, stores, industries and business. Pays 3¢ a word, on acceptance.

THE SPECTATOR—Chestnut & 56th Sts., Philadelphia, Pa. 19139.
Articles on insurance and financial management, 6 to 10 pages, and black-and-white photos. Pays from $35 to $50, on acceptance.

THE SPORTING GOODS DEALER—1212 North Lindbergh, St. Louis, Mo. 63132. Roland Burke, Managing Editor.
News, merchandising ideas, and pictures of sporting goods stores and personalities. Pays 2¢ a word and up, $5 per photo, on publication.

SUPERMARKET MANAGEMENT—209 Dunn Ave., Stamford, Conn. 06905.
Articles, with photos, on assignment only. Pays $50 per published page.

SUPERVISION—424 North Third, Burlington, Iowa 52601. G. B. McKee, Editor.
Self-help articles, 1,500 to 2,000 words, for management executives, particularly supervisors, foremen and production managers. Pays 2¢ a word, on publication.

TENNIS INDUSTRY—14695 Northeast 6th Ave., North Miami, Fla. 33161. Michael Keighley, Editor.
Articles, 1,000 to 2,000 words, on the business end of tennis; tennis products, new court surfaces, recreational center planning, the costs of creating and operating tennis complexes at schools, etc. Pays 5¢ a word, on acceptance. Query.

TENNIS TRADE—3000 France Ave. South, Minneapolis, Minn. 55416. Bob Gillen, Managing Editor.
News and case history articles on successful tennis business enterprises—indoor and outdoor clubs, pro shops, specialty stores, camps, clinics, coaching programs, and recreation. Pays on publication.

TEXTILE INDUSTRIES—1760 Peachtree Rd. N.W., Atlanta, Ga. 30309. George H. Dockray, Editor.
Articles about the management and engineering phases of the textile industry. Photos and drawings. Pays $30 per page, on acceptance, extra for photos. Authors must be qualified to write on textile industry.

TEXTILE WORLD—1375 Peachtree St. N. E., Atlanta, Ga. 30309. L. A. Christiansen, Chief Editor.
Articles, 1,000 to 3,000 words, with photos, on technology of manufacturing and finishing textiles, on increasing textile-mill efficiency, modernizing, management techniques, marketing, etc. Pays on acceptance.

TRAILER/BODY BUILDERS—1602 Harold St., Houston, Texas. 77006. Charles N. Tunnell, Publisher.
Articles on engineering, sales, and management ideas for truck body and truck trailer manufacturers. Pays 4¢ and up a word, on acceptance.

VEND—150 North Wacker Ave., Chicago, Ill. 60606.
Feature material on the automatic merchandising industry. Case studies on vending machine operating companies, mobile catering companies, and use of vending machines in industrial plants, institutions, etc. Length, 250 to 2,000 words. Pays 5¢ a word and up, $5 per photo. Query first.

THE WELDING DISTRIBUTOR—5811 Dempster St., Morton Grove, Ill. 60053. Don Jefferson, Editor.
Articles, 1,000 to 3,500 words, on selling welding and safety equipment and supplies. Merchandising articles; general articles on running a small business, keeping records, etc. Cartoons and photos. Pays 2¢ a word, on publication.

WESTERN OUTFITTER—5314 Bingle Rd., Houston, Tex. 77018. Tad S. Mizwa, Editor.
Articles, 2,000 to 3,000 words, with photos, on merchandising of western wear and equipment; depth pieces on familiar items of sale indicating product knowledge, retail sales and promotion, as slanted towards people in the western business particularly. Pays 3¢ per word, $5 per picture, upon publication. Query necessary as most free-lance subjects are assigned.

WESTERN PAINT REVIEW—1833 West 8th St., Los Angeles, Calif. 90057. E. C. Ansley, Editor.
Articles, 1,000 to 2,000 words, with three or four accompanying photos, on the paint and painting industries in the 13 Western states. Pays 4¢ per word and $3 per photo, on publication. Query.

WINES & VINES—703 Market St., San Francisco, Calif. 94103.
Articles on the wine industry, emphasizing marketing, about 1,000 words, with photos. Pays 3¢ a word, on acceptance.

WOODWORKING & FURNITURE DIGEST—Hitchcock Bldg., Wheaton, Ill. 60187. E. R. Gillis, Editor.

Articles, with photos, dealing with management, production, and engineering problems related to industries using wood as a primary raw material. Prefers "problem-solving" case history manufacturing type articles. No sawmill, logging or forestry. Pays $35 to $45 per published page. Query.

WORLD COFFEE & TEA—McKeand Publications Inc., 636 First Ave., West Haven, Conn. 06516. J. J. Martino, Editor.
Buys only first person stories from overseas areas producing coffee and tea. Pays $200 per page. Query.

WORLD OIL—Gulf Publishing Co., P. O. Box 2608, Houston, Tex. 77001. Donald E. Kliewer, Editorial Director.
Engineering and operations articles on petroleum industry exploration, drilling or producing subjects. Photos or drawings as required to illustrate engineering articles. Pays $17.50 per printed page. Query first.

SPECIALIZED MAGAZINES

HEALTH

ACCENT ON LIVING—P. O. Box 726, Bloomington, Ill. 61701. Raymond C. Cheever, Editor.
Articles on rehabilitation of the handicapped, success stories, and features on self-help devices. Currently interested in humorous articles concerning physical disabilities and articles dealing constructively with prejudice against the handicapped. Pays up to $50, on publication.

AMERICAN BABY (formerly *Mothers-to-be/American Baby*)—10 East 52nd St., New York, N. Y. 10022. Judith Nolte, Editor.
Articles for new and expectant parents, on care of babies one month to three years old, from 400 to 1,500 words. Payment varies.

AMERICAN FAMILY PHYSICIAN—1740 West 92nd St., Kansas City, Mo. 64114. Walter H. Kemp, Managing Editor.
Articles, 1,600 to 3,200 words, primarily on clinical medicine. Accompanying photos or drawings preferred. Pays from $50, on publication. Query.

AMERICAN JOURNAL OF NURSING—10 Columbus Circle, New York, N. Y. 10059. Thelma M. Schorr, Executive Editor.
Articles on nursing and related subjects, 1,500 to 2,000 words. Photographs. Pays $20 per printed page, on publication. Query first.

DENTAL ECONOMICS—P.O. Box 1260, Tulsa, Okla. 74101.
Primarily for dentists. Articles, concerning dental-practice management, 1,200 to 1,500 words. Photos. Pays on publication.

THE EXCEPTIONAL PARENT—P.O. Box 101, Back Bay Annex, Boston, Mass. 02117. Howard Dinin, Assistant Editor.
Articles, 600 to 3,000 words, giving practical guidance, in layman's language, for parents of disabled children. Pays 5¢ a word, on publication. Query.

EXPECTING—Parents' Magazine Enterprises, Inc., 52 Vanderbilt Ave., New York, N. Y. 10017.
Guide for expectant mothers. Medical articles, by R.N.'s and M.D.'s, and knowledgeable personal experience pieces, 700 to 1,500 words. Pays from $50 to $125, on acceptance. Slightly higher rates for specialists, such as M.D.'s. Query first with outline.

FAMILY HEALTH—1271 Ave. of the Americas, New York, N. Y. 10022.
Articles, about 3,000 words, and photo-essays, on health, beauty, physical fitness, marriage, child care, nutrition, etc. Submit outline first. Pays on acceptance.

FITNESS—33 East Minor St., Emmaus, Pa. 18049. John Haberern, Editor.
Articles, to 2,000 words, with photos, on physical fitness and exercise, appealing to the general public. Pays $50 to $120, extra for photos, on acceptance.

HEALTH—212 East Ohio St., Chicago, Ill. 60611. Mary Anne Klein, Associate Editor.
Articles on health and medicine for the lay reader, 1,000 to 2,000 words. Also photos and drawings for articles, and cartoons on medical subjects. Pays 4¢ a word, $5 a photo; $7.50 a cartoon.

HOSPITAL PROGRESS—1438 South Grand Blvd., St. Louis, Mo. 63104. H. R. Bryden, Editor.
Official journal of the Catholic Hospital Association. Hospital management and paramedical features, 1,500 to 5,000 words. Pays $1 per column inch, on publication.

MD—30 East 60th St., New York, N. Y. 10022. Michael Fry, D.Sc., Managing Editor.
Not in the market at the present time.

MEDICAL OPINION—575 Madison Ave., New York, N. Y. 10022. Byron T. Scott, Executive Editor.
As-told-to, expert-bylined, or in-depth articles, 1,000 to 2,500 words, on wide range of medical topics. Strong point of view essential; must interest general practitioner. Pays from $150 to $300, on acceptance.

RN—RN Publications, Oradell, N. J. 07649.
Articles on subjects of interest and practical value to nurses, to 1,500 words. Pays up to 10¢ a word, on publication. Query first.

STRENGTH AND HEALTH—P.O. Box 1707, York, Pa. 17405. Tom Holbrook, Editor.
Articles, 1,500 words and up, on weightlifting and physical fitness. Pays $50 and up, on publication.

TIC—P.O. Box 407, North Chatham, N. Y. 12132. Joseph Strack, Editor.
Articles, 800 to 3,000 words, on subjects of interest to dentists, preferably dealing with practice building and patient management. Pays on acceptance.

TODAY'S HEALTH—535 North Dearborn St., Chicago, Ill. 60610. David A. Sendler, Editor.
Family-angled articles, 2,500 to 3,000 words, on nutrition, recreation, child development, ecology and other health-related problems. Fresh insights on improving the way people interact, health angles on major news events and personalities, well-documented pieces crusading for healthier living. Medical articles must be scientifically accurate. Payment ranges from $500 to $1,000. No unsolicited manuscripts. Query first.

EDUCATION

AMERICAN EDUCATION—400 Maryland Avenue, S.W., Washington, D. C. 20202. Leroy V. Goodman, Editor.
Published by U.S. Office of Education. Informative feature articles, 1,000 to 3,000 words, preferably with photos, on current developments in education—from pre-school through college, as well as adult and vocational education and teacher training. Activities reported must involve Federal education programs. Audience includes educators, school and college administrators, parents, civic leaders. Pay scale varies. Query first, with lead paragraph and outline.

AMERICAN SCHOOL AND UNIVERSITY—134 North 13th St., Philadelphia, Pa. 19107. Henry S. Slesinger, Editor.
Articles and case studies dealing with the design, construction, operation, maintenance, and equipping of the school plant, 1,200 to 1,500 words preferred. Usually no payment. Query first.

AMERICAN SCHOOL BOARD JOURNAL—National School Boards Association, State National Bank Plaza, Evanston, Ill. 60201.
Articles on problems of school administration. Query.

ATHLETIC JOURNAL—1719 Howard St., Evanston, Ill. 60202. John L. Griffith, Editor.
Technical articles on interscholastic athletics by coaches and athletic directors only, to 1,500 words. Photos. Pays $20, on publication.

CANADIAN TEACHER OF THE DEAF—Box 308, Amherst, Nova Scotia, Canada.
Articles, up to 2,000 words, with black-and-white photos, on professional work with deaf children and adults, particularly in Canada. Payment in copies.

THE CATHOLIC SCHOOL EDITOR—1135 West Kilbourn Ave., Milwaukee, Wisc. 53233.
Articles, 1,700 to 3,000 words, with photos, on school publication goals, problems, and procedures. Reviews, 1,500 words, of books of interest to journalists. Pays $15 for reviews, $35 for articles, on publication.

COLLEGE MANAGEMENT—22 West Putnam Ave., Greenwich, Conn. 06830. Campbell Geeslin, Editor.
Case histories of college management problems and their solutions. Pays various rates, on or before publication. Query first.

ELEMENTARY SCHOOL JOURNAL—5835 Kimbark Ave., Chicago, Ill. 60637. Richard H. Hodges, Editor.
Articles dealing with the profession of education, such as classroom procedure, supervision and school administration, 2,000 to 4,000 words. Also black-and-white photos. No payment.

FORECAST FOR HOME ECONOMICS (Teacher Edition of *Co-Ed*)—50 West 44th St., New York, N. Y. 10036. Eleanor Adams, Editor.
Articles slanted to needs of home economics teachers, by specialists in the field. Rates vary, depending on quality and photos.

GRADE TEACHER—See *Teacher*.

THE HORN BOOK MAGAZINE—585 Boylston St., Boston, Mass. 02116. Paul Heins, Editor.
Articles, 600 to 2,000 words, for librarians, teachers, parents, and others connected with the pleasure-reading of children. Pays 1¢ a word, on publication, Query first.

INDUSTRIAL EDUCATION—22 West Putnam Ave., Greenwich, Conn. 06830. John L. Feirer, Editor.
Administrative and instructional material for vocational and industrial arts classes, 1,000 to 2,000 words. Some photos and drawings. Pays $10 to $15 per magazine page, on publication.

THE INSTRUCTOR—Dansville, N. Y. 14437.
Articles on teaching from persons in the teaching field. Elementary school level.
Query first.

MISSOURI ENGLISH BULLETIN—Missouri Association of Teachers of English,
Northeast Missouri State College, Kirksville, Mo. 63501. Hubert T. Moore,
Editor.
Articles, book reviews, poetry for English teachers, elementary through college,
with an emphasis on the jr. and sr. high levels. Length: to 2,500 words, on
teaching techniques, research, successful methods, literary criticism and analysis,
humor, etc. Pays in contributors' copies.

THE NATION'S SCHOOLS—230 West Monroe, Chicago, Ill. 60606.
Articles on school administration, on assignment only.

PARKS & RECREATION—National Recreation and Park Association, 1601 North
Kent St., Arlington, Va. 22209. Sidney G. Lutzin, Editor.
Full-length articles, 1,000 words, and short articles, 400 to 500 words, on
individual or group recreation and/or park programs, how-to-do-it crafts, and
camping, playground and community activities, hobbies, recreation interests for
the new leisure. Photos when possible. No payment.

PHI DELTA KAPPAN—8th St. and Union Ave., Box 789, Bloomington, Ind. 47401.
Articles in the field of education, 1,000 to 4,000 words. Also, cartoons related to
education issues. Fees negotiated—$25 to $250. Query first.

SCHOLASTIC TEACHER—Scholastic Magazines, 50 West 44th St., New York, N. Y.
10036. Loretta Hunt Marion, Editor.
Major features (with a national scope) on controversies, trends and innovations
in education, 1,000 to 2,000 words—*on assignment only*. Please query editor. Pays
$150 and up. Also, some articles about a single innovative program or methods
articles, 1,000 words or less. Pays $40 to $75, on acceptance. Also, teaching tips,
500 words or less. Pays $5 to $20, on publication.

SCHOOL MANAGEMENT—22 West Putnam Ave., Greenwich, Conn. 06830. Paul
K. Cuneo, Editor.
Articles on practical, proven solutions to school management problems; examples
of courageous or dynamic school district leadership; unusual or unusually effective
school programs. Authors should study magazine and query before submitting
manuscripts or photos. Pays 3¢ a word and up.

SCHOOL REVIEW—5835 Kimbark Ave., Chicago, Ill. 60637. Benjamin D. Wright,
Editor.
A voice for research, theory, and philosophical inquiry in education and related
disciplines. No payment.

SCIENCE AND CHILDREN—National Science Teachers Association, 1201 16th St.,
N.W., Washington, D. C. 20036. Robert H. Carleton, Editorial Director.
Informational articles to assist the elementary science school teacher, 800 to 1,200
words. No payment.

TEACHER (formerly *Grade Teacher*)—22 West Putnam Ave., Greenwich, Conn.
06830. Harold Littledale, Editor.
Features for teachers of kindergarten, primary, intermediate and junior high
school grades, on curriculum and methods, classroom-tested units, new teaching
strategies, up to 1,500 words. Pays 1¢ a word and up.

TODAY'S CATHOLIC TEACHER—38 West Fifth St., Dayton, Ohio 45402.

For Catholic elementary school teachers. Articles, 600 to 800 words, and 1,500 to 3,000 words, on teaching curriculum subjects, retarded readers, guidance, testing, parent-teacher relationships, civil rights, new developments in reading and TV teaching, etc. Sample copies on request. Pays from $20 to $80, on acceptance.

WILSON LIBRARY BULLETIN—950 University Ave., Bronx, N. Y. 10452.
Articles, 2,000 to 4,000 words, on book-related material, education, and "informed commentary." Also special library news reports of national interest, and 2,000-word opinion pieces on library issues for the "Overdue" column. Cartoons, photos of library displays, and color slides or original artwork for cover. Pays $50 and up for articles; $35 for cartoons, $10 for display photos, and $100 for cover artwork. Study copies.

AGRICULTURE

AMERICAN AGRICULTURALIST-RURAL NEW YORKER—DeWitt Building, Ithaca, N. Y. 14850. Gordon L. Conklin, Editor.
Articles on farm subjects in the Northeast (New York, New Jersey, northern Pennsylvania, and New England states). Pays on acceptance.

THE AMERICAN FARMER (formerly *Nation's Agriculture*)—225 Touhy Ave., Park Ridge, Ill. 60068.
Feature articles on farm management and economics.

AMERICAN FRUIT GROWER—Willoughby, Ohio 44904. E. G. K. Meister, Publisher.
Articles, preferably under 750 words, on how a commercial grower overcomes specific production or marketing problems. Photos. Pays about 2¢ a word, on acceptance or publication; $3 and up per photo. Same address and requirements for *American Vegetable Grower*.

AMERICAN VEGETABLE GROWER—See *American Fruit Grower*.

BIG FARMER—131 Lincoln Highway, Frankfort, Ill. 60423. Royal Fraedrich, Editor.
Challenging articles for and about high income commercial farmers, to 1,500 words. Dramatic, top-quality photos essential. Short items on new cost-cutting, money-making ideas for top farmers. Pays on acceptance.

FARM JOURNAL—Washington Sq., Philadelphia, Pa. 19105. Lane Palmer, Editor.
Articles, 500 to 1,500 words with photos, on new ideas used in farming to increase profit, save time, or improve living. Occasional humor. Pays 10¢ to 15¢ per word, on acceptance. Query.

FARM SUPPLIER—Mt. Morris, Ill. 61504. Ray Bates, Editor.
Articles and photos giving information on selling and servicing feed, fertilizer, agricultural chemicals, farm supplies, etc., through various types of retail farm trade outlets, 600 to 1,200 words. Also articles on small business management topics. Pays about 7¢ a word, on acceptance; extra for good photos.

THE FURROW—Deere & Co., John Deere Rd., Moline Ill. 61265.
Mostly staff-written. Buys occasional illustrated articles of interest to farmers. Query first. Pays good rates, on acceptance. Send queries to George Sollenberger.

THE GEORGIA FARMER—500 Plasamour Dr. N.E., Atlanta, Ga. 30324. Elmo Hester, Editor.
Illustrated features and shorts, up to 1,000 words, slanted for Georgia farm family readership. Pays on publication.

THE KENTUCKY FARMER—Suite 212, Cutliff Bldg., Bowling Green, Ky. 42101.
General or specialized how-to farming articles, preferably about Kentucky farmers only. Photos. Payment varies, is on publication.

THE NATIONAL FUTURE FARMER—P.O. Box 15130, Alexandria, Va. 22309.
Wilson Carnes, Editor.
For high school students of vocational agriculture, who are members of the Future Farmers of America. Nonfiction, up to 1,000 words on vocational, educational, social, and recreational interests.

ORGANIC GARDENING AND FARMING—Emmaus, Pa. 18049. M. C. Goldman, Managing Editor.
Articles, 1,000 to 2,500 words, on any phase of gardening or farming, ecology, environmental action, etc.; stressing natural gardening techniques: use of organic and ground rock mineral fertilizers, mulching, biological insect control, livestock, house plants, conservation, etc. Also home handicraft, landscaping, orcharding, fruits, wildlife. Photos. Pays $35 to $80; extra for photos. Author's Handbook and sample copy sent on request.

POULTRY MEAT, THE MAGAZINE FOR THE BROILER BUSINESS—Cullman, Ala. 35055. Charles Perry, Editor.
Articles with pictures, giving broiler production, processing and marketing information. Pays $40 to $100, on acceptance, for articles 1,200 to 2,000 words.

POULTRY TRIBUNE—Mt. Morris, Ill. 61054. Milton R. Dunk, Editor.
Egg production, processing, and marketing stories, related to the egg business, 200 to 1,000 words. Pays 2¢ to 5¢ a word, on acceptance.

SUCCESSFUL FARMING—1716 Locust St., Des Moines, Iowa 50303. Dick Hanson, Editor.
Farm articles, with emphasis on management aspects, farming operations and experience stories. Helpful hints for farm shop. Pays various rates.

WALLACES FARMER—Des Moines, Iowa 50305. Alvin F. Bull, Editor.
Short features, 600 to 700 words, on Iowa; interview stories on farming methods, practices, equipment. Pays 4¢ to 5¢ per published word; $10 for cartoons; $7.50 to $15 for black-and-white photos. Mostly staff-written.

THE WESTERN PRODUCER—446 2nd Ave. North Saskatoon, Sask., Canada.
Short stories and articles, up to 2,500 words, on western Canadian subjects, with black-and-white or color photos, to interest intelligent farm and rural readers. Pays up to $75 a page for articles, on acceptance, and $5 to $35 for photos.

THE WYOMING STOCKMAN FARMER—110 East 17th St., Cheyenne, Wyo. 82001. Russell A. Fawcett, Editor.
Ranch and farm newspaper. Factual features, historical or current, on agriculture in the Wyoming-west Nebraska-Rocky Mountain area, to 500 words. Accompanying black-and-white photos. Pays various rates, on publication.

ART, PHOTOGRAPHY, HOBBIES, MUSIC, THE THEATRE

AFTER DARK, THE MAGAZINE OF ENTERTAINMENT—10 Columbus Circle, New York, N. Y. 10019. William Como, Editor.
Covers the whole entertainment scene, including theatre, films, TV, dance, opera, pop music, happenings. Reviews, feature articles on regional theatres, people in the entertainment field, etc. Photos, drawings, occasional fillers. Pays $15 to $25; $5 to $25 for photos, on publication.

AMERICAN AIRCRAFT MODELER—733 15th St., N.W., Washington, D. C. 20005. William Winter, Publisher; Edward C. Sweeney, Jr., Editor.
Articles, 500 to 3,000 words, on model planes and radio control projects, photos and drawings. Pays before publication.

AMERICAN RECORDER—Box 330, Norwich, Vt. 05055. John Koch, Editor.

Articles, 1,000 to 5,000 words, of interest to recorder players, about the instrument itself or music of medieval, Renaissance, baroque, or contemporary period for recorder. Pays in copies.

THE ANTIQUE DEALER—1115 Clifton Ave., Clifton, N. J. 07013. Stella Hall, Editor.
Articles, 1,200 to 2,000 words, on trends, pricing, retailing hints, as well as "hard news" stories, in the antiques trade. Also uses longer features by authorities. Pays 4¢ a word for articles, $30 per page for longer features, on publication; $5 per photo. Query.

ANTIQUES JOURNAL—P.O. Box 88128, Dunwoody, Ga. 30338. John Mebane, Editor.
Illustrated articles about antiques, under 2,000 words. Original professional photos required. Articles must be factual and well-researched. Query first.

ARTS IN SOCIETY—University Exchange, University of Wisconsin, 606 State St., Madison, Wis. 53706.
Articles, 2,500 to 3,500 words, on teaching and learning of the arts; aesthetics and philosophy; social analysis; significant examples of creative expression in media which may be served by printing process. Pays honorarium upon publication.

ARTS MAGAZINE—23 East 26th St., New York, N. Y. 10010.
Occasional free-lance articles on art and architecture, reviews of painting and sculpture exhibitions, book reviews. Preferred length for articles, 1,000 to 2,000 words. Pays on acceptance.

AUDIO—134 North 13th St., Philadelphia, Pa. 19107. G. W. Tillett, Editor.
Semi-technical articles of interest to the hi-fi hobbyist, constructor, and experimenter. Pays $35 a page, on publication.

BOTTLES AND RELICS—See *Collector's World*.

BROADCASTER—77 River St., Toronto 247, Ontario, Canada. Pat Young, Editor.
Canadian-oriented articles, 500 to 2,000 words, illustrating how various communicators conduct their business; profiles or interviews of successful men and women; industry news and technical news in layman's language. Payment from $25, on acceptance. Query.

CB MAGAZINE—250 Park Ave., New York, N. Y. 10017. Leo G. Sands, Editor.
Wants technical articles and case histories, 1,000 to 3,000 words, about use of two-way citizens band radio. Payment varies.

CAMERA 35—61 West 51st St., New York, N. Y. 10019. Jim Hughes, Editor.
Illustrated, instructional articles, 800 to 3,000 words, dealing with the practice and technique of 35 mm photography. Pays $50 per page, on publication.

COLLECTOR'S WORLD (Incorporating *Bottles and Relics*)—P.O. Box 328, Conroe, Tex. 77301.
Wants articles on all types of collectibles and the geneology connected therewith, 1,200 to 1,800 words. Accepts cartoons and photographs and drawings when appropriate to the material. Pays standard rates, on acceptance.

CRAFT HORIZONS—44 West 53rd St., New York, N. Y. 10019. Rose Slivka, Editor.
Nonfiction of high quality in the craft-art fields—ceramics, weaving, wood, metal, 500 to 2,000 words. Payment varies. Query first.

THE CRAFTSMAN—See *Make It with Leather*.

CREATIVE CRAFTS MAGAZINE—P.O. Box 700, Newton, N. J. 07860. Sybil C. Harp, Editor.
One- to six-page how-to features, with photos, on handicrafts of all types. Must tell how authors themselves do craft work. No interview or personality-type articles. Pays various rates, on publication.

DANCE MAGAZINE—10 Columbus Circle, New York, N. Y. 10019. William Como, Editor.
Personality, ideas, informed commentary on the best in all kinds of dancing. Low payment.

DANCE PERSPECTIVES—29 East 9th St., New York, N. Y. 10003. Selma Jeanne Cohen, Editor.
Monographs 15,000 to 20,000 words, on critical or historical aspects of dance. Specialized knowledge of field is essential. Pays $150, on acceptance. Query first.

DESIGN—1100 Waterway Blvd., Indianapolis, Ind. 46202. E. Catherine Cummins, Associate Editor.
Wants articles for the grade school art teacher on new techniques of possibly old mediums, or totally original techniques, suitable for the elementary child. Use only black-and-white glossy photos. Payment is on publication. Send manuscripts with stamped return envelopes.

THE DRAMA REVIEW—School of the Arts, New York University, 32 Washington Place, New York, N. Y. 10003. Michael Kirby, Editor.
Theatre, film, dance, TV, music: criticism, theory, and history. Also original scripts. Pays 2¢ per word, less for translations, on publication; photos.

DRAMATICS—College Hill Station, Box E, Cincinnati, Ohio 45224. R. Glenn Webb, Editor.
Articles on theatre for secondary students and teachers, to 2,500 words, with two black-and-white glossies. Pays $25, on acceptance.

EXHIBIT—P.O. Box 23505, Fort Lauderdale, Fla. 33307.
Articles to about 900 words, on commercial or fine art: how-to's and step-by-step demonstrations on art techniques and methods; profiles of outstanding artists; articles on new ideas in art. Accompanying photos welcome. Pays 5¢ per accepted word, on acceptance.

FM GUIDE—1290 Ave. of the Americas, New York, N. Y. 10019.
Brief articles, fillers, photos, of interest to FM listeners, on music, unique equipment, rock or classical artists, etc. Payment varies.

THE FAMILY HANDYMAN—235 East 45th St., New York, N. Y. 10017.
Non-technical, step-by-step articles, to 1,000 words, with black-and-white photos, on home improvement, repair and maintenance for do-it-yourselfers. Pays $40 to $100, on acceptance. Shorts, 100 to 300 words, with or without photos and rough drawings, on expert tips or shortcuts for do-it-yourselfers. Pays $5 to $15, on acceptance.

FILM QUARTERLY—University of California Press, Berkeley, Calif. 94720.
Reviews of films, historical and critical articles, stories of production projects, etc., up to about 5,000 words. Pays 1¢ a word, on publication. Approach very specialized. Authors must be familiar with magazine. Query.

GEMS AND MINERALS—P.O. Box 687, Mentone, Calif. 92359. Don MacLachlan, Editor and Publisher.
Wants articles with photos or drawings on "how to do it" and "where to find it." Personality pieces are seldom acceptable. Feature articles paid at 50¢ per column inch; full page paid at $15 per page. Unsolicited manuscripts and photographs must be accompanied by self-addressed, stamped envelopes.

GUITAR PLAYER—348 North Santa Cruz Ave., Los Gatos, Calif. 95030.
Guitar-oriented, technical and instructional articles; interviews with guitarist "talking guitar"; coverage of festivals, concerts. Pays in copies.

HAM RADIO—Greenville, N. H. 03048. James R. Fisk, Editor.
Technical and home-construction articles pertaining to amateur radio, up to 2,500 words. No operating news or fiction. Query helpful. Payment up to 5¢ per word.

HIGH FIDELITY—Great Barrington, Mass. 01230. Leonard Marcus, Editor.
Articles about music, records, and sound reproduction, 2,500 to 3,000 words. Pays on acceptance. Query first.

INDUSTRIAL PHOTOGRAPHY—750 Third Ave., New York, N. Y. 10017.
Illustrated articles, 500 to 1,500 words, of interest to industrial photographers and executives. Emphasis on specific case histories with technical data. Pays on publication. Query.

LEICA PHOTOGRAPHY—15 Columbus Circle, New York, N. Y. 10019.
Articles on 35 mm photo techniques, how-to-do-it's on Leica cameras and equipment, 750 to 1,500 words. Photos taken with Leica cameras and lenses. Pays on acceptance. Query first.

McCALL'S NEEDLEWORK AND CRAFTS MAGAZINE—230 Park Ave., New York, N. Y. 10017. Nanina Comstock, Editor.
Wants made-up handcraft items in a variety of techniques with the directions for making them. This is a strictly how-to publication. Payment is in ratio to originality and quality.

MAKE IT WITH LEATHER (formerly *The Craftsman*)—Box 1386, Fort Worth, Tex. 76101.
How-to articles on leathercraft, to 2,000 words, with photos and diagrams. Pays from $10 to $50 per printed page, on publication.

MODEL AIRPLANE NEWS—White Plains Plaza, 1 North Broadway, White Plains, N. Y. 10601. Walter L. Schroder, Publisher; Arthur F. Schroeder, Editor.
Scientific or technical articles and photos on model aviation. Construction projects with drawings, photos, directions. Payment on publication.

MODEL RAILROADER—1027 North 7th St., Milwaukee, Wisc. 53233. Linn H. Westcott, Editor.
Articles on construction or operation of model railroads, with photos of layout and equipment. Firsthand knowledge essential. Pays on acceptance.

MUSICAL AMERICA—1 Astor Plaza, New York, N. Y. 10036.
Nonfiction feature material of authoritative musical interest, 1,000 to 1,500 words.

NEWSPAPER COLLECTOR'S GAZETTE—2164 East Broadmor, Tempe, Ariz. 85282.
Wants articles on history of journalism: early newspapers, newsmen, newspaper collecting, 1,800 words maximum. Will consider photographs or drawings, if pertinent. Usually reports within 48 hours. Payment is 1¢ a word to $12; cartoons $3; features $1 to $3, on acceptance. Send 45¢ for a sample copy and spec sheet.

OLD BOTTLE MAGAZINE—Box 243, Bend, Ore. 97701. Shirley Asher, Editor.
Articles of moderate length (to 2,000 words) pertaining to the various aspects of the bottle collecting hobby, with photos. Pays to $50 per article; $5 for photos with captions and drawings submitted separately, on acceptance.

OPERA NEWS—The Metropolitan Opera Guild, 1865 Broadway, New York, N. Y. 10023. Frank Merkling, Editor.
Articles on all aspects of lyric theatre today; also pre-publication chapters of books, humorous anecdotes and offbeat associations between writer and subject, 600 to 3,500 words. Pays 8¢ a word and up.

PLAYBILL—485 Lexington Ave., New York, N. Y. 10017. Joan Rubin, Editor.
Short, sophisticated articles on theatre subjects or general subjects of interest to the theatre-going public, 800 to 2,000 words. Accompanying photos welcome. Pays $100 to $300.

POPULAR CERAMICS—6011 Santa Monica Blvd., Los Angeles, Calif. 90038.
Step-by-step instructional articles on hobby ceramics, 300 to 1,000 words. Photos. No payment.

POPULAR CRAFTS—7950 Deering Ave., Canoga Park, Calif. 91304.
Articles, 250 to 1,500 words, with photos and/or drawings, on all areas of crafts, including complete, step-by-step instruction and materials. Pays from $50 to $150, on publication.

POPULAR PHOTOGRAPHY MAGAZINE—One Park Ave., New York, N. Y. 10016.
Articles for the amateur photographer. How-to-do-it features with illustrations. For queries, include one-page outline, mentioning pictures available. Length, 500 to 2,000 words. Payment is $75 and up for complete word-and-picture articles; $10 for illustrated "Photo Tips."

PROFITABLE CRAFT MERCHANDISING—Pleasantville, N. Y. 10570. Jack Wax, Editor.
Articles on craft retailers who have developed successful merchandising or sales technique which can be emulated by other dealers. Black-and-white photos to illustrate articles. Pays 3¢ a word, and $5 per photo, upon publication.

R/C MODELER MAGAZINE—P.O. Box 487, Sierra Madre, Calif. 91024. Don Dewey, Editor.
A "how-to" type publication for the hobbyist in the model aircraft field. Wants technical and semitechnical articles on radio controlled model aircraft. Pays $25 to $400, 30 days after publication. Query first and ask for sample copy of publication.

RAILROAD MODEL CRAFTSMAN—P.O. Box 700, Newton, N. J. 07860.
How-to-do-it features on scale model railroading: cars, structures, operation, scenery, locos, etc. Also "how I built my layout" features. Authors must be railroad modelers. Pays on publication.

RELICS—P.O. Box 3338, Austin, Tex. 78704. Robert Stout, Editor.
Wants articles, 500 to 2,000 words, concerning frontier relics, historical Americana, amateur collecting, old items of American origin rather than European, helpful information slanted to collectors who love old things. Photographs and drawings will be returned after publication. Pays 2¢ a word, on acceptance. Query first.

REVUE DES BEAUX ARTS—P.O. Box 23505, Fort Lauderdale, Fla. 33307. Marie Stilkind, Editor.
Articles to about 900 words, of interest to art connoisseurs; profiles of famous artists, art methods and history. Accompanying photos welcome. Pays 5¢ a word, on publication.

ROCK AND GEM—Behn-Miller Publishers, Inc., 16001 Ventura Blvd., Encino, Calif. 91316.
How-to-do-it articles, 2,000 words, with photos, on the lapidary field. Pays $40 per printed page, on publication.

SHOWCASE—Chicago Sun-Times, 401 North Wabash Ave., Chicago, Ill. 60611.

Articles to 1,500 words, with black-and-white photos or drawings, on serious and lively arts. Also profiles, interviews. Pays up to 10¢ a word, on acceptance.

SOUTHERN THEATRE—Box 12559, Gainesville, Fla. 32601. Ralph N. Swanson, Editor.
Uses special interest articles, to 3,000 words, on all types of theatre organizations. Also needs criticism and reviews to 1,500 words. No payment. Query.

STEREO QUARTERLY—State Rd., Great Barrington, Mass. 01230.
Factual articles, to 4,000 words, on stereo music system and related equipment; humor; descriptions and photos of attractive installations. Pays up to 10¢ a word, on acceptance. Query.

WESTART—Box 1396, Auburn, Calif. 95603.
Artists' newspaper primarily concerned with current news items in the West Coast arts field. Features of exceptional interest, 350 to 500 words, in the field of crafts and fine arts. No hobbies. Pays 30¢ per column inch for pictures and/or copy.

WINE WORLD—7555 Woodley Ave., Van Nuys, Calif. 91406. Roy Brady, Editor.
Articles on wine, wine makers, travel, restaurants, history, choosing and serving wine, home wine cellars, etc. written for all who enjoy wine. Uses many black-and-white and some color photos. Pays up to $5 for black-and-white photos and $100 per article, on publication. Query.

TECHNICAL AND SCIENTIFIC

For High Fidelity magazines, see listings under *Art, Photography, Hobbies, Music, Theatre*. Many *Trade and Business Magazines* also use technical articles in their specific fields.

THE AOPA PILOT—7315 Wisconsin Ave., Bethesda, Md. 20014.
Private and business aviation articles, with human interest. First-person and how-to-do-it articles. Photos or sketches with articles. Short items, 100 to 300 words, one photo, about a personality or a new development of interest. Pays 5¢ a word, on acceptance; $5 to $10 for photos.

AIR PROGRESS—437 Madison Ave., New York, N. Y. 10022. Richard B. Weeghman, Editor.
Articles and photos on aviation subjects. Pays about $100 up per article, on acceptance.

CARS—1560 Broadway, New York, N. Y. 10036. Martyn L. Schorr, Editor.
Articles for people interested in performance of new cars and in increasing performance of their cars, with know-how and equipment to make engine and custom modifications. Photos, 5 x 7 or larger, with captions, should accompany articles. Pays $35 a page, $50 to $100 a color page, and $100 a color cover. Payment is within two weeks of publication.

COMPUTER DECISIONS—50 Essex St., Rochelle Park, N. Y. 07662. Robert Haavind, Editor.
Articles, 800 to 4,000 words, on generic uses of computer systems, and filler-length computer games, including program and explanation of program. Pays $30 to $50 per published page.

ELECTRONICS ILLUSTRATED—See *Mechanix Illustrated*.

ENVIRONMENT—438 North Skinker Blvd., St. Louis, Mo. 63130. Sheldon Novick, Editor.
Factual articles, 5,000 to 7,000 words, presenting technical information in layman's

terms on environment pollution, effects of technology. Pays $100. Submit brief proposal first.

MECHANIX ILLUSTRATED (Incorporating *Electronics Illustrated*)—1515 Broadway, New York, N. Y. 10036. Robert G. Beason, Editor.
Strong lead articles; articles on controversial subjects. Pays $500 and up for feature articles, 1,500 to 2,500 words; $75 to $250 for short articles or picture sets of one or two pages; up to $400 for how-to projects; $10 to $20 for useful tips with photo or drawing, $5 if un-illustrated; $10 to $25 for single photos with captions.

NEW ENGINEER—MBA Enterprises, 555 Madison Ave., New York, N. Y. 10022. Steven S. Ross, Editor.
Articles, 1,500 to 5,000 words, about the engineering profession, technical projects of wide interest, the common ground between engineering and other professions. Query. Pays $50 per published page, on acceptance.

PACIFIC DISCOVERY--California Academy of Sciences, Golden Gate Park, San Francisco, Calif. 94118. Bruce Finson, Editor.
Natural history articles, 1,500 to 3,000 words, with extensive photo coverage, addressed to the scientist and seriously interested layman. Pays 5¢ a word; $10 a picture, on publication. Query.

POLLUTION CONTROL JOURNAL—144 West 12th St., Denver, Colo. 80204.
Factual news articles on pollution subjects, 2,500 to 3,000 words. Black-and-white photos or color transparencies to accompany articles. Pays $25 to $200, on publication.

POPULAR ELECTRONICS—One Park Ave., New York, N. Y. 10016. Milton S. Snitzer, Editor.
Looking for state-of-the-art reports and tutorial-length feature articles on modern electronics technology. Editorial policy aimed toward the seriously-interested electronics hobbyist, technician and engineer with an avocational interest in electronics. Pays up to $500 for feature-length articles and for construction articles.

POPULAR MECHANICS—224 West 57th St., New York, N. Y. 10019. Robert P. Crossley, Editor.
Features on scientific, mechanical, and industrial subjects, with action or adventure elements; occasional articles on almost any subject of general interest to men, including sports. Material in automotive and housing fields. Also how-to-do-it pieces on craft projects and shop work. Good illustrations required. Photo shorts with up to 250 words of copy and one or two photos. Pays $300 to $500 for top-quality features; $12 and up for shorts.

POPULAR SCIENCE MONTHLY—355 Lexington Ave., New York, N. Y. 10017. Hubert P. Luckett, Editor.
Timely material on new developments in applied science and technology, well-illustrated with photographs, 2,000 words or less. Short illustrated articles describing new inventions and discoveries.

RADIO-ELECTRONICS—200 Park Ave. South, New York, N. Y. 10003.
Illustrated technical articles, 2,000 to 3,000 words, authoritative, easy to read, and interesting. Photos should be 8 x 10 glossies. Pays good rates, on acceptance.

SCIENCE AND MECHANICS—229 Park Ave. South, New York, N. Y. 10003. Tony Hogg, Editor.
How-it-works articles in layman's language; articles on new and unusual developments in the physical sciences which lend themselves to art treatment, 1,000 to 1,500 words. Pays good rates, on acceptance. Queries preferred.

SCIENCE DIGEST—224 West 57th St., New York, N. Y. 10019. Richard F. Dempewolff, Editor.
Scientifically accurate articles 1,500 to 2,500 words, for the average reader, on any of the sciences; picture stories; human-interest photos. Occasional cartoons. Pays from $50 to $350 per article. Query first on all articles ideas.

SEA FRONTIERS—The International Oceanographic Foundation, 1 Rickenbacker Causeway, Virginia Key, Miami, Fla. 33149. F. G. Walton Smith, Editor.
Articles for the layman on recent scientific advances and discoveries related to the sea, 2,000 words. Also uses general articles on interesting life or phenomena of the sea, and economic and industrial applications of marine sciences. Illustrations, black-and-white and color, preferably photographs, required. Pays 5¢ a word and up, on acceptance. Query.

POETRY MARKETS

The following list is divided into four categories: general magazines; college, literary, little magazines and magazines which use only poetry; religious or denominational magazines, and greeting card markets. Each tends to use a certain type of poetry, but many poems may meet the requirements of markets in more than one of the groups. Markets for both serious and light verse are included in each category.

In addition to the markets listed here, many daily and weekly newspapers use occasional verse. Though they may not specifically seek poetry from free-lance writers, the papers often print verse submitted to them, especially on holidays and other special occasions.

The markets for juvenile poetry are listed under *Juvenile, Teen-Age and Young Adult Magazines* and markets for book-length poems or collections of poems are under *Book Publishers*.

GENERAL MAGAZINES

THE AMERICAN LEGION MAGAZINE—1345 Ave. of the Americas, New York, N. Y. 10019.
Humorous verse, up to 16 lines. No serious poetry accepted. Pays $10 and up, on acceptance. Submit to "Parting Shots Editor."

THE AMERICAN-SCANDINAVIAN REVIEW—127 East 73rd St., New York, N. Y. 10021. Erik J. Friis, Editor.
Verse, 10 to 30 lines, about Scandinavia. Payment is $5 to $10, on acceptance.

THE AMERICAN SCHOLAR—1811 Q Street, N.W., Washington, D. C. 20009. Hiram Haydn, Editor.
Uses some distinguished verse. Pays from $35 to $75.

THE ATLANTIC—8 Arlington St., Boston, Mass. 02116. Robert Manning, Editor.
Highest quality. Limited market; prints only one or two poems an issue. Special interest in young poets. Some light verse.

THE ATLANTIC ADVOCATE—Gleaner Bldg., Phoenix Square, Fredericton, N. B., Canada.
High quality, short poetry, sonnet length or less. Payment on publication.

BABY CARE—52 Vanderbilt Ave., New York, N. Y. 10017.
Occasionally uses poetry. Payment varies.

BLACK TIMES: VOICES OF THE NATIONAL COMMUNITY—Box 10246, Palo Alto, Calif. 94303.
Welcomes poetry. Sample copies are 50¢.

CARTOON PARADE—See *Humorama, Inc.*

CAT FANCY—11760 Sorrento Valley Rd., San Diego, Calif. 92121. Leslie S. Smith, Editor.
Uses well-written poems about cats. Pays $10 and up, on publication.

CATS MAGAZINE—P.O. Box 4106, Pittsburgh, Pa. 15202.
Poems about cats, up to 30 lines. Payment, 20¢ a line, on publication.

CHATELAINE—481 University Ave., Toronto, Ont., Canada. Doris Anderson, Editor.
Uses short verse. Pays on acceptance.

THE CHRISTIAN SCIENCE MONITOR—One Norway St., Boston, Mass. 02115.
Fresh, vigorous, clearly focused poems of high literary standard and positive constructive content accepted. Subject matter may vary widely. Pays shortly after publication. Address: Home Forum Page.

ESSENCE—102 East 30th St., New York, New York 10016. Sharyn J. Skeeter, Fiction and Poetry Editor.
Poetry to 40 lines. Pays $25 and up, after publication.

THE EXCEPTIONAL PARENT—P.O. Box 101, Back Bay Annex, Boston, Mass. 02117. Howard Dinin, Assistant Editor.
Poems, 5 to 50 lines long, appropriate for parents of disabled children. Query.

FAMILY WEEKLY—641 Lexington Ave., New York, N. Y. 10022.
Sunday supplement. Uses humorous verse for humor page, "Quips and Quotes." Pays $20 to $35, on acceptance.

GOLF DIGEST MAGAZINE—297 Westport Ave., Norwalk, Conn. 06856.
Light verse, preferably short. Pays $5 to $20, on acceptance.

GOLF MAGAZINE—235 East 45th St., New York, N. Y. 10017.
Can use humorous verse. Payment is $10 and up, on publication.

GOOD HOUSEKEEPING—959 Eighth Ave., New York, N. Y. 10019.
Good serious poetry of any length. Subject matter should be of interest to women. Send to Poetry Editor. Short, light verse should be sent to Delores Hudson, Assistant Editor, for Light Housekeeping page. Pays $5 a line and up, on acceptance.

GOURMET MAGAZINE—777 Third Ave., New York, N. Y. 10017.
Light verse with a sophisticated food or drink angle. Verse should avoid mention of dieting, calories, etc. Payment is on acceptance.

HARPER'S MAGAZINE—2 Park Ave., New York, N. Y. 10016. Robert Shnayerson, Editor.
Uses only a limited amount of poetry. Pays on acceptance. Please include stamped return envelope.

THE HARTFORD COURANT—285 Broad St., Hartford, Conn. 06101. Malcolm L. Johnson, Poetry Column Editor.
Verse up to 50 lines, from out-of-state as well as Connecticut residents. No payment. Tear sheets sent to contributors.

HUMORAMA, INC.—100 North Village Ave., Rockville Center, N. Y. 11570. Ernest N. Devver.

Breezy, fast, and humorous verse from 4 to 48 lines. Pays 40¢ a line, before publication. Same address and requirements for *Laugh Riot, Joker, Cartoon Parade, Jest, Quips, Stare, Romp.*

IN WYOMING—Box 2108, Casper, Wyo. 82601. Grace Curl Cochran, Poetry Editor. Verse of 14 to 16 lines. Pays 50¢ a line, upon publication.

JEST—See *Humorama, Inc.*

JOKER—See *Humorama, Inc.*

LADIES' HOME JOURNAL—641 Lexington Ave., New York, N. Y. 10022. Not currently in the market for poetry.

LAUGH RIOT—See *Humorama, Inc.*

LEATHERNECK—P.O. Box 1918, Quantico, Va. 22134. Ronald D. Lyons, Managing Editor. Serious poems should be spirited, stirring, impassioned even, but never melancholy. Humorous poems should not be risqué. Themes should have to do with the Marines. Minimum payment is $10, on acceptance.

MADEMOISELLE—350 Madison Ave., New York, N. Y. 10017. Ellen A. Stoianoff, Fiction and Poetry Editor. Outstanding poetry of high literary quality, up to 65 lines. Payment begins at $25.

MODERN BRIDE—One Park Ave., New York, N. Y. 10016. Short verse appealing to the bride and groom. Pays on acceptance.

MUSIC EDUCATORS JOURNAL—Music Educators National Conference, 1201 16th St. N. W., Washington, D. C. 20036. Malcolm E. Bessom, Editor. Occasional poetry on music, to 25 lines. Pays in copies.

NEW-ENGLAND GALAXY—Old Sturbridge Village, Sturbridge, Mass. 01566. Catherine Fennelly, Editor. High quality poetry, to 30 lines, of New England interest. Pays $50, on publication.

THE NEW YORKER—25 West 43rd St., New York, N. Y. 10036. Light verse (topical, satirical or humorous) and serious poetry. Pays top rates, on acceptance. Address all communications to "The Editors."

THE OHIO MOTORIST—6000 South Marginal Rd., Cleveland, Ohio 44103. A. K. Murway, Editor. Short humorous poems on motoring, automotive and vacation topics (foreign and domestic), preferably 4 to 6 lines. Payment is $5 to $6.

OREGONIAN VERSE—*The Oregonian,* Portland, Ore. 97201. Howard McKinley Corning, Editor. Weekly column. Quality verse only. Short lyrics preferred. Poems of image and meaning, written out of experience, with a fresh use of language. Seasonal poems should be submitted several weeks in advance. Pays $5 per poem, following publication; also sends clippings to contributors.

PEN—444 Sherman St., Denver, Colo. 80203. Jean Blair Ryan, Editor. Uses humorous poetry and light verse. Some serious poems, for holiday issues. Length, to 16 lines. Pays 50¢ a line, on acceptance.

PEOPLE AND PLACES—Box 47, Grand Marais, Mich. 49839. Rose Mary Bridger, Editor. Poetry of all kinds. Payment varies. Send one dollar for two typical issues.

QUIPS—See *Humorama, Inc.*

QUOTE—Box 4073, Sta. B., Anderson, S. C. 29621.
Buys epigrams and 4-line verse of interest to public speakers. Material must be original. Payment is on acceptance.

RAMPARTS—2054 University Ave., Berkeley, Calif. 94704.
Rarely prints poetry. Highest literary quality only. Pays 75¢ a line, on publication. Query.

THE RHODE ISLANDER—75 Fountain St., Providence, R. I. 02902. Ted Holmberg, Editor.
Poetry. Pays on publication.

ROLL CALL—636 Pennsylvania Ave., S.E., Washington, D.C. 20003.
"The Newspaper of Capitol Hill." Short light verse on political subjects. Payment on publication.

ROMP—See *Humorama, Inc.*

THE ROTARIAN—1600 Ridge Ave., Evanston, Ill. 60201. Karl K. Krueger, Editor.
Occasionally uses humorous or philosophical bits of verse having special appeal for businessmen. Pays fair rates, on acceptance.

ROUNDUP—The Denver *Post,* 650 15th St., Denver, Colo. 80201.
Poems, not over 20 lines. Pays $2, on acceptance. Address mail to "The Poetry Forum," Henry Hough, Editor.

THE SATURDAY EVENING POST—1100 Waterway Blvd., Indianapolis, Ind. 46202. Frederic A. Birmingham, Managing Editor.
Poetry of any length, modern preferred to traditional techniques. No restrictions on form. Pays competitive rates.

STARE—See *Humorama, Inc.*

SUCCESSFUL FARMING—1716 Locust St., Des Moines, Iowa 50303.
Uses a very limited amount of light verse, not more than 4 lines in length. Payment is $5 to $10, on publication.

SURFER MAGAZINE—Box 1028, Dana Point, Calif. 92629. Steve Pezman, Editor.
Accepts poetry related to subject of surfing. Send stamped, self-addressed envelope.

TORONTO LIFE—56 The Esplanade, Toronto 1, Ontarior, Canada. Gary Ross, Poetry Editor.
Poems of high quality, 40 lines or less, set in Toronto or a comparable city, to interest Toronto readers. Pays from $5 per poem.

UNDERSTANDING—P.O. Box 206, Merlin, Ore. 96522. Dr. Daniel W. Fry, Editor.
Uses a limited amount of poetry, to 36 lines, expressing good will. Pays 10¢ a line, on publication.

WESTWAYS—Box 2890, Terminal Annex, Los Angeles, Calif. 90051.
Serious, high-quality verse of not more than 24 lines, preferably with a Western mood or theme; e.g., travel, history, conservation or contemporary events. No poems dealing exclusively with, for example, Iowa grain-fields. Uses 10 to 12

poems· each year; pays $25 minimum, on acceptance. Heavily overstocked at present. Please submit no more than five poems for consideration.

YANKEE—Dublin, N. H. 03444.
Serious poetry of high quality under 30 lines. Pays $25 per poem. Submit all poetry to Jean Burden, Poetry Editor.

COLLEGE, LITERARY, AND POETRY MAGAZINES

AMANUENSIS—Dept. of English, University of Kentucky, Lexington, Ky. 40506. James Gash, Editor.
Poetry. Pays in copies.

THE ANTIGONISH REVIEW—Dept. of English, St. Francis Xavier University, Antigonish, N.S., Canada. R. J. MacSween, Editor.
Quality poetry on any subject. Pays in copies.

THE ANTIOCH REVIEW—P.O. Box 148, Yellow Springs, Ohio 45387. Eric Horsting, Poetry Editor.
Quality poetry, especially with clear content and form. Pays $8 a poem or per page for longer poems.

ARIZONA QUARTERLY—University of Arizona, Tucson, Ariz. 85721. Albert F. Gegenheimer, Editor.
Uses poetry. No payment. Annual award.

THE ARK RIVER REVIEW—440 North Yale, Wichita, Kan. 67208.
Contemporary and experimental poetry, any length. Pays 20¢ a line or $5 per poem, whichever is greater.

BALL STATE UNIVERSITY FORUM—Ball State University, Muncie, Ind. 47306. Merrill Rippy and Frances Mayhew Rippy, Editors.
Poetry 4 to 200 lines. Uses 2 to 20 poems per issue. Payment in copies only.

BARDIC ECHOES—1036 Emerald Ave. N. E., Grand Rapids, Mich. 49503. Clarence L. Weaver, Editor.
Publishes poetry in any form, not over 40 lines; shorter poems preferred. Reports within a month. Overstocked until mid-1972. Pays in copies. Single copy 50¢.

BELOIT POETRY JOURNAL—Box 2, Beloit, Wis. 53511.
Quality poetry of any length, experimental or traditional. Occasional special chap-books. Pays in copies.

BEYOND BAROQUE—P.O. Box 806, Venice, Calif. 90291.
Avant-garde poetry.

BITTERROOT—Box 51, Blythebourne Sta., Brooklyn, N. Y. 11219. Menke Katz, Editor. Sol Karp, Assistant Editor.
Quarterly poetry magazine.

CARDINAL POETRY QUARTERLY—10418 West Drummond Pl., Melrose Park, Ill. 60164. Eda Casciani, Editor.
Traditional or modern poems, to 35 lines. Essays, to 350 words, on poetry or poets. Also uses artwork. Pays in copies. Annual awards.

CAROLINA QUARTERLY—Box 1117, Chapel Hill, N. C. 27514. Junius Grimes, Editor.
Quality poetry, all forms, lengths, and subjects. Payment is $5 per poem.

CHARAS—1224 North J, Tacoma, Wash. 98403. Claire Levenhagen, Editor.
Traditional and modern poetry of any length. Pays in copies.

THE CHICAGO REVIEW—The University of Chicago, Chicago, Ill. 60637. Sol Sepsenwol, Poetry Editor.
Uses verse, verse translations, experimental poetry, and verse plays.

CIMARRON REVIEW—Oklahoma State University, Stillwater, Okla. 74074. Jeanne Adams Wray, Managing Editor.
Poetry of any length. No payment.

CONTEMPORA—P.O. Box 673, Atlanta, Ga. 30301.
Poetry. Payment upon publication.

THE COOPERATOR—17819 Roscoe Blvd., Northbridge, Calif. 91324.
Wants poetry which fosters the emergence of a new universal man and civilization based upon unity in diversity among all peoples. Length, to 40 lines. Pays in copies.

COUNTER/MEASURES—Box 431, Bedford, Mass. 01730.
Poems in rhyme and/or meter. Payment is in subscriptions.

CRAZY HORSE—Southwest Minnesota State College, Marshall, Minn. 56258. Philip Dacey, Editor.
Quality modern poems of any length. All subjects and styles. Stamped, self-addressed envelopes should accompany manuscripts. Prompt reply. Pays in copies.

DASEIN—G.P.O. Box 2121, New York, N. Y. 10001. Percy Johnston, Editor.
Poetry of any length. No light verse. No payment.

THE DEKALB LITERARY ARTS JOURNAL—DeKalb College, 555 Indian Creek Dr., Clarkston, Ga. 30021. Mel McKee, Editor.
High quality poetry. Pays in copies.

DESCANT—Texas Christian University, T. C. U. Station, Fort Worth, Tex. 76129. Betsy Colquitt, Editor.
Poetry of any length; short poetry preferred. Payment in copies only.

EPOCH—251 Goldwin Smith Hall, Cornell University, Ithaca, N. Y. 14850.
Verse of high quality; not necessarily experimental, but expressive of contemporary experience. Payment is in contributors' copies.

EPOS—Crescent City, Fla. 32012. Will Tullos and Evelyn Thorne, Editors.
"Excellence is our only requirement." Prompt reports. Pays in copies.

ESSENCE—26 Fowler St., New Haven, Conn. 06515. Joseph Payne Brennan, Editor.
Short lyric poems with impact and originality. Must send stamped return envelope. Pays in copies.

EXTENSIONS—P.O. Box 383, Cathedral Station, New York, N. Y. 10025. Suzanne Zavrian and Joachim Neugroschel, Editors.
Experimental poetry and translations. Pays in copies. See magazine before submitting.

THE FALCON—Mansfield State College, Mansfield, Pa. 16933. W. A. Blais, Poetry Editor.
Surrealistic and prose-poems. Accepts very little traditional poetry. Pays in copies

but cash payment for exceptional work. Send stamped, self-addressed envelope with manuscripts.

THE FIDDLEHEAD—Dept. of English, University of New Brunswick, Fredericton, N.B., Canada. Robert Gibbs, Editor.
Very high quality poetry, preferably short. Emphasis on Canadian writing. Usually pays $5 per page, on publication.

FIELD—Rice Hall, Oberlin College,·Oberlin, Ohio 44074. David P. Young, Editor.
Poetry of highest quality from established and unknown poets. Pays $10 per page. Study sample issue.

FORUM—The University of Houston, Houston, Texas 77004. William Lee Pryor, Editor. Archibald Henderson, Poetry Editor.
Quality poetry. No payment.

FOUR QUARTERS—LaSalle College, Philadelphia, Pa. 19141. John Keenan, Editor.
Shorter poems (under 30 lines) preferred. $5 honorarium (except for 3-line fillers).

THE FREE LANCE—6005 Grand Ave., Cleveland, Ohio 44104. Casper LeRoy Jordan and Russell Atkins, Editors.
Poetry of any length. Avant-garde material welcome. Pays in copies.

GEORGIA REVIEW—University of Georgia, Athens, Ga. 30601. Edward Krickel, Poetry Editor.
Poetry to any length.

GHOST DANCE—ATL, Michigan State University, Lansing, Mich. 48823.
Experimental poetry: Eclectic. Pays in copies.

THE GREEN RIVER REVIEW—P.O. Box 594, Owensboro, Ky. 42301. Raymond Tyner and Emil Ahnell, Editors.
Poetry to 500 lines. Pays in copies.

THE GREENFIELD REVIEW—Greenfield Centre, N. Y. 12833. Joseph Bruchac III, Editor.
Contemporary poetry, of any length, by established poets, new writers and third world writers. Also translations. Pays in copies.

HAIKU HIGHLIGHTS—Box 15, Kanona, N. Y. 14856. Jean Calkins, Editor.
Verse to 8 lines. Cash and book awards. Sample copy 35¢.

HIRAM POETRY REVIEW—P.O. Box 162, Hiram, Ohio 44234.
Quality poetry of any length. Pays in copies and subscription.

IRONWOOD—P.O. Box 49023, Tucson, Ariz. 85717.
Poetry, any length, with stress on perception, vision and clarity. Also, translations of important contemporary poets and interviews with leading American poets. No payment.

JEAN'S JOURNAL—274 Arlington Ave., Brooklyn, N. Y. 11208.
Verse of any type and length. Cash and book awards. Sample copy 35¢.

KANSAS QUARTERLY—Dept. of English, Kansas State University, Manhattan, Kansas 66502.
Poetry of all types. No payment.

THE LITERARY REVIEW—Fairleigh Dickinson University, Rutherford, N. J. 07070. Charles Angoff, Editor.
Poetry of high literary quality, any length. Payment in copies only.

THE LITTLE MAGAZINE—P.O. Box 207, Cathedral Station, New York, N. Y. 10025. Thomas Beeler and David G. Hartwell, Editors.
Uses poetry of any length. Pays in copies.

THE LYRIC—Bremo Bluff, Va. 23022. Ruby Altizer Roberts and John Nixon, Jr., Editors.
Traditional poetry. High standards. Leans toward the optimistic viewpoint. No payment, but cash prizes, and annual college contest.

MACABRE—26 Fowler St., New Haven, Conn. 06515. Joseph Payne Brennan, Editor.
Short verse on eerie, macabre, supernatural subject matter. No science fiction or light verse. Payment in copies only.

MICHIGAN QUARTERLY REVIEW—3032 Rockham Bldg., University of Mich., Ann Arbor, Mich. 48104.
Poetry, from 4 to 30 lines. Occasionally uses longer poems. Pays 50¢ a line, after acceptance.

THE MIDWEST QUARTERLY—Kansas State College, Pittsburg, Kans. 66762. Rebecca Patterson, Editor.
Serious poetry of all types, preferably short; 50-line maximum. No payment.

MISSISSIPPI REVIEW—Dept. of English, Southern Sta., Box 37, University of Southern Mississippi, Hattiesburg, Miss. 39401.
Poetry of high quality, to 100 lines. Pays in copies.

MISSOURI TODAY—School of Journalism, University of Missouri, Columbia, Mo. 65201.
Poetry of high quality. No payment. Query.

MUNDUS ARTIUM—Ellis Hall, Ohio University, Athens, Ohio 45701. Rainer Schulte, Editor.
International bilingual poetry. Looking for highly conceptual quality rather than descriptive material. Inspection copies, $1.50.

MUSTANG REVIEW—212 South Broadway, Denver, Colo. 80209. Karl Edd, Editor.
Uses imagist poetry, preferably 12 to 20 lines. Pays in copies.

NEW ORLEANS REVIEW—Loyola University, New Orleans, La. 70118.
Pays $10 for poems.

NEW YORK QUARTERLY—Room 603, Columbia University Club, 4 West 43rd St., New York, N. Y. 10036.
Poetry of all schools and genres, no length limit, and critical essays on craft and technique of poetry, 800 to 2,000 words. Pays $5 per poem, and by arrangement for articles.

NIMROD—University of Tulsa, Tulsa, Okla. 74104.
Serious poetry. Token payment.

NORTH AMERICAN REVIEW—University of Northern Iowa, Cedar Falls, Iowa 50613. Peter Cooley, Poetry Editor.
Highest quality verse only. Pays 50¢ a line, on publication.

OCCIDENT—Eshleman Hall, University of California, Berkeley, Calif. 94720.
Poetry. Pays in copies.

OYEZ!—Roosevelt University, 430 South Michigan Ave., Chicago, Ill. 60605. Charlotte Carter, Editor.
Poetry, 50 to 60 lines. No payment.

PARTISAN REVIEW—Rutgers, 1 Richardson St., New Brunswick, N. J. 08903. William Phillips, Editor.
No length limit on verse. Manuscripts are held for consideration for at least four months. Include stamped return envelope. Payment 1½¢ per word, on publication.

PEBBLE—118 South Boswell Ave., Crete, Nebr. 68333. Greg Kuzma, Editor.
Poems, any length, reviews of poetry books, and essays on poetry. Pays $2 per page.

PERSPECTIVE—Washington University P.O., St. Louis, Mo. 63130. Jarvis Thurston and Mona Van Duyn, Editors.
High-quality serious poetry; no restrictions as to form or length. No payment.

POEM—Box 1247, West Station, Huntsville, Ala. 35807. H. E. Francis, Editor.
Highest quality poetry, any length. Pays $5 a poem.

POET LORE—Box 688, Westport, Conn. 06880.
Conventional and experimental poetry of all types, both original and in translation. Also uses plays. No payment. Annual prizes for best poem published in four categories: Narrative ($100), Descriptive ($75), Subjective ($75), Translation ($50).

POETRY—1228 North Dearborn Pkwy., Chicago, Ill. 60610. Daryl Hine, Editor.
Considers poems written on any theme. Any length, except the rare poem which is too long for a single issue. Very high standard. Pays $1 a line, on publication.

POETRY NORTHWEST—University of Washington, Seattle, Wash. 98105. David Wagoner, Editor.
Poetry. Pays five contributors' copies plus a year's free subscription.

PRAIRIE SCHOONER—Andrews Hall 219, University of Nebraska, Lincoln, Nebr. 68508. Bernice Slote, Editor.
Verse of any length. Accepts free verse. Payment is in copies and reprints.

PRISM INTERNATIONAL—c/o Creative Writing, University of British Columbia, Vancouver 8, B. C., Canada.
Experimental poetry of high quality; no length limit. Pays $5 per magazine page, upon publication.

PSYCHOLOGICAL PERSPECTIVES—595 East Colorado Blvd., Suite 503, Pasadena, Calif. 91101.
Interested only in quality short poems on contemporary issues, events, figures, etc., that "ask" to be examined in a psychological light.

QUARTERLY REVIEW OF LITERATURE—26 Haslet Ave., Princeton, N. J. 08540. T. Weiss, Editor.
Uses verse of varying lengths. Prefers experimentation, but considers any verse of quality. Author should be familiar with magazine before submitting.

QUARTET—1119 Neal Pickett Dr. College Station, Tex. 77840.
Poetry as a fresh act of language. Highly literate audience. Pays in copies. Often sends editors' criticisms.

ROANOKE REVIEW—English Dept., Roanoke College, Salem, Va. 24153. R. R. Walter, Editor.
Quality poetry in all forms. Pays in copies.

SATIRE NEWSLETTER—State University of New York College, Oneonta, N. Y. 13820.
Poetry, satirical in nature or relating to satire. Pays in copies.

THE SECOND WAVE—Box 344, Cambridge A, Cambridge, Mass. 02139.
Poetry dealing with women's lives and problems, preferably with a feminist slant. Editors prefer work by women. Pays in copies.

SEVEN—21 North Harvey (Terminal Arcade), Oklahoma City, Okla. 73102. James
Neill Northe, Editor.
Will use seven high-quality, original poems, any form; free verse only if genuine
and not chopped prose. See magazine before submitting. Pays $3 per poem, on
acceptance.

SEWANEE REVIEW—Sewanee, Tenn. 37375. Andrew Lytle, Editor.
Uses serious verse of high quality in any length.

SHANTIH—P.O. Box 542, New York, N. Y. 10016. John S. Friedman and Irving
Gottesman, Editors.
Poetry, including translations. No payment.

THE SMITH—5 Beekman St., New York, N. Y. 10038. Harry Smith, Editor.
General interest poetry of any length. Modest payment.

SNOWY EGRET—17 Usher Rd., West Medford, Mass. 02155. Alan Seaburg, Poetry
Editor.
Interested in poems related to natural history. Send stamped, self-addressed enve-
lope. Payment is minimum of $2 to $4 per magazine page, on publication.

SOUTH AND WEST—2601 South Phoenix St., Fort Smith, Ark. 72901. Sue Abbott
Boyd, Editor.
Publishes all types of poetry, up to 40 lines; vignettes and book reviews. $250 in
annual awards.

SOUTH DAKOTA REVIEW—Box 111, University Exchange, Vermillion, S. D. 57069.
John R. Milton, Editor.
Publishes occasional verse of experimental nature. Payment is in copies.

SOUTHERN HUMANITIES REVIEW—Auburn University, Auburn, Ala. 36803.
Poems, no longer than two pages. Pays in copies.

SOUTHERN REVIEW—Drawer D, University Sta., Baton Rouge, La. 70803. Lewis
P. Simpson and Donald E. Stanford, Editors.
Poetry, 1 to 4 pages, of lasting literary merit. Pays $20 per page, on acceptance.

SOUTHWEST REVIEW—Southern Methodist University, Dallas, Texas 75222. Margaret L. Hartley, Editor.
Uses some short verse and occasional longer pieces. Pays $5 per poem, on publi-
cation.

THE SPARROW—103 Waldron St., West Lafayette, Ind. 47906.
High-quality poems and translations, in any style. No restrictions on length. Pays
in copies. Also publishes *Vagrom Chap Books.*

SPECTRUM—Virginia Commonwealth University, 901 West Franklin St., Richmond,
Va. 23220.
Uses high-quality poetry and "serious" light verse, no specifications on length.
Enclose stamped, self-addressed envelope. Pays in copies.

SPIRIT—Seton Hall University, South Orange, N. J. 07079. David Rogers, Editor.
Poetry of all forms and lengths.

THE SUNSTONE REVIEW—P.O. Box 2321, Santa Fe, New Mexico 87501. Jody
Ellis, Editor.
Poems of any length. Pays in copies.

TAMARACK REVIEW—Box 159, Postal Station K, Toronto 12, Ont., Canada. Robert Weaver, Editor.
Literary poetry. Chiefly Canadian contributors, but occasionally includes U.S.
writers. Payment is $10 per page, on publication.

TRIQUARTERLY—University Hall 101, Northwestern University, Evanston, Ill. 60201.
Highest quality verse. Pays various rates. Query first.

UNIVERSITY OF DENVER QUARTERLY—University of Denver, Denver, Colo. 80210. Burton Feldman, Editor.
Uses quality verse. No length limitations. Pays $10 per page.

UNIVERSITY OF WINDSOR REVIEW—Dept. of English, University of Windsor, Ont., Canada.
Limited amount of poetry used. Pays in copies and offprints.

THE VILLAGER—135 Midland Ave., Bronxville, N. Y. 10708. Mrs. Lee A. Beiard, Poetry Editor.
Uses short verse. No payment.

VIRGINIA QUARTERLY REVIEW—1 West Range, Charlottesville, Va. 22903. Charlotte Kohler, Editor.
Poetry selected without regard for "schools." Material from both nationally known poets and promising newcomers. Material must have permanent literary value to be acceptable.

WEST COAST REVIEW—Simon Fraser University, Burnaby 2, B. C., Canada.
Verse of any length. Pays from $5 to $25, on acceptance.

WESTERN HUMANITIES REVIEW—OSH 316, University of Utah, Salt Lake City, Utah 84112. Jack Garlington, Editor.
High-quality verse of any length. Pays in reprints and contributors' copies.

WIND—RFD Route No. 1, Box 810, Pikeville, Ky. 41501. Quentin R. Howard, Editor.
Poems under 30 lines. Payment in contributors' copies. Stamped, self-addressed envelopes with manuscripts are required. Sample copy $1.25.

WISCONSIN POETRY MAGAZINE—P.O. Box 187, Milwaukee, Wis. 53201. A. M. Sterk, Editor.
Only the most skillfully written poems are accepted. Accompanying art work also considered. No payment, but frequent prizes, and radio readings of best poems.

WISCONSIN REVIEW—Wisconsin State University, Oshkosh, Wis. 54901.
Poetry, 50 lines or fewer. Pays in copies.

THE WORMWOOD REVIEW—P.O. Box 8840, Stockton, Calif. 95204. Marvin Malone, Editor.
Poems and prose poems; four-page maximum. "The form may be traditional or avant-garde, the tone serious or flip, the content conservative or taboo." Payment in copies or cash.

YALE REVIEW—28 Hillhouse Ave., New Haven, Conn. 06520. J. E. Palmer, Editor.
Limited market for exceptional poetry. Pays on publication.

YES, A MAGAZINE OF POETRY—Smith Pond, R.D. 1, Avoca, N. Y. 14809. Virginia Elson and Beverlee Hughes, Editors.
Quality poetry of all types; 30 to 40 lines preferred. Payment is in copies. Stamped, self-addressed envelope must accompany manuscripts.

ZAHIR—English Dept., University of New Hampshire, Durham, N. H. 03324. Diane Kruchkow, Editor.
Poetry, Pays in copies.

RELIGIOUS AND DENOMINATIONAL MAGAZINES

AMERICAN ZIONIST—145 East 32nd St., New York, N. Y. 10016. Elias Cooper, Editor.
Poetry on themes relating to Israel, Jewish issues in the United States and elsewhere. Pays on publication.

CATHOLIC RURAL LIFE—3801 Grand Ave., Des Moines, Iowa 50312. Msgr. E. W. O'Rourke, Editor.
Pays $2 to $5, shortly after acceptance, for verse with spiritual emphasis and rural slant, up to one page.

CATHOLIC WORLD—1865 Broadway, New York, N. Y. 10023.
Uses short verse only, 4 to 22 lines.

THE CHRISTIAN—See *The Disciple.*

THE CHRISTIAN CENTURY—407 South Dearborn St., Chicago, Ill. 60605. Kyle Haselden, Editor.
Protestant ("Ecumenical"). Verse, up to 20 lines. No payment.

CHRISTIAN HERALD—27 East 39th St., New York, N. Y. 10016. Kenneth L. Wilson, Executive Editor.
Interdenominational. Limited need for short verse.

THE CHRISTIAN HOME—201 Eighth Ave. South, Nashville, Tenn. 37203. Helen F. Couch, Editor.
Methodist. Seasonal, inspirational, or humorous verse, to 16 lines, of interest to parents. Pays 50¢ a line, on acceptance.

CHURCH MANAGEMENT—115 North Main St., Mt. Holly, N. C. 28120. Norman L. Hersey, Editor.
Two- or three-verse poems of interest to Protestant ministers. No payment.

CONQUEST—6401 The Paseo, Kansas City, Mo. 64131. Paul Miller, Editor.
Church of the Nazarene. Devotional and inspirational poetry, up to 20 lines. Pays 10¢ a line, on acceptance.

DAILY MEDITATION—Box 2710, San Antonio, Tex. 78206. Ruth S. Paterson, Editor.
Some inspirational verse. Pays 14¢ a line, on acceptance.

THE DISCIPLE (Combining *The Christian* and *World Call*)—Box 179, St. Louis, Mo. 63166.
Disciples of Christ. Pays $2.50 to $5 for poetry.

THE EVANGEL (formerly *Light and Life Evangel*)—999 College Ave., Winona Lake, Ind. 46590.
Free Methodist. Serious poetry, 8 to 12 lines. Pays 25¢ a line.

FACE-TO-FACE—201 Eighth Ave. South, Nashville, Tenn. 37203. Mrs. Sharilyn S. Adair, Editor.
United Methodist. Traditional and avant garde poetry, 10 to 150 lines. Pays 25¢ a line.

GOSPEL HERALD—Scottdale, Pa. 15683. John M. Drescher, Editor.
Mennonite. Poetry, up to 10 lines, on Christian experience and concerns. Pays up to 1½¢ a word, on acceptance.

HOME LIFE—127 Ninth Ave. North, Nashville, Tenn. 37203. Dr. Joe W. Burton, Editor.
Southern Baptist. Short, lyrical poems with family angle; also humorous verse. Pays on acceptance.

THE LINK—122 Maryland Ave. N.E., Washington, D. C. 20002. Edward I. Swanson, Editor.
Interdenominational. Short poetry, of interest to young men and women in military service..Payment on acceptance.

MATURE YEARS—201 Eighth Ave. South, Nashville, Tenn. 37203. Daisy D. Warren, Editor.
United Methodist. For older adults. Poetry (12 lines or less) $1 per line.

THE MIRACULOUS MEDAL—475 East Chelten Ave., Philadelphia, Pa. 19144. Rev. Donald L. Doyle, C.M., Editorial Director.
Catholic. Short verse, 20-line maximum. Religious theme—preferably about the Virgin Mary. Pays 50¢ a line and up, on acceptance.

NEW/WORLD OUTLOOK—475 Riverside Dr., New York, N. Y. 10027. Arthur J. Moore, Jr., Editor.
Occasional poetry, up to 16 lines. Pays 2¢ a word.

THE ORPHAN'S MESSENGER—81 York St., Jersey City, N. J. 07302. Sister Eleanor Quin, C.S.J. Editor.
Catholic. Verse of 4 to 40 lines.

PEOPLE—1312 Massachusetts Ave., N. W., Washington, D. C. 2005. Carolyn Sherman, Editor.
Catholic. Poetry.

PURPOSE—610 Walnut Ave., Scottdale, Pa. 15683. Paul M. Schrock, Editor.
Verse from 8 to 24 lines. Pays $2.50 to $5. Free sample copies on request.

QUEEN—40 South Saxon Ave., Bay Shore, N. Y. 11706. Rev. James McMillan, S.M.M., Editor.
Poems with a Marian theme. Payment on acceptance.

THE RECONSTRUCTIONIST—15 West 86th St., New York, N. Y. 10024. Dr. Ira Eisenstein, Editor.
Verse dedicated to the advancement of Judaism. Payment on publication.

REVIEW FOR RELIGIOUS—612 Humboldt Bldg., 539 N. Grand Blvd., St. Louis, Mo. 63103.
Verse of interest to religious men and women; any length. Pays $5 per printed page at time of publication.

VISTA—Box 2000, Marion, Ind. 46952.
Poems from 4 to 16 lines. Pays 25¢ a line.

THE GREETING CARD MARKET

AMERICAN GREETINGS CORPORATION—10500 American Road, Cleveland, Ohio 44144.
Buys fresh and highly original ideas for promotions, books, humorous cards, studio cards. Send studio cards to Hi Brow Dept.; humorous and book material to Editorial Dept. No conventional verse. Pays top rates.

BARKER GREETING CARD CO.—P.O. Box 9010, Cincinnati, Ohio 45209. George Wilson, Editor.
Needs fresh, original ideas for Humorous, Studio, Juvenile, and Novelty greeting cards. Special interest in ideas using attachments or mechanical action. Publishes both Everyday and Seasonal lines. Pays also bonus money for attachment and

mechanical ideas. Monthly Market Letter on request when stamped, self-addressed envelope is included.

CURTIS CONTEMPORARY CARDS—Curtis Circulation Co., 841 Chestnut St., Philadelphia, Pa. 19105.
Humorous studio cards only. Uses no traditional sweet verse. Needs ideas for Birthday, Get-Well, Anniversary, Friendship, Christmas, Valentine, Mother's Day, Father's Day, Graduation, astrology, ski cards and local imprints for resorts, colleges, military bases. Prompt decisions and payment, at above average rates. All art assigned. Market letter sent on request.

DAVID PRINTS, INC.—P.O. Box 502, Miller Place, N. Y. 11764.
Ideas, art work and copy for general occasion cards.

FEITH, STRAUSS AND ASSOCIATES, INC.—530 Ft. Washington Ave., New York, N. Y. 10033.
Happy Birthday, Thank You, Get Well copy for line called "Flubbies." Pays $10 after acceptance.

D. FORER & COMPANY, INC.—18 West 18th St., New York, N. Y. 10011.
Cute everyday ideas, all titles. $15 per idea. Also designs for Studio, Everyday and Christmas lines. $35 for finished art work to start. Suggests writer and artist be familiar with company's style. Stamped, self-addressed envelope must be enclosed for return.

FRAN MAR GREETING CARDS, LTD.—630 South Columbus Ave., Mt. Vernon, N. Y. 10550.
Needs greeting card verse or copy, preferably no more than 4 lines. All copy should be on the cute side, and short and whimsical, preferably not verse. It should appeal to the teen and college market; no juvenile copy. Publishes Birthday (general and relative), Get Well, Anniversary, and Friendship cards, and special titles. Seasonal ideas for St. Patrick's Day, Valentine's Day, Easter, Mother's Day, Christmas, etc., may be submitted at any time. Pays $10 per idea within 30 days. Reports promptly. Stamped, self-addressed envelope must be enclosed.

FRAVESSI-LAMONT, INC.—11 Edison Place, Springfield, N. J. 07081.
Short verses, mostly humorous; Studio cards with witty prose; a few sentimental verses; no Christmas material. Payment varies. Address the Editor.

GALLANT GREETING CORPORATION—2725 West Fullerton, Chicago, Ill. 60647.
Ideas for humorous greeting cards. Submit on 3 x 5 cards. Pays $12 to $15 per idea.

GIBSON GREETING CARDS, INC.—2100 Section Rd., Cincinnati, Ohio 45237.
Interested in outstanding studio, humorous, and general material. Minimum rates —$20 humorous ($25 when submitted in usable dummy form), $25 studio. Prices increase when accompanied with unusual design and/or mechanical ideas such as trick folds, die cuts, shapes, or attachments with little or no reworking required. Straight verse, $1.50 per line and up, depending on originality and suitability for publication with little or no editing. Pays on acceptance. Reports within 10 days.

HALLMARK CARDS, INC.—Kansas City, Mo. 64141. Kent DeVore, Contemporary Editor.
General greeting card ideas on assignment only. Interested in contemporary card ideas only at the present time. Material must express strong new idea. Does not buy art work. Pays $25 to $50 per idea.

KEEP 'N TOUCH GREETING CARDS, INC.—P.O. Box 912, Framingham, Mass. 01702. Ruth Fishel, Art Department.
A Studio card line that is punchy, cheerful, and complimentary. No conventional poetry, sarcasm, off-color cards, or overly sweet "hearts and flowers" ideas. Looking for sophisticated cards that say something nice in a humorous way. Also interested in collegiate situations but must have a reason for sending. Ideas should be typed on 3 x 5 cards or sketched in Studio card form. Art ideas accepted but

no common cartoons. Pays $15 to $20 for art, $12 to $15 per idea, $20 to $30 for art and idea combined, depending on the amount of staff work needed. Also interested in sensitive photography. Pays on publication. Newsletter always available to contributors. Enclose self-addressed, stamped envelope.

ALFRED MAINZER, INC.—39-33 29th St., Long Island City, N. Y. 11101. Mr. Ronald O. Mainzer, Editor.
Everyday, Easter, Christmas, Mother's Day verses.

MILLER DESIGNS—9 Ackerman Ave., Emerson, N. J. 07630. Joseph Schulman, Editor.
Short, simple ideas for sophisticated animal cards: birthday, anniversary, get well. Include stamped, self-addressed envelope. Reports in two weeks. Payment open.

MISTER B GREETING CARD CO., INC.—3500 N.W. 52nd St., Miami, Fla. 33142. Alvin Barker, Editor.
Interested in humorous or novelty ideas; no serious, conventional or sentimental material. Prefers ideas that are short, preferably no more than 4 lines. Can use material for Anniversary, Birthday, Mother's and Father's Day, Graduation, Valentine's Day, St. Patrick's Day, Christmas, Get Well, Miss You—almost all types except Easter or religious and sentimental cards. Illustration optional. Payment varies.

NORCROSS, INC.—244 Madison Ave., New York, N. Y. 10016.
Everyday and seasonal verse. Pays $1.50 and $3 a line. Also studio and humorous ideas. Pays $20 to $50. Include stamped, self-addressed envelope.

NOVO CARD PUBLISHERS, INC.—3855 Lincoln Ave., Chicago, Ill. 60613.
Only interested in Humorous, Cute, Studio, novelty greeting cards for all occasions, "with a real comic punch or kick." Partial to ideas with a double meaning. Does not buy sentimental-type verse. Ideas should be submitted in the form of a rough sketch. Accepts verse and art combinations. Send material to "Editor." Query first.

THE PARAMOUNT LINE, INC.—Box 678, Pawtucket, R. I. 02862. Dorothy M. Nelson, Editor.
Interested in humorous ideas and rough dummies. Buys four and eight line verses, both Everydays and Seasonals. Also interested in copy for "Images," both Everyday and Seasonals. Prefers material that is conversational and casual rather than sentimental. Family captions especially welcome. Reports promptly.

REED STARLINE CARD CO.—3331 Sunset Blvd., Los Angeles, Calif. 90026. Reed Stevens, Editor.
Needs short, witty Studio card copy, conversational in tone, for sophisticated adults. Must have messgae; no verse or jingles. Everyday copy accepted throughout the year, with emphasis on Birthday cards. Also uses Friendship, Get Well, Anniversary, Thank You, Travel and Congratulations. Valentine's and St. Patrick's Day deadline February 28. Submit each idea on 3 x 5 card. Include stamped return envelope. Pays $40 per idea, on acceptance. Also cash prizes for top-sellers.

ROTH GREETING CARDS—P.O. Box 1455, 7900 Deering Ave., Canoga Park, Calif. 91304. Charles Roth, Editor.
Humorous Studio cards. Ideas for all occasions may be submitted throughout the year. Submit each idea on 3 x 5 card and enclose stamped self-addressed envelope with all work submitted. Pays $20 for original ideas, on acceptance.

RUST CRAFT PUBLISHERS—Rust Craft Park, Dedham, Mass. 02026. Dolores Anderson, Editor-in-Chief.
Buys general and religious verse, $1.25 per line for fresh, new ideas. $10 for informal cards with strong illustration possibilities, $10 for prose sentiments, $25 for Studio Card ideas, $30 for rhymed humorous, and $30 for juvenile novelties.

Pays on acceptance. Replies promptly. Market Letter available on request. Send stamped, self-addressed envelope.

STONE HOUSE, INC.—800 Park Ave., Keene, N. H. 03431.
In the market for material for their sensitivity line called "Expressions."

THOUGHT FACTORY—P.O. Box 5515, Sherman Oaks, Calif. 91413.
Greeting and note cards in sensitivity line, for "Love Thoughts" cards and "Nature Thoughts" posters.

UNITED CARD CO.—1101 Carnegie, Rolling Meadows, Ill. 60008. Ed Letwenko, Creative Director.
Humorous contemporary Studio greeting cards, with seasonal or year-round application. Submissions may be in any form, but no finished art work wanted. Pays from $10 to $35 and $50 per idea. Reports in about three weeks.

VAGABOND CREATIONS—2560 Lance Dr., Dayton, Ohio 45409. George F. Stanley, Jr., Editor.
Publishes Birthday, Everyday, Valentine, Christmas, and Graduation Studio cards. Needs Studio card copy in good taste with surprise inside punch line. Humor slanted to younger age group with no references to age itself. Mild risqué humor acceptable. Seasonal material may be submitted at any time. Pays $10 on acceptance. Prompt decisions.

WARNER PRESS, INC.—Anderson, Ind. 46011. Mrs. Dorothy Smith, Verse Editor.
Creators of the "Sunshine Line." Religious greeting card verse only, with suggested Scripture text for each verse (no extra pay for texts). Prefers verses from 4 to 6 lines. Begins reading Everyday sentiments September 1; Christmas sentiments, November 1. Pays $1 a line.

FILLERS AND HUMOR

Included in this list are those magazines which are noted for their excellent filler departments, plus a cross-section of other representative publications that use fillers. However, almost all magazines use some type of filler material, and writers can find dozens of markets by studying sample copies of magazines at a library or newsstand.
Many magazines do not return filler material. In such cases, writers can assume that ninety days is a long enough period to wait; after that, a filler may be submitted to another market.

ALASKA, MAGAZINE OF LIFE ON THE LAST FRONTIER—Box 4-EEE, Anchorage, Alaska 99503.
Uses short features with photos on Alaska by Alaskans.

ALIVE!—Christian Board of Publication, Box 179, St. Louis, Mo. 63166.
For young teens. Uses suitable cartoons, puzzles, brain-teasers, word games, and short poetry.

THE AMERICAN FIELD—222 West Adams St., Chicago, Ill. 60606.
Short fact items and anecdotes on outdoor sports, recreational activities, and field trials for bird dogs. Payment varies and is on acceptance.

AMERICAN FRUIT GROWER—37841 Euclid Ave., Willoughby, Ohio 44094.
Short, personal experiences dealing with commercial production and/or selling fruit. Pays 1¢ per word. Photos with information caption: $5.

AMERICAN LEGION MAGAZINE—1345 Ave. of the Americas, New York, N. Y. 10019.
Wants original anecdotes (up to 300 words), epigrams, humorous and light verse (up to 16 lines). Pays $2.50 per line of verse, $10 per epigram, and $20 per anecdote. Address manuscripts to "Parting Shots" Editor.

THE AMERICAN ROSE MAGAZINE—4048 Roselea Place, Columbus, Ohio 43214.
Magazine for home gardeners. Uses fillers. No payment.

AMERICAN VEGETABLE GROWER—Willoughby, Ohio 44094.
For commercial vegetable growers. Fact items pertaining to production and marketing of vegetables, on a commercial basis—spraying, fertilizing, irrigating, etc. Also items about machinery used by growers; innovator ideas, where a grower has developed equipment especially for his needs. Length: 200 to 500 words. Pays about 1¢ a word, on acceptance.

THE AMERICAN WEST—599 College Ave., Palo Alto, Calif. 94306.
One filler department: "Portraits for a Western Album," 1,000 words, about unusual people, places or events in the Old West, constructed around full-page illustration which author should furnish. Pays $75.

ARGOSY—420 Lexington Ave., New York, N. Y. 10017.
"Hunting and Fishing Tips" Department uses fillers from 25 to 30 words. Pays $5.

ARIZONA—Arizona *Republic*, 120 East Van Buren St., Phoenix, Ariz. 85004.
Short fillers and humor, must be on subjects related to Arizona. Also uses cartoons. Pays before publication.

THE ATLANTIC—8 Arlington St., Boston, Mass. 02116.
Will consider sophisticated humorous or satirical pieces, one or two pages long. Some light poetry. Authors should study magazine before submitting. Rates vary according to length. Payment is on acceptance.

BABY CARE—52 Vanderbilt Ave., New York, N. Y. 10017. Mrs. Maja Bernath, Editor.
Short items for columns: "Focus on You" (500 words), pays $25; "Family Corner" (100 words), pays $10. Study magazine before submitting. No fillers, but occasionally accepts short poetry and cartoons.

BABY TALK—66 East 34th St., New York, N. Y. 10016.
Uses short features on child care.

BETTER CAMPING—500 Hyacinth Pl., Highland Park, Ill. 60035.
"Overflow," a page of short, humorous camping anecdotes and poems, under 250 words preferred. Pays $5 to $10. "Over an Open Fire," recipes for the outdoors, pays $3 and up, depending on length. "Voice of Experience," tips from readers on camping shortcuts, safety, good practices, pays $3 and up.

BITS AND PIECES—The Economics Press, Inc., 12 Daniel Rd., Fairfield, N. J. 07006. Marvin G. Gregory, Editor.
Real or imaginary anecdotes, 50 to 500 words, written in the third person, about living and working with people. May be humorous or serious. Pays 15¢ a word, on acceptance.

BITS AND PIECES—Box 746, Newcastle, Wyo. 82701. Mabel E. Brown, Editor.
Short fillers on the history of Wyoming and the surrounding states. Source of
information must be given. Length: 500 to 1,000 words. Pays in copies.

BLACK BELT—5455 Wilshire Blvd., Los Angeles, Calif. 90036.
Articles and news shorts, 200 to 2,000 words, preferably with photos, on judo, ju-
jitsu, karate, aikido, kendo, and other Oriental arts and sports of self-defense. Also
international tournament coverage. Payment rates vary, on publication.

BOOT & SHOE RECORDER—Chilton Way, Radnor, Pa. 19089.
Buys obituaries, anecdotes concerning almost any footwear topic. Length: to 3
paragraphs. Pays about $1.00 per item, after publication.

BOY'S LIFE—North Brunswick, N. J. 08903.
Short how-to-do-it features on hobbies, crafts, science, outdoor skills. Text articles under 1,000 words on same topics, plus off-beat and interesting material on
history, sports, and subjects of interest to boys.

CAMPING AND TRAILERING GUIDE—P.O. Box 1014, Grass Valley, Calif. 95945.
Magazine dealing with practical aspects of family camping. Uses occasional one-
picture how-to's, 300 to 800 words, usually about travel objectives and with
information about camping at the scene or close by. Pays $25, on publication.

CAR AND DRIVER—One Park Ave., New York, N. Y. 10016.
For automotive enthusiasts. Uses news stories on automotive events, and foibles
of the industry, to 300 words. No warranty/dealer/insurance gripes. Pays $20 and
up, on publication.

CARTOON PARADE—See *Humorama, Inc.*

CATALYST—Christian Board of Publication, Box 179, St. Louis, Mo. 63166.
Magazine for senior high school students. Uses poems and cartoons. Pays up to
25¢ a line for poetry, $6 and up for cartoons.

CATHOLIC DIGEST—P.O. Box 3090, St. Paul, Minn. 55101.
For "Hearts are Trumps" feature, wants original accounts, under 300 words, of
true cases where unseeking kindness was rewarded. For "The Open Door," true
incidents by which persons were brought into the Church. For "The Perfect Assist," original reports of tactful remarks or actions. $50 for each item. Also needed
is material for "People Are Like That," illustrating instinctive goodness of human
nature, and amusing or inspiring tales for "In Our Parish" and "In Our House."
Pays $20 for each item. Pays $4 for acceptable "Flights of Fancy," picturesque
figures of speech, with exact source given. All payments on publication. Fillers
not acknowledged or returned.

CATS—P.O. Box 4106, Pittsburgh, Pa. 15202.
Poems, preferably light, about cats, up to 30 lines. Pays 20¢ a line, on acceptance.

CHANGING TIMES: THE KIPLINGER MAGAZINE—1729 H St., N. W., Wash-
ington, D. C. 20006.
Epigrams and topical quips, one or two sentences, for "Notes on These Changing
Times" page. Payment is $5 per item.

CHATELAINE—481 University Ave., Toronto 2, Ont., Canada.
Light verse. Pays $10 to $15.

CHEVRON USA—P.O. Box 6227, San Jose, Calif. 95150.
Humorous anecdotes, 100 to 250 words, related to travel in the U.S. West, with emphasis on automobile trips. Cartoons. Pays $25 to $50, on acceptance.

CHILD LIFE—1100 Waterway Blvd., Indianapolis, Ind. 46202.
For children, ages 7 to 12. Uses verse, puzzles, games, mazes, and tricks. Pays about 3¢ a word for prose, 25¢ a line for poetry, on publication.

CHILDREN'S PLAYMATE—1100 Waterway Blvd., Indianapolis, Ind. 46202.
For children, ages 3 to 8. Uses verse, puzzles, games, mazes and tricks. Pays about 3¢ a word for prose, 25¢ a line for poetry, on publication.

THE CHRISTIAN ADVENTURER—Messenger Publishing House, P.O. Box 850, Joplin, Mo. 64802.
Weekly Sunday school paper for teen-agers. Uses inspirational fillers and suitable jokes. Pays ¼¢ a word, on publication.

THE CHRISTIAN BOOKSELLER—Gundersen Dr. and Schmale Rd., Wheaton, Ill. 61087.
Business magazine for religious bookstore dealers and owners. Uses cartoons, humorous pieces about incidents occurring in bookstores or publishing houses, and short items on new products for booksellers. Length: 100 to 300 words. Pays $15 to $50, on publication.

CHRISTIAN HERALD—27 East 39th St., New York, N. Y. 10016.
Uses short poems, 4 to 8 lines, church bulletin board photos with significant messages, brief personal experiences with a point, to 500 words. Also unusual original anecdotes. Pays $5 to $10.

THE CHRISTIAN HOME—201 Eighth Ave., South, Nashville, Tenn. 37203.
United Methodist: for parents. Will consider material on almost any subject related to family living. Length: 800 to 1,000 words. Also seasonal, inspirational, or humorous verse, to 16 lines. Pays 50¢ a line for poetry, $10 to $15 for prose, on acceptance.

THE CHRISTIAN SCIENCE MONITOR—One Norway St., Boston, Mass. 02115.
Address material to People Page. Fillers: shorts (not fact fillers) ; anecdotes; true accounts of outstanding courage, kindness, good-neighbor policy, for "Sundial" feature. Payment twice a month, covering material accepted or used in the preceding two weeks.

CLIMB—Warner Press Inc., Publication Board of the Church of God, Anderson, Ind. 46011.
Church school paper for junior boys and girls. Puzzles, 50 to 100 words; also stories or articles, 300 to 500 words, on Bible persons or themes. Pays $7.50 per thousand words, on acceptance.

COLORADO—7190 West 14th Ave., Denver, Colo. 80215. David Sumner, Editor.
For Alpinehaus feature, articles to 1,000 words, on mountain homes in Rocky Mountain West, with photos. Pays $150. Pays $75 for "Out-of-the-Way-West" features, 750-word articles about unusual spots off main highways in Rocky Mountain states. Pays $50 for Snowmobile Adventure Trails, 500-word articles about snowmobile routes in West.

COLUMBIA—Box 1670, New Haven, Conn. 06507.
Official journal of the Knights of Columbus. Uses short humor or satire features,

to 1,000 words, fillers of about 100 words, and cartoons. Pays up to $100 for short humor, $10 for fillers, $25 for cartoons, on acceptance.

CONFIDENTIAL CONFESSIONS—Dauntless Books, Inc., 1120 Ave. of the Americas, New York, N. Y. 10036.
Fillers on marriage, courtship, personality, and child care, up to 700 words. Pays 3¢ a word and up for fillers, on acceptance. Same address and requirements for *Daring Romances, Exciting Confessions, Revealing Romances* and *Secrets.*

DAVID C. COOK PUBLISHING CO.—850 North Grove Ave., Elgin, Ill. 60120.
Puzzles, games, cartoons, how-to-make-it features, anecdotes about famous people, word origins, etc., for junior through adult Protestant evangelical Sunday schools. Pays 2¢ to 4¢ a word.

COSMOPOLITAN—224 West 57th St., New York, N. Y. 10019.
Not in the market for fillers. Authors should watch magazine for announcements of special columns which buy short items.

THE CRAFTSMAN—See *Make It With Leather.*

CREEM—P.O. Box 202, Walled Lake, Mich. 48088. David R. Marsh, Editor.
Crossword Puzzles, cartoons and fillers. Payment varies.

CURRENT COMEDY—1529 East 19th St., Brooklyn, N. Y. 11230.
Send manuscripts to Robert Orben, 67-00 192 St. Flushing, N. Y. 11365. Uses funny, performable one-liners and brief jokes related to news, fads, trends, topical subjects. Pays $2 per item, at end of month. No material returned without stamped, self-addressed envelope.

CYCLE WORLD—1499 Monrovia Ave., P.O. Box 1757, Newport Beach, Calif. 92663.
Humor of interest to motorcycle enthusiasts, 1,500 to 2,000 words. Also uses racing reports, 400 to 600 words, with photos; cartoons; news of motorcycle industry, legislation, and trends. Pays minimum of 5¢ a word, on publication.

DARING ROMANCES—See *Confidential Confessions.*

DIXIE-ROTO—*The Times-Picayune,* New Orleans, La. 70140.
Humorous original shorts involving children, from Louisiana or Mississippi (published in collection under title, "Bright Talk"). Also documented historical anecdotes related to the South. Shorts, $2 to $3. Anecdotes, $20.

DOWN EAST—Camden, Maine 04843.
True anecdotes and stories about Maine, up to 300 words, for "It Happened Down East." Pays $5.

EBONY—820 South Michigan Ave., Chicago, Ill. 60605.
"Speaking of People" column accepts items up to 200 words, on Negroes in jobs heretofore closed to Negroes. Material must describe job, how obtained, training, etc. Human interest angle helpful. Payment is $20 and up, on publication.

ELKS MAGAZINE—425 West Diversey Parkway, Chicago, Ill. 60614.
Short humorous material, 1,000 words. Very sophisticated or lowbrow material should be avoided. Payment starts at 10¢ a word, on acceptance.

THE EMPIRE MAGAZINE—*Denver Post,* Denver, Colo. 80201.
Weekly rotogravure supplement. Photo-illustrated shorts or fillers on subjects of interest to Rocky Mountain readers. Pays 4¢ to 5¢ a word, plus $5 for each photo.

ESQUIRE—488 Madison Ave., New York, N. Y. 10022.
Short humor, short fact items, and extended letters (for "Aftermath") on articles in the magazine. Payment on acceptance.

EVENT—Baptist Sunday School Board, 127 Ninth Ave. North, Nashville, Tenn. 37203.
For Southern Baptist youth. Puzzles and cartoons, poetry to 16 lines. Pays $5 to $15.

EVERYWOMAN—6516 West 83rd St., Los Angles, Calif. 90045.
Fillers and short humor. Pays in copies.

EXCITING CONFESSIONS—See *Confidential Confessions.*

EXPECTING—Parents' Magazine Enterprises, Inc., 52 Vanderbilt Ave., New York, N. Y. 10017.
"Happenings," anecdotes about pregnancy. Also sophisticated light verse. Pays $10 per item; $5 for verse.

FAMILY CIRCLE—488 Madison Ave., New York, N. Y. 10022.
Short humor, 1,500 words. Also household and child care fillers for departments. How-to and inspirational items. Pays $100 to $500.

FATE—500 Hyacinth Pl., Highland Park, Ill. 60035.
Fact fillers of 200 words or less on strange, psychic, or unexplained happenings. Also buys true stories of 300 words or less on psychic or mystic personal experiences. Pays $3 for fact fillers, $5 for true stories, on acceptance.

FIELD AND STREAM—383 Madison Ave., New York, N. Y. 10017.
Short features on unusual outdoor subjects, basically how-to, up to 1,000 words. Also humorous articles, to 2,000 words. Pays $150 and up, on acceptance for fillers; more for humor.

FUNNY FUNNY WORLD—407 Commercial Center St., Beverly Hills, Calif. 90210. Martin A. Ragaway, Editor.
Humorous and funny news happenings around the world. Also, new witty lines and anecdotes. Payment varies. Query. Enclose stamped return envelope for free sample copy.

GARCIA FISHING ANNUAL—329 Alfred Ave., Teaneck, N. J. 07666. Robert E. Stankus, Editor.
Uses humorous pieces dealing with fishing. Pays on acceptance.

GIRLTALK—380 Madison Ave., New York, N. Y. 10017.
Uses fillers and poetry of interest to women. Payment is 8¢ a word for filler articles.

GOLF—235 East 45th St., New York, N. Y. 10017.
Uses short humor. Pays on acceptance. Query.

GOLF DIGEST MAGAZINE—297 Westport Ave., Norwalk, Conn. 06856.
Short fact items, anecdotes, quips, jokes, and light verse. For "Links Laughs," wants true humorous or odd incidents, up to 200 words. Pays 20¢ a word minimum, on acceptance; $15 for "Links Laughs."

GOOD HOUSEKEEPING—959 Eighth Ave., New York, N. Y. 10019. Robert Liles, Features Editor.
Pays $5 and up a line for light verse. Also very short humorous prose items for humor page and back of the book fillers. Payment is $10 to $100.

GOURMET MAGAZINE—777 Third Ave., New York, N. Y. 10017.
Light verse with a sophisticated food or drink angle. Payment is on acceptance.

GUIDEPOSTS—3 West 29th St., New York, N. Y. 10001.
Short features, to 250 words, for "Calendar of Holidays and Holy Days," "Fragile Moments," and other short items. Pays $25 to $50.

GUNS AND AMMO—8490 Sunset Blvd., Los Angeles, Calif. 90069.
1,500-word features of do-it-yourself tips pertaining to sporting firearms. Pays 5¢ per word.

HARDWARE AGE—Chilton Way, Radnor, Pa. 19089. John J. Sullivan, Editor.
Fillers and photos, describing unique or successful hardware store operations. Pays $10 and up.

HOME LIFE—127 Ninth Ave, North, Nashville, Tenn. 37203.
Southern Baptist. Addressed to parents. Uses fillers, 100 to 500 words, on anything that points up family relationships. Pays 2½¢ a word, on acceptance.

HOSPITAL PHYSICIAN—550 Kinderkamack, Oradell, N. J. 07649.
Anecdotes by doctor readers. Pays $25.

HUMORAMA, INC.—100 North Village Ave., Rockville Center, N. Y. 11570.
Topical satire, epigrams, humorous fillers, up to 1,000 words. Light verse, up to 48 lines. Pays $1 for one-line fillers, 45¢ a line for verse and 3¾¢ a word for prose, just before publication. Same address and requirements for *Cartoon Parade, Pop Cartoons, Pop Jokes, Jest, Joker, Laugh Riot, Quips.*

INSECT WORLD DIGEST—Route 1, Box 161, Tallahassee, Fla. 32303. Ross Arnett, Editor.
Uses some humor dealing with insects in the broad sense. Magazine aimed at entomologists, conservationists, teachers and the educated public. Pays 2¢ a word, on acceptance. Query; request editorial guidelines sheet.

JACK AND JILL—1100 Waterway Blvd., Indianapolis, Ind. 46202.
For children 4 to 12. Poems, puzzles, jokes, riddles, word games. Payment varies, upon publication.

JEST—See *Humorama, Inc.*

THE JEWELERS' CIRCULAR-KEYSTONE—Chilton Way, Radnor, Pa. 19089.
Uses 200- to 300-word shorts, focusing sharply on some single activity that built traffic and sales or cut costs for a jeweler or jewelry department in a department store. Pays $10, on acceptance.

JOKER—See *Humorama, Inc.*

THE JUNIOR MUSICIAN—See *Young Musicians.*

LADY'S CIRCLE—21 West 26th St., New York, N. Y. 10010.
"Sound-Off" Department pays $25; "Cut-Out Cookbook" $5 for each recipe used.

LAUGH RIOT—See *Humorama, Inc.*

THE LINK—122 Maryland Ave., N. E., Washington, D. C. 20002.
Religious magazine for military personnel. Uses short inspirational and helpful material, 1 to 4 lines. Also material for "Lift Up Your Heart," inspirational column. Pays $1 per item.

McCALL'S MAGAZINE—230 Park Ave., New York, N. Y. 10017.
Uses some quality poetry, of lengths from 4 lines up to approximately 30. Top rates. Send to Eileen Shapiro, Poetry Editor.

MAKE IT WITH LEATHER—(formerly *The Craftsman*)—Box 1386, Fort Worth, Tex. 76101.
"Tips and Hints" uses a few lines pertaining to leathercraft. Pays $3 to $10.

MALE—575 Madison Ave., New York, N. Y. 10022.
Uses jokes of interest to men. Submissions must be typewritten or legible, and cannot be returned. No poetry. Pays $5 per joke, on acceptance. Same address and requirements for *Men, Man's World,* and *True Action.*

MAN'S WORLD—See *Male.*

MARRIAGE: THE MAGAZINE FOR HUSBAND AND WIFE—St. Meinrad, Ind. 47577.
For "We Tried This," wants short, personal accounts, up to 400 words, telling about original solutions to family problems. For "At Our House," wants short, personal accounts of unusual or amusing incidents of family living, up to 400 words. Pays $15, on acceptance.

MATURE YEARS—Methodist Publishing House, 201 Eighth Ave. South, Nashville, Tenn. 37202.
For older adults. Uses poems, cartoons, and puzzles. Also anecdotes, to 300 words, fact items of about 600 words, and jokes. Pays 3¢ per word, on acceptance.

MECHANIX ILLUSTRATED—1515 Broadway, New York, N. Y. 10036.
Buys single photos with captions, tips illustrated by rough drawings, or un-illustrated tips for short cuts in the shop, garage, or home. Departments include Home Kinks, Home & Shop Shorts, Freddie Fumbles (cartoon strip), Farmer's Page, Inventions Wanted (ideas for inventions from readers), and MIMI (unusual new products shown with girl "product tester"). Also buys cartoons and short one-column and half-column fillers, to 500 words. Rates: captioned photos, $20; tips with drawing, to $15; un-illustrated tips, $5; cartoons $30; Inventions Wanted ideas, $5; Freddie Fumbles ideas, $10; finder's fee for MIMI products, $50; one-column fillers, $75.

MEN—See *Male.*

MODERN BRIDE—One Park Ave., New York, N. Y. 10017.
Poems and short humorous pieces directed to the about-to-be or newly-married bride, 500 to 1,500 words. Payment is on acceptance.

MODERN PHOTOGRAPHY—165 West 46th St., New York, N. Y. 10036.
Buys photographic how-to-do-its, 250 to 300 words. Pays $10 to $15 for test and photograph, on acceptance.

MOTOR BOATING & SAILING—224 West 57th St., New York, N. Y. 10019.
Seeking short items of strong boating or water sports interest, including anecdotes, humor, news, shorts, fillers, and cartoons. Pays varying but competitive rates, on acceptance.

MUSIC JOURNAL—200 West 57th St., New York, N. Y. 10019.
Fillers and short items on some aspect of music. No payment available except for a limited number of feature articles on music and $5 for poems on music.

THE NATIONAL GUARDSMAN—1 Massachusetts Ave., N. W., Washington, D. C. 20001.
Army National Guard and Air National Guard magazine. For "Tales from the Troops," wants military anecdotes, 150 to 250 words. Payment is $10, on publication.

NATIONAL LAMPOON—635 Madison Ave., New York, N. Y. 10022.
Monthly magazine of humor and satire with a predominantly college-age readership. Parodies, satires, humorous fiction, amusing articles and other funny stuff, preferably under 2,500 words. Pays 10¢ a word for basic text pieces; other articles on a page rate basis.

THE NATIONAL OBSERVER—11501 Columbia Pike, Silver Spring, Md. 20910.
Humorous pieces, about 600 words. Pays $50 per item. Address "Reflections" Editor.

NATIONAL REVIEW—150 East 35th St., New York, N. Y. 10016.
Conservative political journal. Uses short satirical poems, 4 to 30 lines, and short prose satire, up to 900 words. Payment is $10 to $35, on publication.

NEBRASKALAND—2200 North 33rd St., Lincoln, Nebr. 68503. Dick H. Schaffer, Editor.
Verse and cartoons of interest to Nebraska. No payment.

THE NEW ENGLAND GUIDE—Box 108, Concord, N. H. 03301.
Humorous essays, personal experiences and observations, to 800 words, on New England subjects only. Pays $40, on publication. One-paragraph fillers, New England subjects, $5.

THE NEW YORKER—25 West 43rd St., New York, N. Y. 10036.
Buys light verse, amusing bits printed in newspapers, books, magazines, etc., and entertaining anecdotes. Pays a minimum of $5, on acceptance; extra payment is made for titles and/or tag lines. Address the Editors.

THE OHIO MOTORIST—6000 South Marginal Rd., Cleveland, Ohio 44103.
Short humorous poems on motoring, automotive and vacation topics (foreign and domestic), preferably 4 to 6 lines. Pays $5 to $6.

OKLAHOMA RANCH AND FARM WORLD—Box 1770, Tulsa, Okla. 74102.
Monthly Sunday supplement of the Tulsa Sunday World. Farm, suburban and homemaking fillers to 200 words. Pays $7.50 per column, on publication. Authors must query.

OKLAHOMA TODAY—Will Rogers Memorial Bldg., State Capitol, Oklahoma City, Okla. 73105.
Humor, to 1,500 words, on Oklahoma topics. Pays 5¢ a word, on publication.

ON THE LINE—Mennonite Publishing House, Scottsdale, Pa. 15683.
Children's story paper. Light verse to 24 lines, some cartoons, human interest

photos with brief explanations. Pays $3 and up for puzzles, quizzes, and verse, $5 to $10 for photo features. Sample copies available on request.

ORGANIC GARDENING AND FARMING—Emmaus, Pa. 18049.
Fillers dealing with actual garden experience: how-to's, solution of problems, etc. Also uses material for department and news items. Length: 100 to 500 words. Pays from $5 to $25, before publication.

THE ORPHAN'S MESSENGER—P.O. Box 288, Jersey City, N. J. 07303.
Humorous fillers, 90 to 100 words, and verse, 4 to 40 lines in length. Pays 2¢ to 3¢ per word, on acceptance.

OUTDOOR LIFE—355 Lexington Ave., New York, N. Y. 10017.
Buys short fact items and hints on hunting, fishing, camping, and the care and repair of firearms, fishing tackle, motor boats, and similar outdoor equipment. Pays on acceptance.

PARENTS' MAGAZINE—52 Vandebilt Ave., New York, N. Y. 10017.
Imaginative, humorous children's sayings for "Out of the Mouths of Babes," pays $5 per item; short items on sensible solution of some problem in child care or family relations (allowances, nap-taking, eating problems, etc.) for "Family Clinic," pays $10 per item. Payment is on publication.

PEN—444 Sherman St., Denver, Colo. 80203.
Uses humorous or informative fillers, up to 350 words, of general interest. Pays 3¢ a word.

PLAYBOY—919 North Michigan Ave., Chicago, Ill. 60611.
High-quality entertainment magazine for urban men. Buys jokes for $50; "After Hours" items (brief amusing paragraphs on topical subjects) for $50 to $250. Address appropriate submission to Party Jokes Editor or After Hours Editor.

PLAYGIRL—1801 Century Park East, Suite 2300, Century City, Los Angeles, Calif. 90067.
For contemporary women. Fillers, 500 to 800 words. Humor, especially satire. Pays various rates.

POP CARTOONS—See *Humorama, Inc.*

POP JOKES—See *Humorama, Inc.*

POPULAR PHOTOGRAPHY—One Park Ave., New York, N. Y. 10016.
Interested in material for "Photo Tips" and "Movie Tips" departments. Pays $10 for each illustrated "Tip." Payment is on acceptance.

POPULAR SCIENCE MONTHLY—355 Lexington Ave., New York, N. Y. 10017.
Short fact items and hints for special sections: "Hints from the Model Garage" (auto upkeep); "Short Cuts and Tips" (home shop hints and techniques); "I'd Like to See Them Make . . ." (pet ideas for gadgets readers would like to see in general use). If possible, glossy photos or rough sketches should accompany material. Pays $25 for shorts, on acceptance.

PROCEEDINGS—U. S. Naval Institute, Annapolis, Md. 21402. Commander Robert P. Brewer, USN (Retired), Editor.
Short, humorous naval anecdotes to interest those involved in naval and maritime fields. Pays $10.00 per anecdote, on acceptance.

QUIPS—See *Humorama, Inc.*

REACHOUT—Light and Life Press, Winona Lake, Ind. 46590.
Sunday school take-home paper for young teens. Uses some verse, 8 to 16 lines. Pays 20¢ a line, on acceptance.

READER'S DIGEST—Pleasantville, N. Y. 10570.
Buys contributions for "Life in These United States," "Humor in Uniform," "Toward More Picturesque Speech," "Laughter, the Best Medicine," "Quotable Quotes," "Personal Glimpses," "Campus Comedy," etc. Contributors should watch magazine for announcements of other departments. Address submissions to the Editor of each department. Payment for previously unpublished anecdotes used in "Life in These United States," "Campus Comedy," and "Humor in Uniform" is $100, on publication. Payment for other original filler items is $10 per *Digest* two-column line on publication. No fillers can be acknowledged or returned.

REVEALING ROMANCES—See *Confidential Confessions.*

THE RHODE ISLANDER—Providence Sunday *Journal*, Providence, R. I. 02902.
Sunday paper supplement. Uses short articles, not over 1,000 words, relating to Rhode Island, with photos. Also light features and essays. Pays $35 to $200.

ROLL CALL: THE NEWSPAPER OF CAPITOL HILL—636 Pennsylvania Ave., S. E., Washington, D. C. 20003.
Short, humorous items concerning Congress and Congressmen, anecdotes, puzzles, quips on political subjects. Payment on acceptance.

ROTARIAN—1600 Ridge Ave., Evanston, Ill. 60201. Karl K. Krueger, Editor.
Humorous articles of interest to business and professional men, 1,200 words. Query first. Pays first-class rates on acceptance.

RV WORLD—16200 Ventura Blvd., Encino, Calif. 91316.
First-person humor with a recreational vehicle slant, to 1,800 words. Pays $50 per printed page, on publication. Query.

Rx SPORTS AND TRAVEL—447 South Main St., Hillsboro, Ill. 62049. Tom D. Harris, Editor.
Participation sports tips, humorous sports happenings and other filler material, from 250 to 750 words, of interest to physicians. Payment is upon acceptance.

SAN FRANCISCO—120 Green St., San Francisco, Calif. 94111.
Cartoons. Pays $15 and up, on publication.

SCIENCE DIGEST—224 West 57th St., New York, N. Y. 10019.
Uses interesting editorial items on scientific developments, preferably with good photos. Pays $20 to $50.

SECRETS—See *Confidential Confessions.*

THE SENTINEL MAGAZINE—c/o Organizational Services Corp., 1616 Soldiers Field Rd., Boston, Mass. 02135.
Publication of the Massachusetts Police Association. Uses some humorous short articles and fillers. Pays 5¢ a word, on acceptance.

SEVENTEEN—320 Park Ave., New York, N. Y. 10022.
Fashion and service magazine for teen-age girls. Short articles for "Face to Face" column; pays $100 to $150. Also buys photos and information for "Teen Scene." Payment varies, on acceptance. Query first.

SEVENTY-SIX MAGAZINE—P.O. Box 7600, Los Angeles, Calif. 90054.
Union Oil Company of California house organ. Short pieces on employees, with an unusual twist, 500 to 750 words. Pays 10¢ a word and up.

SICK—919 Third Ave., New York, N. Y. 10022. Paul Laikin, Editor.
Zany-type articles that fit magazine's format. No lengthy prose pieces. Study magazine before submitting. Pays within a month of acceptance.

SKIING MAGAZINE—One Park Ave., New York, N. Y. 10016.
Short articles on skiing of the past; significant personal anecdotes that add to the lore and history of skiing; humorous vignettes. Length: 900 to 1,200 words. Also "Letter From" column, detailing a skiing experience in a distant place, 1,200 to 1,500 words. Pays $100 to $150, on acceptance. Query.

SMALL WORLD—Volkswagen of America, 818 Sylvan Ave., Englewood Cliffs, N. J. 07632.
Anecdotes about Volkswagen owners' experiences, cartoons, and photos about Volkswagens. Length: to 100 words. Pays $15 minimum, on acceptance.

SNOTRACK—534 North Broadway, Milwaukee, Wis. 53202. Dorothy Deer, Associate Editor.
Official magazine of United States Snowmobile Association. Uses short humor and cartoons. Pays $25 for single cartoon, other payments vary.

SPORTS AFIELD—250 West 55th St., New York, N. Y. 10019.
Fillers on hunting, fishing, camping, boating, shooting, 100 to 700 words. Photographs are almost a must. Unusual and useful gimmicks and tips for sportsmen are the most acceptable. Rates up to $100, on acceptance.

SUCCESSFUL FARMING—1716 Locust St., Des Moines, Iowa 50336.
Buys light verse, hints, recipes, quips and jokes. Special departments: "Successful Recipes," "All Around the House" (hints), "All Around the Farm" (hints), and "Tips for the Cook" (hints). Pays $3 to $5, on acceptance, for jokes and newsbreaks for the "Laughing at Life" humor column. Newsbreaks must be actual tear sheets, including name of paper. Other payment on publication. Material cannot be returned.

SUNDANCE—1913 Filmore St., San Francisco, Calif. 94115.
Poetry, fillers, jokes and news shorts. Pays 4¢ per word, within 30 days of publication. Query.

SUNDAY DIGEST—850 North Grove Ave., Elgin, Ill. 60120.
Weekly Protestant publication for older youth and adults. Original anecdotes to 500 words, inspirational or humorous. Pays $2 to $15. Timely vignettes, quizzes, quotations, to 300 words. Seasonal and holiday material must be submitted nine months in advance. Pays up to $10. Short, pithy, original epigrams pinpointing Christian virtues or frailties. Pays $2.50 to $5. All payment is on acceptance. Material will be returned if stamped, self-addressed envelope is enclosed.

SURFER MAGAZINE—Box 1028, Dana Point, Calif. 92629.
Surfing magazine. Humor, humorous poems, cartoons, news items. Must relate to surfing. "Pipeline" uses news items and photos. Length: 50 words. Pays 4¢ to 10¢ a word, on publication.

TV GUIDE—Radnor, Pa. 19088.
Short humor pertaining to television for one-page "TV Jibe" feature. Items must fit on one *TV Guide* page or may be shorter. Payment varies.

TEACH—Box 1591, Glendale, Calif. 91209.
Uses short humor from real life on children, preferably in a church context. Pays $1 per anecdote, on acceptance.

TODAY'S CHRISTIAN MOTHER—8121 Hamilton Ave., Cincinnati, Ohio 45231.
A guide for Christian child training. Uses material for fathers' page, and pages with creative children's activities. Quips and short poems. "How We Did It" page uses brief suggestions from mothers about their methods of building Christian homes. Length: to 25 words for quips, to 16 lines for poems. Pays various rates, on acceptance.

TOGETHER—1661 North Northwest Hwy., Park Ridge, Ill. 60068.
For Methodist families. Uses true personal incidents, short humor, and short verse. "Getting Along Together" pays $5 for short, true anecdotes about events which "brightened a day or lightened a heart." Payment for other items varies.

TRUE—1515 Broadway, New York, N. Y. 10036.
Adventure magazine for men. Buys fillers about sports for "It Happened in Sports" feature, and humor for "This Funny Life." Also needs material, 1,000 to 5,000 words, for "In This Corner," a monthly controversial or humorous essay; "Man and His Money" (financial service feature); "Man and His Health" (medical feature); "True Views the Lively Arts" (arts and theater essay). Pays good rates.

TRUE ACTION—See *Male*.

TRUE CONFESSIONS—205 East 42nd St., New York, N. Y. 10017.
Buys a limited number of seriously-handled self-help and inspirational fillers, 300 to 800 words, using "you" approach. Home-making material is handled by staff. Pays 5¢ a word, on acceptance.

TRUE ROMANCE—205 East 42nd St., New York, N. Y. 10017.
Pays $10 for short personal-experience items for columns: "Laughs in Your Life," "Pet Peeves," "Family Album" and "Space Set Says": same rates for photos submitted for "Cute Kids" column.

TRUE STORY—P.O. Box 1448, Grand Central Sta., New York, N. Y. 10017.
"Women are Wonderful" uses short personal experiences, humorous or inspirational features relating to home and children, and light verse. Pays 5¢ a word.

TRUE TREASURE—P.O. Drawer L, Conroe, Tex. 77301.
Bimonthly magazine about lost mines, buried or sunken treasure. Uses short "Treasure Nuggets," 100 to 250 words. Pays $12.50 for fillers.

WEIGHT WATCHERS MAGAZINE—635 Madison Ave., New York, N. Y. 10022.
Fiction, humor, jokes, quizzes and cartoons. No poetry or puzzles. Pays on acceptance.

WESTART—Box 1396, Auburn, Calif. 95603.
Artists' newspaper. Primarily concerned with current news items in the arts field.
Uses short features, 350 to 500 words, of exceptional interest in the field of crafts
and fine arts. No hobbies. Pays 30¢ per column inch, on publication.

WOMAN'S DAY—1515 Broadway, New York, N. Y. 10036.
For "Neighbors" department needs items relating some family experience which
will benefit others, also brief practical suggestions for homemakers. Pays $25 for
each letter published, $5 for suggestions. Photographs are welcome.

THE WORKBASKET—4251 Pennsylvania, Kansas City, Mo. 64111.
Uses how-to articles, 300 to 500 words, with completed models or good black-and-
white photos, and clear instructions. Pays 2¢ per word, on acceptance. "Women
Who Make Cents" column uses short instructions concerning a specific item women
can make and sell (include selling price). Pays 2¢ per item, on acceptance.

YACHTING MAGAZINE—50 West 44th St., New York, N. Y. 10036. William W.
Robinson, Editor.
Occasional short fillers and anecdotes. Nominal payment, on publication.

YANKEE MAGAZINE—Dublin, N. H. 03444.
Monthly magazine about New England. Uses unusual short articles, around 500
words, on subjects relating to New England. Photos wanted if possible. "Small
Business & Crafts" column uses items under 400 words about New England's small
business and/or hobbies. Payment is $15 for "Small Business & Crafts" items. Pays
$25 to $400 for articles and fiction; $15 to $25 for photos.

THE YOUNG JUDEAN—817 Broadway, New York, N. Y. 10003.
Cartoons and anecdotes suitable for boys and girls about modern Israel, American Jewish child life, Jewish parents; also items about Hebrew school, etc. Poems
on important Zionist events and personalities for readers, 8 to 14 years old. Pays
up to $10.

YOUNG MISS—52 Vanderbilt Ave., New York, N. Y. 10017.
Teen-age magazine. Wants how-to hints for young teen-age girls, especially things
to make out of odds and ends, up to 100 words. Pays $5 per item, on acceptance.

YOUNG MUSICIANS (formerly *The Junior Musician*)—127 Ninth Ave., North,
Nashville, Tenn. 37203. Jimmy R. Key, Editor.
Publishes music puzzles, games, quizzes, cartoons. Also uses miscellaneous filler
items relating to church music for children, ages 9-11, and illustrated material on
making simple instruments, sound experiments.

JUVENILE, TEEN-AGE AND YOUNG ADULT MAGAZINES

Magazines for both children and teen-agers are listed here. Markets for book-length
juvenile fiction and nonfiction are listed under *Book Publishers*.

JUVENILE MAGAZINES

ADVENTURE—Baptist Sunday School Board, 127 Ninth Ave. North, Nashville,
Tenn. 37203.
Fiction, 900 to 1,200 words; articles, up to 900 words; puzzles, cartoons, and
poems, up to 16 lines, to appeal to children 8 to 11. Also articles with photos. Pays
2½¢ a word, on acceptance.

AMERICAN RED CROSS YOUTH NEWS—American National Red Cross, Washington, D. C. 20006.
600-word stories for primary children and 1,000- to 1,200-word stories for children through sixth grade, on children of other lands, holidays, contemporary U.S. children. Articles of 1,200 words on science, nature, and social studies topics. Pays $50 to $125, on acceptance.

BROWNIE READER—830 Third Ave., New York, N. Y. 10022. Elisabeth Brower, Editor-in-Chief.
Uses fiction, 500 words; articles, to 500 words with photos, and poetry, to 30 lines, of interest to 6-, 7- and 8-year-old Brownie Girl Scouts. Pays to $25, on publication.

CHILD LIFE—1100 Waterway Blvd., Indianapolis, Indiana 46202. E. Catherine Cummins, Editor.
For children 7 to 12. Fiction to 900 words. Beginner reading material, 400 to 500 words. Games, puzzles, projects, etc. Short plays for classroom and living room production. Pays approximately 3¢ a word for stories and 25¢ a line for verse, on publication. Reports in 8 to 10 weeks.

CHILDREN'S PLAYMATE MAGAZINE—1100 Waterway Blvd., Indianapolis, Ind. 46202. Mrs. Beth W. Thomas, Editor.
For children ages 3 to 8. Short stories, to 600 words. Also poetry, beginning science, puzzles, easy projects. Pays about 3¢ a word, on publication.

THE CHRISTIAN SCIENCE MONITOR—One Norway St., Boston, Mass. 02115.
Uses a story of 600 to 900 words for children 10 years and under, once a week. Pays $30. No serials. Address "Editor for Children."

CLIMB—Box 2499, Fifth and Chestnut Sts., Anderson, Ind. 46011.
For children ages 8 to 11. Character-building and religious stories, 900 to 1,200 words; fiction and nonfiction. Pays $7.50 per 1,000 words, on acceptance.

CRICKET—Open Court Publishing Co., Box 599, La Salle, Ill. 61301.
Fiction and articles, 200 to 2,000 words, poems, plays, crafts, etc., for ages 6 to 10. Pays 25¢ a word for prose, $3 a line for poetry.

CRUSADER—1548 Poplar Ave., Memphis, Tenn. 38104. Lee Hollaway, Editor.
Brotherhood Commission of the Southern Baptist Convention. Uses material of interest to boys ages 6 to 11: fiction and nonfiction (especially hobbies, games, handicrafts) to 1,000 words. Pays 2¢ a word, on acceptance.

DISCOVERY—Light and Life Press, Winona Lake, Ind. 46590.
Fiction, 1,800 to 2,000 words, for 8- to 11-year-olds. Also how-to-do-it features, 500 to 1,000 words, and verse. Seasonal material wanted. Pays 2¢ a word for prose; 25¢ a line for poetry, after acceptance.

EBONY JR!—1820 South Michigan Ave., Chicago, Ill. 60616. John H. Johnson, Editor.
Factual articles, 400 to 1,500 words for children aged 6 to 12, dealing with blacks in science, and biographies and stories about childhoods of prominent blacks. Realistic, well-plotted action fiction dealing with children in black communities and children's emotional growth. Also fantasy, humor, mystery, West Indian and African folklore. Welcomes rhyming verse, clearly and simply written skits, short plays, puzzles, projects, riddles and jokes, games that feature aspects of black-heritage. Material should not include death or violence. Pays on acceptance. Include stamped, self-addressed envelope.

EXPLORE—Christian Board of Publication, Box 179, St. Louis, Mo. 63166.
For grades 1 and 2. Short stories to 600 words, and poems, to 12 lines. Also feature articles, to 400 words (include source of information). Pays on acceptance. For specifications and sample copies, send 25¢.

FIVE/SIX—201 Eighth Ave. South, Nashville, Tenn. 37203.

For fifth and sixth graders. Can use stories up to 1,250 words. Some poetry. Pays from 2¢ to 4¢ a word for stories; $1 a line for poetry.

THE FRIEND—50 East North Temple, Salt Lake City, Utah 84150. Mrs. Lucile C. Reading, Managing Editor.
Stories for children to 1,000 words, with character-building ideals; suspense, adventure, holiday, humor. "Tiny tot" stories, 300 to 500 words. Needs stories and verse for holidays, younger children, girls. Payment for fiction is up to 4¢ a word; for poetry, 25¢ to 50¢ a line, on acceptance; occasional bonuses.

FUN FOR MIDDLERS—American Baptist Board of Education and Publication, Valley Forge, Pa. 19481. Gracie Adkins, Editor.
Fiction, to 1,200 words, for children 8 to 9. Biographies, articles on current issues, reports on noteworthy activities of children. Also poetry, projects, puzzles, cartoons. Pays up to 2¢ a word, on acceptance.

HIGHLIGHTS FOR CHILDREN—803 Church St., Honesdale, Pa. 18431. Garry Cleveland Myers, Editor-in-Chief.
Stories for children, 3 to 12, under 1,000 words. Humor, struggle, self-sacrifice for an ideal preferred. Particularly needs easy-to-read stories (400 to 600 words) with strong plot. Also urban settings or characters from American ethnic groups. Overstocked on verse. Pays 6¢ a word and up, on acceptance.

HUMPTY DUMPTY'S MAGAZINE—52 Vanderbilt Ave., New York, N. Y. 10017.
Uses three kinds of stories: (1) Picture stories for Beginning Readers, usually on assignment. (2) Read-Aloud Stories: typical picture book stories up to 900 words. Third- or fourth-grade vocabulary. (3) Tell-Me Stories, designed to be read by the parent and retold to the child, up to 1,000 words. Pays $50, on acceptance.

JACK AND JILL—1110 Waterway Blvd., Indianapolis, Ind. 46202.
Fiction from 300 to 1,500 words, factual articles, puzzles, plays, songs, games, riddles and jokes, poems and creative activities. Reports in about three weeks. Pays on publication.

JET CADET—8121 Hamilton Ave., Cincinnati, Ohio 45231. Dana Eynon, Editor.
Sunday school weekly for children 9 to 12. Christian character-building (not "preachy") stories, 900 to 1,200 words, of young teen-agers in situations involving mystery, animals, sports, adventure, school, travel, relationships with parents and friends. Two-part serials to 2,000 words. Articles, 400 to 500 words, on hobbies, animals, nature, life in other lands, sports, seasonal subjects, with religious emphasis. Poems, to 12 lines. Puzzles, cartoons. Pays 25¢ to 35¢ a line for poetry, up to 1½¢ a word for stories and articles, on acceptance.

JUNIOR DISCOVERIES—6401 The Paseo, Kansas City, Mo. 64131. Maureen H. Box, Editor.
For Sunday School children 9 to 11. Fiction, 1,000 to 1,400 words, with Christian emphasis, Bible background. Features, 500 to 800 words, on nature, travel, history, çrafts, science, devotional, biographical topics; illustrations; cartoons. Poetry, 4 to 20 lines. Pays 1½¢ per word for prose, 10¢ a line for poetry, on acceptance.

JUNIOR TRAILS—1445 Boonville Ave., Springfield, Mo. 65802. Dorothy Morris, Editor.
For boys and girls 10 to 12. Stories, 1,200 to 1,500 words, showing how to put Bible principles into action in everyday living. Pays on acceptance.

KIDSTUFF—3000 Winton Rd. South, Rochester, N. Y. 14623.
Articles, 500 to 1,500 words, on children's art and craft projects, nature, and science, and children involved in unusual activities. Color photo-features on places of interest to young readers. Pays $50 to $100.

THE KINDERGARTNER—Graded Press, 201 Eighth Ave. South, Nashville, Tenn. 37202. Mrs. Ernestine Calhoun, Editor.
Methodist church-related story paper for kindergarten. Length, to 300 words. Poems. Payment on acceptance.

MERRY-GO-ROUND—Scholastic Magazines, Inc., 50 West 44th St., New York, N. Y. 10036.
Stories of about 280 words, with early 2nd grade vocabulary; or stories of about 375 words, for upper 2nd grade vocabulary. Must have style, real plot, strong appeal. Most fiction done on assignment. Submit sample stories. Pays from $75 to $100, on acceptance. Address, Manuscript Editor.

MORE—Baptist Sunday School Board, 127 Ninth Ave. North, Nashville, Tenn. 37203. Muriel F. Blackwell, Editor.
Stories, to 500 words, for beginning readers. Also, nonfiction articles, of interest to children, to 500 words. Needs simple puzzles, poems up to 16 lines. Pays 2½¢ a word, on acceptance.

NEWS EXPLORER—Scholastic Magazines, 50 West 44th St., New York, N. Y. 10036.
Stories, 900 to 1,000 words, for children 9 or 10. Suspenseful two-part serials, to 2,000 words. Topics: boys and girls of today or other times, other peoples, school, hobbies, humor, pets, mysteries, legends, adventure, etc. Well plotted. Pays from $75, on acceptance. Address Manuscript Editor.

NEWSTIME—Scholastic Magazines, 50 West 44th St., New York, N. Y. 10036.
Stories for children ages 11 to 12, 600 words; 1,200 to 1,500 words; 2,000 words. Well plotted, thought-provoking, crammed with incident—humor, mystery, family life, folklore, etc., but no war, violence, dating, obvious moralizing, or involved psychological problems. Pays $50 and up. Address Manuscript Editor.

NEWS TRAILS—Scholastic Magazines, 50 West 44th St., New York, N. Y. 10036.
For children 8 and 9. Stories from 800 to 1,000 words about boys and girls of today or of other times, in our country or in other lands. Subjects: school situations, pets, holidays, and general children's interests. Should use average 3rd grade vocabulary. Action and dialogue should move story. Pays from $75, on acceptance. Address Manuscript Editor.

NURSERY DAYS—Graded Press, 201 Eighth Ave. South, Nashville, Tenn. 37202. Miss Evelyn Andre, Editor.
Methodist story paper for nursery children, 2 and 3 years old. Ideas mainly on church, family, friends, God's world, Bible, Jesus. Length, 300 words. Poems. Pays on acceptance.

OUR LITTLE FRIEND—Pacific Press Publishing Assoc., 1350 Villa St., Mountain View, Calif. 94040. Louis Schutter, Editor.
Seventh-day Adventist weekly for children 2 to 6. Stories, 800 to 1,500 words, "slanted to our religious standards." Also verse, 8 to 12 lines, puzzles, photos, drawings. Pays 1¢ a word for stories, 10¢ a line for verse.

PRIMARY TREASURE—Pacific Press Publishing Assoc., 1350 Villa St., Mountain View, Calif. 94040. Louis Schutter, Editor.
Seventh-day Adventist weekly for children 7 to 9. Stories, 800 to 1,500 words; "must be slanted to our religious standards." Verse (8 to 12 lines), puzzles, photos, drawings. Query on serials. Pays 1¢ a word for stories, 10¢ a line for verse.

QUEST—Christian Board of Publication, Box 179, St. Louis, Mo. 63166. Lee Miller, Editor.
For grades 5 and 6. Short stories, to 1,200 words, and verse, to 20 lines. Also feature articles, to 600 words (include source). Pays on acceptance. Sample copies 25¢.

RANGER RICK'S NATURE MAGAZINE—Publisher's Services, Inc., 1518 Walnut St., Philadelphia, Pa. 19102. Trudy Dye Farrand, Editor.
Articles, to 900 words, that will help young people enjoy nature. Material must be related to nature, natural science, ecology, or conservation. Pays from $5 to $200, shortly before publication.

ROADRUNNER—American Baptist Board of Education and Publication, Valley Forge, Pa. 19481. Nina M. Booth, Editor.
Stories, biographies, articles, 200 to 700 words, for children 6 to 7. Also puzzles, poetry, projects welcome. Pays up to 2¢ a word, on acceptance.

STONE SOUP—Box 83, Santa Cruz, Calif. 95063. William Rubel, Editor.
Prints stories, poems, plays, book reviews, games, and illustrations by children under 13. Manuscripts should be in original form; dictated works should be indicated as such. Some adult work. Pays in copies.

STORY FRIENDS—Mennonite Publishing House, Scottdale, Pa. 15683. Alice Hershberger, Editor.
Story paper for children 4 to 8, containing stories which relate faith to everyday experiences; stories on family, school, church life; stories about nature, special days, friendship and building love for all races. Length: 400 to 900 words. Pays up to 2¢ a word for first rights, on acceptance.

SUMMERTIME—Scholastic Magazines, 50 West 44th St., New York, N. Y. 10036.
Stories for children ages 11 to 13, 750 to 800 words; 1,700 words; 2,800 words. Should be well ploted and filled with incident. May be mysteries, humorous, deal with sports, family life, folklore, etc., but no war, violence, dating, obvious moralizing. Query for serial ideas. Pays $50 and up, on acceptance. Address Manuscript Editor.

THREE/FOUR—201 Eighth Ave. South, Nashville, Tenn. 37203. Betty M. Buerki, Editor.
Weekly magazine for third and fourth graders. Short stories of about 1,000 words, poetry, puzzles, quizzes. Short informational articles. Pays 4¢ a word for stories; 50¢ to $1 a line for poetry.

TRAILS—Box 788, Wheaton, Ill. 60187. Carole Sherman, Editor.
Published by Pioneer Girls for girls, 8 to 12. Short stories and articles, up to 2,000 words. Looking for high-caliber writing consistent with Christian teaching. Pays up to $35, on acceptance. Also uses photos and cartoons.

VACATION FUN—Scholastic Magazines, 50 West 44th St., New York, N. Y. 10036.
Stories for children 8 to 10, to 1,000 words; longer if they have enough suspense to be divided into two parts. Stories should be well plotted, and within the average 3rd and 4th grader's vocabulary. May be about boys and girls of today or other times, pets; also adventure, legends, etc. Pays from $75, on acceptance. Address Manuscript Editor.

WEE WISDOM—Unity Village, Mo. 64063. Thomas N. Hopper, Editor.
Character-building magazine for boys and girls. Wants short, lively stories; science, nature stories, projects; creative craft ideas (especially for boys). Avoid sermonizing.

WHENEVER WHATEVER—American Baptist Board of Education and Publication, Valley Forge, Pa. 19481. Gracie Adkins, Editor.
Fiction, to 1,800 words, for children 10 to 11. Biographies, reports on noteworthy

activities of boys and girls, articles on current events. Also poetry, How-to-Do-It projects, puzzles, cartoons. Pays up to 2¢ a word, on acceptance.

WONDER TIME—6401 The Paseo, Kansas City, Mo. 64131. Elizabeth B. Jones, Editor.
For Sunday school boys and girls under nine. Fiction, 200 to 750 words. Christian emphasis. Features, 200 to 500 words: nature, travel, simple crafts, Bible background. Poetry, 4 to 16 lines. Payment on acceptance: prose, 2¢ per word; verse, 12½¢ per line and up.

WOODMEN OF THE WORLD MAGAZINE—1700 Farnam St., Omaha, Nebr. 68102. Leland A. Larson, Editor.
Stories, 400 to 1,200 words, of interest to boys and girls 8 to 19. Pays 2¢ a word, on acceptance.

YOUNG CRUSADER—1730 Chicago Ave., Evanston, Ill. 60201. Lillian Luney, Editor.
Character-building stories, 600 to 850 words, for readers ages 6 to 12. Pays ½¢ a word, on acceptance.

YOUNG WORLD—1100 Waterway Blvd., Box 567B, Indianapolis, Ind. 46206. Ellen Taggart Tull, Editor.
Stories and articles appealing to boys and girls 10 to 14; some verse. Length and subject matter flexible. Needs articles dealing with contemporary situations—teenagers in community action, in sports, in entertainment, etc. Also articles on popular sports and entertainment personalities; on fashion, beauty, school and family, music, crafts. Pays 2¢ to 3¢ a word for prose, $10 and up for poetry, $2.50 each for black-and-white photos used with articles, $5 for color slides or transparencies, on publication.

TEEN-AGE, YOUNG ADULT MAGAZINES

ACCENT ON YOUTH—201 Eighth Ave. South, Nashville, Tenn. 37203. Margaret Barnhart, Editor.
Short stories to 2,500 words; articles and photos: nature lore, biography, camping, family life, hobbies, religion, photo features, etc. Pays 3¢ a word and up, on acceptance.

ALIVE!—Christian Board of Publication, Beaumont and Pine Blvd., St. Louis, Mo. 63166. Darrell Faires, Editor.
Fiction, 1,800 to 2,200 words, appealing to junior high youth. Articles, to 1,500 words; first-person articles on outstanding youth, projects and activities, with photos. Cartoons for teens. Also puzzles, word games, brain-teasers, and poetry to 16 lines. Pays 1½¢ per word for fiction and articles, extra for photos and illustrations. Pays 25¢ per line for poetry. Query for articles. Sample copy 25¢.

AMERICAN GIRL—830 Third Ave., New York, N. Y. 10022. Pat di Sernia, Editor.
Published by the Girl Scouts for all girls 10 to 16. Nonfiction, 500 to 1,500 words, covering teen-age interests. Fiction, 1,000 to 3,000 words, and two- to six-part serials. Mystery and adventure stories, tales of school and family life, sports, careers, friendship and romance, etc. Pays on acceptance. Query for articles.

AMERICAN NEWSPAPER BOY—915 Carolina Ave., N.W., Winston-Salem, N. C. 27101. Charles Moester, Editor.
Light fiction, mystery, character-building and adventure stories for newsboys, 14 to 17 (1,800 to 2,000 words). Also inspirational articles, editorials, articles on newspaper routes. Payment varies; normally $10 to $25.

BOYS' LIFE—North Brunswick, N. J. 08902. Robert E. Hood, Editor.
For boys 10 to 17. Short stories, 800 to 2,500 words. Pays high rates, on acceptance. Nonfiction: Short articles, 750–1,200 words; payment, $150–$300. Feature articles: 2,500 words; payment, $500–$1,000, depending upon quality of writing and reputation of contributor. Photo essays: black-and-white photos, $100 per page minimum; color photos, $200 per page minimum. Query. "Information for Authors" and sample copy available on request. Limited market at present.

CAMPUS LIFE—Box 419, Wheaton, Ill. 60187. Harold Myra, Editor.
Slanted to 16 to 19 age group. Fiction and articles, about 1,500 words; stories of outstanding Christian young people; factual stories on teen-age life; how-to-do-it pieces. Pays 2¢ a word and up. Most needed: photo stories of teens in wholesome, unique activities. Also *teen-slanted* cartoons. Query—most articles assigned.

CATALYST—Christian Board of Publication, Beaumont and Pine Blvd., St. Louis, Mo. 63166. Jerry O'Malley, Editor.
Articles on religion or social issues, or what high school youth are doing in these areas. Fiction, 1,500 to 2,000 words, for intelligent teens. Uses poetry to 16 lines about problems of the day. Also cartoons and photos. Humor, especially satire, will be appreciated. Pays 1½¢ a word and up for prose, 25¢ a line for poetry, $6 and up for cartoons. Sample copy 25¢.

CO-ED—Scholastic Magazines, 50 West 44th St., New York, N. Y. 10036.
Stories to 5,000 words for girls 14 to 18, dealing with problems of contemporary teen-agers: home, family, love, personal relationships, boy-girl situations. Humor welcome. Fall, winter, or spring settings preferred. Pays from $150, on acceptance. Address Manuscript Editor.

CONQUEST—6401 The Paseo, Kansas City, Mo. 64131. Paul Miller, Editor.
A denominational magazine for teen-agers. Religious articles, short stories, and verse. Fiction, to 2,500 words; nonfiction, 500 to 1,200 words. Poetry, to 20 lines. Pays 1½¢ per word, on acceptance.

CONTACT—44 East Franklin St., Room 302, Huntington, Ind. 46750. Stanley Peters, Editor.
United Brethren in Christ. Christ-centered fiction and articles for teens and adults, true stories of notable Christians, up to 1,500 words. Pays ¾¢ a word for first rights; ⅔¢ a word for second rights.

ENCOUNTER—Sunday School Magazines, The Wesleyan Church, Box 2000, Marion, Ind. 46952.
For older teen-agers, ages 15 to 18. Uses fiction, 800 to 2,500 words, with Christian emphasis. Serials, 6 to 8 chapters, 800 to 2,500 words per chapter. Nonfiction, 500 to 1,500 words—nature, travel, history, science, devotional, informational. Poems 4 to 16 lines. Pays 2¢ per word for quality prose, 25¢ per line for poetry.

ETC.—6401 The Paseo, Kansas City, Mo. 64131, Paul Miller, Editor.
A denominational monthly for the 18- to 24-year-old. Religious articles, 500 to 1,200 words. Poetry to 20 lines. Pays 1½¢ a word, on acceptance.

EVENT—Baptist Sunday School Board, 127 Ninth Ave. North, Nashville, Tenn. 37203. Linda Lawson, Editor.
For Southern Baptist youth, 12 to 17. Stories, 1,000 to 3,000 words, and articles, to 1,500 words. Contemporary poetry, any length. Pays 2½¢ a word for all rights, on acceptance for prose, slightly more for poetry.

FACE-TO-FACE—201 Eighth Ave. South, Nashville, Tenn. 37202. Kenneth Winston, Editor.
United Methodist. Fiction, 2,500 to 3,000 words, on problems and concerns of older

teens. No straight moral fiction. Illustrated articles, 1,500 to 1,800 words. Pays 2¢ a word and up, on acceptance. Query.

FOR TEENS ONLY—235 Park Ave. South, New York, N. Y. 10003. Rena Adler, Editor.
Teen-slanted short stories, to 4,000 words, including mysteries. Pays $50, on acceptance.

FREE WAY—Scripture Press Publications, 1825 College Ave., Wheaton, Ill. 60187. Anne Harrington, Editor.
For ages 15-19. Nonfiction, to 2,000 words, about young people who have experienced a dramatic, life-changing encounter with Christ, or overcome danger, frustration, etc. by relying on faith in Christ. Photos help. Query first. Only top-notch fiction. Pays up to $60, upon acceptance; more for photos. Samples on request.

GRIT—Williamsport, Pa. 17701. Kenneth D. Loss, Feature Editor.
Articles, black-and-white photos and color transparencies on personalities and small towns for Teen pages. Pays on acceptance.

HICALL—1445 Boonville Ave., Springfield, Mo. 65802. Dorothy Morris, Editor.
Fiction and nonfiction with evangelical emphasis, for young people, 12 to 21. Fiction, 1,200 to 1,500 words. Nonfiction, 500 to 1,000 words: Christian biography, true stories from mission fields, features slanted to teen-agers. Pays on acceptance.

HIGH—Harvest Publications, 1233 Central, Evanston, Ill. 60201. David Olson, Editor.
Illustrated feature articles (on evangelical persons and activities), 500 to 1,500 words, plus photos. Evangelical Christian fiction, 1,200 to 1,500 words, for teenagers. Query advisable. Samples and information available on *High* and other agegroup papers. Pays 3¢ a word and up, on acceptance. Photos, $4 and up.

INGENUE—See *The New Ingenue.*

JUNIOR SCHOLASTIC—Scholastic Magazines, Inc., 50 West 44th St., New York, N. Y. 10036.
For grades 7 and 8 (ages 12 to 14). Fiction: 1,000 to 2,000-word original plays and stories; occasional nonfiction features, 500 to 2,000 words, about young teenagers: hobbies, community activities, various achievements. Pays from $50 to $100, and up, on acceptance. Address Manuscript Editor. Query.

LETTERMAN—Box 804, Wheaton, Ill. 60187. Paul Nyberg, Editor.
Local news and features, sports how-to's, 500 to 2,000 words, on high school athletes, as well as short stories on sports, 1,500 words. Photos of athletes and school needed with articles. Also anecdotes, fillers on sports. Pays by arrangement.

LIGHTED PATHWAY—1080 Montgomery Ave., Cleveland, Tenn. 37311. Clyne W. Buxton, Editor.
Uses religious nonfiction, 400 to 700 words. Pays ½¢ per word, on acceptance; $7.50 for photos used for covers; $1.50 for photos used with articles.

LITERARY CAVALCADE—Scholastic Magazines, 50 West 44th St., New York, N. Y. 10036.
Fiction (reprint only), 1,500 to 3,500 words, on an adult level, with universal themes. "Must be some *story*" which may be about young people. No mood pieces or high school romance. Pays from $150.

THE NATIONAL FUTURE FARMER—Box 15130, Alexandria, Va. 22309. Wilson Carnes, Editor.
Written for high school students of vocational agriculture, average age 17. Nonfiction, to 1,000 words, on activities of the Future Farmers of America, new developments in agriculture, and leadership and citizenship subjects. Pays up to 4¢ a word, on acceptance. Cartoons, $7.50.

THE NEW INGENUE—635 Madison Ave., New York, N. Y. 10022. Joanna Brown, Editor.
Wants adult fiction for teen-agers, dealing with their problems and interests. Also articles—controversial, news, psychological, entertainment—relating to contemporary teens. Pays $100 to $500 for articles and $175 to $400 for fiction, on acceptance. Query.

ON THE LINE—610 Walnut Ave., Scottdale, Pa. 15683. Helen Alderfer, Editor.
Weekly story paper for children 9 to 14. Stories and articles, 750 to 1,000 words, that help children see God at work in the world around them. Poetry, quizzes, puzzles, and cartoons. Pays up to 2¢ a word, less for second rights. Sample copies and "When You Write" leaflet free on request.

PROBE—1548 Poplar Ave., Memphis, Tenn. 38104. Mike Davis, Editor.
Brotherhood Commission of the Southern Baptist Convention. Uses material of interest to boys, ages 12 to 17: fiction and nonfiction (especially hobbies, games, handicrafts) to 1,000 words. Pays 2¢ a word, on acceptance.

REACHOUT—Light and Life Press, Winona Lake, Ind. 46590.
Uses two short stories an issue, between 1,800 and 2,500 words. Also uses human interest, hobby, and career articles from 800 to 1,500 words, fillers and occasional poetry. All fiction should be religious in tone. Seasonal material wanted. Pays 2¢ per word.

REFLECTION—Box 788, Wheaton, Ill. 60187. Carole Sherman, Editor.
Published by Pioneer Girls for girls, 13 to 18. Short stories and articles, up to 2,000 words. Looking for high-caliber writing consistent with Christian teaching. Pays up to $35, on acceptance. Also uses photos and cartoons.

SCHOLASTIC SCOPE—Scholastic Magazines, 50 West 44th St., New York, N. Y. 10036.
For 4th to 6th grade reading level; 15 to 18 age level. Fiction, 400 to 1,200 words; plays to 3,000 words, on problems of urban students, relationships (inter-racial, adult-teen, employer-employee), etc. Strives for realism, action, depth of characterization. Also realistic stories from viewpoint of minority member; not necessarily about race relations. Wants action stories, but not crime fiction. Pays from $150. Also articles, 400 to 800 words, on youths with jobs not requiring a college education, and open to minority groups. Include requirements, pay, where to write for information, etc. Articles on teens who have overcome great odds also welcome. Pays $50 per printed page, $10 per photo used.

SCHOLASTIC SEARCH—50 West 44th St., New York, N. Y. 10036.
For readers 14 to 17 with 4th to 6th grade reading level. Fiction and articles, 400 to 1,200 words, plays to 3,000 words, on relationships between people, in family, job, and home. Pays $100 to $150. See issues before submitting.

SCHOLASTIC VOICE—Scholastic Magazines, 50 West 44th St., New York, N. Y. 10036.
For readers 14 through 17. Stories, plays, 1,500 to 3,000 words; short-shorts, 500 to 1,000 words, about teen-agers, strong on plot and characterization. Adventure, mystery, science fiction, family situations, sports, teen-age problems. Avoid formula stories about puppy love. Plays should be suitable both for reading aloud and stage presentation. Pays from $150 ($100 for short-shorts), on acceptance. Address Manuscript Editor.

SCIENCE WORLD—Scholastic Magazines, 50 West 44th St., New York, N. Y. 10036.
For grades 7 through 12. Overstocked at present.

SEVENTEEN—320 Park Ave., New York, N. Y. 10022. Babette Rosmond, Fiction Editor.
Well-written fiction, adult in its techniques and conception, but limited to situations involving young people, adolescent "growing up" experiences. Pays good rates, on acceptance.

STRAIGHT—8121 Hamilton Ave., Cincinnati, Ohio 45231. Mrs. Bee Nelson, Editor.
Fiction: character-building stories, about 1,500 words, with teen-age characters. Possible subjects: Christian athletes, church work, school incidents, family situations, teen problems, mystery, etc. Immediate need for articles emphasizing Christian approach to current events and problems. Feature articles, 1,000 to 1,200 words. Pays up to $35.

'TEEN MAGAZINE—8831 Sunset Blvd., Los Angeles, Calif. 90069. Carole Ann Tucker, Managing Editor.
Good picture-feature stories for teen-agers, under 1,500 words. Fiction, 2,500 to 4,000 words, teen-age slanted; pays $150 and up.

TEENS TODAY—6401 The Paseo, Kansas City, Mo. 64131. Wesley Tracy, Editor.
Contemporary, hard-hitting stories and articles to challenge teens. Also articles on central truths of Christian faith, biographical pieces. Fiction to 2,500 words; articles to 1,500 words; some poetry. Pays 2¢ per word, on acceptance. Reports in four weeks.

UNION GOSPEL PRESS—Box 6059, Cleveland, Ohio 44101.
Publishers of Sunday school literature. Factual articles with a religious emphasis for teens and young adults, 925 to 1,425 words. Also short pieces, 300 words. Pays 2¢ a word. Samples on request.

VENTURE—Christian Service Brigade, P.O. Box 150, Wheaton, Ill. 60187. Daniel C. Jessen, Editor-in-Chief.
Occasionally uses fiction directed to boys 8 to 18. Other features designed to help boys develop a Bible-based life style are usually used. Biographical stories and incidents of Christian men and/or boys considered. Preferred length: 1,000 to 1,500 words. Pays $25 to $100 per article, on publication.

WIND—Box 2000, Marion, Ind. 46952. David L. Keith, Executive Editor.
Newspaper published by The Wesleyan Church. Religious or educational articles, to 1,000 words, for teens. Pays 1¢ a word, $2.50 each for photos and cartoons.

WORLD OVER—426 West 58th St., New York, N. Y. 10019. Ezekiel Schloss, Dr. Morris Epstein, Editors.
Fiction of Jewish interest, historical or contemporary, aimed at children 9 to 14. Jewish content (holidays, etc.) essential. Pays 4¢ to 5¢ a word, on acceptance, for a story of 600 or 1,200 words; $175 to $225 for a serial (5 chapters, 1,200 words per chapter). More for exceptional material. Query.

YOUNG AMBASSADOR—Box 82808, Lincoln, Nebr. 68501. Ruth Johnson Jay, Associate Editor.
Fiction, about 1,800 words, with spiritual tone, but not preachy, for young teenagers. Pays 1½¢ a word.

YOUNG JUDAEAN—817 Broadway, New York, N. Y. 10003. Doris B. Gold, Editor.
"Especially for Inters" pages, for readers 12 to 14, uses news of Jewish music on records, plays, and Israel-U.S.A. current topics. Also poems and humor of Jewish youth vs. parents. Pays 2¢ a word; rates arranged for humor and poetry. Authors' copies 25¢. Study before submitting.

YOUNG MISS—52 Vanderbilt Ave., New York, N. Y. 10017. Rubie Saunders, Editor.
Stories, 2,000 to 2,300 words; articles on sports, careers, crafts, personal problems, 1,000 to 2,000 words. For girls 10 to 14. Query on articles. Also interested in novelettes, about 6,000 to 6,500 words. Pays $50 to $100 for short fiction, $100 to $150 for novelettes, $10 to $50 for articles on acceptance.

YOUTH ALIVE—1445 Boonville Ave., Springfield, Mo. 65802.
For mid- and late teens. Photo features, photos, interviews, forums, biographical features, reports on outstanding Christian youth, how-to-do-it features, fiction (some), satire, humor, anecdotes, poems, puzzles, news, motivational articles, seasonal material, personal experiences. Length: 800 to 1,000 words. Pays 1¢ per word, on acceptance. Free sample copy and writer's guide available on request.

YOUTH IN ACTION—Winona Lake, Ind. 46590.
Official publication of Free Methodist Youth. Emphasis on guidance in Christian living for teen-agers. Needs fiction, 500 to 1,500 words, and nonfiction, 500 to 1,500 words. Also needs articles to encourage and strengthen servicemen. Buys good quality, black-and-white photos. Pays 1¢ a word.

REPRINT MAGAZINES

If a writer has sold an article or story to a magazine and retains the reprint rights, he may submit the piece to a reprint publication. The following list gives a few of these reprint or digest magazines.

Many of the smaller and more specialized magazines listed elsewhere as markets for unpublished material occasionally buy reprint rights. A writer can submit a copy of a published article or story to another magazine, together with information about when and where the material has been published, if he is certain that he has the permission of the original publisher.

CATHOLIC DIGEST—P.O. Box 3090, St. Paul, Minn. 55101.

CHILDREN'S DIGEST—52 Vanderbilt Ave., New York, N. Y. 10017.

READER'S DIGEST—Pleasantville, N. Y. 10570.

TELEVISION AND PLAYS

This section includes markets for dramatic material: television, publishers of plays for the amateur stage, community and college theatres, and literary magazines that occasionally buy plays.

Changes are taking place continually in the television world. New shows are always being tried out; old shows go off the air or become inactive script markets. Therefore, the following list of programs should not be considered complete or permanent.

If the address of a particular program is not available, write to the program's Script Editor, in care of the local television station program director, or to the story editor of the national network televising the program. It is always wise to query first, especially in the case of a new program or a program that has not definitely stated it is buying free-lance scripts.

There are relatively few markets for free-lance material in radio at the present time. For full information, write to the major networks listed below.

Publishers of plays for school, community, and church groups offer a hospitable market for free-lance writers. This field has rewards and pleasures of its own, and playwrights who are interested in writing for television and the professional theatre will find the amateur stage a good proving ground.

A number of community theatres, college dramatics groups, and little theatres are actively in the market for plays by free-lance writers for stage production. Payment is seldom great, but usually college and community theatres buy only the right to produce a play and all further rights revert to the author.

As a rule, Broadway producers will not read plays sent in by an unknown playwright. Writers with plays they wish to have considered for Broadway production should query one of the recognized literary agents listed on page 808.

Several literary, university and "little" magazines are occasionally interested in publishing plays. They are not an active play market because of space limitations; dramatic material can appear only infrequently if at all. However, they may be good markets for experimental drama, or plays which have little chance of appearing in more popular media.

MAJOR TELEVISION AND RADIO NETWORKS

AMERICAN BROADCASTING CO., INC.—1330 Avenue of the Americas, New York, N. Y. 10019.

COLUMBIA BROADCASTING SYSTEM—51 West 52nd St., New York, N. Y. 10019.

NATIONAL BROADCASTING CO.—RCA Bldg., 30 Rockefeller Plaza, New York, N. Y. 10020.

PUBLIC BROADCASTING SERVICE—955 L'Enfant Plaza North, S.W., Washington, D. C. 20024.

TELEVISION PROGRAMS

ADAM-12—*Network:* NBC-TV. *Length:* 30 minutes.
Script: Police drama about Los Angeles patrol car officers Peter Malloy and Jim Reed. Scripts are developed by writers working on assignment with officers of the L.A. Police Dept. *Contact:* Bryan Joseph, Executive Story Consultant, *Adam-12* Office, Universal Studios, Universal City, Calif. 91608.

ALL IN THE FAMILY—*Network:* CBS-TV. *Length:* 30 minutes.
Script: Situation comedy series about an opinionated middle-class husband and father and his family. Scripts through recognized agents only. *Contact:* Norman Lear, Producer, Tandem Productions, CBS Television City, 7800 Beverly Blvd., Los Angeles, Calif. 90036.

BARNABY JONES—*Network:* CBS-TV. *Length:* 1 hour.
Script: Suspense drama starring Buddy Ebsen as a veteran private investigator working in Los Angeles and Southern California. Scripts on assignment through recognized agents only. *Contact:* Gerald Sanford, Associate Producer, QM Productions, Samuel Goldwyn Studios, 1041 N. Formosa, Los Angeles, Calif. 90046.

BOB NEWHART SHOW—*Network:* CBS-TV. *Length:* 30 minutes.
Script: Situation comedy about a psychologist in Chicago and his wife. Scripts on assignment through recognized agents only. Contact: Tom Patchett and Jay Tarses, Story Editors, MTM Enterprises, Inc., CBS Studio Center, 7800 Beverly Blvd., Los Angeles, Calif. 90038.

THE BRADY BUNCH—*Network:* ABC-TV. *Length:* 30 minutes.
Script: Family comedy about a widower with three sons, a widow with three daughters, and their amusing maid. Scripts through recognized agents only. *Contact:* Story Editor, Paramount TV, 5451 Marathon, Hollywood, Calif. 90038.

CANADIAN BROADCASTING CORPORATION—National Script Dept., P.O. Box 500, Postal Terminal A, Toronto, Ontario, Canada.
Will consider quality submissions from anywhere, preferably in dramatic form, TV drama, 30 and 90 minutes in length, and radio drama, one hour in length; may be mysteries, melodramas, psychological dramas, family situation comedies, or plays based on important current themes. Fee is by individual negotiation.

CANNON—*Network:* CBS-TV. *Length:* 1 hour.
Script: Suspense dramas about a former police lieutenant, now a private investigator handling major cases with a variety of interests. Scripts on assignment through recognized agents only. *Contact:* Paul Playdon, Associate Producer, or David Moessinger, Script Consultant, QM Productions, Samuel Goldwyn Studios, 1041 North Formosa, Los Angeles, Calif. 90046.

CHASE—*Network:* NBC-TV. *Length:* 1 hour.
Script: Police drama about 3-member undercover unit with special skills. Scripts on assignment through recognized agents only. *Contact:* Robert A. Cinader, Executive Producer, Mark VII, Ltd. with Universal Television, Universal City Studios, Universal City, Calif. 91608.

COLUMBO—See *Sunday Mystery Movie.*

DIRECTIONS—*Network:* ABC-TV. *Length:* 30 minutes.
Scripts: Programs designed to be endorsed by the Catholic, Jewish, Protestant and minority faiths. Themes can be religious, presenting perspectives of the faiths and how they affect people today. Themes can also deal with any current social problems of concern to the various faith groups. Scripts on assignment only. *Contact:* Sid Darion, Manager of Public Affairs, ABC-TV News, 1926 Broadway, New York, N. Y. 10023.

EMERGENCY—*Network:* NBC-TV. *Length:* 1 hour.
Script: Dramas concerning hospital emergency unit and Fire Department's Paramedic Unit. Scripts on assignment through recognized agents only. *Contact:* Executive Producer, Mark VII, Ltd., Universal City Studios, Universal City, Calif. 91608.

THE FBI—*Network:* ABC-TV. *Length:* 1 hour.
Script: Drama series centering on F.B.I. chief in Washington, D. C., whose cases take him and his staff throughout the United States. All stories are based on actual case histories and are assigned to specific writers. *Contact:* Philip Saltzman, Producer, QM Productions, Warner Bros. Studios, 4000 Warner Blvd., Burbank, Calif. 91505.

GUNSMOKE—*Network:* CBS-TV. *Length:* 1 hour.
Script: Western adventure series, using period dramas with straight story lines. Story locale is Dodge City in the 1870's. Scripts must be accompanied by standard release form. *Contact:* Jack Miller, CBS-TV at Studio Center, North Hollywood, Calif. 91604.

HAWAII 5-0—*Network:* CBS-TV. *Length:* 1 hour.
Script: Police adventure, set in Hawaii. Scripts on assignment through recognized agents only. *Contact:* Will Lorin, Story Editor, Leonard Freeman Productions, CBS Studio Center, 4030 Radford, North Hollywood, Calif. 91604.

HEC. RAMSEY—See *Sunday Mystery Movie.*

IRONSIDE—*Network:* NBC-TV. *Length:* 1 hour.
Script: Police drama series, starring Raymond Burr as Ironside, former chief of detectives, now a paraplegic, who serves as consultant to the Detective Bureau of the San Francisco Police Dept., with two police aides and an aide-companion. Scripts are originals on assignment only. Unsolicited scripts are accepted but will be read only if accompanied by standard release form. *Contact:* Albert Aley, Story Editor, Universal City Studios, Universal City, Calif. 91608.

KUNG FU—*Network:* ABC-TV. *Length:* 1 hour.
Script: Drama about a Chinese-American in the frontier West who possesses a knowledge of the oriental philosophy of kung fu. Scripts on assignment through recognized agents. *Contact:* Producer, Warner Brothers TV, 4000 Warner Blvd., Burbank, Calif. 91505.

LOTSA LUCK—*Network:* NBC-TV. *Length:* 30 minutes.
Script: Dom DeLuise plays a Brooklyn bachelor who lives with and supports his mother, sister, and brother-in-law. Scripts on assignment through recognized agents only. *Contact:* Norman Barasch, Carroll Moore, Don Van Atta, Producers, Concept II Productions, NBC Studios, 3000 West Alameda Blvd., Burbank, Calif. 91503.

THE MAGICIAN—*Network:* NBC-TV. *Length:* 1 hour.
Script: Suspense dramas about Anthony Blake, a professional magician who helps people in trouble, using the tricks of his trade. Scripts on assignment through recognized agents only. *Contact:* Story Editor, Paramount Television, 5451 Marathon St., Hollywood, Calif. 90038.

MANNIX—*Network:* CBS-TV. *Length:* 1 hour.
Script: Detective series concerning an independent private investigator with a young widowed secretary. Scripts are originals, on assignment only, through recognized agents. *Contact:* Story Editor, Paramount-TV, 780 North Gower, Los Angeles, Calif. 90038.

THE MARY TYLER MOORE SHOW—*Network:* CBS-TV. *Length:* 30 minutes.
Script: Situation comedy starring Mary Tyler Moore as a 30-year-old career girl working in television, and hoping to get married. Original scripts on assignment through recognized agents only. *Contact:* David Davis, Producer, Lorenzo Music, Story Consultant, CBS Studio Center 4024 Radford Ave., Studio City, Calif. 91604.

M*A*S*H—*Network:* CBS-TV. *Length:* 30 minutes.
Script: Stories of the high-jinks of two accomplished Army surgeons between their duty hours of combat surgery. Scripts on assignment through recognized agents only. *Contact:* Larry Gelbart, Co-Producer, 20th Century-Fox TV, 10201 West Pico, Los Angeles, Calif. 90064.

MAUDE—*Network:* CBS-TV. *Length:* 30 minutes.
Script: Beatrice Arthur plays Maude, who thinks of herself as a liberated woman. Scripts on assignment through recognized agents only. *Contact:* Alan J. Levitt, Story Editor, Tandem Productions, CBS Television City, 7800 Beverly Blvd., Los Angeles, Calif. 90036.

McCLOUD—See *Sunday Mystery Movie.*

McMILLAN AND WIFE—See *Sunday Mystery Movie.*

MEDICAL CENTER—*Network:* CBS-TV. *Length:* 1 hour.
Script: Medical dramas about medicine and research at a large university medical center. Scripts on assignment through recognized agents only. *Contact:* Story Editor, Alfra Productions, MGM Studios, 10202 West Washington Blvd., Culver City, Calif. 90230.

OWEN MARSHALL: COUNSELOR AT LAW—*Network:* ABC-TV. *Length:* 1 hour.
Script: Legal dramas about the cases of a dedicated lawyer. Scripts through recognized agents only. *Contact:* Jerry McNeely, Story Editor, Universal City Studios, 100 Universal City Plaza, Universal City, Calif. 91608.

THE PARTRIDGE FAMILY—*Network:* ABC-TV. *Length:* 30 minutes.
Script: Comedy with music, starring Shirley Jones as widowed mother of five who becomes lead singer of her kids' pop singing group. Original scripts on assignment only, through recognized agents. *Contact:* Larry Rosen, Dale McRaven, Producers, Screen Gems, 1334 North Beachwood, Hollywood, Calif. 90028.,

SANFORD AND SON—*Network:* NBC-TV. *Length:* 30 minutes.
Script: Situation comedy about an aging black junk dealer and his son. Scripts on assignment through recognized agents only. *Contact:* Aaron Ruben, Producer, Tandem Productions, NBC Television, 3000 West Alameda Blvd., Burbank, Calif. 91503.

SHAFT—*Network:* CBS-TV. *Length:* 90 minutes.
Script: Detective series with Richard Roundtree as a flamboyant private detective. Scripts on assignment through recognized agents only. *Contact:* Allan Balter or William Woodfield, Executive Producers, MGM Television, MGM Studios, 10202 West Washington Blvd., Culver City, Calif. 90230.

THE STREETS OF SAN FRANCISCO—*Network:* ABC-TV. *Length:* 1 hour.
Script: Human dramas about people whose problems bring them into contact with the San Francisco Police Department. Scripts on assignment through recognized agents only. *Contact:* Cliff Gould, Producer, or John Wilder, Executive Story Consultant, QM Productions, 4000 Warner Blvd., Burbank, Calif. 91505.

SUNDAY MYSTERY MOVIE—*Network:* NBC-TV. *Length:* 90 minutes.
Script: Four police dramas in rotation: COLUMBO is about a police lieutenant (Peter Falk); McCLOUD stars Dennis Weaver as a New Mexico lawman in New York City; McMILLAN AND WIFE is about a San Francisco Police Commissioner (Rock Hudson); HEC RAMSEY, about a turn-of-the-century gunfighter turned crime fighter (Richard Boone). Scripts on assignment through recognized agents only. *Contact:* Executive Producer, Universal City Studios, 100 Universal City Plaza, Universal City, Calif. 91608.

THE NEW DICK VAN DYKE SHOW—*Network:* CBS-TV. *Length:* 30 minutes.
Script: Situation comedy series about the host of a local TV variety-talk show in Phoenix, Arizona. Scripts through recognized agents only. *Contact:* Story Editor, Cave Creek Enterprises, Graham Studios, Carefree, Arizona 85331.

MARCUS WELBY, M.D.—*Network:* ABC-TV. *Length:* 1 hour.
Script: Medical dramas concerning the practice of a general practitioner in Santa Monica, Calif. Scripts on assignment only, through recognized agents. *Contact:* Story Editor, Universal City Studios, 100 Universal City Plaza, Universal City, Calif. 91608.

THE WALTONS—*Network:* CBS-TV. *Length:* 1 hour.
Script: Family dramas about a mountain family in the Blue Ridge Mountains of Virginia during the depression years. Scripts through recognized agents only. *Contact:* Story Editor, Lorimar Productions, 4000 Warner Blvd., Burbank, Calif. 91505.

THE WONDERFUL WORLD OF DISNEY—*Network:* NBC-TV. *Length:* 1 hour.
Script: Variety of subject matter with elements (not juvenile) which will appeal to all age groups: suspense, adventure, nature comedy. Free-lance and staff-written; agent contact required. *Contact:* William B. Dover, Executive Story Editor, Walt Disney Productions, 500 South Buena Vista St., Burbank, Calif. 91503.

PLAY PUBLISHERS

ART CRAFT PLAY COMPANY—Box 1058, Cedar Rapids, Iowa 52406.
Plays suited for production by high schools, colleges, and little theatres. Those with one interior setting are most popular. Also one-act dramas for contest use. Write for free leaflet "Pointers to Writers of Amateur Plays."

WALTER H. BAKER COMPANY (BAKER'S PLAYS)—100 Summer St., Boston, Mass. 02110.

"You will always find us ready and willing to read any manuscript that is submitted . . . provided it is in the field of dramatics."

CHILD LIFE MAGAZINE—1100 Waterway Blvd., Indianapolis, Ind. 46206.
Short plays, 300 to 700 words, for classroom and living room production, suitable for children 5 to 12. Pays approximately 3¢ a word, on publication.

CHILDREN'S PLAYMATE MAGAZINE—1100 Waterway Blvd., Indianapolis, Ind. 46206.
Short plays, 300 to 700 words, for classroom and living room production, suitable for children 3 to 8. Pays approximately 3¢ a word, on publication.

CONTEMPORARY DRAMA SERVICE—Box 457, Downers Grove, Ill. 60515. Arthur L. Zapel, Editor.
Needs original musical comedy productions suitable for school and church use, and documentary dramas for high school classroom use. Also uses simple comedy and skit material. Current needs include: one-act plays for Lent and Easter; Old Testament Bible story Christian education playlets for grade school level; puppet play scripts. All materials should not exceed 17 typewritten pages in length. Payment by arrangement on a royalty basis.

DRAMATIC PUBLISHING CO.—86 East Randolph St., Chicago, Ill. 60601.
Three-act and one-act plays and musical comedies for amateur groups: children's theatre, high schools, plays for colleges, clubs, churches, summer and community theatres. Any theme is welcome: serious drama, mysteries, comedies, or "just a piece of fluff." The most profitable plays tend to be those that appeal to the high school market. Payment by royalty contract, on acceptance. Free catalog on request.

DRAMATICS—College Hill Station, Box E, Cincinnati, Ohio 45224.
One-act plays of interest to high schools, 2,500 words or less. Photos of productions are helpful. Pays between $15 and $25, on publication.

ELDRIDGE PUBLISHING CO.—Franklin, Ohio 45005.
The type of material used depends on the year's publishing schedule, but always includes three-act and one-act plays for schools, churches, community groups, etc., stunts, novelties, etc. "We are always glad to consider one-act Thanksgiving and three-act Christmas comedies, also one-act Christmas sacred plays and pageants. We prefer to have material submitted between October and early spring, but good manuscripts will be considered any time during the year." Address Kay Myerly, Editorial Department.

SAMUEL FRENCH, INC.—25 West 45th St., New York, N. Y. 10036.
Publishes plays for all markets: stock, community theatre, colleges, high schools, children's theatre, churches, organizations. Editorial Department interested primarily in plays for Broadway and off-Broadway production; secondarily in packages for television series. Also welcomes one- and three-act play scripts designed for the non-professional market. Contracts are usually on royalty basis.

GRADE TEACHER—See *Teacher.*

HEUER PUBLISHING CO.—Drawer 248, Cedar Rapids, Iowa 52406. Edward I. Heuer, Editor.
"We are interested in good, clean one- and three-act plays that appeal to high school, church, and general community groups." Pays on acceptance. Prompt reports.

THE INSTRUCTOR—Dansville, N. Y. 14437.
Plays for elementary schools, about 2,000 words. Particularly wants plays for very young children and for grades 3 through 6; considers very few for grades 7 and 8. "Each month we try to emphasize holidays, special weeks, and occasions. Play

frameworks or stories which children can dramatize creatively are desired." Pays from $15 to $50.

JACK AND JILL—P.O. Box 528B, 1110 Waterway Blvd., Indianapolis, Ind. 46206. Plays for children; humor desired. Pays on publication.

DAVID McKAY, CO., INC.—750 Third Ave., New York, N. Y. 10017.
Three-act and one-act comedies and dramas of good quality which have been first tried out in local production, or which have won or gained favorable recognition in playwriting contests. One set preferred. Each play is considered individually as to payment.

PLAYS, THE DRAMA MAGAZINE FOR YOUNG PEOPLE—8 Arlington, St., Boston, Mass. 02116. A. S. Burack, Editor.
One-act plays with simple settings, suitable for production by young people from seven to seventeen. Casts may be mixed, all-male or all-female. Plays with one scene preferred. Subjects: holiday, historical, biographical, patriotic, comedy, etc. Maximum lengths: lower grades, 8–10 double-spaced typewritten pages; middle grades, 15 double-spaced typewritten pages; junior high and older groups, 25 double-spaced typewritten pages. If possible, plays shorter than these maximum lengths are preferred. No musical plays or pageants. Manuscript specification sheet available on request. Pays good rates, on acceptance.

SCHOLASTIC SCOPE—Scholastic Magazines, Inc., 50 West 44th St., New York, N. Y. 10036. Norma Ainsworth, Manuscript Editor.
For ages 15 to 18, with 4th to 6th grade reading level. Plays up to 3,000 words, dealing with the interests of today's students, relationships between people (interracial, adult-teen-age, employer-employee, etc.) in family, job, school situations. Strive for honesty, directness, realism, and action, preferably carried through dialogue rather than exposition, and depth of characterization in at least one character. Realistic stories, written from viewpoint of a member of one of our minority peoples, not necessarily focusing on race relations, would be helpful. Avoid too many coincidences and random happenings. Even though *Scope* wants action stories, this is not a market for crime fiction. Pays good rates, on acceptance.

SCHOLASTIC VOICE—Scholastic Magazines, Inc., 50 West 44th St., New York, N. Y. 10036.
For ages 14 to 17. Uses stories and plays, 1,500 to 3,000 words, strong on plot and characterization and dealing with problems of interest to teen-agers. Authors should steer clear of teen-age stereotypes. Good subjects are boy-girl situations (avoid formula stories about puppy love), school situations, adventure, mystery, science fiction, family situations, sports. Problems that confront teen-agers, like finding one's own identity, setting standards of conduct, reconciling ideals and reality, bridging the generation gap, etc., are good. Pays good rates, on accepance. Address Editor of Manuscript Dept.

TEACHER (formerly *Grade Teacher*)—22 West Putnam Ave., Greenwich, Conn. 06830. Harold Littledale, Editor.
Needs tested school entertainment material—plays, assembly programs and seasonal celebrations. Plays should have plot and emotional appeal. Especially welcome are incomplete plays that set up a situation, start dialogue, and then suggest ways in which children and teachers can complete them; also plays allowing children to improvise (rather than memorize) lines. Plays should have a flexible cast, preferably ten or more characters. Pays $25 minimum, on acceptance.

COMMUNITY AND COLLEGE THEATRES

ACADEMY THEATRE—3213 Roswell Rd., N.E., Atlanta, Ga. 30305. Peter Scupham, Director for New Scripts.
Plays of highest quality always considered: full-length, experimental, drama, comedy, musical, etc. Writer-in-residence program.

ALPHA-OMEGA PLAYERS—Repertory Theatre of America, P.O. Box 8192, Dallas, Tex. 75205.
Will consider new plays for repertory, with small casts and simple production style. Always interested in stage adaptations of works by famous authors, preferably American. Pays royalty of $10 per performance; a popular play will be kept for several seasons, at about 200 performances per season.

BOWIE STATE COLLEGE—Bowie, Md. 20715. Address Perry Schwartz, Speech and Theatre Department.
Particularly interested in experimental plays and in new black plays of all types. Pays on royalty basis.

CHELSEA THEATRE CENTER—Brooklyn Academy of Music, 30 Lafayette Ave., Brooklyn, N. Y. 11217.
Full-length (and occasionally one-act) plays, saying something new or using the theatre in a new way. Payment is based on Standard Dramatists Guild contract, as applied to off-Broadway productions.

THE CLEVELAND PLAY HOUSE—2040 East 86th St., Cleveland, Ohio 44106.
Considers scripts of finished plays by writers in any section of the country, for possible production. Manuscripts should be clean and securely bound, and a stamped, self-addressed envelope must be included.

EARPLAY—WHA Radio, Vilas Communication Hall, 821 University Ave., Madison, Wisc. 53706.
Radio plays of literary quality, all lengths. Purchases and produces plays for three years unlimited use on 500 public radio stations in U. S. Pays from $200 for 10-minute scripts to $500 for 30-minute scripts, on acceptance.

HOFSTRA UNIVERSITY—Dept. of Drama, Hempstead, N. Y. 11550.
Scripts that are contemporary in feeling and form, appropriate for undergraduate actors. Payment arranged.

HONOLULU THEATRE FOR YOUTH—Box 3257, Honolulu, Hawaii 96801.
Looking for good, intelligently written children's plays by new or established playwrights, approximately one hour in length, for presentation to school-age audiences (pre-school to high school) by predominantly adult casts. Authors should write to Executive Director for detailed information about requirements. Royalties paid by arrangement.

MARK TAPER FORUM—Center Theatre Group, 135 North Grand Ave., Los Angeles, Calif. 90012.
Plays on any subject, of any length, for an experimental theatre program. Enclose self-addressed, stamped envelope. Evaluation process takes about six weeks. Send only one play.

OFFICE FOR ADVANCED DRAMATIC RESEARCH—3526 Humboldt Ave., South, Minneapolis, Minn. 55408. Arthur H. Ballet, Director.
Unproduced plays by an American author may be submitted for consideration. No adaptations or musicals accepted. Recommends and underwrites about 40 plays each year for production in theatres throughout United States. Transportation expenses and royalty paid.

EUGENE O'NEILL MEMORIAL THEATRE CENTER—305 Great Neck Rd., Waterford, Conn. New York Office: Suite 1012, 1860 Broadway, New York, N. Y. 10023.
Considers new plays between September 15 and December 15 *only* for possible production at the Annual National Playwrights' Conference in Waterford. Playwrights may submit only one play (two copies) to New York Office, with return postage. Expenses are paid for playwrights whose work is produced.

SOUTHWEST THEATRE CONFERENCE NEW PLAYS LIBRARY SERVICE— Dept. of Speech, Louisiana State University, Baton Rouge, La. 70803.
Current catalog, available without charge, lists plays and contains procedures for use of NPLS by new playwrights and by production groups. Address all inquiries to Clinton W. Bradford, Director.

UNIVERSITY OF ALABAMA—University Theatre, Box 1965, University, Ala. 35486.
Plays of all types considered for production. Pays playwright's expenses to attend rehearsals, or standard catalog royalty.

UNIVERSITY OF DENVER—Dept. of Theatre, Denver, Colo. 80210.
Will consider comedies, dramas, musicals, adaptations and new types of plays. No payment.

LITERARY MAGAZINES

CHELSEA—Box 5880, G. C. Station, New York, N. Y. 10017.
Occasional short plays of high quality. Pays in copies.

THE DEKALB LITERARY ARTS JOURNAL—DeKalb College, 555 Indian Creek Dr., Clarkston, Ga. 30021. Mel McKee, Editor.
One-act plays. Pays in copies.

THE FREE LANCE—6005 Grand Ave., Cleveland, Ohio 44104. Casper LeRoy Jordan, Adelaide Simon, and Russell Atkins, Editors.
One-act plays. Avante-garde material only. Pays in copies.

JANUS—314 Bayview Ave., Seaside Park, N. J. 08752. Pat Jasin, Editor.
One-act plays from new, unpublished playwrights. Articles on new theatre groups, produced playwrights, off-Broadway theatres. Query. Pays in copies.

THE LITERARY REVIEW—Fairleigh Dickinson University, Rutherford, N. J. 07070. Charles Angoff, Editor.
Literary plays. Also radio and television plays. No payment.

THE NEW RENAISSANCE—9 Heath Rd., Arlington, Mass. 02174.
One-act plays, primarily for reading. Overstocked. Manuscripts will not be returned unless accompanied by a stamped, self-addressed envelope.

POET LORE—52 Cranbury Rd., Westport, Conn. 06880.
Verse plays. No payment.

QUARTERLY REVIEW OF LITERATURE—26 Haslet Ave., Princeton, N. J. 08540.
Publishes verse plays occasionally, when exceptionally good. Several issues should be studied before material is submitted.

WIND—RFD Rte. No. 1, Box 810, Pikesville, Ky. 41501.
Uses one one-act play each year. Pays in copies.

BOOK PUBLISHERS

Three lists are included here: general book publishers, who publish primarily hard-cover editions; firms that accept original manuscripts for paperback editions; and university presses, which usually publish specialized books or books by authorities in a given field.

Royalty rates usually start at about ten per cent of the retail price of the book, and increase after a certain number of copies have been sold. The publishing company usually pays the author an advance against royalties when the book contract is signed or when the finished manuscript is received.

Book manuscripts may be sent by Railway Express or by first-class mail, but the most inexpensive and commonly used method at present is by "Special Fourth Class

Rate—Manuscript." For a summary of postal regulations for the "Special Fourth Class Rate—Manuscript," see Chapter 100, *Manuscript Preparation and Submission,* and for complete details of this postal rate, insurance, etc., inquire at your local post office.

GENERAL BOOK PUBLISHERS

ABBEY PRESS, INC.—St. Meinrad, Ind. 47577. John J. McHale, Editor.
   Books about marriage and family life for an ecumenical audience. Pays advance against royalties.

ABELARD-SCHUMAN LIMITED (A division of *Intext Educational Publishers*)—
   257 Park Ave. S., New York, N. Y. 10010. Mrs. Frances Schwartz, Senior Editor, Children's Books. John Brimer, Senior Editor, Adult Books.
   Fiction, nonfiction, science, biography, garden, cookbooks, mysteries, children's books.

ABINGDON PRESS—201 Eighth Ave. South, Nashville, Tenn. 37203. Emory S. Bucke, Senior Editor.
   Religious books, juveniles, college texts, and general nonfiction; biography, Americana, marriage and family, social issues and recreation. Reports in two months on juveniles, all others in one month. Query first with outline and sample chapters. Pays on royalty basis.

ADDISON-WESLEY PUBLISHING CO.—Reading, Mass. 01867. Juvenile Division. Harry B. Stanton, Vice-President. Ray Broekel, Editor.
   Picture books and all types of fiction and nonfiction for 4- to 16-year-olds. Pays by standard royalty rates.

ALLYN AND BACON, INC.—470 Atlantic Ave., Boston, Mass. 02110.
   Textbooks for classes from kindergarten through college. Philip Parson, Editor-in-Chief, elementary-high school texts; Wayne Barcomb, Editor-in-Chief, college texts. Pays on royalty basis.

AMERICAN BOOK COMPANY (A division of *Litton Educational Publishing Inc.*)—
   Litton Industries, 450 West 33rd St., New York, N. Y. 10001.
   Textbooks and educational materials for schools and colleges.

AMERICAN HERITAGE PRESS—Incorporated into *McGraw-Hill.*

AMERICAN WEST PUBLISHING CO.—599 College Ave., Palo Alto, Calif. 94306. Donald E. Bower, Editor.
   Specialized, high-quality nonfiction on the West, both natural history and human history. Pays standard royalty rates. Query first.

AMIS PUBLISHING CO., INC. (including *Sabra Books*)—38 West 32nd St., New York, N. Y. 10001. Harold Miller, President.
   General trade nonfiction. Backlist primarily Jewish and Israeli themes. Standard royalty contracts. Query before submitting manuscript. Also juvenile nonfiction.

ARBOR HOUSE PUBLISHING CO., INC.—600 Third Ave., New York, N. Y. 10016.
   General fiction and nonfiction. Query.

ARCO PUBLISHING CO.—219 Park Ave. South, New York, N. Y. 10003. Dave Goodnough, Editor.
   How-to-do-it books; how to pass tests of all types; tests and testing; books on business, sports, hobbies; general nonfiction. Prefers queries or outlines first. Pays outright and by contract.

ARKHAM HOUSE—Sauk City, Wis. 53583.
   Macabre fiction and verse, 25,000 to 80,000 words. Pays by standard royalty rates. Query first, overstocked at present.

ARLINGTON HOUSE, INC.—81 Centre Ave., New Rochelle, N. Y. 10801. Malcolm Wright, Editor.
Nonfiction. Mail order self-help books, books for political conservatives, and nostalgic books on the 1920-1950 era. Query first.

ASSOCIATION PRESS—291 Broadway, New York, N. Y. 10007. Robert W. Hill, Director.
Booklength manuscripts of general nonfiction, recreation, group leadership, sports, social and behavioral sciences, family life and marriage education, and religious--ethical problems. Payment by royalty. Query first.

ASTOR-HONOR, INC.—P. O. Box 89, Stamford, Conn. 06904.
General trade and nonfiction books. Also publishes juvenile line, *Astor Books,* and quality paperback line, *Honor Books.* Query first.

ATHENEUM PUBLISHERS—122 East 42nd St., New York, N. Y. 10017. Simon Michael Bessie, President. Alfred Knopf, Jr., Chairman.
Quality fiction and nonfiction, including biography, history, books on current affairs, belles-lettres, juveniles, and books for a general audience. Also quality paperbacks. Pays on royalty basis.

THE ATLANTIC MONTHLY PRESS—8 Arlington St., Boston, Mass. 02116. Peter Davison, Director.
Fiction, biography, history, social sciences, belles-lettres, poetry, general nonfiction, juveniles. The editorial board often tries to link part-serialization in *The Atlantic* with book publication. Publishes books in association with *Little, Brown & Co.*

AUGSBURG PUBLISHING HOUSE—426 South Fifth St., Minneapolis, Minn. 55415. Roland Seboldt, Book Editor.
Fiction and nonfiction on Christian themes or related topics; juveniles. Pays on a regular royalty basis for most books; some manuscripts bought outright.

AURORA PUBLISHERS, INC.—118—16th Ave. South, Nashville, Tenn. 37203.
Hardcover and paperback publishers; juveniles (from earliest ages through young adult). Query. Payment by standard royalty rate.

BAKER BOOK HOUSE—1019 Wealthy St., S.E., Grand Rapids, Mich. 49506. Cornelius Zylstra, Editor.
Nonfiction from 30,000 to 60,000 words: Bible study aids, homiletic literature, Christian solutions to contemporary problems. Payment on royalty basis.

BARLENMIR HOUSE, PUBLISHERS—413 City Island Ave., New York, N. Y. 10064.
Books on fine arts; also dealing with psychology of art, etc. Royalty contract. Query.

A. S. BARNES & CO., INC.—Box 421, Cranbury, N. J. 08512.
Books on sports, outdoors, dancing and recreation. Also fiction; nonfiction, in the specialized fields of boating, electronics, aviation, photography, automobiles, and subjects of interest to women. Pays on royalty basis.

BASIC BOOKS, INC., PUBLISHERS—10 East 53rd St., New York, N. Y. 10022.
Books on behavioral, social, political and physical sciences; belles-lettres; history; science and general nonfiction for readers 14 years old and up. Pays on royalty basis.

THE BEACON PRESS—25 Beacon St., Boston, Mass. 02108.
General nonfiction with emphasis on current events and major problems of American society. Also, scholarly works supporting this interest in contemporary affairs, and liberal religious works. Pays on royalty basis. Always query first.

CHAS. A. BENNETT CO., INC.—809 West Detweiller Dr., Peoria, Ill. 61614. Paul Van Winkle, Senior Editor.
Books on high school and junior college home economics and industrial education.

BINFORDS & MORT—2505 S.E. 11th Ave., Portland, Ore. 97242. L. K. Phillips, Editor.
Books about the Pacific Northwest, preferably nonfiction, about 70,000 words. Pays on royalty basis.

BLOCH PUBLISHING CO., INC.—915 Broadway, New York, N. Y. 10010. Solomon Kerstein, Vice President and Editor, *Bloch's Book Bulletin.*
Books of Jewish content.

THE BOBBS-MERRILL CO., INC.—4 West 58th St., New York, N. Y. 10019.
Full-length novels, biographies, autobiographies, popular science, crafts, history, music, religion. Juvenile fiction or nonfiction for all age levels, all lengths. Pays by royalty contracts. Considers queries only.

THOMAS BOUREGY & CO., INC.—22 East 60th St., New York, N. Y. 10022.
Light, wholesome romances, westerns, mysteries, and science fiction, up to 55,000 words. Pays on a royalty basis.

BRADBURY PRESS, INC.—2 Overhill Rd., Scarsdale, N. Y. 10583. Richard W. Jackson, Editor-in-Chief.
Fiction about fully-characterized people or animals, for children from 2 to 12. Book lengths vary: picture books about 2 typewritten pages; story books from 25 to 50 typed pages; novels from about 75 to 150 typed pages. Royalty basis. Query.

CHARLES T. BRANFORD CO.—28 Union St., Newton Centre, Mass. 02159. Ilse F. Jacobs, Editor.
Nonfiction: art books, natural history, how-to-do-it, hobby and crafts books. No fiction or verse. Payment on royalty basis. Query before submitting material.

GEORGE BRAZILLER, INC.—One Park Ave., New York, N. Y. 10016. Edwin Seaver, Editor.
Literature, history, philosophy, science, art, drama, social science books; exceptional fiction.

BROADMAN PRESS—127 Ninth Ave. North, Nashville, Tenn. 37203.
William J. Fallis, Editor, general religious nonfiction; W. S. Cannon, Editor, inspirational and fiction; R. Lane Easterly, Editor, juvenile fiction, biography and picture books. Usually pays on royalty basis. Query.

BRUCE—8701 Wilshire Blvd., Beverly Hills, Calif. 90211.
Textbooks: high school, college, vocational education, industrial arts. Payment on royalty basis. Query.

THE CAXTON PRINTERS, LTD.—Box 700, Caldwell, Idaho 83605.
Most interested in authentic Americana, with emphasis on frontier and Western materials, but considers other types which are authentic and outstanding. Particularly interested in work of new writers. No fiction. Payment on royalty basis. Query first.

CHARTERHOUSE BOOKS—750 Third Ave., New York, N. Y. 10017.
Fiction and nonfiction. Standard royalties. Query.

CHILDREN'S PRESS—1224 West Van Buren St., Chicago, Ill. 60607. Mrs. Margaret R. Friskey, Editor.
Juvenile books, in line with school curriculum. More nonfiction than fiction.

CHILTON BOOK COMPANY—Radnor, Pa. 19089.
General nonfiction. Books on arts and crafts, sports, science. Welcomes free-lance manuscripts, outlines, and proposals. Regular royalty payments.

CHRONICLE BOOKS—807 Market St., San Francisco, Calif. 94103.
Western regional books to 100,000 words, some with photos and drawings used. Pays standard royalty rates. Query Editor before submitting manuscript.

THE CITADEL PRESS—120 Enterprise Ave., Secaucus, N. J. 07094. Allan J. Wilson, Editor-in-Chief.
In the market for all types of nonfiction. Some fiction.

CITATION PRESS—Scholastic Books, 50 West 44th St., New York, N. Y. 10036.
Professional books in education (paperback and hardcover) for teachers, administrators, and college students in teacher education. Editorial focus is on trends, innovations and new programs in education at all levels. Address Mrs. Norma Ainsworth, Editor of Manuscript Dept.

CONCORDIA PUBLISHING HOUSE—3558 South Jefferson Ave., St. Louis, Mo. 63118.
Fiction and nonfiction with moral or religious tone, for adults. Also juvenile and teen-age books. Minimum length for adult books is 25,000 words; no minimum for juveniles. Regular royalty payments.

CORNELL MARITIME PRESS, INC.—Cambridge, Md. 21613. Mrs. Mary Jane Cornell, Editor.
Specialized. Maritime technical, professional, and how-to books. *Tidewater Publishers*—Chesapeake Bay, Md., Va., subjects. Royalty basis. Query with outline.

COWARD, McCANN & GEOGHEGAN—200 Madison Ave., New York, N. Y. 10016. John J. Geoghegan, President and Editor-in-Chief.
Fiction, preferably of the more solid type; quality suspense. All types of nonfiction except purely technical books. High-grade juveniles: fiction and nonfiction for nursery school age to teen-age. Payment on royalty basis. Writers must query first, with description of book.

CREATIVE HOME LIBRARY—See *Meredith Corporation.*

CRITERION BOOKS (Division of *Intext Press*)—257 Park Ave. South, New York, N. Y. 10010.
Fiction and nonfiction, children's books. Query.

THOMAS Y. CROWELL CO.—666 Fifth Avenue., New York, N. Y. 10019.
Nonfiction books of knowledge, reference books and children's books. College textbooks. Regular royalty payments. Query first.

CROWN PUBLISHERS, INC.—419 Park Ave. South, New York, N. Y. 10016. Herbert Michelman, Editor-in-Chief.
All types of fiction and nonfiction.

THE DARTNELL CORPORATION—4660 Ravenswood Ave., Chicago, Ill. 60640.
Books on business topics, from 50,000 to 100,000 words. Payment on royalty basis.

JONATHAN DAVID PUBLISHERS, INC.—68-22 Eliot Ave., Middle Village, N. Y. 11379. Alfred J. Kolatch, Editor-in-Chief.
Predominantly nonfiction of interest to the Jewish book-buying market. Also juveniles and texts. Some general books. Royalty or outright purchase.

JOHN DAY COMPANY, INC.—257 Park Ave. South, New York, N. Y. 10010.
Richard J. Walsh, Jr., President.
Book-length fiction and nonfiction. No verse. Payment on royalty basis.

JOHN DE GRAFF, INC.—34 Oak Ave., Tuckahoe, N. Y. 10707.
Interested in nonfiction, particularly on nautical subjects, such as marine and
pleasure boating.

T. S. DENISON & CO.—5100 West 82nd St., Minneapolis, Minn. 55431.
Interested in all types of books except fiction. Emphasis on how-to-do-it subjects,
inspirational and religious books, game and party books, children's illustrated
stories suitable for school use, teachers' texts, etc.

THE DEVIN-ADAIR CO.—143 Sound Beach Ave., Old Greenwich, Conn. 06870.
Serious nonfiction. Religious, political, Irish, farming, and nature topics. Pays on
royalty basis. Always query first.

THE DIAL PRESS—1 Dag Hammarskjöld Plaza, 245 East 47th St., New York, N. Y.
10017. Richard Marek, Editor-in-Chief. Mrs. Phyllis Fogelman, Juvenile Editor.
General fiction and nonfiction of lasting importance. No mysteries, westerns, verse,
romances, or highly technical works. Payment in regular royalties and advances.

DIMENSION BOOKS, INC.—P.O. Box 811, Denville, N. J. 07834. Thomas Coffey,
Editor.
Nonfiction, Catholic books, children's books and travel. Query.

DODD, MEAD & COMPANY, INC.—79 Madison Ave., New York, N. Y. 10016.
Limited fiction list. General nonfiction. Seldom publishes verse. Juveniles. All
types and all lengths. Payment is on royalty basis. Please query first.

DOUBLEDAY & CO., INC.—245 Park Ave., New York, N. Y. 10017.
Interested in good books of all types: biography, history, travel, religious, science,
juvenile; limited numbers of novels, poetry collections. "We have reluctantly arrived at a decision to return unopened and unread all complete manuscripts—
novels and nonfiction—submitted to us. There is an exception—we will accept
appropriate manuscripts addressed to the following: Editor, Mysteries; Editor,
Science Fiction; Editor, Westerns. In all other categories we are requesting writers
to query us with a complete description." Pays on royalty basis.

DOW JONES-IRWIN, INC.—1818 Ridge Rd., Homewood, Ill. 60430. Norman F.
Guess, Editor.
Specialized; business books only. Pays by royalty rates.

E. P. DUTTON & CO., INC.—201 Park Ave. South, New York, N. Y. 10003.
General nonfiction of all kinds, fiction, mysteries, children's books, quality paperbacks. Pays on royalty basis.

WM. EERDMANS PUBLISHING CO.—255 Jefferson Ave., S.E., Grand Rapids, Mich.
49503.
Adult and juvenile nonfiction of a Christian religious character. Pays on royalty
basis.

ELK GROVE PRESS—Box 1637, Whittier, Calif. 90609. Ruth Shaw Radlauer, Editor.
Social studies-area books, for kindergarten through eighth grade. Standard royalty
contract. Query first.

EMERSON BOOKS, INC.—Reynolds Lane, Buchanan, N. Y. 10511.
Interested in how-to, puzzle, and math books with popular appeal. Self-help
books, collecting books, and books on gems and jewelry. Reference books. Royalty
payment.

PAUL S. ERIKSSON, INC.—119 West 57th St., New York, N. Y. 10019.
Adult fiction, juveniles, general nonfiction, biography, etc. Payment by usual royalty agreement. Query first.

M. EVANS & CO., INC.—216 East 49th St., New York, N. Y. 10017.
General fiction, nonfiction, juveniles. Query.

FARRAR, STRAUS AND GIROUX—19 Union Square West, New York, N. Y. 10003.
General publishers of both fiction and nonfiction. *Noonday Press,* paperbacks. *Octagon Books,* scholarly reprints.

FREDERICK FELL, INC.—386 Park Ave. South, New York, N. Y. 10016.
Fell's Guide Series, handicraft and hobbies—query Roger Blair, Editor. *Fell's Business and Financial Book Shelf,* business and finance—query Frederick Fell. *Fell's Better Health Series,* physical and mental health—query Roger Blair, Health Editor. Also nonfiction on current social topics, mysticism and the occult, and biography and autobiography. Query Margaret Brilant, Editor, with outline and sample chapters. Royalty basis.

FIDES PUBLISHERS, INC.—Notre Dame, Ind. 46556. James F. Burns, Editor.
Religious-oriented books, and books on modern education, Montessori applications. Royalty basis.

FLEET PRESS CORPORATION—160 Fifth Ave., New York, N. Y. 10010. D. Schiff, Editor.
Nonfiction, excluding scientific and technical manuscripts. No fiction. Query first. *Fleet Academic Editions, Inc.*—Humanities and social sciences. Query first.

FOLLETT PUBLISHING COMPANY—1010 West Washington Blvd., Chicago, Ill. 60607.
Quality juvenile fiction and nonfiction manuscripts, adult reference, general nonfiction and sports.

FORTRESS PRESS (incorporating *Muhlenberg Press, Augustana Press*)—2900 Queen Lane, Philadelphia, Pa. 19129. Helmut T. Lehmann, Editor-in-Chief.
Books on theology, for the layman, the student, the minister, the scholar. Payment is by standard royalty agreement.

FOUR WINDS PRESS—Scholastic Magazines, Inc., 50 West 44th St., New York, N. Y. 10036.
Original fiction and nonfiction. Juvenile, young adult. Submit outline and sample chapters for nonfiction, complete manuscript for fiction. Pays on royalty basis.

THE FREE PRESS (A division of *The Macmillan Company*)—866 Third Ave., New York, N. Y. 10022.
Nonfiction: college-level texts and professional books in the social sciences and humanities. Payment by royalty agreement.

FUNK & WAGNALLS (A division of *Reader's Digest Books, Inc.*)—866 Third Ave., New York, N. Y. 10019.
Adult nonfiction, English usage books, reference books, current affairs, science, biography, how-to and handbooks: address Gordon Carruth, Editor. Pays on royalty basis.

GAMBIT, INC.—437 Boylston St., Boston, Mass. 02108.
General fiction and nonfiction.

BERNARD GEIS ASSOCIATES—128 East 56th St., New York, N. Y. 10022.
Biographies, general nonfiction, fiction. Publishes a limited number of titles per year. Query first.

GINN AND COMPANY—191 Spring St., Lexington, Mass. 02173.
Publishes textbooks for use in schools and colleges.

GOLDEN PRESS, INC.—850 Third Ave., New York, N. Y. 10022.
Fiction and nonfiction for children, adult nonfiction, reference books.

THE STEPHEN GREENE PRESS—Box 1000, Brattleboro, Vt. 05301.
Quality nonfiction and regional (New England) books. Query first with table of contents and not more than two chapters. Pays on royalty basis.

GROSSET & DUNLAP, INC.—51 Madison Ave., New York, N. Y. 10010.
History, biography, literature, science, fine arts; also practical and self-help nonfiction, cookbooks, reference books and general nonfiction for adults. Various lines of picture story books, informational and activity books for young children. Fiction, history, biography and informational books for teen-agers. Queries only.

GROVE PRESS, INC.—53 East 11th St., New York, N. Y. 10003. Barney Rosset, Editor and Publisher.
General high-quality fiction and nonfiction. Also *Evergeen Books,* paperback series. Pays on royalty basis. Query first.

HARCOURT BRACE JOVANOVICH, INC.—757 Third Ave., New York, N. Y. 10017. Julian P. Muller, Editor-in-Chief.
General fiction and nonfiction, 60,000 words and up. Mimi Epstein, Juvenile Editor. Fiction and nonfiction manuscripts for beginning readers through the young teen-ager, 5,000 to 60,000 words.

HARPER & ROW, PUBLISHERS—10 East 53rd St., New York, N. Y. 10016.
General fiction and nonfiction, elementary, high school and college texts, social and economic books, religious books, medical books, and juveniles. Miss Ursula Nordstrom, Juvenile Editor. Interested in all types of manuscripts for boys and girls, from picture and story books for the youngest up to fiction and nonfiction for the teens. Payment by royalty contract.

HARPER'S MAGAZINE PRESS—2 Park Ave., New York, N. Y. 10016. Lawrence Freundlich, Editor.
Fiction and nonfiction, 60,000 to 100,000 words. Standard royalty contract. Query first.

HARVEY HOUSE, INC.—Irvington-on-Hudson, N. Y. 10533. Jeanne Gardner, Editor.
Picture books, fiction and nonfiction. Strong on science and/or informational books for young readers, grades 2-5 and 5-8.

HASTINGS HOUSE, PUBLISHERS, INC.—10 East 40th St., New York, N. Y. 10016. Walter Frese, Editor.
General nonfiction: Americana, biography, travel, guide and photographic picture books, books on cooking and wines. Juveniles: Miss Judy Donnelly, Editor. Communication arts (including films, television and radio), graphic and visual arts: Russell F. Neale, Editor. Pays on royalty basis.

HAWTHORN BOOKS—260 Madison Ave., New York, N. Y. 10016.
General nonfiction; religious books for all faiths. Also, reference works, books on cooking, art, self-help. Query first with outline and sample chapter. Pays by royalty contract.

HEARTHSIDE PRESS, INC.—445 Northern Blvd., Great Neck, N. Y. 10021. Nedda C. Anders, Editor.
Home, needlecraft, antiques, and garden books. Pays on royalty basis.

D. C. HEATH (Division of Raytheon Company)—125 Spring St., Lexington, Mass. 02173.
Textbooks only for elementary schools, high schools and colleges.

HILL AND WANG, INC.—19 Union Sq. West, New York, N. Y. 10003. Arthur W. Wang, Editor.

Fiction. Nonfiction: science, history, drama, and social history. Standard royalty contracts. Query before submitting.

HOBBS/CONTEXT—Rm. 1505, 52 Vanderbilt Ave., New York, N. Y. 10017.
Educational texts and supplementary reading; technical reports; how-to-do-it material. Query first.

HOLIDAY HOUSE—18 East 56th St., New York, N. Y. 10022. Eunice Holsaert, Editor.
Juvenile books of high merit. Science and nature books with fresh angles wanted for kindergarten to teen-age. Query first with ideas or outline and sample chapter; address Edward Lindemann, Science Editor.

HOLT, RINEHART AND WINSTON, INC.—383 Madison Ave., New York, N. Y. 10017.
General fiction and nonfiction; religious nonfiction; also juveniles. Pays royalties twice yearly. Query first with outline and sample chapters. Write to Trade Editor.

HORIZON PRESS—156 Fifth Ave., New York, N. Y. 10010. Ben Raeburn, Editor.
General trade books, nonfiction, art, architecture, science, and reference books; some fiction. Standard royalty agreement.

HOUGHTON MIFFLIN CO.—2 Park St., Boston, Mass. 02107. Richard B. McAdoo, Editor.
Fiction, stressing contemporary themes and issues, American or foreign background; historical; general. Nonfiction: history, natural history and important biography; books on sociopolitical subjects; humor; general. Literary Fellowships to finance work in progress. General juvenile and teen-age books.

HOWELL BOOK HOUSE, INC.—730 Fifth Ave., New York, N. Y. 10019.
Nonfiction, informative works on care, training, breeding, etc., of pure-bred dogs. How-to books, histories, behavior and other aspects of dog knowledge. Minimum length about 20,000 words. Pays by standard royalty rates.

HOWELL-NORTH BOOKS—1050 Parker St., Berkeley, Calif. 94710. F. D. North, Editor.
Specialized—railroad histories, Western Americana, pictorials mainly. Pays royalties, no advance. Query.

INTERNATIONAL MARINE PUBLISHING CO.—21 Elm St., Camden, Me. 04843. Roger C. Taylor, President and Editor.
Marine subjects, including maritime history, oceanography, sea ecology, sailing, motorboating, etc. Creative pictorial studies welcomed. Pays standard royalty rates.

JEWISH PUBLICATION SOCIETY—1528 Walnut St., Philadelphia, Pa. 19102. Dr. Chaim Potok, Editor.
Nonfiction, fiction, and juveniles. All material must have a bearing on Jewish life, literature, history, biography, etc. Occasionally publishes translations. Pays on royalty basis.

JUDSON PRESS—Valley Forge, Pa. 19481. Harold L. Twiss, Editor.
Religious. Current moral and social issues, inspirational and devotional material. Pays by royalty rates.

P. J. KENEDY & SONS—866 Third Ave., New York, N. Y. 10022.
Liturgical books, books on moral and religious issues, Bibles and related books. Pays on royalty basis.

ROBERT R. KNAPP, PUBLISHER—Box 7234, San Diego, Calif. 92107.
Professional reference, and textbooks: the humanities and social sciences, especially psychology, psychiatry, and statistics. Query first. Pays on royalty basis.

ALFRED A. KNOPF, INC.—201 East 50th St., New York, N. Y. 10022. Ashbel Green, Managing Editor.

Book-length fiction of above-average quality. Nonfiction: should not be too technical. Prefers letters describing subject matter and qualifications of author. College texts in humanities and the social sciences. Juveniles: Virginie Fowler, Juvenile Editor. All types: picture books, fiction and nonfiction. Picture books: 3,000 to 5,000 words. Royalty basis.

JOHN KNOX—341 Ponce de Leon Ave., N. E., Atlanta, Ga. 30308.
Books on the ethical, social, or cultural dimensions of religion. Pays by royalty rates. Query first.

LANTERN PRESS—354 Hussey Rd., Mt. Vernon, N. Y. 10552.
Juvenile fiction and nonfiction; adult nonfiction. Query first.

SEYMOUR LAWRENCE, INC.—90 Beacon St., Boston, Mass. 02108.
Works of fiction of literary distinction; books on child care and child development; children's books. Pays standard royalty rates. Query first on nonfiction; submit completed manuscript of fiction.

LENOX HILL PRESS—419 Park Ave. South, New York, N. Y. 10016. Alice Sachs, Editor.
Light romances, science fiction, westerns, 55,000 to 60,000 words. No manuscripts with an emphasis on sex and violence. Pays $250 for romances, $150 for westerns, $200 for science fiction, on receipt of signed contract.

LERNER PUBLICATIONS CO.—241 First Ave. North, Minneapolis, Minn. 55401. W. J. Kauffmann, Editorial Director.
Fiction and nonfiction for children, from 20 to 50 typewritten pages. Photographs or drawings. Usually 3 payments per contract, $300 to $700; no initial royalties.

LION BOOKS—111 East 39th St., New York, N. Y. 10016. Sayre Ross, Editor-in-Chief.
Young adult-juveniles. General publishing in picture books, minority novels, social studies, activities books, science and nature books, up to 60,000 words. Children's verse, up to 72 pages. Royalty basis.

J. B. LIPPINCOTT COMPANY—521 Fifth Ave., New York, N. Y. 10017. Edward L. Burlingame, Editor-in-Chief.
Adult and juvenile fiction and general nonfiction. Areas of special interest: biography, social history, nature, contemporary affairs, sports and humor. Submit juvenile manuscripts to Dorothy Briley. Contracts and royalty payments competitive with other major publishers.

LITTLE, BROWN & CO.—34 Beacon St., Boston, Mass. 02106. J. Randall Williams, Editor; John G. Keller, Juvenile Editor.
Fiction, general nonfiction and juveniles.

LIVERIGHT PUBLISHING CORP.—386 Park Ave. South, New York, N. Y. 10016.
Interested in nonfiction and books on psychology and sociology for intelligent layman and student. Uses some how-to books; occasionally unusual fiction, 50,000 words and up. Submit synopses and biographical sketches in advance. Payment is usually on royalty basis.

ROBERT B. LUCE, INC.—2000 N St., N. W., Washington, D. C. 20036. Robert D. Van Roijen, President.
Preference for the nonfiction, public affairs book, but will accept a limited amount of fiction. Payment by usual royalty agreement with an advance.

McGRAW-HILL BOOK CO. —Trade Dept. 1221 Ave. of the Americas, New York, N. Y. 10020.
Fiction and general nonfiction, including biography, history, humor, and popular science, religion, business, reference, how-to books. No verse or plays. Payment on royalty basis. *McGraw-Hill Junior Books:* fiction and nonfiction in the fields of history, biography, science, guidance and related subjects, for younger readers. Art Book Dept. wants works in all areas related to art.

DAVID McKAY CO., INC.—750 Third Ave., New York, N. Y. 10017. Kenneth L. Rawson, President and Editor-in-Chief.
Adult nonfiction in all areas, with strong emphasis on contemporary concerns: human behavior, science, medicine and health. Adult fiction with strong promotable central theme, substantial interesting backgrounds. College texts covering wide range.

MACMILLAN PUBLISHING COMPANY—866 Third Ave., New York, N. Y. 10022.
Fiction; general nonfiction; children's books; religious, medical and health, business, technical, and textbooks on all levels. Address fiction and general nonfiction to Trade Department; children's books to Children's Book Department; textbooks to the College or School Departments. Query first.

MACRAE SMITH CO.—225 South 15th St., Philadelphia, Pa. 19102. Donald P. Macrae, Editor-in-Chief.
Adult trade books: nonfiction, reference and fiction. Juvenile and young adult, ages 9 to 11, 12 to 16: nonfiction, reference, and fiction.

MEREDITH CORPORATION, CONSUMER BOOK DIVISION—1716 Locust St., Des Moines, Iowa 50303. Don Dooley, Editorial Director.
Better Homes and Gardens Books; Creative Home Library. Outlines first, then manuscripts for the following high-interest subjects: sewing, health, decorating, gardening, money management, home entertaining, cars in the family, building. Study other *BH&G* books. Query. Address manuscripts to the Editors. Pays flat fees or royalties.

JULIAN MESSNER (Division of Simon and Schuster)—1 West 39th St., New York, N. Y. 10018.
Books, 50,000 words and up, for ages 12 to 17. Special interest in biography and curriculum-oriented nonfiction; novels with strong themes showing personal adjustment; career fiction. Lee Hoffman, Editor, Books for Boys and Girls. Nonfiction, curriculum-oriented for grades 4 to 6: social studies; ethnic backgrounds; collective biography. 10,000–15,000 words.

MOODY PRESS—820 North LaSalle St., Chicago, Ill. 60610. Leslie H. Stobbe, Editor.
Evangelical publishing house associated with Moody Bible Institute. Fiction and nonfiction, reflecting conservative doctrinal position. Pays standard royalties for hardcover books; outright purchase of paperback manuscripts.

MOREHOUSE-BARLOW CO., INC.—14 East 41st St., New York, N. Y. 10017.
Nonfiction, especially adult and children's religious books and curriculum-oriented texts. No fiction or poetry. Pays on royalty basis. Outline and sample chapter with first inquiry.

WILLIAM MORROW AND COMPANY, INC.—105 Madison Ave., New York, N. Y. 10016.
Fiction and nonfiction of general interest. Constance C. Epstein, Editor of *Morrow Junior Books.* Junior books for all ages except the pre-school child. Pays on royalty basis.

NASH PUBLISHING—9255 Sunset Blvd., Los Angeles, Calif. 90069.
Controversial nonfiction books on current issues; how-to titles; self-improvement; psychological subjects. Pays by flat fee or standard royalty rates. Queries only.

THOMAS NELSON & SONS—30 East 42nd St., New York, N. Y. 10017.
Adult nonfiction; juvenile and young adult fiction and nonfiction.

NELSON-HALL PUBLISHERS—325 West Jackson Blvd., Chicago, Ill. 60606. V. Peter Ferrara, Editor.
Applied psychology, sociology and other practical topics in the behavioral sciences, for areas of home, employment, community. Author must be an authority on subject of book. Pays by standard royalty contracts.

W. W. NORTON & COMPANY, INC.—500 Fifth Ave., New York, N. Y. 10036.
Fiction and all nonfiction. Pays on royalty basis.

OCEANA PUBLICATIONS, INC.—75 Main St., Dobbs Ferry, N. Y. 10522. W. W. Cowan, Managing Editor.
Law and public policy. Query first. Pays flat fee for small titles, standard royalty contract for others.

ODDO PUBLISHING, INC.—Box 68, Beauregard Blvd., Fayetteville, Ga. 30214.
Juveniles for school and library use, kindergarten to junior high, on reading, speech improvement, conservation, math, basic science. Remedial reading series for grades 2 to 6 with 10- to 16-year-old interest level. Royalty and outright purchase.

OHARA PUBLICATIONS—5455 Wilshire Blvd., Los Angeles, Calif. 90036.
Oriental philosophy subjects, well-documented, intelligently written. Query first with synopsis or description of manuscript, plus resumé of published books or articles. Pays standard royalty rates.

OUTERBRIDGE & LAZARD, INC.—Merged with *E. P. Dutton Co.*

OPEN COURT PUBLISHING CO.—Box 599, LaSalle, Ill. 61301.
Nonfiction: education, philosophy, religion. Query.

OXFORD UNIVERSITY PRESS—200 Madison Ave., New York, N. Y. 10016.
Authoritative books on literature, history, religion, philosophy, biography, government, economics, science, art, music; college textbooks, medical books, etc. No fiction. Query before submitting.

PANTHEON BOOKS—201 East 50th St., New York, N. Y. 10022.
Fiction, nonfiction, art, history, and juveniles.

PARENTS' MAGAZINE PRESS—52 Vanderbilt Ave., New York, N. Y. 10017.
Manuscripts, 500 to 1,500 words, for picture books for children, 4 to 8. Simplicity of style and possibilities for illustration essential.

PARNASSUS PRESS—2721 Parker St., Berkeley, Calif. 94704.
Children's books, from pre-school to teen-age; picture books and full-length teen-age novels. Accepts queries only for adult fiction and nonfiction. Pays by royalties and advance.

PAULIST/NEWMAN PRESS—1865 Broadway, New York, N. Y. 10023. Kevin A. Lynch, C.S.P., Editor.
Catholic book publishers interested in religious education materials, theology, philosophy, liturgical and spiritual writing. Welcomes and gives prompt attention to unsolicited manuscripts.

PFLAUM/STANDARD—2285 Arbor Blvd., Dayton, Ohio 45439. John M. Heher, Director.

Books and materials in the areas of film study, mental health and personal guidance, religious education, and teacher training. Pays on royalty basis.

S. G. PHILLIPS, INC.—305 West 86th St., New York, N. Y. 10024. Sidney Phillips, Editor.
Fiction and nonfiction with contemporary themes relevant to the interests and concerns of today's young people. Especially interested in biographies, politics, history, archaeology, anthropology, social sciences, architecture, city planning, as well as outstanding fiction on all subjects for all age groups. No unsolicited manuscripts—query the editor.

PITMAN PUBLISHING CORP.—6 East 43rd St., New York, N. Y. 10017.
Nonfiction on business and business education; art; arts and crafts, economics, education, history, psychology, Russian language. General nonfiction. No fiction or verse. Pays on royalty basis.

THE PLATT & MUNK CO., INC.—1055 Bronx River Ave., Bronx, N. Y. 10472. Don Stern, Editorial Director.
Mass-market juvenile books for ages 1–14.

PLAYBOY PRESS—747 Third Ave., New York, N. Y. 10017. Bill Adler, Senior Editor.
High-quality, book-length fiction and nonfiction. Query.

CLARKSON N. POTTER, INC.—419 Park Ave. South, New York, N. Y. 10016. Clarkson N. Potter, Editor.
General trade books, fiction and nonfiction; especially on Americana, science, art, the contemporary scene. Pays on usual royalty basis. Query before submitting.

PRAEGER PUBLISHERS, INC.—111 Fourth Ave., New York, N. Y. 10003. Arnold Dolin, Executive Editor.
Nonfiction on contemporary issues, international relations, history, military affairs, political and social science, urban affairs, education, art, architecture, archaeology, design. Pays on royalty basis. Query first.

PRENTICE-HALL, INC.—Englewood Cliffs, N. J. 07632.
Very select fiction and nonfiction manuscripts. Special interest in biography, history, politics. No westerns, mysteries, drama, poetry or popular romances. Interested in fiction and nonfiction for children under 12; no poetry or picture books. Query before submitting. Other book publishing divisions are College Books, Educational Textbooks, Business, and Professional Books.

PRICE/STERN/SLOAN PUBLISHERS, INC.—410 North La Cienega Blvd., Los Angeles, Calif. 90048.
Short, humorous "non-books." Query first.

PRUETT PUBLISHING COMPANY—P.O. Box 1560, Boulder, Colo. 80302.
Books about the history and development of the American West; railroads; outdoor books for the Rocky Mt. region; hiking, camping, mountain climbing. No fiction. Query Gerald Keenan. Also interested in textbooks and fiction for slow readers. Query Elizabeth Opal.

PUBLIC AFFAIRS PRESS—419 New Jesey Ave., S.E., Washington, D. C. 20003.
Nonfiction: current affairs and social sciences. Payment varies.

G. P. PUTNAM'S SONS—200 Madison Ave., New York, N. Y. 10016. William Targ, Editor-in-Chief. Tom MacPherson, Editor-in-Chief, Juvenile Books.
Fiction and nonfiction for adults and children of all ages. Payment on royalty basis.

QUADRANGLE/THE NEW YORK TIMES BOOK CO.—10 East 53rd St., New York, N. Y. 10022. Herbert Nagourney, President.
Serious nonfiction by recognized authorities. Query first.

RANDOM HOUSE, INC.—201 East 50th St., New York, N. Y. 10022.
Fiction and nonfiction, juveniles and adult.

FLEMING H. REVELL COMPANY—Old Tappan, N. J. 07675. Dr. Frank S. Mead,
Editor-in-Chief. Mr. Richard Baltzell, Editorial Director.
Revell Books—Inspirational and devotional religious books, self-help, personality
biographies. Reports after at least one month. Payment on royalty basis.

THE WARD RITCHIE PRESS—3044 Riverside Dr., Los Angeles, Calif. 90039.
Cookbooks, Western Americana, juveniles, Western travel. Standard royalty rates.

THE RONALD PRESS CO.—79 Madison Ave., New York, N. Y. 10016.
General nonfiction, professional reference books, and college texts.

RICHARDS ROSEN PRESS, INC.—29 East 21st St., New York, N. Y. 10010. Ruth
C. Rosen, Editor.
Nonfiction books on teen-age guidance, to 40,000 words. Payment to be arranged.

ROY PUBLISHERS, INC.—30 East 74th St., New York, N. Y. 10021. Hanna Kister,
Editor.
General fiction, nonfiction and juveniles with emphasis on international interests.
Query first; manuscripts sent without permission will be refused.

RUTLEDGE BOOKS, INC.—17 East 45th St., New York, N. Y. 10017.
All types of unusual adult nonfiction of high quality, plus juvenile fiction and
nonfiction. Cookbooks a specialty. Query first with outline. Payment is in advances and royalties.

SAGE BOOKS—1139 South Wabash, Chicago, Ill. 60605.
Nonfiction books about the American West. Pays regular royalty rates. See *Swallow Press.*

ST. MARTIN'S PRESS, INC.—175 Fifth Ave., New York, N. Y. 10010.
Fiction, general nonfiction and juveniles. History, political science, biography,
college textbooks, scholarly, technical books. Pays on royalty basis.

SATURDAY REVIEW PRESS—230 Park Ave., New York, N. Y. 10017.
General fiction and nonfiction, especially contemporary and historical fiction,
social issues, history and biography, popular science. Pays by royalty rates.

SCHOLASTIC BOOKS—50 West 44th St., New York, N. Y. 10036. Mrs. Norma
Ainsworth, Editor of Manuscript Dept.
Book clubs for grades 1–12 use picture books, science, biography, mystery, how-to,
teen-age interests, beauty and grooming, young adult mystery and suspense. Also
fiction for teen-agers who read at 2nd to 4th grade level. Query.

CHARLES SCRIBNER'S SONS—597 Fifth Ave., New York, N. Y. 10017.
Books of all kinds, including juveniles. Authors should not submit manuscripts
without prior correspondence.

SEABURY PRESS—815 Second Ave., New York, N. Y. 10017. Arthur R. Buckley,
Adult Editor. James C. Giblin, Editor, Books for Young People.
Official publishing house of the Episcopal Church. Interested primarily in sociological and religious nonfiction on the adult level, and in picture book manuscripts for
ages 5–8 and fiction and nonfiction for ages 8–12 and ages 12 up in the juvenile
area. Payment is arranged by royalty contract.

SHEED & WARD, INC.—475 Fifth Ave., New York, N. Y. 10017.
Specializes in philosophy, theology, psychology, and history, with religious interest.

SHERBOURNE PRESS—1640 South La Cienega, Los Angeles, Calif. 90035. Shelly Lowenkopf, Editor.
Contemporary fiction, science fiction, mystery-suspense. No espionage. General nonfiction, with emphasis on self-help, exposé, and consumer protection. Also solidly-plotted, motivated, juveniles for ages 12-16. Hardcover only—no paperbacks.

SIERRA CLUB BOOKS—Mills Tower, San Francisco, Calif. 94104.
Specialized conservation, natural history, outdoor guidebooks, recreation, etc. Query.

SIMON AND SCHUSTER—630 Fifth Ave., New York, N. Y. 10020. Michael V. Korda, Editor-in-Chief; Jonathan Dolger, Mrs. Evelyn Gendel, Daniel Moses, Mrs. Alix Nelson, Editors. Miss Barbara Norville, Inner Sanctum Mystery Editor.
General fiction, nonfiction, mysteries. "We now return unread all unsolicited manuscripts not addressed to an editor by name." Pays standard royalty rates.

STACKPOLE BOOKS—Cameron and Kelker Sts., Harrisburg, Pa. 17105.
Manuscripts, 20,000 words and up, covering anything dealing with the outdoors, military services, guns, sports, camping, political-military affairs, leisure-oriented ideas, international relations, citizenship, education, and general nonfiction. Pays on royalty basis. Query first.

STECK-VAUGHN CO.—Box 2028, Austin, Tex. 78767. Paul C. Craig, Executive Editor.
Juveniles, textbooks.

STEIN AND DAY—Scarborough House, Briarcliff Manor, N. Y. 10510. Rennie Browne, Editor.
All types of nonfiction except technical material. Quality fiction. No unsolicited manuscripts will be considered. Nonfiction authors should first submit a summary or outline and sample chapter of their work; novelists should submit first chapter only. Pays on royalty basis.

STERLING PUBLISHING CO.—419 Park Ave. South, New York, N. Y. 10016. David A. Boehm, President.
How-to's, general information, sports and science books for adults and young people. Payment is sometimes on a royalty basis, usually by outright purchase. Always query before submitting.

STRAIGHT ARROW BOOKS—625 Third St., San Francisco, Calif. 94107. Alan Rinzler, Editor.
Publishes hardcover books and paperbacks, on history, politics, how-to-do-it books for self-sufficient living, music, religion and spiritualism, fiction and reference. Pays standard royalty rates. Query Editor before submitting.

SWALLOW PRESS—1139 South Wabash, Chicago, Ill. 60605. Durrett Wagner, Editor.
General nonfiction. Pays regular royalty rates. Publishers of *Sage Books*.

TUDOR PUBLISHING CO.—221 Park Ave. South, New York, N. Y. 10003.
General nonfiction, books on fine and practical art, philosophy. Payment generally by royalty agreement. Address manuscripts to Norman Blaustein.

UNION OF AMERICAN HEBREW CONGREGATIONS—838 Fifth Ave., New York, N. Y. 10021.
Book manuscripts in the fields of Jewish religion, the application of the principles of Reform Judaism in everyday life, history, biography, literature, and current problems affecting Jews. Children's books.

UNITED CHURCH PRESS—1505 Race St., Philadelphia, Pa. 19102. David F. Marshall, Editor-in-Chief.
Nonfiction, with particular appeal for college- and university-connected audiences: politics, government, humanities, social sciences, etc. Pays standard royalty rates. Query first with sample chapter and extensive outline.

THE VANGUARD PRESS, INC.—424 Madison Ave., New York, N. Y. 10017. Bernice Woll, Editor.
Strong interest in fiction of all kinds, about 50,000 words and up. Nonfiction of all kinds, especially books of a provocative nature, on democracy, biography, history, politics, economics, humor, how-to-do, adventure, personal experience, etc. Large juvenile list of all categories, emphasizing nonfiction in new fields. Occasional special books. Pays on royalty basis. Particularly interested in new writers of promise and ability.

VAN NOSTRAND REINHOLD COMPANY (A division of *Litton Educational Publishing, Inc.*)—450 West 33rd St., New York, N. Y. 10001.
Adult trade books; informative nonfiction of all sorts; arts, crafts, and design; juvenile and informational; reference, technical, scientific; business; college textbooks. Query for current needs.

THE VIKING PRESS, INC.—625 Madison Ave., New York, N. Y. 10022.
Book-length novels of literary quality (not ordinary popular fiction). Biography, general works on history, science, sociology, etc., for the layman. Art and travel (*Studio Books*). Higher types of juveniles (*Junior Books*). Paperbound (*Viking Compass Books, Viking Seafarer Books*). *Viking Portable Library.* Payment by usual royalty rates.

HENRY Z. WALCK, INC.—19 Union Sq. West, New York, N. Y. 10003. Refna Wilkin, Senior Editor.
Juvenile books. Query.

WALKER AND COMPANY—720 Fifth Ave., New York, N. Y. 10019.
General adult fiction and nonfiction. Juvenile fiction and nonfiction for ages 12 and up. Query first.

FREDERICK WARNE & CO., INC.—101 Fifth Ave., New York, N. Y. 10003.
Books for children and young adults. Query first for current needs.

IVES WASHBURN, INC.—750 Third Ave., New York, N. Y. 10017.
A selected small list of fiction, nonfiction and junior books.

WATSON-GUPTILL PUBLICATIONS, INC.—1515 Broadway, New York, N. Y. 10036.
How-to-do-it books for artists, art teachers, art students and hobbyists. Subjects include painting, sculpture, printmaking, drawing, commercial art, crafts, art education. Books emphasize techniques, step-by-step demonstrations. Pays on royalty basis.

FRANKLIN WATTS, INC.—730 Fifth Ave., New York, N. Y. 10019.
Interested in fiction on contemporary themes, and nonfiction books for children, especially at elementary school age level. Please query.

WESTERN PUBLISHING COMPANY, INC.—Juvenile picture-storybook division, 1220 Mound Ave., Racine, Wis. 53404.
Whitman Books, some *Golden.Books.* Picture-storybook manuscripts under 800 words; childhood experiences, animal stories, mechanical subjects. Humor welcomed. Novels 35,000 words and up, for pre-teen and early-teen readers; query with synopsis. Payment by arrangement.

THE WESTMINSTER PRESS—900 Witherspoon Bldg., Philadelphia, Pa. 19107. Barbara Bates, Children's Book Editor.
Juvenile fiction and nonfiction for age 8 and up. Payment on royalty basis.

WEYBRIGHT AND TALLEY—750 Third Ave., New York, N. Y. 10017.
Quality nonfiction. Query first.

WILDERNESS PRESS—2440 Bancroft Way, Berkeley, Calif. 94704. Thomas Winnett, Editor.
Guides to Western outdoor areas; other outdoor manuscripts slanted toward hikers and backpackers. Length, 200 to 300 pages. Pays royalties of 8% to 10% on book sales semiannually. Query.

JOHN WILEY & SONS, INC.—605 Third Ave., New York, N. Y. 10016. Robert Polhemus, Editorial Director.
Technical, scientific, and business books. Pays on royalty basis. Query first.

WORD BOOKS—4800 West Waco Drive, Waco, Tex. 76703. Floyd W. Thatcher, Editor.
All types of religious nonfiction, 160-200 typed pages. Standard royalty payments.

YOUNG SCOTT BOOKS—See *Addison-Wesley.*

ZONDERVAN PUBLISHING HOUSE—1415 Lake Drive, S.E., Grand Rapids, Mich. 49506. T, Alton Bryant, Editor.
Protestant religious subjects. Inspirational and devotional themes for young people and adults; textbooks and handbooks for schools and clergymen; juvenile, teen, and adult fiction and biography with moral and religious content. Books on religious subjects from a psychological orientation.

PAPERBACK BOOK PUBLISHERS

ACE BOOKS—1120 Avenue of the Americas, New York, N. Y. 10036.
Original science fiction and western novels, about 50,000 words; nurse romance novels, some women-slanted suspense novels, women's "Gothic" suspense romances, and occasional general fiction. Some nonfiction. Pays up to $2,000 advance against standard royalties.

ARCHWAY PAPERBACKS (A division of *Simon & Schuster, Inc.*)—630 Fifth Ave., New York, N. Y. 10020. Patricia MacDonald, Editor.
Fiction (mysteries, animal stories, adventure, young romance, humor, sports, etc.) and nonfiction (biographies) for young readers, 8 to 14. Query first.

ARCO BOOKS, INC.—219 Park Ave. South, New York, N. Y. 10003. David Goodnough, Editor.
Nonfiction originals and reprints, 50,000 words and up. Outright purchase and standard royalty payment.

AVON BOOKS—959 Eighth Ave., New York, N. Y. 10019. Peter M. Mayer, Editor-in-Chief.
Modern fiction with a commercial slant. Also educational nonfiction. Length, from 60,000 to 200,000 words. Prefers works by previously published writers, but looks at all. Query first. Good royalties against an advance on signing of contract.

BALLANTINE BOOKS, INC.—201 East 50th St., New York, N. Y. 10022.
Contemporary fiction, some historical fiction, westerns and science fiction, suspense and mystery novels. Also nonfiction on topics of widespread interest. Query before submitting. Pays on royalty basis.

BANTAM BOOKS, INC.—666 Fifth Ave., New York, N. Y. 10019.
Accepts material through agents and publishers only.

BELMONT PRODUCTIONS, INC.—185 Madison Ave., New York, N. Y. 10016. Cynthia U. Kutz, Editor-in-Chief. Jennifer B. Haring, Senior Editor.
Mysteries, westerns, science fiction, gothics, general modern novels, novels with powerful sex emphasis, 50,000 to 60,000 words. Query first with outline and sample chapter. Pays standard royalties.

BERKLEY PUBLISHING CORPORATION—200 Madison Ave., New York, N. Y. 10016. Thomas A. Dardis, Vice-President.
Science fiction, mysteries, suspense and espionage novels, but no adventure novels. Overstocked on westerns at the present time. Query first in detail. Payment rates vary.

CAMELOT BOOKS (A division of *Avon Books*)—959 Eighth Ave., New York, N. Y. 10019. Nancy Coffey, Editor.
Fiction and nonfiction for young readers, 10 to 15. Payment is negotiable. Query first.

COLLIER BOOKS—866 Third Ave., New York, N. Y. 10022.
Can use a wide variety of nonfiction of any length. No original fiction is published. Pays on royalty basis. Query first.

CORNERSTONE LIBRARY, INC.—630 Fifth Ave., New York, N. Y. 10020.
Basic books in leisure-time fields (chess, tennis, golf, bridge); guide books to various subjects; how-to-do-its in all areas; some inspirational books. Pays in advances and royalties.

DAW BOOKS, INC.—c/o New American Library, 1301 Avenue of the Americas, New York, N. Y. 10019. Donald A. Wollheim, Publisher.
Paperback science fiction covering the entire field of the science fiction/fantasy novel. Pays $1,500 advance against royalties of 4% and 6%.

DELL BOOKS—245 East 47th St., New York, N. Y. 10017. Mrs. Peggy Roth, Executive Editor.
Fiction and nonfiction, 60,000 words and up. Queries preferred.

DELTA BOOKS—Dell Publishing Co., 1 Dag Hammarskjöld Plaza, 245 East 47th St., New York, N. Y. 10017. Richard Huett, Editor-in-Chief.
Selected fiction. Nonfiction of general and academic interest, especially in the areas of history, psychology, science, literature, philosophy. Query first.

THE DOUBLEDAY/NATURAL HISTORY PRESS—Publisher for The American Museum of Natural History, 277 Park Ave., New York, N. Y. 10017.
Adult trade books, children's books, and illustrated editions of all areas of natural history, including anthropology, ecology and astronomy.

FAWCETT WORLD LIBRARY—1515 Broadway, New York, N. Y. 10003.
Fawcett Crest Books: Fiction and nonfiction reprints. Pays on royalty basis. Query first. *Fawett Premier Books:* Reprints and originals for secondary schools and colleges; supplementary reading. Pays on royalty basis.

GOLD MEDAL BOOKS (A division of *Fawcett World Library*)—1515 Broadway, New York, N. Y. 10003. Walter Fultz, Editor.
Wants first-rate suspense novels, westerns, humorous novels, anthologies, and cartoon books. Also Gothic novels and books in the science fiction and occult fields; topical text-and-photo books with mass market potential. Query first; reports on manuscripts in three to six weeks. Royalties paid on amount of copies printed.

LAUREL EDITIONS—Dell Publishing Co., 750 Third Ave., New York, N. Y. 10017. Richard Huett, Editor-in-Chief.
Nonfiction of general and academic interest. Original writings or anthologies in fields of history, psychology, science, literature, philosophy, etc. Queries preferred.

THE NATURAL HISTORY PRESS—See *The Doubleday/Natural History Press.*

NEW AMERICAN LIBRARY—1301 Avenue of the Americas, New York, N. Y. 10019. Edward T. Chase, Editorial Vice-President.
Signet Books are largely novels with strong, contemporary themes; lively nonfiction. Considers originals from query and outline only. Query first. Standard royalty contract.

101 PRODUCTIONS—834 Mission St., San Francisco, Calif. 94103.
Cookbooks, home, travel. Manuscripts of 100-200 pages. Standard royalties after publication.

PAPERBACK LIBRARY—See *Warner Paperback Library.*

POCKET BOOKS (A division of *Simon & Schuster, Inc.*)—630 Fifth Ave., New York, N. Y. 10020.
Cardinal and *Pocket Books* are chiefly reprint. Some originals published.

POPULAR LIBRARY, INC.—600 Third Ave., New York, N. Y. 10016. Juris Jurjevics, Senior Editor.
Some originals, of a topical or timely nature. General fiction, mystery, suspense novels, adventure and espionage, historical fiction, westerns, and some humor and science fiction. Minimum length, 40,000 words. Pays on royalty basis. Query first.

PREMIER BOOKS—See *Fawcett World Library.*

PYRAMID BOOKS—919 Third Ave., New York, N. Y. 10022.
Fiction and nonfiction. Publishes reprints and originals. Query first.

TEMPO BOOKS—51 Madison Ave., New York, N. Y. 10010. Ronald Buehl, Editor.
Fiction and nonfiction for teen-agers, 40,000 to 80,000 words. Primarily reprints, but some originals. Payment is by standard paperback arrangement with advance against royalties Prefers query or outline first.

WARNER PAPERBACK LIBRARY—75 Rockefeller Plaza, New York, N. Y. 10019.
Jerry Gross, Editorial Director.
Romantic historical novels, mystery series with a continuing hero, Gothic novels, and novels that reveal the inner workings of an industry, profession, life-style, etc. Also controversial nonfiction. Length, from 50,000 to 125,000 words. Query first with outline and two sample chapters. Pays on advance and royalty basis.

WASHINGTON SQUARE PRESS (A division of *Pocket Books*)—630 Fifth Ave., New York, N. Y. 10020.
Specializes in paperback books of educational and scholarly interest for schools and the general public. Pays standard royalties.

WILSHIRE BOOK CO.—12015 Sherman Rd., North Hollywood, Calif. 91605.
Specialized—astrology, inspirational, psychological self-help books (e.g. psychocybernetics). Length, 35,000 to 70,000 words. Pays standard royalties.

UNIVERSITY PRESSES

BROWN UNIVERSITY PRESS—71 George St., Providence, R. I. 02912.

CAMBRIDGE UNIVERSITY PRESS—32 East 57th St., New York, N. Y. 10022.

THE CATHOLIC UNIVERSITY OF AMERICA PRESS—620 Michigan Ave., N.E., Washington, D. C. 20017.

COLUMBIA UNIVERSITY PRESS—562 West 113th St., New York, N. Y. 10025.

CORNELL UNIVERSITY PRESS—124 Roberts Pl., Ithaca, N. Y. 14850.

DUKE UNIVERSITY PRESS—Box 6697, College Station, Durham, N. C. 27708.

DUQUESNE UNIVERSITY PRESS—Pittsburgh, Pa. 15219.

FORDHAM UNIVERSITY PRESS—441 East Fordham Rd., Bronx, N. Y. 10458.

HARVARD UNIVERSITY PRESS—79 Garden St., Cambridge, Mass. 02138.

INDIANA UNIVERSITY PRESS—10th and Morton Sts., Bloomington, Ind. 47401.

IOWA STATE UNIVERSITY PRESS—Press Bldg., Ames, Iowa 50010.

THE JOHNS HOPKINS PRESS—Baltimore, Md. 21218.

LOUISIANA STATE UNIVERSITY PRESS—Baton Rouge, La. 70803.

LOYOLA UNIVERSITY PRESS—3441 North Ashland Ave., Chicago, Ill. 60657.

MARQUETTE UNIVERSITY PRESS—1131 West Wisconsin Ave., Milwaukee, Wis. 53233.

THE M.I.T. PRESS—50 Ames St., Cambridge, Mass. 02142.

MICHIGAN STATE UNIVERSITY PRESS—Box 550, East Lansing, Mich. 48824.

NEW YORK UNIVERSITY PRESS—32 Washington Place, New York, N. Y. 10003.

NORTHWESTERN UNIVERSITY PRESS—1735 Benson Ave., Evanston, Ill. 60201.

OHIO STATE UNIVERSITY PRESS—Hitchcock Hall, 2070 Neil Ave., Columbus, Ohio 43210.

OHIO UNIVERSITY PRESS—301 Davis Hall, Athens, Ohio 45701.

OREGON STATE UNIVERSITY PRESS—101 Waldo Hall, Corvallis, Ore. 97331.

OXFORD UNIVERSITY PRESS—200 Madison Ave., New York, N. Y. 10016.

THE PENNSYLVANIA STATE UNIVERSITY PRESS—University Press Bldg., University Park, Pa. 16802.

THE PRESS OF CASE WESTERN RESERVE UNIVERSITY—11000 Cedar Rd., Cleveland, Ohio 44106.

PRINCETON UNIVERSITY PRESS—Princeton, N. J. 08540.

RUTGERS UNIVERSITY PRESS—30 College Ave., New Brunswick, N. J. 08903.

ST. JOHN'S UNIVERSITY PRESS—Grand Central and Utopia Parkways, Jamaica, N. Y. 11432.

SOUTHERN ILLINOIS UNIVERSITY PRESS—Carbondale, Ill. 62901.

SOUTHERN METHODIST UNIVERSITY PRESS—Dallas, Texas 75222.

STANFORD UNIVERSITY PRESS—Stanford, Calif. 94305.

SYRACUSE UNIVERSITY PRESS—Box 87, University Station, Syracuse, N. Y. 13210.

THE UNITED STATES NAVAL INSTITUTE—Annapolis, Md. 21402.

UNIVERSITY OF ALABAMA PRESS—Drawer 2877, University, Ala. 35486.

UNIVERSITY OF ARIZONA PRESS—Box 3398, College Station, Tucson, Ariz. 85700.

UNIVERSITY OF CALIFORNIA PRESS—Berkeley, Calif. 94720.

UNIVERSITY OF CHICAGO PRESS—5750 Ellis Ave., Chicago, Ill. 60637.

UNIVERSITY OF COLORADO PRESS—Regent Hall, Box 22, Boulder, Colo. 80302.

UNIVERSITY OF FLORIDA PRESS—15 N.W. 15th St., Gainesville, Fla. 32601.

UNIVERSITY OF GEORGIA PRESS—Athens, Ga. 30601.

UNIVERSITY OF HAWAII PRESS—535 Ward Ave., Honolulu, Hawaii 96814.

UNIVERSITY OF ILLINOIS PRESS—Urbana, Ill. 61801.

UNIVERSITY OF MASSACHUSETTS PRESS—Munson Hall, Amherst, Mass. 01002.

UNIVERSITY OF MIAMI PRESS—Drawer 9088, Coral Gables, Fla. 33124.

UNIVERSITY OF MICHIGAN PRESS—Ann Arbor, Mich. 48106.

UNIVERSITY OF MINNESOTA PRESS—2037 University Ave., S.E., Minneapolis, Minn. 55455.

UNIVERSITY OF MISSOURI PRESS—Columbia, Mo. 65201.

UNIVERSITY OF NEBRASKA PRESS—Lincoln, Nebr. 68508.

UNIVERSITY OF NEW MEXICO PRESS—Albuquerque, N. M. 87106.

UNIVERSITY OF NORTH CAROLINA PRESS—Chapel Hill, N. C. 27515.

UNIVERSITY OF NOTRE DAME PRESS—Notre Dame, Ind. 45556.

UNIVERSITY OF OKLAHOMA PRESS—Norman, Okla. 73069.

UNIVERSITY OF PENNSYLVANIA PRESS—3933 Walnut St., Philadelphia, Pa. 19104.

UNIVERSITY OF PITTSBURGH PRESS—Social Sciences Bldg., Pittsburgh, Pa. 15213.

UNIVERSITY OF SOUTH CAROLINA PRESS—USC Campus, Columbia, S. C. 29208.

UNIVERSITY OF TENNESSEE PRESS—Publications Bldg., Knoxville, Tenn. 37916.

UNIVERSITY OF TEXAS PRESS—Box 7819, University Station, Austin, Texas 78712.

UNIVERSITY OF UTAH PRESS—Bldg. 301, Salt Lake City, Utah 84112.

UNIVERSITY OF WASHINGTON PRESS—Seattle, Wash. 98105.

UNIVERSITY OF WISCONSIN PRESS—Box 1379, Madison, Wis. 53701.

THE UNIVERSITY PRESS OF KANSAS—358 Watson, Lawrence, Kans. 66044.

THE UNIVERSITY PRESS OF KENTUCKY—Lafferty Hall, Lexington, Ky. 40506.

THE UNIVERSITY PRESS OF VIRGINIA—Box 3608, University Sta., Charlottesville, Va. 22903.

VANDERBILT UNIVERSITY PRESS—Nashville, Tenn. 37203.

WAYNE STATE UNIVERSITY PRESS—5980 Cass, Detroit, Mich. 48202.

WESLEYAN UNIVERSITY PRESS—100 Riverview Center, Middletown, Conn. 06457.

YALE UNIVERSITY PRESS—149 York St., New Haven, Conn. 06511.

THE SYNDICATE MARKET

This list includes major syndicates which are in the market for free-lance material at the present time. It is always best to query syndicates before sending in manuscripts. For a complete list of all syndicates, see the *Editor and Publisher Directory of Syndicated Features*, which may be purchased from *Editor and Publisher*, 850 Third Ave., New York, N. Y. 10022.

B P SINGER FEATURES INC.—3164 West Tyler Ave., Anaheim, Calif. 92801. Jane Sherrod, Editor.
Fiction, all lengths, previously published and on universal themes; biography and woman interest material, all lengths. Illustrated columns and short humor. Books for foreign reprint. Also color transparencies, cartoons and comic strips. Buys outright or pays on percentage basis.

CHICAGO TRIBUNE-NEW YORK TIMES SYNDICATE INC.—220 East 42nd St., New York, N. Y. 10017. Arthur Laro, Editor.
Nonfiction. Newsworthy subjects desired, seven installments, 1,200 words each. Rates negotiated, payment is on publication.

CITY DESK FEATURES—310 East 75th St., New York, N. Y. 10021. Sylvia Fenmore, Editor.
Columns on varied topics, timely, carefully researched, of national interest, possessing that extra spark, 500–700 words. Manner of payment: 50% basis. Will return material if accompanied by stamped, self-addressed envelope.

ENTERPRISE SCIENCE SERVICE—Newspaper Enterprise Assn., 230 Park Ave., New York, N. Y. 10017.
Science feature material, 800 to 1,000 words, by experienced science and medical writers. Photos necessary. Pays $40 and up, on publication.

THE HOLLYWOOD INFORMER SYNDICATE—Box 3094, Hollywood, Calif. 90028. John Austin, Director.
Feature material, 1,000 to 1,500 words, on TV and motion picture personalities, knowledgeably written. Pays on percentage basis.

HOLLYWOOD PRESS SYNDICATE—6605 Hollywood Blvd., Hollywood Calif. 90028. J. B. Polonsky, Editor.
Feature-length articles. Interviews with important personalities, popular science articles, etc. Good human-interest photos. No fiction. Pays on a fifty-fifty basis.

INTERCITY NEWS SERVICE—103 Park Ave., New York, N. Y. 10017. John Kelly, Editor; Ed Nassauer, General Manager.
Business, financial and trade press articles; also syndicated columns and special correspondence by assigned staff writers only.

KING FEATURES SYNDICATE—235 East 45th St., New York, N. Y. 10017. Milton J. Kaplan, General Manager. Neal Freeman, Executive Editor. Louis Messolonghites, Senior Editor for picture pages.
Columns, comic features of all types. Most contributors are on contract. Payment varies.

THE LEDGER SYNDICATE, INC.—110 West 40th St., New York, N. Y. 10018.
Series on current, front-page news subjects, 750 to 1,100 words per installment,
6 to 12 installments per series. Considers published writers only. Pays 50 per cent
of net.

LOS ANGELES TIMES SYNDICATE—Times Mirror Square, Los Angeles, Calif.
90053. Patrick McHugh, Chief Editor.
Features on a long-range program basis, such as comic strips, panels, daily columns, etc. No short stories or spot releases.

McNAUGHT SYNDICATE, INC.—60 East 42nd St., New York, N. Y. 10017.
William A. Kennedy, Editor.
Humorous material; drawings and ideas for syndication. Pays on acceptance.

NATIONAL CATHOLIC NEWS SERVICE—1312 Massachusetts Ave. N. W., Washington, D. C. 20005. Patrick Joyce, News Editor.
Serves Catholic diocesan weekly newspapers in U. S. and Canada. Articles about
Catholic Church or issues of special interest to Catholics, and photos. Pays up to
5¢ a published word, after publication.

NATIONAL NEWSPAPER SYNDICATE—National Newspaper Syndicate, Inc. of,
America, 20 North Wacker Dr., Chicago, Ill. 60606. R. Kirkwood Brodie III,
Editor.
Write for further details.

NEWSPAPER ENTERPRISE ASSOCIATION, INC.—230 Park Ave., New York,
N. Y. 10017. Robert Lochnar, Executive Editor.
News features, background material, feature stories concerning current news. Most
material is staff-written, or done by writers under contract.

NORTH AMERICAN NEWSPAPER ALLIANCE—220 East 42nd St., New York,
N. Y. 10017. Sheldon Englemayer, Editor.
News and feature stories of nationwide interest, to 450 words. Special Sunday
articles, to 1,500 words. Series of two to five articles. Decision within a few days.
Payment is usually $25, immediately after distribution.

PUBLISHERS-HALL SYNDICATE, INC.—401 North Wabash Ave., Chicago, Ill.
60611. Robert M. Hall, President; Robert Cowles, Executive Vice President
and General Manager; Richard Sherry, Editor.
Comic strips; cartoon features.

THE REGISTER AND TRIBUNE SYNDICATE—715 Locust St., Des Moines, Iowa
50304. Dennis R. Allen, President.
Ideas for regular newspaper columns, comic strips, and any continuing features
for newspapers. Decision based on 6 or 12 releases and an explanatory outline.
Pays percentage of collections. Query first.

RELIGIOUS NEWS SERVICE—43 West 57th St., New York, N. Y. 10019. Lillian
R. Block, Managing Editor.
Nonfiction only; spot religious news stories and features. Pays 2¢ a word, beginning of each month. Also good, clear, glossy photos on religious subjects. Pays $5
and up for photos, on acceptance.

TRANSWORLD FEATURE SYNDICATE, INC.—141 East 44th St., New York, N. Y.
10017. Mary Schilling, Editor.
Feature material for overseas markets. Query first.

UNITED FEATURE SYNDICATE—220 East 42nd St., New York, N. Y. 10017.
James L. Freeman, Managing Editor.
Comics, columns, and an occasional special series of articles. Pays on a 50–50
basis.

UNIVERSAL SCIENCE NEWS (formerly *World Book Encyclopedia Science Service*)
—314 West Commerce, Tomball, Tex. 77375. William J. Cromie, Editor.
Authoritative, well-written articles on science and science-related subjects. Final
length: 500 to 2,500 words. News-oriented. Query first with brief suggestions and
qualifications.

UNIVERSAL TRADE PRESS SYNDICATE—37-20 Ferry Hts., Fair Lawn, N. J.
07410. Leon D. Gruberg, Director.
Services trade papers with spot news and feature articles. Free-lancers should query
first in 50 words. Payment is 65 to 80 per cent of receipts. Query first.

THE WASHINGTON STAR SYNDICATE—444 Madison Ave., New York, N. Y.
10022. Harry Elmlark, Executive Editor.
Features of various kinds. Most of the material used is handled under yearly
contract.

HOUSE MAGAZINES AND COMPANY PUBLICATIONS

House magazines (also called company publications) are published by a company
or corporation to promote good will, familiarize readers with the company's services
and products, and interest customers in these products. A large percentage of the
material published in house organs is frankly promotional—but editors also look for
general-interest articles, travel or regional features, humor, and, surprisingly enough,
some short stories. These magazines are also an excellent market for photographs.

The house magazines on the following list represent only a sampling of the many
publications in the field. For a complete listing of house magazines—both those that
buy free-lance material and those that do not—see the *Gebbie House Magazine
Directory*, published by the House Magazine Publishing Co. (Sioux City, Iowa
51102), available in most libraries.

AIR FORCE MAGAZINE—1750 Pennsylvania Ave. N. W., Washington, D. C. 20006.
John Frisbee, Executive Editor.
Articles, 1,500 to 3,000 words, on military aviation and aerospace; current, his-
torical and semi-technical subjects. Query. Pays 7¢ a word, on acceptance, and
$10 for true items of Air Force life, 250 words.

AIR LINE PILOT—Air Line Pilots Association International, 1625 Massachusetts Ave.,
N.W., Washington, D. C. 20036. Lou Davis, Editor.
Aviation-oriented articles, to 5,000 words, stressing the pilot's point of view. Safety
articles on aircraft, airports, and equipment, and articles relating to stewards and
stewardesses also needed. Payment varies, is on publication.

ALOFT—4025 Ponce de Leon Blvd., Coral Gables, Fla. 33146. Karl Y. Wickstrom,
Editor.
National Airlines in-flight magazine. Uses articles, about 1,300 words, giving fresh
approaches to cities along the National route. Off-beat angles on places to go;

sports or show business personality profiles. Pays $150 to $200 for articles. Query first.

THE AMERICAN WAY—420 Lexington Ave., New York, N. Y. 10017.
American Airlines magazine. Thoughtful, authoritative articles, 2,000 to 2,500 words, written by experts. Pays $200 to $400, one month after acceptance. Not now soliciting material. Query.

ARCO SPARK—Atlantic Richfield Company, 515 South Flower St., Los Angeles, Calif. 90071.
Articles up to 2,500 words, with photos; subject must have energy indûstry tie-in, and preferably Atlantic Richfield tie-in. Pays about 10¢ a word, on acceptance. Query.

BAUSCH & LOMB FOCUS—619 St. Paul St., Rochester, N. Y. 14602. Ralph I. Feister, Editor.
Articles about new or novel methods in science teaching, or interesting applications of scientific optical instruments, 3,000 words. Uses accompanying photos. Before submitting, write for pamphlet S-301, "How to Write for Bausch & Lomb *Focus*." Pays 3¢ a word, plus $5 per photo used.

THE BOLEX REPORTER—Paillard Inc., 1900 Lower Road, Linden, N. J. 07036.
Short technical articles and photographs on moviemaking, and travel articles including moviemaking details, preferably featuring Bolex cameras. Pays $50 per published page. Query.

THE CARAVANNER—600 South Commonwealth Ave., Los Angeles, Calif. 90005. Address Frank Quattrocchi, Public Relations.
Articles relating to pleasant, interesting or unusual use of Airstream travel trailers, from 500 to 2,000 words. All articles should be illustrated by one or more black-and-white photographs of the Airstream used. "We are looking for articles about happy people, not hardware." Payment is made after acceptance, and averages $75 for a manuscript plus three photos. Also buys reprints. No fillers or cartoons. Query.

CHANNELS OF BUSINESS COMMUNICATION—Northwestern Bell Telephone Co., Room 910, 100 South 19th St., Omaha, Nebr. 68102. Gerald T. Metcalf, Editor.
Case-history articles on how specific businesses in northwestern states use communications to best advantage (data transmission, computer-to-computer, etc.); articles about communications in the broader sense. Aimed at 27,000 business leaders in Northwest. Preferred length: 500 to 1,200 words. Artwork or photos should accompany manuscripts if possible; cartoons are also used. Pays $100 and up for articles, $10 and up for cartoons. Queries welcomed. Allow one month for reply.

THE COMPASS—Mobile Sales and Supply Corp., 150 East 42nd St., New York, N. Y. 10017. K. V. W. Lawrence, Editor.
Short stories and articles on the sea and deep sea trade, with a historical twist where needed. Items should have an international flavor, since magazine is distributed world-wide. Maximum length for both fiction and nonfiction is 3,500 words. Color photos should accompany manuscripts wherever possible. Rates depend on length and photos, and are up to $250. Query.

THE CONTINENTAL MAGAZINE—Room 950 Central Office Bldg., Ford Motor Company, Dearborn, Mich. 48121. Robert M. Hodesh, Editorial Director.
Service articles, 1,300 to 1,700 words, on travel, entertainment, shopping, sport for the well-to-do. Articles of high quality. Pays on acceptance. Query.

ENTHUSIAST—Harley-Davidson Motor Co., P.O. Box 653, Milwaukee, Wis. 53201. T. C. Bolfert, Editor.
Emphasis on photo-journalism. Fiction and articles, to 2,500 words, on motor-cycling subjects. Travel stories, particularly about places not readily accessible by car. Pays 5¢ a word, $7.50 to $15 per photo, on acceptance.

FLAGSHIP NEWS—American Airlines, Inc., 633 Third Ave., New York, N. Y. 10017. Bill Hunter, Editor.
Distributed to American Airlines employees and travel agents. Articles of varying lengths on humorous or unusual incidents on board American Airlines planes, or features about destination cities on the AA system. Emphasis on the employee angle. Most photos assigned. Pays varying rates, within 30 days of publication.

FORD TIMES—Ford Motor Co., The American Rd., Dearborn, Mich. 48121. Hal Butler, Managing Editor.
Articles of 1,500 words or less, on recreation and travel related to car ownership; humor; unique and little-known places to visit. Pays 10¢ and up a word, on acceptance. Query preferred.

FORD TRUCK TIMES—420 Lexington Ave., New York, N. Y. 10017. Henry J. Zaleski, Editor.
How-to pieces and articles, 500 to 1,000 words of interest to truck owners. Sports, adventure, outdoor, general-interest and business-success stories related to the use of or need for a Ford truck, illustrated with color photos. Pays on publication. Write for details.

FRIENDS—4-213 General Motors Bldg., Detroit, Mich. 48202. Alexander Suczek, Editor.
Photo-articles and photos with caption material. Uses articles on travel, with route and recreation information, sports, personalities, unusual news or recreation events, human-interest articles. Both color and black-and-white photos used; write for information on submitting. Pays from $75 a page to $150 a page, including photos. Query first with outline and photo situations.

THE FURROW—John Deere, John Deere Rd., Moline, Ill. 61265. Ralph Reynolds, Editor.
Nonfiction and humor, to 1,500 words, with emphasis on researched agricultural-technical features and rural social- and economic-trend features. Success stories about small towns and unique solutions to the problems of rural living. Payment is up to $200, on acceptance.

GAYLORD'S TRIANGLE—Gaylord Brothers, Inc., P.O. Box 61, Syracuse, N. Y. 13201. W. F. Hogan, Advertising Manager.
Uses brief articles about new company products, and testimonial photos and write-ups showing products in use.

GOING PLACES—American Express Co., 65 Broadway, New York, N. Y. 10006.
Diane Plummer, Editor.
Occasional travel articles, to 1,000 words. Payment varies, and is made on acceptance.

HARVEST—Campbell Soup Co., Campbell Place, Camden, N. J. 08101.
Uses articles with a company tie-in, or of a general food industry nature—agricultural developments, free enterprise, health and nutrition, safety, food research. Candid photos that help to tell the story are essential: either 35mm or $2\frac{1}{4}$ x $2\frac{1}{4}$ color transparencies or 8 x 10 black-and-white glossies. Payment is made on acceptance, by arrangement. Requirement sheet and sample copy on request. Query.

HUGHES RIGWAY MAGAZINE—Hughes Tool Co., P.O. Box 2539, Houston, Tex. 77001. Address all correspondence to Mark Eversole.
Fact features and topical articles of interest to men in oil-field drilling business; dramatic historical narratives; specialty, novelty, unusual sports and outdoor features of general masculine interest; oilfield fiction. Preferred length: 2,000 to 2,500 words. Pays 10¢ a word, on acceptance.

ILLINOIS CENTRAL GULF NEWS—Illinois Central Gulf Railroad, 135 East 11th Pl., Chicago, Ill. 60605. A. R. Lind, Editor.
Occasionally buys articles, with pictures and captions, on railroads. Also uses travel articles dealing mostly with the Midwest (from Chicago to New Orleans). Length: to 1,500 words. Pays $25, on acceptance.

IMPERIAL OIL FLEET NEWS—111 St. Clair Ave., Toronto 195, Ont., Canada. Gordon R. McKean, Editor.
Articles of interest to tankermen, preferably with a modern or historical Canadian angle. Length: 1,000 to 3,000 words. Photos to illustrate articles are used. Pays $40, on publication. Query.

INLAND—Inland Steel Co., 18 South Home Ave., Park Ridge, Ill. 60068. Sheldon A. Mix, Managing Editor.
Articles, essays, or commentaries on topics of broad current interest in the Middle West; also history, reminiscence. Length is open. Pays about $300, on acceptance.

THE IRON WORKER—Lynchburg Foundry Co., Lynchburg, Va. 24505. B. T. Hillman, Editor.
Well-documented and factual historical articles, Virginia-related Americana, written in depth, from 3,500 to 5,000 words. Payment varies, and is made on acceptance. Query.

KENDALL SPORTS TRAIL—The Kendall Co., Sports Division, 20 Walnut Street, Wellesley Hills, Mass. 02181. John S. O'Neill, Editor.
External house organ for high school and college athletic administrators. Uses articles, to 2,500 words and photos on all phases of athletic department and sports management: game and personnel management, finance, sports, medicine, coaching and athletics administration, etc. Pays 5¢ a word, $5 to $25 for black-and-white photos, $50 to $75 for color transparencies, on acceptance.

THE LOOKOUT—15 State St., New York, N. Y. 10004. Harold G. Petersen, Editor.
Articles, to 1,000 words, relating to old or modern merchant marine. Pays up to $40. Also needs cover photos.

THE LUFKIN LINE—P.O. Box 849, Lufkin, Tex. 75901. Virginia R. Allen, Editor.
Articles on travel in the United States and Canada, 1,000 to 1,200 words, with a minimum of eight 8 x 10 black-and-white photos. Pays $50, on acceptance.

MARATHON WORLD—Marathon Oil Co., 539 South Main St., Findlay, Ohio 45840.
Joe Callanan, Editor.
Petroleum- and business-oriented articles; general-interest and travel articles,
1,500 to 3,000 words, preferably pertaining to the Midwest. "World Outlook"
feature uses 200- to 350-word items on topical petroleum or industrial subjects.
Pays from $150 to $500 for feature-length articles and $25 for shorts. Query
essential.

MILKPAIL—Publications Office, H. P. Hood & Sons, 500 Rutherford Ave., Boston,
Mass. 02129.
Articles pertaining to dairy farming and agriculture, particularly in New England,
and articles about technological developments that have an impact on dairying.
Length: 300 words and up. Also farm or dairy interest fillers, cartoons. Pays from
$5 to $10, on publication.

THE MODERN WOODMEN—Modern Woodmen of America, 1701 First Ave., Rock
Island, Ill. 61201. Robert E. Frank, Editor.
Junior edition, ages 16 and under. General-interest fiction and nonfiction, from
1,500 to 2,000 words, strongly plotted, with accurate foreign or historical setting
when used. 8 x 10 black-and-white glossies with manuscripts or individually. Pays
$25 and up for fiction and articles, more with photos; $25 for cover photos.

NEW HOLLAND—Division of Sperry Rand Corp., New Holland, Pa. 17557. Michael
A. Balas, Editor.
Articles about farmers and farm operations, mentioning New Holland equipment
only as it is used in the farm operation. Length: 4 to 5 double-spaced pages.
Black-and-white action photos, and 4 x 5 color transparencies must accompany
articles. Pays on publication.

NORTHLINER MAGAZINE—1999 Shepard Rd., St. Paul, Minn. 55116. Don Picard,
Editor.
Inflight magazine of North Central Airlines. Uses 1,000- to 2,000-word articles,
with 35mm color transparencies, for travelers in Minnesota-Wisconsin-Michigan-
Illinois area. Pays from $100 to $400, upon acceptance. Query first.

ORBIT—Goodyear International Corporation, 1144 East Market St., Akron, Ohio
44316. Thomas S. Palmer, Jr., Editor.
Articles, 4 to 6 typewritten pages, double-spaced, with high-quality color transparencies or black-and-white glossies, about interesting people, places, or events,
including some mention of Goodyear, written from a non-American viewpoint.
Locale should be outside continental U. S. and Canada. Pays $125 to $300, plus
$50 for a cover feature, on acceptance. "Outline for Writers" is available.

OUTDOORS—Outdoors Bldg., Columbia, Mo. 65201.
Illustrated articles, accompanied by 8 x 10 black-and-white photos, on recreational
subjects, with emphasis on boating. Manuscripts should be informative. Length:
to 1,200 words. Pays $35 to $100, on acceptance.

POINTS—465 West Milwaukee, Detroit, Mich. 48202.
Illustrated articles, 700 to 900 words, on family activities, stressing little-known
or unusual ideas; semi-technical articles concerning first aid, photography, etc.;
hobbies; women's features; arts and crafts. "Features must involve the 'how'
and 'why' of hobbies, sports, and other subjects relating to travel." Color transparencies required. Payment is from $125 to $400 for articles with photos, and
from $60 to $150 for photos alone.

PRINTING SALESMAN'S HERALD—Champion Papers, 245 Park Ave., New York,
N. Y. 10017. Michael P. Corey, Editor.
Knowledgeable articles related to the buying and selling of printing, 500 to 2,500

words, to help to make printing salesmen more effective and useful members of their profession. Pays from $50 to $75 per article, on acceptance.

THE RECORD—Fireman's Fund American Insurance Companies, 3333 California St., San Francisco, Calif. 94120. William F. Lawler, Editor.
Buys one short story with strong Christmas theme, about 3,000 words, each year. Must be a valid piece of fiction, not a reminiscence or collection of anecdotes. Early September deadline. Pays from $300 to $500.

SEASONS—P.O. Box 4040, St. Paul, Minn. 55116. Richard L. Smith, Editor.
Articles aimed at homeowners, 500 to 1,700 words, with black-and-white photos or color transparencies, on home improvements and family activities in the home. Does not accept articles written in first person. Pays up to $200.

SEVENTY-SIX MAGAZINE—Union Oil Co. of California, Box 7600, Los Angeles, Calif. 90051. Peter Craigmoe, Editor.
Dramatizes company operations in terms of the employees who participate in the operations. Prefers emphasis on anecdotes and quotes. No dealer stories. No fillers or poetry. Black-and-white, color photos to illustrate story. Query. Articles range from 750 to 1,750 words. Pays 10¢ to 30¢ a word, extra for photos, on acceptance. Samples and writer's kit gladly sent.

SMALL WORLD—Volkswagen of America, 818 Sylvan Ave., Englewood Cliffs, N. J. 07632. Jonathan Fisher, Editor.
Articles, 600 to 1,400 words, which relate to Volkswagens or Volkswagen owners. Pays $100 per page for text and photos (color transparencies preferred). Also, whimsical anecdotes about Volkswagen owners' experiences, cartoons and photos about Volkswagens. Length: up to 100 words. Pays $15 minimum, on acceptance.

TEXACO TEMPO—Texaco Canada Ltd., 90 Wynford Dr., Don Mills 403, Ont., Canada.
Articles relating to Canadian oil industry in some way, with Texaco Canada interest preferred, 800 to 1,200 words, and photos to accompany manuscripts. Pays from $100 to $150, plus photo costs, on acceptance.

THINK—International Business Machines, Armonk, N. Y. 10504. Howard M. Greenwald, Managing Editor.
In-company magazine. Articles, 2,000 to 4,000 words, on management, science, education, and public affairs. Query first. Pays $500 and up.

TILE AND TILL—Eli Lilly and Company, Indianapolis, Ind. 46206.
Uses management and scientific articles dealing with pharmacy, by qualified writers. Query.

TRAINED MEN—International Correspondence Schools, Scranton, Pa. 18515. Catherine Harrington, Editor.
Articles of interest to middle- and upper-management officials, 1,200 to 3,000 words, on new methods, systems, techniques, etc. Accompanying photos encouraged. Pays 2¢ to 3¢ a word.

THE WATER SKIER—American Water Ski Association, P.O. Box 191, Winter Haven, Fla. 33880. Thomas C. Hardman, Editor.
Occasionally uses off-beat articles to 2,500 words, and/or photo features involving water skiing. Payment varies, and is made on acceptance. Query.

WATERSPORT—Boat Owners Council of America, 534 North Broadway, Milwaukee, Wisc. 53202. A. W. Limburg, Editor.
High-quality articles and photographs of boating and other water sports activity. Pays good rates, on acceptance.

CITY AND REGIONAL MAGAZINES

The following list gives a representative sample of the many city and regional magazines published across the country. These publications offer writers an excellent market for all types of material—general-interest articles, travel features, photofeatures and fillers with photos, and even, occasionally, short stories.

City magazines, usually published by chambers of commerce, are particularly interested in articles and features that build local pride, focusing on business, history, local politics, and cultural and urban affairs.

It's essential for writers to query editors of these publications before sending completed manuscripts, and to enclose a list of photos available, or even a few sample prints or transparencies. Always study past issues of these magazines carefully to learn what has been used recently, and to determine a magazine's style and slant.

ADIRONDACK LIFE—Willsboro, N. Y. 12996. Lionel A. Atwill, Editor.
Articles, 750 to 2,000 words, on artists, personalities, history, events, unusual trips, collectibles, geography, wildlife, etc. related to Adirondacks. Color transparencies, 35mm or larger, black-and-white prints, 4 x 5 or larger, or drawings must accompany articles. Pays $75 to $100 per article. Query.

ALABAMA REVIEW—University of Alabama Press, Drawer 2877, University, Ala. 35486. Malcolm C. McMillan, Editor.
Articles, not over 28 double-spaced pages, containing historical and scholarly material on Alabama and the southern region.

ALASKA JOURNAL—422 Calhoun, Juneau, Alaska 99801. R. N. DeArmond, Editor.
Soundly researched articles on Alaska and Yukon history, 500 to 5,000 words, with black-and-white and color photos, and articles on Alaska artists. Pays about 2¢ a word, upon publication. Query.

ALASKA, THE MAGAZINE OF LIFE ON THE LAST FRONTIER—Box 4-EEE, Anchorage, Alaska 99503. Bob Henning, Editor.
Interested in stories, articles and photos on "Life on the Last Frontier." Short pieces, 100 to 1,000 words; articles and fiction from 1,500 to 3,000 words. All material should be accompanied by photos. Pays $10 to $25 for short pieces, $25 to $100 for regular length. Pays $25 for cover color pictures, $5 to $15 for others. Payment is on publication.

THE AMERICAN WEST—599 College Ave., Palo Alto, Calif. 94306. Donald E. Bower, Editor.
Articles on western history, from 1,000 to 4,000 words. Pays $75 to $300, on publication. Query.

ARIZONA—Arizona *Republic*, 120 East Van Buren St., Phoenix, Ariz. 85004. Bud DeWald, Editor.
Articles, 500 to 2,500 words; short fillers and humor, photos and drawings, and cartoons. All material must be on subjects related to Arizona, except cartoons. Pays $25 to $175, on scheduling for publication.

ARIZONA AND THE WEST—University of Arizona Press, Library 308, University of Arizona, Tucson, Ariz. 85721. Harwood P. Hinton, Editor.
Scholarly articles pertaining to the history of the trans-Mississippi West, and edited original documents. Length: 25 to 30 pages, double spaced. Also uses accompanying photographs and maps. No payment.

ARIZONA HIGHWAYS—2039 West Lewis Ave., Phoenix, Ariz. 85009. Raymond Carlson, Editor.
Articles of about 2,500 words of interest to the traveler or visitor. Queries only.

THE ATLANTIC ADVOCATE—Gleaner Bldg., Phoenix Sq., Fredericton, N.B., Canada. Ken Chisholm, Editor.
Prefers regional articles about Eastern Canada, but also considers general-interest articles, especially unusual, well-researched pieces. Photos. Payment by negotiation. High quality fiction, for family reading, to 2,500 words. Poetry overstocked at present. Pays on publication.

AUSTIN—Austin Chamber of Commerce, Box 1967, Austin, Tex. 78767. George Seagert, Editor.
Articles pertaining to Austin, 800 to 1,000 words; occasional fiction and cartoons. Also uses photos. Rates negotiable. Query.

BALTIMORE MAGAZINE—Baltimore Association of Commerce, 22 Light Street, Baltimore, Md. 21202. William Stump, Editor.
Articles up to 2,500 words, on area problems, aspirations and pleasures. Pays up to $175. Some photos. Query essential.

THE BEAVER—Hudson's Bay House, Winnipeg, Manitoba, R 3C 2R1, Canada. Miss Malvina Bolus, Editor.
Uses fillers, 700 to 1,500 words, and authentic, well-written articles dealing.with historical or modern aspects of the far north and its people. Average length: 3,000 words. Should be accompanied by photos or drawings. Pays about 5¢ a word, on acceptance.

BIRMINGHAM—Birmingham Chamber of Commerce, 1914 Sixth Ave. North, Birmingham, Ala. 35211.
Uses articles of local and regional interest, 1,500 to 3,000 words. Photos are on assignment. Pays on publication; query.

BOSTON MAGAZINE—38 Newbury St., Boston, Mass. 02116. Nancy Love, Editor.
Boston-oriented articles, to 3,000 words. Query first.

BUCKS COUNTY PANORAMA—50 East Court St., Doylestown, Pa. 18901. Sheila W. Martin, Editor.
Regional articles and fiction, 1,000 to 2,500 words, oriented toward Bucks County, Pa., on historical or modern subjects, with photos. Pays $10 to $15 for manusripts.

BUFFALO SPREE MAGAZINE—P.O. Box 38, Buffalo, N. Y. 14226. Richard G. Shotell, Editor.
Stimulating essays, 2,000 to 4,000 words, exploring contemporary social, philosophical, artistic and environmental concerns. Occasional fiction, 2,000 to 4,000 words. High-quality, experimental poetry, 2 to 52 lines. Pays $75 for lead article or story, $1.00 per line for poetry with a $20 maximum.

CALIFORNIA JOURNAL—1617 10th St., Sacramento, Calif. 95814. Ed Salzman, Editor.
Well-written, expert, objective and analytical articles on California state government and politics, of varying length. Pays by arrangement. Study back issues and query.

CALIFORNIA TODAY—750 Ridder Park Dr., San Jose, Calif. 95131. Ted Bredt, Editor.
Sunday magazine of San Jose *Mercury-News*. Wants articles and photo-features with California tie-in, to reflect the "good life", with strong emphasis on sports, outdoors, the leisure home. No fiction or poetry. Pays 5¢ a word and up, on acceptance, for articles, and $35 and up, on acceptance, for short humor and history. $20 each or $50 per page for color or black-and-white photos, on publication.

CANADIAN GEOGRAPHICAL JOURNAL—488 Wilbrod St., Ottawa, Ont., KIN 6M8, Canada. Major-General W. J. Megill, Editor.
Articles and pictorial features about Canada, 2,000 to 3,000 words. Some foreign material accepted. Photos essential. Pays on publication.

CHAMBER CHATTER—P.O. Box 8, Deming, New Mexico 88030. Tom Lund, Editor.
Can use all material concerning community improvement. No payment.

CHEVRON USA—P.O. Box 6227, San Jose, Calif. 95150. Gary A. Williams, Editor.
Interested in articles, 500 to 1,500 words, on travel in the U. S. West, with emphasis on auto trips. Overstocked on Alaska, Hawaii. Pays 15¢ a word and up, on acceptance. Also uses humorous anecdotes, 100 to 250 words; cartoons; black-and-white and color photos, for which payment is $35 to $200.

THE CHICAGO GUIDE—500 North Michigan Ave., Chicago, Ill. 60603.
Nonfiction related to Chicago, 2,500 words. Pays various rates. Query.

THE CHICAGOAN—645 North Michigan Ave., Suite 540, Chicago, Ill. 60611. Richard Christiansen, Editor.
Articles, 1,500 to 5,000 words, on Chicago area—people, places, neighborhoods, newsmakers, events, trends of the times, with or without photos. Also short fiction, poetry, puzzles, cartoons, light essays. Pays $200 to $500, depending on length and quality. Query.

CINCINNATI—309 Vine Street, Greater Cincinnati Chamber of Commerce, Cincinnati, Ohio 45202. Richard L. Gordon, Editor.
Uses only articles about Greater Cincinnati and its residents, 800 to 1,800 words. Pays 8¢ per word, on publication.

COLORADO MAGAZINE—7190 West 14th Ave., Denver, Colo. 80215. David Sumner, Executive Editor.
Exciting adventure, both current and historical, about people and events in the Rocky Mountain West, from 2,500 to 3,000 words. Photos should accompany all articles. Pays 10¢ a word, on acceptance. Query.

COLUMBUS DISPATCH SUNDAY MAGAZINE—Columbus, Ohio 43216. Robert K. Waldron, Editor.
Articles, to 1,800 words, with a strong Ohio slant. Pays 2¢ a word minimum, $3 for photos, tenth of month after publication.

COMMONWEALTH—Virginia State Chamber of Commerce, 611 East Franklin, Richmond, Va. 23219. James S. Wamsley, Editor.
Wants articles with a sophisticated Virginia slant. No stock history or travel pieces. Length: 1,500 to 3,000 words. Average payment, 4¢ to 5¢ per word. Query.

CONNECTICUT MAGAZINE—2505 Main St., Stratford, Conn. 06497.
Connecticut-based articles, 1,000 to 2,500 words. Also profiles, investigative reports. Pays $50–$500.

DALLAS—1507 Pacific Ave., Dallas, Tex. 75201.
Metro-interest articles and features, 4,000 words, to explore the Dallas environment, heritage, growth, and human resources. Query first—all articles written on assignment. Pays $150 and up, on acceptance.

DAYTON, U.S.A.—Dayton Area Chamber of Commerce, 210 North Main St., Dayton, Ohio 45459. Kathleen Turner, Editor.
Published bi-monthly for community decision makers in business, industry, education and home. Article length, 2,000 to 3,000 words. Uses photographs or drawings to illustrate articles or as feature spread. No payment. Query.

DOWN EAST—Camden, Maine 04843. Duane Doolittle, Editor.
Articles, 1,500 to 2,500 words, on subjects related to Maine. Black-and-white photos and 4 x 5 color transparencies only. Pays minimum of 2¢ a word on acceptance, $3 to $5 each for photos.

THE DULUTHIAN—Chamber of Commerce, 220 Medical Arts Building, Duluth, Minn. 55802.
Articles, 750 to 1,500 words, about the Duluth area. Subjects are people, business developments, some civic and social problems or activities and some outdoor or area sports interests. No payment.

EMPIRE MAGAZINE—The Denver *Post*, P.O. Box 1709, Denver, Colo. 80201. Bill Hosokawa, Editor.
Articles with a strong regional peg about people, events, history, adventure, issues. Length: 500 to 3,000 words. Photos may help sell article. Pays about 4¢ a word, on acceptance. Query advisable.

FLORIDA TREND—P.O. Box 2350, 1306 West Kennedy Blvd., Tampa, Fla. 33601.
Articles about Florida business and businessmen, to 3,000 words. Also uses photos. Rates negotiable, average 6¢ a word. Query.

THE FLORIDIAN—St. Petersburg *Times*, Box 1121, St. Petersburg, Fla. 33731.
Florida material. Uses in-depth features—personality profiles, controversial subjects in medicine, law, education, nature, history. Also photos and line drawings. Pays $70 to $150, on acceptance. Query preferred.

FOCUS/MIDWEST—Box 3086, St. Louis, Mo. 63130. Charles I. Klotzer, Editor.
Controversial regional and national articles, 900 to 3,000 words, of direct concern to readers in the Midwest, particularly Missouri and Illinois, on political, social and cultural issues, especially those dealing with urban problems in Chicago, St. Louis, and Kansas City. No taboos. Pays on publication.

FORT WORTH—Fort Worth Chamber of Commerce, 700 Throckmorton, Fort Worth, Texas 76102. Barbara Allen, Editor.
Fort Worth or West Texas articles on subjects or personalities. Query first, as outside material is only on assignment.

GEORGIA MAGAZINE—Box 1047, Decatur, Ga. 30031. Jim Townsend, Editor.
Articles on Georgia, past and present, under 2,000 words. Interested in people, history, scenic beauty, industries, vacation opportunities, and folklore. Pays up to $250, on publication.

GOLDEN GATE NORTH—P. O. Box 3028, Santa Rosa, Calif. 95403.
In-depth articles, 3,000 words, on local and regional issues and personalities, plus interviews and black-and-white photos or photofeatures. Pays 5¢ a word and $10 per photo, on publication.

HOUSTON-CHRONICLE TEXAS MAGAZINE—801 Texas, Houston, Texas 77002. Jack Loftis, Editor.
Texas-oriented photo features of top professional quality.

INCREDIBLE IDAHO—Room 108, Capitol Bldg., Boise, Id. 83707. Dorine Goertzen, Editor.
Wants illustrated articles related to Idaho, from 1,000 to 2,500 words, and poems. Photos should be either 5 x 7 or 8 x 10 black-and-white glossies, or 2¼ x 2¼ to 4 x 5 color transparencies. Payment is in copies. Query essential.

JACKSONVILLE—Jacksonville Chamber of Commerce, P.O. Box 329, Jacksonville, Fla. 32201.
Uses very little free lance material. Articles, 1,000 to 3,000 words, must have local angle, and be accompanied by photos of human interest. Query essential.

LONG ISLAND FORUM—P.O. Box 215, West Islip, N. Y. 11795. Carl A. Starace, Editor.
Uses nonfiction exclusively, photos only when they accompany an article. Interested in Long Island history and folklore, to 2,400 words per single article or installment. No payment. Query essential.

LOS ANGELES MAGAZINE—342 North Rodeo Dr., Beverly Hills, Calif. 90210. David R. Brown, Editor.
Topical articles, of particular relevance to active, affluent Southern Californians, to 2,500 words. Some photo stories and humor. Pays 5¢ to 10¢ a word, on publication. Query.

LOUISVILLE—300 West Liberty St., Louisville, Ky. 40202. Betty Lou Amster, Managing Editor.
Articles, 1,000 to 2,000 words, on community problems, business success stories. Louisville businessmen, aimed at business leaders of Louisville metropolitan area. Some photos and art. Rarely, short verse. Pays $35 and up, on acceptance. Query.

MIAMI MAGAZINE—2825 Oak Ave., Miami, Fla. 33133.
Articles, any length, on South Florida lifestyle. Payment varies.

MIDWEST MAGAZINE—Chicago *Sun-Times,* Chicago, Ill. 60611.
Articles, 1,000 to 1,500 words, preferably geared to Chicago and Chicago-area interest. Pays $35 to $175. Query.

MONTANA: THE MAGAZINE OF WESTERN HISTORY—Montana Historical Society, 225 North Roberts, Helena, Montana 59601. Mrs. Vivian A. Paladin, Editor.
Uses well-written articles, 3,500 to 6,500 words, on history of the American West, preferably lesser-known facets. Must be documented. Also uses authentic photos, drawings, or engravings. Pays 1½¢ a word. Query.

NEBRASKALAND—Nebraska Game and Parks Commission, 2200 North 33rd St., Lincoln, Nebr. 68503. Dick H. Schaefer, Editor.
Material dealing with Nebraska: people, hunting, fishing, travel, tourism, outdoor and historical articles, with 2¼ x 2¼ transparencies preferred, 35 mm or 4 x 5 acceptable. No payment.

NEVADA HIGHWAYS AND PARKS—State of Nevada Dept. of Highways, Carson City, Nev. 89701.
Articles with a Nevada angle—historical, scenic, etc.—1,000 to 2,500 words, and black-and-white glossies, 4 x 5, or 2¼ x 2¼ transparencies. Pays from 5¢ to 8¢ a word for articles, $10 to $40 for photos, upon scheduling.

NEW-ENGLAND GALAXY—Old Sturbridge Village, Sturbridge, Mass. 01566. Catherine Fennelly, Editor.
Well-written nonfiction, to 3,000 words, preferably historical. New England material only. Pays $75 to $150, on publication. Query. Also uses verse, to 32 lines, and photos or drawings.

THE NEW ENGLAND GUIDE—Box 108, Concord, N. H. 03301.
New England subjects only: off-beat historical episodes, little-known people who had an impact. Also humorous essays, personal experiences and observations. Length: to 800 words. Uses photos and art if it illustrates the article. Pays $40, on publication. Query essential. No sample copies.

NEW HAMPSHIRE PROFILES—3 Sheafe St., Portsmouth, N. H. 03801. Peter E. Randall, Editor.
Nonfiction, to 2,000 words, on country living, or pertinent to New Hampshire. Uses 8 x 10 black-and-white photos related to N. H. Payment varies, is on publication. Query.

NEW MEXICO MAGAZINE—113 Washington Ave., Santa Fe, N. M. 87501. Walter Briggs, Editor.
Nonfiction on New Mexico subjects, 1,000 to 5,000 words. Photos, 35 mm and up, of New Mexico locales and activities. Pays $25 to $400 for articles, $10 to $36 for photos. Query.

NEW NORFOLK—269 Boush St., Norfolk, Va. 23510. June S. Morrisette, Editor.
Wants articles, from 500 to 3,000 words, on business, civic or metropolitan-oriented topics. Payment is 20¢ per column inch, upon publication.

NORTHWEST—1320 S. W. Broadway, Portland, Oregon 97201.
Sunday supplement magazine of the *Sunday Oregonian.* J. R. Bianco, Editor. In the market for articles, to 1,500 words, on wildlife, travel in the Pacific Northwest and regional-interest subjects. Black-and-white photos with articles are used. No hunting articles. Payment is $35 per·magazine page, plus $10 for each black-and-white photo, on the 10th of each month. Stamped, self-addressed envelopes must accompany all manuscripts.

OKLAHOMA TODAY—Will Rogers Memorial Bldg., State Capitol, Oklahoma City, Okla. 73105. Bill Burchardt, Editor.
Articles on Oklahoma topics up to 1,500 words. Study past issues carefully before querying. Pays 3¢ a word, on publication, extra for photos.

OLD WEST—See *True West.*

OREGON HISTORICAL QUARTERLY—Oregon Historical Society, 235 S.W. Market St., Portland, Oregon 97201. Thomas Vaughan, Editor.
Nonfiction, 1,000 to 20,000 words on Pacific Northwest regional history of all kinds: diaries, recollections, etc. Interested in new material and new interpretations pertinent to the region, its role in the U.S. or the West. Illustrated articles welcome (both photos and drawings). No payment.

OUTDOOR ARIZONA (formerly *Arizona Wildlife Sportsman*)—1230 East Camelback, Phoenix, Ariz. 85014. Bob Hirsch, Editor.
Articles, 700 to 2,000 words, on almost any outdoor subject oriented to Arizona. Welcomes pieces on nature study, travel, non-game animal and game subjects. Accompanying photos, 8 x 10 black-and-white, almost a must. Pays 2¢ a word for articles, $3 to $4 for pictures. Query.

PHILADELPHIA—1500 Walnut St., Philadelphia, Pa. 19102. Alan Halpern, Editor.
Nonfiction, 1,000 to 20,000 words. Mostly staff-written: interested only in material dealing specifically with the Philadelphia metropolitan area. Pays $50 to $500, on acceptance. Query.

PHILADELPHIA INQUIRER TODAY MAGAZINE—Broad and Callowhill Sts., Philadelphia, Pa. 19101. Howard Coffin, Editor.
Nonfiction, 500 to 3,500 words, on local subjects. Accompanying photos or drawings. Pays on publication, rates vary. Query.

PHOENIX MAGAZINE—1230 East Camelback Rd., Phoenix, Ariz. 85014. Kenneth A. Walsh, Editor.
Locally oriented articles, 1,000 to 2,500 words, with photos or drawings. Pays from $50, on publication. Query.

REAL WEST—Charlton Bldg., Derby, Conn. 06418. Edward T. LeBlanc, Editor.
Nonfiction only, 3,000 to 5,000 words; illustrations essential. Especially interested in pioneering experiences in the West around the turn of the century. Pays 2¢ per word, on acceptance.

THE RHODE ISLANDER—Providence Sunday *Journal,* Providence, R. I. 02902. Ted Holmberg, Sunday Editor.
Rhode Island-oriented articles, 500 to 2,000 words. Pays $35 to $250 on publication. Query.

ROLL CALL: THE NEWSPAPER OF CAPITOL HILL—636 Pennsylvania Ave., S.E., Washington, D. C. 20003.
Magazine for professional politicians, office holders, and political scientists. Articles must be authoritative and accurate; anti-congressional slant is out. Historical pieces with topical significance, personality pieces, humor; good satire most wanted, but not on "issues." Length: 250 to 1,000 words for articles, 500 to 1,000 words for fiction. Pays on acceptance. Slow reports. Prestige high, payment low.

THE ST. LOUISAN—7036 Clayton Ave., St. Louis, Mo. 63117. Bobbi Linkemer, Editor.
Features on St. Louis subjects of interest to residents. Photos and photo-features. Pays after publication. Query.

SAN ANTONIO MAGAZINE—Chamber of Commerce, P.O. Box 1628, San Antonio, Tex. 78206. Roddy Stinson, Editor.
Articles pertaining to San Antonio or the immediate surrounding area. Payment 3¢ per word, upon acceptance.

SAN FRANCISCO—120 Green St., San Francisco, Calif. 94111. Geoffrey Link, Editor.
Wants features and profiles of Bay Area subjects and personalities that are significant, interesting, and written with style. Subject matter is wide open. Length: 1,000 to 3,000 words. Uses many historical features about San Francisco. Prefers narrative, anecdotal style about little-known characters and events from the city's past. Also cartoons. Pays on publication: $5 for fillers, $50 to $200 for articles, $15 minimum for cartoons. Query.

SAN FRANCISCO BUSINESS—Greater San Francisco Chamber of Commerce, 420 Montgomery St., San Francisco, Calif. 94104.
Articles, 1,500 words, on business or area subjects. No payment. Query.

SANDLAPPER: THE MAGAZINE OF SOUTH CAROLINA—Box 1668, Columbia, S. C. 29202.
Articles, 500 to 2,500 words, on people and events in and about South Carolina. Photos. Pays $20 to $100 for articles, extra for photos. Query.

SEATTLE BUSINESS—Seattle Chamber of Commerce, 215 Columbia St., Seattle, Wash. 98104. Ed Sullivan, Editor.
Primarily business-related with particular application to Seattle and the rest of Washington State. Also interested in socio-economic aspects of business. Query.

SEATTLE TIMES SUNDAY MAGAZINE—Box 70, Seattle, Wash. 98111. Richard Johnston, Editor.
Articles, historical or current, dealing with the Pacific Northwest, 800 to 1,200 words. Accompanying illustrations. Pays on publication, $35 to $50. Query helpful.

SOUTHLAND MAGAZINE—Long Beach *Independent Press-Telegram,* 6th and Pine, Long Beach, Calif. 90801. Robert S. Martin, Editor.
Articles, 500 to 2,000 words, dealing mainly with southern California subjects. Some light humor, photos with articles. Pays following publication, about 5¢ a word.

THE STATE—Box 2169, Raleigh, N. C. 27602. Bill Wright, Editor.
Features, 500 to 1,500 words, on subjects related to North Carolina. Pays $10 to $35, on acceptance.

TEXAS PARADE—P.O. Box 12037, Capitol Station, Austin, Texas 78711. Kenneth Lively, Editor.
Needs articles, 1,500 to 2,000 words; with a strong Texas slant. Also photos or drawings. Pays $25 minimum per printed page, 10th of month following publication. Query.

THIS IS WEST TEXAS—West Texas Chamber of Commerce, Box 1561, Abilene, Texas 79604. Jimmie Martin, Editor.
Illustrated articles, 1,500 to 2,000 words, on scenic, historical, industrial, educational, etc., subjects. Must be oriented to West Texas area.

TOLEDO BLADE SUNDAY MAGAZINE—Toledo, Ohio 43604. Mike Tressler, Editor.
Toledo-area material: in-depth personality stories, current news angles, fiction and nonfiction. Accom. ying photos or drawings desirable. Length: to 4,000 words. Pays on publication, $20 to $50 plus $5 each for photos or drawings. Query.

TORONTO LIFE—56 The Esplanade, Toronto 1, Ontario, Canada. Robert Collins, Editor.
Largely staff-written; contributors must be very familar with Toronto. Articles, 1,500 to 2,500 words. Pays $150 to $400. Query essential.

TRENTON—Trenton-Mercer County Chamber of Commerce, 104 North Broad St., Trenton, N. J. 08608. Donald E. Congram, Editor.
Wants articles with local angle or geared to urban problems. Length: 500 to 1,500 words. Photos. Pays $25 to $100 for articles, $5 for photos. Query.

TROPIC—*The Miami Herald,* 1 Herald Plaza, Miami, Fla. 33101. John Parkyn, Editor.
Professionally-written, general-interest articles, 1,500 to 3,000 words, on topics appealing to South Florida readers. Especially interested in high-quality personality profiles. No family situation material. Pays up to $250, on publication. Query.

TRUE WEST—P.O. Box 3338, Austin, Tex. 78704. Pat Wagner, Editor.
Nonfiction articles about the West, 1830–1910, first-hand accounts or otherwise. Documentary, essay style is not encouraged but material must be accurate and accompanied by sources. Length: 500 to 3,500 words preferred. Photos with articles welcome. Originals returned after publication. Pays 2¢ a word, on acceptance. Query. Sample copies available at 50¢ each. Same requirements for *Frontier Times* and *Old West.*

TULSA—Tulsa Chamber of Commerce, 616 South Boston Ave., Tulsa, Oklahoma 74119. Larry P. Silvey, Editor.
Primarily for area businessmen. Uses in-depth, people-oriented articles, 800 to 1,600 words, dealing with Tulsa and vicinity. Articles must be factual, and must tell all sides of question if topic is controversial or provocative. Uses some accompanying illustrations. Pays $25 to $75, on acceptance. Query.

UPCOUNTRY—Eagle Publishing Co., Pittsfield, Mass. 01201. William H. Tague, Managing Editor.
Articles, 500 to 2,500 words with photos, on rural and small town New England: problems faced by city people who move to country; land management and development; social, economic, environmental and other contemporary issues; sports. First person accounts and nostalgia generally not appropriate. Humorous articles considered. Payment varies, on acceptance.

VERMONT LIFE—61 Elm St., Montpelier, Vt. 05602.
Factual articles on Vermont, 2,000 words in length. Uses accompanying photos. Pays 10¢ a word, on acceptance. Query.

THE WASHINGTONIAN—1218 Connecticut Ave., N.W., Washington, D. C. 20036. Laughlin Phillips, Editor.
Most stories commissioned on basis of full story proposal. Uses articles on any subject if it has a strong Washington flavor. Length: 1,000 to 4,000 words. Articles should stimulate, assist, and/or entertain an audience of intelligent and well-informed Washingtonians. Pays 8¢ to 10¢ a word, on acceptance.

WEEKEND MAGAZINE—231 St. James Street West, Montreal 215, Quebec, Canada. Frank Lowe, Editor.
Uses feature material of topical interest to Canadian newspaper readers, both text and photos. Pays on acceptance. Also uses art. Query.

WESTWAYS—Box 2890, Terminal Annex, Los Angeles, Calif. 90054.
Articles, 800 to 2,500 words, on western U.S., Canadian, and Mexican activities: natural science, travel, history, etc. Also prints verse, to 45 lines. Pays 10¢ a word on acceptance, for articles; $25 per black-and-white photo, $50 and up for color photos. Overstocked. Query.

WICHITA—Chamber of Commerce, 350 West Douglas, Wichita, Kan. 67202. Marge Setter, Editor.
Wants articles, from 300 to 600 words, pertaining to Wichita. Payment is from $50 to $100, half paid upon acceptance and half upon publication.

WISCONSIN TRAILS—P.O. Box 5650, Madison, Wis. 53705. Mrs. Jill Dean, Editor. Editor.
Articles, 1,500 to 3,000 words, relating to Wisconsin: history, industry, personalities, recreational possibilities. Articles should inform as well as entertain. Pays $40 to $125 for articles, on publication; $10 for black-and-white photos, $50 for color. Query.

WONDERFUL WEST VIRGINIA—Information and Education Division, Dept. of Natural Resources, Charleston, West Va. 25305. Edward R. Johnson, Editor.
Articles on nature, conservation, natural resources, hunting, fishing, hiking, caves, mountain climbing, forestry, water resources, wildlife, state parks, winter sports, outdoor lore—all with relation to West Virginia. Length: 6 pages typewritten, double-spaced. Fillers; black-and-white photos of native animals and 4 x 5 color transparencies of scenes in West Virginia. Query. No payment.

YANKEE—Dublin, N. H. 03444. Judson D. Hale, Editor.
Articles with New England locale, not over 2,000 words, preferably with black-and-white photos. Pays $25 to $400; average $250 to $300.

THE YANKEE GUIDE TO THE NEW ENGLAND COUNTRYSIDE—143 Newbury St., Boston, Mass. 02116. Georgia Orcutt, Editor.
Biannual guidebook. Articles, 500 to 2,000 words, with photos, on family activities in New England. Also, short features two printed pages long. Pays from $50 to $200. Query a must.

LITERARY PRIZE OFFERS AND AWARDS

Each year many important prize contests are open to free-lance writers. Some of these are conducted regularly. Others are one-time competitions, and writers should watch the newspapers and magazines for announcements of these special contests.

The short summaries given below are intended merely as guides. Closing dates, requirements, and rules are tentative. No manuscript should be submitted to any competition unless the writer has first checked with the Contest Editor and received complete information about a particular contest.

The prizes listed below are offered for unpublished works. For full information about prizes and awards for both published and unpublished works, writers should consult *Literary and Library Prizes* (6th Edition), published by the R. R. Bowker Company, 1180 Avenue of the Americas, New York, N. Y. 10036.

THE ATLANTIC—8 Arlington St., Boston, Mass. 02116.
Offers continuing wards for *"Atlantic Firsts,"* outstanding stories by new writers, 2,000 to 10,000 words. These stories are purchased at the magazine's top rates, and judged at the end of each year for a first prize of $750 and a second prize of $250.

COUNCIL ON INTERRACIAL BOOKS FOR CHILDREN—29 West 15th St., New York, N. Y. 10011.
Offers three prizes of $500 for children's books manuscripts by previously unpublished African-American, Mexican-American, Puerto Rican, American Indian and Asian-American writers. Closes in April.

DOUBLEDAY & CO., INC.—277 Park Ave., New York, N. Y. 10017.
Sponsors the Doubleday Catholic Prize Contest with $5,000 prizes in three fields: fiction, biography (or autobiography), and nonfiction. Contest is biennial, and usually closes in June.

E. P. DUTTON & CO., INC.—201 Park Ave. South, New York, N. Y. 10003.
Offers the Dutton Man in His Environment Book Award for a full-length nonfiction work dealing with past, present or future of man in his environment. The award is a $10,000 advance against royalties.

FOLLETT PUBLISHING CO.—1010 West Washington Blvd., Chicago, Ill. 60607.
Offers Charles W. Follett Award of $3,000 for fiction and nonfiction book-length manuscripts for young people. Closes in July.

HARPER & ROW, PUBLISHERS—10 East 53rd St., New York, N. Y. 10016.
Offers the Harper-Saxton Fellowship to aid talented new writers. The fellowship consists of $7,500, of which $2,500 is an outright grant, and $5,000 is an advance against royalties.

HOUGHTON MIFFLIN CO.—2 Park St., Boston, Mass. 02107.
Offers the Houghton Mifflin Literary Fellowships, awards designed to help promising authors who need financial assistance to complete literary projects in fiction and nonfiction. The amount of the award is $7,500 of which $5,000 is an advance against royalties and $2,500 is an outright grant. There is no fixed closing date.

INTERNATIONAL POETRY FORUM'S UNITED STATES AWARD—University of Pittsburgh Press, Pittsburgh, Pa. 15213.
Offers award of $2,000 plus publication for a first book of poetry by a U.S. citizen. Closes in April. For rules and entry procedures, send stamped, self-addressed envelope.

IOWA SHORT FICTION AWARD—English-Philosophy Bldg., University of Iowa, Iowa City, Iowa 52240.
$1,000 plus publication for book-length collection of short fiction by author who has not published a book of fiction. Closes in September.

THE MACDOWELL COLONY—Peterborough, N. H. 03458.
Offers fellowships for room and board to provide professionals in the arts freedom to concentrate upon creative work. Apply four months in advance.

MADEMOISELLE MAGAZINE—350 Madison Ave., New York, N. Y. 10017.
Conducts College Writing Competitions in Fiction and Poetry open to women college undergraduates. Cash prizes and publication in the magazine are awarded to the winning works. Contests usually close in February.

MARY ROBERTS RINEHART FOUNDATION GRANTS-IN-AID—The Mary Roberts Rinehart Foundation, Room 504, 516 Fifth Ave., New York, N. Y. 10036.
Provides financial assistance to help creative writers complete work definitely projected. Send stamped, self-addressed envelope for further information. No closing date.

O'NEILL FOUNDATION—O'Neill Theater Center, 1860 Broadway, New York, N. Y. 10023.
Holds an annual playwriting contest, with stipends of $150 each for winning plays, plus production at the annual National Playwrights' Conference in Waterford, Connecticut. Plays may be submitted between September and December.

SERGEL DRAMA PRIZE—University of Chicago Theatre, 5706 South University Ave., Chicago, Ill. 60637.
Awards of $3,000 ($1,500 first prize, $1,000 second prize, $500 third prize) to encourage writing of new American plays. Closes in July.

SEVENTEEN MAGAZINE—320 Park Ave., New York, N. Y. 10022.
Offers prizes of up to $500 for short stories by teen-agers. Usually closes in July.

VIRIGINIA QUARTERLY REVIEW—One West Range, Charlottesville, Va. 22903.
Awards the Emily Clark Balch prizes in creative American writing. The annual awards are given in alternate years for short stories and poetry. The first prize for short stories is $1,000 and the first prize for poetry is $500. There are additional prizes, and the winning works will be published in the magazine. The closing date date is usually in March.

WILMETTE CHILDREN'S THEATRE—726 Ridge Rd., Wilmette, Ill. 60091.
Sponsors annual playwriting contest for plays for children. A first prize of $100 and a second prize of $50 are awarded. Contest usually closes in April.

THE YALE UNIVERSITY PRESS—Box 92A, Yale Station, New Haven, Conn. 06520.
The Yale Series of Younger Poets awards are made for manuscripts of poetry by writers under forty who have not had a volume of verse published. The winning manuscript will be published by Yale University Press. The competition opens in March and closes in May.

ORGANIZATIONS FOR WRITERS

AMERICAN TRANSLATORS ASSOCIATION
Box 129,
Croton-on-Hudson,
N. Y. 10520
American Translators Association is a professional society concerned with the interests of practicing translators, and serves as a forum and clearing house to advance the standards of the profession and to promote the intellectual and material interests of translators and interpreters in the United States. Its publications contain material useful to professionals and to aspirants for a career as translators.
Membership is open to any person actively engaged in translating, interpreting, or professionally related work (*Active Member*), or to any person or organization interested in the objectives of the Association (*Associate Member*). Dues for individuals are $15 annually.

THE AUTHORS LEAGUE OF AMERICA, INC.
234 West 44th Street
New York, New York 10036
Mills Ten Eyck, *Executive Secretary*
The Authors League of America is a national membership organization of authors and dramatists, representing them on matters of joint concern, such as copyright, taxes, and freedom of expression. Since reorganization in 1964, an author or dramatist auto-

matically becomes a member of the League upon joining The Authors Guild, Inc., or The Dramatists Guild, Inc., which are themselves corporate members of the League, but are concerned with the protection and promotion of the professional interests of their respective memberships, including contract terms. Because the Dramatists Guild is concerned with playwrights and authors writing for the musical stage, the material presented here deals only with the Authors Guild.

Who is eligible to join The Authors Guild? By resolution of The Authors Guild Council, any author who shall have had a book published by a reputable American publisher within seven years prior to his application; or any author who shall have had three works, fiction or nonfiction, published by a magazine or magazines of general circulation, either national or local, within eighteen months prior to his application; or any author whose professional standing, in the opinion of the Membership Committee, shall entitle him to membership whether or not he shall have had work published as defined above, shall be eligible to join The Authors Guild as an *active* member with voting rights.

The Authors Guild Council has also provided that the Membership Committee may give permission to an author with work in progress but not yet meeting the specifications for active membership to enroll as an *associate* member with all rights except voting rights. The circumstances of such permissions are left to the discretion of the Membership Committee. Many authors become associate members when they are offered a contract by a publisher for their first book.

Both active and associate members pay annual dues of $30.

MYSTERY WRITERS OF AMERICA, INC.
105 East 19th Street
New York, N. Y. 10003
Gloria Amoury, *Executive Secretary*

Mystery Writers of America, Inc., exists for the purpose of raising the prestige of mystery and detective writing, and of defending the rights and increasing the income of all writers in the field of mystery, detection, and fact crime.

There are four chapters of the MWA in the United States: New York, Midwest, Northern California and Southern California, and an At Large membership for those living in the United States but not conveniently near one of the chapters. As of 1967, membership totaled approximately 700 members.

There are four classifications of membership in MWA: 1) *Active*—for anyone who has made a single sale in the field of mystery, suspense, or crime writing (book, magazine, newspaper, motion picture, radio, television). Only *Active* members may vote or hold office. 2) *Associate*—for non-writers who are allied to the mystery field—editors, publishers, critics, literary agents, motion picture, radio or television producers. 3) *Corresponding*—for writers living outside the United States. *Corresponding* members do not need to be American citizens. 4) *Affiliate*—for new writers who have not as yet made a sale, or non-writers who are mystery enthusiasts.

Annual dues for *Active* members are $20; for *Associate* members, $20; for *Corresponding* members, $8; and for *Affiliate* members, $20.

P.E.N.—AMERICAN CENTER
156 Fifth Ave.
New York, New York, 10010
Mrs. Kirsten Michalski, *Executive Secretary*

The P.E.N. Club is a world association of poets, playwrights, essayists, and novelists, and its purpose is to bring about better understanding between nations through the fellowship of the literary community. P.E.N. has 80 centers in Europe, Asia, Africa, Australia, and the Americas.

There is only one classification of membership in the American Center of P.E.N. Membership is open to all qualified writers, editors, and translators who subscribe to the aims of International P.E.N. Membership is by invitation of the Admissions Committee, usually after nomination by another P.E.N. member.

There are three classifications for dues, although no special privileges go with the higher amounts, which simply constitute contributions to P.E.N. *Regular:* $16 per year; *Contributing:* $26 per year; and *Sustaining:* $50 and up per year.

THE POETRY SOCIETY OF AMERICA
15 Gramercy Park,
New York, New York 10003
Charles A. Wagner, *Executive Secretary*

The purpose of The Poetry Society of America is to secure fuller recognition for poetry as one of the important forces making for a higher civilization and to kindle a fuller and more intelligent appreciation of poetry, especially of the work of living American poets, and to encourage and foster American poetry and aid and assist American poets.

Members of the Society shall be elected by the Executive Board. Persons in sympathy with the general purposes of the Society, including poets and students and lovers of poetry, shall be eligible for membership. Members shall be divided into three classes: *Members, Associate* members, and *Honorary* members, all of whom shall be qualified to vote in the elections of officers and of members of the Executive Board or upon a proposed amendment to the Constitution of the Society.

To qualify as *Members,* applicants must submit five short poems, published or unpublished. Poets of standing qualify for membership without the need to submit work. *Associate* membership includes critics, educators, librarians, teachers of English, etc. All such groups qualify automatically. *Honorary* membership is strictly limited to outstanding poets by invitation of the Executive Board.

Dues for all classes of membership are the same—$12 annually.

SCIENCE FICTION WRITERS OF AMERICA
12051 Laurel Terr.,
Studio City, Calif. 91604
Jerry Pournelle, *President*

The purposes of the Science Fiction Writers of America are: 1) to defend the rights of science fiction writers; 2) to enhance the prestige of science fiction writers, and science fiction in general; 3) to disseminate business information; *i.e.,* relevant data regarding trends, contracts, publishers, editors, contests, new markets, are discussed; 4) to promote and maintain the highest possible standards of excellence in writing.

There are two types of membership: *active* and *associate.* Publication or sale of a short story in the field of science fiction serves as the credential for active membership for a period of two years; the same applies for an original science fiction screenplay. A radio play or teleplay provides for one year's active membership, and a novel for five years. All of these requirements satisfy the eligibility credentials for the quoted number of years *following* the year of production, publication, or broadcast. To be an associate member, one need merely have satisfied any of these requirements *at any time.* An associate member, however, may not vote or hold office.

Dues for both active and associate members are $5 per year.

SOCIETY OF MAGAZINE WRITERS
The Town Hall, 123 West 43rd St.
New York, New York 10036
Dorothea Lobsenz, *Executive Secretary*

This is an organization of free-lance nonfiction magazine journalists who depend for their livelihood on the practice of this branch of the writing profession. The Society exists to increase communication among its members, and to enhance their prestige, effectiveness and security.

Membership is carefully limited to professional writers who meet exacting standards. Only nonfiction free-lance writers for magazines of national stature are eligible. Qualifications of applicants are judged by the Membership Committee. Editors, though welcome as guests, are not admitted to membership.

The initiation fee is $20, and annual dues range from $25 to $35, depending upon location.

WESTERN WRITERS OF AMERICA, INC.
1505 West D Street
North Platte, Nebraska 69101
Nellie Yost, *Secretary-Treasurer*

Western Writers of America, Inc., is a non-profit organization of professional writers of fiction and nonfiction pertaining to the traditions, legends, development and history of the American West. Its chief purpose is to promote a more widespread distribution, readership and appreciation of the literature of the West.

There are two types of membership: *Active* and *Associate*. To be eligible for an *Active* membership, a writer must have either three Western books published, or twenty-five Western short stories or articles sold and published, or have credit for twenty original Western teleplays or five original Western screenplays actually produced and presented. Only active members can hold office or vote for officials or changes in the constitution. *Associate* membership is open to writers with one published Western book or five magazine stories or articles. *Associate* membership may also be granted to other persons active in the field of Western literature, such as editors, publishers, literary agents, literary critics, and motion picture and television producers and directors.

Dues are $15 a year.

Awards of merit, WWA Spur Awards, are given each year to the authors of the best Western material in five categories published during the past year.

WRITERS GUILD OF AMERICA, EAST, INC.
1212 Avenue of the Americas
New York, New York 10036.
Evelyn F. Burkey, *Executive Director*

The Writers Guild of America (East and West) represents writers in the fields of radio, television, and motion pictures. For jurisdictional purposes, there are two separate corporations—Writers Guild of America, East, Inc., and Writers Guild of America, West, Inc. (see below). However, in actual operations, as far as contracts, dues, membership, etc., are concerned, the two corporations function together to create a national organization.

The purpose of the Guild is to promote and protect the professional interests of all creators and adaptors of literary, dramatic, and musical material in the radio, television, and motion picture industries, and to represent its members for the purpose of collective bargaining.

In order to qualify for membership, a writer must be presently employed in one of the three fields or have had material produced in one of these three fields within the past two years.

The basic dues are $6.25 a quarter. In addition, there are quarterly dues based on a percentage of the writer's earnings in any of these fields over which the Guild has jurisdiction. The initiation fee is $50.

The Writers Guild has basic agreements with the producers and employers in all of these fields covering free-lance writers and also, in some instances, staff writers.

WRITERS GUILD OF AMERICA, WEST, INC.
8955 Beverly Boulevard
Los Angeles, California 90048.
Michael H. Franklin, *Executive Director*

The Writers Guild of America, West, Inc., represents all screen, television and radio writers in Hollywood (some 2,000 of them) with respect to their contractual relationship with producers, agents and their fellow writers.

The writer's remuneration, his rights, and his working conditions are all of concern to the Guild, which seeks always to spell them out by legal agreement, and also to further his general ascendancy in the industry. Contracts are held by the Guild with practically every producer in Hollywood in all three media.

For this service the writer pays to the Guild $25 annual basic dues and a percentage of his earnings.

Entrance requirements for membership are sale of original literary material to radio, screen, or television within the preceding two-year period, or employment as a writer, in any one of these three fields during the same period of time.

Writers Guild of America, West, is affiliated with the Writers Guild of America, East, which performs the same functions under the same conditions of membership requirements and dues for screen, television, and radio writers east of the Mississippi.

AMERICAN LITERARY AGENTS

Most literary agents do not usually accept new writers as clients. Since the agent's only income is a percentage—usually 10%—of the amount he receives from the sales he makes for his clients, he must have as clients writers who are selling fairly regularly to good markets.

Always query an agent first. Do not send any manuscripts until the agent has asked you to do so.

The following list is only a partial selection of representative agents. Addresses given are in New York City. (Zip codes are given in parentheses.)

Cyrilly Abels, 119 West 57 Street (10019)
Maxwell Aley Associates, 145 East 35th Street (10016)
American Play Company, Inc., 52 Vanderbilt Avenue (10017)
Ashley Famous Agency, Inc.—See *International Famous Agency, Inc.*
Bill Berger Associates, Inc., 535 East 72nd Street (10021)
Lurton Blassingame, 60 East 42nd Street (10017)
Brandt & Brandt, 101 Park Avenue (10017)
Curtis Brown, Ltd., 60 East 56th Street (10022)
James Brown Associates, Inc., 22 East 60th Street (10022)
Collins-Knowlton-Wing, Inc., 60 East 56th Street (10022)
John Cushman Associates, Inc., 25 West 43 Street (10036)
Joan Daves, 515 Madison Avenue (10017)
Ann Elmo Agency, Inc., 52 Vanderbilt Avenue (10017)
Frieda Fishbein, 353 West 57th Street (10019)
Barthold Fles Literary Agency, 507 Fifth Avenue (10017)
Harold Freedman, Brandt & Brandt Dramatic Dept., Inc., 101 Park Avenue (10017)
Samuel French, Inc., 25 West 45th Street (10036)
Sanford Jerome Greenburger, 757 Third Avenue (10017)
Blanche C. Gregory, Inc., 2 Tudor City Place (10017)
Franz J. Horch Associates, Inc., 325 East 57th Street (10022)
International Famous Agency, 1301 Avenue of the Americas (10019)
Margot Johnson Agency, 405 East 54th Street (10022)
Nannine Joseph, 200 West 54th Street (10019)
Lucy Kroll Agency, 390 West End Avenue (10024)
Robert Lantz-Candida Donadio Literary Agency, Inc., 111 West 57th Street (10019)
Lenniger Literary Agency, Inc., 437 Fifth Avenue (10016)
The Sterling Lord Agency, 660 Madison Avenue (10021)
McIntosh, McKee & Dodds, Inc., 22 East 40th Street (10016)
McIntosh & Otis, Inc., 18 East 41st Street (10017)
Elisabeth Marton, 96 Fifth Avenue (10011)
Harold Matson Company, Inc., 22 East 40th Street (10016)
William Morris Agency, Inc., 1350 Avenue of the Americas (10019)
Harold Ober Associates, Inc., 40 East 49th Street (10017)
Paul R. Reynolds, Inc., 599 Fifth Avenue (10017)
Virginia Rice, 301 East 66th Street (10021)
Flora Roberts, Inc., 116 East 59th Street (10022)
Marie Rodell, 141 East 55th Street (10022)
Russell & Volkening, Inc., 551 Fifth Avenue (10017)
Leah Salisbury, Inc., 790 Madison Avenue (10021)
John Schaffner, 425 East 51st Street (10022)
Ad Schulberg Agency, 300 East 57th Street (10022)
Seligmann & Collier, 280 Madison Avenue (10016)
Gunther Stuhlmann, 65 Irving Place (10003)
A. Watkins, Inc., 77 Park Avenue (10016)
Max Wilkinson Associates, Inc., Shelter Island, N. Y. (11964)
Mary Yost Associates, 141 East 55th Street (10022)

INDEX TO MARKETS